PRINCIPLES AND PRACTICE
OF AMERICAN POLITICS

Sixth Edition

SAGE | 50 YEARS

PRINCIPLES AND PRACTICE OF AMERICAN POLITICS

Classic and Contemporary Readings

Sixth Edition

Samuel Kernell
University of California, San Diego

Steven S. Smith
Washington University, St. Louis

Editors

Los Angeles | London | New Delhi
Singapore | Washington DC | Boston

Los Angeles | London | New Delhi
Singapore | Washington DC | Boston

FOR INFORMATION:

CQ Press

An Imprint of SAGE Publications, Inc.

2455 Teller Road

Thousand Oaks, California 91320

E-mail: order@sagepub.com

SAGE Publications Ltd.

1 Oliver's Yard

55 City Road

London EC1Y 1SP

United Kingdom

SAGE Publications India Pvt. Ltd.

B 1/I 1 Mohan Cooperative Industrial Area

Mathura Road, New Delhi 110 044

India

SAGE Publications Asia-Pacific Pte. Ltd.

3 Church Street

#10-04 Samsung Hub

Singapore 049483

Printed in the United States of America

Cataloging-in-publication data is available for this book from the Library of Congress.

ISBN 978-1-4833-1987-2

This book is printed on acid-free paper.

Acquisitions Editor: Sarah Calabi

Senior Development Editor: Nancy Matuszak

Editorial Assistant: Raquel Christie

Production Editor: Laura Barrett

Copy Editor: Megan Granger

Typesetter: C&M Digitals (P) Ltd.

Proofreader: Annie Lubinsky

Cover Designer: Anupama Krishan

Marketing Manager: Amy Whitaker

17 18 19 20 21 10 9 8 7 6 5 4 3

CONTENTS

Preface   xii

About the Editors   xiv

CHAPTER 1. DESIGNING INSTITUTIONS   1

1-1 Mancur Olson Jr. from *The Logic of Collective Action*   1

   *In an excerpt from his classic work of 1965, Mancur Olson
   Jr. explains why groups often have difficulty achieving their
   collective goals, even when agreement among their
   members is widespread.*

1-2 Garrett Hardin The Tragedy of the Commons   9

   *In another classic work, Garrett Hardin uses the idea of the
   tragedy of the commons to explain why public goods are so
   often misused.*

CHAPTER 2. THE CONSTITUTIONAL FRAMEWORK   18

2-1 Brutus *Anti-Federalist* No. 3   18

   *In this essay, published early in the ratification debates,
   Brutus unveils the principal arguments against the
   Constitution.*

2-2 James Madison *Federalist* No. 10   22

   *James Madison argues that a large, diverse republic is not
   only capable of controlling the tyranny of faction but, when
   properly designed, the best means of doing so.*

2-3 James Madison *Federalist* No. 51   27

   *James Madison explains how the Constitution will employ
   checks and balances to prevent the people's representatives
   from exploiting their political power.*

2-4 SAMUEL KERNELL "The True Principles of Republican
Government": Reassessing James Madison's Political Science   29

*Samuel Kernell considers the similarities and differences
between James Madison's* Federalist *Numbers 10 and 51.*

CHAPTER 3. FEDERALISM   47

3-1 DONALD F. KETTL Federalism: Sorting Out Who Does What   47

*Donald F. Kettl explores the lessons of recent natural disasters
for understanding the ever-evolving division of power and
responsibility between the state and federal governments.*

3-2 JONATHAN RAUCH A Separate Peace   65

*Jonathan Rauch states that federalism provides a "safety
valve" to American democracy by allowing the various
states to adopt different policies on issues on which
differences of opinion run deep.*

3-3 THAD KOUSSER How America's "Devolution
Revolution" Reshaped Its Federalism   68

*Thad Kousser considers how the devolution of power to
the states has changed U.S. federalism.*

CHAPTER 4. CIVIL RIGHTS   86

4-1 SUPREME COURT OF THE UNITED STATES Schuette v. Bamn   86

*In this ruling the Supreme Court upheld the
constitutionality of Michigan voters' choice to ban race as a
consideration in university admission decisions.*

4-2 JUSTIN LEVITT from New State Voting Laws:
Barriers to the Ballot?   92

*This essay questions the integrity of recent changes to state
voting laws that may make voting disproportionately more
difficult for racial minorities.*

CHAPTER 5. CIVIL LIBERTIES   99

5-1 CASS R. SUNSTEIN from Republic.com 2.0   99

*The author applies established freedom of speech doctrines
to novel forms of expression in the electronic age.*

5-2 SUPREME COURT OF THE UNITED STATES Roe v. Wade   111

*In this controversial decision, the Supreme Court considers
whether the Constitution protects a woman's right to
terminate her pregnancy against the objections of the State.*

5-3 GERALD N. ROSENBERG The Real World of
Constitutional Rights: The Supreme Court and
the Implementation of the Abortion Decisions 117

*Gerald N. Rosenberg examines the political and legal
environment surrounding abortion policy, which is still a
source of conflict 30 years after* Roe v. Wade.

CHAPTER 6. CONGRESS 138

6-1 STEVEN S. SMITH Congress, the Troubled Institution 138

*Steven S. Smith describes Congress's struggles with
partisanship, filibusters, and scandals as it tackles
momentous issues.*

6-2 SARAH A. BINDER The Politics of Legislative Stalemate 151

*Sarah A. Binder outlines the effects of divided party control
of the institutions of government and partisan polarization
on the policymaking process.*

6-3 JOHN H. ALDRICH AND DAVID W. ROHDE
Congressional Committees in a Continuing Partisan Era 161

*John H. Aldrich and David W. Rohde state that in an era of
polarized parties, party leaders dominate standing
committees in the policymaking process of the House of
Representatives.*

CHAPTER 7. THE PRESIDENCY 177

7-1 RICHARD E. NEUSTADT from *Presidential Power* 177

*Richard E. Neustadt shows that successful presidential
leadership depends on the ability to persuade.*

7-2 SAMUEL KERNELL from *Going Public* 192

*Samuel Kernell observes that modern presidents, in their
efforts to persuade other politicians to adopt their policy
preferences, often "go public": a set of activities borrowed
from presidential election campaigns.*

CHAPTER 8. THE BUREAUCRACY 205

8-1 TERRY M. MOE The Politics of Bureaucratic Structure 205

*Terry M. Moe argues that the federal bureaucracy is not
structured on the basis of a theory of public administration
but instead is the product of politics.*

8-2 DAVID E. LEWIS from *The Politics of Presidential Appointments*   216

This essay states that presidents' strategies for controlling federal departments and agencies have evolved in important ways in recent decades.

CHAPTER 9. THE JUDICIARY   233

9-1 ANTONIN SCALIA from *A Matter of Interpretation: Federal Courts and the Law*   233

In this lecture to law school students, Supreme Court Justice Antonin Scalia makes a strong case for judges to limit their analysis to what laws say instead of exploring their intent.

9-2 STEPHEN BREYER from *Active Liberty*   245

Antonin Scalia's colleague Supreme Court Justice Stephen Breyer argues instead that judges should weigh the implications of their decisions for advancing democracy.

9-3 ALEXANDER HAMILTON *Federalist* No. 78   254

While asserting that the unelected judiciary is the "least dangerous branch," Alexander Hamilton assumes for the Supreme Court the important role of judicial review.

9-4 ROBERT A. CARP AND KENNETH L. MANNING Selecting Justice: The Ideology of Federal Judges Appointed by President Barack Obama   258

This essay argues that all presidents seek judges who share their policy views and offers an early appraisal of the ideology of the federal district judges appointed by President Obama.

CHAPTER 10. PUBLIC OPINION   273

10-1 HERBERT ASHER Analyzing and Interpreting Polls   273

Herbert Asher explains the common ways that polls are misinterpreted and misused.

10-2 JOHN ZALLER AND STANLEY FELDMAN A Simple Theory of the Survey Response: Answering Questions Versus Revealing Preferences   294

This essay argues that people do not hold strong or stable attitudes about most issues and political phenomena, and that their survey responses are instead influenced by circumstances.

10-3 MORRIS P. FIORINA from *Culture War?*
The Myth of a Polarized America   308

*Morris P. Fiorina challenges the popular notion that
Americans are becoming more deeply divided on cultural
issues.*

10-4 ALAN I. ABRAMOWITZ The Polarized Electorate   316

*Alan I. Abramowitz argues that partisan polarization is real
and affects the competitiveness of elections.*

CHAPTER 11. VOTING, CAMPAIGNS, AND ELECTIONS   325

11-1 SAMUEL L. POPKIN from *The Reasoning Voter*   325

*Samuel L. Popkin argues that in a world of imperfect and
incomplete information, voters rely on shortcuts to make
decisions. His depiction of the decision-making processes of
voters helps explain the characteristics of campaigns and
other features of American politics.*

11-2 GARY C. JACOBSON No Compromise:
The Electoral Origins of Legislative Gridlock   330

*Gary C. Jacobson describes the way partisan polarization
and gridlock in American policymaking reflect the disparate
electoral coalitions responsible for electing Democrats and
Republicans to public office.*

11-3 MICHAEL SCHUDSON America's Ignorant Voters   351

*Michael Schudson observes that American voters are not
becoming less knowledgeable about government (contrary
to the conventional wisdom) and, even without all the facts
about politics, are able to make reasonable judgments
about candidates.*

11-4 LYNN VAVRECK U.S. Presidential Election Forecasting: Want a
Better Forecast? Measure the Campaign, Not Just the Economy   357

*Lynn Vavreck argues that 2012 presidential candidate Mitt
Romney miscalculated when he emphasized that the
economic recovery was too slow under incumbent
Democrat Barack Obama.*

CHAPTER 12. POLITICAL PARTIES   362

12-1 JOHN H. ALDRICH from *Why Parties?*   362

*John H. Aldrich describes the political problems that parties
solve for candidates and voters.*

12-2 Larry M. Bartels Partisanship and
Voting Behavior, 1952–1996   371

*Larry M. Bartels describes trends in the party identification
of Americans and explains the importance of these trends
for voting behavior.*

12-3 Morris P. Fiorina Parties as Problem Solvers   380

*According to Morris P. Fiorina, today's centralized, cohesive
parties are no better at solving today's problems than were
the decentralized, disunited parties of a half century ago
and may even make them worse.*

CHAPTER 13. INTEREST GROUPS   391

13-1 E. E. Schattschneider The Scope and Bias of the
Pressure System   391

*In a still-relevant piece from the 1960s, E. E.
Schattschneider argues that moneyed interests dominated
midcentury politics by controlling the agenda and
influencing policymakers.*

13-2 Richard L. Hall and Richard Anderson Issue
Advertising and Legislative Advocacy in Health Politics   398

*This essay describes recent trends and outlines the efforts of
special interest groups to frame issues and mobilize public
support for their causes.*

13-3 Jennifer Nicoll Victor Gridlock Lobbying:
Breaking, Creating, and Maintaining Legislative Stalemate   414

*Jennifer Nicoll Victor shows how the model of a liberal-to-
conservative continuum can be used to help understand
how lobbyists for interest groups adjust their strategies to
the policy preferences of legislators and presidents.*

CHAPTER 14. NEWS MEDIA   431

14-1 James T. Hamilton The Market and the Media   431

*News, James T. Hamilton reminds us, is a consumer
product and as such changes with consumer demands and
market competition.*

14-2 Shanto Iyengar and Kyu S. Hahn Red Media, Blue Media:
Evidence of Ideological Selectivity in Media Use   443

Shanto Iyengar and Kyu S. Hahn suggest that the trend of voters' being able to better identify which party's politicians favor policies closer to their own views may reflect the public's ability in this information age to select their news from producers displaying a stance with which they agree.

Constitution of the United States   **452**

PREFACE

Assembling this set of readings for students of American politics has been a pleasure and a challenge. The pleasure has come in discovering so many articles that illuminate American politics. The challenge has come in finding far more than can be contained in a single volume. Consequently, despite its heft, *Principles and Practice of American Politics* represents a small sampling of the available literature.

Our shared perspective on politics has guided the selection of articles. Political actors pursue goals informed by self-interest. This perspective does not require abandoning all hope that politics can result in public policy that serves the common interests of the public today and for future generations. It says simply that to understand politics we need to understand what different political actors want and how this leads them to engage in various strategies to achieve their goals. For government actors, these goals will largely reflect the offices they hold, the constituents they represent, and the constitutional obligations and opportunities that define their roles. Other major actors—the public, the news media, and activists in political parties and interest groups—are similarly motivated by self-interest. They do not occupy government positions, and so their behavior is regulated by a different constellation of opportunities and limitations. Each chapter's readings introduce the interests, rules, and strategic contexts of political action in a major national political forum.

Conflict over social issues, polarization in Washington and the nation, legislative gridlock, and the tremendous challenges facing policymakers are among the subjects of the new selections for this edition. Our selections reflect the changing federal–state relationship; the growing number of states enacting voter identification laws; the continuing debates over the polarization of the American electorate and Congress; the role of media in influencing public views of politicians and issues; and the ever-evolving state of civil rights and civil liberties.

We have chosen the readings to serve two audiences. Many instructors will employ *Principles and Practice of American Politics* as a supplement to an introductory American politics textbook. For others, this book may constitute the core reading material for a course. For the former, we have selected readings that will animate the institutional processes described in the text. For the latter, we have sought readings that can stand alone and do not assume more than an elementary knowledge of American government and politics. Based on feedback from our reviewers, we have streamlined the articles available in this edition, removing those that saw little use. In this edition, we have added essays that challenge students to think more carefully about alternative institutions and political arrangements. The essays present institutions of majority rule, the nature of racial discrimination, and the proper role of the Court as less settled issues that provide students an opportunity to think through (and discuss) their views on the future direction of American civic life.

Some of the selections are classics that all instructors will recognize; others, which may be less familiar, address contemporary political developments or proposals for reform. Each article adds emphasis and depth to textbook coverage and illustrates an important theme; most also introduce an important writer on American politics. We hope all the articles enrich students' understanding of American politics.

We have taken care to include as much of each original source as possible. We have edited some of the pieces to make them appropriate for classroom use. Ellipses indicate where material has been excised, and brackets enclose editorial interpolations. Other changes are explained in the source note for the reading.

We wish to thank the editorial staff of CQ Press, an imprint of SAGE Publications, for their expertise, energy, and patience in helping us bring this project to completion. Charisse Kiino offered essential encouragement and guidance throughout the effort and provided superb editorial assistance, and Nancy Matuszak persisted in acquiring permission to reprint the selections and managed the project into production. Several anonymous reviewers and the following political scientists provided very helpful comments on our plans for this edition: Scott Adler, University of Colorado; Craig Burnett, Appalachian State University; Marc J. Hetherington, Vanderbilt University; Kenneth L. Manning, University of Massachusetts–Dartmouth; Stephen Nicholson, University of California, Merced; Eric Schickler, University of California, Berkeley; John Shively, Longview Community College; John J. Theis, Lonestar College–Kingwood; and Lynn Vavreck, University of California, Los Angeles.

Samuel Kernell
Steven S. Smith

ABOUT THE EDITORS

Samuel Kernell is professor of political science at the University of California, San Diego, where he has taught since 1977. He taught previously at the University of Mississippi and the University of Minnesota, and served as a senior fellow at the Brookings Institution. Kernell's research interests focus on the presidency, political communication, and American political history. His books include *Going Public: New Strategies of Presidential Leadership*; *James Madison: The Theory and Practice of Republican Government*, an edited collection of essays; and *The Logic of American Politics*, coauthored with Gary C. Jacobson, Thad Kousser, and Lynn Vavreck. His latest book (with Erik J. Engstrom) is *Party Ballots, Reform, and the Transformation of America's Party System* published in 2014.

Steven S. Smith is professor of political science and director of the Weidenbaum Center at Washington University in St. Louis. He has taught at the University of Minnesota, Northwestern University, and George Washington University, and has served as a senior fellow at the Brookings Institution. His research interests include American politics, congressional politics, Russian politics, positive theories of politics, and theories of institutional development. He is author or coauthor of the following: *The Senate Syndrome: The Evolution of Procedural Warfare in the Modern U.S. Senate*; *Party Influence in Congress*; *Politics or Principle: Filibustering in the United States Senate*; *Committees in Congress*; *The American Congress*; *Call to Order: Floor Politics in the House and Senate*; *Managing Uncertainty in the House of Representatives*; and *The Politics of Institutional Choice: The Formation of the Russian State Duma*.

Chapter 1

Designing Institutions

1-1 From *The Logic of Collective Action*

Mancur Olson Jr.

With the publication of The Logic of Collective Action *in 1965, Mancur Olson Jr. introduced the fundamental dilemma of collective action to all who study politics. When members of a group agree to work together to achieve a collective goal, each member as an individual faces powerful disincentives, Olson showed, that can frustrate the efforts of the group as a whole. For example, when each can foresee that his or her relatively small contribution to a collective enterprise will not affect its overall success, many will fail to contribute—a phenomenon known as free riding—and leave to everyone else the burden of supplying the collective good. As a consequence, collective enterprises based on cooperation, and supported by the entire collectivity, nevertheless often fail.*

It is often taken for granted, at least where economic objectives are involved, that groups of individuals with common interests usually attempt to further those common interests. Groups of individuals with common interests are expected to act on behalf of their common interests much as single individuals are often expected to act on behalf of their personal interests. This opinion about group behavior is frequently found not only in popular discussions but also in scholarly writings. Many economists of diverse methodological and ideological traditions have implicitly or explicitly accepted it. This view has, for example, been important in many theories of labor unions, in Marxian theories of class action, in concepts of "countervailing power," and in various discussions of economic institutions. It has, in addition, occupied a prominent place in political science, at least in the United States, where the study of pressure groups has been dominated by a celebrated "group theory" based on the idea that groups will act when necessary to further their common or group goals. Finally, it has played a significant role in many well-known sociological studies.

The view that groups act to serve their interests presumably is based upon the assumption that the individuals in groups act out of self-interest. If the individuals in a group altruistically disregarded their personal welfare, it would not be very likely that collectively they would seek some selfish common or group objective. Such altruism is, however, considered exceptional, and self-interested behavior is usually thought to be the rule, at least when economic issues are at stake; no one is surprised when individual businessmen seek higher profits, when individual workers seek higher wages, or when individual consumers seek lower prices. The idea that groups tend to act in support of their group interests

Source: Reprinted by permission of the publisher from *The Logic of Collective Action: Public Goods and the Theory of Groups* by Mancur Olson, pp. 1-2, 5-8, 8-9, 10-16, Cambridge, Mass.: Harvard University Press, Copyright © 1965, 1971 by the President and Fellows of Harvard College.

is supposed to follow logically from this widely accepted premise of rational, self-interested behavior. In other words, if the members of some group have a common interest or objective, and if they would all be better off if that objective were achieved, it has been thought to follow logically that the individuals in that group would, if they were rational and self-interested, act to achieve that objective.

But it is *not* in fact true that the idea that groups will act in their self-interest follows logically from the premise of rational and self-interested behavior. It does *not* follow . . . that they would act to achieve that objective, even if they were all rational and self-interested. Indeed, unless the number of individuals in a group is quite small, or unless there is coercion or some other special device to make individuals act in their common interest, *rational, self-interested individuals will not act to achieve their common or group interests*. In other words, even if all of the individuals in a large group are rational and self-interested, and would gain if, as a group, they acted to achieve their common interest or objective, they will still not voluntarily act to achieve that common or group interest. The notion that groups of individuals will act to achieve their common or group interests, far from being a logical implication of the assumption that the individuals in a group will rationally further their individual interests, is in fact inconsistent with that assumption. . . .

A Theory of Groups and Organizations

The Purpose of Organization

Since most (though by no means all) of the action taken by or on behalf of groups of individuals is taken through organizations, it will be helpful to consider organizations in a general or theoretical way.[1] The logical place to begin any systematic study of organizations is with their purpose. But there are all types and shapes and sizes of organizations, even of economic organizations, and there is then some question whether there is any single purpose that would be characteristic of organizations generally.

One purpose that is nonetheless characteristic of most organizations, and surely of practically all organizations with an important economic aspect, is the furtherance of the interests of their members. That would seem obvious, at least from the economist's perspective. To be sure, some organizations may out of ignorance fail to further their members' interests, and others may be enticed into serving only the ends of the leadership.[2] But organizations often perish if they do nothing to further the interests of their members, and this factor must severely limit the number of organizations that fail to serve their members.

The idea that organizations or associations exist to further the interests of their members is hardly novel, nor peculiar to economics; it goes back at least to Aristotle, who wrote, "Men journey together with a view to particular advantage, and by way of providing some particular thing needed for the purposes of life, and similarly the political association seems to have come together originally, and to continue in existence, for the sake of the *general* advantages it brings."[3] More recently Professor Leon Festinger, a social psychologist, pointed out that "the attraction of group membership is not so much in sheer belonging, but rather in attaining something by means of this membership."[4] The late Harold Laski, a political scientist, took it for granted that "associations exist to fulfill purposes which a group of men have in common."[5]

The kinds of organizations that are the focus of this study are *expected* to further the interests of their members.[6] Labor unions are expected to strive for higher wages and better working conditions for their members; farm organizations are expected to strive for favorable legislation for their members; cartels are expected to strive for higher prices for participating firms; the corporation is expected to further the interests of its stockholders;[7] and the state is expected to further the common interests of its citizens (though in this nationalistic age the state often has interests and ambitions apart from those of its citizens).

Notice that the interests that all of these diverse types of organizations are expected to further are for the most part *common* interests: the union members' common interest in higher wages, the farmers' common interest in favorable legislation, the cartel members' common interest in higher prices, the stockholders' common interest in higher dividends and stock prices, the citizens' common interest in good government. It is not an accident that the diverse types of organizations listed are all supposed to work primarily for the *common* interests of their members. Purely personal or individual interests can be advanced, and usually advanced most efficiently, by individual, unorganized action. There is obviously no purpose in having an organization when individual, unorganized action can serve the interests of the individual as well as or better than an organization; there would, for example, be no point in forming an organization simply to play solitaire. But when a number of individuals have a common or collective interest—when they share a single purpose or objective—individual, unorganized action (as we shall soon see) will either not be able to advance that common interest at all, or will not be able to advance that interest adequately. Organizations can therefore perform a function when there are common or group interests, and though organizations often also serve purely personal, individual interests, their characteristic and primary function is to advance the common interests of groups of individuals.

The assumption that organizations typically exist to further the common interests of groups of people is implicit in most of the literature about organizations, and two of the writers already cited make this assumption explicit: Harold Laski emphasized that organizations exist to achieve purposes or interests which "a group of men have in common," and Aristotle apparently had a similar notion in mind when he argued that political associations are created and maintained because of the "general advantages" they bring. . . . As Arthur Bentley, the founder of the "group theory" of modern political science, put it, "there is no group without its interest."[8] The social psychologist Raymond

Cattell was equally explicit, and stated that "every group has its interest."[9] This is also the way the word "group" will be used here.

Just as those who belong to an organization or a group can be presumed to have a common interest,[10] so they obviously also have purely individual interests, different from those of the others in the organization or group. All of the members of a labor union, for example, have a common interest in higher wages, but at the same time each worker has a unique interest in his personal income, which depends not only on the rate of wages but also on the length of time that he works.

Public Goods and Large Groups

The combination of individual interests and common interests in an organization suggests an analogy with a competitive market. The firms in a perfectly competitive industry, for example, have a common interest in a higher price for the industry's product. Since a uniform price must prevail in such a market, a firm cannot expect a higher price for itself unless all of the other firms in the industry also have this higher price. But a firm in a competitive market also has an interest in selling as much as it can, until the cost of producing another unit exceeds the price of that unit. In this there is no common interest; each firm's interest is directly opposed to that of every other firm, for the more other firms sell, the lower the price and income for any given firm. In short, while all firms have a common interest in a higher price, they have antagonistic interests where output is concerned. . . .

For these reasons it is now generally understood that if the firms in an industry are maximizing profits, the profits for the industry as a whole will be less than they might otherwise be.[11] And almost everyone would agree that this theoretical conclusion fits the facts for markets characterized by pure competition. The important point is that this is true because, though all the firms have a common interest in a higher price for the industry's product, it is in the interest of each firm that the other firms pay the cost—in terms of the necessary reduction in output—needed to obtain a higher price.

About the only thing that keeps prices from falling in accordance with the process just described in perfectly competitive markets is outside intervention. Government price supports, tariffs, cartel agreements, and the like may keep the firms in a competitive market from acting contrary to their interests. Such aid or intervention is quite common. It is then important to ask how it comes about. How does a competitive industry obtain government assistance in maintaining the price of its product?

Consider a hypothetical, competitive industry, and suppose that most of the producers in that industry desire a tariff, a price-support program, or some other government intervention to increase the price for their product. To obtain any such assistance from the government, the producers in this industry will presumably have to organize a lobbying organization; they will have to become an active pressure group.[12] This lobbying organization may have to conduct a considerable campaign. If significant resistance is encountered, a great amount of money will be required.[13] Public relations experts will be needed to influence the newspapers, and some advertising may be necessary. Professional organizers will probably be needed to organize "spontaneous grass roots" meetings among the distressed producers in the industry, and to get those in the industry to write letters to their congressmen.[14] The campaign for the government assistance will take the time of some of the producers in the industry, as well as their money.

There is a striking parallel between the problem the perfectly competitive industry faces as it strives to obtain government assistance, and the problem it faces in the marketplace when the firms increase output and bring about a fall in price. *Just as it was not rational for a particular producer to restrict his output in order that there might be a higher price for the product of his industry, so it would not be rational for him to sacrifice his time and money to support a lobbying organization to obtain government assistance for the industry. In neither case would it be in the interest of the individual producer to assume any of the costs himself. A lobbying organization, or indeed a labor union or any other organization, working in the interest of a large group of firms or workers in some industry, would get no assistance from the rational, self-interested individuals in that industry.* This would be true even if everyone in the industry were absolutely convinced that the proposed program was in their interest (though in fact some might think otherwise and make the organization's task yet more difficult).

Although the lobbying organization is only one example of the logical analogy between the organization and the market, it is of some practical importance. There are many powerful and well-financed lobbies with mass support in existence now, but these lobbying organizations do not get that support because of their legislative achievements. . . .

Some critics may argue that the rational person will, indeed, support a large organization, like a lobbying organization, that works in his interest, because he knows that if he does not, others will not do so either, and then the organization will fail, and he will be without the benefit that the organization could have provided. This argument shows the need for the analogy with the perfectly competitive market. For it would be quite as reasonable to argue that prices will never fall below the levels a monopoly would have charged in a perfectly competitive market, because if one firm increased its output, other firms would also, and the price would fall; but each firm could foresee this, so it would not start a chain of price-destroying increases in output. In fact, it does not work out this way in a competitive market; nor in a large organization. When the number of firms involved is large, no one will notice the effect on price if one firm increases its output, and so no one will change his plans because of it. Similarly, in a large organization, the loss of one dues payer will not noticeably increase the burden for any other one dues payer, and so a rational person would not believe that if he were to withdraw from an organization he would drive others to do so.

The foregoing argument must at the least have some relevance to economic organizations that are mainly means through which individuals attempt to obtain the same things they obtain through their activities in the market. Labor unions, for example, are organizations through which workers strive to get the same things they get with their individual efforts in the market—higher wages, better working conditions, and the like. It would be strange indeed if the workers did not confront some of the same problems in the union that they meet in the market, since their efforts in both places have some of the same purposes.

However similar the purposes may be, critics may object that attitudes in organizations are not at all like those in markets. In organizations, an emotional or ideological element is often also involved. Does this make the argument offered here practically irrelevant?

A most important type of organization—the national state—will serve to test this objection. Patriotism is probably the strongest non-economic motive for organizational allegiance in modern times. This age is sometimes called the age of nationalism. Many nations draw additional strength and unity from some powerful ideology, such as democracy or communism, as well as from a common religion, language, or cultural inheritance. The state not only has many such powerful sources of support; it also is very important economically. Almost any government is economically beneficial to its citizens, in that the law and order it provides is a prerequisite of all civilized economic activity. But despite the force of patriotism, the appeal of the national ideology, the bond of a common culture, and the indispensability of the system of law and order, no major state in modern history has been able to support itself through voluntary dues or contributions. Philanthropic contributions are not even a significant source of revenue for most countries. Taxes, *compulsory* payments by definition, are needed. Indeed, as the old saying indicates, their necessity is as certain as death itself.

If the state, with all of the emotional resources at its command, cannot finance its most basic and vital activities without resort to compulsion, it would seem that large private organizations might also have difficulty in getting the individuals in the groups whose interests they attempt to advance to make the necessary contributions voluntarily.[15]

The reason the state cannot survive on voluntary dues or payments, but must rely on taxation, is that the most fundamental services a nation-state provides are, in one important respect, like the higher price in a competitive market: they must be available to everyone if they are available to anyone. The basic and most elementary goods or services provided by government, like defense and police protection, and the system of law and order generally, are such that they go to everyone or practically everyone in the nation. It would obviously not be feasible, if indeed it were possible, to deny the protection provided by the military services, the police, and the courts to those who did not voluntarily pay their share of the costs of government, and taxation is accordingly necessary. The common or collective benefits provided by governments are usually called "public goods" by economists, and the concept of public goods is one of the oldest and most important ideas in the study of public finance. A common, collective, or public good is here defined as any good such that, if any person X_i in a group $X_1, \ldots, X_i, \ldots, X_n$ consumes it, it cannot feasibly be withheld from the others in that group.[16] In other words, those who do not purchase or pay for any of the public or collective good cannot be excluded or kept from sharing in the consumption of the good, as they can where noncollective goods are concerned.

Students of public finance have, however, neglected the fact that the achievement of any common goal or the satisfaction of any common interest means that a public or collective good has been provided for that group.[17] The very fact that a goal or purpose is common to a group means that no one in the group is excluded from the benefit or satisfaction brought about by its achievement. As the opening paragraphs of this chapter indicated, almost all groups and organizations have the purpose of serving the common interests of their members. As R. M. MacIver puts it, "Persons . . . have common interests in the degree to which they participate in a cause . . . which indivisibly embraces them all."[18] It is of the essence of an organization that it provides an inseparable, generalized benefit. It follows that the provision of public or collective goods is the fundamental function of organizations generally. A state is first of all an organization that provides public goods for its members, the citizens; and other types of organizations similarly provide collective goods for their members.

And just as a state cannot support itself by voluntary contributions, or by selling its basic services on the market, neither can other large organizations support themselves without providing some sanction, or some attraction distinct from the public good itself, that will lead individuals to help bear the burdens of maintaining the organization. The individual member of the typical large organization is in a position analogous to that of the firm in a perfectly competitive market, or the taxpayer in the state: his own efforts will not have a noticeable effect on the situation of his organization, and he can enjoy any improvements brought about by others whether or not he has worked in support of his organization.

There is no suggestion here that states or other organizations provide *only* public or collective goods. Governments often provide noncollective goods like electric power, for example, and they usually sell such goods on the market much as private firms would do. Moreover . . . large organizations that are not able to make membership compulsory *must also* provide some noncollective goods in order to give potential members an incentive to join. Still, collective goods are the characteristic organizational goods, for ordinary noncollective goods can always be provided by individual action, and only where common purposes or collective goods are concerned is organization or group action ever indispensable.[19]

Notes

1. Economists have for the most part neglected to develop theories of organizations, but there are a few works from an economic point of view on the subject. See, for example, three papers by Jacob Marschak, "Elements for a Theory of Teams," *Management Science,* I (January 1955), 127–137, "Towards an Economic Theory of Organization and Information," in *Decision Processes,* ed. R. M. Thrall, C. H. Combs, and R. L. Davis (New York: John Wiley, 1954), pp. 187–220, and "Efficient and Viable Organization Forms," in *Modern Organization Theory,* ed. Mason Haire (New York: John Wiley, 1959), pp. 307–320; two papers by R. Radner, "Application of Linear Programming to Team Decision Problems," *Management Science,* V (January 1959), 143–150, and "Team Decision Problems," *Annals of Mathematical Statistics,* XXXIII (September 1962), 857–881; C. B. McGuire, "Some Team Models of a Sales Organization," *Management Science,* VII (January 1961), 101–130; Oskar Morgenstern, *Prolegomena to a Theory of Organization* (Santa Monica, Calif.: RAND Research Memorandum 734, 1951); James G. March and Herbert A. Simon, *Organizations* (New York: John Wiley, 1958); Kenneth Boulding, *The Organizational Revolution* (New York: Harper, 1953).

2. Max Weber called attention to the case where an organization continues to exist for some time after it has become meaningless because some official is making a living out of it. See his *Theory of Social and Economic Organization,* trans. Talcott Parsons and A. M. Henderson (New York: Oxford University Press, 1947), p. 318.

3. *Ethics* viii.9.1160a.

4. Leon Festinger, "Group Attraction and Membership," in *Group Dynamics,* ed. Dorwin Cartwright and Alvin Zander (Evanston, Ill.: Row, Peterson, 1953), p. 93.

5. *A Grammar of Politics,* 4th ed. (London: George Allen & Unwin, 1939), p. 67.

6. Philanthropic and religious organizations are not necessarily expected to serve only the interests of their members; such organizations have other purposes that are considered more important, however much their members "need" to belong, or are improved or helped by belonging. But the complexity of such organizations need not be debated at length here, because this study will focus on organizations with a significant economic aspect. The emphasis here will have something in common with what Max Weber called the "associative group"; he called a group associative if

"the orientation of social action with it rests on a rationally motivated agreement." Weber contrasted his "associative group" with the "communal group," which was centered on personal affection, erotic relationships, etc., like the family. (See Weber, pp. 136–139, and Grace Coyle, *Social Process in Organized Groups,* New York: Richard Smith, Inc., 1930, pp. 7–9.) The logic of the theory developed here can be extended to cover communal, religious, and philanthropic organizations, but the theory is not particularly useful in studying such groups. See Olson, pp. 61n17, 159–162.

7. That is, its members. This study does not follow the terminological usage of those organization theorists who describe employees as "members" of the organization for which they work. Here it is more convenient to follow the language of everyday usage instead, and to distinguish the members of, say, a union from the employees of that union. Similarly, the members of the union will be considered employees of the corporation for which they work.

8. Arthur Bentley, *The Process of Government* (Evanston, Ill.: Principia Press, 1949), p. 211. David B. Truman takes a similar approach; see his *The Governmental Process* (New York: Alfred A. Knopf, 1958), pp. 33–35. See also Sidney Verba, *Small Groups and Political Behavior* (Princeton, N.J.: Princeton University Press, 1961), pp. 12–13.

9. Raymond Cattell, "Concepts and Methods in the Measurement of Group Syntality," in *Small Groups,* eds. A. Paul Hare, Edgard F. Borgatta, and Robert F. Bales (New York: Alfred A. Knopf, 1955), p. 115.

10. Any organization or group will of course usually be divided into subgroups or factions that are opposed to one another. This fact does not weaken the assumption made here that organizations exist to serve the common interests of members, for the assumption does not imply that intragroup conflict is neglected. The opposing groups within an organization ordinarily have some interest in common (if not, why would they maintain the organization?), and the members of any subgroup or faction also have a separate common interest of their own. They will indeed often have a common purpose in defeating some other subgroup or faction. The approach used here does not neglect the conflict within groups and organizations, then,

because it considers each organization as a unit only to the extent that it does in fact attempt to serve a common interest, and considers the various subgroups as the relevant units with common interests to analyze the factional strife.

11. For a fuller discussion of this question see Mancur Olson, Jr., and David McFarland, "The Restoration of Pure Monopoly and the Concept of the Industry," *Quarterly Journal of Economics,* LXXVI (November 1962), 613–631.

12. Robert Michels contends in his classic study that "democracy is inconceivable without organization," and that "the principle of organization is an absolutely essential condition for the political struggle of the masses." See his *Political Parties,* trans. Eden and Cedar Paul (New York: Dover Publications, 1959), pp. 21–22. See also Robert A. Brady, *Business as a System of Power* (New York: Columbia University Press, 1943), p. 193.

13. Alexander Heard, *The Costs of Democracy* (Chapel Hill: University of North Carolina Press, 1960), especially note 1, pp. 95–96. For example, in 1947 the National Association of Manufacturers spent over $4.6 million, and over a somewhat longer period the American Medical Association spent as much on a campaign against compulsory health insurance.

14. "If the full truth were ever known . . . lobbying, in all its ramifications, would prove to be a billion dollar industry." U.S. Congress, House, Select Committee on Lobbying Activities, *Report,* 81st Cong., 2nd Sess. (1950), as quoted in the *Congressional Quarterly Almanac,* 81st Cong., 2nd Sess., VI, 764–765.

15. Sociologists as well as economists have observed that ideological motives alone are not sufficient to bring forth the continuing effort of large masses of people. Max Weber provides a notable example:

All economic activity in a market economy is undertaken and carried through by individuals for their own ideal or material interests. This is naturally just as true when economic activity is oriented to the patterns of order of corporate groups. . . .

Even if an economic system were organized on a socialistic basis, there would be no fundamental difference in this respect. . . . The structure of interests and the relevant situation might change; there would be other means of pursuing interests, but this fundamental factor would remain just as relevant as before. It is of course true that economic action which is oriented on purely ideological grounds to the interest of others does exist. But it is even more certain that the mass of men do not act this way, and it is an induction from experience that they cannot do so and never will. . . .

In a market economy the interest in the maximization of income is necessarily the driving force of all economic activity (Weber, pp. 319–320). Talcott Parsons and Neil Smelser go even further in postulating that "performance" throughout society is proportional to the "rewards" and "sanctions" involved. See their Economy and Society (Glencoe, Ill.: Free Press, 1954), pp. 50–69.

16. This simple definition focuses upon two points that are important in the present context. The first point is that most collective goods can only be defined with respect to some specific group. One collective good goes to one group of people, another collective good to another group; one may benefit the whole world, another only two specific people. Moreover, some goods are collective goods to those in one group and at the same time private goods to those in another, because some individuals can be kept from consuming them and others can't. Take for example the parade that is a collective good to all those who live in tall buildings overlooking the parade route, but which appears to be a private good to those who can see it only by buying tickets for a seat in the stands along the way. The second point is that once the relevant group has been defined, the definition used here, like Musgrave's, distinguishes collective good in terms of infeasibility of excluding potential consumers of the good. This approach is used because collective goods produced by organizations of all kinds seem to be such that exclusion is normally not feasible. To be sure, for some collective goods it is physically possible to practice exclusion. But, as Head has shown, it is not necessary that exclusion be technically impossible; it is only necessary that it be infeasible or uneconomic. Head has also shown most clearly that nonexcludability is only one of two basic elements in the traditional understanding of public goods. The other, he points out, is "jointness of supply." A good has "jointness" if making it available to one individual means that it can be easily or freely

supplied to others as well. The polar case of jointness would be Samuelson's pure public good, which is a good such that additional consumption of it by one individual does not diminish the amount available to others. By the definition used here, jointness is not a necessary attribute of a public good. As later parts of this chapter will show, at least one type of collective good considered here exhibits no jointness whatever, and few if any would have the degree of jointness needed to qualify as pure public goods. Nonetheless, most of the collective goods to be studied here do display a large measure of jointness. On the definition and importance of public goods, see John G. Head, "Public Goods and Public Policy," *Public Finance,* vol. XVII, no. 3 (1962), 197–219; Richard Musgrave, *The Theory of Public Finance* (New York: McGraw-Hill, 1959); Paul A. Samuelson, "The Pure Theory of Public Expenditure," "Diagrammatic Exposition of a Theory of Public Expenditure," and "Aspects of Public Expenditure Theories," in *Review of Economics and Statistics,* XXXVI (November 1954), 387–390, XXXVII (November 1955), 350–356, and XL (November 1958), 332–338. For somewhat different opinions about the usefulness of the concept of public goods, see Julius Margolis, "A Comment on the Pure Theory of Public Expenditure," *Review of Economics and Statistics,* XXXVII (November 1955), 347–349, and Gerhard Colm, "Theory of Public Expenditures," *Annals of the American Academy of Political and Social Science,* CLXXXIII (January 1936), 1–11.

17. There is no necessity that a public good to one group in a society is necessarily in the interest of the society as a whole. Just as a tariff could be a public good to the industry that sought it, so the removal of the tariff could be a public good to those who consumed the industry's product. This is equally true when the public-good concept is applied only to governments; for a military expenditure, or a tariff, or an immigration restriction that is a public good to one country could be a "public bad" to another country, and harmful to world society as a whole.

18. R. M. MacIver in *Encyclopaedia of the Social Sciences,* VII (New York: Macmillan, 1932), 147.

19. It does not, however, follow that organized or coordinated group action is *always* necessary to obtain a collective goal.

1-2 The Tragedy of the Commons

Garrett Hardin

In this seminal article, Garrett Hardin identifies another class of collective action problems, the "tragedy of the commons." The concept—a "tragedy" because of the inevitability with which public goods, or the "commons," will be exploited—is generally applied to study cases in which natural resources are being misused. Unlike the problems we have already encountered, which concern the production of public goods, the tragedy of the commons affects their conservation. Because public goods are freely available, members of the community will be tempted to overly consume them—to overfish, to overuse national parks, to pollute public water or air—even as they realize their behavior and that of their neighbors is destroying the goods. Hardin discusses social arrangements that can substitute for the commons, or public ownership of scarce resources, and argues that the tragedy of the commons is becoming a more pressing concern as the population increases. As with the problem of free riding described by Mancur Olson Jr., government authority offers one solution extricating participants from their bind.

At the end of a thoughtful article on the future of nuclear war, Wiesner and York concluded that: "Both sides in the arms race are . . . confronted by the dilemma of steadily increasing military power and steadily decreasing national security. *It is our considered professional judgment that this dilemma has no technical solution.* If the great powers continue to look for solutions in the area of science and technology only, the result will be to worsen the situation."[1]

I would like to focus your attention not on the subject of the article (national security in a nuclear world) but on the kind of conclusion they reached, namely that there is no technical solution to the problem. An implicit and almost universal assumption of discussions published in professional and semipopular scientific journals is that the problem under discussion has a technical solution. A technical solution may be defined as one that requires a change only in the techniques of the natural sciences, demanding little or nothing in the way of change in human values or ideas of morality.

In our day (though not in earlier times) technical solutions are always welcome. . . . [Yet of the] class of human problems which can be called "no technical solution problems" . . . [i]t is easy to show that [it] is not a null class. Recall the game of tick-tack-toe. Consider the problem, "How can I win the game of tick-tack-toe?" It is well known that I cannot, if I assume (in keeping with the conventions of game theory) that my opponent understands the game perfectly. Put another way, there is no "technical solution" to the problem. I can win only by giving a radical meaning to the word "win." I can hit my opponent over the head; or I can drug him; or I can falsify the records. Every way in which I "win" involves, in some sense, an abandonment of the game, as we intuitively understand it. (I can also, of course, openly abandon the game—refuse to play it. This is what most adults do.)

The class of "No technical solution problems" has members. My thesis is that the "population problem," as conventionally conceived, is a member of this class. How it is conventionally conceived needs some comment. It is fair to say that most people who anguish over the population problem are trying to find a way to avoid the evils of overpopulation without relinquishing any of the privileges they now enjoy. They think that farming the seas or developing new strains of wheat will solve the problem—technologically. I try to show here that the solution they seek cannot be found. The population problem cannot be solved in a technical way, any more than can the problem of winning the game of tick-tack-toe.

What Shall We Maximize?

Population, as Malthus said, naturally tends to grow "geometrically," or, as we would now say, exponentially. In a finite world this means that the per capita share of the world's goods must steadily decrease. Is ours a finite world?

A fair defense can be put forward for the view that the world is infinite; or that we do not know that it is not. But, in terms of the practical problems that we must face in the next few generations with the foreseeable technology, it is clear that we will greatly increase human misery if we do not, during the immediate future, assume that the world available to the terrestrial human population is finite. "Space" is no escape.[2]

A finite world can support only a finite population; therefore, population growth must eventually equal zero. . . . When this condition is met, what will be the situation of mankind? Specifically, can [Jeremy] Bentham's goal of "the greatest good for the greatest number" be realized? . . .

The . . . reason [why not] springs directly from biological facts. To live, any organism must have a source of energy (for example, food). This energy is utilized for two purposes: mere maintenance and work. For man, maintenance of life requires about 1600 kilocalories a day ("maintenance calories"). Anything that he does over and above merely staying alive will be defined as work, and is supported by "work calories" which he takes in. Work calories are used not only for what we call work in common speech; they are also required for all forms of enjoyment, from swimming and automobile racing to playing music and writing poetry. If our goal is to maximize population it is obvious what we must do: We must make the work calories per person approach as close to zero as possible. No gourmet meals, no

vacations, no sports, no music, no literature, no art. . . . I think that everyone will grant, without argument or proof, that maximizing population does not maximize goods. Bentham's goal is impossible. . . .

The optimum population is, then, less than the maximum. The difficulty of defining the optimum is enormous; so far as I know, no one has seriously tackled this problem. Reaching an acceptable and stable solution will surely require more than one generation of hard analytical work—and much persuasion. . . .

We can make little progress in working toward optimum population size until we explicitly exorcize the spirit of Adam Smith in the field of practical demography. In economic affairs, *The Wealth of Nations* (1776) popularized the "invisible hand," the idea that an individual who "intends only his own gain," is, as it were, "led by an invisible hand to promote . . . the public interest."[3] Adam Smith did not assert that this was invariably true, and perhaps neither did any of his followers. But he contributed to a dominant tendency of thought that has ever since interfered with positive action based on rational analysis, namely, the tendency to assume that decisions reached individually will, in fact, be the best decisions for an entire society. If this assumption is correct it justifies the continuance of our present policy of laissez-faire in reproduction. If it is correct we can assume that men will control their individual fecundity so as to produce the optimum population. If the assumption is not correct, we need to reexamine our individual freedoms to see which ones are defensible.

Tragedy of Freedom in a Commons

The rebuttal to the invisible hand in population control is to be found in a scenario first sketched in a little-known pamphlet in 1833 by a mathematical amateur named William Forster Lloyd (1794–1852).[4] We may well call it "the tragedy of the commons," using the word "tragedy" as the philosopher Whitehead used it: "The essence of dramatic tragedy is not unhappiness. It resides in the solemnity of the remorseless working of things."[5] He then goes on to say, "This inevitableness of destiny can only be illustrated in terms of human life by incidents which in fact involve unhappiness. For it is only by them that the futility of escape can be made evident in the drama."

The tragedy of the commons develops in this way. Picture a pasture open to all. It is to be expected that each herdsman will try to keep as many cattle as possible on the commons. Such an arrangement may work reasonably satisfactorily for centuries because tribal wars, poaching, and disease keep the numbers of both man and beast well below the carrying capacity of the land. Finally, however, comes the day of reckoning, that is, the day when the long-desired goal of social stability becomes a reality. At this point, the inherent logic of the commons remorselessly generates tragedy.

As a rational being, each herdsman seeks to maximize his gain. Explicitly or implicitly, more or less consciously, he asks, "What is the utility *to me* of adding one more animal to my herd?" This utility has one negative and one positive component.

1. The positive component is a function of the increment of one animal. Since the herdsman receives all the proceeds from the sale of the additional animal, the positive utility is nearly +1.

2. The negative component is a function of the additional overgrazing created by one more animal. Since, however, the effects of overgrazing are shared by all the herdsmen, the negative utility for any particular decision-making herdsman is only a fraction of −1.

Adding together the component partial utilities, the rational herdsman concludes that the only sensible course for him to pursue is to add another animal to his herd. And another. . . . But this is the conclusion reached by each and every rational herdsman sharing a commons. Therein is the tragedy. Each man is locked into a system that compels him to increase his herd without limit—in a world

that is limited. Ruin is the destination toward which all men rush, each pursuing his own best interest in a society that believes in the freedom of the commons. Freedom in a commons brings ruin to all.

Some would say that this is a platitude. Would that it were! In a sense, it was learned thousands of years ago, but natural selection favors the forces of psychological denial.[6] The individual benefits as an individual from his ability to deny the truth even though society as a whole, of which he is a part, suffers. Education can counteract the natural tendency to do the wrong thing, but the inexorable succession of generations requires that the basis for this knowledge be constantly refreshed.

A simple incident that occurred a few years ago in Leominster, Massachusetts, shows how perishable the knowledge is. During the Christmas shopping season the parking meters downtown were covered with plastic bags that bore tags reading: "Do not open until after Christmas. Free parking courtesy of the mayor and city council." In other words, facing the prospect of an increased demand for already scarce space, the city fathers reinstituted the system of the commons. (Cynically, we suspect that they gained more votes than they lost by this retrogressive act.)

In an approximate way, the logic of the commons has been understood for a long time, perhaps since the discovery of agriculture or the invention of private property in real estate. But it is understood mostly only in special cases which are not sufficiently generalized. Even at this late date, cattlemen leasing national land on the western ranges demonstrate no more than an ambivalent understanding, in constantly pressuring federal authorities to increase the head count to the point where overgrazing produces erosion and weed-dominance. Likewise, the oceans of the world continue to suffer from the survival of the philosophy of the commons. Maritime nations still respond automatically to the shibboleth of the "freedom of the seas." Professing to believe in the "inexhaustible resources of the oceans," they bring species after species of fish and whales closer to extinction.[7]

The National Parks present another instance of the working out of the tragedy of the commons. At present, they are open to all, without limit. The parks themselves are limited in extent—there is only one Yosemite Valley—whereas population seems to grow without limit. The values that visitors seek in the parks are steadily eroded. Plainly, we must soon cease to treat the parks as commons or they will be of no value to anyone.

What shall we do? We have several options. We might sell them off as private property. We might keep them as public property, but allocate the right to enter them. The allocation might be on the basis of wealth, by the use of an auction system. It might be on the basis of merit, as defined by some agreed-upon standards. It might be by lottery. Or it might be on a first-come, first-served basis, administered to long queues. These, I think, are all the reasonable possibilities. They are all objectionable. But we must choose—or acquiesce in the destruction of the commons that we call our National Parks.

Pollution

In a reverse way, the tragedy of the commons reappears in problems of pollution. Here it is not a question of taking something out of the commons, but of putting something in—sewage, or chemical, radioactive, and heat wastes into water; noxious and dangerous fumes into the air; and distracting and unpleasant advertising signs into the line of sight. The calculations of utility are much the same as before. The rational man finds that his share of the cost of the wastes he discharges into the commons is less than the cost of purifying his wastes before releasing them. Since this is true for everyone, we are locked into a system of "fouling our own nest," so long as we behave only as independent, rational, free-enterprisers.

The tragedy of the commons as a food basket is averted by private property, or something formally like it. But the air and waters surrounding us cannot readily be fenced, and so the tragedy of the commons as a cesspool must be prevented by different means, by coercive laws or taxing devices that make it cheaper for the polluter to treat his pollutants than to discharge them untreated. We have not progressed as far with the solution of this problem as we have with the first. Indeed, our particular concept of private property, which deters us from exhausting the positive resources of the earth, favors pollution. The owner of a factory on the bank of a stream—whose property extends to the middle of the stream—often has difficulty seeing why it is not his natural right to muddy the waters flowing past his door. The law, always behind the times, requires elaborate stitching and fitting to adapt it to this newly perceived aspect of the commons.

The pollution problem is a consequence of population. It did not much matter how a lonely American frontiersman disposed of his waste. "Flowing water purifies itself every 10 miles," my grandfather used to say, and the myth was near enough to the truth when he was a boy, for there were not too many people. But as population became denser, the natural chemical and biological recycling processes became overloaded, calling for a redefinition of property rights.

How to Legislate Temperance?

Analysis of the pollution problem as a function of population density uncovers a not generally recognized principle of morality, namely: *the morality of an act is a function of the state of the system at the time it is performed.*[8] Using the commons as a cesspool does not harm the general public under frontier conditions, because there is no public; the same behavior in a metropolis is unbearable. A hundred and fifty years ago a plainsman could kill an American bison, cut out only the tongue for his dinner, and discard the rest of the animal. He was not in any important sense being wasteful. Today, with only a few thousand bison left, we would be appalled at such behavior.

In passing, it is worth noting that the morality of an act cannot be determined from a photograph. One does not know whether a man killing an elephant or setting fire to the grassland is harming others until one knows the total system in which his act appears. "One picture is worth a thousand words," said an ancient Chinese; but it may take 10,000 words to validate it. It is as tempting to ecologists as it is to reformers in general to try to persuade others by way of the photographic shortcut. But the essence of an argument cannot be photographed: it must be presented rationally—in words.

That morality is system-sensitive escaped the attention of most codifiers of ethics in the past. "Thou shalt not . . ." is the form of traditional ethical directives which make no allowance for particular circumstances. The laws of our society follow the pattern of ancient ethics, and therefore are poorly suited to governing a complex, crowded, changeable world. Our epicyclic solution is to augment statutory law with administrative law. Since it is practically impossible to spell out all the conditions under which it is safe to burn trash in the back yard or to run an automobile without smog-control, by law we delegate the details to bureaus. The result is administrative law, which is rightly feared for an ancient reason—*Quis custodiet ipsos custodes?*—"Who shall watch the watchers themselves?" John Adams said that we must have "a government of laws and not men." Bureau administrators, trying to evaluate the morality of acts in the total system, are singularly liable to corruption, producing a government by men, not laws.

Prohibition is easy to legislate (though not necessarily to enforce); but how do we legislate temperance? Experience indicates that it can be accomplished best through the mediation of administrative law. We limit possibilities unnecessarily if we suppose that the sentiment of *Quis custodiet* denies us the use of administrative law. We should rather retain the phrase as a perpetual reminder of fearful dangers we cannot avoid. The great challenge facing us now is to invent the corrective feedbacks that are needed to keep custodians honest. We must find ways to legitimate the needed authority of both the custodians and the corrective feedbacks.

Freedom to Breed Is Intolerable

The tragedy of the commons is involved in population problems in another way. In a world governed solely by the principle of "dog eat dog"—if indeed there ever was such a world—how many children a family had would not be a matter of public concern. Parents who bred too exuberantly would leave fewer descendants, not more, because they would be unable to care adequately for their children. David Lack and others have found that such a negative feedback demonstrably controls the fecundity of birds.[9] But men are not birds, and have not acted like them for millenniums, at least.

If each human family were dependent only on its own resources; *if* the children of improvident parents starved to death; *if,* thus, overbreeding brought its own "punishment" to the germ line—*then* there would be no public interest in controlling the breeding of families. But our society is deeply committed to the welfare state,[10] and hence is confronted with another aspect of the tragedy of the commons.

In a welfare state, how shall we deal with the family, the religion, the race, or the class (or indeed any distinguishable and cohesive group) that adopts overbreeding as a policy to secure its own aggrandizement?[11] To couple the concept of freedom to breed with the belief that everyone born has an equal right to the commons is to lock the world into a tragic course of action.

Unfortunately this is just the course of action that is being pursued by the United Nations. In late 1967, some 30 nations agreed to the following: "The Universal Declaration of Human Rights describes the family as the natural and fundamental unit of society. It follows that any choice and decision with regard to the size of the family must irrevocably rest with the family itself, and cannot be made by anyone else."[12] It is painful to have to deny categorically the validity of this right; denying it, one feels as uncomfortable as a resident of Salem, Massachusetts, who denied the reality of witches in the 17th century. At the present time, in liberal quarters, something like a taboo acts to inhibit criticism of the United Nations. There is a feeling that the United Nations is "our last and best hope," that we shouldn't find fault with it; we shouldn't play into the hands of the archconservatives. However, let us not forget what Robert Louis Stevenson said: "The truth that is suppressed by friends is the readiest weapon of the enemy." If we love the truth we must openly deny the validity of the Universal Declaration of Human Rights, even though it is promoted by the United Nations. We should also join with Kingsley Davis in attempting to get Planned Parenthood–World Population to see the error of its ways in embracing the same tragic ideal.[13] . . .

The argument has here been stated in the context of the population problem, but it applies equally well to any instance in which society appeals to an individual exploiting a commons to restrain himself for the general good—by means of his conscience. To make such an appeal is to set up a selective system that works toward the elimination of conscience from the race.

Pathogenic Effects of Conscience

It is a mistake to think that we can control the breeding of mankind in the long run by an appeal to conscience. . . . If we ask a man who is exploiting a commons to desist "in the name of conscience," what are we saying to him? What does he hear?—not only at the moment but also in the wee small hours of the night when, half asleep, he remembers not merely the words we used but also the nonverbal communication cues we gave him unawares? Sooner or later, consciously or subconsciously, he senses that he has received two communications, and that they are contradictory: (i) (intended communication) "If you don't do as we ask, we will openly condemn you for not acting like a responsible citizen"; (ii) (the unintended communication) "If you *do* behave as we ask, we will secretly condemn you for a simpleton who can be shamed into standing aside while the rest of us exploit the commons." . . .

To conjure up a conscience in others is tempting to anyone who wishes to extend his control beyond the legal limits. Leaders at the highest level succumb to this temptation. Has any President during the past generation failed to call on labor unions to moderate voluntarily their demands for higher wages, or to steel companies to honor voluntary guidelines on prices? I can recall none. The rhetoric used on such occasions is designed to produce feelings of guilt in noncooperators.

For centuries it was assumed without proof that guilt was a valuable, perhaps even an indispensable, ingredient of the civilized life. Now, in this post-Freudian world, we doubt it.

Paul Goodman speaks from the modern point of view when he says: "No good has ever come from feeling guilty, neither intelligence, policy, nor compassion. The guilty do not pay attention to the object but only to themselves, and not even to their own interests, which might make sense, but to their anxieties."[14]

One does not have to be a professional psychiatrist to see the consequences of anxiety. We in the Western world are just emerging from a dreadful two-centuries-long Dark Ages of Eros that was sustained partly by prohibition laws, but perhaps more effectively by the anxiety-generating mechanisms of education. Alex Comfort has told the story well in *The Anxiety Makers;* it is not a pretty one.[15]

Since proof is difficult, we may even concede that the results of anxiety may sometimes, from certain points of view, be desirable. The larger question we should ask is whether, as a matter of policy, we should ever encourage the use of a technique the tendency (if not the intention) of which is psychologically pathogenic. We hear much talk these days of responsible parenthood; the coupled words are incorporated into the titles of some organizations devoted to birth control. Some people have proposed massive propaganda campaigns to instill responsibility into the nation's (or the world's) breeders. But what is the meaning of the word responsibility in this context? Is it not merely a synonym for the word conscience? When we use the word responsibility in the absence of substantial sanctions are we not trying to browbeat a free man in a commons into acting against his own interest? Responsibility is a verbal counterfeit for a substantial *quid pro quo.* It is an attempt to get something for nothing.

If the word responsibility is to be used at all, I suggest that it be in the sense Charles Frankel uses it.[16] "Responsibility," says this philosopher, "is the product of definite social arrangements." Notice that Frankel calls for social arrangements—not propaganda.

Mutual Coercion, Mutually Agreed Upon

The social arrangements that produce responsibility are arrangements that create coercion, of some sort. Consider bank-robbing. The man who takes money from a bank acts as if the bank were a commons. How do we prevent such action? Certainly not by trying to control his behavior solely by a verbal appeal to his sense of responsibility. Rather than rely on propaganda we follow Frankel's lead and insist that a bank is not a commons; we seek the definite social arrangements that will keep it from becoming a commons. That we thereby infringe on the freedom of would-be robbers we neither deny nor regret.

The morality of bank-robbing is particularly easy to understand because we accept complete prohibition of this activity. We are willing to say "Thou shalt not rob banks," without providing for exceptions. But temperance also can be created by coercion. Taxing is a good coercive device. To keep downtown shoppers temperate in their use of parking space we introduce parking meters for short periods, and traffic fines for longer ones. We need not actually forbid a citizen to park as long as he wants to; we need merely make it increasingly expensive for him to do so. Not prohibition, but carefully biased options are what we offer him. A Madison Avenue man might call this persuasion; I prefer the greater candor of the word coercion.

Coercion is a dirty word to most liberals now, but it need not forever be so. As with the four-letter words, its dirtiness can be cleansed away by exposure to the light, by saying it over and over without apology or embarrassment. To many, the word coercion implies arbitrary decisions of distant and irresponsible bureaucrats; but this is not a necessary part of its meaning. The only kind of coercion I recommend is mutual coercion, mutually agreed upon by the majority of the people affected.

To say that we mutually agree to coercion is not to say that we are required to enjoy it, or even to pretend we enjoy it. Who enjoys taxes? We all grumble about them. But we accept compulsory taxes because we recognize that voluntary taxes would favor the conscienceless. We institute and (grumblingly) support taxes and other coercive devices to escape the horror of the commons.

An alternative to the commons need not be perfectly just to be preferable. With real estate and other material goods, the alternative we have chosen is the institution of private property coupled with legal inheritance. Is this system perfectly just? As a genetically trained biologist I deny that it is. It seems to me that, if there are to be differences in individual inheritance, legal possession should be perfectly correlated with biological inheritance—that those who are biologically more fit to be the custodians of property and power should legally inherit more. But genetic recombination continually makes a mockery of the doctrine of "like father, like son" implicit in our laws of legal inheritance. An idiot can inherit millions, and a trust fund can keep his estate intact. We must admit that our legal system of private property plus inheritance is unjust—but we put up with it because we are not convinced, at the moment, that anyone has invented a better system. The alternative of the commons is too horrifying to contemplate. Injustice is preferable to total ruin.

It is one of the peculiarities of the warfare between reform and the status quo that it is thoughtlessly governed by a double standard. Whenever a reform measure is proposed it is often defeated when its opponents triumphantly discover a flaw in it. As Kingsley Davis has pointed out,[17] worshippers of the status quo sometimes imply that no reform is possible without unanimous agreement, an implication contrary to historical fact. As nearly as I can make out, automatic rejection of proposed reforms is based on one of two unconscious assumptions: (i) that the status quo is perfect; or (ii) that the choice we face is between reform and no action; if the proposed reform is imperfect, we presumably should take no action at all, while we wait for a perfect proposal.

But we can never do nothing. That which we have done for thousands of years is also action. It also produces evils. Once we are aware that the status quo is action, we can then compare its discoverable advantages and disadvantages with the predicted advantages and disadvantages of the proposed reform, discounting as best we can for our lack of experience. On the basis of such a comparison, we can make a rational decision which will not involve the unworkable assumption that only perfect systems are tolerable.

Recognition of Necessity

Perhaps the simplest summary of this analysis of man's population problems is this: the commons, if justifiable at all, is justifiable only under conditions of low-population density. As the human population has increased, the commons has had to be abandoned in one aspect after another.

First we abandoned the commons in food gathering, enclosing farm land and restricting pastures and hunting and fishing areas. These restrictions are still not complete throughout the world.

Somewhat later we saw that the commons as a place for waste disposal would also have to be abandoned. Restrictions on the disposal of domestic sewage are widely accepted in the Western world; we are still struggling to close the commons to pollution by automobiles, factories, insecticide sprayers, fertilizing operations, and atomic energy installations.

In a still more embryonic state is our recognition of the evils of the commons in matters of pleasure. There is almost no restriction on the propagation of sound waves in the public medium. The shopping public is assaulted with mindless music, without its consent. Our government is paying out billions of dollars to create supersonic transport which will disturb 50,000 people for every one person who is whisked from coast to coast 3 hours faster. Advertisers muddy the airwaves of radio and television and pollute the view of travelers. We are a long way from outlawing the commons in matters of pleasure. Is this because our Puritan inheritance makes us view pleasure as something of a sin, and pain (that is, the pollution of advertising) as the sign of virtue?

Every new enclosure of the commons involves the infringement of somebody's personal liberty. Infringements made in the distant past are accepted because no contemporary complains of a loss. It is the newly proposed infringements that we vigorously oppose; cries of "rights" and "freedom" fill the air. But what does "freedom" mean? When men mutually agreed to pass laws against robbing, mankind became more free, not less so. Individuals locked into the logic of the commons are free only to bring on universal ruin; once they see the necessity of mutual coercion, they become free to pursue other goals. I believe it was Hegel who said, "Freedom is the recognition of necessity."

The most important aspect of necessity that we must now recognize, is the necessity of abandoning the commons in breeding. No technical solution can rescue us from the misery of overpopulation. Freedom to breed will bring ruin to all. At the moment, to avoid hard decisions many of us are tempted to propagandize for conscience and responsible parenthood. The temptation must be resisted, because an appeal to independently acting consciences selects for the disappearance of all conscience in the long run, and an increase in anxiety in the short.

The only way we can preserve and nurture other and more precious freedoms is by relinquishing the freedom to breed, and that very soon. "Freedom is the recognition of necessity"—and it is the role of education to reveal to all the necessity of abandoning the freedom to breed. Only so, can we put an end to this aspect of the tragedy of the commons.

Notes

1. J. B. Wiesner and H. F. York, *Sci. Amer.* 211 (No. 4), 27 (1964).

2. G. Hardin, *J. Hered.* 50, 68 (1959); S. von Hoernor, *Science* 137, 18 (1962).

3. A. Smith, *The Wealth of Nations* (Modern Library, New York, 1937), p. 423.

4. W. F. Lloyd, *Two Lectures on the Checks to Population* (Oxford Univ. Press, Oxford, England, 1833), reprinted (in part) in *Population, Evolution, and Birth Control,* G. Hardin, Ed. (Freeman, San Francisco, 1964), p. 37.

5. A. N. Whitehead, *Science and the Modern World* (Mentor, New York, 1948), p. 17.

6. G. Hardin, Ed. *Population, Evolution and Birth Control* (Freeman, San Francisco, 1964), p. 56.

7. S. McVay, *Sci. Amer.* 216 (No. 8), 13 (1966).

8. J. Fletcher, *Situation Ethics* (Westminster, Philadelphia, 1966).

9. D. Lack, *The Natural Regulation of Animal Numbers* (Clarendon Press, Oxford, 1954).

10. H. Girvetz, *From Wealth to Welfare* (Stanford Univ. Press, Stanford, Calif., 1950).

11. G. Hardin, *Perspec. Biol. Med.* 6, 366 (1963).

12. U. Thant, *Int. Planned Parenthood News,* No. 168 (February 1968), p. 3.

13. K. Davis, *Science* 158, 730 (1967).

14. P. Goodman, *New York Rev. Books* 10(8), 22 (23 May 1968).

15. A. Comfort, *The Anxiety Makers* (Nelson, London, 1967).

16. C. Frankel, *The Case for Modern Man* (Harper, New York, 1955), p. 203.

17. J. D. Roslansky, *Genetics and the Future of Man* (Appleton-Century-Crofts, New York, 1966), p. 177.

Chapter 2

The Constitutional Framework

2-1 *Anti-Federalist* No. 3

Brutus
November 15, 1787

*After the Constitutional Convention, most of the delegates returned home to pro-
mote ratification by their states. Some, however, had opposed the final plan for the
new government. They, along with allies who had boycotted the Convention, began
lobbying their state legislatures to reject ratification. The two sides battled each other
in the nation's newspapers. We celebrate the winners as the Framers, as contemporaries frequently called them.*

*Weeks after the Convention, Alexander Hamilton, James Madison, and John Jay
launched a series of pro-ratification newspaper articles under the pen name Publius;
collectively, they called themselves "Federalists," in order to allay misgivings about
the creation of the new, more resourceful national government. After ratification,
their eighty-five essays were published in book form as* The Federalist, *and subsequently as* The Federalist Papers. *(Thomas Jefferson immediately added it to the
required reading list of all University of Virginia undergraduates.)*

*Their opponents, known as the "Anti-Federalists," were also capable political think-
ers. While history has tended to denigrate them as "men of little faith," it is difficult to
find fault with much of their reasoning. In the essay below—one of sixteen penned by
Brutus (likely New York delegate Robert Yates)—the author highlights some serious
issues with the new Constitution and its plan of "nominal" representation. How can
the presence of a distant, national government advance democracy (popular control)
over that presently provided by the smaller states' own assemblies? Why should a
small, unelected, malapportioned Senate be permitted to veto any proposal arising in
the more democratic institution, the House of Representatives? Both are serious problems which Madison grapples with in his famous "rebuttals" in the next readings.*

To the citizens of the State of New-York.
In the investigation of the constitution, under
your consideration, great care should be taken,
that you do not form your opinions respecting
it, from unimportant provisions, or fallacious
appearances.

On a careful examination, you will find, that
many of its parts, of little moment, are well formed;
in these it has a specious resemblance of a free government—but this is not sufficient to justify the
adoption of it—the gilded pill, is often found to
contain the most deadly poison.

You are not however to expect, a perfect form of government, any more than to meet with perfection in man: your views therefore, ought to be directed to the main pillars upon which a free government is to rest. . . . Under these impressions, it has been my object to turn your attention to the principal defects in this system. . . . I shall now [in this third essay] proceed . . . to examine its parts more minutely, and show that the powers are not properly deposited, for the security of public liberty.

The first important object that presents itself in the organization of this government, is the legislature. This is to be composed of two branches; the first to be called the general assembly [the House of Representatives], and is to be chosen by the people of the respective states, in proportion to the number of their inhabitants, and is to consist of sixty five members, with powers in the legislature to increase the number, not to exceed one for every thirty thousand inhabitants. The second branch is to be called the senate, and is to consist of twenty-six members, two of which are to be chosen by the legislatures of each of the states.

In the former of these there is an appearance of justice, in the appointment of its members—but if the clause, which provides for this branch, be stripped of its ambiguity, it will be found that there is really no equality of representation, even in this house.

The words are "representatives and direct taxes, shall be apportioned among the several states, which may be included in this union, according to their respective numbers, which shall be determined by adding to the whole number of free persons, including those bound to service for a term of years, and excluding Indians not taxed, three fifths of all other persons."—What a strange and unnecessary accumulation of words are here used to conceal from the public eye what might have been expressed in the following concise manner. Representatives are to be proportioned among the states respectively, according to the number of freemen and slaves inhabiting them, counting five slaves for three free men.

"In a free state," says the celebrated Montesquieu, "every man who is supposed to be a free agent, ought to be concerned in his own government. Therefore the legislature should reside in the whole body of the people, or their representatives." But it has never been alleged that those who are not free agents, can, upon any rational principle, have any thing to do in government, either by themselves or others. If they have no share in government, why is the number of members in the assembly, to be increased on their account? Is it because in some of the states, a considerable part of the property of the inhabitants consists in a number of their fellow men, who are held in bondage, in defiance of every idea of benevolence, justice, and religion, and contrary to all the principles of liberty, which have been publicly avowed in the late glorious revolution? If this be a just ground for representation, the horses in some of the states, and the oxen in others, ought to be represented—for a great share of property in some of them consists in these animals; and they have as much control over their own actions, as these poor unhappy creatures, who are intended to be described in the above recited clause, by the words, "all other persons." By this mode of apportionment, the representatives of the different parts of the union will be extremely unequal. . . .

There appears at the first view a manifest inconsistency in the apportionment of representatives in the senate, upon the plan of a consolidated government. On every principle of equity, and propriety, representation in a government should be in exact proportion to the numbers, or the aids afforded by the persons represented. How unreasonable and unjust then is it that Delaware should have a representation in the senate, equal to Massachusetts, or Virginia, the latter of which contains ten times her numbers . . . ? This article of the constitution will appear the more objectionable, if it is considered, that the powers vested in this branch of the legislature are very extensive, and greatly surpass those lodged in the assembly [House of Representatives], not only for general purposes, but in many instances, for the internal police of the states. The Other branch of the legislature, in which, if in either, a faint spark of democracy is to be found, should have been properly organized and established—but upon examination you will find, that this branch does not possess the qualities of a just representation, and that there is no kind of security, imperfect as it is for its remaining in the hands of the people. . . .

The very term, representative, implies, that the person or body chosen for this purpose, should resemble those who appoint them. A representation of the people of America, if it be a true one, must be like the people. It ought to be so constituted, that a person, who is a stranger to the country, might be able to form a just idea of their character, by knowing that of their representatives. . . . Society instituted government to promote the happiness of the whole, and this is the great end always in view in the delegation of powers. It must then have been intended, that those who are placed instead of the people, should possess their sentiments and feelings, and be governed by their interests, or, in other words, should bear the strongest resemblance of those in whose room they are substituted. It is obvious, that for an assembly to be a true likeness of the people of any country, they must be considerably numerous. One man or a few men cannot possibly represent the feelings, opinions, and characters of a great multitude. In this respect, the new constitution is radically defective. The house of assembly, which is intended as a representation of the people of America, will not, nor cannot, in the nature of things, be a proper one. Sixty-five men cannot be found in the United States, who hold the sentiments, possess the feelings, or are acquainted with the wants and interests of this vast country. This extensive continent is made up of a number of different classes of people; and to have a proper representation of them each class ought to have an opportunity of choosing their best informed men for the purpose; but this cannot possibly be the case in so small a number. The state of New York, on the present apportionment, will send six members to the assembly: I will venture to affirm, that number cannot be found in the state, who will bear a just resemblance to the several classes of people who compose it. In this assembly, the farmer, merchant, mechanic and other various orders of people, ought

to be represented according to their respective weight and numbers; and the representatives ought to be intimately acquainted with the wants, understand the interests of the several orders in the society, and feel a proper sense and becoming zeal to promote their prosperity.

I cannot conceive that any six men in this state can be found properly qualified in these respects to discharge such important duties: but supposing it possible to find them, is there the least degree of probability that the choice of the people will fall upon such men? According to the common course of human affairs, the natural aristocracy of the country will be elected. Wealth always creates influence, and this is generally much increased by large family connections: this class in society will for ever have a great number of dependents; besides, they will always favor each other—it is their interest to combine—they will therefore constantly unite their efforts to procure men of their own rank to be elected—they will concentrate all their force in every part of the state into one point, and by acting together, will most generally carry their election. It is probable, that but few of the merchants, and those most opulent and ambitious, will have a representation from their body. Few of them are characters sufficiently conspicuous to attract the notice of the electors of the state in so limited a representation. The great body of the yeomen of the country cannot expect any of their order in this assembly. The station will be too elevated for them to aspire to. The distance between the people and their representatives will be so very great that there is no probability that a farmer, however respectable, will be chosen. The mechanics of every branch, must expect to be excluded from a seat in this Body. It will and must be esteemed a station too high and exalted to be filled by any but the first men in the state, in point of fortune; so that in reality there will be no part of the people represented, but the rich, even in that branch of the legislature, which is called the democratic. The well born, and highest orders in life, as they term themselves, will be ignorant of the sentiments of the middling class of citizens, strangers to their ability,

not enough representatives
of all interests

wants, and difficulties, and void of sympathy, and fellow feeling. This branch of the legislature will not only be an imperfect representation, but there will be no security in so small a body, against bribery, and corruption. It will consist at first, of sixty-five, and can never exceed one for every thirty thousand inhabitants; a majority of these, that is, thirty-three, are a quorum, and a majority of which, or seventeen, may pass any law—so that twenty-five men, will have the power to give away all the property of the citizens of these states. What security therefore can there be for the people, where their liberties and property are at the disposal of so few men? It will literally be a government in the hands of the few to oppress and plunder the many. . . . The rulers of this country must be composed of very different materials . . . if the majority of the legislature are not, before many years, entirely at the devotion of the executive. . . .

The more I reflect on this subject, the more firmly am I persuaded, that the representation is merely nominal—a mere burlesque; and that no security is provided against corruption and undue influence. No free people on earth, who have elected persons to legislate for them, ever reposed that confidence in so small a number. The British house of commons consists of five hundred and fifty-eight members; the number of inhabitants in Great Britain is computed at eight millions. This gives one member for a little more than fourteen thousand, which exceeds double the proportion this country can ever have: and yet we require a larger representation in proportion to our numbers, than Great Britain, because this country is much more extensive, and differs more in its productions, interests, manners, and habits. The democratic branch of the legislatures of the several states in the union consists, I believe at present, of near two thousand; and this number was not thought too large for the security of liberty by the framers of our state constitutions: some of the states may have erred in this respect, but the difference between two thousand, and sixty-five, is so very great, that it will bear no comparison.

Other objections offer themselves against this part of the constitution. I shall reserve them for a future paper, when I shall show, defective as this representation is, no security is provided that even this shadow of the right will remain with the people.

2-2 *Federalist* No. 10

James Madison
November 22, 1787

When one reads this tightly reasoned, highly conceptual essay, it is easy to forget that it was published in a New York newspaper with the purpose of persuading that state's ratification convention to endorse the Constitution. Although after ratification this essay went unnoticed for more than a century, today it stands atop virtually every scholar's ranking of The Federalist *essays. Written in November 1787, it was James Madison's first contribution to the ratification debate. In responding to Brutus's claim that only small democracies are viable, Madison develops a persuasive rationale for a large, diverse republic—one that he had employed several times in debates at the Convention and that his pro-ratification allies had popularized. The modern reader can appreciate how it resonates with the nation's diversity of interests in the twenty-first century. And everyone, then and now, can admire the solid logic employed by this intelligent man, who begins with a few unobjectionable assumptions and derives from them the counterintuitive conclusion that the surest way to avoid the tyranny of faction is to design a political system in which factions are numerous and none can dominate. This essay repays careful reading.*

Among the numerous advantages promised by a well-constructed Union, none deserves to be more accurately developed than its tendency to break and control the violence of faction. The friend of popular governments never finds himself so much alarmed for their character and fate, as when he contemplates their propensity to this dangerous vice. He will not fail, therefore, to set a due value on any plan which, without violating the principles to which he is attached, provides a proper cure for it. The instability, injustice, and confusion introduced into the public councils, have, in truth, been the mortal diseases under which popular governments have everywhere perished; as they continue to be the favorite and fruitful topics from which the adversaries to liberty derive their most specious declamations. The valuable improvements made by the American constitutions on the popular models, both ancient and modern, cannot certainly be too much admired; but it would be an unwarrantable partiality, to contend that they have as effectually

obviated the danger on this side, as was wished and expected. Complaints are everywhere heard from our most considerate and virtuous citizens, equally the friends of public and private faith, and of public and personal liberty, that our governments are too unstable, that the public good is disregarded in the conflicts of rival parties, and that measures are too often decided, not according to the rules of justice and the rights of the minor party, but by the superior force of an interested and overbearing majority. However anxiously we may wish that these complaints had no foundation, the evidence, of known facts will not permit us to deny that they are in some degree true. It will be found, indeed, on a candid review of our situation, that some of the distresses under which we labor have been erroneously charged on the operation of our governments; but it will be found, at the same time, that other causes will not alone account for many of our heaviest misfortunes; and, particularly, for that prevailing and increasing distrust of public engagements, and alarm for private rights, which are echoed from one end of the continent to the other. These must be chiefly, if not wholly, effects of the unsteadiness and injustice with which a factious spirit has tainted our public administrations.

By a faction, I understand a number of citizens, whether amounting to a majority or a minority of the whole, who are united and actuated by some common impulse of passion, or of interest, adversed to the rights of other citizens, or to the permanent and aggregate interests of the community.

There are two methods of curing the mischiefs of faction: the one, by removing its causes; the other, by controlling its effects. There are again two methods of removing the causes of faction: the one, by destroying the liberty which is essential to its existence; the other, by giving to every citizen the same opinions, the same passions, and the same interests.

It could never be more truly said than of the first remedy, that it was worse than the disease. Liberty is to faction what air is to fire, an aliment without which it instantly expires. But it could not be less folly to abolish liberty, which is essential to political life, because it nourishes faction, than it would be to wish the annihilation of air, which is essential to animal life, because it imparts to fire its destructive agency.

The second expedient is as impracticable as the first would be unwise. As long as the reason of man continues fallible, and he is at liberty to exercise it, different opinions will be formed. As long as the connection subsists between his reason and his self-love, his opinions and his passions will have a reciprocal influence on each other; and the former will be objects to which the latter will attach themselves. The diversity in the faculties of men, from which the rights of property originate, is not less an insuperable obstacle to a uniformity of interests. The protection of these faculties is the first object of government. From the protection of different and unequal faculties of acquiring property, the possession of different degrees and kinds of property immediately results; and from the influence of these on the sentiments and views of the respective proprietors, ensues a division of the society into different interests and parties.

The latent causes of faction are thus sown in the nature of man; and we see them everywhere brought into different degrees of activity, according to the different circumstances of civil society. A zeal for different opinions concerning religion, concerning government, and many other points, as well of speculation as of practice; an attachment to different leaders ambitiously contending for pre-eminence and power; or to persons of other descriptions whose fortunes have been interesting to the human passions, have, in turn, divided mankind into parties, inflamed them with mutual animosity, and rendered them much more disposed to vex and oppress each other than to co-operate for their common good. So strong is this propensity of mankind to fall into mutual animosities, that where no substantial occasion presents itself, the most frivolous and fanciful distinctions have been sufficient to kindle their unfriendly passions and excite their most violent conflicts. But the most common and durable source of factions has been the various and unequal distribution of property. Those who hold and those who are without property have ever formed distinct interests in society. Those who are creditors, and those who are debtors, fall under a like discrimination. A landed interest, a manufacturing interest, a mercantile interest, a moneyed interest, with many lesser interests, grow up of necessity in civilized nations, and divide them into different classes, actuated by different sentiments and views. The regulation of these various and interfering interests forms the principal task of modern legislation, and involves the spirit of party and faction in the necessary and ordinary operations of the government.

No man is allowed to be a judge in his own cause, because his interest would certainly bias his judgment, and, not improbably, corrupt his integrity. With equal, nay with greater reason, a body of men are unfit to be both judges and parties at the same time; yet what are many of the most important acts of legislation, but so many judicial determinations, not indeed concerning the rights of single persons, but concerning the rights of large bodies of citizens? And what are the different classes of legislators but advocates and parties to the causes which they determine? Is a law proposed concerning private debts? It is a question to which the creditors are parties on one side and the debtors on the other. Justice ought to hold the balance between them. Yet the parties are, and must be, themselves the judges; and the most numerous party, or, in other words, the most powerful faction must be expected to prevail. Shall domestic manufactures be encouraged, and in what degree, by restrictions on foreign manufactures? are questions which would be differently decided by the landed and the manufacturing classes, and probably by neither with a sole regard to justice and the public good. The apportionment of taxes on the various descriptions of property is an act which seems to require the most exact impartiality; yet there is, perhaps, no legislative act in which greater opportunity and temptation are given to a predominant party to trample on the rules of justice. Every shilling with which they overburden the inferior number, is a shilling saved to their own pockets.

It is in vain to say that enlightened statesmen will be able to adjust these clashing interests, and render them all subservient to the public good. Enlightened statesmen will not always be at the helm. Nor, in many cases, can such an adjustment be made at all without taking into view indirect and remote considerations, which will rarely prevail over the immediate interest which one party may find in disregarding the rights of another or the good of the whole. The inference to which we are brought is, that the causes of faction cannot be removed, and that relief is only to be sought in the means of controlling its effects.

If a faction consists of less than a majority, relief is supplied by the republican principle, which enables the majority to defeat its sinister views by regular vote. It may clog the administration, it may convulse the society; but it will be unable to execute and mask its violence under the forms of the Constitution. When a majority is included in a faction, the form of popular government, on the other hand, enables it to sacrifice to its ruling passion or interest both the public good and the rights of other citizens. To

secure the public good and private rights against the danger of such a faction, and at the same time to preserve the spirit and the form of popular government, is then the great object to which our inquiries are directed. Let me add that it is the great desideratum by which this form of government can be rescued from the opprobrium under which it has so long labored, and be recommended to the esteem and adoption of mankind.

By what means is this object attainable? Evidently by one of two only. Either the existence of the same passion or interest in a majority at the same time must be prevented, or the majority, having such coexistent passion or interest, must be rendered, by their number and local situation, unable to concert and carry into effect schemes of oppression. If the impulse and the opportunity be suffered to coincide, we well know that neither moral nor religious motives can be relied on as an adequate control. They are not found to be such on the injustice and violence of individuals, and lose their efficacy in proportion to the number combined together, that is, in proportion as their efficacy becomes needful.

From this view of the subject it may be concluded that a pure democracy, by which I mean a society consisting of a small number of citizens, who assemble and administer the government in person, can admit of no cure for the mischiefs of faction. A common passion or interest will, in almost every case, be felt by a majority of the whole; a communication and concert result from the form of government itself; and there is nothing to check the inducements to sacrifice the weaker party or an obnoxious individual. Hence it is that such democracies have ever been spectacles of turbulence and contention; have ever been found incompatible with personal security or the rights of property; and have in general been as short in their lives as they have been violent in their deaths. Theoretic politicians, who have patronized this species of government, have erroneously supposed that by reducing mankind to a perfect equality in their political rights, they would, at the same time, be perfectly equalized and assimilated in their possessions, their opinions, and their passions.

lots of interests

A republic, by which I mean a government in which the scheme of representation takes place, opens a different prospect, and promises the cure for which we are seeking. Let us examine the points in which it varies from pure democracy, and we shall comprehend both the nature of the cure and the efficacy which it must derive from the Union.

The two great points of difference between a democracy and a republic are: first, the delegation of the government, in the latter, to a small number of citizens elected by the rest; secondly, the greater number of citizens, and greater sphere of country, over which the latter may be extended. The effect of the first difference is, on the one hand, to refine and enlarge the public views, by passing them through the medium of a chosen body of citizens, whose wisdom may best discern the true interest of their country, and whose patriotism and love of justice will be least likely to sacrifice it to temporary or partial considerations. Under such a regulation, it may well happen that the public voice, pronounced by the representatives of the people, will be more consonant to the public good than if pronounced by the people themselves, convened for the purpose. On the other hand, the effect may be inverted. Men of factious tempers, of local prejudices, or of sinister designs, may, by intrigue, by corruption, or by other means, first obtain the suffrages, and then betray the interests, of the people. The question resulting is, whether small or extensive republics are more favorable to the election of proper guardians of the public weal; and it is clearly decided in favor of the latter by two obvious considerations.

In the first place, it is to be remarked that, however small the republic may be, the representatives must be raised to a certain number, in order to guard against the cabals of a few; and that, however large it may be, they must be limited to a certain number, in order to guard against the confusion of a multitude. Hence, the number of representatives in the two cases not being in proportion to that of the two constituents, and being proportionally greater in the small republic, it follows that, if the proportion of fit characters be not less in the large than in the small republic, the former will present a greater option, and consequently a greater probability of a fit choice.

In the next place, as each representative will be chosen by a greater number of citizens in the large than in the small republic, it will be more difficult for unworthy candidates to practice with success the vicious arts by which elections are too often carried; and the suffrages of the people being more free, will be more likely to centre in men who possess the most attractive merit and the most diffusive and established characters.

It must be confessed that in this, as in most other cases, there is a mean, on both sides of which inconveniences will be found to lie. By enlarging too much the number of electors, you render the representatives too little acquainted with all their local circumstances and lesser interests; as by reducing it too much, you render him unduly attached to these, and too little fit to comprehend and pursue great and national objects. The federal Constitution forms a happy combination in this respect; the great and aggregate interests being referred to the national, the local and particular to the State legislatures.

The other point of difference is, the greater number of citizens and extent of territory which may be brought within the compass of republican than of democratic government; and it is this circumstance principally which renders factious combinations less to be dreaded in the former than in the latter. The smaller the society, the fewer probably will be the distinct parties and interests composing it; the fewer the distinct parties and interests, the more frequently will a majority be found of the same party; and the smaller the number of individuals composing a majority, and the smaller the compass within which they are placed, the more easily will they concert and execute their plans of oppression. Extend the sphere, and you take in a greater variety of parties and interests; you make it less probable that a majority of the whole will have a common motive to invade the rights of other citizens; or if such a common motive exists, it will be more difficult for all who feel it to discover their own strength, and to act in unison with each other. Besides other impediments, it may be remarked that, where there is a consciousness of unjust or dishonorable purposes, communication is always checked by distrust in proportion to the number whose concurrence is necessary.

Hence, it clearly appears, that the same advantage which a republic has over a democracy, in controlling the effects of faction, is enjoyed by a large over a small republic,—is enjoyed by the Union over the States composing it. Does the advantage consist in the substitution of representatives whose enlightened views and virtuous sentiments render them superior to local prejudices and schemes of injustice? It will not be denied that the representation of the Union will be most likely to possess these requisite endowments. Does it consist in the greater security afforded by a greater variety of parties, against the event of any one party being able to outnumber and oppress the rest? In an equal degree does the increased variety of parties comprised within the Union, increase this security. Does it, in fine, consist in the greater obstacles opposed to the concert and accomplishment of the secret wishes of an unjust and interested majority? Here, again, the extent of the Union gives it the most palpable advantage.

The influence of factious leaders may kindle a flame within their particular States, but will be unable to spread a general conflagration through the other States. A religious sect may degenerate into a political faction in a part of the Confederacy; but the variety of sects dispersed over the entire face of it must secure the national councils against any danger from that source. A rage for paper money, for an abolition of debts, for an equal division of property, or for any other improper or wicked project, will be less apt to pervade the whole body of the Union than a particular member of it; in the same proportion as such a malady is more likely to taint a particular county or district, than an entire State.

In the extent and proper structure of the Union, therefore, we behold a republican remedy for the diseases most incident to republican government. And according to the degree of pleasure and pride we feel in being republicans, ought to be our zeal in cherishing the spirit and supporting the character of Federalists.

2-3 *Federalist* No. 51

James Madison

February 8, 1788

Where Federalist No. 10 finds solution to tyranny in the way society is organized, No. 51 turns its attention to the Constitution. In a representative democracy citizens must delegate authority to their representatives. But what is to prevent these ambitious politicians from feathering their own nests or usurping power altogether at their constituencies' expense? The solution, according to James Madison, is to be found in "pitting ambition against ambition," just as the solution in No. 10 lay in pitting interest against interest. In this essay, Madison explains how the Constitution's system of checks and balances will accomplish this goal. Note that he does not try to refute Brutus directly by defending the design of the Senate, which would have been a tough argument. Rather he assumes a different premise—namely, the popularly elected House of Representatives will push the envelope of its authority. He then avers that the Senate and the executive may find the House irresistible, requiring some future Convention to strengthen these institutions to buttress separation of powers.

To what expedient, then, shall we finally resort, for maintaining in practice the necessary partition of power among the several departments, as laid down in the Constitution? The only answer that can be given is, that as all these exterior provisions are found to be inadequate, the defect must be supplied, by so contriving the interior structure of the government as that its several constituent parts may, by their mutual relations, be the means of keeping each other in their proper places. Without presuming to undertake a full development of this important idea, I will hazard a few general observations, which may perhaps place it in a clearer light, and enable us to form a more correct judgment of the principles and structure of the government planned by the convention.

In order to lay a due foundation for that separate and distinct exercise of the different powers of government, which to a certain extent is admitted on all hands to be essential to the preservation of liberty, it is evident that each department should have a will of its own; and consequently should be so constituted that the members of each should have as little agency as possible in the appointment of the members of the others. Were this principle rigorously adhered to, it would require that all the appointments for the supreme executive, legislative, and judiciary magistracies should be drawn from the same fountain of authority, the people, through channels having no communication whatever with one another. Perhaps such a plan of constructing the several departments would be less difficult in practice than it may in contemplation appear. Some difficulties, however, and some additional expense would attend the execution of it. Some deviations, therefore, from the principle must be admitted. In the constitution of the judiciary department in particular, it might be inexpedient to insist rigorously on the principle: first, because peculiar qualifications being essential in the members, the primary consideration ought to be to select that mode of choice which best secures these qualifications; secondly, because the permanent tenure by which the appointments are held in that department, must soon destroy all sense of dependence on the authority conferring them.

It is equally evident, that the members of each department should be as little dependent as possible on those of the others, for the emoluments annexed to their offices. Were the executive magistrate, or the judges, not independent of the legislature in this particular, their independence in every other would be merely nominal.

But the great security against a gradual concentration of the several powers in the same department, consists in giving to those who administer each department the necessary constitutional means and personal motives to resist encroachments of the others. The provision for defense must in this, as in all other cases, be made commensurate to the danger of attack. Ambition must be made to counteract ambition. The interest of the man must be connected with the constitutional rights of the place. It may be a reflection on human nature, that such devices should be necessary to control the abuses of government. But what is government itself, but the greatest of all reflections on human nature? If men were angels, no government would be necessary. If angels were to govern men, neither external nor internal controls on government would be necessary. In framing a government which is to be administered by men over men, the great difficulty lies in this: you must first enable the government to control the governed; and in the next place oblige it to control itself. A dependence on the people is, no doubt, the primary control on the government; but experience has taught mankind the necessity of auxiliary precautions.

This policy of supplying, by opposite and rival interests, the defect of better motives, might be traced through the whole system of human affairs, private as well as public. We see it particularly displayed in all the subordinate distributions of power, where the constant aim is to divide and arrange the several offices in such a manner as that each may be a check on the other; that the private interest of every individual may be a sentinel over the public rights. These inventions of prudence cannot be less requisite in the distribution of the supreme powers of the State.

But it is not possible to give to each department an equal power of self-defense. In republican government, the legislative authority necessarily predominates. The remedy for this inconveniency is to divide the legislature into different branches; and to render them, by different modes of election and different principles of action, as little connected with each other as the nature of their common functions and their common dependence on the society will admit. It may even be necessary to guard against dangerous encroachments by still further precautions. As the weight of the legislative authority requires that it should be thus divided, the weakness of the executive may require, on the other hand, that it should be fortified. An absolute negative on the legislature appears, at first view, to be the natural defense with which the executive magistrate should be armed. But perhaps it would be neither altogether safe nor alone sufficient. On ordinary occasions it might not be exerted with the requisite firmness, and on extraordinary occasions it might be perfidiously abused. May not this defect of an absolute negative be supplied by some qualified connection between this weaker department and the weaker branch of the stronger department, by which the latter may be led to support the constitutional rights of the former, without being too much detached from the rights of its own department? . . .

2-4 "The True Principles of Republican Government": Reassessing James Madison's Political Science

Samuel Kernell

On casual reading, Federalist *Numbers 10 and 51 so resemble each other, one might well view them as parts of the same argument. In both, James Madison, writing as Publius, considers how government can be configured to prevent politicians in power from keeping it by tyrannizing their opponents. In Number 10, we read how the solution rests with a legislature whose members represent a large, diverse nation. In Number 51, the secret lies in dispersing government power across the legislative, executive, and judicial branches. In this essay, Samuel Kernell argues that the resemblance between Numbers 10 and 51 is deceptive. The government system designed to mitigate active tyranny in Number 10 works at odds with the separation of powers in Number 51. In the former, all that is required to protect liberty is the healthy political competition found in a well-designed, popularly elected assembly—really, the House of Representatives. In the latter, however, Publius worries that the president and Senate might be too weak to keep the House of Representatives in its proper place. After examining Madison's views expressed at the Constitutional Convention and elsewhere, Kernell concludes that Number 10 reflects Madison's sincere views on the subject, while Number 51 marshals the best case for ratifying the Constitution that he (or anyone) could muster.*

Since Thomas Jefferson made *The Federalist* required reading for all University of Virginia students, professors have enlisted these essays to instruct each generation of undergraduates in the principles of American government. The two favorites in today's classroom are James Madison's *Federalist* Numbers 10 and 51. Each essay identifies an essential and distinguishing characteristic of the American political system. Number 10 offers an ingenious rationale for the nation's pluralist politics, while Number 51 dissects the formal constitutional system. The first grapples with the tyrannical impulses of society's factions and the second with self-interested politicians who might be tempted to usurp their authority. In both cases concentration is the threat for which Madison finds similar solutions in "divide and conquer," a principle he had once described as the "reprobated axiom of tyrants." In Number 10 his solution takes the form of an extended republic containing numerous, diverse factions whose representatives reconcile their competing interests in a well designed, deliberative national legislature. In Number 51 a republican equilibrium requires a strong form of separation of powers containing checks and balances. Given that factional competition and checks and balances are based on the same strategic idea and the fact that Number 51 closes with a recapitulation of the main points of Number 10, it is not hard to see that these twin principles should be regarded as establishing the theoretical foundation of the Constitution.

Harder to understand is how this "Madisonian model" went unrecognized for so long, from shortly after ratification until Charles A. Beard reintroduced it more than a century later in his classic *An Economic Interpretation of the Constitution of the United States* (1913). According to Beard, Madison and his nationalist allies fused these principles in a scheme to hamstring government action and prevent national majorities from raiding the purses of the propertied class. While Beard was not the first to level these charges, he appears to have been the first since the ratification campaign to fashion these two principles into a unified theoretical model.[1] Beard's class conspiracy long ago lost favor, but the Madisonian model and its conservative bias remain the conventional wisdom of modern scholarship on James Madison and the Constitution's founding.

Subsequent scholars, many of whom rank among the Who's Who of twentieth-century political science, have relied on Beard to berate the Madison model. "If the multiplicity of interests in a large republic makes tyrannical majorities impossible," complained E. E. Schattschneider (1942), "the principal theoretical prop of the separation of powers has been demolished." By the 1950s, even those students of American pluralism who might be expected to number among Madison's most faithful boosters had joined the ranks of critics. Citing the presumed duplication of these principles, Robert A. Dahl (1956) concluded that the Constitution goes "about as far as . . . possible [in frustrating majority control] while still remaining within the rubric of democracy." And a few years later James MacGregor Burns (1963) joined the chorus, again charging that Madison "thrust barricade after barricade against popular majorities." . . .

. . . The Madisonian model is a misnomer. It does not represent Madison's sincere theoretical views on the Constitution—at least before and during the Constitutional Convention, when they were consequential. Instead, the Madisonian model was formulated after the fact, specifically in *Federalist* Number 51 and its companion essays, in order to promote the Constitution's ratification. In parrying the nearly apocalyptic Anti-Federalist charges that the Constitution took a short path to tyranny, the nationalist campaign needed desperately to show that the new plan was constructed on sound republican principles and assuage the worries of fence-sitting delegates to the states' ratification conventions. The Madisonian model fulfilled that need.

I arrive at this conclusion after examination of several kinds of evidence—the internal validity of the central arguments of Numbers 10 and 51 and the consistency between them; similarities and differences between the Madisonian model and Madison's previous political science . . . ; and the model's value as campaign rhetoric during the ratification debates. In the next section (I), I argue that the Madisonian model is fundamentally flawed. Beyond the familiar charges of duplication—which, after all, may amount to no more than "too much of a good thing"—the Madison model contains a serious contradiction between its core principles. One simply cannot design a constitution that optimizes the performance of both factional competition and checks and balances. While the former prescribes essentially a majoritarian solution to the potential dilemma of majority tyranny, separation of powers—as implemented with the Constitution's strong checks and balances described in Number 51—succeeds only to the extent it frustrates this same majority control. . . . This raises the question of how Madison could embrace a contradictory argument. The answer is simply that he did not. A review in Section II of Madison's relevant writings and activities fails to turn up an instance where he combined these principles prior to Number 51.

The joint appearance of factional competition and checks and balances in his *Federalist* essays might, as some have argued (Banning 1995), reflect the continuing development of Madison's theoretical views. Perhaps so, but there is little evidence from Madison's subsequent writings that he seriously revised his theoretical views on institutional design from those he took to the Convention (Riley 2001, 176–82). At least as strong an argument can be made that Number 51 springs from a strategic desire to dress up the Constitution in familiar principles in order to reassure delegates who were deliberating its fate at their states' ratification conventions. In section III I test this possibility by examining its value as campaign rhetoric. The Madisonian model presents a compelling case for ratification that is both different from the standard nationalist position and one Anti-Federalists probably found difficult to refute.

I conclude that Madison went to Philadelphia committed to replacing the Articles of Confederation with a constitutional system capable of positive action, both responsive to national majorities and protective of minorities in the states. He left Philadelphia with something quite different in hand. Despite privately expressing disappointment and lingering misgivings with the Constitution, he accepted it as superior to the Confederation and defended it vigorously in the ratification campaign. In doing so he combined the principles of factional competition and separation of powers into a rationale for legitimizing a Constitution born of politics and its contradictions.

I. The Disparate Logics of Number 10 and Number 51

The *Federalist* Numbers 10 and 51 are canon. And yet, I argue, they contradict each other. Nowhere is this more evident and destructive for the Madisonian model than in these essays' treatment of the House of Representatives. In Number 10, Publius unconditionally reposes government authority in a well designed legislature, which closely resembles the House of Representatives in all of its essential features—membership composition, size and extent of its constituencies. . . . Yet writing Number 51 several months later, Publius singles out the House as posing the greatest potential threat to liberty and against which the Constitution must array the full force of checks

and balances. To understand how these principles could generate such contradictory prescriptions, we need to understand their disparate logics.

I.A. Number 10: Institutionalizing Factional Competition

Madison opens this famous essay by declaring that the chief virtue of a "well-constructed Union" lies in "its tendency to break and control the violence of faction." He defines faction as "a number of citizens, whether amounting to a majority or minority of the whole, who are united and actuated by some common impulse of passion or of interest, adverse to the rights of other citizens, or to the permanent and aggregate interests of the community." After exploring its properties, Madison concludes: "The inference to which we are brought is that the *causes* of faction cannot be removed, and that relief is only to be sought in the means of controlling its *effects*." This lays the groundwork for a government founded on factional competition.

Madison then constructs a constitutional system from some simple, mostly unobjectionable assumptions about the effects of size and diversity. He begins by noting that the advantage of representative over direct democracy lies in conveniently incorporating a large number of citizens. Greater numbers mean greater variety of interests, or factions, that will participate in the nation's collective decisions. As factions compete they hold each other in check and enact only those policies that command broad support. It is a simple yet profound idea. In that an extended republic supplies the diversity of interests vital for keeping factional tyranny in check, this argument allowed Publius to counter the favorite Anti-Federalist shibboleth that only small republics could endure.

As for institutional design, Number 10 presents two mechanisms for containing and aggregating preferences of numerous, potentially "turbulent" factions. These are representation and a deliberative legislature. On the former, Madison introduces a theoretical novelty, "a scheme of representation" that "promises the cure for [faction] which we are seeking." Republican theorists had traditionally regarded representatives as serving essentially as agents of a particular interest. Members of Britain's House of Lords, Montesquieu explained, were selected in such a manner as to guarantee their undistracted representation of the aristocracy. When Alexander Hamilton and John Adams explored possible constitutional arrangements in America, they had held fast to this conventional republican principle in formulating an American variant of "mixed government" in which the lower house of the legislature would represent the poor; the upper, the rich; and at least for Hamilton, the disinterested executive, the public good. For Madison, however, multiple-cleavaged constituencies implied a more complex role for politicians. These actors, he sensed, would embody "a change in the principle of representation" (Hunt 1900, 338). Like present-day members of the House of Representatives, but unlike all models of representation that preceded this essay, Madison's politicians succeeded electorally by building consensus (i.e., coalitions) across factions by discovering common policies that served their constituencies' competing interests.

On the legislative process, Madison again enlists pluralism to take the rough edges off factionalism. He is clearly sanguine about the moderating effects of this new scheme of representation but allows that even were representatives "of factious tempers, of local prejudices, or of sinister designs" elected, they would be constrained by their need to coalesce with differently minded representatives. The only additional ingredient required was a sufficient variety of interests so that none could dominate. This fortuitously came in precisely the form that responded to the Anti-Federalist fears of a large republic. "Extend the sphere," Publius reassures us, "and you take in a greater variety of parties and interests; you make it less probable that a majority of the whole will have a common motive to invade the rights of other citizens." All three of Number 10's key features—representation, a well-proportioned legislature, and an extended republic—follow logically from the presence of multiple factions whose divergent and conflicting interests must be represented and combined. Moreover, by identifying these institutional attributes as desirable, the argument served the ratification cause by highlighting prominent features of the House of Representatives as well as by rendering the Constitution suitable for a growing nation.

. . . Certainly if factional competition *is* the solution, then it should be the criterion for judging the internal design and power relations among the other branches of government as well. Of course, the Constitution did not implement the logic of factional competition beyond the House of Representatives, which undoubtedly explains why Publius failed to continue his exercise beyond a well-proportioned, popularly elected legislature. After all, the presidency, the Supreme Court, and even the Senate fall far short of satisfying the design requirements identified in Number 10 for generating moderate policy. This raises the question, how in the absence of factional competition do these other branches avoid capture by some faction or inappropriately configured coalition bent on pursuing immoderate policies? The answer, at least for the second part of the question, is offered in Number 51's checks and balances.

I.B. Number 51: Institutionalizing Separation Of Powers

Where Number 10 makes a tightly reasoned, deductive argument, Number 51 approaches its task in a more empirical, discursive, and speculative fashion. Experience and widely accepted republican notions of good government are summoned to endorse the Constitution's provisions and to rule out governmental arrangements that do not survive in the final plan. Consequently, the constituent parts of Number 51's overall argument depend less on one another than did those in Number 10. Where all of Number 10 rests or falls on the integrity of factional competition, here particular claims or causal statements stand more on their own. . . .

This essay proceeds from a definition (stated in Number 47) that tyranny is tantamount to the "accumulation" of government power. Madison does not initially explain just why this should be so, but later in Number 51 he elliptically hints at two possible reasons. First, despite factional competition, aggrandizing majorities might occasionally materialize to endanger the civil rights of those factions in the minority. . . . Second, politicians pursue their self-interests, just as do their constituents, and if left unchecked, they will exploit their authority to the detriment of the general welfare. So, "first government must control the populace and then control itself." In the language of modern principal-agency theory, the problem of tyranny from politicians represents a severe form of "agency loss." This is an apt expression capturing Madison's conception of citizens as principals who delegate authority to representatives who act as their agents.[2] We adopt it here to distinguish it from Number 10's majority tyranny.

For the most part, Publius concentrates on agency tyranny in fashioning checks and balances as a system of "auxiliary" controls. . . . Publius acknowledges that in a democracy direct popular election is the preferred method for keeping politicians responsive to the citizenry. This passing homage to democratic creed immediately throws into question the need for separation of powers and, ultimately, wreaks havoc on the seemingly neat division of labor between Numbers 10 and 51. Why not minimize agency loss by simply electing everyone? Indeed, this was standard practice in the states at the time and . . . remained so decades later. Moreover, in his essay "The Vices of the Political System of the United States," written shortly before the Constitutional Convention, Madison appeared to judge direct and indirect elections as fully adequate to the task of checking agency tyranny. After distinguishing these two forms of tyranny in much the same way as he would in Number 51, Madison observes that though agency tyranny is a particular curse of monarchies, republics may not be immune from it either.[3] Yet it is less likely to pose a serious threat to republics because "the melioration of the Republican form is such a process of elections as will most certainly extract from the mass of the Society the . . . noblest characters . . . [who] will at once feel most strongly the proper motives to pursue the end of their appointment, and be most capable to devise the proper means of attaining it." Elections are at the core of Madison's new scheme of representation developed in this pre-Philadelphia essay—just as they are in Number 10, but not in Number 51—and are presented as adequate for solving the agency problem. . . .

Writing Number 51 eight months later, Publius finds elections to be problematic. The difficulty they present has more to do, I suspect, with political strategy than with any newly discovered theoretical concerns. Specifically, if elections sufficed to keep politicians in line, they would threaten to terminate the argument before Publius can make his case for the Constitution's checks and balances. Clearly, if Number 51 were to promote ratification, Madison had to get past the electoral solution to the one actually provided in the Constitution. He tries to extricate himself from this bind with what must be one of the most anemic (and charitably ignored) arguments Madison ever authored. He discounts the utility of universal elections as causing "some difficulties" and "additional expense." . . .

He forges on, but a little later . . . returns to elections as if to suggest a reconciliation. Again, Madison the democrat reminds us that elections must constitute the "primary" control mechanism in a republic, but here, . . . he applies these "auxiliary" controls exclusively to the only branch of the new American government that will already be subject to direct elections, the House of Representatives. Publius endorses a presidential veto that can be sustained by a one-third minority of the Senate. Even this check, he cautions, might prove inadequate to rein in a House of Representatives inclined, by virtue of its singular popular mandate, to act "with an intrepid confidence in its own strength." In sum, writing as Publius, Madison developed a rationale for a strong

checks + balances

form of separation of powers best suited for checking the ambitions of unelected politicians in the executive and judiciary, but then, he turned it against the popularly elected House of Representatives. . . .

Where does the Constitution's separation of powers leave factional competition as *the* "republican solution?" It is unclear that factional competition will have more than an incidental, moderating influence on national policy. Given the vetoes held by the Senate and presidency, successful policy will have to pass through these institutions whose members are neither selected via the carefully configured representational scheme of Number 10 nor subject to the countervailing pressures from politicians representing other interests. Policies arising from the Senate and presidency can be expected to deviate frequently from the preferences of the median member of the House of Representatives, and where they do they will be less desirable. The likely results are gridlock and bad public policy.

. . . If the inconsistencies of the Madisonian model reappear in his earlier political science, they might confirm Dahl's assessment of Madison as a brilliant politician but a second-rate theorist. But if Madison's previous political science turns up free from the flaws revealed here, we would be on firmer ground in suspecting that under the guise of Publius, Madison promulgated these contradictory principles to promote ratification. There are several episodes that deserve close investigation occurring in the mid-1780s when Madison crossed swords with Virginia's political leader Patrick Henry over religious subsidies and revision of that state's constitution and involving Madison's proposals for a new national constitution.

II. James Madison's Political Science Prior to Publius

. . . Even as the youngest member of Congress during the Revolution, he gained colleagues' notice for his compelling arguments in behalf of a strengthened national government. These included proposals to give the government coercive authority to remedy states' chronic shirking of their contributions to the war effort and beefed up executive agencies to which Congress could delegate important administrative decisions (e.g., the number of uniforms to purchase), thus freeing its time for making war policy. Not until he was back in Virginia in the mid-1780s, however, did he find himself confronting systematic institutional reform.

II.A. Virginia's Religious Wars: An Education in Factional Competition

On his return to Virginia after the war Madison discovered Patrick Henry firmly in control of the state through his leadership in the Assembly and in turn through that chamber's domination of the other branches. The contrast with his recent experiences in the feeble national Congress was stark and instructive. And it helps explain the resolve with which Madison headed to Philadelphia in 1787 to strengthen national authority and set it up as a check on majority power in the states.

In the spring of 1784, Patrick Henry proposed a general tax on Virginians to support "teachers of the Christian religion." When a legislative majority appeared poised to pass this legislation, Madison rallied Methodist, Baptist, and Presbyterian leaders who had chaffed under years of Virginia's tax subsidy for the Episcopal Church and were understandably wary of any new proposals that would reintroduce state subsidies of religion (Ketcham 1971, 162–68). In the fall election they successfully challenged some of the bill's chief boosters and sent a message to other would-be supporters of the legislation. When the assembly returned to session the next spring, the leadership quietly dropped the measure.[4] Reporting candidly on the home front to Jefferson in Paris in August 1785, Madison (*The Papers of James Madison* [hereafter MP] 8,345) noted, perhaps for the first time, the political benefits of factional competition: "The mutual hatred of these sects has been much inflamed . . . . I am far from being sorry for it, as a coalition between them could alone endanger our religious rights."

During the next several years leading up to the Convention, Madison frequently returned to this theme. According to his first biographer and next door neighbor, Madison often recited Voltaire: "If one religion only were allowed in England, the government would possibly be arbitrary; if there were but two, the people would cut each other's throats; but, as there are such a multitude, they all live happy and in peace" (Ketcham 1971, 166). Not until the spring of 1787, however, in his penetrating essay "Vices of the Political System of the United States," did Madison fully secularize this principle: "The Society becomes broken into a greater variety of interests, of pursuits, of passions, which check each other, whilst those who may feel a common sentiment have less opportunity of communication and concert." Establishing the desirability of a "greater variety of interests" allowed Madison to then conclude that an "extended" republic would limit the power of imprudent majorities.

James Madison was not the first to offer this rationale favoring large over small republics. Credit for that belongs to David Hume, who had made a similar argument nearly a half-century earlier. Until Douglass Adair (1974) identified striking similarities between the language of several of Hume's essays and Number 10, however, few scholars fully appreciated Madison's debt to this Scottish philosopher. So similar are some passages of Number 10—particularly, those defining factions—with those in Hume's essays "Of Parties in General" and "Idea of a Perfect Commonwealth," one might be tempted to conclude that without Hume's coaching Madison might not have made the transition from sects to factions or recognized the advantages of a large republic.

Hume undoubtedly influenced Madison's thinking, probably beginning with his undergraduate course work at Princeton under Professor John Witherspoon, a student of the Scottish Enlightenment. Yet Hume did not lead Madison toward factional competition as offering the "republican solution" to the conundrum of majority tyranny. To appreciate the development of Madison's political science and its original contribution to republican theory, consider what Hume had to offer on the subject and where his thinking stopped. Declaring "democracies are turbulent," Hume proposed an elaborate (and to Madison nonsensical) constitutional order designed to isolate society's different interests from one another as much as possible. The representatives to the political institutions that ultimately controlled decisions would not meet, but would vote from their communities, as if in a referendum. For Hume the virtue of an extended republic lay exclusively in its expanse (Hume 1985 [1777], 528): "The parts are so distant and remote, that it is very difficult, either by intrigue, prejudice, or passion, to hurry them into any measures against the public interest." Only by disengaging politics could a peaceful republic, "steady and uniform without tumult and faction," be realized.[5]

In a little noted passage of "The Perfect Commonwealth," Hume caught a glimpse of the path Madison would take nearly a half-century later. "The chief support of the British government is," Hume admits, "the opposition of interests; but that, though in the main serviceable, breeds endless factions." His own scheme (ibid., 525), conversely, "does all the good without any of the harm." This passage offers a rare instance in which an earlier generation theorist, locked in a paradigm based on the cultivation of virtue rather than interest, discerns a critical, anomalous fact but does not know what to make of it. Whether standing on Hume's shoulders or not, Madison is the first to examine pluralism unflinchingly and to discover within it the "remedy for the diseases most incident to republican government." He traveled to the Convention armed with this insight and a plan for the new government derived from it.

. . .

At the Constitutional Convention, Madison can be read as having promoted two distinct constitutional plans neither of which corresponds to the Madisonian model. From the opening day until July 14, he ardently pursued the Virginia Plan. This constitutional blueprint closely follows the logic of factional competition with only modest employment of checks and balances. After its defeat with the adoption of the Grand Compromise, Madison abruptly switched principles. With a Senate controlled by the states, he began to search for ways to salvage independent national authority and fence in the Senate's jurisdiction; he found it in checks and balances. At the same time factional competition became irrelevant and disappeared from Madison's discourse for the remainder of the summer.

II.B. The Virginia Plan

In the spring of 1787, after months of scholarly research and with the Convention drawing near, Madison approached fellow Virginia delegates on the need to prepare a substitute plan of government that would be capable of "positive" action. Madison's correspondence sketches out a popularly elected legislature whose members would be apportioned across the states by population. This legislature would possess unequivocal authority to veto state laws to prevent them from "oppressing the minority within themselves by paper money and other unrighteous measures which favor the interests of the majority."[6] This passage and others like it show Madison arriving at Philadelphia, preoccupied with immoderate factional majorities in the states. In none of this preparatory correspondence does he address agency tyranny, the problem that subsequently motivates much of his discussion in Number 51. Madison arranged for the Virginia delegation to assemble in Philadelphia a few days early to draft a reform proposal and probably to plot strategy. The product of their collaboration (Matthews 1995) soon came to be known as the Virginia Plan.[7]

In this plan Madison envisioned a government organized around an elective, bicameral National Legislature with representation to both chambers based on population. Members of the second chamber—soon to be referred to as the Senate—would be elected by those in the first from nominations provided by the state legislatures. Each chamber could originate laws "to legislate in all cases to which the separate states are incompetent." This included the authority "to negative [veto] all laws passed by the several States, contravening in the opinion of the National Legislature the articles of the Union; and to call forth the force of the Union" against any state failing to perform its constitutional duties.

Nowhere is the National Legislature's supremacy more apparent than in the organization of the other branches diagrammed in Figure 1. The National Legislature would elect the National Executive for a fixed term and without eligibility for re-election. This officer (or officers) would exercise general authority to administer national laws. Similarly, the National Legislature would create a national judiciary and elect its members, who would then serve for a term of good behavior. Together, the executive and a "convenient number of judges" would constitute a Council of Revision with the sole task of vetoing imprudent legislation.[8] If legislative selection of the executive and judiciary did not ensure the Council's sympathetic oversight, the National Legislature's ultimate authority was secure in a provision for a veto override.[9]

Remarkably, the vast literature on Madison's contribution to the Constitution's development fails to credit the Virginia Plan with faithfully and extensively implementing the principle of factional competition. Perhaps the five-month interval between presentation of the plan and Number 10 obscures their association. Yet at the Convention, Madison offered early, partially developed versions of Number 10's argument in defense of the Virginia Plan. In one of his most important and, for us, theoretically revealing speeches, Madison employed factional competition to counter claims by Delaware's John Dickinson and others that tyranny could be avoided only through strict separation of powers with "the legislative, executive and judiciary departments . . . as independent as possible."

Figure 1   The Virginia Plan

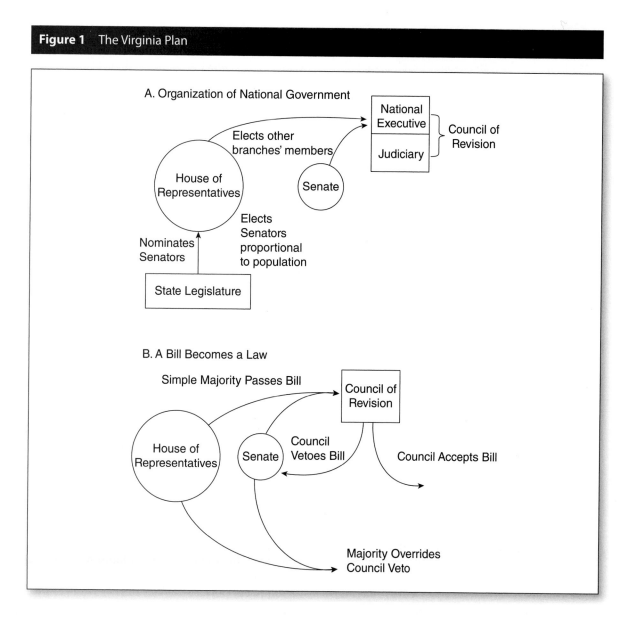

A. Organization of National Government

B. A Bill Becomes a Law

Madison beat back strict separation of powers and defended legislative supremacy with factional competition.[10] During floor debates on June 4, Madison unveiled the argument that would become Number 10. William Pierce from South Carolina discerned in it "a very able and ingenious" outline of "the whole scheme of government" (Rakove 1996, 61). During the next four days, Madison repeated the argument no less than four times, and fellow nationalists picked it up in their speeches. At one point, after listening to the familiar recitation of the small state arguments, James Wilson (1990, 67) reminded everyone: "No answer has been given to the observations of [Madison] on the subject."

Madison, no less than anyone else, also wanted to associate his proposals with separation of powers, but during these early deliberations, he employed it mostly to describe the division of labor that would strengthen the capacity of the new national government. Reminding his colleagues of the wartime Congress's dismal performance in administering the government with legislative committees, Madison commended separation of power as fostering government efficiency.

There are elements of checks and balances in the Virginia Plan. These remained implicit in the general outline in "Vices," but Madison drew them out more explicitly during the Convention's deliberations. In that these mild checks were tendered in response to other delegates' insistence for creating truly "separate" branches, one might be tempted to dismiss them as rhetorical embroidery offered to allay some small state delegates' misgivings. Yet, the weak form of checks and balances Madison offers at the Convention is wholly consistent with the Virginia Plan's legislative supremacy. The two constitutional features that Madison emphasized as checks are the Council of Revision with its weak veto and the Senate with nearly coequal legislative authority. . . . Clearly, in Madison's view the checking benefits from the Senate derived not from representing different interests, since these men would in fact be elected by the "popular branch." Rather it came by representing the same interests in a different deliberative setting. "Enlarge their number," added Madison in the next sentence, "you communicate to them the vices which they are meant to correct." The upper chamber's "coolness" and "system" buys time and opportunity for reconsideration. . . .

With the demise of the Virginia Plan, Madison's interest in separation of powers turns from efficiency and a system of modest checks to a radically different form of checks and balances. He had worked against a hemmed in Congress when the Virginia Plan was under consideration, but now

needing a means to quarantine the state-infested Senate he switched to a dispersion of governmental authority—stronger on some checking provisions, in fact, than those contained in the final Constitution.

II.C. After the Grand Compromise

After losing the legislature and the national veto over the states in the Grand Compromise, Madison sought unfettered national authority in a more independent executive and judiciary.[11] To achieve this Madison continued to invoke separation of powers during the second half of the Convention and apparently succeeded in that no one in the sometimes heated exchanges accused him of changing his mind.[12] From Madison's numerous statements, proposals and votes during this period one can fashion a second plan—a plan that does not so much add up to a formal system of government as a collection of provisions that consistently worked to shift authority away from the poorly designed Congress. Most directly, he endorsed the proposed enumeration of powers for Congress, an idea he had resisted during consideration of his Virginia Plan. When the states' rights delegates advocated state election of the president, Madison countered with direct national election. The result was yet another compromise, the Electoral College. Similarly, some states' rights supporters wanted the president to serve at the pleasure of Congress. Madison had equivocated on this matter earlier, but now he insisted that separation of powers required a fixed term without term limits. Others wanted administrative and judicial officials appointed by Congress, but Madison, sounding increasingly like Hamilton, countered that the appointment power struck to the core of executive responsibility. By late July this recent proponent of legislative supremacy was fashioning an independent, assertive president. Noting the tendency of a "legislature to absorb all power in its vortex," Madison (MP 2, 586–87) defended a veto with a three-fourths override provision as necessary "to check legislative injustice and encroachments."

When it came to the judiciary, neither side appears to have decided which arrangement best served its interest. Early on, the nationalists won adoption of a judicially enforceable supremacy clause—consolation, they were reminded, for losing the national veto over state laws. Subsequently, Madison and his allies faced down a half-hearted attempt to leave constitutional interpretation and enforcement of federal laws to the separate state judiciaries. During the late days of the Convention, . . . Madison used these numerous, small victories to fend off additional state incursions and to stamp onto the Constitution his nationalist preferences, at least as best one could with the negative instruments of checks and balances.

. . .

III. Federalist Number 51 as Campaign Rhetoric

Right up to the time he began writing his *Federalist* essays, Madison privately expressed reservations about the Constitution and could bring himself to muster only tepid support for the overall plan. In his letter (MP 10, 163–64) to Jefferson on September 6, 1787, in which he explains the Convention's work during the summer, Madison devoted more space to excusing the Constitution's deficiencies than to celebrating its strengths. The new national government will "neither effectually answer its national object nor prevent the local mischiefs which everywhere excite disgusts against the state governments."[13] This and other private statements reveal Madison working for ratification mostly from an aversion to the Articles of Confederation. They certainly give a hollow ring to Publius's boosterism.

From his private views and public activities before and during the Convention one can reasonably surmise that Madison's *sincere* public endorsement of the Constitution would have gone something like this: "The nation is presented with a choice between two imperfect governmental systems. Unquestionably,

the Constitution is superior to the Articles of Confederation and therefore, deserves ratification. Its advantages include a popularly elected and fairly apportioned House of Representatives, federal taxation authority, and provisions for amendment that will allow it to be strengthened as the need arises." This halfhearted endorsement would have befitted Madison's modest won-lost record at the Convention, but it would not, of course, have served the ratification cause.[14] All this adds up to an image of Madison wanting Publius to succeed, but not having much to offer in the way of compelling, sincere arguments.

Normally, politicians' issue stances are anchored in the vicinity of core constituency commitments and by the threatened loss of credibility were they to drift too far from their established positions. But the guise of Publius relaxed these constraints and freed Madison to tailor his message closely to the preferences of his audience. Thomas Jefferson (*The Papers of Thomas Jefferson* [hereafter JP] 11, 353) thought he had detected such strategic writing in Madison's *Federalist* essays and averred to his friend: "In some parts it is discoverable that the author means only to say what may be best said in defense of opinions in which he did not concur." If so, the contradiction that arises in Number 10 and Number 51 might reflect Madison's need to modify his sincere views with campaign rhetoric to appeal to fence-sitting voters and delegates.

The absence of public opinion data for this eighteenth-century, national election severely handicaps our ability to assess the relative merits of campaign arguments. The situation is not hopeless, however. If one assumes that each side's campaign strategists knowledgeably adapted their issue stances to the median voter or delegate, we can by tracking the course of campaign rhetoric discover which issue stances received the greatest play and required a response from the other side. By examining the shifting positions and issues over the seven-month campaign we can evaluate the merits of Number 10 and Number 51 as campaign statements.

The data for this exercise comes from William H. Riker (1991, 1996), who systematically compiled and analyzed all of the pro and con arguments that appeared in the nation's newspapers during the ratification campaign.[15] The antiratification side conducted essentially a negative, single-issue campaign. More than 90 percent of their published arguments raised the specter of tyranny.[16] Clearly, the untested Constitution gave the Anti-Federalists superior material for imagining hypothetical dangers, and wherever they searched among the Constitution's provisions, they uncovered a potential source of tyranny.[17] Ultimately, the Federalist had to answer these charges. "Just as the plaintiff-like position of the Anti-Federalists forced them to be negative," observed Riker (1996, 244), "so the defendant-like position of the Federalists forced them to be positive in the sense that they had to refute the Anti-Federalists' criticisms." The Constitution's provision for a standing army supplied early fodder for Anti-Federalist attack. They dropped it after the nationalists successfully answered that with America flanked by three foreign powers, this feature of the Constitution remedied one of the glaring vulnerabilities of the defenseless confederation. A little later the antiratification forces discovered that the missing Bill of Rights exposed a major chink in the nationalists' armor. After initial insistence that "paper guarantees" were neither effective nor necessary in a limited government, Madison and his allies recognized that these responses were not working and agreed to introduce appropriate constitutional amendments as soon as the new government was under way.

A careful examination of the charges and countercharges flying back and forth when Numbers 10 and 51 were written shows both essays directly responding to a variant of the tyranny currently being advanced by the Constitution's opponents.[18] On October 17, 1787, Brutus (probably Robert Yates, who served as one of New York's delegates to the Constitutional Convention) published an article in a New York paper charging "a free republic cannot succeed over a country of such immense extent, containing such a number of inhabitants, and these

encreasing in such rapid progression." Hamilton quickly countered (Ball 1988, 162) with *Federalist* Number 9, arguing that Montesquieu's prescriptions, on which Brutus relied, were based on societies with aristocracies that had to be accommodated. Shortly thereafter, Madison issued Number 10. Fortunately for Madison, Brutus's essay limited its attack to the "extended republic" variant of tyranny and did not venture into the structure of new national government for which factional competition could offer no justification. Brutus's narrow argument allowed Madison to truncate his factional competition discussion precisely at the point where this principle's institutional prescriptions diverge from the Constitution's provisions.

Later in the fall, the Anti-Federalist campaign began hammering the new government as providing insufficient checks and balances against national tyranny. The arguments took a variety of forms, from name-calling to informed theoretical exposition. One widely reprinted Anti-Federalist article, "Dissent of Pennsylvania Minority," stated a familiar mainstay of the opposition to which the ratification forces clearly needed to respond.

> The constitution presents . . . undue mixture of the powers of government: the same body possessing legislative, executive, and judicial powers. The senate is a constituent branch of the legislature, it has judicial power in judging on impeachment, and in this case unites in some measure the character of judge and party, as all the principal officers are appointed by the president-general, with the concurrence of the senate and therefore they derive their offices in part from the senate . . . . Such various, extensive, and important powers combined in one body of men, are inconsistent with all freedom; the celebrated Montesquieu tells us, that "when the legislative and executive powers are united in the same person, or in the same body of magistrates, there can be no liberty." . . . The president general is dangerously connected with the

senate; his coincidence with the views of the ruling junta in that body, is made essential to his weight and importance in the government, which will destroy all independence and purity in the executive department. (*Debate* 1993, 1, 546)

Of the various charges in "Dissent," possibly the most damaging is the image of a "junta" forming between the president and the Senate. Riker (1996) logged more Anti-Federalist references to a presidency that might evolve into an elective monarchy than any other dire scenario. As with the extended republic variant on the tyranny argument, one can imagine a couple of rebuttals available to proratification strategists. They could, as did Hamilton in Number 9, deny the premise from which tyranny could be deduced. In the following passage, fellow nationalist Americanus (John Stevens, Jr.) adopts this approach and ices it with a vivid ad hominem.

> Montesquieu's *Spirit of the Laws* is certainly a work of great merit . . . . On an attentive perusal, however, of this celebrated performance, it will manifestly appear, that the main object of the author, and what he seems ever to have most at heart, was to mollify the rigors of Monarchy, and render this species of Government in some degree compatible with Liberty . . . . But tho' his work has been of infinite service to his country, yet the principles he has endeavored to establish will by no means stand the test of the rigid rules of philosophic precision . . . . It ever has been the fate of *system mongers* to mistake the productions of their own imaginations, for those of nature herself. (*Debate* 1993, 1, 487–93, emphasis added)

Madison could have sincerely signed his name to this argument, including the slap at Montesquieu.[19] Instead Publius takes a more ambitious, if circuitous, approach by reconciling Montesquieu and separation of powers doctrine with the Constitution. The volume and variety of pro-ratification campaign arguments suggest that this issue had to be neutralized, but could it be by simply denying its validity for the American case?

Consider, in comparison, the gambit Number 51 offers. After elevating Montesquieu as "the oracle who is always consulted," Publius stipulates that tyranny is indeed a serious threat for which a well configured separation of powers is the preferred solution. No problem so far, since he has matched Anti-Federalist arguments almost word for word. Only late into the argument does Publius depart from the path taken by the Constitution's opponents. Sizing up the distribution of authority across the branches differently, he reassures readers that they need not worry about a coalition forming between the president and a Senate junta. These politicians, if they are lucky, might manage to stave off an overreaching House of Representatives prone to act with "intrepid confidence." If they are not so lucky, the Constitution might need to be amended to bring interbranch relations into balance. But certainly, one need not worry that the executive and judiciary possess the kind of authority that would allow them to usurp a democratic government.

This is a terrific campaign argument. First, Publius shifts the debate to safer ground for engaging his adversaries. He takes exception to Anti-Federalist conjecture over the operation of a hypothetical government rather than by arguing against the universally accepted separation-of-powers principle and needlessly picking a fight with the illustrious Montesquieu. Second, Publius adroitly configures his argument to avoid a variety of possible Anti-Federalist rebuttals. He might, alternatively, have invoked the judicial branch in its acknowledged role—with or without judicial review—as referee over jurisdictional disputes, but he would have opened the door to a favorite Anti-Federalist retort that Publius was prepared to entrust the fate of the Republic on unelected justices. . . . But instead, he minimizes the president-Senate threat by introducing the possibility that all of its authority might be insufficient to withstand an overreaching House of Representatives. He knows full well, as Riker's analysis verifies, that the Anti-Federalists will not attack the House of Representatives, the one popular branch.

Whatever difficulties Number 51 presents Madison's political science, its strategic value cannot be doubted. Clearly, the generality of separation of powers doctrine opened the way for this tactic, but its success depended on a sophisticated understanding of subtle, institutional design arguments, a talent for which Madison was peerless. He, more than anyone else, could figure out a way to abduct Montesquieu and steal the separation-of-powers issue from the opposition.[20]

. . .

IV. Conclusion: Madison, a Nationalist and Pluralist

Several weeks after the close of the Constitutional Convention in September 1787, James Madison (MP 10, 163–65) wrote a long letter to Jefferson in Paris reporting the results of the recently concluded Constitutional Convention. After singling out various provisions of the new Constitution for praise and criticism, Madison noted that on balance private rights would be more secure "under the Guardianship of the General Government than under the State Governments." Madison then posed to his friend a riddle: why should this be so, assuming both levels are "founded on the republican principle which refers the ultimate decision to the will of the majority, and are distinguished . . . by extent . . . than by any material difference in their structure?" Solving this puzzle, Madison averred, would "unfold the true principles of Republican Government." Indeed it does. Without explicitly solving the puzzle, Madison proceeded to lay out the rationale for factional competition. The puzzle fully encapsulates the goal orientation of Madison's political science. The stated goal of republican government is to protect private rights while empowering majority rule. Moreover, the

"principles" for achieving this goal are found less in the "interior" design of institutions (as in Number 51) than in the quality of pluralism. Where this condition is satisfied, the task of institutional design is to harness this pluralism with factional competition.

This is a riddle composed by a nationalist and pluralist. The former label is a familiar one for Madison. His nationalist credentials were well established among his contemporaries. Calling Madison a pluralist is more controversial. It squarely disputes familiar critiques of Madison and the Constitution that began most prominently with Beard and continued with Dahl (1956), both of whom judged Madison as embracing "the goal of avoiding majority control." He "goes about as far as possible," Dahl added, without having to drop the republican label, but in reality he belongs "in the camp of the great antidemocratic theorists." Both critiques rely chiefly on Number 51.

Madison's pluralism does not make him a majoritarian democrat in the modern sense of the phrase. He accepted unfettered representative democracy only in circumstances that imposed serious collective action problems for the formation of governing majorities. These conditions could be satisfied in an extended republic in which governmental institutions gave full expression to the nation's pluralism. When these conditions were met, the design requirements of America's national government could be simple: representation that reflected the preferences of the population and a fairly apportioned, well designed national legislature. This Madison implemented, not in the Constitution, but in the Virginia Plan. . . .

Where does this leave the Madisonian model, the presumed theory behind the Constitution? First, associating it with Madison is a misnomer, since Madison does not offer it until late in the ratification campaign in Number 51, and then only behind the cloak of Publius. It might not represent Madison's political science, but the model does describe the Constitution. Number 51's combination of factional competition and checks and balances should be recognized as

Madison's brilliant effort to justify theoretically a Constitution born of politics and facing an uncertain future. The Madisonian model (or perhaps more felicitously, the "Publius model") rationalizes a plan created from numerous logrolls and compromises that reconciled competing interests. . . . To conclude, Numbers 10 and 51 carry a division of labor quite different from that with which we opened the discussion. Number 10 states James Madison's prescriptions for republican government, when the necessary conditions are present, while Number 51 explains the Constitution.

Notes

1. Beard reintroduced readers to the long neglected Number 10, "the most philosophical examination of the foundations of political science"; then, several pages later he grafted it onto the already famous checks and balances provisions of Number 51. Beard characterized Number 51's argument as "fundamental theory . . . the basis of the original American conception of the balance of powers."

2. One familiar passage of Number 10 illustrates Madison's agency perspective. In distinguishing democracy from republic Madison notes "t h e delegation of the government, in the latter, to a small number of citizens elected by the rest." Wood (1969, 543–53) cites numerous instances of the widespread use of agency theory at the Philadelphia convention and in the ratification debates. In the Virginia ratification convention, John Marshall maintained that since the citizenry could not "exercise the powers of the government personally," they "must trust to agents."

3. "The great desideratum in Government is such a modification of the Sovereignty as will render it sufficiently neutral between the different interests and factions, to controul one part of the Society from invading the rights of another, and at the same time sufficiently controuled itself, from setting up an interest adverse to that of the whole Society."

4. Sensing his sudden advantage in the backlash, Madison dusted off Jefferson's stalled "Bill for Establishing Religious Freedom" and won its speedy enactment. Three years later at the Virginia ratification convention, Madison (Miller 1992) reminded delegates of this recent controversy while defending the absence of a bill of rights from the Constitution. Declarations are merely "parchment barriers." "The utmost freedom of religion" rests with the "multiplicity of sects . . . which is the best and only security for religious liberty in any society."

5. Adair p. 148. David Epstein (1984, p, 102) also stresses the fundamental dissimilarities of Madison and Hume. To achieve such a solution, Hume constructs a dubious, three-tiered system of government. The nation is divided into 100 equally populous counties whose citizens elect 100 county representatives (for 10,000 in all), who in turn elect eleven county magistrates and one senator. Only the 100 senators ever convene as a deliberative body, and any policy they adopt must be ratified by a majority of the county magistrates or representatives meeting in their separate locales. Ultimate authority would reside with officeholders who never meet.

6. Madison listed other advantages of the "negative" over state policies: resolve state boundaries; "guard the national rights and interests against invasion"; and restrain the states from "molesting each other" (Papers, March 19, 1787, 9: 318–19). In his subsequent letter to Randolph, Madison suggests that the veto be lodged with the upper chamber (the Senate) because its membership would be more divorced from politics (Papers, April 8, 1787, 9:369). Hobson (1979) persuasively places this frequently neglected federal veto at the center of Madison's republican theory.

7. Historians agree (Miller 1992; Ketcham 1990) that it represents Madison's ideas for the new Constitution.

8. Madison's paternal preference for the Virginia plan is revealed in the extent to which he resisted proposed changes. Early on, he opposed the convention's decision to substitute a presidential veto for the Council of Revision. He subsequently sought to reinstate it. See Farrand (1937, 1:236 and 2:74, 298).

9. Unlike Madison's endorsement of a three-fourths supermajority override rule later in the summer, after the Great Compromise, the Virginia Plan did not broach a supermajority requirement.

10. Moreover, he used this tactic on other occasions, but once the Great Compromise was narrowly adopted,

he dropped the argument until Number 10. In his record of the day's events, William Pierce of Georgia described it as "a very able and ingenious speech." (Farrand 1937: 1, p. 110). On June 26 Madison returned to this argument in defending a population basis for representation in the Senate. Jillson and Eubanks (1984) examine the theoretical novelty of Madison's ideas.

11. The loss of the national veto came in two stages. Over Madison's objection, the Convention limited it to instances when national and state authority intersected. Then the *coup de grace* came when any mention of this essential feature was left out of the Grand Compromise.

12. His success continues today as scholars locate Madison's *Federalist* arguments in his Convention speeches but fail to recognize that he was enlisting the same language to promote much different conceptions of the Constitution. Carey (1978), for example, enlists passages of Madison's June Convention speeches in behalf of the Virginia Plan to validate for Madison's support in Number 51 for provisions of the Constitution that are inimical to the Virginia Plan.

13. It would probably soon require fixing, he added. In fashioning a rationale for the actual Constitution—whether designed to be persuasive or not—many of Madison's sincere views on republican governance were simply irrelevant. In *Federalist* Number 37, he speculates, "the convention must have been compelled to sacrifice theoretical propriety to the force of extraneous considerations."

14. Lance Banning (1995), one of the few scholars to confront the striking inconsistencies between Madison's earlier writings and his Federalist essays, asserts that this is precisely what happened. "Madison's opinions changed as he was working on the series," Banning (1995, 400) concludes, "a possibility that ought to seem entirely likely to anyone who has completed a major piece of writing." The main evidence Banning offers for this claim is that Madison never subsequently retracted or contradicted positions taken in these essays. The absence of evidence, however, does not offer a very compelling case for anything other than a null hypothesis. Moreover, this explanation does not resolve the contradictions that appear within Madison's Federalist essays.

15. Riker's analysis covered some 617 entries ranging from "minor squibs" to *The Federalist*. These he decomposed into 3268 segments which he then weighted according to the frequency with which they were reprinted across the states.

16. Riker's (1996) classification found 49% of Anti-Federalists' appeals concerned tyranny: General threat stated: 14%; With respect to civil liberties: 14%; With respect to governmental structure: 14%; With respect to national authority: 7%; Total: 49%.

17. In a frequently cited essay, Cecilia Kenyon (1955) judged Anti-Federalists to be "men of little faith." If one considers the decision facing the nation, a negative campaign has a lot of strategic merit. Why make promises, on which Anti-Federalists might disagree, when a negative campaign succeeds in keeping one's adversaries on the defensive? This, and not the absence of core beliefs about the character of government, might explain the distinct differences that emerged across the two sides' campaigns. Perhaps the best known Federalist effort at scare tactics is John Jay's *Federalist* Number 2 in which he predicted the nation would splinter into regional, competing confederacies if the national government were not strengthened.

18. New York's support was critical and yet most of the delegates elected in the fall had publicly stated varying degrees of displeasure with the Constitution. When the Anti-Federalist governor, George Clinton, delayed consideration in the hope that Virginia and other states would vote down ratification, making it easier to do so, the state became one of the most hotly contested battlegrounds of ratification. Campaign editorials, essays and letters flowed daily through New York City's five newspapers—three of which were declared supporters of ratification, one opposing and one neutral. In addition to reprinting articles published outside the state, the New York campaign spawned substantial local campaign writing enterprises that included some of the most persuasive and theoretically ambitious essays from both sides of the issue. See Eubanks (1989).

19. In the February 18, 1792, issue of the *National Gazette*, Madison was more reserved: "Montesquieu was in politics not a Newton or a Locke, who established immortal systems, the one in matter, the other in mind. He was in his particular science what Bacon was in universal science: He lifted the veil from the venerable errors which enslaved opinion, and pointed the way to those luminous truths of which he had but a glimpse himself." See MP 14: 233–34.

20. This is not all the nationalists stole. They had beaten the more deserving opposition to the Federalist label, occasioning Patrick Henry's complaint that the nationalists would be better named the "Rats," presumably because they favored ratification.

References

Adair, Douglass G. l974. "'That Politics May Be Reduced to a Science': David Hume, James Madison and the Tenth Federalist," in *Fame and the Founding Fathers*, 93-106. New York: WW Norton.

Ball, Terence. 1988. "'A Republic – If You Can Keep It,'" in *Conceptual Change and the Constitution*, ed. Terence Ball and J. G. A. Pocock, 137-64. Lawrence: University of Kansas Press.

Banning, Lance. 1995. The *Sacred Fire of Liberty: James Madison and the Founding of the Federal Republic.* Ithaca, NY: Cornell University Press.

Beard, Charles. 1913. *An Economic Interpretation of the Constitution of the United States.* New York: Macmillan.

Burns, James MacGregor. 1963. *The Deadlock of Democracy.* Englewood Cliffs, NJ: Prentice-Hall.

Carey, George W. 1978. "Separation of Powers and the Madisonian Model: A Reply to Critics." *American Political Science Review* 72 (Mar.): 151-64.

Dahl, Robert A. 1956. *A Preface to Democratic Theory.* New Haven: Yale University Press.

The Debate on the Constitution: Federalist and Antifederalist Speeches, Articles, and Letters during the Struggle over Ratification. 1993. 2 vols. New York: Library of America.

Epstein, David. 1984. *The Political Theory of the Federalist.* Chicago: University of Chicago Press.

Eubanks, Cecil L. 1989. "New York: Federalism and the Political Economy of Union," in *Ratifying the Constitution,* ed. Michael Allen Gillespie and Michael Lienesch. Lawrence: University of Kansas Press.

Farrand, Max, ed. 1966. *The Records of the Federal Convention of 1787.* 4 vols. New Haven: Yale University Press.

Hume, David. 1985 [1777]. *Essays, Moral, Political, and Literary.* Indianapolis: Liberty Classics.

Hunt, Galliard. 1900. *The Writings of James Madison.* New York: G.P. Putnam's Sons.

Jefferson, Thomas. 1950-. *The Papers of Thomas Jefferson,* Ed. Julian P. Boyd. Princeton: Princeton University Press.

Jillson, Calvin C., and Cecil L. Eubanks. 1984. "The Political Structure of Constitution Making: The Federal Convention of 1787." *American Journal of Political Science* 28 (Aug.): 435-58.

Kenyon, Cecilia. 1955. "Men of Little Faith: The Antifederalists on the Nature of Representative Government." *William and Mary Quarterly,* third ser., 12: 3-43.

Ketcham, Ralph. 1971. *James Madison: A Biography.* Charlottesville: University Press of Virginia.

Madison, James. 1969-85. *The Papers of James Madison.* 15 vols. Various eds. (William M. E. Rachel, Robert A. Rutland, Charles F. Hobson, and others). Chicago: University of Chicago Press; Charlottesville: University Press of Virginia.

Matthews, Richard K. 1995· *If Men Were Angels: James Madison and the Heartless Empire of Reason.* Lawrence: University Press of Kansas.

Miller, William Lee. 1992. The *Business of May Next: James Madison and the Founding.* Charlottesville: University Press of Virginia.

Rakove, Jack. 1996. *Original Meanings: Politics and Ideas in the Making of the Constitution.* New York: Alfred A. Knopf.

Riker, William H. 1991. "Why Negative Campaigning Is Rational: The Rhetoric of the Ratification Campaign of 1787-1788." *American Political Development 5* (fall): 224-83.

———. 1996. *The Strategy of Rhetoric: Campaigning for the American Constitution.* New Haven: Yale University Press.

Riley, Johnathan. 2001. "Imagining Another Madisonian Republic." in John Ferejohn, Jack N. Rakove and Jonathan Riley, eds., *Constitutional Culture and Democratic Rule,* 170-204. Cambridge: Cambridge University Press.

Schattschneider, E. E. 1942. *Party Government.* New York: Farrar and Rinehart.

Wilson, James Q. 1990. "Interests and Deliberation in the American Republic, or, Why James Madison Would Never Have Received the James Madison Award." *PS: Political Science and Politics* (Dec.): 558-62.

Wood, Gordon S. 1969. *The Creation of the American Republic.* Chapel Hill: University of North Carolina Press.

Chapter 3

Federalism

3-1 Federalism: Sorting Out Who Does What

Donald F. Kettl

The phrase separation of powers *refers to the division of authority across the institutions of the national government;* federalism *refers to the vertical division of authority and responsibility between Washington and the states. The Constitution keeps state authority separate and distinct, but its framers did not build walls separating these governments into exclusive domains of policy. Instead, American federalism, like separation of powers, is a system of shared powers. During the 20th century, power and responsibility have undoubtedly shifted to the national (or, as it is commonly called, federal) government. Yet the states remain key participants, meaning that successful programs involve continuous coordination across these levels of government. Mostly the arrangement works reasonably well. But as events related to a Washington State mudslide in 2014 and Hurricane Katrina in 2005 have demonstrated, America's federalism is anything but a finely tuned machine. In the following essay, Donald F. Kettl, one of the nation's authorities on the subject, finds the difficult lessons these disasters have taught the public and policymakers.*

It didn't take long after the tragedy of the Oso mudslide in March 2014 for everyone to wonder: Should local officials have done more to prevent people from building in harm's way? For the citizens of this small town tucked into a picturesque hollow in Washington State, it was a time to search for lessons in the middle of an unspeakable tragedy that took the lives of 41 people, with two others missing under mountains of mud. The victims ranged from a 4-month-old baby to a 91-year-old resident who had lived in the community for decades. The slide hit suddenly and gave its victims no time to flee.

The local emergency management director, John Pennington, was grief-stricken. Struggling to respond to tough questions about why the local government had not prevented the victims from settling in harm's way, he told reporters, "We did everything we could." He added, "Sometimes big events just happen. Sometimes large events that nobody sees happen. And this just happened."[1]

A retired architect who had a weekend home in the path of the slide—and who lost many of his neighbors—told *The Seattle Times*, "We are not a bunch of stupid people ignoring warnings." He explained, "We all make risk assessments every day of our lives. But you cannot make a risk assessment on information you do not have."[2]

Source: This piece is an original essay commissioned for this volume. Some of the material in this reading first appeared in the author's "Potomac Chronicle" column, which is featured every other month in *Governing* magazine, a publication for state and local governments.

That quickly became the backstory. Residents would not have built homes in the area if they had known the risks. The slide was unpredictable, and local officials had done all they could. And then a freakish act of nature took scores of lives.

Critics sharply disagreed. They pointed to a long pattern of logging above the slide and to previous slides in 1949, 1951, and 2006 in the same area. Soon after the 2006 slide, in fact, local officials allowed new construction to resume. New residents moved in, apparently unaware that they were settling in harm's way.

International landslide expert Dave Petley, a professor of hazard and risk at Durham University in the United Kingdom, was sure the slide was predictable. He wrote in his *Landslide Blog* on the American Geophysical Union's website, "I'll nail my colours to the mast—to my mind this was a foreseeable event, and as such the disaster represents a failure of hazard management."[3]

He's not alone. In 1999, private geomorphologist Daniel Miller wrote a report for the U.S. Army Corps of Engineers that warned of the possibility of "large catastrophic failure."[4] In a post he wrote for CNN, he said, "As a scientist, I knew that material [on the hill above] would someday be on the valley floor."[5]

This all paints a dilemma that constantly plays out across the country. Federal government officials often know a great deal about the risks that local residents face, but they don't have the authority to act because most building policies are local. Local governments have the authority to act, especially through zoning requirements, but they often don't have the capacity to collect all the technical information—and sometimes don't have the will to interfere in local development.

New Orleans officials for decades had known their citizens were at risk from big storms. Just a year before Katrina struck in 2005, a Federal Emergency Management Agency simulation, Hurricane Pam, pointed to the devastation that a Category 3 storm would cause. Evacuating the city, the exercise found, would be a huge problem. But when the storm hit, the city was woefully unprepared.

Along the northeast coast, the National Oceanographic and Atmospheric Administration had long predicted that low-lying areas were vulnerable to storms, and the UN Intergovernmental Panel on Climate Change backed up the warnings. Superstorm Sandy's devastating wallop in 2013 confirmed that too many residents had built too many properties on land that was too vulnerable.

That doesn't prevent citizens from looking to government as the insurer of last resort. When natural disasters devastate local communities, a warm-hearted nation invariably provides help. Even small-government conservatives rally around government aid when their communities are affected, and such emergency aid is one of government's most important roles: banding all together to help the few in need. Such short-term federal relief efforts, however, have often planted the seeds for future disasters. By helping local communities rebuild, federal programs have often created targets for the next natural disaster in an ongoing cycle of devastate–rebuild–devastate.

Since the mid-2000s, that's started to change. The federal government's recovery aid after both Katrina and Sandy has included tough new zoning and flood insurance requirements, including raising living quarters above flood levels and prohibiting any rebuilding in the most endangered areas. But the underlying policy dilemma remains: whether to make the federal government the insurer of last resort, with the responsibility for salvaging the housing decisions made by individual citizens and zoning policies set by individual communities.

"Risk management" might sound boring, until it's your house affected by a mudslide or a hurricane.[6] Nothing could be more important then. It can also seem light-years away from the Founding Fathers' thoughts about federalism, but it's increasingly right at the center of relations among the federal, state, and local governments.

Everyone wants a small government, but every natural disaster brings calls for more governmental help for the afflicted and tighter governmental rules to prevent problems from recurring. That inevitably leads to the searching questions about whether government could (and should) have prevented individuals from making decisions that put them in harm's way. It also leads to fundamental debates about which level of government should have what responsibility. The debates are enormously important, but we often ask the toughest questions at the worst possible time, trying to frame smart long-term strategies in the face of unspeakable human tragedy—and that's a difficult way to make good policy.

Stronger alliances among the parts of the federal system are making progress. The new risk-based zoning and flood-insurance policies that appeared after Katrina and Sandy are steering investments away from the areas at greatest risk. But we still have a long way to go in sorting out just who ought to be in charge of what. We can't stop natural disasters, but we need to do much better in setting the policies—at the federal, state, and local levels—that help people figure out how much risk to take and what kind of help government will provide when disasters strike. The debate about federalism is as old as the American republic. Its consequences are front and center today, often where we're not looking.

In the complex world of American politics, it never takes long for the powers, responsibilities, and obligations of different levels of government to collide. Arizona and Mississippi have challenged federal immigration policy by passing tougher laws than the federal standard. Washington and Colorado passed laws on recreational use of marijuana that flew in the face of long-standing federal drug-control policies. The Obama administration bypassed wildly disparate state policies by pushing through Congress a health reform law that required all citizens to get health insurance and all states to create health exchanges to help their citizens buy policies—against which opponents promptly filed a vigorous challenge that went all the way to the U.S. Supreme Court, where the Obama administration won.

The constitutional principles, on a strict reading of the document, seem clear. The Tenth Amendment states, "The powers not delegated to the United States by the Constitution, nor prohibited by it to the States, are reserved to the States respectively, or to the people." Put simply, if the Constitution does not allow the federal government to take action, power rests with the states and their citizens. But that has scarcely prohibited an enormous expansion

of federal power since the ratification of the Tenth Amendment in 1791. In fact, it has led to the drawing of battle lines in sorting out who does what, and these lines have been the trenches for unending conflict in American federalism.

The nation's founders, of course, did not intend to create an eternal struggle. They were pragmatic people trying to find a delicate balance between large and small states, maritime and agricultural states. Their goal was compromise, not conflict. No one knows who came up with the name, but the founders coalesced around the idea of a "united states of America," individual colonies that retained their identities but joined in a single new American nation. The choice of name helped create a national identity, but it scarcely resolved the debate. We are located in America, but few problems are purely America-based any longer. We are a collection of states, but we are uneasily united in a single nation. The founders could have pushed hard to resolve the issue, but that would have produced disunited states and no nation; so they finessed the issue, seizing on a name that suggested unity. They roughed out the boundaries without creating sharp lines.

Throughout the nation's history, that's led to debates about the Louisiana Purchase, slavery, the Civil War, the nation's currency, civil rights, health care, and immigration. The issues continue to play out in problems large and small. Federalism is, at once, a basic principle of American democracy and an arena in which some of democracy's most basic tensions have, for more than 235 years, played themselves out.

Shifting Boundaries

New York Times columnist Maureen Dowd got more than she bargained for when she visited Denver in mid-2014 to report on the sale of legalized marijuana. It began innocently enough, with a visit to a local pot shop to buy—legally—a caramel-chocolate flavored candy bar. She tried a couple of bites and felt nothing. But after an hour and a room-service dinner, she wrote, "I felt a scary shudder go through my body and brain. I barely made it from the desk to the bed, where I lay curled up in a hallucinatory state for the next eight hours." She became paranoid, at first not able to remember where she was or what she was wearing and eventually "convinced that I had died and no one was telling me."[7]

When the buzz finally wore off the next day, an interview with a medical consultant revealed what had happened. There was no labeling on the candy bar to warn her to use only small bites—16 pieces for novices who hadn't determined how the edible pot would affect them. Five months after marijuana became eligible for recreational use, Dowd concluded, "some kinks need to be ironed out with the intoxicating open bar at the Mile High Club."[8]

The regulatory issues were growing ever more important, especially since Colorado was becoming a destination for those seeking to enjoy more than the view and the skiing. The Colorado Symphony Orchestra staged a "'Classically Cannabis' fundraiser with joints and Debussy," Dowd explained. After eating a cannabis cookie, a Wyoming college student jumped off a Denver hotel balcony. A Denver resident ate Karma Kandy, laced with marijuana; he lost control of his judgment, got a handgun from a safe, and killed his wife. Edible pot was sending growing numbers of people on bad trips. Large numbers of new users, inexperienced with the effects of marijuana—especially edible versions—pushed past the boundaries of existing government regulations.[9]

Of course, there *were* government regulations. Federal law is clear and inflexible. According to the national drug policy, pot remains a Schedule 1 drug, along with heroin, ecstasy, and LSD, with "no currently accepted medical use in the United States" and "a high potential for abuse." And that has left the Obama administration nothing but tough choices: invoking federal preemption and taking a tough enforcement stand, which would anger many members of the base that just returned the president to the White House; winking at people getting baked and feeding their munchies; or artfully threading their way through the dilemma of strong state support for decisions in opposition to national policy. But the legalization of marijuana, beginning in Washington State and Colorado, created tough dilemmas. Should the federal government step in and challenge the decisions of state voters, who approved referenda to make pot legal? Or should the feds step back, allow the states to follow the will of their voters, and hope that the states will create regulations to ensure the safety of this surprising new industry?

The controversy, in fact, left some observers of federalism to wonder whether Seattle's police department had adopted as its new poster child "The Dude" character, played by Jeff Bridges in the movie *The Big Lebowski*. On the day in December 2012 when using small quantities of marijuana became legal in Washington State, the city's police department posted Bridges's picture on its website, with the caption "The Dude abides, and says 'take it inside.'"[10] Under the referendum passed by voters in November, citizens could possess small amounts of pot but not in public. The advice: "Under state law, you may responsibly get baked, order some pizzas and enjoy a Lord of the Rings marathon in the privacy of your own home, if you want to." The police calculated that invoking *The Big Lebowski* might connect more with users than would formal posters.

Breckenridge, Colorado, may have beaten them to it. Voters in that state also voted to legalize the possession of small quantities of pot. "The Amsterdam of the Rockies," some reporters called the town as, years before, some residents quietly encouraged tourists to come for "our great outdoor beauty—and then relax with a joint at the end of the day."

For governments everywhere, the tugs on toking set up some exceptionally tough issues. How far should the federal government go in enforcing laws out of sync with local voters? How can local officials slide around national policies so they stay in sync with their citizens? In the Netherlands, which has a central government, local governments, no system of federalism, and Amsterdam—famous for its "coffee shops" where visitors can enjoy both java and ganja—national officials tried to dance artfully between its national policy against drug use and the local drug trade. Neighboring governments in France and Germany insisted they would keep their pot bans in place, and the Danish government refused a request from Copenhagen's city council to experiment with

Amsterdam-style deregulation. In the Czech Republic, Portugal, and Switzerland, the national government has taken a more Breckenridge-like position. In all these cases, national policy rules—to the degree national officials can deal with intransigent local officials and the habits of their citizens.

In the United States, federalism puts an emphasis on local enforcement of laws. The dilemma comes when local laws—and practice—fall out of sync with national laws. Seattle's police dealt with this problem by suggesting that users not "flagrantly roll up a mega-spliff and light up in the middle of the street"[11] and, instead, manage their munchies in the quiet of their own homes. The Obama administration decided not to accept state legalization of marijuana—but it also chose not to enforce federal policy in the face of local opposition.

Governing everywhere is much more about finding a common ground between policy goals and different levels—and charting a road to reconcile what officials want and what citizens will actually do. Our system of federalism, as always, adds a special twist. Whether the issue is mudslides or marijuana, who is ultimately responsible for "life, liberty and the pursuit of happiness," as the Declaration of Independence puts it?

Federalism's Arenas

In case after case, federalism plays itself out in complex ways. The issue is always in part about federalism: With so many different players at all levels involved in the difficult process, the struggle for control as well as for finger-pointing and blame-shifting becomes inevitable. In part, the issue is often fiscal: Who has the prime responsibility for paying for at least a minimum level of services across the nation's communities? The issue is also partially administrative: How can the federal, state, and local governments provide a coordinated, effective response?

Consider the Medicaid program, passed by Congress in 1965 to pay for health coverage for low-income Americans. Forty years later, soaring costs led the nation's governors to push hard for fundamental changes in the program. From 1998 to 2003, Medicaid spending increased 62 percent, almost

twice the rate for Medicare, the other major federal health program, which pays doctor and hospital bills for seniors. Experts estimated that over the next 15 years, Medicaid's cost would grow 145 percent, an annual growth rate of 8.2 percent for the states.[12] For most governors, Medicaid was the fastest-growing item in the budget, and they looked for help in funding an initiative that, after all, was mostly federal. "Governors believe that Medicaid reform must be driven by good public policy and not by the federal budget process," the National Governors Association concluded in a 2005 report.[13] That was impossible, of course. Analysts at the Centers for Medicare and Medicaid Services estimate that by 2020, the federal government will account for half of all health care spending. Medicaid alone is projected to grow from 15 percent of all health care spending in 2009 to 20 percent in 2020.[14]

Governors around the country worried that the escalating costs were becoming a serious drain on state budgets. Several conservative governors argued that the federal government ought to convert the program into a block grant, in which the states would get the federal money and have flexibility in how to spend it. Several liberal governors expanded Medicaid coverage. Some federal officials were concerned that state decisions were making claims on federal budgets, and others worried that state-based decisions were increasing state health care disparities.[15] At the core of the debate were new twists on the central, enduring questions: Which problems are national ones that require federal-level solutions? Which issues are local ones that properly belong with state and local governments? What support should the federal government provide state and local governments to help them accomplish federal goals—and how much support should the federal government give to even out differences in the capacity of state and local governments to tackle important problems? To what degree should state and local governments be seen as independent and free-standing governments—and in what measure are they operating as administrators of federal programs?

These issues were white hot in the Medicaid debate, and they became even more important in the implementation of the Obama administration's signature program, the Affordable Care Act. That program, enacted in 2009, gave states the choice of creating their own health insurance marketplaces or relying on a national one, managed by the federal government. Fourteen states, including the District of Columbia, created their own exchanges, but when the program launched in 2014, some states proved much more successful than others in getting the program running. Oregon gave up and sent its citizens to the federal government's Healthcare.gov website. Maryland and Massachusetts, which both planned an enthusiastic embrace of the new law, encountered big problems. In many states where public officials resisted the program, the federal exchange was the only option; the irony was that state opposition to the program led to a stronger federal role. Opponents warned of a massive federal takeover of health care. In reality, the Affordable Care Act, most fundamentally, created a requirement that all citizens have health insurance and provided subsidies to make that possible. The political battles were over what coverage citizens ought to have—and how best to provide it. The states were central in the health care revolution, but the program took shape in a way that reflected the historic battles of federalism that have so long shaped a vast swath of domestic policies in the United States.

The centrality of these questions is scarcely surprising, since one of the most important questions with which the nation's founders struggled in Philadelphia was the balance between national and state power. However, they did not really intend for this American invention of "federalism" to be a bold, sweeping innovation. They were supremely practical men (women were not invited to Philadelphia to help frame the new nation) with a supremely practical problem. Northern states did not trust southern states. Farmers did not trust merchants. Most of all, larger states did not trust smaller states and vice versa. The fledgling nation's army won independence from Great Britain, but the notables gathered in Philadelphia in 1787 needed to find some glue to hold the new country together. If they had failed, the

individual states would have been too small to endure—and would surely have proved easy pickings for European nations eager to expand.

The system of federalism that the founders created had few rules and fewer fixed boundaries. As federalism has developed over the centuries, however, two important facts about the system have become clear. First, federalism's very strength comes from its enormous flexibility—its ability to adapt to new problems and political cross-pressures. Second, it creates alternative venues for political action. Interests that fight and lose at the state level have been able to find clever ways of taking their battles to the national government. Losers at the national level have been able to refight their wars in the states.

Throughout American history, we have frequently looked on federalism as a rather sterile scheme for determining who is in charge of what in our governmental system. But that misses most of what makes federalism important and exciting. It makes far more sense to view federalism as an ever-evolving, flexible system for creating arenas for political action. Americans have long celebrated their basic document of government as a "living Constitution." No part of it has lived more—indeed, changed more—than that involving the relationship between the national and the state governments and the relationships among the states. This can be seen clearly in the rich variations on the three recurring themes of American federalism: political, fiscal, and administrative.

Political Federalism

In the 1990s, some South Carolina business owners launched the *Tropic Sea* as a casino boat for "cruises to nowhere." However, the enterprise soon became a cruise to a very important somewhere by raising the question: Just how far can—and should—federal power intrude on the prerogatives of the states?

This balance-of-power question is as old as the American republic. In fact, it predates the Constitution. When the colonies declared their independence from King George III, they formed a loose confederation. It proved barely strong enough to win the war and not nearly strong enough to help govern the new nation. Problems with the country's Articles of Confederation led the nation's leaders to gather in Philadelphia to draft a new constitution. At the core of their debate was the question of how much power to give the national government and how much to reserve to the states. The founders followed a time-honored tradition in resolving such tough issues—they sidestepped it. The Constitution is silent on the question, and the Tenth Amendment simply reinforces the obvious: The national government has only the powers that the Constitution gives it. By leaving the details vague, the authors of the Constitution avoided a wrenching political battle. They also ensured that generations of Americans after them would refight the same battles—most often with legal stratagems in the nation's courts but sometimes, as in the Civil War, with blood.

A Cruise to Somewhere?

The *Tropic Sea* sailed into an ongoing struggle in South Carolina politics. Although developers loved gambling ships such as the *Tropic Sea,* which lured tourists to the state, several legislators and local officials did not, and they had been actively campaigning against the ships. As a result, when the *Tropic Sea* asked permission to dock at Charleston's State Ports Authority (SPA) pier terminal, the SPA said no. The boat ended up at anchor in the harbor while its owners sought help from the Federal Maritime Commission (FMC). The FMC sided with the boat owners but was overturned by a federal appeals court. The case eventually ended up in the U.S. Supreme Court.

South Carolina argued that, as a state government, it wasn't subject to the FMC's jurisdiction, and in a bitter 5-to-4 decision at the end of its 2002 term, the Supreme Court agreed. Writing for the majority, Justice Clarence Thomas looked past the usual foundation of political struggles over state power, the Tenth Amendment, and instead built his argument on the little-noticed Eleventh Amendment, ratified in 1798, which specifies that the judicial power of the federal government does not extend to the states. This amendment supported the notion of

dual federalism—separate spheres of federal and state action. In the decades after its ratification, however, the dual federalism argument gradually eroded, especially after 1868, under the weight of the "equal protection" clause of the Fourteenth Amendment. That amendment asserts that all citizens have the right to equal treatment under the law. In establishing a national standard, the Fourteenth Amendment gave the courts power to enforce national policy over state objections. That pushed away the dual federalism concept and helped shift the balance of power to the national government. After William Rehnquist became chief justice in 1986, however, dual federalism resurfaced and surged ahead again.

In ruling for South Carolina, Justice Thomas admitted that there was little textual evidence to support his position. Rather, he said, dual federalism was "embedded in our constitutional structure." The concept helped uphold the "dignity" of the states as dual sovereigns. That, he said, was the core of the decision.[16]

Asserting the dignity of the states is a new constitutional standard. The Eleventh Amendment explicitly applies to federal courts, not federal administrators, such as employees of the FMC. Conservatives, of course, had long criticized liberals for making law from the bench. In this case, however, it was the conservatives on the Court who crafted a new principle, which they used to push back the scope of the national government's power.

Federalism Means War

The Supreme Court under Rehnquist gradually chipped away at national power and aggressively worked to strengthen the role of the states. The major federalism decisions were all by votes of 5 to 4, built on the conservative bloc of William Rehnquist, Clarence Thomas, Anthony Kennedy, Sandra Day O'Connor, and Antonin Scalia. The disputes, on the Court as well as off, have become increasingly intense. As *New York Times* reporter Linda Greenhouse put it, "These days, federalism means war."[17]

The battles became so sharp that candidates' views on federalism were critical in the battles over new appointments to the Supreme Court, especially those of Chief Justice John Roberts and Justice Samuel Alito. Given the ages of several other justices, more appointment battles are certain—and so are questions about the Court's role in reframing federalism. Will the Court remain on its dual federalism course? Staying that course raises two very difficult questions.

First, just how far is the Court prepared to go in pursuing dual federalism? In the past it has ruled that workers cannot sue states for discrimination under federal age and disability standards. It has also protected states from suits by people who claimed unfair competition from state activities in the marketplace, such as photocopying by state universities. Bit by bit the Court has extended state power at the expense of the national government's jurisdiction.

At some point, however, the pursuit of state "dignity" will collide with national standards for equal protection. At some point, state protection against national labor standards will crash into national protection of civil rights and civil liberties. That point might come in debates over family leave or prescription drugs, over voting rights or transportation of nuclear waste—but a collision is certain. From the Fourteenth Amendment, there is a long tradition of asserting national power over the states. From the Rehnquist court, there is a new legal argument for reasserting state power. In the Roberts court, the fundamental questions about the federal government's power to shape state health policy are likely to cast a very long shadow over the power balance in American federalism.

Neither argument is an absolute. In some issues (such as civil rights), there is a strong case for national preeminence. In other issues (such as the states' own systems of law), there is a strong case for state preeminence. Still other issues (such as gambling boats) rest squarely in the middle. And in some issues (such as headlight flashing), federal issues are dragged in to push changes in state and local policy.

The nation then has to determine how best to balance competing policy goals and constitutional principles. Sometimes those battles are fought out in the legislative and executive branches, but most often, they are contested in the courts.

Since the dawn of Roosevelt's New Deal in the 1930s, national power has grown at the expense of the states. Now, with an uncommon purpose, the conservatives on the Supreme Court are pushing that line back. The Roberts court can continue the campaign to reassert the power of the states, but clearly, at some point, it will have to hold national interests paramount. What is less clear is where and how the Court will draw that line.

The second question that the Court's pro–dual federalism course raises is even tougher: How far can the Court advance state-centered federalism without running headlong into the new campaign for homeland security, which demands a strong national role? It is one thing for the Court to pursue the principles of state sovereignty and dignity, but beefing up homeland security inevitably means strengthening federal power. There is a vital national interest in ensuring that state and local governments protect critical infrastructure, such as water systems and harbors. The nation needs not only a strong intelligence apparatus but also a powerful emergency response system.

Federalism and the Living Constitution

Relatively few Americans may care about whether a gambling boat can dock at a South Carolina port. But the basic issue—where to draw the line between national and state power and who ought to draw it—is an issue that all Americans care about, even if they spend little time thinking about it in those terms. It has been the stuff of bloody battles and endless debate. As political scientist Howard Gillman told *The New York Times*, federalism has become "the biggest and deepest disagreement about the nature of our constitutional system."[18] The equal protection and homeland security issues will only intensify that disagreement as we wade deeper into the real meaning of the states' "dignity."

These issues are scarcely ones that the founders could have anticipated when they wrote the Constitution and the Bill of Rights. Few present-day Americans, after all, had heard the term *homeland security* before September 11, 2001. Few Americans stop to think about the relative roles of the federal, state, and local governments—as well as the private and nonprofit sectors—in providing their health care. That, however, is an enormous financial and political issue, as a senior citizen with heart pains calls the local 911 number, talks with a county dispatcher, and is transported in a municipal ambulance, perhaps to a state university hospital where the care is funded by the federal government's Medicare program. The genius of the founders was that they recognized the importance of federalism, that they put broad boundaries around it, but did not try to resolve it for all time. They created a mechanism for Americans in subsequent generations to adjust the balance, subtly—sometimes loudly— and continually.

It was no easy matter to recognize the key questions out of thousands that engaged the members of the Constitutional Convention in Philadelphia. It was even tougher to resolve the questions just sufficiently to win the Constitution's adoption without pushing so hard as to deepen the divisions. And it was quite remarkable to do so in a way that has allowed us to reshape the balance in our time. Federalism is, at its core, a political question. In tackling these political questions, however, state and local governments have often found themselves just one more lobby struggling for influence in an increasingly hyperpoliticized national capital. The National Governors Association (NGA) was once one of the nation's most important and powerful interest groups. Some Republican governors have cut their support for the association, as part of a broader effort to cut government. Governors in both parties who want to advance a political point can often find a host of other Washington-based interest groups and think tanks where they can champion their causes. As the former executive director of the NGA put it, "Now NGA is just one of the organizations, not *the* organization." These political changes are due, in no small part, to the rising importance of fiscal issues.[19]

Fiscal Federalism

These grand debates are what most Americans think of when they think of "federalism." They are the stuff of high school civics classes and the enduring classics of American history. For national, state, and local policymakers, however, the soft underbelly of federalism is much more often the question of who pays for what.

That has not always been the case. But in the 1950s, as the nation—and the national government—became much more ambitious about domestic policy, fiscal federalism became increasingly important. During that period, citizens and national policymakers wanted the country to undertake new, large-scale projects, such as building a national network of highways and tearing down decaying slums. State and local governments could not, or would not, move ahead on such matters. Often they simply did not have the funds to do so; sometimes local political forces opposed the policies. Even without those impediments, state and local governments almost always lacked the ability to coordinate the creation of such complex systems as effective high-speed highways with other jurisdictions. (Who would want to drive on a modern, four-lane road only to hit a two-lane gravel path at the state line? As it is, drivers often complain that snow plowing sometimes stops at municipal boundaries.) Therefore, citizens and national policymakers pressed to empower the national government to undertake the projects.

National Goals Through Intergovernmental Grants

The national government tackled the problem of getting local and state governments to do what it wanted done by offering them grants. If local governments lacked the resources to tear down dilapidated housing, the national government could create an "urban renewal" program and provide the money, thus avoiding the constitutional problem that would have come with national coercion. The national government did not *make* local governments accept the money or tear down the slums. But few local officials could resist a national program that helped them do what they, too—or at least many of their constituents—wanted done.

The same was true at the state level. In the 1950s, Americans were buying cars in record numbers, but they found the roads increasingly clogged. Long-distance driving often proved a special chore, because road systems did not connect well and the quality of the roads fell far below the performance ability of the cars driving on them. During the Eisenhower administration, the national government decided to tackle that problem by creating a new program—the interstate highway system—and inducing states to join it by funding 90 percent of the construction costs. With motorists demanding better roads, the offer was too good to refuse. Since this was occurring amid the hottest moments of the Cold War, President Dwight D. Eisenhower reinforced the idea of a national interest by arguing that the system served both transportation and defense goals—it would allow troops to move quickly to wherever they might be needed. (Wags have since joked that the system could best serve the national defense by luring Russian tanks onto the Beltway around Washington, D.C., and challenging them to cope with the traffic and find the right exit.)

The strategy continued to be used through the 1960s. When Lyndon B. Johnson announced his War on Poverty, he decided to fight it primarily through national grants to state and local governments. He created the Model Cities program, which provided aid to local communities trying to uproot poverty and rebuild urban neighborhoods, and established other programs to provide better housing for poor Americans. He founded Medicaid, which provided grants to state governments so that they, in turn, could provide health care to the poor. More grants followed to support job training, criminal justice, public health, and a host of other national goals.

It was a clever strategy in a number of ways. For one, it sidestepped constitutional limitations on

national interference in state and local issues: The national government did not force state and local governments to join the programs; it simply made them financially irresistible. No state or local officials wanted to have to explain to constituents why they left cheap money on the table, especially when their neighbors were benefiting from the programs.

This approach sidestepped another tough constitutional problem as well: the national government's dealing directly with local governments. Through long-standing constitutional interpretation and practice, local governments are considered creatures of the states, not the national government. The states created the national government; so constitutionally the national government must deal with the states. Hence, the states alone have the power to control what local governments can—and cannot—do. Before Johnson's program, local governments struggled with increasing problems of poverty, substandard housing, and other human needs. They often found themselves without power or enough money to attack the problems. Few state governments themselves had adequate resources to address these serious issues, and in many states, political forces prevented the creation of new programs that might have helped. As Figure 1 shows, federal grants to state and local governments remained relatively flat since the early 1990s, until the Great Recession of the late 2000s led the federal government to create a big stimulus program to assist state and local governments. With the end of the stimulus program, however, federal aid as a share of the federal government began sagging again.

Many analysts concluded that the only solution was to create a direct link between the national and local governments—a link that bypassed the states. But given both constitutional limits and political conflicts, how could such a link be established? Federal grants to local governments proved the answer. Across the nation, state governments gave permission for local governments to receive the money. If the national government agreed to take on the problems and keep state officials out of the process, the programs seemed an attractive proposition to state and local officials alike.

Figure 1   Federal Aid to State and Local Governments

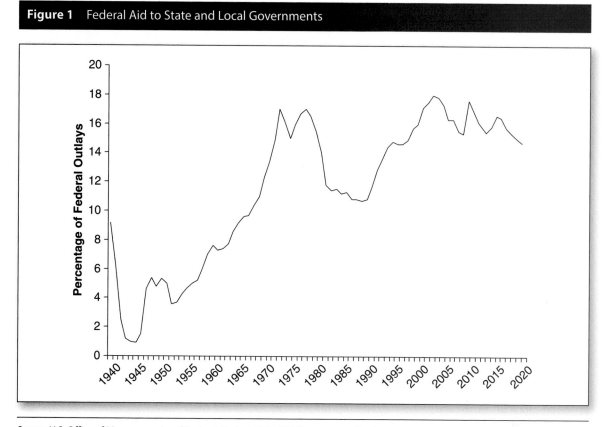

Source: U.S. Office of Management and Budget, *Budget of the U.S. Government, Fiscal Year 2015: Historical Tables,* Table 12.1, http://www .whitehouse.gov/omb/budget/Historicals. Figures for 2014 through 2019 are estimates.

From the 1950s through the 1970s, these inter-governmental aid programs became increasingly popular and important. They not only grew in size but also became ever more vital elements of state and local government financing. In 1938, federal aid had amounted to just 8.7 percent of state and local revenue. It surged to 22 percent—more than 1 out of every 5 dollars raised by state and local governments—in 1978, at the high-water mark of federal aid.

As the national government used its funds to support state and local governments and to induce them to do things they might not have done otherwise, federal aid became not only an increasingly important part of the policy system but also something on which those governments became ever more dependent. When the national government began tightening its fiscal belt in the late 1970s, state and local governments felt the effects keenly. In 1980, federal aid was 40 percent of all spending by state and local governments from their own sources. A decade later, it dropped to 25 percent. Federal aid bounced back to 37 percent of state and local government spending from their own sources in 2010, but that was the product of big budget cuts by state and local governments because of the recession and the federal government's stimulus program to boost the economy. With the stimulus ending in

2011, however, tough budget times for state and local governments remained with no additional help from the feds.[20] Years after the worst months of the collapse, many state and local governments continued to struggle economically.

Few federal programs were abolished. Rather, the national government simply cut back support—leaving state and local governments to deal with ongoing commitments and, in many cases, powerful supporters who fought hard to keep the programs alive. In the federal highway program, federal support mostly provided aid for construction, not maintenance. As highways aged, state governments found themselves with huge bills for repairing crumbling bridges and old roadbeds. Similar problems rippled throughout state and local government budgets. The Government Accountability Office concluded in 2013 that state and local governments face big challenges—and that they will only grow in the coming decades.[21] That left many state and local officials wondering if they were on their own—and when they could count on the feds for help.

No News Was Bad News

When recession hit in 2002, state and local governments looked expectantly to Washington for some hope—and help. The nation's governors, in particular, were hoping for good news when President George W. Bush began 2003 by announcing his plans for a $670 billion tax cut. They hoped the speech would contain at least some help for their ailing budgets. Except for a modest proposal on unemployment insurance, however, they found themselves left out in the January cold.

With their budgets in the biggest crisis since World War II, governors had been lobbying hard for national help. They hoped for a short-term resuscitation of revenue sharing, the federal government's program of distributing broad grants to state and local governments to use as they wished. The program ended in 1982, but they wanted to bring it back. Failing that, they pressed for at least some tinkering with the formula for reimbursing Medicaid spending, the fastest-growing program in many state budgets and one, as noted earlier, that was originally launched through the incentive of national grants. Changes in the Medicaid formulas, the governors hoped, would ease their budget worries.

Ignoring most of the states' pleas, Bush instead advanced a bold stroke to restructure the national tax system. The administration did suggest some changes to Medicaid, but the changes proposed would have reduced aid (or increased costs) for the poor, and they immediately incited opposition from groups struggling to protect the program. The states were left on their own with a $90 billion budget shortfall that threatened to soak up all the short-term economic stimulus Bush was proposing, and more. The net effect promised to be an economic wash surrounded by political conflict.

Who is at fault here? The feds, for failing to extend a helping hand when the states needed it most? Or the states, for digging themselves into the hole and whining when Bush refused to help them out? As with most questions of fault, the answer is, both.

If Bush truly had been interested in jump-starting the economy, pumping money through the states would quickly have done just that. But the president was concerned more with long-term revision of the tax code than with short-term economic stimulus, especially through the states. As for the states, their fault lies in having hitched their spending to the booming economy of the 1990s. They forgot "Stein's Law," derived by the late Herbert Stein, once chair of the president's Council of Economic Advisers: "Things that can't go on forever—won't."[22] When the boom collapsed, the states found themselves hooked on spending increases they could not support. The episode sharply framed the fundamental issues that surround the complex financial puzzles of federalism—starting with who is responsible for what.

Exploding Health Care Costs

In the 1990s, national aid to state and local governments had actually resumed its upward course (see Figure 1) but not because the national government

Figure 2   Grants for Payments to Individuals as a Share of All Grants

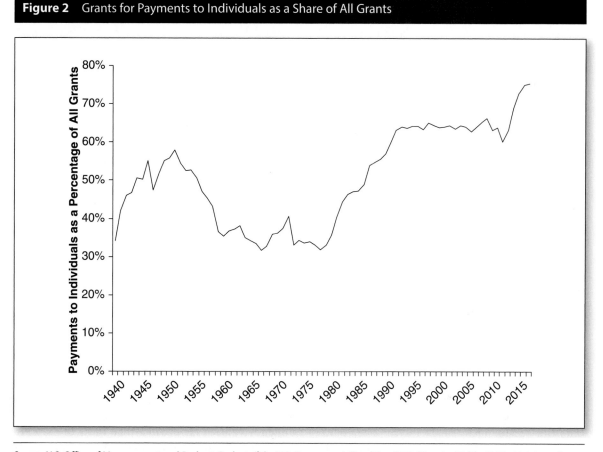

Source: U.S. Office of Management and Budget, *Budget of the U.S. Government, Fiscal Year 2015: Historical Tables,* Table 12.1, http://www .whitehouse.gov/omb/budget/Historicals. Figures for 2014 through 2019 are estimates.

had decided to resume its generosity to state and local governments. Rather, the reason was that national aid for payments to individuals—mostly through Medicaid—suddenly accelerated, as the benefits became more generous and health care costs began to grow rapidly. Grants for all other purposes had leveled off or shrunk, but national aid for health care had swung quickly upward, as had state governments' own spending for their matching share of the costs. In 1960, federal grants for payments to individuals amounted to 31 percent of all grants. The federal government experts estimate that this figure will swell to 78 percent by 2019 (see Figure 2). There will be little federal aid for anything but payments to individuals, and most of those payments will be for Medicaid.

As the new century began, health care costs (particularly under Medicaid) exploded at precisely the same moment that state revenues collapsed. Spending for doctor visits, hospital care, and especially prescription drugs swelled at the highest rate in a decade, growing to 30 percent of state spending, and it could not have come at a worse time for state governments. It has swamped the states' efforts to control the rest of their budgets and aggravated their financial hemorrhage. The monster in the states' budgetary basement has become health care: treating the uninsured, providing long-term care for the elderly, and buying prescription drugs. With the baby boomers reaching retirement age, the budgetary problem promises to get worse.

State spending pegged to unsustainable revenue growth and the sudden increase in health care costs threaten a continuing, profound crisis for state policymakers. Aggravating it is the projection by most economists that economic growth will not proceed fast enough to bail out the states any time soon. It's little wonder that in some states, Democrats were quietly rooting for Republican governors to make the hard budgetary decisions and vice versa. If the states are the laboratories of democracy, the lurching of budgetary Frankenstein's monsters could litter broken test tubes across the floor. This is a long way from the 1960s and early 1970s, when the feds then saw state and local problems as their own and invested substantial federal money to fix them. Democrats and Republicans joined together to provide national funds to leverage state and local action. The partnership might have been paternalistic, but it shaped policy for decades. When budget cuts hit in the late 1970s and early 1980s, national–state ties became increasingly frayed. They unraveled further with the Bush administration's 2002 loosening of air pollution regulations, which complicated the job many states faced in meeting pollution standards and frayed some more with the administration's capital gains tax plan. During the Obama administration, officials first announced tougher rules and then rolled them back following loud protests.

The states can—indeed, they have to—deal with some of these problems by putting their spending back into balance with a realistic view of their revenues. They need to update their revenue systems. But they cannot solve their fundamental fiscal problems without a new partnership between the states and the federal system. And that will be hard to realize as long as the two groups move in such different orbits

that the fundamental problems they share never come together. The many political issues posed by the Affordable Care Act only magnify the financial puzzles that health policy raises.

Administrative Federalism

A close corollary of the rise of fiscal federalism has been the growing importance of state and local governments as administrative agents of national programs. As close observers of Washington politics know, the national government has increased its spending without increasing the number of bureaucrats. How has it been able to do so? The national government has leveraged the activity of state and local governments as agents to do much of its work. As is the case in fiscal federalism, the states usually have discretion about whether to enlist as national agents, but the construction of programs typically leaves them little choice. Consider, for example, the case of environmental policy. Under national environmental laws, state governments have substantial responsibility for issuing permits and monitoring emissions.

The Environmental Protection Agency (EPA) relies heavily on state governments for much of the frontline work. In the process, however, some states have used that role to set their own policies, which often have been far broader than those of the EPA. An up-from-the-bottom style of federalism has meant that some states have, in practice, set policy for the entire nation.

Policymaking for the Nation—in Sacramento

Top officials in the nation's capital have been increasingly consumed by a war about the air, and there is a good chance that a decade from now, the EPA administrator will not be setting much environmental policy. Recent agency administrators, both Republican and Democratic, have been pinned down in a fierce guerrilla battle between some congressional members who are trying to lighten the burden of environmental regulations and others who are trying to toughen pollution standards and reduce global warming. The administrator's job increasingly has been to chart the EPA's course through the political crossfire. As the melee has raged in Washington, the policy initiative has shifted to the states and to foreign governments.

It is little wonder that California has been so aggressive in campaigning to reduce air pollution. Pollution problems in the Los Angeles basin are legendary. Medical research has shown that kids growing up in the area suffer a 10 to 15 percent decrease in lung function and suffer more from asthma and respiratory infections than do their counterparts elsewhere in the country. Autopsies of 152 young people who died suddenly from crime or health problems revealed that all of them had inflamed airways and 27 percent had severe lung damage.

The state has set tougher standards than federal regulations required, and in the past 25 years, the results have been remarkable. The number of health advisories for high levels of ozone shrank from 166 in 1976 to just 15 in 2001.

In July 2002, California took another tough step. The legislature passed a bill requiring that all cars sold in California after 2009 meet tough standards for greenhouse gases, the carbon-based emissions scientists believe promote global warming. In signing the bill, Governor Gray Davis chided the national government for "failing to ratify the Kyoto treaty on global warming." They "missed their opportunity to do the right thing," Davis said. "So it is left to California, the nation's most populous state and the world's fifth largest economy, to take the lead." California was proud to "join the long-standing and successful effort of European nations against global warming."[23]

With its legislation, California rendered moot President Bush's March 2001 decision to withdraw the United States from the Kyoto treaty, at least with respect to carbon dioxide pollution from cars. Carmakers had waged a fierce battle against the California bill, but in the end, they could not beat the forces of environmentalists and citizens worried about public health. They found themselves trooping off to Sacramento to haggle over the details of the new regulations.

No automaker can afford to ignore California and its huge market, as was clear after the state's earlier decision to mandate cleaner gas and catalytic converters. When California mandated catalytic converters to scrub auto exhaust, it soon became impossible to buy cars in Wisconsin or Texas that did not contain the device as well. As California goes, at least in air pollution, so goes the nation.

For California regulators, the aggressive antipollution campaign has not been a one-way street. The new California law requires regulators to reduce not only smog but also greenhouse gases, such as carbon dioxide. New-generation diesel engines are more fuel efficient than many gasoline-powered engines. That means less fuel and lower carbon dioxide emissions. And that, in turn, has brought California regulators into close negotiations with automakers about encouraging production of diesel-powered cars.

For those who have long seen diesels as blue-smoke–belching behemoths, the idea that diesel power might be a pollution-reducing strategy may seem preposterous. It may seem even more unlikely that government would be encouraging a shift to diesel engines or that government regulators would be in conversations with automakers hammering out deals to do so. Above all, it may seem incredible that the government taking the action would be a state government. But that is exactly what is happening in California.

All this, in turn, has led to budding ties between state regulators and the European Union. European nations have been working as hard and as long on global warming as anyone. The European Union's aggressive efforts to reduce greenhouse gases have stimulated new diesel technologies; so California regulators find themselves steering in the same direction as their counterparts abroad. Put together, this means that American policy for auto emissions is subtly shifting course, driven by activities at the state and international levels.

State governments have long prided themselves on being the nation's policy laboratories, and healthy competition among them might produce new breakthroughs. But there is also a profound risk that the nation could find its policy strategies increasingly evolving through accidental bits and bumps, without a national debate about what is truly in the national interest. The trend is already briskly under way. General Electric chief executive Jeffrey Immelt has said that 99 percent of all new regulations the company faces are, over time, coming not from the national government but from the European Union.[24] The states are vigorously developing new pollution standards. Meanwhile, as Washington policymakers focus on the interest group battles that constantly consume them, they risk fighting more and more about less and less.

Conclusion

If James Madison today rode his horse to Washington, down the interstate from an exit near his Virginia estate at Montpelier, would he recognize the system of federalism he helped craft? (And would Americans remember that he, more than any of the other founders, was the architect of the system of federalism we have today?) He would undoubtedly be stunned at the very idea of using federalism to work out problems of ship-based gambling, health care for the poor, and climate change. He might even be surprised that the interstate on which he rode his horse had been paid for mostly by the federal government.

However, after a few moments' reflection—and perhaps after a bit of conversation to get up to speed on the stunning policy predicaments of the 21st century and to activate his smartphone—he would see in these puzzles echoes of the issues he and his colleagues dealt with at the end of the 18th century. He would surely recognize the conflicts over who is in charge of promoting the general welfare in areas at risk from mudslides. He would understand the struggles at the core of the Affordable Care Act, because they are little different in tone from the ones he and his colleagues waged in Philadelphia. And he might quietly smile in discovering that the founders' deliberate strategy of constructive tension along the fault lines of American politics—and American federalism—has proven so resilient over the centuries.

The glue holding together America's special—and peculiar—democratic system comes from a unique blending of federal, state, and local responsibilities. Early Americans faced a fundamental, dramatic choice: to assign those responsibilities clearly to different levels of government and then write rules for governments to coordinate their inevitable differences or to allow governments to share responsibilities and then negotiate their differences through a political process. The latter is the cornerstone of American federalism.

Federalism is a much-revered constitutional principle, rooted deeply in the American tradition, which draws its life from political bargaining. It is tempting to read the Constitution, think of the stirring rhetoric of the founders, and celebrate federalism as a set of rules. In reality, federalism is a puzzle of politics, played out in a series of political arenas. It is far less an institution than a living organism, one that breathes, grows, shrinks, and changes in response to the forces pressing upon it.

Federalism has helped Americans survive the pressures that led to the Civil War, and it has often made possible programs and policies that might not otherwise have existed. It would be hard, for example, to imagine the national government itself taking on the job of building the massive interstate highway system. Only through federalism did this crucial system come into being, as federalism introduced the possibility of a political, fiscal, and administrative partnership that made possible a program no one government alone could have produced. By the same means, federalism has transformed American cities (for better or worse) through urban renewal, launched a war on poverty, helped clean the environment, and produced a health care program for the nation's poor.

Of course, this partnership has not always been a happy or peaceful one. Governors are never convinced that the national government provides enough money, and national policymakers constantly find it difficult to corral 50 different states—and tens of thousands of local governments—into a coherent policy system. When Hurricane Katrina devastated the Gulf Coast in

2005, federalism created a series of roadblocks that vastly complicated the job of getting critical relief to suffering citizens. New Orleans's mayor blamed Louisiana's governor. The governor called on the federal government to send everything it had, but the feds said that the governor had not requested the information in the right way. When the process of rebuilding began, New Orleans residents complained that the feds were slow in providing everything from new maps of the flood plain to trailers for displaced residents. Louisiana residents complained that citizens in Mississippi, the state next door, received more money per capita.

In the storm's wake, study after study pointed to failures of leadership and coordination. It is no exaggeration to conclude that the struggle to coordinate the intergovernmental system cost some people their lives. When quick, coordinated governmental response is needed, federalism has sometimes proved slow and disjointed. It is a system far better equipped to broaden participation in the political process than to produce efficient government.

Of course, if we had wanted that kind of government, we would long ago have sided with Alexander Hamilton in his effort to bring energy to the executive, strengthen presidential power, and centralize power in Washington. Other founders rejected his argument, and the resulting political system has proved remarkably resilient. The system's flexibility and constructive tension has not only made it possible to work out accommodations for the tough issues; it has also created arenas in which Americans with many different points of view can continue to contest the future of the nation's public policy. But the new challenges of homeland security, Katrina-like disasters, health reform, and climate change all raise tough questions about how to ensure that the quest for responsiveness does not prove administratively chaotic.

Notes

1. Jim Brunner and Michael J. Berens, "County's Own 2010 Report Called Slide Area Dangerous," *Seattle Times,* March 25, 2014, http://www.seattletimes .nwsource.com/html/localnews/2023225415_mud slidecounty1xml.html.

2. Mike Baker, Craig Welch, and Ken Armstrong, "Worried About Possible Deaths, County Weighed Buying Out Homes," *Seattle Times,* April 2, 2014, http:// seattletimes.com/html/localnews/2023288058_mud-slidebuyoutxml.html.

3. Dave Petley, "The Oso (Steelhead) Landslide in Washington State—Could It Have Been Foreseen?" *Landslide Blog,* April 2, 2014, http://blogsdev.agu.org/landslide blog/2014/04/02/steelhead-landslide-in-washington/.

4. Daniel Miller, "Hazel/Gold Basin Landslides: Geomorphic Review Draft Report," October 18, 1999, http://www.nws.usace.army.mil/Portals/27/docs/civil works/projects/Hazel-GoldBasinLandslidesGeomor phicReviewDraft.pdf.

5. Daniel Miller, "Deadly Mudslide, a Disaster That Didn't Have to Happen," *CNN Opinion,* April 1, 2014, http://www.cnn.com/2014/04/01/opinion/miller-landslide-washington/index.html?iref=allsearch.

6. For a broader discussion, see Thomas H. Stanton and Douglas W. Webster, *Managing Risk and Performance: A Guide for Government Decision Makers* (Hoboken, NJ: Wiley, 2014).

7. Maureen Dowd, "Don't Harsh Our Mellow, Dude," *New York Times,* June 3, 2014, http://www.nytimes .com/2014/06/04/opinion/dowd-dont-harsh-our-mellow-dude.html.

8. Ibid.

9. Ibid.

10. Jonah Spangenthal-Lee, "'Officers Shall Not Take Any Enforcement Action—Other Than to Issue a Verbal Warning—for a Violation of I-502,'" *SPD Blotter,* Seattle Police Department, December 5, 2012, http://spdblotter.seattle.gov/2012/12/05/officers-shall-not-take-any-enforcement-action-other-than-to-issue-a-verbal-warning-for-a-violation-of-i-502/.

11. Ibid.

12. Bipartisan Commission on Medicaid Reform, "The Medicaid Commission," September 1, 2005, 8.

13. National Governors Association, "Medicaid Reform: A Preliminary Report," June 15, 2005, 1, http://www .finance.senate.gov/imo/media/doc/mwhtestrpt 601505.pdf.

14. Centers for Medicare and Medicaid Services, "National Health Expenditure Projections 2010–2020," https://

www.cms.gov/Research-Statistics-Data-and-Systems/Statistics-Trends-and-Reports/NationalHealthExpend Data/downloads/proj2010.pdf.

15. Stephen B. Thomas, Sandra Crouse Quinn, James Butler, Craig S. Fryer, and Mary A. Garza, "Toward a Fourth Generation of Disparities Research to Achieve Health Equity," *Annual Review of Public Health* 32, no. 1 (2011): 399–416.

16. *Federal Maritime Commission v. South Carolina Ports Authority,* 535 U.S. 743 (2002). See Linda Greenhouse, "Justices Expand States' Immunity in Federalism Case," *New York Times,* May 29, 2002, sec. A.

17. Linda Greenhouse, "The Nation: 5-to-4, Now and Forever; At the Court, Dissent Over States' Rights Is Now War," *New York Times,* June 9, 2002, sec. 4.

18. Ibid.

19. J. B. Wogan, "States and Localities Are Losing Their Influence in Washington," *Governing,* June 2014, http://www.governing.com/topics/politics/gov-states-localities-losing-influence.html.

20. U.S. Census Bureau, *Statistical Abstract of the United States, 2012* (Washington, DC: Government Printing Office), Table 431.

21. U.S. Government Accountability Office, "State and Local Governments Fiscal Outlook," updated April 2013, http://www.gao.gov/assets/660/654255.pdf.

22. Herbert Stein, interview with the author.

23. Gray Davis, "California Takes on Air Pollution," *Washington Post,* July 22, 2002, sec. A.

24. Brandon Mitchener, "Increasingly, Rules of Global Economy Are Set in Brussels," *Wall Street Journal,* April 23, 2002, sec. A.

3-2 A Separate Peace

Jonathan Rauch

The previous essay presents American federalism the way it is typically por-trayed—as an amalgam of state and federal responsibilities whose separate adminis-tration challenges effective coordination. Disaster policy, for example, has gravitated from the states to the federal government. Secondary education has witnessed an expanded federal role, but primary responsibility remains with the states. Both areas, however, exhibit serious friction between these levels of government. Jonathan Rauch considers in this essay another commonly expressed virtue of federalism: the states' capacity to act independently allows many different policy approaches to be tested simultaneously. Successes tend to be copied by other states and frequently serve as models for national policy. Rauch finds an additional virtue in independent state action: it moderates easily inflamed cultural issues. In the case of abortion, the issue became highly contentious after the Supreme Court proclaimed in Roe v. Wade *the right to an abortion to be a national privacy right. But with gay marriage, the national government has stayed clear. As states pass their own laws, mostly banning gay marriage, the issue has remained defused.*

Mitt Romney, the former governor of Massachu setts and a 2008 Republican presidential candi-date, is a thoughtful politician, for a politician. So it was not surprising to find him recently debating one of the country's core conundrums. It was a little surprising, though, to find him debating himself.

Romney believes abortion is wrong, but he thinks the decision on whether to allow it should be left to the states. In February, *National Journal* asked him if he favored a constitutional amendment banning abortion. No, he replied:

What I've indicated is that I am pro-life and that my hope is that the Supreme Court will give to the states . . . their own ability to make their own decisions with regard to their own abor-tion law. . . . My view is not to impose a single federal rule on the entire nation, a one-size fits all approach, but instead allow states to make their own decisions in this regard.

Romney also believes gay marriage is wrong, but he thinks the decision on whether to allow it should *not* be left to the states. Last year, he poured scorn on Senator John McCain, who (like Romney) opposes gay marriage, but who (unlike Romney) opposes a U.S. constitutional amend-ment banning it. "Look," Romney said, "if some-body says they're in favor of gay marriage, I respect that view. If someone says—like I do—that I oppose same-sex marriage, I respect that view. But those who try and pretend to have it both ways, I find it to be disingenuous."

Taking the two quotations side by side, one could be excused for supposing Romney was trying to have it both ways. However, in fairness to him, now is not the first time Republicans have argued with themselves over moral federalism—or, what may be a better term, moral pluralism: leaving states free to go their separate ways when a national moral consensus is lacking.

In 1973, when the Supreme Court (in Roe v. Wade) declared abortion to be a constitutional right, conservatives were outraged. But what to do? Republicans were divided. Abortion opponents wanted the practice banned by a constitutional amendment, and supporters of Ronald Reagan soon took up the cause. Reagan, of course, was preparing a conservative primary challenge to the politically vulnerable and ideologically moderate Republican president, Gerald Ford—and Ford was in a bind, because his wife, Betty, had already endorsed Roe ("a great, great decision").

Ford's response was also to call for a constitutional amendment—but one that would return authority over abortion to the states, not impose a federal ban. In the end, Ford won the presidential nomination but lost the struggle within his party: The 1976 Republican platform called for "enactment of a constitutional amendment to restore protection of the right to life for unborn children."

The more things change, the more they stay the same: In this decade, Vice President Cheney—a Ford administration alumnus, as it happens—has called for the gay-marriage issue to be left to the states. But his party's cultural right has insisted on a national ban: not one gay marriage on U.S. soil! When President [George W.] Bush sided with the right, he effectively cast the deciding vote, and moral pluralism lost.

Who was right, Cheney or Bush? Ford or Reagan? Romney or Romney? A priori, the answer isn't obvious, but the country has recently run, in effect, a laboratory experiment. On abortion, it went with a uniform national rule. On gay marriage, it has gone the other way.

Abortion started in the state legislatures, where it was sometimes contentious but hardly the stuff of a nationwide culture war. Neither party's national political platform had an abortion plank until 1976. In the late 1960s and early 1970s, some liberal-minded states began easing restrictive abortion laws. When the Supreme Court nationalized the issue, in 1973, it short-circuited a debate that was only just getting started.

By doing that, it moved abortion out of the realm of normal politics, which cuts deals and develops consensus, and into the realm of protest politics, which rejects compromise and fosters radicalism. Outraged abortion opponents mobilized; alarmed abortion-rights advocates countermobilized; the political parties migrated to extreme positions and entrenched themselves there; the Supreme Court became a punching bag; and abortion became an indigestible mass in the pit of the country's political stomach.

Gay marriage started out looking similarly intractable and inflammable. As with abortion, a few liberal states began breaking with tradition, thereby initiating a broader moral debate; and, as with abortion, purists on both extremes denounced the middle as unsustainable or intolerable, saying that gay marriage (like abortion) must be illegal (or legal) everywhere in order to be effectively illegal (or legal) anywhere. The purists got help when two important actors preemptively rejected compromise. The Massachusetts Supreme Judicial Court ordered same-sex marriage in 2003, and then refused even to consider civil unions. That decision provoked President Bush's equally provocative endorsement of a constitutional ban on gay marriage. The battle lines appeared to have been drawn for a national culture war, waged by extremes of left and right over the heads of a marginalized center.

But the political system, and the public, refused to be hustled. Congress rejected a federal constitutional ban. The federal courts stayed out of the argument (and Bush's appointment of two conservative Supreme Court justices who look favorably on states' rights probably ensures that the Court will keep its distance). With the federal government standing aside, the states got busy. All but a handful passed bans on gay marriage. Several adopted civil unions instead of gay marriage. One, Massachusetts, is tussling over efforts to revoke gay marriage.

The result is a diversity of practice that mirrors the diversity of opinion. And gay marriage, not incidentally, is moving out of the realm of protest politics and into the realm of normal politics; in the 2006 elections, the issue was distinctly less inflammatory than two years earlier. It is also moving out of the courts. According to Carrie Evans, the state legislative director of the Human Rights Campaign (a gay-rights organization), most gay-marriage litigation has already passed through the judicial pipeline; only four states have cases under way, and few other plausible venues remain. "It's all going to shift to the state legislatures," she says. "The state and national groups will have to go there."

Barring the unexpected, then, same-sex marriage began in the courts and will wind up in the state legislatures and on state ballots: the abortion tape runs backward. The issue will remain controversial, producing its share of flare-ups and fireworks; but it will become more tractable over time, as the country works its way toward a consensus. As a political issue, gay marriage will be around for years, but as a catalyst for culture war, it has already peaked.

Although I bow to no one in my support for gay marriage—society needs more marriages, not fewer, and gay couples need the protections and obligations of marriage, and gay individuals need the hope and promise of marriage—the last few years have provided a potent demonstration of the power of moral pluralism to act as a political shock absorber. Even moral absolutists—people who believe gay marriage is a basic human right or, for that matter, people who believe abortion is murder—should grudgingly support pluralism, because it makes the world safe for their moral activism by keeping the cultural peace. Someone should tell Mitt Romney. Maybe Mitt Romney could tell him.

3-3 How America's "Devolution Revolution" Reshaped Its Federalism

Thad Kousser

From the arrival of Franklin D. Roosevelt's New Deal policies to fight the Depression in the early 1930s until the wane of Lyndon B. Johnson's Great Society initiatives to end poverty in the late 1960s, federalism was in steady retreat. States appeared destined to become the administrative units of the national government. Although they administered most social welfare policies, they followed strict federal guidelines in spending mostly federal dollars. Beginning in the 1990s, the trend has reversed—what Thad Kousser refers to in this essay as the "devolution revolution." This recent history reminds us that federalism is solidly implanted in the Constitution, awaiting the efforts of those with a stake in strong state control to invoke its provisions. During the past two decades, Republicans opposed to many of the social policies coming out of Washington have done so, with success.

For the first few minutes after the Supreme Court issued its opinion in the case challenging President Obama's universal healthcare law—a constitutional battle fought over whether the federal government could order individuals to buy health insurance, launched by state governments that opposed such mandates—America's leading media outlets got the news wrong. Fox News and CNN incorrectly reported that the health care mandate had been overturned, misleading even the president himself.[1] Reading the first few pages of the opinion, in which the Court took the side of the states in sharply limiting the power of the federal government to regulate commerce, reporters first believed that the healthcare law had been overturned. Reading further, they saw that Court upheld most parts of the law, interpreting the health care mandate as a "tax" which Congress was free to levy. When they read further still, reporters discovered that the opinion struck down the requirement that states dramatically expand the healthcare program (known as Medicaid) that provides care for the poor and elderly or lose all federal funding for

these services. This returned to governors and state legislatures the power to decide how wide their social safety nets should be cast.

The frantic, confused news cycle on the morning of June 28, 2012 serves as a microcosm of the shifting story of American federalism. Exactly which powers belong to the federal government and which are reserved to the states has been fought out in constitutional conventions, in courtrooms, and on battlegrounds. Victories have never been complete and resolutions are never final, but the impacts of these fights have always had a profound effect on vital policies governing millions of Americans. This essay focuses on one critical episode in the evolution of American federalism and how it has shaped health care and social service policy.

I. American Federalism in Flux

Throughout its development as a nation, the United States has seen its formal governing structures and informal lines of authority redrawn over and over again through the constantly contested

Source: Translated from Kousser Thad, Géant Laure, « La « dévolution » : une reformulation du fédéralisme américain », Revue française de science politique 2/ 2014 (Vol. 64), p. 265-287 © Presses de Sciences Po.

evolution of American federalism. Conflicts over which powers should belong to the national government and which belong to the states are as American as apple pie, the Star Spangled Banner, and Levi's jeans. America's failed first government under the Articles of Confederation collapsed in large part because the federal government was not given enough authority. The debates over the new Constitution in Philadelphia in 1787 often focused on the key question of federalism, with the Founders constructing patchwork solutions such as state-based representation in the US Senate and the population-based House to bring states large and small into agreement. Since then, two of the nation's most profound and bloodiest internal conflicts—the Civil War from 1861–65 and the civil rights movement nearly a century later—have been fought over the intersecting issues of race and states' rights. Because the national government and states often take opposing positions in areas as fundamental as slavery, civil rights, abortion rights, and the scope of government, shifting authority from one level to another shifts policy in profound ways. "From the start," one scholar of the history of American federalism notes, "political opponents have fought about federalism because it affects who wins and who loses a particular fight" (Robertson 2012, p. 8).

In recent decades, battles over federalism have shifted into less hostile but still critically important venues. The federal courts are the final arbiter of what is and what is not a state right, and also serve as the final arbiter in the disputes between the fifty sovereign states that are inevitable in America's "horizontal federalism" (Zimmerman 2011). Recent landmark cases have shifted power in different directions. In the 2010 *McDonald v. Chicago* case, the US Supreme Court struck down a Chicago, Illinois handgun ban, ruling that the Constitution's 2nd Amendment right to bear arms constrained state gun control legislation. Yet the national government does not always win in federal courts. The Supreme Court's June 28, 2012 decision in the *National Federation of Independent Business v. Sebelius* case, while upholding much of President Obama's healthcare law, was nonetheless a victory for states because it so sharply circumscribed

what the federal government could do to regulate commerce and to compel states to expand programs like Medicaid that are jointly funded by states and by the national government.

The back and forth of modern federalism has played out most clearly in an area of government that is central to both the budgets of federal, state, and local governments and to the lives of tens of millions of Americans: the social safety net. Power over the design and funding of welfare and health-care programs has been in constant and consequential flux over the past generation. These social services were first provided by individual states with some federal assistance, then standardized into the joint federal-state programs of Franklin D. Roosevelt's "New Deal" and Lyndon B. Johnson's "Great Society" legislation, and more recently have come to be shaped more and more by state forces.

These changes have over and again rewritten the rules of federalism. One longtime observer of and participant in these battles, who served as an intergovernmental affairs advisor to President Richard Nixon, titled a recent essay, "There Will Always Be a New Federalism" (Nathan 2006). The newest federalism was created in the mid-1990s through the "devolution revolution," which gave states tremendous power to rewrite the rules of their welfare programs, changed the fiscal incentives that states face, and initiated a massive health insurance expansion funded primarily the federal government but implemented, with great latitude, by states.

In this essay, I ask how the devolution revolution has reshaped federalism in the United States. My focus is on services because its stakes are so high—with joint federal and state expenditures totaling $405 billion dollars in 2009[2]—and because it is in this realm that policy choices and implementation by the two levels of government are most deeply intertwined. I look at how the newest "new federalism"— including the devolution of authority over welfare and the children's health insurance program, as well as new intergovernmental fiscal incentives—has altered both state policy and the federal-state relationship. I begin by explaining how federalism now works in the realm of social service policy, describing how federal laws shape the level of state flexibility and the variation in policy choices across states. To illustrate how abstract regulations affect concrete political decisions, I turn a close focus to how the devolution revolution played out in the nation's largest state, California. I then draw upon recent data from all states in order to two central theses:

1. The way that federal aid to states is structured has profound fiscal and political effects, determining how fast the social service safety net will expand. When Washington, DC began funding state welfare programs through block grant, this shift in the structure of aid predictably caused growth in state spending on welfare to slow dramatically. By contrast, generous matching grants for Medicaid and children's health insurance have put states on a fiscal escalator that has been hard to get off even during recessions.

2. Shifts in which level of government funds a social service program have a profound effect on which types of Americans pay its bills. When the federal government supports a program, the highly progressive structure of federal taxation ensures that more affluent Americans provide most of the funding for redistribution. When states pay more, the burden of welfare funding falls more heavily on middle-and low-income residents because state taxes in the US are generally regressive.

After demonstrating these points, I conclude by putting my findings in the broader context of the literature on federalism and on political representation, and by speculating about the lessons they hold for future policy devolution.

II. The Devolution Revolution in Social Services

The construction of America's social safety net—the healthcare, welfare, and pensions provided to the aged, the needy, and the disabled—is a complex story of federal and state policymakers working together to provide services that are funded both by government and by the private sector (see Hacker's 2002 *The Divided Welfare State*) and delivered both through bureaucracies and through private actors (see Morgan and Campbell's 2011 *The Delegated Welfare State*). Any brief summary of its history necessarily omits important details. Still, I begin this section by outlining how the development of America's welfare state interacts with federalism, and then devote the rest of the section to a close look at one critical period: the "devolution revolution" in social services that took place during the 1990s. I discuss the political debate over their safety nets and how to change the funding formulas that structure intergovernmental aid. I then analyze how those formulas shape the incentives of state policymakers. To illustrate the ways in which the new authority and new incentives affected state policy choices, I provide a case study that focuses on how the devolution revolution led to the expansion of one program but the contraction of another in California.

The American welfare state has its roots in the pensions provided for veterans of the nation's Civil War during the late nineteenth century and in the payments granted to impoverished single women with children in the early twentieth century (Skocpol 1992). The veterans' pensions were federally funded, but state governments played an important cooperative role in the early development of social service programs (Johnson 2007). For instance, California's 1941 budget included $38 million in federal assistance payments to the aged, blind and children, matched by $22 million in state funds. The two landmark expansions of these joint state-federal social services came with the "New Deal" policies passed under President Franklin D. Roosevelt in the 1930s and the "Great Society" policies passed by President Lyndon B. Johnson in the 1960s. The New Deal established pensions for the elderly and systematized welfare payments to the poor through what became known as the Aid to Families with Dependent Children (AFDC) program. The Great Society created, among other programs, the Medicaid program to fund health care for the poor, the elderly in nursing homes, and the disabled. Both Medicaid and AFDC would be administered by the states, with the federal government paying at least half of the cost through "matching grants" and more than half of the cost in passed new laws giving states the opportunity to expand their safety nets (Congressional Research Service 1993, Coughlin, Ku, and Holahan 1994). Because the matching grants offered them such a good deal, which I detail below, most states took advantage of this opportunity and widened their safety nets. Then, in the devolution revolution of the 1990s, lawmakers in Washington, DC changed the funding relationship between the federal and state governments, giving states more autonomy but at the same time halting the growth of one of these social service programs.

II.A. Roots of the Revolution

In the mid-1990s, the roots of this revolution were planted by two trends, one economic and one political. First, a national recession put tremendous fiscal pressure on states, especially in the area of social services. Though the recession lasted only from July 1990 through March 1991[3], the slow recovery created major deficits in state budgets for years to follow. Twenty-nine states were forced to cut their budgets in 1991, and thirty-five states made budget cuts totaling $4.5 billion in 1992.[4] California's budget did not pass until months past the constitutional deadline in 1993, and even as late as 1995, eight states, including New York, were still forced to make cuts.[5]

Why did the recession hit states so hard? One reason is that nearly all American states have strict balanced budget requirements,[6] a rule that is notably lacking at the federal level. Presidents and Congress can react to deficits by increasing spending and cutting taxes, as President Obama and the Democratic Congress did with the 2009 stimulus package. States, by contrast, must balance their books through painful cuts and tax increases. A second reason is that because states administer so many of the nation's safety net services, any financial downturn has a two-sided effect on their budgets. The supply of tax revenues goes down, but the demand for social services like Medicaid and welfare rises.

A contemporary report by the National Association of Budget Officers at the time demonstrated how these supply and demand dynamics threw state budgets out of balance: "Both the modest budget growth and the midyear budget adjustments reflect the tepid economy as well as pressures from double-digit growth in Medicaid spending and increased welfare caseloads."[7] The statements of state leaders testify to how they saw these trends. Medicaid was called the "Pac-man" of state budgets, a reference to the video game character who ate up everything around him, and Georgia governor Zell Miller compared it to the state's quick-spreading kudzu plant (Weissert 1992). State officials chafed at what they perceived as a lack of flexibility to make major Medicaid and welfare cuts, and called upon Washington, DC to give states great power over these increasingly expensive programs.

After the 1994 elections, Congress became much more receptive to such demands. The Newt Gingrich-led "Republican Revolution," in which the GOP took control of the House of Representatives for the first time in a generation, set the stage for the devolution revolution. This shift in party control came in the midst of the growing political polarization between the two parties in America (see McCarty, Poole, and Rosenthal 2006). Whether the sharp disagreement between Democrats and Republicans on issues such as the optimal size of the safety net was due more to shifts among elected leaders (Fiorina 2005) or among voters, it was clear during the 1994 elections that the partisan divide was vast. After winning those elections, Gingrich and many other Republicans pushed for a switch from federal matching grants for social services to "block grants," a proposal that had also been made by Ronald Reagan. This was a proposal as much about ideology as it was about federalism, since all sides expected that block grants would lead to smaller government. "Block grants aim to provide greater federal budget certainty and a stronger state incentive to contain program costs," according to Lambrew (2005, p. 1). They do so by giving states both a fixed annual sum from the federal government to run a social service program (increasing predictability) and by making states responsible for any and all funding above that sum (providing them with the incentive to cut costs). In 1995, Speaker Gingrich pushed to switch the Medicaid program into a block grant to states, but lost in a political battle that revived the electoral fortunes of President Bill Clinton.

The Democratic president had steadfastly opposed major changes in Medicaid, but throughout his career had called for "an end to welfare as we have come to know it."[8] He vetoed two early welfare reform bills pushed by Republicans, but as the 1996 election approached, Clinton took a centrist position by cutting a deal with Gingrich on a major welfare reform package in August of that year. The new law transformed the Aid to Families with Dependent Children program, renaming it Temporary Assistance for Needy Families, proposing a five-year lifetime limit on benefits, requiring that welfare recipients go back to work after two years on the rolls, and providing more child care for working recipients.[9] The law also changed federalism by making welfare a block grant, and giving states tremendous control over how to spend the grant. No longer did states receive matching dollars from the federal government, giving them the greater incentives to cut costs that Gingrich had favored for Medicaid. States were also given great freedom to craft their new programs; they could make their lifetime limits either shorter or longer than the federal baseline of a five-year limit, they could set the length of the workweek required of welfare recipients, and could create other limits or extensions. Whether states wished to build a program that was more conservative or more liberal than the federal guidelines, they had the flexibility to do so (Kousser 2005, Ch. 7).

Another major deal cut between Clinton and Gingrich the next year completed the devolution revolution. The creation of the state Children's Health Insurance Program (CHIP) as part of a budget deal in 1997 put states in charge of building a new healthcare program for the children of the working poor and, at state discretion, their parents. Reaching families with incomes too high to qualify for Medicaid but too low to purchase private insurance, the program could be offered through Medicaid, through the plan that covered state employees, or through a new program that met specific benchmarks (Health Care Financing Administration 1998). State legislatures and governors were left to decide. In this way, the CHIP program gave states another great source of authority. However, in its funding structure, it resembled Medicaid, with matching rates giving the federal government the ability to influence state decisions.

While the move in the mid-1990s to shift policy and fiscal control of social services to the states may have been an incomplete victory for the advocates of states' rights, it still constituted a revolution. Though Medicaid remained generally unchanged, the new CHIP program gave states policy control of a program with fiscal incentives still managed by the federal government, and the TANF program transformed welfare into a system with policies and purse strings firmly under state control.

In the battles over each of these programs, Democratic and Republican leaders in Washington, DC clearly understood that the major policy dimension that polarizes American parties—the battle over whether to expand or to shrink government—was at stake in the debate over whether to devolve authority and restructure grants. Federalism, to paraphrase Robertson's (2012) words, would determine who won and who lost the fight over health care costs and welfare generosity. Republican support for decentralization of social policy, as Béland and de Chantal (2003) have observed, was driven primarily by ideological opposition to big government. To understand completely the link between devolution and the size of the safety net, it is necessary to look close at how federal funding formulas can influence state decisions.

II.B. How Federal Funding Formulas Reshape State Incentives

In the joint federal-state programs that compose America's healthcare and welfare programs, the national government has used both regulations and inducements to motivate states to broaden their safety nets. The regulations have come in the requirement that states dramatically expand their welfare (beginning in the 1930s) and healthcare programs (starting in the 1960s) to meet new nationwide standards. The inducements have been the federal dollars sent to pay much of the cost of these new mandates, structured in a way that gave states a clear incentive to meet and often to go beyond the national baseline. Federal grants were intentionally designed to push states toward more generous services than they might otherwise provide. If Washington, DC had sent states block grants of a fixed amount, most states would spent all of the federal money while trying hard to minimize state costs paid in addition to the block grant. Instead, federal lawmakers designed matching rates that required states to spend their own dollars in order to bring in federal money. The more a state spent of its own, the more money it would bring in from Washington, DC, a formula for growth in social service provision.

The rationale for this system, from economic theories of fiscal federalism, is that matching grants should "be employed where the provision of local services generates benefits for residents of other jurisdictions (Oates 1999, p. 1127)." That is, because the advantages of providing for the welfare and healthcare of residents in one state spill over into other states and the nation as a whole, those benefits should be internalized into the decision calculus of lawmakers in each state. It did not hurt that Democrats in Congress at the time favored higher social service spending, and realized that matching grants would create a powerful incentive for states, even ones that had traditionally been frugal, to move in this direction. Importantly, the federal matching rate varied across states, and always provided at least one federal dollar for each state dollar spent.

Table 1	Federal Matching Rates for Social Service Programs	

State	Medicaid	CHIP
Arkansas	$4.31	$4.25
California	$1.60	$1.86
Kansas	$2.30	$2.61
Mississippi	$5.61	$4.87
Montana	$3.54	$3.38
New York	$1.60	$1.86
New Mexico	$4.13	$3.99
Texas	$2.44	$2.46

Notes: Entries indicate how many dollars will be transferred by the federal government to match one dollar of state spending, by program and by state. Medicaid and CHIP figures are from the 2010 fiscal year, both taken from Kaiser Family Foundation (2011) and Families USA (2011).

Table 1 shows the matching rates that an illustrative sample of states receives today in Medicaid and in the CHIP program. It shows that poorer states like Mississippi and New Mexico received a higher match than rich states such as California and New York, a deliberate feature of the funding formula designed to give state lawmakers in states with tight budgets the ability to provide generous services.

Consider the effects of this grant structure on the decision calculus of governors and state legislators writing their budgets. For a program like the Children's Health Insurance Program, in New York the nearly two-to-one match means that in good times, the state can increase its budget by $100 million dollars and deliver, thanks to the federal grant, an additional $286 million in healthcare services to poor families. When the state budget is flush, this acts like an escalator, providing a great incentive to spend a surplus on the CHIP program because lawmakers get so much "bang for the buck" in this program area. But just as the federal match makes it easy to increase spending in this area during good times, it also makes it hard to cut healthcare spending in bad times. When New York is in deficit, in order to reduce its state deficit by $100 million, lawmakers must eliminate $286 million worth of services. This effectively sends $186 million back to the federal government, never an attractive option to state policymakers. This makes cutting healthcare to working families much more difficult, in both political and policy terms, than cutting other areas of government like higher education, prisons, or primary education that are almost entirely state funded. Because matching grants push states to increase healthcare provision in good times and make it hard to cut in bad times, they should be thought of— whether one favors or opposes generous social services—as a lever of federal control over state decisions that reduces state autonomy.

In a poor state such as Mississippi, the federal matching rate is even higher. This gives the state an even better fiscal deal, at the same time that it makes the federal level of control even stronger. For $100 million in new state spending, Mississippi lawmakers can secure an extra $487 in federal CHIP funds, but of course they would have to sacrifice that much in order to trim their state budget by $100 million. Washington, DC structured grants this way during times when Democrats controlled government, knowing that the arrangement would lead to social service expansion, while Newt Gingrich and other Republicans sought to change the formulas in order to shrink government.

The partisan politics of matching grants have also come into play in the wake of the Supreme Court's decision, referenced at the beginning of this essay, on the health care reform effort led by President Obama. This episode has demonstrated the limits of the federal government's legal and fiscal power. The Affordable Care Act originally mandated that states expand their Medicaid programs to cover the working poor by January, 2014, with the federal government paying all of the costs initially and then giving every state a generous matching rate (paying 90%– 95% of the costs) in the following years. The Supreme Court overturned this mandate, and the reaction by many states showed that even this enormous fiscal incentive could not compel them to act. Two dozen states, led primarily by Republican governors, refused the Medicaid expansion out of ideological opposition to the growth of social services and political opposition to the president. This halted the implementation of a key part of Obamacare in many areas of the country, leaving the federal government powerless to coerce the states.

Yet sometimes lost in debates about the overall size of government is the important redistribution of federal tax dollars across states accomplished by the varying matching rates detailed in Table 1. Pointing out the disparities in these matching grants rates paints a portrait of an "equalizing" federalism that is at odds with the conventional idea that America's national government treats all states uniformly. "In all other federal systems," Robertson (2012, p. 2) writes, "the national government deliberately equalizes regional resources by redistributing more financial aid to the poorest regions. The United States is the only federal system that does not equalize state resources in this way" (see also Watts, 2006). In Medicaid, a massive program in which the federal government distributes $318 billion in aid across the states annually (Bureau of the Census 2012, Table 152), the aid is spread out unequally, with the most generous grants going to the poorest states. At least in this realm, American federalism is not exceptional; it redistributes money from rich to poor states just as federalism does in other nations.

II.C. Implementing the Devolution Revolution in California

Leaders in each state capitol had little time to ponder such distributional concerns in the late 1990s, because the devolution revolution gave them important decisions to make. Every state's autonomous control over its welfare programs dramatically increased after the federal passage of welfare reform in 1996. While the freedom granted by this devolution sent states in different directions, the experience of one state can teach general lessons about how the shift in power and the new fiscal relationship played out in state capitols around the country. The nation's social services have diffused across the rest of the nation (Walker 1969, Gray 1973). The state's government at the time was split between the nation's two political parties, with a Republican governor negotiating policy with a legislature controlled by Democrats. Like the rest of America, the Golden State was just coming out of the deep recession, giving policymakers some money to spend on expanding social services but leaving them cautious about how such generosity would threaten the state budget when lean years returned. Though never a "typical state," California's political and fiscal conditions at this time were reflective of what was occurring in many other states.

In California, 1997 was the year of welfare reform, with Washington DC's actions of the previous year putting this issue at the top of the agenda for state officials at the state's capitol in Sacramento. Governor Pete Wilson, a moderate Republican who had been elected on a platform of expanding "preventive" social services like child care and prenatal health, but who had been forced by the state's struggling economy to push for budget cuts in these and other areas, saw this as a chance to leave a major policy legacy. The Democrats who controlled the two houses of the state's legislature worried that any welfare reform meant welfare cuts to the constituents whom many Democrats represented. Yet while legislators have a monopoly over the power to introduce bills in California, as in all American legislatures, they felt pressured to respond to the federal mandate for reform as well as to the way that block grants changed state fiscal incentives. As the following account shows, this led to one of the paradoxical patterns of federalism: while devolution gives states freedom, it also forces decisions upon them and allows the federal government to dictate state policy agendas.

When California's legislature convened for the beginning of its session in January, 1997, one influential newspaper columnist wrote that the capitol's hallways were filled with talk of many issues, but that "there was, however, one topic that overshadowed all others in terms of magnitude, uncertainty and urgency: welfare reform. Under new federal welfare-reform legislation, Republican Gov. Pete Wilson and the Democrat-controlled Legislature have six months to develop an overhaul of the system that consumes nearly a fifth of the state budget and supports nearly 5 million Californians, about 20 percent of the nation's welfare burden."[10] The extent to which state action was forced by federal devolution was illustrated by another columnist's quote: "The challenge the state faces to come up with a new welfare system is enormous, dictated by the federal welfare reform bill President Clinton signed last summer."[11]

Does this mean that devolution pushed the state in a direction that its leaders did not want to go? In the legislature's case, it certainly did. Prominent leaders like Senate Health and Human Services Committee Chair Diane Watson, a Democrat representing an inner city Los Angeles district with many welfare recipients, certainly would have preferred not to change the existing system. But Gov. Wilson clearly did want change, and seized the political opportunity created by federal action. In the spring of 1997, he gave speeches across the state in support of his reform plan, which went beyond the federal guidelines by putting a one-year limit on welfare enrollment, cutting the size of monthly checks to recipients, and requiring them to work 35 hours a week in job training or education programs to receive the checks.[12]

Democratic legislative leaders, quite predictably, pushed back against the governor's proposal. When the bills containing them, authored by Republican legislators, reached the Assembly Human Services Committee, the Democratic majority on the committee stripped out their key provisions—the one-year time limit, the grant reductions, and the 35-hour workweek—on votes that broke down along party lines. "I would suggest that's gutting the bill to almost nothing," said Republican Assemblyman Keith Olberg, author of one of the bills.[13] Yet legislators knew that the governor possessed the key power of the veto, giving him the power to kill any welfare deal that the Democrats themselves reached and thus assuring that the state's reaction to federal devolution would be a compromise between what California Democrats and Republican Gov. Pete Wilson wanted. Dion Aroner, the state Assembly's Human Services Chair, spoke about welfare reform in a tone that was at once resigned to the fact that federal action worked against her policy preferences but also optimistic that it opened up new opportunities for positive state innovations. "We will do significant damage to lots of families and seniors and kids who will be hurt by what the federal government did." Aroner said. "We can't fix that . . . But if the system becomes more focused on helping people get off welfare and finding them jobs, . . . that will be historic reform."[14]

In order to craft a compromise that might garner both legislative approval and the governor's signature, top leaders created a conference committee that brought together 18 members of the Assembly and Senate, many of whom were political moderates not closely tied to either side of the issue. After liberals on the committee pushed for a plan that "went as far as it legally could to maintain the status quo . . . Speaker Cruz Bustamante intervened, and he and Senate President Pro Tem Bill Lockyer directed Democratic members of a welfare conference committee to tone down their plan and make it at least marginally acceptable to moderates."[15]

After Gov. Wilson vetoed the first set of welfare bills sent to him at the beginning of the summer, in August he signed a compromise package crafted in the conference committee. Passed on votes of 65–11 in the Assembly and 33–5 in the Senate, with liberal Democrats objecting, the plan included an 18-month time limit and a 20-hour work requirement, splitting the difference between the governor's plan and the legislature's proposals.[16] Just as importantly for the state, it slowed the growth of welfare spending, with all of the savings going to other California programs because the funding was sent through a block grant. The devolution of power from the federal government had spurred state action, but the new policy bore the imprint of both branches of state government and put all of the savings back into California's budget.

Welfare was not the only power passed along to the states by Clinton and the Republican in Congress. In late 1997, after the welfare reform debate was resolved in California, state lawmakers were given authority over a newly created program to provide health insurance for the children of the working poor through the Children's Health Insurance Program. Unlike welfare reform, this program was a clear expansion of the social safety net, a concession that President Clinton won from Newt Gingrich that thrilled Democrats in state capitols across the country and calmed the fears of fiscal conservatives with its generous federal matching rate. Because every dollar of California spending was matched with nearly two federal dollars, Republican Governor Wilson and legislative Democrats both agreed on expanding coverage.

While they could have done so through Medicaid or the government employees' healthcare program, California lawmakers took advantage of the federal option to craft a completely new program which they called "Healthy Families." The privately administered, publicly funded insurance program would be available to 580,000 children whose parents paid a premium of about $27 per month, costing the state $478 million and the federal government $875 million.[17] The governor proposed a plan that Democratic leaders immediately embraced. While a handful of conservative lawmakers criticized the plan as too costly for the state and some Democrats worried that the premiums charged would be too expensive for the poor, it passed within weeks with overwhelming bipartisan support.[18]

The lessons of this California case study are clear, and confirm the strategies that Gingrich and Clinton pursued in Washington, DC. Giving states more autonomy through block grants in welfare led California to contract its welfare services and spending, even though the federal law did not strictly mandate such retrenchment. In the Children's Health Insurance Program, by contrast, the generous matching grants combined with state autonomy was a gift that California's Republican governor and Democratic legislators eagerly accepted. They designed a new program, putting a Californian imprint on the national idea, but happily took Washington's money to expand their health coverage of the working poor. Devolving power through different funding structures caused the healthcare safety net to widen while the welfare safety net shrank.

III. The Long-Term Effects of the Devolution Revolution

While every state's reaction to the devolution revolution differed in its details, the broad spending trends in health care and welfare across the states mirror California's pattern. This section examines broad spending patterns to show that healthcare expenditures rose consistently after the devolution revolution, while welfare spending has often been flat. This illustrates the argument that grant structures help to shape the size of government. After looking at how much is spent, I then ask which citizens pay for safety net spending when more responsibility is sent to the states. Looking at tax distributions at different levels of government supports the thesis that devolutions to the states quietly shift the fiscal burden of supporting the safety net towards lower-and middle-income Americans.

III.A. State Spending Patterns Since the 1990s

Just as California's response to powers devolved from the national government was shaped by the state's partisan configuration, policy needs, and fiscal capacity, other states took the devolved responsibilities in different directions. Their governments crafted policies that "fit their states," in the term often used by advocates of devolution, or at least reflected contemporary demands and the preferences of state leaders at the time. To structure their CHIP plans, 13 states offered plans similar to the plans provided to state employees, but 35 did what California did: they created their own new systems, verified as "equivalent" to the benchmark but with

state-specific details (Kousser 2005, Ch. 7). When it came to reforming their state welfare systems, 36 states adopted the federal default of a five-year lifetime limit on benefits, but nine states adopted shorter limits and five states enacted longer limits. In both policy areas, states picked policies that generally fit the preferences of the parties holding their governorships and state legislatures. States with more "professional" legislatures—those paying full-time salaries, meeting year-round, and employing large staffs—were more likely to move beyond the default options and craft innovative programs (Kousser 2005, Ch. 7).

At the same time that the devolution revolution changed the shape of state social safety nets, it also changed their scope. State spending on healthcare and welfare both shifted. Importantly, they went in different directions, a divergence that can be explained by the differing funding formulas chosen for each policy area. In health care, where generous federal matching grants created an incentive for states to spend a bit more of their own money to capture many federal dollars, spending rose sharply. By definition, CHIP spending rose as the new program came into being.

But Figure 1 shows just how much the Medicaid matching rates, preserved in the 1995 budget battle that fended off the transition to a block grant, gave states both the motivation and the means to spend ever-larger sums on health care for the poor, aged, blind, and disabled. Medicaid spending was already high in the early 1990s, but since the mid-1990s it rose sharply as medical costs soared and as states frequently added recipients and services to their programs. This growth generally slowed when a stronger economy meant that fewer Americans qualified to receive health care coverage, but grew nonetheless. Total state and federal Medicaid spending more than doubled from $161 billion in 1997 to $374 billion in 2009.

By contrast, the rise in welfare spending was sharply curtailed through the welfare reforms of 1996. As Figure 2 shows, after an initial increase in federal expenditures to provide services such as child care and job training in the immediate aftermath

Figure 1   Growth in Federal, State, and Total Medicaid Spending Since "Devolution Revolution" (in Billions)

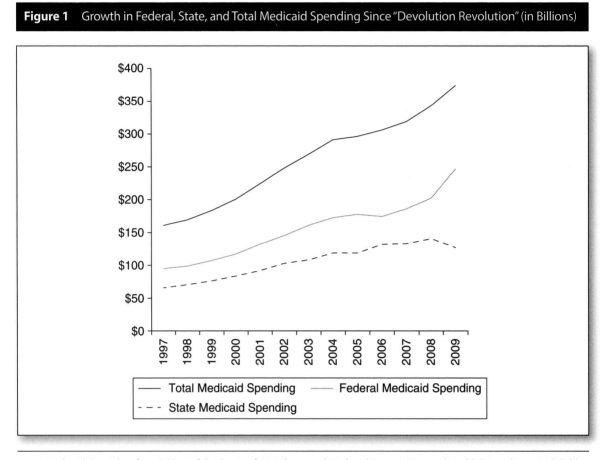

Notes: Medicaid data taken from Table 3 of the Centers for Medicare and Medicaid Services' National Health Expenditures Web Tables, accessed at https://www.cms.gov/NationalHealthExpendData/downloads/tables.pdf in November, 2011.

of welfare reform, spending on this safety net program has been flat or decreasing over the past decade. Since the numbers reported for both Medicaid and welfare here are not adjusted for inflation, they indicate a clear retrenchment in this portion of the American safety net. This is a function of two trends. First, the default guidelines passed down from the federal government to the states tightened up welfare eligibility through policies such as weekly work requirements and, most importantly, the lifetime limit on benefits. Although the federal welfare reform did also encourage more spending in areas such as child care, and the federal legislation did not dictate any reduction in monthly benefit checks, many states were able to contain their costs by trimming their welfare rolls once recipients had reached their lifetime benefit limits. The second factor at work here was the shift to a block grant funding structure. When states cut welfare after 1997, they could (subject to "maintenance of effort" requirements[19]) keep much of the savings, and this no doubt played a role in the many benefit cuts that have come during tough fiscal times over the past decade.

Figure 2 Growth in Federal, State, and Total Welfare Spending Since "Devolution Revolution" (in Billions)

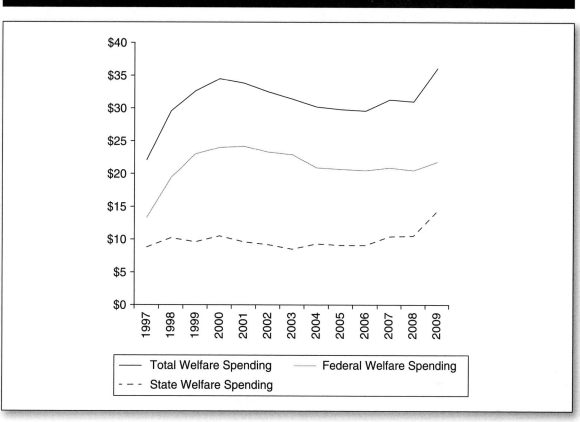

Notes: "Welfare" spending defined as Temporary Aid to Needy Family (TANF) total federal and total state maintenance of effort spending. Welfare data taken from appropriate tables in the US Department of Health and Human Services' TANF Financial Data Archives, accessed at http://www.acf.hhs.gov/programs/ofs/data/archives.html in November, 2011.

Overall, the devolution revolution has been a tale of two programs. Once Newt Gingrich's proposal to block grant Medicaid was defeated, the program saw no major policy or funding formula changes. As a result, this program continued to grow through state and primarily federal funds, and was augmented by the Children's Health Insurance Program with its generous matching grants. In welfare, both policy reforms and a shift to block grant funding set the program on a path to retrenchment. Though one could still debate whether the compromise reached by Speaker Gingrich and President Clinton led to "an end to welfare as we have come to know it," both the state and national governments have been able to curtail the growth of welfare spending. States have been able to shape the program's new rules to the policy preferences of their elected officials, and as many states meet the bare minimum spending requirements, the federal government has paid an increasingly large role in funding welfare.

III.B. Changing "Who Decides?" Changes "Who Pays?"

The shares of funding for a program that is paid by the federal government and by the states is important for those concerned with redistribution. One fact of federalism that is seldom discussed but which deserves serious contemplation is that shifting the responsibility for funding programs to the states also shifts the burden of paying for them to less affluent Americans. This is a result of the way that tax structures differ across different levels of government. The federal government relies primarily on a progressive income tax and other payroll taxes to fund its programs.[20] Because money is raised this way, higher income Americans generally pay a larger share of their incomes in federal taxes than middle and low income Americans do. States vary dramatically in the sources of their funding. Legislators, governors, and direct democracy voters have set up fiscal systems that rely in different measures on income taxes, sales taxes, and property taxes. There is no single state tax structure. What is generally true, though, is that state taxes all across the country are less progressive than federal taxes.

A "progressive" tax system is one in which higher income households pay a higher tax rate. By contrast, the less affluent must pay a larger portion of their incomes in taxes than the rich in a "regressive" system. Analyses of the tax rates paid by Americans in different income groups show that federal taxes are strongly progressive, while nearly every state has, instead, a regressive tax system. Figure 3 reports the tax rates paid by different income groups, beginning with the poorest 20% of Americans at the top and continuing through to the richest 1% at the bottom. Moving down the chart, we see that Americans who make more money pay higher tax rates. The least affluent income groups pay 3.9% and 9.1% of their incomes in federal taxes, because the tax rates on their incomes are so low and because many qualify for the earned income tax credit (EITC), a rebate given to those with low incomes to make up for the fact that Social Security taxes are withheld from their monthly paychecks. As incomes rise, eligibility for the EITC goes away and those in the third group, the middle class, pay 13.9% of their income in taxes. The upper middle class pays 17.3% and the richest Americans pay tax rates of about

20%, with the rate edging up at every income level. Overall, taxes paid to the federal government take much more from the rich than from the poor.

The pattern in the states is radically different. As Figure 4 shows, state and local[21] tax rates are highest on the least affluent. States rely on three general types of taxes. First, many raise money from personal and corporate income taxes, but state income tax rates are generally less progressive than federal rates and some states, such as Texas and Florida, have no personal income tax at all. Second, most states[22] fill their coffers with sales taxes, which charge a flat rate on the purchase of products. Since poorer Americans spend more of their incomes on these purchases than rich Americans, who are generally able to save more money, sales taxes hit the poor especially hard. Finally, states charge property taxes, paid by homeowners and passed along, by market forces, to renters. These rates—which range from 0.40 in Hawaii to 2.57 in Texas[23]—are flat across property values, and thus generally hit lower income earners harder than the affluent. Although states vary widely in which of these three areas they rely most upon for their tax revenues, the cumulative effect is that states charge higher rates to poorer residents, acting like the folklore character Robin Hood in reverse.

Figure 4 reports tax rates by income group for Texas (a relatively low-tax, strongly regressive state), California (a high tax, less regressive state) and for the average across all states. In each case, state residents in the lowest income group pay the highest rate: 10.2% in California, 12.2% in Texas, and 10.9% across all states. By contrast, the top 1% of earners only pay 7.4% of their income in state taxes in California, a mere 3.0% in Texas, and 5.2% nationally. Averaging across all states, tax rates go down as income levels rise, just the opposite of the pattern for federal taxes. Why is this the case? In Texas, taxes are so clearly regressive because the state imposes no personal income tax and instead taxes the sales and housing expenses that cost the poor so much of their incomes. California does impose an income tax, which

Figure 3   Fraction of Income Paid in Federal Taxes, by Income Group

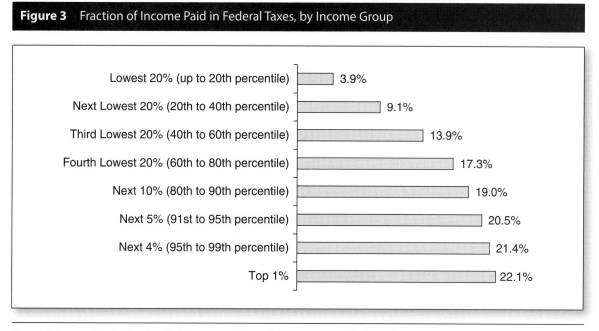

Source: Citizens for Tax Justice, *America's Tax System Is Not as Progressive as You Think,* April 2011. Based on the Institute on Taxation and Economic Policy Tax Model.

explains why it is less regressive than Texas and the state average. Yet because the Golden State's famous Proposition 13 dramatically reduced property tax receipts, it relies on a steep sales tax that taxes the poor heavily.

Overall, federal taxes take the most from the wealthiest, while state tax policies give some of this redistribution back. The implications for federalism are clear. Any shift in program responsibility from the federal to state governments shifts the burden of paying for these programs increasingly to the less affluent. Devolution, in this respect, works against redistribution. By contrast, federal "bailouts" of the states are paid for much more by high-income earners than tax increases enacted at the state level. Recognizing this does not imply a normative judgment about such shifts—there have been strenuous arguments made in favor of both progressive and regressive tax structures. What is hard to debate, however, is that changing who decides on a

policy by shifting control of it from one level of government to another also changes who pays for it.

IV. Conclusion: Perspectives on Devolution

While modern America may have been created through a war against England, its national structure has been formed and reshaped not through fights with external powers but by internal conflicts among states and between states and the federal government. The battles to define American federalism were once carried out in a war and in lunch counter sit-ins, but have now shifted to the courts and to federal funding formulas. These venues may be less dramatic, but they are no less important. As Théret (1992) makes clear, federal systems need not be static, with the actual practice of federalism—including whether or not the central government equalizes resources across subnational units—determining whether the form of the federation will endure, centralize, or dissolve. Though a bloodless

Figure 4   Fraction of Income Paid in State and Local Taxes, by Income Group

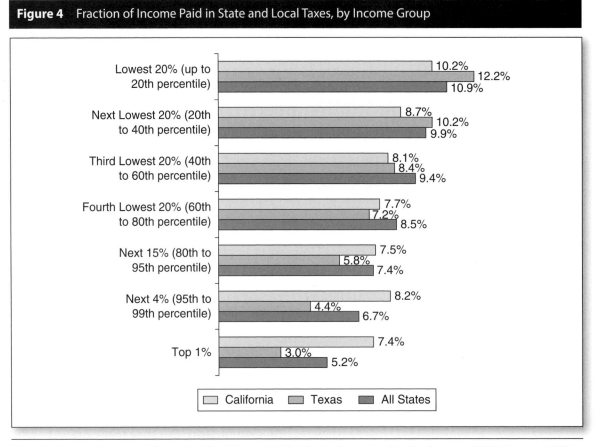

Source: Institute on Taxation and Economic Policy, Who Pays? A Distributional Analysis of the Tax Systems of All 50 States, 3rd Edition, November 2009. Percentages reflect net payments by non-elderly families in 2007 after federal deductibility of some state taxes in calculating federal income taxes.

revolution, the "devolution revolution" nonetheless changed the structure of the federal-state relationship and the scope of the social service safety net.

Were these changes for the better? The fiscal federalism literature has long argued for an increased role for states in fitting policies to local needs and demands. "In our 'ideal' model," declared influential economist Wallace Oates, "the central government provides the efficient out-put of the national public good, while numerous local governments offer individuals a wide variety of output of the local public

good" (Oates 1968, 54). The devolution revolution clearly gave states more authority over their welfare programs, and provided the opportunity to create new health care programs and much of the money to fund them.

Did this give Americans the structure of government that they wanted? A recent survey asking respondents about what level of government should address specific policy challenges found that voters wanted to see the federal government address health care, but that state and local governments should assist the poor (Schneider et al. 2010, 9). Because the devolutions of the 1990s provided the most latitude to states in the welfare realm, both in the freedom to craft policy and through the funding mechanism of block grants, this move appears consistent with public opinion.

Does devolution give residents of each state the programs and policies that they desire? While much research has shown the impact that the preferences of state elected officials has on policy choices, a new study based on a breakthrough in the ability to measure state public opinion shows that these choices do not always reflect voter demands. Not all states respond equally to public demands, and some do such a poor job matching policy with public opinion that there is a potential "democratic deficit" in the states (Lax and Phillips 2011). Combined with Wlezien and Soroka's (2010) recent research showing the challenges that Canadian federalism poses for public responsiveness, this recent stream of research raises questions about whether giving more authority to states truly brings government closer to the people.

Looking toward the future of federalism in America, how do the lessons of this essay combine to tell us anything about what might happen if more control over the safety net is devolved to the states? Just as Newt Gingrich pushed to create Medicaid block grants in 1995, Republican candidate Mitt Romney called for block grants during the 2012 presidential campaign.[24] If this new round of devolution comes to pass, how will states react? The lessons of the devolution revolution suggest that growth in Medicaid spending will slow dramatically if states have to pay all of the costs of program expansion and are allowed to keep all of the savings of program cuts. Medicaid expenditures may flatten out in the way that welfare spending has evened out since over the past decade. This pattern will not be uniform across states, of course. Because the two parties take clearly different positions on this issue, statehouses controlled by Republicans will be much more likely to use their newfound autonomy to cut Medicaid than Democratic-led states.

The analysis in this essay, put in the context of recent findings from the cross-national study of welfare states, also suggests that the distribution of tax burdens could also shape how state policy might shift. Kato (2003) shows that, during the economic downturns of the 1980s, nations with generous social services turned to consumption taxes—a regressive yet stable source of income—in order to retain funding for their welfare states. In the American states, taxes are already much more regressive than they are at the federal level. If the next round of devolution forces states to provide more of the funding for social services, health care and welfare programs might be preserved only by raising regressive taxes such as the sales tax. If the United States thus follows the European path, social service programs will be funded through taxes that burden poor and middle class taxpayers most heavily (as a proportion of their incomes). The redistributive impact of Medicaid and welfare would be counterbalanced by a more regressive funding, all because of a quirk of American federalism.

Notes

1. Neetzan Zimmerman, "President Obama Thought SCOTUS Struck Down Individual Mandate Because CNN and Fox News Said So." June 28, 2012. *Gawker*.

2. In 2009, joint state and federal expenditures on social services included $374 billion for Medicaid, $11 billion for the Children's Health Insurance Program, and $20 billion in Temporary Aid to Needy Families (Bureau of the Census 2012, Tables 135 and 540).

3. National Bureau of Economic Research, "NBER Business Cycle Dating Committee Determines that Recession Ended in March 1991." Accessed in October 2011.

4. National Association of State Budget Officers, *The Fiscal Survey of the States: October 1992*, Washington, DC: National Governors Association.

5. National Association of State Budget Officers, *The Fiscal Survey of the States: October 1995*, Washington, DC: National Governors Association.

6. For full detail on the nature of these requirements, see National Conference of State Legislatures, *NCSL*

Fiscal Brief: State Balance Budget Provisions, Denver, CO: National Conference of State Legislatures, October 2010.

7. Quoted from page 7 of National Association of State Budget Officers, *The Fiscal Survey of the States: October 1992*, Washington, DC: National Governors Association.

8. Bill Clinton, "The New Covenant: Responsibility and Rebuilding the American Community. Remarks to Students at Georgetown University," October 23, 1991.

9. CNN All Politics, "Clinton Signs Welfare Reform Bill, Angers Liberals," *CNN All Politics*, August 22, 1996.

10. Dan Walters, "The Welfare Unknown," *Sacramento Bee*, January 8, 1997, p. 6B.

11. John Jacobs, "Movement on Welfare Reform," *Sacramento Bee*, March 25, 1997, p. 6B.

12. John Jacobs, "Movement on Welfare Reform," *Sacramento Bee*, March 25, 1997, p. 6B.

13. Dana Wilkie, "Democrats gut Wilson proposal to cut welfare: Assembly panel leaves only shell, but it's not dead yet," *San Diego Union-Tribune*, April 2, 1997, p. A3.

14. Quoted in John Jacobs, "Movement on Welfare Reform," *Sacramento Bee*, March 25, 1997, p. 6B.

15. Dan Walters, "Demos' Welfare Plan Backfires," *Sacramento Bee*, June 30, 1997, p. A1.

16. Brad Hayward and Dan Smith, "Wilson Gets Landmark Welfare Bill," *Sacramento Bee*, p. A1.

17. John Maurelius, "Wilson Optimistic on Kids' Health Coverage," August 28, 1997, *San Diego Union Tribune*, p. A3.

18. Bill Ainsworth, "Kids Health Plan Could Get OK Today," *San Diego Union Tribune*, September 12, 1997, p. A1.

19. See Mark Greenberg, "The TANF Maintenance of Effort Requirement," Center for Law and Social Policy, accessed at http://www.policyarchive.org/handle/10207/bitstreams/14041.pdf in November, 2011.

20. In 2010, 90% of the federal government's $2.163 trillion budget came from these sources: $899 billion from personal income taxes, $191 billion from corporate income taxes, and $857 billion from Medicare, Social Security, and unemployment insurance taxes (which are not structured in the progressive way that income taxes are structured but which are still less regressive than state sales taxes). See Table S3 from the Summary Tables of the Budget of the United States Government, Fiscal Year 2012, accessed at http://www.whitehouse.gov/sites/default/files/omb/budget/fy2012/assets/tables.pdf in October, 2011.

21. Fiscal analyses that compare states frequently combine state and local receipts because, while some states collect more money at the local level than others and some states administer more programs than others at the local level, the combined receipts and programs of these two closely interconnected levels of government represent the full package of taxes and policies that make states comparable to each other.

22. Again, some states—Alaska, Delaware, New Hampshire, Montana, and Oregon—do not charge sales taxes at all. See Federation of Tax Administrators, "State Sales Tax Rates," February 2011, accessed at http://www.taxadmin.org/fta/rate/sales.pdf in October 2011.

23. See *New York Times*, State-by-State Property-Tax Rates, April 10, 2011, accessed at http://www.nytimes.com/2007/04/10/business/11leonhardt-avgproptaxrates.html in October 2011.

24. Sam Baker, "Romney plan calls for Medicaid block grants, repeal of Obama health law," *The Hill*, September 6, 2011.

References

Béland, Daniel and François Vergniolle de Chantal. 2004. "Fighting 'Big Government': Frames, Federalism, and Social Policy Reform in the United States". *Canadian Journal of Sociology* 29(2): 241–264.

Bureau of the Census. 2012. *The 2012 Statistical Abstract*, accessed at http://www.census.gov/compendia/statab/2012edition.html in August 2012.

Congressional Research Service. 1993. *Medicaid Source Book: Background Data and Analysis*. Washington, DC: Congressional Research Service.

Coughlin, T. A., L. Ku, and J. Holahan. 1994. *Medicaid Since 1980: Costs, Coverage, and the Shifting Alliance Between the Federal Government and the States*. Washington, DC: The Urban Institute Press.

Families USA. 2011. Federal Matching Rates for Medicaid and the State Children's Health Insurance Program (CHIP).

Accessed at http://www.familiesusa.org/assets/pdfs/fmap-for-medicaid-and-chip.pdf in October, 2011.

Fiorina, Morris P. 2005. *Culture War? The Myth of a Polarized America.* New York: Pearson-Longman.

Gray, Virginia. 1973. "Innovation in the States: A Diffusion Study." *American Political Science Review* 67:1174–1185.

Hacker, Jacob S. 2002. *The Divided Welfare State: The Battle over Public and Private Social Benefits in the United States.* Cambridge, UK: Cambridge University Press.

Health Care Financing Administration. 1998. *The Children's Health Insurance Program* (CHIP). Press release issued by HCFA on July 17, 1998.

Johnson, Kimberly S. 2007. *Governing the American State: Congress and the New Federalism, 1877–1929.* Princeton, NJ: Princeton University Press.

Lambrew, Jeanne M. 2005. "Making Medicaid a Block Grant Program: An Analysis of the Implications of Past Proposals." *Millbank Quarterly*, January 2005.

Kaiser Family Foundation. 2011. Federal Medical Assistance Percentage (FMAP) for Medicaid and Multiplier. Accessed at http://www.statehealthfacts. org/comparetable. jsp?typ=1&ind=184&cat=4&sub=47 in October, 2011.

Kato, Junko. 2003. *Regressive Taxation and the Welfare State.* Cambridge, UK: Cambridge University Press.

Kousser, Thad. 2005. *Term Limits and the Dismantling of Legislative Professionalism.* New York: Cambridge University Press.

Lax, Jeffrey R. and Justin H. Phillips. 2011. "The Democratic Deficit in the States." *American Journal of Political Science* 56(1): 148–166.

McCarty, Nolan, Keith T. Poole, and Howard Rosenthal. 2006. *Polarized America: The Dance or Ideology and Unequal Riches.* Cambridge: Massachusetts Institute of Technology Press.

Morgan, Kimberly J., and Andrea Louise Campbell. 2011. *The Delegated Welfare State: Medicare, Markets, and the Governance of Social Policy.* New York, NY: Oxford University Press.

Nathan, Richard P. 2006. "There Will Always Be a New Federalism." *Journal of Public Administration Research and Theory* 16(4): 499–510.

Oates, Wallace E. 1968. "The Theory of Public Finance in a Federal System." *The Canadian Journal of Economics* 1(1): 37–54.

Oates, Wallace E. 1999. "An Essay on Fiscal Federalism," *Journal of Economic Literature* 37(3): 1120–1149.

Robertson, David Brian. 2012. *Federalism and the Making of America.* New York and London: Routledge.

Schneider, Sandra K, William G. Jacoby, and Daniel C. Lewis. 2010. "Public Opinion Toward Intergovernmental Policy Responsibilities." *Publius* 41(1): 1–30.

Skocpol T. 1992. *Protecting Soldiers and Mothers: The Political Origins of Social Policy in the United States.* Cambridge, MA: The Belknap Press of Harvard University Press.

Théret, Bruno. 1999. "Regionalism and Federalism: a Comparative Analysis of the Regulation of Economic Tensions between Regions by Canadian and American Federal Intergovernmental Transfer Programmes." *International Journal of Urban and Regional Research* 23(3): 479–512.

Walker, Jack. 1969. "The Diffusion of Innovations Among the American States." *American Political Science Review* 63:880–899.

Watts, Ronald L. 2006. "Comparative Conclusions," in Akhtar Majeed, Ronald L. Watts, and Douglas M. Brown, editors, *Distribution of Powers and Responsibilities in Federal Countries.* Montreal, Canada: McGill-Queens University Press.

Weissert, Carol S. 1992. "Medicaid in the 1990s: Trends, Innovations, and the Future of the 'PAC-Man' of State Budgets." *Publius* 22:93–109.

Wlezien, Christopher, and Stuart N. Soroka. 2010. "Federalism and Public Responsiveness to Policy." *Publius* 41(1): 31–52.

Zimmerman, Joseph F. 2011. *Horizontal Federalism: Interstate Relations.* Albany, NY: State University of New York Press.

Chapter 4

Civil Rights

4-1 *Schuette v. Bamn*

Supreme Court of the United States

> After the Supreme Court ruled in 2003 that the University of Michigan could consider race in admitting undergraduates and law school students, voters passed an amendment to the state constitution (Proposition 26) banning consideration of race in admission decisions to the state's public universities. During the spring of 2014, the Supreme Court upheld the constitutionality of Michigan voters' decision in a 6-to-2 vote (with one abstention). The key issue in this much-anticipated decision was not the constitutionality of using race but, rather, whether voters could revoke from admission officials the discretion to enlist race as a criterion. In Chapter 9, justices Antonin Scalia and Stephen Breyer describe the reasoning they follow in deciding a case. Their very different approaches are well illustrated in their opinions below.

SCHUETTE, ATTORNEY GENERAL OF MICHIGAN *v.*

COALITION TO DEFEND AFFIRMATIVE ACTION,

INTEGRATION AND IMMIGRATION RIGHTS AND FIGHT FOR

EQUALITY BY ANY MEANS NECESSARY (BAMN) ET AL.[1]

JUSTICE KENNEDY announced the judgment of the Court and delivered an opinion, in which THE CHIEF JUSTICE and JUSTICE ALITO join.

The Court in this case must determine whether an amendment to the Constitution of the State of Michigan, approved and enacted by its voters, is invalid under the Equal Protection Clause of the Fourteenth Amendment to the Constitution of the United States.

In 2003 the Court reviewed the constitutionality of two admissions systems at the University of Michigan, one for its undergraduate class and one for its law school. The undergraduate admissions plan was addressed in *Gratz* v. *Bollinger*. The law school admission plan was addressed in *Grutter* v. *Bollinger*. Each admissions process permitted the explicit consideration of an applicant's race. In *Gratz*, the Court invalidated the undergraduate plan as a violation of the Equal Protection Clause. In *Grutter*, the Court found no constitutional flaw in the law school admission plan's more limited use of race-based preferences.

In response to the Court's decision in *Gratz*, the university revised its undergraduate admissions process, but the revision still allowed limited use of race-based preferences. After a statewide debate on the question of racial preferences in the context of governmental decisionmaking, the voters, in 2006, adopted an amendment to the State Constitution prohibiting state and other governmental entities in Michigan from granting certain preferences, including race-based preferences, in a wide range of actions and decisions. Under the terms of the amendment, race-based preferences cannot be part of the admissions process for state universities. That particular prohibition is central to the instant case.

The ballot proposal was called Proposal 2 and, after it passed by a margin of 58 percent to 42 percent, the resulting enactment became Article I, §26, of the Michigan Constitution. As noted, the amendment is in broad terms. Section 26 states, in relevant part, as follows:

"(1) The University of Michigan, Michigan State University, Wayne State University, and any other public college or university, community college, or school district shall not discriminate against, or grant preferential treatment to, any individual or group on the basis of race, sex, color, ethnicity, or national origin in the operation of public employment, public education, or public contracting.

"(2) The state shall not discriminate against, or grant preferential treatment to, any individual or group on the basis of race, sex, color, ethnicity, or national origin in the operation of public employment, public education, or public contracting.

. . .

Before the Court addresses the question presented, it is important to note what this case is not about. It is not about the constitutionality, or the merits, of race-conscious admissions policies in higher education. The consideration of race in admissions presents complex questions, in part addressed last Term in *Fisher* v. *University of Texas at Austin*. In *Fisher*,

the Court did not disturb the principle that the consideration of race in admissions is permissible, provided that certain conditions are met. In this case, as in *Fisher*, that principle is not challenged. The question here concerns not the permissibility of race-conscious admissions policies under the Constitution but whether, and in what manner, voters in the States may choose to prohibit the consideration of racial preferences in governmental decisions, in particular with respect to school admissions. . . . While this case arises in Michigan, the decision by the State's voters reflects in part the national dialogue regarding the wisdom and practicality of race-conscious admissions policies in higher education.

. . .

Here Michigan voters acted in concert and statewide to seek consensus and adopt a policy on a difficult subject against a historical background of race in America that has been a source of tragedy and persisting injustice. That history demands that we continue to learn, to listen, and to remain open to new approaches if we are to aspire always to a constitutional order in which all persons are treated with fairness and equal dignity. Were the Court to rule that the question addressed by Michigan voters is too sensitive or complex to be within the grasp of the electorate; or that the policies at issue remain too delicate to be resolved save by university officials or faculties, acting at some remove from immediate public scrutiny and control; or that these matters are so arcane that the electorate's power must be limited because the people cannot prudently exercise that power even after a full debate, that holding would be an unprecedented restriction on the exercise of a fundamental right held not just by one person but by all in common. It is the right to speak and debate and learn and then, as a matter of political will, to act through a lawful electoral process.

The respondents in this case insist that a difficult question of public policy must be taken from the reach of the voters, and thus removed from the realm of public discussion, dialogue, and debate in an election campaign. Quite in addition to the serious First Amendment implications of that position with respect to any particular election, it is inconsistent with the underlying premises of a responsible, functioning democracy. One of those premises is that a democracy has the capacity—and the duty—to learn from its past mistakes; to discover and confront persisting biases; and by respectful, rational deliberation to rise above those flaws and injustices. That process is impeded, not advanced, by court decrees based on the proposition that the public cannot have the requisite repose to discuss certain issues. It is demeaning to the democratic process to presume that the voters are not capable of deciding an issue of this sensitivity on decent and rational grounds. The process of public discourse and political debate should not be foreclosed even if there is a risk that during a public campaign there will be those, on both sides, who seek to use racial division and discord to their own political advantage. An informed public can, and must, rise above this. The idea of democracy is that it can, and must, mature. Freedom embraces the right, indeed the duty, to engage in a rational, civic discourse in order to determine how best to form a consensus to shape the destiny of the Nation and its people. These First Amendment dynamics would be disserved if this Court were to say that the question here at issue is beyond the capacity of the voters to debate and then to determine.

This case is not about how the debate about racial preferences should be resolved. It is about who may resolve it. There is no authority in the Constitution of the United States or in this Court's precedents for the Judiciary to set aside Michigan laws that commit this policy determination to the voters. . . . Deliberative debate on sensitive issues such as racial preferences all too often may shade into rancor. But that does not justify removing certain court-determined issues from the voters' reach. Democracy does not presume that some subjects are either too divisive or too profound for public debate.

The judgment of the Court of Appeals for the Sixth Circuit is reversed.

It is so ordered.

Justice Scalia's concurring opinion (joined by Clarence Thomas).

It has come to this. Called upon to explore the jurisprudential twilight zone between two errant lines of precedent, we confront a frighteningly bizarre question: Does the Equal Protection Clause of the Fourteenth Amendment *forbid* what its text plainly *requires*? Needless to say (except that this case obliges us to say it), the question answers itself. "The Constitution proscribes government discrimination on the basis of race, and state-provided education is no exception." . . . It is precisely this understanding—the correct understanding—of the federal Equal Protection Clause that the people of the State of Michigan have adopted for their own fundamental law. By adopting it, they did not simultaneously *offend* it.

Even taking this Court's sorry line of race-based admissions cases as a given, I find the question presented only slightly less strange: Does the Equal Protection Clause forbid a State from banning a practice that the Clause barely—and only provisionally—permits? Reacting to those race-based-admissions decisions, some States—whether deterred by the prospect of costly litigation; aware that *Grutter*'s bell may soon toll simply opposed in principle to the notion of "benign" racial discrimination—have gotten out of the racial-preferences business altogether. And with our express encouragement: "Universities in California, Florida, and Washington State, where racial preferences in admissions are prohibited by state law, are currently engaging in experimenting with a wide variety of alternative approaches. Universities in other States can *and should* draw on the most promising aspects of these race-neutral alternatives as they develop." Respondents seem to think this admonition was merely in jest.[1] The experiment, they maintain, is not only over; it never rightly began. Neither the people of the States nor their legislatures ever had the option of directing subordinate public-university officials to cease considering the race of applicants, since that would deny members of those minority groups the option of enacting a policy designed to further their interest, thus denying them the equal protection of the laws. Never mind that it is hotly disputed whether the practice of race-based admissions is *ever* in a racial minority's interest. . . . And never mind that, were a public university to stake its defense of a race-based-admissions policy on the ground that it was *designed* to benefit primarily minorities (as opposed to all students, regardless of color, by enhancing diversity), *we would hold the policy unconstitutional.*

But the battleground for this case is not the constitutionality of race-based admissions—at least, not quite. Rather, it is the so-called political-process doctrine. . . . The problems with the political-process doctrine begin with its triggering prong, which assigns to a court the task of determining whether a law that reallocates policy-making authority concerns a "racial issue." . . . It suggests that an issue is racial if adopting one position on the question would "at bottom inur[e] primarily to the benefit of the minority, and is designed for that purpose." . . . It is irrelevant that . . . both the racial minority and the racial majority benefit from the policy in question, and members of both groups favor it. Judges should instead focus their guesswork on their own juridical sense of what is primarily for the benefit of minorities. . . . On second thought, maybe judges need only ask this question: Is it possible "that minorities may consider" the policy in question to be "in their interest"? . . . If so, you can be sure that you are dealing with a "racial issue." No good can come of such random judicial musing. . . . Fundamentally, it misreads the Equal Protection Clause to protect "particular group[s]," a construction that we have tirelessly repudiated in a "long line of cases understanding equal protection as a personal right."

Taken to the limits of its logic, . . . [the political process doctrine] nearly swallows the rule of structural state sovereignty. If indeed the Fourteenth Amendment forbids States to "place effective decision making authority over" racial issues at "different level[s] of government," then . . . a subordinate entity (suppose it is a city council) could itself take action on the issue, action either favorable or unfavorable to minorities. It could even reverse itself

later. What it could not do, however, is redelegate its power to an even lower level of state government (such as a city council committee) without forfeiting it, since the necessary effect of wresting it back would be to put an additional obstacle in the path of minorities. Likewise, no entity or official higher up the state chain (*e.g.,* a county board) could exercise authority over the issue. Nor, even, could the state legislature, or the people by constitutional amendment, revoke the legislative conferral of power to the subordinate, whether the city council, its subcommittee, or the county board. [Its] logic would create affirmative-action safe havens wherever subordinate officials in public universities (1) traditionally have enjoyed "effective decision making authority" over admissions policy but (2) have not yet used that authority to prohibit race-conscious admissions decisions. The mere existence of a subordinate's discretion over the matter would work a kind of reverse pre-emption. It is "a strange notion—alien to our system—that local governmental bodies can forever pre-empt the ability of a State—the sovereign power—to address a matter of compelling concern to the State."

––––––––––––

Justice Breyer, concurring in the judgment.

. . . We here focus on the prohibition of "grant[ing] . . . preferential treatment . . . on the basis of race . . . in . . . public education." I agree with the plurality that the amendment is consistent with the Federal Equal Protection Clause. U. S. Const., Amdt. 14. But I believe this for different reasons.

First, we do not address the amendment insofar as it forbids the use of race-conscious admissions programs designed to remedy past exclusionary racial discrimination or the direct effects of that discrimination. Application of the amendment in that context would present different questions which may demand different answers. Rather, we here address the amendment only as it applies to, and forbids, programs that . . . rest upon "one justification": using "race in the admissions process" solely in order to "obtai[n] the educational benefits that flow from a diverse student body. . . .

Second, . . . the Constitution allows local, state, and national communities to adopt narrowly tailored race-conscious programs designed to bring about greater inclusion and diversity. But the Constitution foresees the ballot box, not the courts, as the normal instrument for resolving differences and debates about the merits of these programs. . . . In short, the "Constitution creates a democratic political system through which the people themselves must together find answers" to disagreements of this kind.

Third, . . . this case, in contrast, does not involve a reordering of the *political* process; it does not in fact involve the movement of decisionmaking from one political level to another. Rather, here, Michigan law delegated broad policymaking authority to elected university boards, but those boards delegated admissions-related decisionmaking authority to unelected university faculty members and administrators. . . . Thus, unelected faculty members and administrators, not voters or their elected representatives, adopted the race-conscious admissions programs affected by Michigan's constitutional amendment. The amendment took decisionmaking authority away from these unelected actors and placed it in the hands of the voters.

Why does this matter? . . . The administrative process encompasses vast numbers of decisionmakers answering numerous policy questions in hosts of different fields. . . . Administrative bodies modify programs in detail, and decisionmaking authority within the administrative process frequently moves around—due to amendments to statutes, new administrative rules, and evolving agency practice. It is thus particularly difficult in this context for judges to determine when a change in the locus of decisionmaking authority places a comparative structural burden on a racial minority. . . .

As I have said, my discussion here is limited to circumstances in which decisionmaking is moved from an unelected administrative body to a politically responsive one, and in which the targeted race-conscious admissions programs consider race solely in order to obtain the educational benefits of a diverse student body. We need now decide no more

than whether the Federal Constitution permits Michigan to apply its constitutional amendment in those circumstances. I would hold that it does. Therefore, I concur in the judgment of the Court.

Justice Sotomayor dissenting (joined by Ruth Bader Ginsburg).

. . . Under our Constitution, majority rule is not without limit. Our system of government is predicated on an equilibrium between the notion that a majority of citizens may determine governmental policy through legislation enacted by their elected representatives, and the overriding principle that there are nonetheless some things the Constitution forbids even a majority of citizens to do. The political-process doctrine, grounded in the Fourteenth Amendment, is a central check on majority rule.

The Fourteenth Amendment instructs that all who act for the government may not "deny to any person . . . the equal protection of the laws." We often think of equal protection as a guarantee that the government will apply the law in an equal fashion—that it will not intentionally discriminate against minority groups. But equal protection of the laws means more than that; it also secures the right of all citizens to participate meaningfully and equally in the process through which laws are created. Few rights are as fundamental as the right to participate meaningfully and equally in the process of government. . . . That right is the bedrock of our democracy, recognized from its very inception. . . .

This should come as no surprise. The political process is the channel of change. . . . It is the means by which citizens may both obtain desirable legislation and repeal undesirable legislation. Of course, we do not expect minority members of our society to obtain every single result they seek through the political process—not, at least, when their views conflict with those of the majority. The minority plainly does not have a right to prevail over majority groups in any given political contest. But the minority does have a right to play by the same rules as the majority. . . .

Our cases recognize at least three features of the right to meaningful participation in the political process. Two of them, thankfully, are uncontroversial. First, every eligible citizen has a right to vote. . . . This, woefully, has not always been the case. But it is a right no one would take issue with today. Second, the majority may not make it more difficult for the minority to exercise the right to vote. This, too, is widely accepted. After all, the Court has invalidated grandfather clauses, good character requirements, poll taxes, and gerrymandering provisions. The third feature, the one the plurality dismantles today, is that a majority may not reconfigure the existing political process in a manner that creates a two-tiered system of political change, subjecting laws designed to protect or benefit discrete and insular minorities to a more burdensome political process than all other laws. . . .

My colleagues would stop at the second. The plurality embraces the freedom of "self-government" without limits. . . . The wrong sought to be corrected by the political-process doctrine, they say, is not one that should concern us and is in any event beyond the reach of the Fourteenth Amendment. As they see it, the Court's role in protecting the political process ends once we have removed certain barriers to the minority's participation in that process. Then, they say, we must sit back and let the majority rule. . . .

To accept the first two features of the right to meaningful participation in the political process, while renouncing the third, paves the way for the majority to do what it has done time and again throughout our Nation's history: afford the minority the opportunity to participate, yet manipulate the ground rules so as to ensure the minority's defeat. This is entirely at odds with our idea of equality under the law.

To reiterate, none of this is to say that the political-process doctrine prohibits the exercise of democratic self-government. Nothing prevents a majority of citizens from pursuing or obtaining its preferred outcome in a political contest. Here, for instance, I agree with the plurality that Michiganders who were unhappy with *Grutter* were free to pursue an end to race-sensitive admissions policies in their State. . . . They were free to elect governing boards that opposed race-sensitive admissions policies or, through public discourse and dialogue, to lobby the existing boards toward that end. They were also free to remove from the boards the authority to make any decisions with respect to admissions policies, as opposed to only decisions concerning race-sensitive admissions policies. But what the majority could not do, consistent with the Constitution, is change the ground rules of the political process in a manner that makes it more difficult for racial minorities alone to achieve their goals. In doing so, the majority effectively rigs the contest to guarantee a particular outcome. That is the very wrong the political-process doctrine seeks to remedy. . . .

To be clear, I do not mean to suggest that the virtues of adopting race-sensitive admissions policies should inform the legal question before the Court today regarding the constitutionality of [proposition] 26. But I cannot ignore the unfortunate outcome of today's decision: Short of amending the State Constitution, a Herculean task, racial minorities in Michigan are deprived of even an opportunity to convince Michigan's public colleges and universities to consider race in their admissions plans when other attempts to achieve racial diversity have proved unworkable, and those institutions are unnecessarily hobbled in their pursuit of a diverse student body.

Today's decision eviscerates an important strand of our equal protection jurisprudence. For members of historically marginalized groups, which rely on the federal courts to protect their constitutional rights, the decision can hardly bolster hope for a vision of democracy that preserves for all the right to participate meaningfully and equally in self-government.

I respectfully dissent.

Note

1. We excerpted the text of the decision here and omitted case law citation for readability. For the full decision, see http://www.supremecourt.gov/opinions/13pdf/12-682_8759.pdf.

4-2 From *New State Voting Laws: Barriers to the Ballot?*

Justin Levitt

> *The following essay represents excerpts compiled from Justin Levitt's testimony before the Senate Judiciary Committee in 2011. In it he criticizes recent changes in half a dozen states' voting laws. The expressed purpose of these reforms is to prevent voter fraud. The changes include mandatory photo identification, restrictions on voter registration drives, and a ban on Sunday voting. Given that all were passed by Republican legislatures and should make voting disproportionately more difficult for racial minorities, Professor Levitt questions the integrity of these laws. Since his testimony, numerous additional states have continued to tighten registration and voting laws. The federal courts have variously ruled them constitutional and unconstitutional, which will surely draw the U.S. Supreme Court into this thicket of state regulations.*

. . . As has been repeatedly recognized, voting, the right preservative of all other rights, "is of the most fundamental significance under our constitutional structure. . . . Unfortunately, a spate of recent state regulations seem headed in the wrong direction. These laws exact real burdens on real Americans, making it more difficult for citizens to exercise their rights to vote. Crucially, these burdens are not only real but unnecessary, which renders them suspect as a matter of constitutional law, and fundamentally flawed as a matter of public policy. Not only do they make it more difficult for Americans to vote, but they do so without any meaningful benefit. Indeed, in several circumstances, the new laws are directly counterproductive.

There are several types of state laws or policies that deserve attention. . . . The first involves new limits on the ability to help citizens register to vote. The second involves new limits on citizens' ability to cast ballots before election day. And the third involves new limits on citizens' ability to establish their identity at the polls on election day itself. Getting on the rolls, early voting, and voting on election day: all have been subject to new, and unjustified, limits.

Restrictions on Registration

First, there have recently been renewed efforts to restrict the ability of citizens to offer their colleagues assistance in registering to vote. These efforts are exemplified by troublesome provisions of HB 1355. . . . Florida's latest in a series of attempts to restrict voter registration over the past few years . . . In 2005, ostensibly concerned by organizations withholding registration forms that they collected, the legislature imposed . . . substantial restrictions on organizations conducting voter registration drives. These restrictions included substantial fines, with both individual and organizational liability, for each and every form delivered to elections officials more than 10 days after the form was completed. The fine structure was sufficiently severe to cause the nonpartisan

Source: Subcommittee on Constitution, Civil Rights and Human Rights of the Committee on the Judiciary, U.S. Senate. *New State Voting Laws: Barriers to the Ballot?* 112th Cong., 1st sess., September 8, 2011, statement of Justin Levitt, associate professor of law, Loyola Law School, Los Angeles, California. http://www.gpo.gov/fdsys/pkg/CHRG-112shrg71326/html/CHRG-112shrg71326.htm.

League of Women Voters—concerned citizens volunteering their time to help other eligible citizens register to vote—to stop its Florida voter registration activity for the very first time in the organization's 67-year history.

In subsequent litigation, a federal court rightly recognized that voter registration drives entail core political speech, protected by the First Amendment and inextricably intertwined with efforts to "persuade others to vote, educate potential voters about upcoming political issues, communicate their political support for particular issues, and otherwise enlist like-minded citizens in promoting shared political, economic, and social positions." And it rightly recognized that undue efforts to restrict registration drives impermissibly limit both political speech and association. The court explained that Florida had not "provided any evidence[,] much less an explanation," supporting the need for its fine structure—and preliminarily enjoined the implementation of this portion of the law.

One year later, the legislature enacted an amended law . . . , HB 1355. . . . It requires any person—any individual or group—to fill out an official state form before offering to help distribute, collect, and submit the registration form of anyone other than immediate family; this registration includes the name, address, and sworn declaration of every single individual soliciting or collecting registration forms, whether employee or casual volunteer. . . .

. . .

Given its burdens, the law will have some predictable effects—few of which increase the reliability of the registration system in any meaningful respect. Instead, the law has caused both Democracia USA, one of the larger civic engagement organizations in Florida dedicated to empowering the Latino electorate, and the League of Women Voters, a nonpartisan civic engagement enterprise of unparalleled lineage, to declare a halt to all voter registration activity within the state.

When voter registration drives are unable to offer their assistance, citizens lose one vital means to ensure that they are properly registered to vote—not merely new registrants, but also the 14% of Floridians who move within the state and need to re-register.[1] Moreover, the population impacted by such restrictions is not evenly distributed. According to the U.S. Census Bureau's Current Population Survey, minority citizens disproportionately register and re-register through voter registration drives: . . . in 2010, 6% of non-Hispanic white voters reported registering through a voter registration drive, compared to 14% of Hispanic voters and 12% of non-Hispanic African-American voters.

What is particularly galling to many is that the new restrictions on civic participation put Florida's League of Women Voters out of the voter registration business unnecessarily. That is, there is no compelling public policy need for such prerequisite burdens on informal voter registration drives on campuses, in houses of worship, and in the many other circumstances in which individuals assist their fellow citizens without first creating a bureaucratic documentation, reporting, and tracking apparatus. Florida already had legal provisions requiring voter registration forms to be delivered in timely fashion. Florida already had legal provisions vigorously defended in court as ensuring the accuracy of registration form information. Florida already had legal provisions penalizing any intentional wrongdoing in the registration process. The new regulations impose a burden out of proportion to their incremental benefit.

. . .

Restrictions on Early Voting

Second, there have recently been efforts to limit opportunities for citizens to cast valid ballots in advance of Election Day. Here too, Florida's HB 1355 provides an example.

At least since 1998, Florida has allowed electors to vote ballots in-person before Election Day. . . . HB 1355 would change the early voting schedule again, restricting local authority. . . . The most significant restriction is that jurisdictions would no longer have the option to offer early voting on the Sunday before Election Day. This was an option that several counties offered in the past, as a service to their constituents, many of whom work long hours during the week, are more available on the weekend, and are most energized just before Election Day. The list of jurisdictions choosing to offer early voting on the Sunday before Election Day in the past includes the state's largest, most urban, and most diverse counties. . . . Under HB 1355, they do not have this latitude.

The change has a direct impact on a particularly notable form of mobilization in Florida: many houses of worship, particularly in minority communities, encourage their congregations in nonpartisan fashion to discharge their civic obligations after fulfilling their spiritual ones. So after Sunday morning church services, many congregants would travel to the polls, in the counties that offered Sunday voting. After HB 1355, this is no longer an option.

As with the restriction on registration drives, the elimination of early voting on the Sunday before the election does not fall evenly on the population as a whole. In the past, minority citizens disproportionately voted on the final Sunday before Election Day.[2] In 2008, for example, African-Americans represented 13% of the total voters, and 22% of the early voters, but *31%* of the total voters on the final Sunday; Hispanic citizens represented 11% of the total voters, and 11% of the early voters, but *22%* of the total voters on the final Sunday. Notably, the pattern is similar in 2010: African-Americans represented 12% of the total voters, and 13% of the early voters, but *23%* of the voters on the final Sunday; Hispanics represented 9% of the total voters, and 8% of the early voters, but *16%* of the voters on the final Sunday.

Restrictions at the Polls

. . .

Before 2011, only two states in the country—Indiana and Georgia—required government-issued photo identification in order to cast a ballot at the polls that can be counted. The five additional states mentioned above represent disturbing additions, but they remain, together, only a small minority of jurisdictions.

Instead, the vast majority of states allow legitimate citizens a broader set of options to prove their identity. . . . The alternatives range from signature comparisons, to sworn affidavits, to identification documents like utility bills, bank statements, employee IDs, and the like. Some of these other states ask those without government-issued photo identification to vote provisional ballots, which can be further investigated if there arises additional doubt about a voter's identity. . . . And all of these identification provisions are layered atop the considerable security safeguards of the federal Help America Vote Act of 2002 ("HAVA"), which requires that each of a jurisdiction's first-time voters registering by mail have her identity confirmed—either by verifying her social security digits or driver's license number against reliable lists, or by presenting reliable documentation from a long and inclusive menu—before her ballot may be counted. These other 44 states offer alternatives for a reason. They recognize that there are some legitimate, eligible American citizens who do not possess government-issued photo identification cards. . . .

The Harm of Restrictive Identification Rules

There is no question that government-issued photo identification makes many common practices easier. Those who do not have such ID are likely to find it more difficult to take advantage of many of the privileges of modern society. It is true, for example, that you have to show photo identification to buy full-strength Sudafed.[3] It is also deeply beside the point. No American ever gave her life for the fundamental right to buy decongestants.

There is also no question that most eligible citizens have government-issued photo identification. It is likely that each of the individuals attending today's hearing has some form of government-issued photo identification. But the right of the franchise—and the responsibility to ensure its continued reasonable access—is not limited to the individuals attending today's hearing, or even to the majority of the American public. Voting is a fundamental right for more than just most of us. It is a right that must be zealously safeguarded for every eligible American citizen. . . .

There have recently been renewed efforts to limit opportunities for citizens to cast a valid ballot at the polls, most notably in the form of new restrictions on how those citizens may demonstrate their identity. In 2011, four states—Kansas, Tennessee, Texas, and Wisconsin—passed new restrictive laws requiring most citizens to show particular types of government-issued photo identification cards in order to cast a ballot at the polls that can be counted. . . .

There have been several surveys asking eligible Americans about the documentation they possess, with some varying conclusions. . . . A 2008 survey found that 4.9% of *registered voters* responding nationwide did not have current government-issued photo identification; an additional 3.1% of respondents did not have current government-issued photo identification listing their full legal name (rather than, for example, a nickname or maiden name).[4] Another 2008 survey found that 5.7% of *registered voters* nationwide did not have a current valid driver's license or passport; an additional 1.1% of respondents had those documents, but not listing their full legal name.[5] . . . Still another 2008 survey found that 1.2% of *registered voters* in Indiana, Maryland, and Mississippi did not have any government-issued photo identification, but did not inquire whether the subjects' ID was current or reflected the same name on the registration rolls.[6] . . . A 2006 survey found that 12% of *actual midterm voters* in California, New Mexico, and Washington did not have a valid state driver's license, but did not inquire whether the subjects had a non-driver's government-issued photo identification card.

Other research surveys voting-age American citizens, whether currently registered or not. A 2007 survey found that 16.1% of *voting-age citizens* in Indiana did not have current government-issued photo identification; an additional 2.8% of respondents did not have current identification listing their full legal name. And a 2006 survey found that 11% of *voting-age citizens* nationwide did not have current government-issued photo identification.[7]

. . .

It is important to note that even choosing the most conservative estimate—a survey targeting registered voters in select states, rather than the electorate as a whole—1.2% of registered voters do not have the identification required by the most restrictive states. Even this substantially conservative result amounts to an impact reaching more than *two million* registered voters if applied nationwide. And the larger estimates show an impact reaching more than *twenty-two million* voting-age citizens.[8]

Moreover, *every* study to have examined the issue has found that those without government-issued photo identification are not evenly spread across the electorate. Just as the surveys differ in their overall assessment of the magnitude of the problem, they differ in their assessment of magnitude of the disparate impact. But the available data clearly show that those without government-issued photo identification are more likely to be nonwhite, more likely to be either younger voters or seniors, more likely to be from low-income households, and more likely to have less formal education. . . .

These impacts are both substantial and statistically significant. For example, one 2008 survey found that while 3.7% of responding white *registered voters* nationwide did not have current valid government-issued photo identification, 7.3% of Latino voters and 9.5% of African-American voters lacked this ID. And among *voting-age citizens* rather than registered voters, a 2006 national survey found that 8% of white citizens but 16% of Latino voting-age citizens and 25% of African-American voting-age citizens do not have current, valid, government-issued photo identification. While other studies differ in the precise magnitude of these (and other) differential ID rates, all show a substantial effect, with historically underrepresented groups much less likely to have current government-issued photo identification.

These statistics are not merely important for their reflection of the status quo, but for their reflection of significant impact into the future. It often takes ID to get ID. For example, most native-born citizens in

Arkansas seem to require an official copy of a birth certificate to get a government-issued photo identification card ... and seem to require government-issued photo identification to get an official copy of a birth certificate.

Even without this sort of vicious loop, those without current government-issued photo identification often face some difficulty in procuring it. All states of which I am aware require documentation to procure state-issued identification. Even when the identification card itself is offered free of charge, an individual without identification must collect this documentation, which involves time and expense, and travel (without driving) to a government office open during limited (working) hours, which involves time and expense. Official copies of birth certificates cost between $7 and $30 depending on the state, with a median of $15; expedited processing will cost more. A passport costs at least $55, and a replacement naturalization certificate costs $345.

. . .

These eligible Americans have names. Dr. Brenda Williams, of Sumter, South Carolina, has recently been attempting to assist some of her patients in getting the government-issued photo identification required by South Carolina's new law. Her comments to the Department of Justice show that she has spent hundreds of dollars helping her patients attempt to get the necessary ID. And still some have been stymied. For example, Dr. Williams wrote to the Department of Justice about Mrs. Naomi Gordon and her brother, Mr. Raymond Rutherford.[9] Mrs. Gordon's first name was apparently misspelled "Llnoie" by a midwife; a midwife also apparently misspelled Mr. Rutherford's first name "Ramon." The misspellings appear on both of their birth certificates; Mr. Rutherford has the particular difficulty of possessing a birth certificate with an incorrect spelling and a Social Security card with a correct spelling. They have been told that they have to have their names changed through the courts before they will be able to get government-issued photo

identification; neither has yet been able to procure the appropriate ID.

Nora Elze, in Savannah, Georgia, is 88, and has been married for 65 years. But because the name on her birth certificate (her maiden name) and the name on her out-of-state ID (her married name) don't match, she has to produce a 65-year-old marriage license in order to get government-issued photo identification. At last report, she had not found the license, and had not been able to acquire the necessary identification.

. . .

Agnes Cowan and her husband lost many of their personal documents in a fire, including her husband's veterans' ID card. At 81 in 2008, and confined to a wheelchair, Ms. Cowan said that it was virtually impossible for her to cobble together replacement documentation in order to get a government-issued photo ID before Georgia's 2008 primary election, making it the first major election that Ms. Cowan had missed in 63 years.

Among the Indiana citizens prevented from voting a valid ballot in 2007 was 61-year old Republican Valerie Williams. Ms. Williams brought her telephone bill, a Social Security letter, and an expired state driver's license to the polls—but she did not have the current government-issued photo ID that Indiana required. Her provisional ballot was never counted.

. . .

Chris Conley, a 50-year-old veteran of the Navy and Marines, tried to vote in Indiana's 2008 primary, but his Veterans Administration photo ID card did not have an expiration date, and therefore did not meet the state requirements.

Birdie Owen was displaced from Louisiana after Hurricane Katrina, where her birth certificate was lost in the storm. Without a birth certificate, she found herself unable to get a state-issued photo identification card in Missouri.[10]

The stories above represent just a selection of the reports of individuals—real American citizens—without government-issued photo identification. Reliable statistics indicate that there are many others.

The Lack of Justification for Restrictive Identification Rules

As with the other restrictions discussed above, the heavy costs on Mrs. Gordon and other eligible American citizens are not justified by any substantial benefit. Laws preventing citizens from proving their identity at the polls by anything other than certain government-issued photo identification cards are often justified by the need to prevent election fraud. Here too, there appear to be particularly pernicious misconceptions.

Requirements to present certain identification at the polls provide even theoretical protection against *only* one form of fraud: someone who arrives at the polls and pretends to be someone else. . . . All of the available evidence demonstrates that the incidence of any fraud that identification rules could prevent is extraordinarily rare. Though it does occur, there are only a handful of recent accounts, even fewer of which have been substantiated. During this same period, hundreds of millions of ballots have been cast. The most notable significance of the incidents that have surfaced is how rare they appear to be.

In order to assess the incidence of fraud that identification rules could possibly prevent, it is first necessary to cut through a large amount of noise. Some reports or allegations of fraud are simply mislabeled; the substance of a newspaper story simply does not support a headline claim of "fraud." Other reports claim fraud but instead reveal straightforward administrative errors, or administrative practices that concern some, but are not errors at all.

Some of these reports actually do present worrisome evidence of fraud—but not any sort of fraud that identification rules could prevent. Instead, they allege schemes involving fraudulent absentee ballots; or absentee voters who have been coerced;[11] or conspiracies to buy votes;[12] or efforts to tamper with ballots or machines or counting systems.[13] There are occasional reports of double-voting, by individuals voting in their own names and without appropriating another's identity.[14] There are occasional schemes

of insider complicity and/or forgery;[15] when pollworkers and officials are willing to break the law, or miscreants are willing to forge documents, additional requirements for pollworkers to review official documentation cannot prevent the wrongdoing. It is impossible to stop local bosses intent on breaking the law by giving them a new law to break.

There are also reports of fraudulent registration forms, though they involve rogue workers hoping to cheat nonprofit organizations out of an honest effort to register real citizens.[16] These forms are usually subject to the safeguards of HAVA, which flags potentially invalid registration forms for further security measures before a corresponding ballot can be cast. I am aware of no recent substantiated case in which such registration fraud has resulted in a fraudulent vote.

. . .

In sum, my research confirms that there are hundreds of reports of alleged fraud, in thousands of elections, with millions of ballots cast. Yet after wading through the unreliable and irrelevant reports categorized above, only a handful of reports remain that even *allege*, much less substantiate, instances of fraud that increased identification requirements at the polls could prevent.[17]

. . .

Conclusion

This testimony reviews several new state laws impacting the voting process before and on Election Day. There are others of concern as well, beyond the scope of my testimony today—including repeals of election-day registration and repeals of practices easing the restoration of civil rights for those who have been convicted. As a theoretical matter, none of above policies make it impossible to vote. Neither did the poll tax, when it was in place. But in practice, these barriers increase the burdens to eligible citizens of exercising the franchise. More disturbing, the restrictions are unnecessary and unjustified, and even potentially counterproductive. Our most fundamental constitutional right deserves better.

Notes

1. U.S. Census Bureau, 2005–2009 American Community Survey, tbl. B07003, at http://1.usa.gov/nh331s.
2. In order to determine the race and ethnicity of early voters by day, I retrieved the individual early vote information from county Early Voting Reports, at https://doe.dos.state.fl.us/fvrscountyballotreports/FVRSAvailableFiles.aspx, and matched voters' unique registration numbers to the registration records on Florida's voter file, which list self-reported race and ethnicity. . . .
3. Lizette Alvarez, *G.O.P. Legislators Move to Tighten Rules on Voting*, N.Y. TIMES, May 29, 2011 ("'If you have to show a picture ID to buy Sudafed, . . . you should show a picture ID when you vote,' Gov. Nikki Haley said this month when she signed the bill into law in South Carolina, using a common refrain among Republicans.") . . .
4. 2008 Collaborative Multi-Racial Post-Election Study (CMPS), questions D21-D21A, at http://cmpstudy.com/; Matt A. Barreto, New Empirical Evidence on Access to Photo ID (visited Sept. 6, 2011), at http://faculty.washington.edu/mbarreto/research/voterid_090611.pdf.
5. Email from Charles Stewart III, MIT, to Justin Levitt, Loyola Law School (Sept. 6, 2011, 13:27 PST); R. Michael Alvarez et al., 2008 Survey of the Performance of American Elections, Final Report, at http://www.vote.caltech.edu/drupal/files/report/Final%20report20090218.pdf.
6. Robert A. Pastor et al., *Voting and ID Requirements: A Survey of Registered Voters in Three States*, 40 AM. REV. PUB. ADMIN. 461 (2010).
7. *See* Brennan Center for Justice, Citizens Without Proof: A Survey of Americans' Possession of Documentary Proof of Citizenship and Photo Identification 3 (2006), *available at* http://www.brennancenter.org/dynamic/subpages/download_file_39242.pdf.
8. *See* U.S. Census Bureau, 2006 American Community Survey tbl. B05003 (reporting 206,287,902 voting-age citizens as of the 2006 survey period).
9. *See, e.g.,* Email from Dr. Brenda Williams to Chief, Voting Section, re File #2011-2495 (Aug. 14, 2011, 18:59 ET).
10. Robin Carnahan, *Elections Can't Really be Fair, Free and Accurate if Eligible Voters Can't Vote*, HUFFINGTON POST, May 9, 2008.
11. *See, e.g.,* Anastasia Hendrix, *City Workers: We Were Told To Vote, Work for Newsom*, S.F. CHRONICLE, Jan. 15, 2004; Matthew Purdy, *5 Bronx School Officials Are Indicted in Absentee Ballot Fraud*, N.Y. TIMES, Apr. 25, 1996.
12. *See, e.g.,* Beth Musgrave, *Three Sentenced in Bath Vote Fraud*, LEXINGTON HERALD-LEADER, Sept. 25, 2007; Nicklaus Lovelady, *Investigation Into Vote Fraud in Benton County Nets 14th Arrest*, MISS. CLARION-LEDGER, Aug. 31, 2007; Tom Searls, *Six To Learn Fate in Lincoln Vote Buying Case*, CHARLESTON GAZETTE (W.Va.), May 3, 2006, at 1C; Michael E. Ruane, *FBI's Sham Candidate Crawled Under W. Va's Political Rock*, WASH. POST, Dec. 2, 2005, at A1.
13. *See, e.g.,* John M. Glionna, *S.F., State Wade Into Vote Count Controversy*, L.A. TIMES, Nov. 21, 2001.
14. *See, e.g.,* Criminal Complaint, Wisconsin v. Gunka, Case No. 2010ML005173 (Wis. Circuit Ct., Milwaukee County Mar. 8, 2010).
15. *See, e.g.,* Eva Ruth Moravec, *Woman, 81, Jailed in Vote-Fraud Case*, SAN ANTONIO EXPRESS-NEWS, Oct. 5, 2010; Hans A. von Spakovsky, *Where There's Smoke, There's Fire: 100,000 Stolen Votes in Chicago* (Heritage Foundation Legal Memorandum No. 23), Apr. 16, 2008; . . . Michael Cass, *Poll Worker Indicted in Vote Probe*, THE TENNESSEAN, Dec. 20, 2007; Manny Garcia & Tom Dubucq, *Unregistered Voters Cast Ballots in Dade: Dead Man's Vote, Scores of Others Were Allowed Illegally, Herald Finds*, MIAMI HERALD, Dec. 24, 2000 . . .
16. *See, e.g.,* Todd C. Frankel, *8 Charged in StL Voter Fraud*, ST. LOUIS POST-DISPATCH, Dec. 21, 2007; Keith Ervin, *Felony Charges Filed Against 7 in State's Biggest Case of Voter-Registration Fraud*, SEATTLE TIMES, July 26, 2007; Carlos Campos, *Bogus Voter Forms Pop Up in Fulton*, ATLANTA J.-CONST., Oct. 21, 2004.
17. Other scholars' thorough research confirms these conclusions. *See, e.g.,* Lorraine C. Minnite, *The Myth of Voter Fraud* (2010).

Chapter 5

Civil Liberties

5-1 From *Republic.com 2.0*

Cass R. Sunstein

It is difficult to think of more universal and absolute language concerning free speech than the First Amendment's provision: "Congress shall make no law . . . abridging the freedom of speech." Yet, jurists have long noted that it cannot be absolute. Justice Oliver Wendell Holmes famously observed that the amendment does not allow a person to yell "Fire!" in a crowded theater. In this essay, Cass Sunstein cites numerous circumstances— many involving new communications technologies—that appear equally problematic. Where and how should the line be drawn between speech that is protected and speech that is not? He presents and assesses two competing principles of free speech. One is a kind of libertarian, "consumerist" principle that individuals and organizations invoke to protect whatever speech they want to say or sponsor. The alternative, favored by Sunstein, is the democratic principle that holds some speech to be more sacrosanct than other speech. In this scheme, the most protected speech is that which affects democratic control of government; government is allowed to regulate other forms of speech, such as statements that are patently harmful.

Were those responsible for the I LOVE YOU virus protected by the free-speech principle? It would be silly to say that they are. But if this form of speech may be regulated, what are the limits on government's power?

Consider a case involving not email but a website—a case that may, in some ways, turn out to be emblematic of the future. The site in question had a dramatic name: "The Nuremberg Files." It began, "A coalition of concerned citizens throughout the USA is cooperating in collecting dossiers on abortionists in anticipation that one day we may be able to hold them on trial for crimes against humanity." The site contained a long list of "Alleged Abortionists and Their Accomplices," with the explicit goal of recording "the name of every person working in the baby slaughter business in the United States of America." The list included the names, home addresses, and license-plate numbers of many doctors who performed abortions, and also included the names of their spouses and children.

So far, perhaps, so good. But three of these doctors had been killed. Whenever a doctor was killed, the website showed a line drawn through his name. The site also included a set of "wanted posters," Old West–style, with photographs of doctors with the word "Wanted" under each one. A group of doctors brought suit, contending the practices of which this site was a part amounted in practice to "a hit list" with death threats and intimidation. The jury awarded them over $100 million in damages; the verdict was upheld on

Source: Cass R. Sunstein, from "Freedom of Speech," in *Republic.com 2.0,* by Cass R. Sunstein (Princeton, N.J.: Princeton University Press, 2007), 165–189. © 2001 Princeton University Press. Reprinted by permission of Princeton University Press.

appeal, though the dollar award was reduced substantially (it remained in the millions of dollars).

Should the free-speech principle have protected the Nuremberg Files? Maybe it should have. But if you think so, would you allow a website to post names and addresses of doctors who performed abortions, with explicit instructions about how and where to kill them? Would you allow a website to post bomb-making instructions? To post such instructions alongside advice about how and where to use the bombs? To show terrorists exactly where and how to strike? As we have seen, there is nothing fanciful about these questions. Dozens of sites now contain instructions about how to make bombs—though to my knowledge, none of them tells people how and where to use them. If you have no problem with bomb-making instructions on websites, you might consider some other questions. Does your understanding of free speech allow people to work together at a site called pricefixing.com, through which competitors can agree to set prices and engage in other anticompetitive practices? (I made that one up.) Does your understanding of free speech allow people to make unauthorized copies of movies, music, and books, and to give or sell those copies to dozens, thousands, or millions of others? (I didn't make that one up.)

My basic argument here is that the free-speech principle, properly understood, is not an absolute and that it allows government to undertake a wide range of restrictions on what people want to say on the Internet. However the hardest questions should be resolved, the government can regulate computer viruses, criminal conspiracy, and explicit incitement to engage in criminal acts, at least if the incitement is likely to be effective. In my view, it would also be acceptable for government to require broadcasters to provide educational programming for children on television, as in fact it now does; to mandate free air time for candidates for public office; and to regulate contributions to and expenditures on political campaigns, at least within certain boundaries.

This is not the place for a full discussion of constitutional doctrines relating to freedom of expression. But in the process of showing the democratic roots of the system of free expression, I attempt to provide an outline of the basic constitutional principles.[1]

Emerging Wisdom? Televisions as Toasters

An emerging view is that the First Amendment to the Constitution requires government to respect consumer sovereignty. Indeed, the First Amendment is often treated as if it incorporates the economic ideal—as if it is based on the view that consumer choice is what the system of communications is all about. Although it is foreign to the original conception of the free-speech principle, this view can be found in many places in current law.

For one thing, it helps to explain the constitutional protection given to commercial advertising. This protection is exceedingly recent. Until 1976,[2] the consensus within the Supreme Court and the legal culture in general was that the First Amendment did not protect commercial speech at all. Since that time, commercial speech has come to be treated more and more like ordinary speech, to the point where Justice Thomas has even doubted whether the law should distinguish at all between commercial and political speech.[3] To date, Justice Thomas has not prevailed on this count. But the Court's commercial-speech decisions often strike down restrictions on advertising, and for that reason, those decisions are best seen as a way of connecting the idea of consumer sovereignty with the First Amendment itself.

Belonging in the same category is the frequent constitutional hostility to campaign-finance regulation. The Supreme Court has held that financial expenditures on behalf of political candidates are generally protected by the free-speech principle—and in what seems to me an act of considerable hubris, the Court has also held that it is illegitimate for government to try to promote political equality by imposing ceilings on permissible expenditures.[4] The inequality that comes from divergences in wealth is not, [i]n the Court's view, a proper subject for democratic control. According to the Court, campaign-finance restrictions cannot be justified by reference to equality at all. It is for this reason that candidate *expenditures* from candidates' personal funds may not be regulated. It is also for this reason that restrictions on campaign *contributions* from one person to a candidate can be regulated only as a way of preventing the reality or appearance of corruption.

The constitutional debate over campaign-finance regulation remains complex and unresolved, and the members of the Supreme Court are badly divided.[5] Some of the justices would further reduce the government's existing authority to regulate campaign contributions, on the theory that such contributions lie at the heart of what the free-speech principle protects. Here too an idea of consumer sovereignty seems to be at work. In many of the debates over campaign expenditures and contributions, the political process itself is being treated as a kind of market in which citizens are seen as consumers, expressing their will not only through votes and statements but also through money. I do not mean to suggest that the government should be able to impose whatever restrictions it wishes. I mean only to notice, and to question, the idea that the political domain should be seen as a market and the influential claim that government is entirely disabled from responding to the translation of economic inequality into political equality.

Even more relevant for present purposes is the widespread suggestion, with some support in current constitutional law, that the free-speech principle forbids government from interfering with the communications market by, for example, attempting to draw people's attention to serious issues or regulating the content of what appears on television networks.[6] To be sure, everyone agrees that the government is permitted to create and protect property rights, even if this means that speech will be regulated as a result. We have seen that the government may give property rights to websites and broadcasters; there is no constitutional problem with that. Everyone also agrees that the government is permitted to control monopolistic behavior and thus to enforce antitrust law, which is designed to ensure genuinely free markets in communications. Structural regulation, not involving direct control of speech but intended to make sure that the market works well, is usually unobjectionable. Hence government can create copyright law and, at least within limits, forbid unauthorized copying. (There is, however, an extremely important and active debate about how to reconcile copyright law and the free-speech principle.)[7] But if government attempts to require television broadcasters to cover public issues, or to provide free air time for candidates, or to ensure a certain level of high-quality programming for children, many people will claim that the First Amendment is being violated. What lies beneath the surface of these debates?

Two Free-Speech Principles

We might distinguish here between the free-speech principle as it operates in courts and the free-speech principle as it operates in public debate. As far as courts are concerned, there is as yet no clear answer to many of the constitutional questions that would be raised by government efforts to make the speech market work better. For example, we do not really know, as a matter of constitutional law, whether government can require educational and public-affairs programming on television. The Court allowed such regulation when three or four television stations dominated the scene, but it has left open the question of whether such regulation would be legitimate today.[8] As a matter of prediction, the most that can be said is that there is a reasonable chance that the Court would permit government to adopt modest initiatives, so long as it was promoting goals associated with deliberative democracy.

Indeed the Court has been very cautious, and self-consciously so, about laying down firm rules governing the role of the free-speech principle on new technologies. The Court is aware that things are changing rapidly and that there is much that it does not know. Because issues of fact and value are in a state of flux, it has tended to offer narrow, case-specific rulings that offer little guidance, and constraint, for the future.[9]

But the free-speech principle has an independent life outside of the courtroom. It is often invoked, sometimes strategically though sometimes as a matter of principle, in such a way as to discourage government initiatives that might make the communications market serve democratic goals. Outside of the law, and inside the offices of lobbyists, newspapers, radio stations, and recording studios, as well as even in ordinary households, the First Amendment has a large *cultural* presence. This is no less important than its technical role in courts. Here the identification of the free-speech principle with consumer sovereignty is becoming all the tighter. Worst of all, the emerging cultural understanding severs the link between the First Amendment and democratic self-rule.

Recall here Bill Gates's words: "It's already getting a little unwieldy. When you turn on DirectTV and you step through every channel—well, there's three minutes of your life. When you walk into your living room six years from now, you'll be able to just say what you're interested in, and have the screen help you pick out a video that you care about. It's not going to be 'Let's look at channels 4, 5, and 7.'" Taken to its logical extreme, the emerging wisdom would identify the First Amendment with the dream of unlimited consumer sovereignty with respect to speech. It would see the First Amendment in precisely Gates's terms. It would transform the First Amendment into a constitutional guarantee of consumer sovereignty in the domain of communications.

I have had some experience with the conception of the First Amendment as an embodiment of consumer sovereignty, and it may be useful to offer a brief account of that experience. From 1997 to 1998, I served on the President's Advisory Committee on the Public Interest Obligations of Digital Television Broadcasters. Our task was to consider whether and how television broadcasters should be required to promote public-interest goals—through, for example, closed captioning for the hearing-impaired, emergency warnings, educational programming for children, and free air time for candidates. About half of the committee's members were broadcasters, and most of them were entirely happy to challenge proposed government regulation as intrusive and indefensible. One of the two co-chairs was the redoubtable Leslie Moonves, president of CBS. Moonves is an obviously intelligent, public-spirited man but also the furthest thing from a shrinking violet, and he is, to say the least, attuned to the economic interests of the television networks. Because of its composition, this group was not about to recommend anything dramatic. On the contrary, it was bound to be highly respectful of the prerogatives of television broadcasters. In any case the Advisory Committee was just that—an advisory committee—and we had power only to write a report, and no authority to impose any duties on anyone at all.

Nonetheless, the committee was subject to a sustained, intense, high-profile, and evidently well-funded lobbying effort by economic interests, generally associated with the broadcasting industry, seeking to invoke the First Amendment to suggest that any and all public-interest obligations should and would be found unconstitutional. An elegantly dressed and high-priced Washington lawyer testified before us for an endless hour, making quite outlandish claims about the meaning of the First Amendment. A long stream of legal documents was generated and sent to all of us, most of them arguing that (for example) a requirement of free air time for candidates would offend the Constitution. At our meetings, the most obvious (omni) presence was Jack Goodman, the lawyer for the National Association of Broadcasters (NAB), the lobbying and litigating arm of the broadcast industry, which wields the First Amendment as a kind of protectionist weapon against almost everything that government tries to do. To say that Goodman and the NAB would invoke the free-speech principle at the drop of a hat, or the faintest step of a Federal Communications Commission official in the distance, is only a slight exaggeration.

Of course all this was an entirely legitimate exercise of free speech. But when the President's Advisory Committee on the Public Interest Obligations of Digital Television Broadcasters already consists, in large part, of broadcasters, and when that very committee is besieged with tendentious and implausible interpretations of the First Amendment, something does seem amiss. There is a more general point. The National Association of Broadcasters and others with similar economic interests typically use the First Amendment in precisely the same way that the National Rifle Association uses the Second Amendment. We should think of the two camps as jurisprudential twins. The National Association of Broadcasters is prepared to make self-serving and outlandish claims about the First Amendment before the public and before courts, and to pay lawyers and publicists a lot of money to help establish those claims. (Perhaps they will ultimately succeed.) The National Rifle Association does the same thing with the Second Amendment. In both cases, those whose social and economic interests are at stake are prepared to use the Constitution, however implausibly invoked, in order to give a veneer of principle and respectability to arguments that would otherwise seem hopelessly partisan and self-interested.

Indeed our advisory committee heard a great deal about the First Amendment, and about marginally relevant Supreme Court decisions, and about footnotes in lower-court opinions, but exceedingly little, in fact close to nothing, about the pragmatic and empirical issues on which many of our inquiries should have turned. If educational programming for children is required on CBS, NBC, and ABC, how many children will end up watching? What would they watch, or do, instead? Would educational programming help them? When educational programming is required, how much do the networks lose in dollars, and who pays the tab—advertisers, consumers, network employees, or someone else? What would be the real-world effects, on citizens and fund-raising alike, of free air time for candidates? Would such a requirement produce more substantial attention to serious issues? Would it reduce current pressures to raise money? What are the consequences of violence on television for both children and adults? Does television violence actually increase violence in the real world? Does it make children anxious in a way that creates genuine psychological harm? How, exactly, are the hard-of-hearing affected when captions are absent?

We can go further still. In the early part of the twentieth century, the due process clause of the Fourteenth Amendment was used to forbid government from regulating the labor market through, for example, minimum-wage and maximum-hour legislation.[10] The Court thought that the Constitution allowed workers and employers to set wages and hours as they "choose," without regulatory constraints. This is one of the most notorious periods in the entire history of the Supreme Court. Judicial use of the Fourteenth Amendment for these purposes is now almost universally agreed to have been a grotesque abuse of power. Nearly everyone now sees that the underlying questions were democratic ones, not ones for the judiciary. The Court should not have forbidden democratic experimentation that would, plausibly at least, have done considerable good.

In fact a central animating idea, in these now-discredited decisions, was that of consumer sovereignty—ensuring that government would not "interfere" with the terms produced by workers, employers, and consumers. (The word "interfere" has to be in quotation marks because the government was there already; the law of property, contract, and torts helps account for how much workers receive, how long they work, and how much consumers pay.) But in the early part of the twenty-first century, the First Amendment is serving a similar purpose in popular debate and sometimes in courts as well. All too often, it is being invoked on behalf of consumer sovereignty in a way that prevents the democratic process from resolving complex questions that turn on issues of fact and value that are ill-suited to judicial resolution.

To say this is not to say that the First Amendment should play no role at all. On the contrary, it imposes serious limits on what might be done. But some imaginable initiatives, responding to the problems I have discussed thus far, are fully consistent with the free-speech guarantee. Indeed, they would promote its highest aspirations.

Free Speech Is Not an Absolute

We can identify some flaws in the emerging view of the First Amendment by investigating the idea that the free-speech guarantee is "an absolute" in the specific sense that government may not regulate speech at all. This view plays a large role in public debate, and in some ways it is a salutary myth. Certainly the idea that the First Amendment is an absolute helps to discourage government from doing things that it ought not to do. At the same time it gives greater rhetorical power to critics of illegitimate government censorship. But a myth, even if in some ways salutary, remains a myth; and any publicly influential myth is likely to create many problems.

There should be no ambiguity on the point: free speech is not an absolute. We have seen that the government is allowed to regulate speech by imposing neutral rules of property law, telling would-be speakers that they may not have access to certain speech outlets. But this is only the beginning. Government is permitted to regulate computer viruses; unlicensed medical advice; attempted bribery; perjury; criminal conspiracies ("let's fix prices!"); threats to assassinate the president; blackmail ("I'll tell everyone the truth about your private life unless you give me $100"); criminal solicitation ("might you help me rob this bank?"); child pornography; violations of the copyright law; false advertising; purely verbal fraud ("this stock is worth $100,000"); and much more. Many of these forms of speech will not be especially harmful. A fruitless and doomed attempt to solicit someone to commit a crime, for example, is still criminal solicitation; a pitifully executed attempt at fraud is still fraud; sending a computer virus that doesn't actually work is still against the law.

Perhaps you disagree with the view, settled as a matter of current American law (and so settled in most other nations as well), that *all* of these forms of speech are unprotected by the free-speech principle. There is certainly a good argument that some current uses of the copyright law impose unnecessary and unjustifiable restrictions on free speech—and that these restrictions are especially troublesome in the era of the Internet.[11] But you are not a free-speech absolutist unless you believe that *each* of these forms of speech should be protected by that principle. And

if this is your belief, you are a most unusual person (and you will have a lot of explaining to do).

This is not the place for a full account of the reach of the First Amendment of the American Constitution.[12] But it is plain that some distinctions must be made among different kinds of speech. It is important, for example, to distinguish between speech that can be shown to be quite harmful and speech that is relatively harmless. As a general rule, the government should not be able to regulate the latter. We might also distinguish between speech that bears on democratic self-government and speech that does not; certainly an especially severe burden should be placed on any government efforts to regulate political speech. Less simply, we might want to distinguish among the *kinds of lines* that government is drawing in terms of the likelihood that government is acting on the basis of illegitimate reasons (a point to which I will return).

These ideas could be combined in various ways, and indeed the fabric of modern free-speech law in America reflects one such combination. Despite the increasing prominence of the idea that the free-speech principle requires unrestricted choices by individual consumers, the Court continues to say that political speech receives the highest protection and that government may regulate (for example) commercial advertising, obscenity, and libel of ordinary people without meeting the especially stringent burden of justification required for political speech. But for present purposes, all that is necessary is to say that no one really believes that the free-speech principle, or the First Amendment, is an absolute. We should be very thankful for that.

The First Amendment and Democratic Deliberation

The fundamental concern of this book is to see how unlimited consumer options might compromise the preconditions of a system of freedom of expression, which include unchosen exposures and shared experiences. To understand the nature of this concern, we will make most progress if we insist that the free-speech principle should be read in light of the commitment to democratic deliberation. In other words, a central point of the free-speech principle is to carry out that commitment.

There are profound differences between those who emphasize consumer sovereignty and those who stress the democratic roots of the free-speech principle. For the latter, government efforts to regulate commercial advertising need not be objectionable. Certainly false and misleading commercial advertising is more readily subject to government control than false and misleading political speech. For those who believe that the free-speech principle has democratic foundations and is not fundamentally about consumer sovereignty, government regulation of television, radio, and the Internet is not always objectionable, at least so long as it is reasonably taken as an effort to promote democratic goals.

Suppose, for example, that government proposes to require television broadcasters (as indeed it now does) to provide three hours per week of educational programming for children. Or suppose that government decides to require television broadcasters to provide a certain amount of free air time for candidates for public office, or a certain amount of time on coverage of elections. For those who believe in consumer sovereignty, these requirements are quite troublesome, indeed they seem like a core violation of the free-speech guarantee. For those who associate the free-speech principle with democratic goals, these requirements are fully consistent with its highest aspirations. Indeed in many democracies—including, for example, Germany and Italy—it is well understood that the mass media can be regulated in the interest of improving democratic self-government.[13]

There is nothing novel or iconoclastic in the democratic conception of free speech. On the contrary, this conception lay at the heart of the original understanding of freedom of speech in America. In attacking the Alien and Sedition Acts, for example, James Madison claimed that they were inconsistent with the free-speech principle, which he linked explicitly to the American transformation of the concept of political sovereignty. In England, Madison noted, sovereignty was vested in the King. But "in the

United States, the case is altogether different. The People, not the Government, possess the absolute sovereignty." It was on this foundation that any "Sedition Act" must be judged illegitimate. "[T]he right of electing the members of the Government constitutes . . . the essence of a free and responsible government," and "the value and efficacy of this right depends on the knowledge of the comparative merits and demerits of the candidates for the public trust."[14] It was for this reason that the power represented by a Sedition Act ought, "more than any other, to produce universal alarm; because it is levelled against that right of freely examining public characters and measures, and of free communication among the people thereon, which has ever been justly deemed the only effectual guardian of every other right."

In this way Madison saw "free communication among the people" not as an exercise in consumer sovereignty, in which speech was treated as a kind of commodity, but instead as a central part of self-government, the "only effectual guardian of every other right." Here Madison's conception of free speech was a close cousin of that of Justice Louis Brandeis, who . . . saw public discussion as a "political duty" and believed that the greatest menace to liberty would be "an inert people." A central part of the American constitutional tradition, then, places a high premium on speech that is critical to democratic processes, and centers the First Amendment on the goal of self-government. If history is our guide, it follows that government efforts to promote a well-functioning system of free expression, as through extensions of the public-forum idea, may well be acceptable. It also follows that government faces special burdens when it attempts to regulate political speech, burdens that are somewhat more severe than those it faces when it attempts to regulate other forms of speech.

American history is not the only basis for seeing the First Amendment in light of the commitment to democratic deliberation. The argument can be justified by basic principle as well.[15]

Consider the question whether the free-speech principle should be taken to forbid efforts to make communications markets work better from the democratic point of view. Return to our standard examples: educational programming for children, free air time for candidates for public office, closed-captioning for the hearing-impaired. (I am putting the Internet to one side for now because it raises distinctive questions.) Perhaps some of these proposals would do little or no good, or even harm; but from what standpoint should they be judged inconsistent with the free-speech guarantee?

If we believe that the Constitution gives all owners of speech outlets an unbridgeable right to decide what appears on "their" outlets, the answer is clear: government could require none of these things. But why should we believe that? If government is not favoring any point of view, and if it is really improving the operation of democratic processes, it is hard to find a legitimate basis for complaint. Indeed, the Supreme Court has expressly held that the owner of shopping centers—areas where a great deal of speech occurs—may be required to keep their property open for expressive activity.[16] Shopping centers are not television broadcasters; but if a democratic government is attempting to build on the idea of a public forum so as to increase the likelihood of exposure to and debate about diverse views, is there really a reasonable objection from the standpoint of free speech itself?

In a similar vein, it makes sense to say that speech that is political in character, in the sense that it relates to democratic self-government, cannot be regulated without an especially strong showing of government justification—and that commercial advertising, obscenity, and other speech that is not political in that sense can be regulated on the basis of a somewhat weaker government justification. I will not attempt here to offer a full defense of this idea, which of course raises some hard line-drawing problems. But in light of the importance of the question to imaginable government regulation of new technologies, there are three points that deserve brief mention.

First, an insistence that government's burden is greatest when it is regulating political speech emerges from a sensible understanding of government's own incentives. It is here that government is most likely to

be acting on the basis of illegitimate considerations, such as self-protection, or giving assistance to powerful private groups. Government is least trustworthy when it is attempting to control speech that might harm its own interests; and when speech is political, government's own interests are almost certainly at stake. This is not to deny that government is often untrustworthy when it is regulating commercial speech, art, or other speech that does not relate to democratic self-government. But we have the strongest reasons to distrust government regulation when political issues are involved.

Second, an emphasis on democratic deliberation protects speech not only when regulation is most likely to be biased, but also when regulation is most likely to be harmful. If government regulates child pornography on the Internet or requires educational programming for children on television, it remains possible to invoke the normal democratic channels to protest these forms of regulation as ineffectual, intrusive, or worse. But when government forbids criticism of an ongoing war effort, the normal channels are foreclosed, in an important sense, by the very regulation at issue. Controls on public debate are uniquely damaging because they impair the process of deliberation that is a precondition for political legitimacy.

Third, an emphasis on democratic deliberation is likely to fit, far better than any alternative, with the most reasonable views about particular free-speech problems. However much we disagree about the most difficult speech problems, we are likely to believe that at a minimum, the free-speech principle protects political expression unless government has exceedingly strong grounds for regulating it. On the other hand, forms of speech such as perjury, attempted bribery, threats, unlicensed medical advice, and criminal solicitation are not likely to seem to be at the heart of the free-speech guarantee.

An understanding of this kind certainly does not answer all constitutional questions. It does not provide a clear test for distinguishing between political and nonpolitical speech, a predictably vexing question.[17] (To those who believe that the absence of a clear test is decisive against the distinction itself, the best response is that any alternative test will lead to line-drawing problems of its own. Because everyone agrees that some forms of speech are regulable, line drawing is literally inevitable. If you're skeptical, try to think of a test that eliminates problems of this kind.) It does not say whether and when government may regulate art or literature, sexually explicit speech, or libelous speech. In all cases, government is required to have a strong justification for regulating speech, political or not. But the approach I am defending does help to orient inquiry. When government is regulating false or fraudulent commercial advertising, libel of private persons, or child pornography, it is likely to be on firm ground. When government is attempting to control criminal conspiracy or speech that contains direct threats of violence aimed at particular people, it need not meet the stringent standards required for regulation of political dissent. What I have suggested here, without fully defending the point, is that a conception of the First Amendment that is rooted in democratic deliberation is an exceedingly good place to start.

Forms of Neutrality

None of this means that the government is permitted to regulate the emerging communications market however it wishes. To know whether to object to what government is doing, it is important to know what *kind* of line it is drawing.[18] There are three possibilities here.

- The government might be regulating speech in a way that is *neutral with respect to the content of the speech at issue*. This is the least objectionable way of regulating speech. For example, government is permitted to say that people may not use loudspeakers on the public streets after midnight or that speakers cannot have access to the front lawn immediately in front of the White House. A regulation of this kind imposes no controls on speech of any particular content. An Internet example: if government says that no

one may use the website of CNN unless CNN gives permission, it is acting in a way that is entirely neutral with respect to speech content. So too with restrictions on sending computer viruses. The government bans the ILOVEYOU virus, but it also bans the IHATEYOU virus and the IAMINDIFFERENTTOYOU virus. What is against the law is sending viruses; their content is irrelevant.

- The government might regulate speech in a way that depends on the content of what is said, but without discriminating against any particular point of view. Suppose, for example, that government bans commercial speech on the subways but allows all other forms of speech on the subways. In the technical language of First Amendment law, this form of regulation is "content-based" but "viewpoint-neutral." Consider the old fairness doctrine, which required broadcasters to cover public issues and to allow speech by those with opposing views. Here the content of speech is highly relevant to what government is requiring, but no specific point of view is benefited or punished. The same can be said for the damages award against the Nuremburg Trials website; the content of the speech definitely mattered, but no particular point of view was being punished. The same award would be given against a website that treated pro-life people in the same way that the Nuremburg Trials treated doctors. In the same category would be a regulation saying that in certain areas, sexually explicit speech must be made inaccessible to children. In these cases, no lines are being drawn directly on the basis of point of view.

- The government might regulate a point of view that it fears or dislikes. This form of regulation is often called "viewpoint discrimination." Government might say, for example, that no one may criticize a decision to go to war, or that no one may claim that one racial group is inferior to another, or that no one may advocate violent overthrow of government. Here the government is singling out a point of view that it wants to ban, perhaps because it believes that the particular point of view is especially dangerous.

It makes sense to say that these three kinds of regulations should be treated differently, on the Internet as elsewhere. Viewpoint discrimination is the most objectionable. Content-neutral regulation is the least objectionable. If officials are regulating speech because of the point of view that it contains, their action is almost certainly unconstitutional. Government should not be allowed to censor arguments and positions merely because it fears or disapproves of them. If officials are banning a disfavored viewpoint, they ought to be required to show, at the very least, that the viewpoint really creates serious risks that cannot be adequately combated with more speech. Officials ought also be required to explain, in altogether convincing terms, why they are punishing one point of view and not its opposite.

A content-neutral regulation is at the opposite extreme, and such regulations are often legitimate. If the government has acted in a content-neutral way, courts usually do not and should not intervene, at least if the basic channels of communications remain open, and if government has a solid reason for the regulation. Of course a gratuitous or purposeless regulation must be struck down even if it is content-neutral. Suppose that government says that the public streets—or for that matter the Internet—may be used for expressive activity, but only between 8 p.m. and 8:30 p.m. If so, the neutrality of the regulation is no defense. But content-neutral regulations are frequently easy to justify; their very neutrality, and hence breadth, ensures that there is a good reason for them. The government is unlikely to ban expressive activity from 8:30 p.m. until 7:59 a.m. because so many people would resist the ban. The more likely regulation prohibits noisy demonstrations when people are trying to sleep, and there is nothing wrong with such prohibitions.

Now consider the intermediate case. When government is regulating in a way that is based on content but neutral with respect to point of view, there are two issues. The first is whether the particular line being drawn suggests lurking viewpoint discrimination—a hidden but detectable desire to ban a certain point of view. When it does, the law should probably be struck down. If government says that the most recent war, or abortion, may not be discussed on television, it is, as a technical matter, discriminating against a whole topic, not against any particular point of view; but there is pretty good reason to suspect government's motivations. A ban on discussion of the most recent war is probably an effort to protect the government from criticism.

The second and perhaps more fundamental issue is whether government is able to invoke strong, content-neutral grounds for engaging in this form of regulation. A ban on televised discussion of the most recent war should be struck down for this reason. The ban seems to have no real point, aside from forbidding certain points of view from being expressed. But the government has a stronger argument if, for example, it is requiring broadcasters to offer three hours of educational programming for children. In that case, it is trying to ensure that television serves children, an entirely legitimate interest.

Of course some cases may test the line between discrimination on the basis of content and discrimination on the basis of viewpoint. If government is regulating sexually explicit speech when that speech offends contemporary community standards, is it regulating on the basis of viewpoint or merely content? This is not an easy question, and many people have argued over the right answer. But an understanding of the three categories discussed here should be sufficient to make sense out of the bulk of imaginable free-speech challenges—and should provide some help in approaching the rest of them as well.

Penalties and Subsidies

Of course government can do a range of things to improve the system of free speech. Here it is important to make a further distinction, between "subsidies" on the one hand and "penalties" on the other. Government is likely to have a great deal of trouble when it is imposing penalties on speech. Such penalties are the model of what a system of free expression avoids. Government will have more room to maneuver if it is giving out selective subsidies. Public officials are not required to give money out to all speakers, and if they are giving money to some people but not to others, they may well be on firm ground. But the distinction between the penalties and subsidies is not always obvious.

The most conspicuous penalties are criminal and civil punishments. If government makes it a crime to libel people over the Internet or imposes civil fines on television broadcasters who do not provide free air time for candidates for office, it is punishing speech. The analysis of these penalties should depend on the considerations discussed thus far—whether political speech is involved, what kind of line the government is drawing, and so forth.

Somewhat trickier, but belonging in the same category, are cases in which government is *withdrawing a benefit to which people would otherwise be entitled* when the reason for the withdrawal is the government's view about the appropriate content of speech. Suppose, for example, that government gives an annual cash subsidy to all speakers of a certain kind—say, those networks that agree to provide educational programming for children. But suppose that government withdraws the subsidy from those networks that provide speech of which the government disapproves. Imagine, for example, that the government withdraws the subsidy from networks whose news shows are critical of the president. For the most part, these sorts of penalties should be analyzed in exactly the same way as criminal or civil punishment. When benefits are being withdrawn, just as when ordinary punishment is being imposed, government is depriving people of goods to which they would otherwise be entitled, and we probably have excellent reason to distrust its motives. If government responds to dissenters by taking away benefits that they would otherwise receive, it is violating the free-speech principle.

But a quite different issue is posed when government gives out selective subsidies to speakers. It often does this by, for example, funding some museums and artists but not others, and generally through the National Endowment for the Arts and the Public Broadcasting System. Imagine a situation in which government is willing to fund educational programming for children and pays a station to air that programming on Saturday morning—without also funding situation comedies or game shows. Or imagine that government funds a series of historical exhibits on the Civil War without also funding exhibits on the Vietnam War, or on World War II, or on the history of sex equality in America. What is most important here can be stated very simply: *under current law in the United States (and generally elsewhere), government is permitted to subsidize speech however it wishes.*[19]

Government often is a speaker, and as such, it is permitted to say whatever it likes. No one thinks that there is a problem if officials endorse one view and reject another. And if government seeks to use taxpayer funds to subsidize certain projects and enterprises, there is usually no basis for constitutional complaint. The only exception to this principle is that if government is allocating funds to private speakers in a way that discriminates on the basis of viewpoint, there might be a First Amendment problem.[20] The precise nature of this exception remains unclear. But it would certainly be possible to challenge, on constitutional grounds, a decision by government to fund the Republican Party website without also funding the Democratic Party website.

Of course this kind of discrimination goes far beyond anything that I shall be suggesting here. What is important, then, is that government has a great deal of room to maneuver insofar as it is not penalizing speech but instead subsidizing it.

A Restrained, Prudent First Amendment

This chapter has dealt with a range of free-speech issues, some of them briskly, and it is important not to lose the forest for the trees. My basic claims have been that the First Amendment in large part embodies a democratic ideal, that it should not be identified with the notion of consumer sovereignty, and that it is not an absolute. The core requirement of the free-speech principle is that with respect to politics, government must remain neutral among points of view. Content regulation is disfavored; viewpoint discrimination is almost always out of bounds. A key task is to ensure compliance with these requirements in the contemporary environment.

Notes

1. For more detailed treatments, see Cass R. Sunstein, *Democracy and the Problem of Free Speech* (New York: Free Press, 1993); Alexander Meiklejohn, *Free Speech and its Relation to Self-Government* (New York: Harper, 1948); and C. Edwin Baker, *Human Liberty and Freedom of Speech* (New York: Oxford University Press, 1995).

2. *Virginia State Bd. of Pharmacy v. Virginia Citizens Consumer Council,* 425 U.S. 748 (1976).

3. 44 *Liquormart, Inc. v. Rhode Island,* 517 U.S. 484 (1996).

4. See *Buckley v. Valeo,* 424 U.S. 1 (1979).

5. See, e.g., *Randall v. Sorrell,* 126 S. Ct. 2479 (2006); *McConnell v. FEC,* 540 U.S. 93 (2003).

6. See, e.g., Thomas Krattenmaker and L. A. Powe, "Converging First Amendment Principles for Converging Communications Media," *Yale LJ* 104 (1995): 1719, 1725.

7. For discussion, see Lessig, *Free Culture*; Benkler, *Wealth of Networks.*

8. The old case, allowing government action, is *Red Lion Broadcasting v. FCC,* 395 U.S. 367 (1969).

9. See, e.g., *Denver Area Educational Telecommunications Consortium, Inc. v. FCC,* 518 U.S. 727 (1996). The

Court's caution is defended in Cass R. Sunstein, *One Case at a Time* (Cambridge, Mass.: Harvard University Press, 1999).

10. See *Lochner v. New York,* 198 U.S. 45 (1905).

11. See Lessig, *Free Culture*; Benkler, *Wealth of Networks.*

12. For an effort in this direction, see Sunstein, *Democracy and the Problem of Free Speech.*

13. See ibid., 77–81, for an overview.

14. James Madison, "Report on the Virginia Resolution, January 1800," in *Writings of James Madison* vol. 6, ed. Gaillard Hunt (New York: Putnam, 1906), 385–401.

15. I draw here on Sunstein, *Democracy and the Problem of Free Speech*, 132–36.

16. *Pruneyard Shopping Center v. Robins,* 447 U.S. 74 (1980).

17. I attempt to answer it in Sunstein, *Democracy and the Problem of Free Speech,* 121–65.

18. The best discussion is Geoffrey Stone, "Content Regulation and the First Amendment," *Wm. & Mary L. Rev. 25* (1983): 189.

19. See *Rumsfeld v. Forum for Academic and Institutional Rights,* 126 S. Ct. 1297 (2006).

20. The murkiness of current law is illustrated by the Court's decisions in ibid., in which the Court unanimously upheld the Solomon Amendment, withdrawing federal funding from educational institutions that refused to provide equal access to the United States military; and in *National Endowment for the Arts v. Finley,* 524 U.S. 569 (1998), in which a sharply divided Court upheld a statute directing the NEA, when making funding decisions, to consider "general standards of decency and respect for the diverse beliefs and values of the American public." In the NEA case, the Court suggested that it would have ruled differently if the statute had discriminated on the basis of viewpoint.

5-2 *Roe v. Wade*

Supreme Court of the United States

To what extent can rights perceived by the people, but not explicitly protected by the Constitution, be recognized as constitutional principles by the courts? Judges often disagree on where the lines should be drawn. This question arose in Roe v. Wade, *the Supreme Court's 1973 decision on abortion. The specific issue was, does the Constitution embrace a woman's right to terminate her pregnancy by abortion? A 5–4 majority on the Supreme Court held that a woman's right to an abortion fell within the right to privacy protected by the Fourteenth Amendment. The decision gave a woman autonomy over the pregnancy during the first trimester and defined different levels of state interest for the second and third trimesters. The Court's ruling affected the laws of forty-six states. Justice Harry Blackmun, arguing for the majority, insisted that the Court had recognized such a right in a long series of cases and that it was appropriate to extend the right to a woman's decision to terminate a pregnancy. In a dissenting opinion, Justice William Rehnquist, who later became chief justice, argued that because abortion was not considered an implicit right at the time the Fourteenth Amendment, states must be allowed to regulate it.*

ROE ET AL. V. WADE, DISTRICT ATTORNEY OF DALLAS COUNTY

410 U.S. 113

APPEAL FROM THE UNITED STATES DISTRICT COURT FOR THE NORTHERN DISTRICT OF TEXAS.

Decided January 22, 1973.

MR. JUSTICE BLACKMUN delivered the opinion of the Court.

This Texas federal appeal and its Georgia companion, *Doe v. Bolton*, post, . . . present constitutional challenges to state criminal abortion legislation. The Texas statutes under attack here are typical of those that have been in effect in many States for approximately a century. . . .

We forthwith acknowledge our awareness of the sensitive and emotional nature of the abortion controversy, of the vigorous opposing views, even among physicians, and of the deep and seemingly absolute convictions that the subject inspires. One's philosophy, one's experiences, one's exposure to the raw edges of human existence, one's religious training, one's attitudes toward life and family and their values, and the moral standards one establishes and seeks to observe, are all likely to influence and to color one's thinking and conclusions about abortion. . . .

Our task, of course, is to resolve the issue by constitutional measurement, free of emotion and of predilection. We seek earnestly to do this, and, because we do, we have inquired into, and in this opinion place some emphasis upon, medical and medical-legal history and what that history reveals about man's attitudes toward the abortion procedure over the centuries. We bear in mind, too, Mr. Justice Holmes' admonition in his now-vindicated dissent in *Lochner v. New York,* 198 U. S. 45, 76 (1905):

[The Constitution] is made for people of fundamentally differing views, and the accident of our finding certain opinions natural and familiar or novel and even shocking ought not to conclude our judgment upon the question whether statutes embodying them conflict with the Constitution of the United States.

. . . Jane Roe [a pseudonym used to protect the identity of the woman], a single woman who was residing in Dallas County, Texas, instituted this federal action in March 1970 against the District Attorney of the county. She sought a declaratory judgment that the Texas criminal abortion statutes were unconstitutional on their face, and an injunction restraining the defendant from enforcing the statutes.

Roe alleged that she was unmarried and pregnant; that she wished to terminate her pregnancy by an abortion "performed by a competent, licensed physician, under safe clinical conditions"; that she was unable to get a "legal" abortion in Texas because her life did not appear to be threatened by the continuation of her pregnancy; and that she could not afford to travel to another jurisdiction in order to secure a legal abortion under safe conditions. She claimed that the Texas statutes were unconstitutionally vague and that they abridged her right of personal privacy, protected by the First, Fourth, Fifth, Ninth, and Fourteenth Amendments. By an amendment to her complaint Roe purported to sue "on behalf of herself and all other women" similarly situated. . . .

The principal thrust of appellant's attack on the Texas statutes is that they improperly invade a right, said to be possessed by the pregnant woman, to choose to terminate her pregnancy. Appellant would discover this right in the concept of personal "liberty" embodied in the Fourteenth Amendment's Due Process Clause; or in personal, marital, familial, and sexual privacy said to be protected by the Bill of Rights or its penumbras, . . . or among those rights reserved to the people by the Ninth Amendment. . . .

It perhaps is not generally appreciated that the restrictive criminal abortion laws in effect in a majority of States today are of relatively recent vintage. Those laws, generally proscribing abortion or its attempt at any time during pregnancy except when necessary to preserve the pregnant woman's life, are not of ancient or even of common-law origin. Instead, they derive from statutory changes effected, for the most part, in the latter half of the 19th century. . . .

It is thus apparent that at common law, at the time of the adoption of our Constitution, and throughout the major portion of the 19th century, abortion was viewed with less disfavor than under most American statutes currently in effect. Phrasing it another way, a woman enjoyed a substantially broader right to terminate a pregnancy than she does in most States today. At least with respect to the early stage of pregnancy, and very possibly without such a limitation, the opportunity to make this choice was present in this country well into the 19th century. Even later, the law continued for some time to treat less punitively an abortion procured in early pregnancy. . . .

The Constitution does not explicitly mention any right of privacy. In a line of decisions, however, going back perhaps as far as *Union Pacific R. Co. v. Botsford* . . . (1891), the Court has recognized that a right of personal privacy, or a guarantee of certain areas or zones of privacy, does exist under the Constitution. In varying contexts, the Court or individual Justices have, indeed, found at least the roots of that right in the First Amendment . . . ; in the Fourth and Fifth Amendments . . . ; in the penumbras of the Bill of Rights . . . ; in the Ninth Amendment . . . ; or in the concept of liberty guaranteed by the first section of the Fourteenth Amendment. . . . These decisions make it clear that only personal rights that can be deemed "fundamental" or "implicit in the concept of ordered liberty," . . . are included in this guarantee of personal privacy. They also make it clear that the right has some extension to activities relating to marriage . . . ; procreation . . . ; contraception . . . ; family relationships . . . ; and child rearing and education. . . .

This right of privacy, whether it be founded in the Fourteenth Amendment's concept of personal liberty and restrictions upon state action, as we feel it is, or, as the District Court determined, in the Ninth Amendment's reservation of rights to the people, is broad enough to encompass a woman's decision whether or not to terminate her pregnancy. The detriment that the State would impose upon the pregnant woman by denying this choice altogether is apparent. Specific and direct harm medically diagnosable even in early pregnancy may be involved. Maternity, or additional offspring, may force upon the woman a distressful life and future. Psychological harm may be imminent. Mental and physical health may be taxed by child care. There is also the distress, for all concerned, associated with the unwanted child, and there is the problem of bringing a child into a family already unable, psychologically and otherwise, to care for it. In other cases, as in this one, the additional difficulties and continuing stigma of unwed motherhood may be involved. All these are factors the woman and her responsible physician necessarily will consider in consultation.

On the basis of elements such as these, appellant and some *amici* argue that the woman's right is absolute and that she is entitled to terminate her pregnancy at whatever time, in whatever way, and for whatever reason she alone chooses. With this we do not agree. Appellant's arguments that Texas either has no valid interest at all in regulating the abortion decision, or no interest strong enough to support any limitation upon the woman's sole determination, are unpersuasive. The Court's decisions recognizing a right of privacy also acknowledge that some state regulation in areas protected by that right is appropriate. As noted above, a State may properly assert important interests in safeguarding health, in maintaining medical standards, and in protecting potential life. At some point in pregnancy, these respective interests become sufficiently compelling to sustain regulation of the factors that govern the abortion decision. The privacy right involved, therefore, cannot be said to be absolute. . . .

We, therefore, conclude that the right of personal privacy includes the abortion decision, but that this right is not unqualified and must be considered against important state interests in regulation. . . .

Where certain "fundamental rights" are involved, the Court has held that regulation limiting these rights may be justified only by a "compelling state interest," . . . and that legislative enactments must be narrowly drawn to express only the legitimate state interests at stake. . . .

In the recent abortion cases . . . courts have recognized these principles. Those striking down state laws have generally scrutinized the State's interests in protecting health and potential life, and have concluded that neither interest justified broad limitations on the reasons for which a physician and his pregnant patient might decide that she should have an abortion in the early stages of pregnancy. Courts sustaining state laws have held that the State's determinations to protect health or prenatal life are dominant and constitutionally justifiable. . . .

The District Court held that the appellee [the district attorney, defending the Texas law] failed to meet his burden of demonstrating that the Texas statute's infringement upon Roe's rights was necessary to support a compelling state interest, and that, although the appellee presented "several compelling justifications for state presence in the area of abortions," the statutes outstripped these justifications and swept "far beyond any areas of compelling state interest." 314 F. Supp., at 1222–1223. Appellant and appellee both contest that holding. Appellant, as has been indicated, claims an absolute right that bars any state imposition of criminal penalties in the area. Appellee argues that the State's determination to recognize and protect prenatal life from and after conception constitutes a compelling state interest. As noted above, we do not agree fully with either formulation.

A. The appellee and certain *amici* argue that the fetus is a "person" within the language and meaning of the Fourteenth Amendment. In support of this, they outline at length and in detail the well-known facts of fetal development. If this suggestion of personhood is established, the appellant's case, of course, collapses, for the fetus' right to life would then be guaranteed specifically by the Amendment. The appellant conceded as much on reargument. On the other hand, the appellee conceded on reargument that no case could be cited that holds that a fetus is a person within the meaning of the Fourteenth Amendment.

The Constitution does not define "person" in so many words. Section 1 of the Fourteenth Amendment contains three references to "person." The first, in defining "citizens," speaks of "persons born or naturalized in the United States." The word also appears both in the Due Process Clause and in the Equal Protection Clause. "Person" is used in other places in the Constitution: in the listing of qualifications for Representatives and Senators, Art. I, § 2, cl. 2, and § 3, cl. 3; in the Apportionment Clause, Art. I, § 2, cl. 3; in the Migration and Importation provision, Art. I, § 9, cl. 1; in the Emolument Clause, Art. I, § 9, cl. 8; in the Electors provisions, Art. II, § 1, cl. 2, and the superseded cl. 3; in the provision outlining qualifications for the office of President, Art. II, § 1, cl. 5; in the Extradition provisions, Art. IV, § 2, cl. 2, and the superseded Fugitive Slave Clause 3; and in the Fifth, Twelfth, and Twenty-second Amendments, as well as in §§ 2 and 3 of the Fourteenth Amendment. But in nearly all these instances, the use of the word is such that it has application only postnatally. None indicates, with any assurance, that it has any possible pre-natal application.

All this, together with our observation, *supra,* that throughout the major portion of the 19th century prevailing legal abortion practices were far freer than they are today, persuades us that the word "person," as used in the Fourteenth Amendment, does not include the unborn. This is in accord with the results reached in those few cases where the issue has been squarely presented. . . . Indeed, our decision in *United States v. Vuitch,* 402 U. S. 62 (1971), inferentially is to the same effect, for we there would not have indulged in statutory interpretation favorable to abortion in specified circumstances if the necessary consequence was the termination of life entitled to Fourteenth Amendment protection.

This conclusion, however, does not of itself fully answer the contentions raised by Texas, and we pass on to other considerations.

B. The pregnant woman cannot be isolated in her privacy. She carries an embryo and, later, a fetus, if one accepts the medical definitions of the developing young in the human uterus. . . . As we have intimated above, it is reasonable and appropriate for a State to decide that at some point in time another interest, that of health of the mother or that of potential human life, becomes significantly involved. The woman's privacy is no longer sole and any right of privacy she possesses must be measured accordingly.

Texas urges that, apart from the Fourteenth Amendment, life begins at conception and is present throughout pregnancy, and that, therefore, the State has a compelling interest in protecting that life from and after conception. We need not resolve the difficult question of when life begins. When those trained in the respective disciplines of medicine, philosophy, and theology are unable to arrive at any consensus, the judiciary, at this point in the development of man's knowledge, is not in a position to speculate as to the answer.

It should be sufficient to note briefly the wide divergence of thinking on this most sensitive and difficult question. There has always been strong support for the view that life does not begin until live birth. This was the belief of the Stoics. It appears to be the predominant, though not the unanimous, attitude of the Jewish faith. It may be taken to represent also the position of a large segment of the Protestant community, insofar as that can be ascertained; organized groups that have taken a formal position on the abortion issue have generally regarded abortion as a matter for the conscience of the individual and her family. As we have noted, the common law found greater significance in quickening. Physicians and their scientific colleagues have regarded that event with less interest and have tended to focus either upon conception, upon live birth, or upon the interim point at which the fetus becomes "viable," that is, potentially able to live outside the mother's womb, albeit with artificial aid. Viability is usually placed at about seven months (28 weeks) but may occur earlier, even at 24 weeks. The Aristotelian theory of "mediate animation," that held sway throughout the Middle Ages and the Renaissance in Europe, continued to be official Roman Catholic dogma until the 19th century, despite opposition to this "ensoulment" theory from those in the Church who would recognize the existence of life from the moment of conception. The latter is now, of course, the official belief of the Catholic Church. As one brief *amicus* discloses, this is a view strongly held by many non-Catholics as well, and by many physicians. Substantial problems for precise definition of this view are posed, however, by new embryological data that purport to indicate that conception is a "process" over time, rather than an event, and by new medical techniques such as menstrual extraction, the "morning-after" pill, implantation of embryos, artificial insemination, and even artificial wombs. . . .

In view of all this, we do not agree that, by adopting one theory of life, Texas may override the rights of the pregnant woman that are at stake. We repeat, however, that the State does have an important and legitimate interest in preserving and protecting the health of the pregnant woman, whether she be a resident of the State or a nonresident who seeks medical consultation and treatment there, and that it has still *another* important and legitimate interest in protecting the potentiality of human life. These interests are separate and distinct. Each grows in substantiality as the woman approaches term and, at a point during pregnancy, each becomes "compelling." . . .

The judgment of the District Court as to intervenor Hallford is reversed, and Dr. Hallford's complaint in intervention is dismissed. In all other respects, the judgment of the District Court is affirmed. Costs are allowed to the appellee.

It is so ordered.

MR. JUSTICE REHNQUIST, dissenting.

The Court's opinion brings to the decision of this troubling question both extensive historical fact and a wealth of legal scholarship. While the opinion thus commands my respect, I find myself nonetheless in fundamental disagreement with those parts of it that invalidate the Texas statute in question, and therefore dissent. . . .

. . . I have difficulty in concluding, as the Court does, that the right of "privacy" is involved in this case. Texas, by the statute here challenged, bars the performance of a medical abortion by a licensed physician on a plaintiff such as Roe. A transaction resulting in an operation such as this is not "private" in the ordinary usage of that word. Nor is the "privacy" that the Court finds here even a distant relative of the freedom from searches and seizures protected by the Fourth Amendment to the Constitution, which the Court has referred to as embodying a right to privacy. *Katz v. United States,* 389 U. S. 347 (1967).

If the Court means by the term "privacy" no more than that the claim of a person to be free from unwanted state regulation of consensual transactions may be a form of "liberty" protected by the Fourteenth Amendment, there is no doubt that similar claims have been upheld in our earlier decisions on the basis of that liberty. I agree with the statement of MR. JUSTICE STEWART in his concurring opinion that the "liberty," against deprivation of which without due process the Fourteenth Amendment protects, embraces more than the rights found in the Bill of Rights. But that liberty is not guaranteed absolutely against deprivation, only against deprivation without due process of law. The test traditionally applied in the area of social and economic legislation is whether or not a law such as that challenged has a rational relation to a valid state objective. . . . The Due Process Clause of the Fourteenth Amendment undoubtedly does place a limit, albeit a broad one, on legislative power to enact laws such as this. If the Texas statute were to prohibit an abortion even where the mother's life is in jeopardy, I have little doubt that such a statute would lack a rational relation to a valid state objective under the test stated in *Williamson, supra.* But the Court's sweeping invalidation of any restrictions on abortion during the first trimester is impossible to justify under that standard, and the conscious weighing of competing factors that the Court's opinion apparently substitutes for the established test is far more appropriate to a legislative judgment than to a judicial one.

The Court eschews the history of the Fourteenth Amendment in its reliance on the "compelling state interest" test. . . . But the Court adds a new wrinkle to this test by transposing it from the legal considerations associated with the Equal Protection Clause of the Fourteenth Amendment to this case arising under the Due Process Clause of the Fourteenth Amendment. Unless I misapprehend the consequences of this transplanting of the "compelling state interest test," the Court's opinion will accomplish the seemingly impossible feat of leaving this area of the law more confused than it found it.

While the Court's opinion quotes from the dissent of Mr. Justice Holmes in *Lochner v. New York* . . . (1905), the result it reaches is more closely attuned to the majority opinion of Mr. Justice Peckham in that case. As in *Lochner* and similar cases applying substantive due process standards to economic and social welfare legislation, the adoption of the compelling state interest standard will inevitably require this Court to examine the legislative policies and pass on the wisdom of these policies in the very process of deciding whether a particular state interest put forward may or may not be "compelling." The decision here to break pregnancy into three distinct terms and to outline the permissible restrictions the State may impose in each one, for example, partakes more of judicial legislation than it does of a determination of the intent of the drafters of the Fourteenth Amendment.

The fact that a majority of the States reflecting, after all, the majority sentiment in those States, have had restrictions on abortions for at least a century is a strong indication, it seems to me, that the asserted right to an abortion is not "so rooted in the traditions and conscience of our people as to be ranked as fundamental," *Snyder v. Massachusetts* . . . (1934). Even today, when society's views on abortion are changing, the very existence of the debate is evidence that the "right" to an abortion is not so universally accepted as the appellant would have us believe.

To reach its result the Court necessarily has had to find within the scope of the Fourteenth Amendment a right that was apparently completely unknown to the drafters of the Amendment. As early as 1821, the first state law dealing directly with abortion was enacted by the Connecticut Legislature . . . . By the time of the adoption of the Fourteenth Amendment in 1868, there were at least 36 laws enacted by state or territorial legislatures limiting abortion. While many States have amended or updated their laws, 21 of the laws on the books in 1868 remain in effect today. Indeed, the Texas statute struck down today was, as the majority notes, first enacted in 1857 and "has remained substantially unchanged to the present time." . . .

There apparently was no question concerning the validity of this provision or of any of the other state statutes when the Fourteenth Amendment was adopted. The only conclusion possible from this history is that the drafters did not intend to have the Fourteenth Amendment withdraw from the States the power to legislate with respect to this matter . . . .

For all of the foregoing reasons, I respectfully dissent.

5-3 The Real World of Constitutional Rights: The Supreme Court and the Implementation of the Abortion Decisions

Gerald N. Rosenberg

When one considers how exposed the Constitution's "religious establishment" clause is to continuous revision, it is not surprising to find other, less established rights deeply enmeshed in politics as well. The next essay examines the right to an abortion, a controversial aspect of civil liberties policy that has been defended as an application of the "right to privacy."

The Supreme Court began asserting the right to privacy in earnest with Griswold v. Connecticut *in 1965, when it ruled that a married couple's decision to use birth control lay beyond the purview of the government. The 1973* Roe v. Wade *decision establishing a woman's right to an abortion—the best known and most controversial privacy right—has further established privacy as a class of rights implicit in the Bill of Rights. But, as Gerald N. Rosenberg explains,* Roe v. Wade *left many aspects of abortion rights unresolved, and a lively public debate on the subject continues today.*

In *Roe v. Wade* and *Doe v. Bolton* (1973) the Supreme Court held unconstitutional Texas and Georgia laws prohibiting abortions except for "the purpose of saving the life of the mother" (Texas) and where "pregnancy would endanger the life of the pregnant mother or would seriously and permanently injure her health" (Georgia). The Court asserted that women had a fundamental right of privacy to decide whether or not to bear a child. Dividing pregnancy roughly into three trimesters, the Court held that in the first trimester the choice of abortion was a woman's alone, in consultation with a physician. During the second trimester, states could regulate abortion for the preservation and protection of women's health, and in approximately the third trimester, after fetal viability, could ban abortions outright, except where necessary to preserve a woman's life or health. Although responding specifically to the laws of Texas and Georgia, the broad scope of the Court's constitutional interpretation invalidated the abortion laws of almost every state and the District of Columbia.[1]

According to one critic, *Roe* and *Doe* "may stand as the most radical decisions ever issued by the Supreme Court" (Noonan 1973, 261).

Roe and *Doe* are generally considered leading examples of judicial action in support of relatively powerless groups unable to win legislative victories. In these cases, women were that politically disadvantaged group; indeed, it has been claimed, "No victory for women's rights since enactment of the 19th Amendment has been greater than the one achieved" in *Roe* and *Doe* ("A Woman's Right" 1973, A4). But women are not the only disadvantaged interests who have attempted to use litigation to achieve policy ends. Starting with the famous cases brought by civil rights groups, and spreading to issues raised by environmental groups, consumer groups, and others, reformers have over the past decades looked to the courts as important producers of political and social change. Yet, during the same period, students of judicial politics have learned that court opinions are not always implemented with the speed and directness

Source: Gerald N. Rosenberg, "The Real World of Constitutional Rights: The Supreme Court and the Implementation of the Abortion Decisions," in *Contemplating Courts,* ed. Lee Epstein (Washington, D.C.: CQ Press, 1995), 390–419. Some notes and bibliographic references appearing in the original have been deleted.

that rule by law assumes. This is particularly the case with decisions that touch on controversial, emotional issues or deeply held beliefs, such as abortion.

This chapter contains an exploration of the effect of the Court's abortion decisions, both *Roe* and *Doe*, and the key decisions based on them. How did the public, politicians, medical professionals, and interest groups react to them? Were the decisions implemented? Did they bring safe and legal abortions to all American women? To some American women? If the answer turns out to be only some, then I want to know why. What are the factors that have led a constitutional right to be unevenly available? More generally, are there conditions under which Court decisions on behalf of relatively powerless groups are more or less likely to be implemented.[2]

The analysis presented here shows that the effect and implementation of the Court's abortion decisions have been neither straightforward nor simple. Political response has varied and access to legal and safe abortion has increased, but in an uneven and nonuniform way. These findings are best explained by two related factors. First, at the time of the initial decisions there was widespread support for legal abortion from several sets of actors, including relevant political and professional elites on both the national and local level, the public at large, and activists. Second, the Court's decisions, by allowing clinics to perform abortions, made it possible for women to obtain abortions in some places where hospitals refused to provide them. Implementation by private clinics, however, has led to uneven availability of abortion services and has encouraged local political opposition.

The Abortion Cases

Roe and *Doe* were the Court's first major abortion decisions, but they were not its last.[3] In response to these decisions, many states rewrote their abortion laws, ostensibly to conform with the Court's constitutional mandate but actually with the goal of restricting the newly created right. Cases quickly arose, and continue to arise, challenging state laws as inconsistent with the Court's ruling, if not openly and clearly

hostile to it. In general, the Court's response has been to preserve the core holding of *Roe* and *Doe* that a woman has a virtually unfettered constitutional right to an abortion before fetal viability, but to defer to legislation in areas not explicitly dealt with in those decisions. These cases require brief mention.

Areas of Litigation

Since *Roe* and *Doe*, the Court has heard three kinds of cases on abortion. One type involves state and federal funding for abortion. Here, the Court has consistently upheld the right of government not to fund abortion services and to prohibit the provision of abortions in public hospitals, unless the abortion is medically necessary. In perhaps the most important case, *Harris v. McRae* (1980), the Court upheld the most restrictive version of the so-called Hyde Amendment, which barred the use of federal funds for even medically necessary abortions, including those involving pregnancies due to rape or incest.

A second area that has provoked a great deal of litigation is the degree of participation in the abortion decision constitutionally allowed to the spouse of a pregnant married woman or the parents of a pregnant single minor. The Court has consistently struck down laws requiring spousal involvement but has upheld laws requiring parental notification or consent, as long as there is a "judicial bypass" option allowing minors to bypass their parents and obtain permission from a court.

A third area generating litigation involves the procedural requirements that states can impose for abortions. Most of these cases have arisen from state attempts to make abortion as difficult as possible to obtain. Regulations include requiring all post-first trimester abortions to be performed in hospitals; the informed, written consent of a woman before an abortion can be performed; a twenty-four-hour waiting period before an abortion can be performed; a pathology report for each abortion and the presence of a second physician at abortions occurring after potential viability; the preservation by physicians of the life of viable fetuses; and restrictions on the disposal of fetal remains. The Court's most recent pronouncement on these issues, *Planned Parenthood of Southeastern Pennsylvania v. Casey* (1992), found informed consent, a twenty-four-hour waiting period, and certain reporting requirements constitutional.

Trends in Court Treatment of Abortion Cases

Since the late 1980s, as *Casey* suggests, the Court has upheld more restrictions on the abortion right. In *Webster v. Reproductive Health Services* (1989), the Court upheld a 1986 restrictive Missouri law, and in 1991, in *Rust v. Sullivan,* it upheld government regulations prohibiting family-planning organizations that receive federal funds from counseling patients about abortion or providing abortion referrals. Most important, in *Casey* the Court abandoned the trimester framework of *Roe.* Although the justices did not agree on the proper constitutional standard for assessing state restrictions on abortion, Justices Sandra Day O'Connor, Anthony M. Kennedy, and David H. Souter adopted an "undue burden" standard. Under this standard, states may regulate abortion but may not place an undue burden on women seeking an abortion of a nonviable fetus.

Many commentators expected *Casey* to generate an avalanche of litigation centering directly on the abortion rights. Given the ambiguity of the undue burden standard, they expected expanded state activity to limit abortion. These expectations may yet be fulfilled, but, interestingly, Court cases since *Casey* have not specifically focused on the abortion right per se. Rather, in recent litigation the Court has been asked to resolve questions concerning access to abortion; namely, what steps can courts take to prevent antiabortion advocates from interfering with public access to family-planning and abortion clinics. The reason these kinds of questions arose is not difficult to discern; the 1990s has seen the rise of militant tactics—ranging from boisterous protests to harassment of clinic workers and even to the murder of physicians performing abortions—by certain segments of the antiabortion movement.

These "access" cases have generated mixed Court rulings. In *Bray v. Alexandria Women's Health Clinic*

(1993), the Court rejected an attempt by pro-choice groups to use the 1871 Ku Klux Klan Act as a way to bring federal courts into this area. But, in *Madsen v. Women's Health Center* (1994), the Court upheld parts of a Florida trial court injunction permanently enjoining antiabortion protesters from blocking access to an abortion clinic and from physically harassing persons leaving or entering it. With the enactment by Congress of the Freedom of Access to Clinic Entrances Act in 1994, and the immediate filing of a legal challenge, it is likely that the Court will have another opportunity to address this issue.

Implementing Constitutional Rights

How have the public, politicians, medical professionals, and interest groups reacted to the Court decisions since *Roe* and *Doe*? How has access to legal and safe abortion changed in the wake of these decisions? In other words, when the Supreme Court announces a new constitutional right, what happens?

Legal Abortions: The Numbers

An obvious way to consider this question, at least in the abortion realm, is to look at the number of legal abortions performed before and after the 1973 decisions. For, if the Court has had an important effect on society in this area, we might expect to find dramatic increases in the number of legal abortions obtained after 1973. Collecting statistics on legal abortion, however, is not an easy task. Record keeping is not as precise and complete as one would hope. Two organizations, the public Centers for Disease Control and Prevention in Atlanta and the private Alan Guttmacher Institute in New York, are the most thorough and reliable collectors of the information. The data they have collected on the number of legal abortions performed between 1966 and 1992 and the yearly percentage change are shown in Figure 1.

Interestingly, these data present a mixed picture of the effect of the abortion decisions. On the one hand, they suggest that after *Roe* the number of legal abortions increased at a strong pace throughout the 1970s (the solid line in Figure 1). On the other hand, they reveal that the changes after 1973 were part of a trend

Figure 1   Legal Abortions, 1966–1992

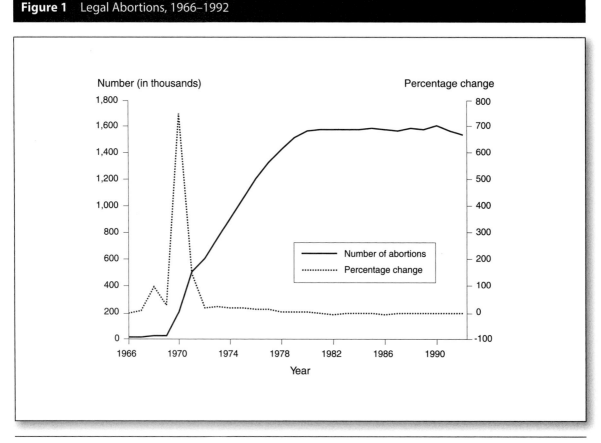

Sources: Estimates by the Alan Guttmacher Institute and the Centers for Disease Control and Prevention in Henshaw and Van Vort 1994, 100–106, 112; Lader 1973, 209; U.S. Congress 1974, 1976; Weinstock et al. 1975, 23. When sources differed, I have relied on data from the Alan Guttmacher Institute since its estimates are based on surveys of all known abortion providers and are generally more complete. Data points for 1983, 1986, and 1990 are estimates based on interpolations made by the Alan Guttmacher Institute.

that started in 1970, three years before the Court acted. Strikingly, the largest increase in the number of legal abortions occurs between 1970 and 1971, two years before *Roe*! In raw numerical terms, the increase between 1972 and 1973 is 157,800, a full 134,500 fewer than the pre-*Roe* increase in 1970–1971. It is possible, of course, that the effect of *Roe* was not felt in 1973. Even though the decision was handed down in January, perhaps the 1973–1974 comparison gives a more accurate picture. If this is the

case, the increase, 154,000, is still substantially smaller than the change during 1970–1971. And while the number of legal abortions continued to increase in the years immediately after 1974, that rate eventually stabilized and by the 1990s had actually declined. The dotted line in Figure 1 (representing the percentage change in the number of legal abortions performed from one year to the next) shows, too, that the largest increases in the number of legal abortions occurred in the years prior to *Roe* . . . .

The data presented above show that the largest numerical increases in legal abortions occurred in the years prior to initial Supreme Court action . . . . There was no steep or unusual increase in the number of legal abortions following *Roe*. To be sure, it is possible that without constitutional protection for abortion no more states would have liberalized or repealed their laws and those that had done so might have overturned their previous efforts. And the fact that the number of legal abortions continued to increase after 1973 suggests that the Court was effective in easing access to safe and legal abortion. But those increases, while large, were smaller than those of previous years. Hence, the growth in the number of legal abortions can be only partially attributed to the Court; it might even be the case that the increases would have continued without the Court's 1973 decisions.

What Happened?

Particularly interesting about the data presented above is that they suggest that *Roe* itself failed to generate major changes in the number of legal abortions. This finding is compatible with political science literature, in which it is argued that Supreme Court decisions, particularly ones dealing with emotional and controversial issues, are not automatically and completely implemented. It also appears to fit nicely with an argument I have made elsewhere (Rosenberg 1991), which suggests that several factors must be present for new constitutional rights to be implemented. These include widespread support from political and professional elites on both the national and local level, from the public at large, and from activists and a willingness on the part of those called on to implement the decision to act accordingly. This is true, as Alexander Hamilton pointed out two centuries ago, because courts lack the power of "either the sword or the purse." To a greater extent than other government institutions, courts are dependent on both elite and popular support for their decisions to be implemented.

To fill out my argument in greater detail, I examine both pre- and post-1973 actions as they relate to the implementation of the abortion right. In so doing, I reach two important conclusions. First, by the time the Court reached its decisions in 1973, little political opposition to abortion existed on the federal level, relevant professional elites and social activists gave it widespread support, it was practiced on a large scale (see Figure 1), and public support for it was growing. These positions placed abortion reform in the American mainstream. Second, in the years after 1973, opposition to abortion strengthened and grew.

Pre-*Roe* Support

In the decade or so prior to *Roe*, there was a sea change in the public position of abortion in American life. At the start of the 1960s, abortion was not a political issue. Abortions, illegal as they were, were performed clandestinely, and women who underwent the procedure did not talk about it.[4] By 1972, however, abortion had become a public and political issue. While little legislative or administrative action was taken on the federal level, a social movement, organized in the mid- and late 1960s, to reform and repeal prohibitions on abortion met with some success at the state level, and public opinion swung dramatically from opposition to abortion in most cases to substantial support.

Elites and Social Activists

Although abortions have always been performed, public discussion did not surface until the 1950s. In 1962 the American Law Institute (ALI) published its Model Penal Code on abortion, permitting abortion if continuing the pregnancy would adversely affect the physical or mental health of the woman, if there was risk of birth defects, or if the pregnancy resulted from rape or incest. Publicity about birth defects caused by Thalidomide, a drug prescribed in the 1960s to cure infertility, and a German measles epidemic in the years 1962–1965 kept the issue prominent. By November 1965 the American Medical Association Board of Trustees approved a report urging adoption of the ALI law.

In 1966, reform activists began making numerous radio and television appearances.[5] By then there were several pro-choice groups, including the Society for Humane Abortion in California; the Association for the Study of Abortion in New York, a prestigious board of doctors and lawyers; and the Illinois Committee for Medical Control of Abortion, which advocated repeal of all abortion laws. Abortion referral services were also started. Previously, pro-choice activists had made private referrals to competent doctors in the United States and Mexico, who performed illegal but safe abortions. But by the late 1960s, abortion referral groups operated publicly. In New York City, in 1967, twenty-two clergy announced the formation of their group, gaining front-page coverage in the *New York Times* (Fiske 1967). The Chicago referral service took out a full page ad in the *Sun-Times* announcing its services. In Los Angeles, the referral service was serving more than a thousand women per month. By the late 1960s pro-choice organizations, including abortion-referral services, were operating in many major U.S. cities. And by 1971, the clergy referral service operated publicly in eighteen states with a staff of about 700 clergy and lay people (Hole and Levine 1971, 299).

In order to tap this emerging support, the National Association for the Repeal of Abortion Laws (NARAL) was founded.[6] Protesting in the streets, lecturing, and organizing "days of anger" began to have an effect. Women who had undergone illegal abortions wrote and spoke openly about them. Seventy-five leading national groups endorsed the repeal of all abortion laws between 1967 and the end of 1972, including twenty-eight religious and twenty-one medical groups. Among the religious groups, support ranged from the American Jewish Congress to the American Baptist Convention. Medical groups included the American Public Health Association, the American Psychiatric Association, the American Medical Association, the National Council of Obstetrics-Gynecology, and the American College of Obstetricians and Gynecologists. Among other groups, support included the American Bar Association and a host of liberal organizations. Even the YWCA supported repeal (U.S. Congress 1976, 4:53–91).

The Federal Government

In the late 1960s, while the abortion law reform battle was being fought in the states, the federal arena was quiet. For example, although states with less restrictive laws received Medicaid funds that paid for some abortions, for "six years after 1967, not a single bill was introduced, much less considered, in Congress to curtail the use of federal funds for abortion" (Rosoff 1975, 13). The pace momentarily quickened in 1968 when the Presidential Advisory Council on the Status of Women, appointed by President Lyndon Johnson, recommended the repeal of all abortion laws (Lader 1973, 81–82).

Still, abortion was not a major issue in the 1968 presidential campaign. Despite his personal beliefs, the newly elected president, Richard M. Nixon, did not take active steps to limit abortion, and the U.S. government did not enter *Roe* nor, after the decision, did it give support to congressional efforts to limit abortion.[7] Although it is true that in 1973 and 1974 President Nixon was occupied with other matters, his administration essentially avoided the abortion issue.

In Congress there was virtually no abortion activity prior to 1973. In April 1970, Sen. Bob Packwood (R-Ore.) introduced a National Abortion Act designed to "guarantee and protect" the "fundamental constitutional right" of a woman "to control her own fertility" (U.S. Congress 1970a). He also introduced a bill to liberalize the District of Columbia's abortion law (U.S. Congress 1970b). Otherwise, Congress remained essentially inactive on the abortion issue.

The States

It is not at all surprising that the president and Congress did not involve themselves in the abortion reform movement of the 1960s. Laws banning abortion were state laws, so most of the early abortion law reform activity was directed at state governments. In the early and middle parts of the decade there was some legislative discussion in California, New

Hampshire, and New York. By 1967, reform bills were introduced in twenty-eight states, including California, Colorado, Delaware, Florida, Georgia, Maryland, Oklahoma, New Jersey, New York, North Carolina, and Pennsylvania (Rubin 1982). The first successful liberalization drive was in Colorado, which adopted a reform bill, modeled on the ALI's Model Penal Code. Interestingly, another early reform state was California, where Gov. Ronald Reagan, despite intense opposition, signed a reform bill.

These victories further propelled the reform movement, and in 1968, abortion legislation was pending in some thirty states. During 1968–1969 seven states—Arkansas, Delaware, Georgia, Kansas, Maryland, New Mexico, and Oregon—enacted reform laws based on or similar to the ALI model (Lader 1973, 84). In 1970, four states went even further. In chronological order, Hawaii, New York, Alaska, and Washington essentially repealed prohibitions on abortions in the first two trimesters.

To sum up, in the five or so years prior to the Supreme Court's decisions, reform and repeal bills had been debated in most states, and seventeen plus the District of Columbia acted to liberalize their laws (Craig and O'Brien 1993, 75). State action had removed some obstacles to abortion, and safe and legal abortions were thus available in scattered states. And, as indicated in Figure 1, in 1972, nearly 600,000 legal abortions were performed. Activity was widespread, vocal, and effective.

Public Opinion

Another important element in the effectiveness of the Court is the amount of support from the population at large. By the eve of the Court's decision in 1973, public opinion had dramatically shifted from opposition to abortion in most cases to substantial, if not majority, support. Indeed, in the decades that have followed, opinion on abortion has remained remarkably stable.[8]

Looking at the 1960s as a whole, Blake (1971, 543, 544) found that opinions on discretionary abortion were "changing rapidly over time" and polls were recording "rapidly growing support." For example,

relying on data from Gallup polls, Blake (1977b, 49) found that support for elective abortion increased approximately two and one-half times from 1968 to 1972. One set of Gallup polls recorded a fifteen-point drop in the percentage of respondents disapproving of abortions for financial reasons in the eight months between October 1969 and June 1970 (Blake 1977a, 58)....In 1971, a national poll taken for the Commission on Population Growth and the American Future found 50 percent of its respondents agreeing with the statement that the abortion "decision should be left up to persons involved and their doctor" (Rosenthal 1971, 22). Thus, in the words of one study, "[b]y the time the Supreme Court made its ruling, there was strong public support behind the legalization of abortion" (Ebaugh and Haney 1980, 493).

Much of the reason for the growth in support for the repeal of the laws on abortion, both from the public and from organizations, may have come from changes in opinion by the professional elite. Polls throughout the late 1960s reported that important subgroups of the American population were increasingly supportive of abortion law reform and repeal. Several nonscientific polls of doctors, for example, suggested a great deal of support for abortion reform. A scientific poll of nearly thirteen thousand respondents in nursing, medical, and social work schools in the autumn and winter of 1971 showed strong support for repeal. The poll found split opinions among nursing students and faculty but found that 69 percent of medical students, 71 percent of medical faculty, 76 percent of social work students, and 75 percent of social work faculty supported "freely accessible abortion" (Rosen et al. 1974, 165). And a poll by the American Council of Education of 180,000 college freshmen in 1970 found that 83 percent favored the legalization of abortion (Currivan 1970). It is clear that in the late 1960s and early 1970s, the public was becoming increasingly supportive of legal abortion.

Post-*Roe* Activity

The relative quiet of the early 1960s has yet to return to the abortion arena. Rather than settling the issue, the Court's decisions added even more controversy.

On the federal level, legislative and administrative action dealing with abortion has swung back and forth, from more or less benign neglect prior to 1973 to open antipathy to modest support. State action has followed a different course. Legislative efforts in the 1960s and early 1970s to reform and repeal abortion laws gave way to efforts to limit access to abortions. Public opinion remained stable until the *Webster* decision, after which there was a noticeable shift toward the pro-choice position. Finally, the antiabortion movement grew both more vocal and more violent.

The Federal Government: The President

On the presidential level, little changed in the years immediately after *Roe.* Nixon, as noted, took no action, and Gerald R. Ford, during his short term, said little about abortion until the presidential campaign in 1976, when he took a middle-of-the-road, antiabortion position, supporting local option, the law before *Roe,* and opposing federal funding of abortion (Craig and O'Brien 1993, 160–161). His Justice Department, however, did not enter the case of *Planned Parenthood of Central Missouri v. Danforth,* in which numerous state restrictions on the provision of abortion were challenged, and the Ford administration took no major steps to help the antiabortion forces.[9]

The Carter administration, unlike its Republican predecessors, did act to limit access to abortion. As a presidential candidate Carter opposed federal spending for abortion, and as president, during a press conference in June 1977, he stated his support for the Supreme Court's decisions allowing states to refuse Medicaid funding for abortions (Rubin 1982, 107). The Carter administration also sent its solicitor general into the Supreme Court to defend the Hyde Amendment.

Ronald Reagan was publicly committed to ending legal abortion. Opposition to *Roe* was said to be a litmus test for federal judicial appointments, and Reagan repeatedly used his formidable rhetorical skills in support of antiabortion activists. Under his presidency, antiabortion laws enacted included prohibiting fetal tissue research by federal scientists, banning most abortions at military hospitals, and denying funding to organizations that counseled or provided abortion services abroad. His administration submitted amicus curiae cases in all the Court's abortion cases, and in two (*Thornburgh v. American College of Obstetricians and Gynecologists,* 1986, and *Webster*) urged that *Roe* be overturned. Yet, despite the rhetoric and the symbolism, these actions had little effect on the abortion rate. As Craig and O'Brien (1993, 190) put it, "in spite of almost eight years of antiabortion rhetoric, Reagan had accomplished little in curbing abortion."

The administration of George Bush was as, if not more, hostile to the constitutional right to abortion as its predecessor. It filed antiabortion briefs in several abortion cases and urged that *Roe* be overturned. During Bush's presidency, the Food and Drug Administration placed RU-486, a French abortion drug, on the list of unapproved drugs, making it ineligible to be imported for personal use. And, in the administration's most celebrated antiabortion action, the secretary of the Health and Human Services Department, Louis W. Sullivan, issued regulations prohibiting family-planning organizations that received federal funds from counseling patients about abortion or providing referrals (the "gag rule" upheld in *Rust*).

President Bill Clinton brought a sea change to the abortion issue. As the first pro-choice president since *Roe,* he acted quickly to reverse decisions of his predecessors. In particular, on the third day of his administration, and the twentieth anniversary of *Roe,* Clinton issued five abortion-related memos.

1. He rescinded the ban on abortion counseling at federally financed clinics (negating *Rust*).

2. He rescinded restrictions on federal financing of fetal tissue research.

3. He eased U.S. policy on abortions in military hospitals.

4. He reversed Reagan policy on aid to international family planning programs involved in abortion-related activities.

5. He called for review of the ban on RU-486, the French abortion pill (Toner 1993).

In addition, in late May 1994, he signed the Freedom of Access to Clinic Entrances Act, giving federal protection to facilities and personnel providing abortion services. And, in early August 1994, the U.S. Justice Department sent U.S. marshals to help guard abortion clinics in at least twelve communities around the country (Thomas 1994). Furthermore, his two Supreme Court appointees as of 1994, Ruth Bader Ginsburg and Stephen Breyer, are apparently both pro-choice.

The Federal Government: Congress

In contrast to the executive branch, Congress engaged in a great deal of antiabortion activity after 1973, although almost none of it was successful, and some supportive activity actually occurred in the late 1980s and early 1990s. By means of legislation designed to overturn *Roe,* riders to various spending bills, and constitutional amendments, many members of Congress made their opposition to abortion clear. Perhaps the most important congressional action was the passage of the Hyde Amendment, which restricted federal funding of abortion: First passed in 1976, and then in subsequent years, the amendment prohibited the use of federal funds for abortion except in extremely limited circumstances. Although the wording varied in some years, the least limited version allowed funding only to save the life of the woman, when rape or incest had occurred, or when some long-lasting health damage, certified by two physicians, would result from the pregnancy. The amendment has been effective and the number of federally funded abortions fell from 294,600 in 1977 to 267 in 1992 (Daley and Gold 1994, 250).

Despite the amount of congressional activity, the Hyde Amendment was the only serious piece of antiabortion legislation enacted.[10] And, in 1994, Congress actually enacted legislation granting federal protection to abortion clinics. Thus, Congress was hostile in words but cautious in action with abortion. While not supporting the Court and the right to abortion, congressional action did not bar legal abortion.[11]

The States

Prior to 1973 the states had been the main arena for the abortion battle, and Court action did not do much to change that. In the wake of the Court decisions, all but a few states had to rewrite their abortion laws to conform to the Court's constitutional mandate. Their reactions, like those on the federal level, varied enormously. Some states acted to bring their laws into conformity with the Court's ruling, while others reenacted their former restrictive laws or enacted regulations designed to impede access to abortion. Since abortion is a state matter, the potential for state action affecting the availability of legal abortion was high.

At the outset, a national survey reported that state governments "moved with extreme caution in implementing the Supreme Court's ruling" (Brody 1973, A1). By the end of 1973, Blake (1977b, 46) reports, 260 abortion-related bills had been introduced in state legislatures and 39 enacted. In 1974, 189 bills were introduced and 19 enacted. In total, in the two years immediately following the Court decisions, 62 laws relating to abortion were enacted by 32 states. And state activity continued, with more abortion laws enacted in 1977 than in any year since 1973 (Rubin 1982, 126, 136).

Many of these laws were hostile to abortion. "Perhaps the major share," Blake (1977b, 61 n. 2) believes, was "obstructive and unconstitutional." They included spousal and parental consent requirements, tedious written-consent forms describing the "horrors" of abortion, funding limitations, waiting periods, hospitalization requirements, elaborate statistical reporting requirements, and burdensome medical procedures. Other action undertaken by states was simple and directly to the point. North Dakota and Rhode Island, for example, responded to the Court's decisions by enacting laws allowing abortion only to preserve the life of the woman (Weinstock et al. 1975, 28; "Rhode Island" 1973). Virginia rejected a bill bringing its statutes into conformity with the Court's order (Brody 1973, 46). Arkansas enforced a state law allowing abortion only if the pregnancy threatened the life or health of the woman ("Abortions Legal for Year" 1973, A14). In Louisiana, the attorney general threatened to take away the license of any physician performing an abortion, and the state medical society declared that any physician who performed an abortion, except to save the woman's life, violated the ethical principles of medicine (Weinstock et al. 1975, 28). The Louisiana State Board of Medical Examiners also pledged to prevent physicians from performing abortions (Brody 1973). In Pennsylvania, the state medical society announced that it did "not condone abortion on demand" and retained its strict standards (King 1973, 35). And in Saint Louis, the city attorney threatened to arrest any physician who performed an abortion (King 1973). Given this kind of activity, it can be concluded that in many states the Court's intent was "widely and purposely frustrated" (Blake 1977b, 60–61).

Variation in state response to the constitutional right to an abortion continues to this day. Although legal abortions are performed in all states, the availability of abortion services varies enormously. As noted, a variety of restrictions on abortion have been enacted across the country. In the wake of the Court's decision in *Webster* (1989), which upheld a restrictive Missouri law, a new round of state restrictions on abortion was generally expected. Indeed, within two years of the decision nine states and Guam enacted restrictions. Nevertheless, four states enacted legislation protecting a woman's right to abortion (Craig and O'Brien 1993, 280). The Pennsylvania enactments were challenged in *Casey* (1992), in which the "undue burden" standard was announced. The lack of clarity in this standard virtually ensures that restrictions will continue to be enacted.

Public Opinion

As shown in Figure 2, public opinion changed little from the early 1970s (pre-*Roe*) until the *Webster* decision in 1989, after which a small but important growth in pro-choice support occurred. Although differently worded questions produce different results, it is clear that the American public remains strongly supportive of abortion when the woman's health is endangered by continuing the pregnancy, when there is a strong chance of a serious fetal defect, and when the pregnancy is the result of rape or incest. The public is more divided when abortion is sought for economic reasons, by single unmarried women unwilling to marry, and by married women who do not want more children. "The overall picture that emerges is that a majority supports leaving abortion legal and available to women unfortunate enough to need it, though many in the majority remain concerned about the moral implications" (Craig and O'Brien 1993, 269). . . .

Anti-Abortion Activity

Organized opposition to abortion increased dramatically in the years following the Court's initial decisions. National groups such as the American Life Lobby, Americans United for Life, the National Right to Life Committee, the Pro-Life Action League, and Operation Rescue and numerous local groups have adopted some of the tactics of the reformers. They have marched, lobbied, and protested, urging that abortion be made illegal in most or all circumstances. In addition, in the 1980s, groups like Operation Rescue began to adopt more violent tactics. And, since 1982, the U.S. Bureau of Alcohol, Tobacco and Firearms has reported 146 incidents of bombing, arson, or attempts against clinics and related sites in thirty states, causing more than $12 million in damages (Thomas 1994). The high level of harassment of abortion clinics is shown in Table 1.

The level of harassment appears to have increased over time. In just 1992 and 1993 the U.S. Bureau of Alcohol, Tobacco and Firearms recorded thirty-six incidents, which resulted in an estimated $3.8 million in damages (Thomas 1994). The National Abortion Federation, representing roughly half of the nation's clinics, noted that incidents of reported vandalism at its clinics more than doubled from 1991 to 1992 (Barringer 1993). From May 1992 to August 1993 the U.S. Bureau of Alcohol, Tobacco

Figure 2 Public Opinion and Abortion, Selected Years, 1975–1992

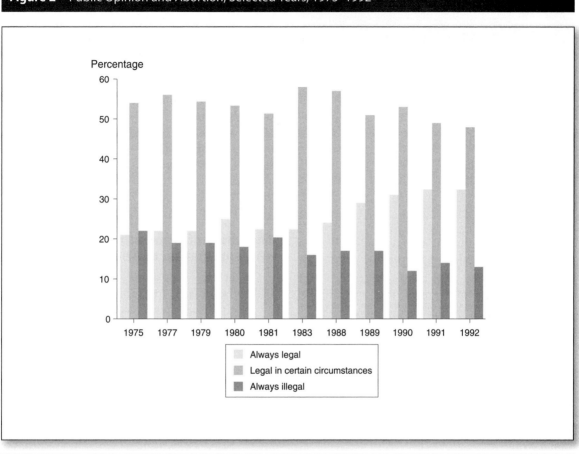

Source: Newport and McAneny 1992, 51–52.

Note: "No opinion" omitted.

and Firearms reported that 123 family-planning clinics were bombed or burned (Baum 1993). In 1992 more than forty clinics were attacked with butyric acid (a chemical injected through key holes, under doors, or into ventilation shafts) forcing clinic closures and requiring costly repairs (Anderson and Binstein 1993, C27). One of the aims of this violence appears to be to raise the cost of operating abortion clinics to such an extent as to force their closure. In 1992 and 1993, for example, arson destroyed clinics

in Missoula and Helena, Montana, and in Boise, Idaho. The clinics have either been unable to reopen or have had great difficulty in doing so because of the difficulty of finding owners willing to rent to them and obtaining insurance coverage. In 1990, in the wake of such violence, one major insurer, Traveler's Insurance Company, decided not to insure any abortion-related concerns (Baum 1993).

Another tactic aimed at shutting down abortion clinics is to conduct large, sustained protests. During

Table 1 Abortion Clinics Reporting Harassment, 1985 and 1988 (in percentage)

Activity	1985	1988
Picketing	80	81
Picketing with physical contact or blocking	47	46
Demonstrations resulting in arrests	—	38
Bomb threats	48	36
Vandalism	28	34
Picketing homes of staff members	16	17

Source: Surveys of all abortion providers taken by the Alan Guttmacher Institute in Henshaw (1991, 246–252, 263).

Note: Dash = question not asked.

the summer of 1991, for example, Operation Rescue staged forty-six days of protest in Wichita, Kansas, resulting in the arrest of approximately 2,700 people. During the summer of 1993, Operation Rescue launched a seven-city campaign with similar aims. In addition, there have been individual acts of violence against abortion providers. Dr. David Gunn was murdered in March 1993 outside an abortion clinic in Pensacola, Florida; Dr. George Tiller was shot in August 1993 in Wichita, Kansas; and Dr. John Britton and his escort, James Barrett, a retired air force lieutenant colonel, were murdered in late July 1994, also in Pensacola. Commenting on the murders of Dr. Britton and James Barrett, Don Treshman, director of the antiabortion group Rescue America, issued an ominous warning: "Up to now, the killings have been on one side, with 30 million dead babies and hundreds of dead and maimed mothers. On the other side, there are two dead doctors. Maybe the balance is going to shift" (quoted in Lewin 1994,

A7).[12] In sum, as Forrest and Henshaw (1987, 13) concluded, "antiabortion harassment in the United States is widespread and frequent."

Two important facts can be gleaned from the foregoing discussion. First, at the time of the 1973 abortion decisions, large segments of the political and professional elite were either indifferent to or supported abortion reform. Second, after the decisions, many political leaders vociferously opposed abortion. Congress enacted antiabortion legislation as did some of the states. In addition, activist opposition was growing. How this opposition affected the implementation of the decisions is the focus of the next section.

The Effect of Opposition on the Implementation of Abortion Rights

On the eve of the abortion decisions, there was widespread support from critical professional elites, growing public support, successful reform in many states, and indifference from most national politicians. Is this sufficient for the implementation of constitutional rights?

Constitutional rights are not self-implementing. That is, to make a right a reality, the behavior of individuals and the policies of the institutions in which they work must change. Because abortion is a medical procedure, and because safe abortion requires trained personnel, the implementation of abortion rights depends on the medical profession to provide abortion services. When done properly, first-term and most second-term abortions can be performed on an outpatient basis, and there is less risk of death in the procedure than there is in childbirth or in such routine operations as tonsillectomies. Thus, no medical or technical reasons stand in the way of the provision of abortion services. Following Supreme Court action, however, the medical profession moved with "extreme caution" in making abortion available (Brody 1973, 1). Coupled with the hostility of some state legislatures, barriers to legal abortion remained.

These barriers have proved to be strong. Perhaps the strongest barrier has been opposition from hospitals. In Table 2, I track the response of hospitals to the Court's decisions. The results are staggering. Despite the relative ease and safety of the abortion procedure, and the unambiguous holding of the Court, both public and private hospitals throughout America have refused to perform abortions. *The vast majority of public and private hospitals have never performed an abortion!* In 1973 and the first quarter of 1974, for example, slightly more than three-quarters of public and private non-Catholic general care short-term hospitals did not perform a single abortion (Weinstock et al. 1975, 31). As illustrated in the table, the passage of time has not improved the situation. By 1976,

three years after the decision, at least 70 percent of hospitals provided no abortion services. By 1992 the situation had further deteriorated: only 18 percent of private non-Catholic general care short-term hospitals and only 13 percent of public hospitals provided abortions. As Stanley Henshaw (1986, 253, emphasis added) concluded, reviewing the data in 1986, "most hospitals have *never* performed abortions."

These figures mask the fact that even the limited availability of hospital abortions detailed here varies widely across states. In 1973, for example, only 4 percent of all abortions were performed in the eight states that make up the East South Central and West South Central census divisions (Weinstock et al. 1975, 25).[13] Two states, on the other hand, New York and California (which are home to about 20 percent of all U.S. women), accounted for 37 percent of all abortions in 1974 (Alan Guttmacher Institute 1976). In eleven states, "not a single public hospital reported performance of a single abortion for any purpose whatsoever in all of 1973" (Weinstock et al. 1975, 31). By 1976, three years after Court action, no hospitals, public or private, in Louisiana, North Dakota, and South Dakota performed abortions. The Dakotas alone had thirty public and sixty-two private hospitals. In five other states, which had a total of eighty-two public hospitals, not one performed an abortion. In thirteen additional states, less than 10 percent of each state's public hospitals reported performing any abortions (Forrest, Sullivan, and Tietze 1979, 46). Only in the states of California, Hawaii, New York, and North Carolina and in the District of Columbia did more than half the public hospitals perform any abortions during 1974–1975 (Alan Guttmacher Institute 1976, 30). By 1992, the situation was little better, with five states (California, New York, Texas, Florida, and Illinois) accounting for 49 percent of all legal abortions (Henshaw and Van Vort 1994, 102).

This refusal of hospitals to perform abortions means that women seeking them, particularly from rural areas, have to travel, often a great distance, to exercise their constitutional rights. In 1973, for

| Table 2 | Hospitals Providing Abortions, Selected Years, 1973–1992 (percentage) |

Year	Private, short-term, non-Catholic, general	Public
1973	24	—
1974	27	17
1975	30	—
1976	31	20
1977	31	21
1978	29	—
1979	28	—
1980	27	17
1982	26	16
1985	23	17
1988	21	15
1992	18	13

Sources: Forrest, Sullivan, and Tietze 1978, table 5; Henshaw 1986, 253; Henshaw et al. 1982, table 7; Henshaw, Forrest, and Van Vort 1987, 68; Henshaw and Van Vort 1990, 102–108, 142; Henshaw and Van Vort 1994, 100–106, 122; Rubin 1982, 154; Sullivan, Tietze, and Dryfoos, 1977, figure 10; Weinstock et al. 1975, 32.

Note: Dash = unavailable.

example, 150,000 women traveled out of their state of residence to obtain abortions. By 1982 the numbers had dropped, but more than 100,000 women were still forced to travel to another state for abortion services. . . .

Even when women can obtain abortions within their states of residence, they may still have to travel a great distance to do so. In 1974, the year after *Roe,* the Guttmacher Institute found that between 300,000 and 400,000 women left their home communities to obtain abortions (Alan Guttmacher Institute 1976). In 1980, across the United States, more than one-quarter (27 percent) of all women who had abortions had them outside of their home counties (Henshaw and O'Reilly 1983, 5). And in 1988, fifteen years after *Roe,* an estimated 430,000 (27 percent) women who had abortions in nonhospital settings traveled more than fifty miles from their home to reach their abortion provider. This includes over 140,000 women who traveled more than 100 miles to obtain a legal abortion (Henshaw 1991, 248).[14]

The general problem that faces women who seek to exercise their constitutional right to abortion is the paucity of abortion providers. From the legalization of abortion in 1973 to the present, at least 77 percent of all U.S. counties have been without abortion providers. And the problem is not merely rural. In 1980, seven years after Court action, there were still fifty-nine metropolitan areas in which no facilities could be identified that provided abortions (Henshaw et al. 1982, 5). The most recent data suggest that the problem is worsening. In 1992, 84 percent of all U.S. counties, home to 30 percent of all women of reproductive age, had no abortion providers. Ninety-one of the country's 320 metropolitan (28 percent) areas have no identified abortion provider, and an additional 14 (4 percent) have providers who perform fewer than fifty abortions per year. . . .

Even when abortion service is available, providers have tended to ignore the time periods set out in the Court's opinions. In 1988, fifteen years after the decisions, only 43 percent of all providers perform abortions after the first trimester. More than half (55 percent) of the hospitals that perform abortions have refused to perform second-trimester procedures, a time in pregnancy at which hospital services may be medically necessary. Only at abortion clinics have a majority of providers been willing to perform abortions after the first trimester. Indeed, in 1988 a startling 22 percent of all providers refused to perform abortions past the tenth week of pregnancy, several weeks within the first trimester, during which, according to the Court, a woman's constitutional right is virtually all-encompassing (Henshaw 1991, 251).

Finally, although abortion is "the most common surgical procedure that women undergo" (Darney et al. 1987, 161) and is reportedly the most common surgical procedure performed in the United States, an *increasing* percentage of residency programs in obstetrics and gynecology do not provide training for it. A survey taken in 1985 of all such residency programs found that 28 percent of them offered no training at all, a nearly fourfold increase since 1976. According to the results of the survey, approximately one-half of the programs made training available as an option, while only 23 percent included it routinely (Darney et al. 1987, 160). By 1992 the percentage of programs requiring abortion training had dropped nearly to half, to 12 percent (Baum 1993). In a study done in 1992 of 216 of 271 residency programs, it was found that almost half (47 percent) of graduating residents had never performed a first-trimester abortion, and only 7 percent had ever performed one in the second trimester (Cooper 1993). At least part of the reason for the increasing lack of training is harassment by antiabortion activists. "Anti-abortion groups say these numbers prove that harassment of doctors, and in turn, medical schools which train residents in abortion procedures, is an effective tactic," Cooper reported. "'You humiliate the school. . . . We hope that in 10 years, there'll be none' that train residents how to perform abortions" (Randall Terry, founder of Operation Rescue, quoted in Cooper 1993, B3). . . .

It is clear that hospital administrators, both public and private, refused to change their abortion policies in reaction to the Court decisions. In the years since the Court's decisions, abortion services have remained centered in metropolitan areas and in those states that reformed their abortion laws and regulations prior to the Court's decisions. In 1976 the Alan Guttmacher Institute (1976, 13) concluded that "[t]he response of hospitals to the legalization of abortion continues to be so limited . . . as to be tantamount to no response." Jaffe, Lindheim, and Lee (1981, 15) concluded that "the delivery pattern for abortion services that has emerged since 1973 is distorted beyond precedent." Reviewing the data in the mid-1980s, Henshaw, Forrest, and Blaine (1984, 122) summed up the situation this way: "There is abundant evidence that many women still find it difficult or impossible to obtain abortion services because of the distance of their home to the nearest provider, the cost, a lack of information on where to go, and limitations on the circumstances under which a provider will make abortions available." Most recently, Henshaw (1991, 253) concluded that "an American woman seeking abortion services will find it increasingly difficult to find a provider who will serve her in an accessible location and at an affordable cost."

Implementing Constitutional Rights: The Market

The foregoing discussion presents a seeming dilemma. There has been hostility to abortion from some politicians, most hospital administrators, many doctors, and parts of the public. On the whole, in response to the Court, hospitals did not change their policies to permit abortions. Yet, as demonstrated in Figure 1, the number of legal abortions performed in the United States continued to grow. How is it, for example, that congressional and state hostility seemed effectively to prevent progress in civil rights in the 1950s and early 1960s but did not prevent abortion in the 1970s? The answer to this question not only removes the dilemma but also illustrates why the Court's abortion decisions were effective in making legal abortion more easily available. The answer, in a word, is *clinics*.

The Court's decisions prohibited the states from interfering with a woman's right to choose an abortion,

at least in the first trimester. They did not uphold hospitalization requirements, and later cases explicitly rejected hospitalization requirements for second-trimester abortions.[15] Room was left for abortion reformers, population control groups, women's groups, and individual physicians to set up clinics to perform abortions. The refusal of many hospitals, then, to perform abortions could be countered by the creation of clinics willing to do the job. And that's exactly what happened.

In the wake of the Court's decisions the number of abortion providers sharply increased. In the first year after the decisions, the number of providers grew by nearly 25 percent. Over the first three years the percentage increase was almost 58 percent. The number of providers reached a peak in 1982 and has declined more than 18 percent since then. These raw data, however, do not indicate who these providers were.

. . . [T]he number of abortion providers increased because of the increase in the number of clinics. To fill the void that hospitals had left, clinics opened in large numbers. Between 1973 and 1974, for example, the number of nonhospital abortion providers grew 61 percent. Overall, between 1973 and 1976 the number of nonhospital providers grew 152 percent, nearly five times the rate of growth of hospital providers. In metropolitan areas . . . the growth rate was 140 percent between 1973 and 1976, five times the rate for hospital providers; in nonmetropolitan areas it was a staggering 304 percent, also about five times the growth rate for nonmetropolitan hospitals.

The growth in the number of abortion clinics was matched by the increase in the number of abortions performed by them. By 1974, nonhospital clinics were performing approximately 51 percent of all abortions, and nearly an additional 3 percent were being performed in physicians' offices. Between 1973 and 1974, the number of abortions performed in hospitals rose 5 percent, while the number performed in clinics rose 39 percent. By 1976, clinics accounted for 62 percent of all reported abortions, despite the fact that they were only 17 percent of all providers (Forrest, Sullivan, and Tietze 1979). From 1973 to 1976, the years immediately following Court action, the number of abortions performed in hospitals increased by only 8 percent, whereas the number performed in clinics and physicians' offices increased by a whopping 113 percent (Forrest et al. 1979).[16] The percentages continued to rise, and by 1992, 93 percent of all abortions were performed in nonhospital settings. Clinics satisfied the need that hospitals, despite the Court's actions, refused to meet.

In permitting abortions to be performed in clinics as well as hospitals, the Court's decisions granted a way around the intransigence of hospitals. The decisions allowed individuals committed to safe and legal abortion to make use of the market and create their own structures to meet the demand. They also provided a financial incentive for services to be provided. At least some clinics were formed solely as money-making ventures. As the legal activist Janice Goodman put it, "Some doctors are going to see a very substantial amount of money to be made on this" (quoted in Goodman, Schoenbrod, and Stearns 1973, 31). Nancy Stearns, who filed a pro-choice amicus brief in *Roe,* agreed: "[In the abortion cases] the people that are necessary to effect the decision are doctors, most of whom are not opposed, probably don't give a damn, and in fact have a whole lot to gain . . . because of the amount of money they can make" (quoted in Goodman et al. 1973, 29). Even the glacial growth of hospital abortion providers in the early and mid-1970s may be due, in part, to financial considerations. In a study of thirty-six general hospitals in Harris County (Houston), Texas, the need for increased income was found to be an important determinant of whether hospitals performed abortions. Hospitals with low occupancy rates, and therefore low income, the study reported, "saw changing abortion policy as a way to fill beds and raise income" (Kemp, Carp, and Brady 1978, 27).

Although the law of the land was that the choice of an abortion was not to be denied a woman in the first trimester, and regulated only to the extent necessary to preserve a woman's health in the second trimester, American hospitals, on the whole, do not honor the law. By allowing the market to meet the need, however, the Court's decisions resulted in at least a continuation of some availability of safe and legal abortion. Although no one can be sure what might have happened if clinics had not been allowed, if the sole burden for implementing the decisions had been on hospitals, hospital practice suggests that resistance would have been strong. After all, the Court did find abortion constitutionally protected, and most hospitals simply refused to accept that decision.

The implementation of constitutional rights, then, may depend a great deal on the beliefs of those necessary to implement them. The data suggest that without clinics the Court's decisions, constitutional rights notwithstanding, would have been frustrated.

Court Decisions and Political Action

It is generally believed that winning a major Supreme Court case is an invaluable political resource. The victorious side can use the decision to dramatize the issue, encourage political mobilization, and ignite a political movement. In an older view, however, this connection is dubious. Writing at the beginning of the twentieth century, Thayer (1901) suggested that reliance on litigation weakens political organizing. Because there have been more than twenty years of litigation in regard to abortion, the issue provides a good test of these competing views.

The evidence suggests that *Roe* and *Doe* may have seriously weakened the political effectiveness of the winners—pro-choice forces—and inspired the losers. After the 1973 decisions, many pro-choice activists simply assumed they had won and stopped their activity. According to J. Hugh Anwyl, then the executive director of Planned Parenthood of Los Angeles, pro-choice activists went "on a long siesta" after the abortion decisions (quoted in Johnston 1977, 1). Alfred F. Moran, an executive vice president at Planned Parenthood of New York, put it this way: "Most of us really believed that was the end of the controversy. The Supreme Court had spoken, and while some disagreement would remain, the issue had been tried, tested and laid to rest" (Brozan 1983, A17). These views were joined by a NARAL activist, Janet Beals: "Everyone assumed that when the Supreme Court made its decision in 1973 that we'd got what we wanted and the battle was over. The movement afterwards lost steam" (quoted in Phillips 1980, 3). By 1977 a survey of pro-choice and antiabortion activity in thirteen states nationwide revealed that abortion rights advocates had failed to match the activity of their opponents (Johnston 1977).[17] The political organization and momentum that had changed laws nationwide dissipated in reaction to Court victory. This may help explain why abortion services remain so unevenly available.

Reliance on Court action seems to have harmed the pro-choice movement in a second way. The most restrictive version of the Hyde Amendment, banning federal funding of abortions even where abortion is necessary to save the life of the woman, was passed with the help of a parliamentary maneuver by pro-choice legislators. Their strategy, as reported the following day on the front pages of the *New York Times* and the *Washington Post,* was to pass such a conservative bill that the Court would have no choice but to overturn it (Russell 1977; Tolchin 1977). This reliance on the Court was totally unfounded. With hindsight, Karen Mulhauser, a former director of NARAL, suggested that "had we made more gains through the legislative and referendum processes, and taken a little longer at it, the public would have moved with us" (quoted in Williams 1979, 12). By winning a Court case "without the organization needed to cope with a powerful opposition" (Rubin 1982, 169), pro-choice forces vastly overestimated the power and influence of the Court.

By the time of *Webster* (1989), however, pro-choice forces seemed to have learned from their mistakes, while right-to-life activists miscalculated. In early August 1989, just after *Webster,* a spokesperson for the National Right to Life Committee proclaimed: "[F]or the first time since 1973, we are clearly in a position of strength" (Shribman 1989, A8). Pro-choice forces, however, went on the offensive by generating a massive political response. Commenting on *Webster,* Nancy Broff, NARAL's legislative and political director, noted, "It finally gave us the smoking gun we needed to mobilize people" (quoted in Kornhauser 1989, 11). Membership and financial support grew rapidly. "In the year after *Webster,* membership in the National Abortion Rights Action League jumped from 150,000 to 400,000; in the National Organization for Women [NOW], from 170,000 to 250,000" (Craig and O'Brien 1993, 296). Furthermore, NARAL "nearly tripled" its income in 1989, and NOW "nearly doubled" its income, as did the Planned Parenthood Federation of America (Shribman 1989, A8). In May 1989 alone, NARAL raised $1 million (Kornhauser 1989).

This newfound energy was turned toward political action. In gubernatorial elections in Virginia and New Jersey in the fall of 1989, pro-choice forces played an important role in electing the pro-choice candidates L. Douglas Wilder and James J. Florio over antiabortion opponents. Antiabortion legislation was defeated in Florida, where Gov. Bob Martinez, an opponent of abortion, called a special session of the legislature to enact it. Congress passed legislation that allowed the District of Columbia to use its own tax revenues to pay for abortions and that essentially repealed the so-called gag rule, but President Bush vetoed both bills, and the House of Representatives failed to override the vetoes. As Paige Cunningham, of the antiabortion group Americans United for Life, put it: "The pro-life movement has been organized and active for twenty years, and some of us are tired. The pro-choice movement is fresh so they're operating with a much greater energy reserve. They've really rallied in light of *Webster*" (quoted in Berke 1989, 1).

This new understanding was also seen in *Casey.* Although pro-choice forces had seen antiabortion restrictions upheld in *Webster* and *Rust,* and the sure antiabortion vote of Justice Clarence Thomas had replaced the pro-choice vote of Justice Thurgood Marshall on the Supreme Court in the interim, pro-choice forces appealed the lower-court decision to the Supreme Court. As the *New York Times* reported, this was "a calculated move to intensify the political debate on abortion before the 1992 election" (Berke 1989, 1). Further increasing the stakes, they asked the Court either to reaffirm women's fundamental right to abortion or to overturn *Roe*. Berke (1991, B8) declared that "[t]he action marked an adjustment in strategy by the abortion rights groups, who seem now to be looking to the Court as a political foil rather than a source of redress."

All this suggests that Thayer may have the stronger case. That is, Court decisions do seem to have a mobilizing potential, but for the losers![18] Both winners and losers appear to assume that Court decisions announcing or upholding constitutional rights will be implemented, but they behave in different ways. Winners celebrate and relax, whereas losers redouble their efforts. Note, too, that in the wake of *Webster,* public opinion moved in a pro-choice direction, counter to the tenor of the opinion. Court decisions do matter, but in complicated ways.

Conclusion

"It does no good to have the [abortion] procedure be legal if women can't get it," stated Gwenyth Mapes, the executive director of the Missoula (Montana) Blue Mountain Clinic destroyed by arson in March 1993 (quoted in Baum 1993, A1).

Courts do not exist in a vacuum. Supreme Court decisions, even those finding constitutional rights, are not implemented automatically or in any straightforward or simple way. They are merely one part of the broader political picture. At best, they can contribute to the process of change. In and of themselves, they accomplish little.

The implementation of the Court's abortion decisions, partial though it has been, owes its success to the fact that the decisions have been made in a time when the role of women in American life is changing dramatically. Out of the social turmoil of the 1960s grew a women's movement that continues to press politically, socially, and culturally for ending restrictions on women's opportunities. Access to safe and legal abortion is part of this movement. In 1973 the Supreme Court lent its support by finding a constitutional right to abortion. And in the years since, it has maintained its support for that core constitutional right. Yet, I have argued that far more important in making safe and legal abortion available are

the beliefs of politicians, relevant professionals, and the public. When these groups are supportive of abortion choice, that choice is available. Where they have opposed abortion, they have fought against the Court's decisions, successfully minimizing access to abortion. Lack of support from hospital administrators and some politicians and intense opposition from a small group of politicians and activists have limited the availability of abortion services. On the whole, in states that were supportive of abortion choice before Court action, access remains good. In the states that had the most restrictive abortion laws before *Roe,* abortion services are available but remain difficult to obtain. As Gwenyth Mapes put it, "It does no good to have the [abortion] procedure be legal if women can't get it."

This analysis suggests that in general, constitutional rights have a greater likelihood of being implemented when they reflect the preexisting beliefs of politicians, relevant professionals, and the public. When at least some of these groups are opposed, locally or nationally, implementation is less likely. The assumption that the implementation of Court decisions and constitutional rights is unproblematic both reifies and removes courts from the political, social, cultural, and economic systems in which they operate. Courts are political institutions, and their role must be understood accordingly. Examining their decisions without making the political world central to that examination may make for fine reading in constitutional-law textbooks, but it tells the reader very little about the lives people lead.

Notes

1. Alaska, Hawaii, New York, and Washington had previously liberalized their laws. The constitutional requirements set forth in *Roe* and *Doe* were basically, although not completely, met by these state laws.
2. For a fuller examination, see Rosenberg 1991.
3. In 1971, before *Roe* and *Doe*, the Court heard an abortion case (*United States v. Vuitch*) from Washington, D.C. The decision, however, did not settle the constitutional issues involved in the abortion controversy.

4. Estimates of the number of legal abortions performed each year prior to *Roe* vary enormously, ranging from 50,000 to nearly 2 million. See Rosenberg 1991, 353–355.

5. The following discussion, except where noted, is based on Lader 1973.

6. After the 1973 decisions, NARAL kept its acronym but changed its name to the National Abortion Rights Action League.

7. Nixon's "own personal views" were that "unrestricted abortion policies, or abortion on demand" could not be squared with his "personal belief in the sanctity of human life" (quoted in Lader 1973, 176–177).

8. Franklin and Kosaki (1989, 762) argue that in the wake of *Roe* opinions hardened. That is, those who were pro-choice before the decision became even more so after; the same held true for those opposed to abortion. Court action did not change opinions; abortion opponents did not become abortion supporters (and vice versa). See Epstein and Kobylka 1992, 203.

9. Ford did veto the 1977 appropriations bill containing the Hyde Amendment. He stated that he did so for budgetary reasons (the bill was $4 billion over his budget request) and reasserted his support for "restrictions on the use of federal funds for abortion" (quoted in Craig and O'Brien 1993, 161).

10. The Congressional Research Service reports that Congress enacted thirty restrictive abortion statutes during 1973–1982 (Davidson 1983).

11. The growth in violent attacks on abortion clinics, and illegal, harassing demonstrations in front of them, may demonstrate a growing awareness of this point by the foes of abortion.

12. Treshman is not the only antiabortion activist to express such views. Goodstein (1994, A1) writes that "there is a sizable faction among the antiabortion movement's activists ... who have applauded Hill [the convicted killer of Dr. Britton and Mr. Barrett] as a righteous defender of babies."

13. The East South Central states are Kentucky, Tennessee, Alabama, and Mississippi. The West South Central states are Arkansas, Louisiana, Oklahoma, and Texas. Together, these eight states contained 16 percent of the U.S. population in 1973.

14. It is possible, of course, that some women had personal reasons for not obtaining an abortion in their home town. Still, that seems an unlikely explanation as to why 100,000 women each year would leave their home states to obtain abortions.

15. *Akron v. Akron Center for Reproductive Health* (1983); *Planned Parenthood v. Ashcroft* (1983). The vast majority of abortions in the United States are performed in the first trimester. As early as 1976, the figure was 90 percent. See Forrest et al. 1979, 32.

16. The percentage for clinics is not artificially high because there were only a small number of clinic abortions in the years preceding Court action. In 1973, clinics performed more than 330,000 abortions, or about 45 percent of all abortions (see Alan Guttmacher Institute 1976, 27).

17. Others in agreement with this analysis include Tatalovich and Daynes (1981, 101, 164), participants in a symposium at the Brookings Institution (in Steiner 1983), and Jackson and Vinovskis (1983, 73), who found that after the decisions "state-level pro-choice grounds disbanded, victory seemingly achieved."

18. This also appears to have been the case in 1954 with the Court's school desegregation decision, *Brown v. Board of Education*. After that decision, the Ku Klux Klan was reinvigorated and the White Citizen's Councils were formed, with the aim of preserving racial segregation through violence and intimidation.

REFERENCES

"Abortions Legal for Year, Performed for Thousands." 1973. *New York Times,* December 31, Sec. A.

Alan Guttmacher Institute. 1976. *Abortion 1974–1975: Need and Services in the United States, Each State and Metropolitan Area.* New York: Planned Parenthood Federation of America.

Anderson, Jack, and Michael Binstein. 1993. "Violent Shift in Abortion Battle." *Washington Post,* March 18, Sec. C.

Barringer, Felicity. 1993. "Abortion Clinics Said to Be in Peril." *New York Times,* March 6, Sec. A.

Baum, Dan. 1993. "Violence Is Driving Away Rural Abortion Clinics." *Chicago Tribune,* August 21, Sec. A.

Berke, Richard L. 1989. "The Abortion Rights Movement Has Its Day." *New York Times,* October 15, Sec. 4.

_____.1991. "Groups Backing Abortion Rights Ask Court to Act." *New York Times,* November 8, Sec. A.

Blake, Judith. 1971. "Abortion and Public Opinion: The 1960–1970 Decade." *Science,* February 12.

_____.1977a. "The Abortion Decisions: Judicial Review and Public Opinion." In *Abortion: New Directions for Policy Studies,* edited by Edward Manier, William Liu, and David Solomon. Notre Dame, Ind.: University of Notre Dame Press.

_____.1977b. "The Supreme Court's Abortion Decisions and Public Opinion in the United States." *Population and Development Review* 3:45–62.

Brody, Jane E. 1973. "States and Doctors Wary on Eased Abortion Ruling." *New York Times,* February 16, Sec. A.

Brozan, Nadine. 1983. "Abortion Ruling: 10 Years of Bitter Conflict." *New York Times,* January 15, Sec. A.

Cooper, Helene. 1993. "Medical Schools, Students Shun Abortion Study." *Wall Street Journal,* Midwest edition, March 12, Sec. B.

Craig, Barbara Hinkson, and David M. O'Brien. 1993. *Abortion and American Politics.* Chatham, N.J.: Chatham House.

Currivan, Gene. 1970. "Poll Finds Shift to Left among College Freshmen." *New York Times,* December 20, Sec. 1.

Daley, Daniel, and Rachel Benson Gold. 1994. "Public Funding for Contraceptive, Sterilization, and Abortion Services, Fiscal Year 1992." *Family Planning Perspectives* 25:244–251.

Darney, Philip D., Uta Landy, Sara MacPherson, and Richard L. Sweet. 1987. "Abortion Training in U.S. Obstetrics and Gynecology Residency Programs." *Family Planning Perspectives* 19:158–162.

Davidson, Roger H. 1983. "Procedures and Politics in Congress." In *The Abortion Dispute and the American System,* edited by Gilbert Y. Steiner. Washington, D.C.: Brookings Institution.

Ebaugh, Helen Rose Fuchs, and C. Allen Haney. 1980. "Shifts in Abortion Attitudes: 1972–1978." *Journal of Marriage and the Family* 42:491–499.

Epstein, Lee, and Joseph F. Kobylka. 1992. *The Supreme Court and Legal Change.* Chapel Hill: University of North Carolina Press.

Fiske, Edward B. 1967. "Clergymen Offer Abortion Advice." *New York Times,* May 22, Sec. A.

Forrest, Jacqueline Darroch, and Stanley K. Henshaw. 1987. "The Harassment of U.S. Abortion Providers." *Family Planning Perspectives* 19:9–13.

Forrest, Jacqueline Darroch, Ellen Sullivan, and Christopher Tietze. 1978. "Abortion in the United States, 1976–1977." *Family Planning Perspectives* 10:271–279.

_____. 1979. *Abortion 1976–1977: Need and Services in the United States, Each State and Metropolitan Area.* New York: Alan Guttmacher Institute.

Franklin, Charles H., and Liane C. Kosaki. 1989. "Republican Schoolmaster: The U.S. Supreme Court, Public Opinion, and Abortion." *American Political Science Review* 83:751–771.

Goodman, Janice, Rhonda Copelon Schoenbrod, and Nancy Stearns. 1973. "Doe and Roe." *Women's Rights Law Reporter* 1:20–38.

Goodstein, Laurie. 1994. "Life and Death Choices: Antiabortion Faction Tries to Justify Homicide." *Washington Post,* August 13, Sec. A.

Henshaw, Stanley K. 1986. "Induced Abortion: A Worldwide Perspective." *Family Planning Perspectives* 18:250–254.

_____. 1991. "The Accessibility of Abortion Services in the United States." *Family Planning Perspectives* 23:246–252, 263.

Henshaw, Stanley K., and Kevin O'Reilly. 1983. "Characteristics of Abortion Patients in the United States, 1979 and 1980." *Family Planning Perspectives* 15:5.

Henshaw, Stanley K., and Jennifer Van Vort. 1990. "Abortion Services in the United States, 1987 and 1988." *Family Planning Perspectives* 22:102–108, 142.

_____. 1994. "Abortion Services in the United States, 1991 and 1992." *Family Planning Perspectives* 26:100–106, 122.

Henshaw, Stanley K., Jacqueline Darroch Forrest, and Ellen Blaine. 1984. "Abortion Services in the United States, 1981 and 1982." *Family Planning Perspectives* 16:119–127.

Henshaw, Stanley K., Jacqueline Darroch Forrest, and Jennifer Van Vort. 1987. "Abortion Services in the United States, 1984 and 1985." *Family Planning Perspectives* 19:63–70.

Henshaw, Stanley K., Jacqueline Darroch Forrest, Ellen Sullivan, and Christopher Tietze. 1982. "Abortion Services in the United States, 1979 and 1980." *Family Planning Perspectives* 14:5–15.

Henshaw, Stanley K., Lisa M. Koonin, and Jack C. Smith. 1991. "Characteristics of U.S. Women Having Abortions, 1987." *Family Planning Perspectives* 23:75–81.

Hole, Judith, and Ellen Levine. 1971. *Rebirth of Feminism.* New York: Quadrangle.

Jackson, John E., and Maris A. Vinovskis. 1983. "Public Opinion, Elections, and the 'Single-Issue' Issue." In *The Abortion Dispute and the American System,* edited by Gilbert Y. Steiner. Washington, D.C.: Brookings Institution.

Jaffe, Frederick S., Barbara L. Lindheim, and Phillip R. Lee. 1981. *Abortion Politics.* New York: McGraw-Hill.

Johnston, Laurie. 1977. "Abortion Foes Gain Support as They Intensify Campaign." *New York Times,* October 23, Sec. 1.

Kemp, Kathleen A., Robert A. Carp, and David W. Brady. 1978. "The Supreme Court and Social Change: The Case of Abortion." *Western Political Quarterly* 31:19–31.

King, Wayne. 1973. "Despite Court Ruling, Problems Persist in Gaining Abortions." *New York Times,* May 20, Sec. 1.

Kornhauser, Anne. 1989. "Abortion Case Has Been Boon to Both Sides." *Legal Times,* July 3.

Lader, Lawrence. 1973. *Abortion II: Making the Revolution.* Boston: Beacon Press.

Lewin, Tamar. 1994. "A Cause Worth Killing For? Debate Splits Abortion Foes." *New York Times,* July 30, Sec. A.

Newport, Frank, and Leslie McAneny. 1992. "Whose Court Is It Anyhow? O'Connor, Kennedy, Souter Position Reflects Abortion Views of Most Americans." *Gallup Poll Monthly* 322 (July): 51–53.

Noonan, John T., Jr. 1973. "Raw Judicial Power." *National Review,* March 2.

Phillips, Richard. 1980. "The Shooting War over 'Choice' or 'Life' Is Beginning Again." *Chicago Tribune,* April 20, Sec. 12.

"Rhode Island Abortion Law Is Declared Unconstitutional." 1973. *New York Times,* May 17, Sec. A.

Rosen, R. A. Hudson, H.W. Werley Jr., J. W. Ager, and F.P. Shea. 1974. "Health Professionals' Attitudes toward Abortion." *Public Opinion Quarterly* 38:159–173.

Rosenberg, Gerald N. 1991. *The Hollow Hope: Can Courts Bring About Social Change?* Chicago: University of Chicago Press.

Rosenthal, Jack. 1971. "Survey Finds 50% Back Liberalization of Abortion Policy." *New York Times,* October 28, Sec. A.

Rosoff, Jeannie I. 1975. "Is Support for Abortion Political Suicide?" *Family Planning Perspectives* 7:13–22.

Rubin, Eva R. 1982. *Abortion, Politics, and the Courts.* Westport, Conn.: Greenwood Press.

Russell, Mary. 1977. "House Bars Use of U.S. Funds in Abortion Cases." *Washington Post,* June 18, Sec. A.

Shribman, David. 1989. "Abortion-Issue Foes, Preaching to the Converted in No Uncertain Terms, Step Up Funding Pleas." *Wall Street Journal,* December 26, Sec. A.

Steiner, Gilbert Y., ed. 1983. *The Abortion Dispute and the American System.* Washington, D.C.: Brookings Institution.

Sullivan, Ellen, Christopher Tietze, and Joy G. Dryfoos. 1977. "Legal Abortion in the United States, 1975–1976." *Family Planning Perspectives* 9:116.

Tatalovich, Raymond, and Byron W. Daynes. 1981. *The Politics of Abortion.* New York: Praeger.

Thayer, James Bradley. 1901. *John Marshall.* Boston: Houghton, Mifflin.

Thomas, Pierre. 1994. "U.S. Marshals Dispatched to Guard Abortion Clinics." *Washington Post,* August 2, Sec. A.

Tolchin, Martin. 1977. "House Bars Medicaid Abortions and Funds for Enforcing Quotas." *New York Times,* June 18, Sec. A.

Toner, Robin. 1993. "Clinton Orders Reversal of Abortion Restrictions Left by Reagan and Bush." *New York Times,* January 23, Sec. A.

United States. Congress. Senate. 1970a. *Congressional Record.* Daily ed. 91st Cong., 2d sess. April 23, S3746.

_____. 1970b. *Congressional Record.* Daily ed. 91st Cong., 2d sess. February 24, S3501.

_____. 1974. Committee on the Judiciary. *Hearings before the Subcommittee on Constitutional Amendments.* Vol. 2. 93d Cong., 2d sess.

_____. 1976. Committee on the Judiciary. *Hearings before the Subcommittee on Constitutional Amendments.* Vol. 4. 94d Cong., 1st sess.

Weinstock, Edward, Christopher Tietze, Frederick S. Jaffe, and Joy G. Dryfoos. 1975. "Legal Abortions in the United States since the 1973 Supreme Court Decisions." *Family Planning Perspectives* 7:23–31.

Williams, Roger M. 1979. "The Power of Fetal Politics." *Saturday Review,* June 9.

"A Woman's Right." 1973. *Evening Star* (Washington, D.C.), January 27, Sec. A

Chapter 6

Congress

6-1 Congress, the Troubled Institution

Steven S. Smith

Political scientist Steven S. Smith outlines major trends in congressional politics—the polarization of Congress, the abuse of congressional procedures by the parties, the flow of power from Congress to the president, and the low public esteem of Congress. He shows how these developments are related to one another and concludes that while some reforms would improve Congress, the underlying polarization will require a more basic change in American politics.

CONGRESS IS A troubled institution. It usually is. At the moment, Congress appears handcuffed by deep partisan polarization, seems to thwart the will of the people in failing to act on important problems, looks weak in comparison with the president and other executive officials, and is held in low esteem by most Americans. Presidents of both parties complain about its slowness; the media highlights "earmarks," "pork," and other characterizations of what some consider wasteful spending; and scandals involving members of Congress surface on a seemingly regular basis. Even legislators who retire from Congress carp about the institution to which they so frequently sought reelection.

It also is true that Congress is the most powerful national legislature in the world. It is formally independent of the chief executive, its jurisdiction is very broad and sets its own agenda, and its members are elected independently of the executive. The executive and judicial branches cannot spend money without its approval, the president needs the approval of the Senate to appoint senior executive officials and

judges and to implement treaties, and Congress has wide-ranging powers to investigate the executive branch.

Nevertheless, in everyday politics Congress is at a severe disadvantage in its relationship with the president and the courts. Congress does not speak with one voice, cannot move quickly most of the time, and is quite permeable to outside influence. Unlike the executive branch, Congress is not led by a single leader who can deliberate in private and articulate a single policy for the institution. Instead, it has two houses (each of which assigns an equal vote to every member) that must negotiate their differences on legislation. Unlike any federal court, Congress is large and unwieldy, it is bicameral, its deliberations are quite visible, and its floor proceedings are televised. Citizens, including lobbyists, are free to roam the halls of Congress's office buildings and visit the offices of members. Outside groups are instrumental to legislators' seeking funding for the campaigns they must mount to retain their jobs.

Source: This piece is an original essay commissioned for this volume.

Congress's political weaknesses have been exposed in recent years. Partisanship, deadlock on key issues, readiness to defer to the president in a crisis, and public despair with its performance have plagued Congress. This essay outlines and evaluates those weaknesses.

A Polarized Congress

The partisan tone of legislators may be the most conspicuous feature of congressional politics over the past quarter century. There is more to it than the derisive nature of the legislators' rhetoric. Deep and wide differences exist between the parties, and it is obvious in legislators' floor voting behavior. In Figure 1, I show the distribution of members of the House and Senate on a liberal–conservative scale. The scale is based on a statistical analysis of all roll-call votes. Here, I show the distribution for two Congresses: the 92nd (1971–1972) and the 112th (2011–2012).

In the early 1970s, Democrats were far more liberal than Republicans on average but there were both conservative Democrats and liberal Republicans. In the House, nearly half the membership fell between the most liberal Republican and most conservative Democrat. In the Senate, more than a third of the membership occupied the overlapping region. These large blocs of legislators in the middle of the policy spectrum dictated outcomes on most important issues.

The pattern has been different since the late 1980s. The middle has been vacated, with the

Figure 1   Liberal–Conservative Scores in Selected Congresses

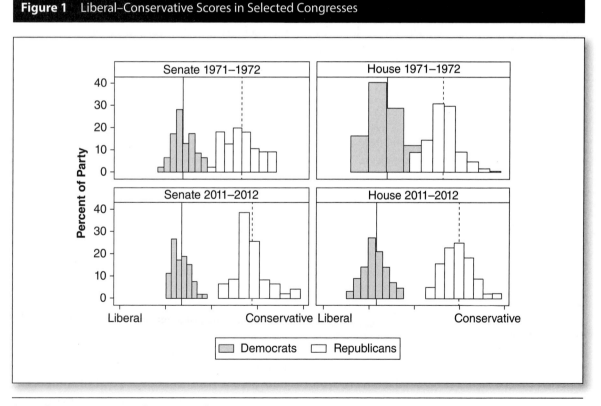

Source: Common space scores (voteview.com).

Republicans moving more to the right than Democrats moved to the left. No longer is there a sizable group of moderate legislators to whom party and committee leaders must appeal to build a majority coalition on most important measures. By behavior, not just rhetoric, the parties are sharply polarized.

The polarization of congressional parties was the product of multiple forces in American politics. The 1960s and early 1970s was a period of social upheaval. The civil rights movement, the women's movement, the Vietnam War, the youth culture, and other developments generated a reaction that attracted the support of conservatives of both parties, particularly in rural America and the South. *Roe v. Wade,* the 1973 Supreme Court decision on abortion, seemed to catalyze Christian conservatives (formerly a dormant group in American politics), who mobilized within the Republican Party in most parts of the country. Republican candidates and strategists recognized an opportunity to join economic and social conservatives in a larger coalition that could upset the long-standing Democratic majorities, comprising northern liberals and southern conservatives.

The realignment of political values and party preferences that started in the late 1960s began to alter the composition of Congress in the 1970s. In the South, many conservative Democrats were replaced by Republicans, making the congressional Democrats more uniformly liberal and reinforcing the conservative forces among congressional Republicans. In the Northeast, Midwest, and West Coast, Republicans (many of whom occupied the moderate region of the policy spectrum) lost to Democrats (most of whom were liberal), which reinforced the liberal trend among congressional Democrats and the conservative trend among Republicans. In the 1980s, the Republicans began to elect conservative leaders from the South, and the Democrats lost the mix of southern leaders who were important to the party in the mid-20th century.

As the composition of the party elites changed, the electorate began to sort itself so that political attitudes on economic and social issues were more strongly aligned with party preferences. In nearly every part of the country, the electorate supporting Democrats became more liberal and the electorate supporting Republicans became more conservative. The result was that political pressures from home became more uniform among the legislators of each party. It became more difficult for moderates to win primary elections, particularly on the Republican side, and make it to the general election ballot.

The successive elections of the 1970s, 1980s, and 1990s brought in legislators more polarized by party. This polarization was enhanced by the strategies of party leaders, first among Republicans and then among Democrats. Republicans in the House, led by Georgia's Newt Gingrich, sought disciplined voting within the party to force Democratic leaders to draw support from conservative Democrats to win floor votes. Conservative Democrats, in turn, would have more difficulty gaining reelection in their conservative districts and states.

These developments were mutually reinforcing. As each party became more cohesive, its leadership could become more assertive and more pressure could be put on misfits within the party. As national party leaders, local party activists, and the electorate sorted themselves, primary election winners became more polarized and the electorate was more frequently given a choice between quite liberal Democrats and quite conservative Republicans. Only liberal legislators had a chance to be elected as a leader among congressional Democrats; only conservative legislators had a chance to be elected as a leader among congressional Republicans. The congressional parties became more polarized, and their leaders were pressured to pursue more aggressive partisan strategies.

It bears noting that drawing district lines to stack House districts with the partisans of one party does not explain the polarization we have witnessed. The Senate, for which state lines are never changed, suffers from the same party polarization as the House. Instead, a sorting of the electorate and legislators into parties with distinctive political attitudes is what has accounted for the durable pattern of the past two decades.

Legislative Pathologies in Congress

The consequences of partisan polarization in Congress are quite different in the two houses. Polarization in the House has yielded a streamlined, centralized process that can speed legislation to passage, but this is a process that often excludes the minority party in ways that intensify minority frustration and partisan passions. In contrast, polarized parties and supermajority rule in the Senate is a recipe for delay and inaction, an outcome that encourages both parties to engage in a blame game that frustrates everyone. Because both houses must approve legislation, Senate obstructionism is enough to kill many bills.

Let's begin with the House. The House majority party is able to control the floor agenda and pass legislation as long as it is reasonably cohesive. This is the product of several features of the modern House:

- The Speaker, as leader of the majority party, serves as the presiding officer and can freely recognize members to make motions on the floor, such as calling up bills for consideration.
- The Committee on Rules, which has been under the control of the Speaker since the early 1970s, can report resolutions that, if adopted by a House majority, can bring bills and conference reports to the floor and limit debate and amendments. A cohesive majority party can get these resolutions, called *special rules*, adopted.
- The Speaker appoints conference committees and can structure their membership to suit his party's needs.

Polarized parties mean that a majority party, which is cohesive when the parties are polarized, can readily gain House approval of special rules, limit minority opportunities to offer proposals, pass legislation, and control conference committee negotiations with the Senate. These features of a polarized House speed legislative action.

Unfortunately for the House minority party, partisan polarization also tends to produce a process so dominated by majority party members that minority party members get excluded from meaningful participation. Both Democratic and Republican majority parties have moved decisions on the most important policies from standing committees (where the minority is represented proportionately in most cases) to the leadership and informal work groups of the majority party (where the minority is not represented at all). Both Democratic and Republican majority parties have so restricted floor amendments on major bills that the minority party often does not have a meaningful opportunity to propose alternatives and attract some support for them among majority party members.

In contrast, the Senate has the following features:

- The majority party's leader does not preside and instead attempts to move the Senate by making motions from the floor.
- Most motions can be filibustered—that is, subjected to unending debate—and so the minority can attempt to obstruct action on bills it dislikes.
- To overcome a filibuster or threatened filibuster of most bills, a three-fifths majority of all elected senators (60 when 99 or 100 seats are filled) is required to invoke cloture (close debate) and get a vote to pass a bill.
- The ability of the minority to filibuster proposals to change the rules means that the majority party cannot put in place rules similar to those that so advantage a House majority party. A two-thirds majority of senator voting (67 when 100 senators are voting) is required to invoke cloture on legislation that changes the rules.

Polarized parties mean that a sizable minority party—one that has 41 or more members—can block majority party legislation on the floor. This feature of a polarized Senate can delay or even kill legislation.

For the Senate, public expectations that the majority party can pass its legislation often fail to reflect the fact that the minority party possesses the parliamentary tools to prevent that from happening. And the minority party has been exploiting those parliamentary tools with greater frequency. Figure 2

Figure 2   Number of Measures and Nominations Subject to Cloture Motions, 1961–2014

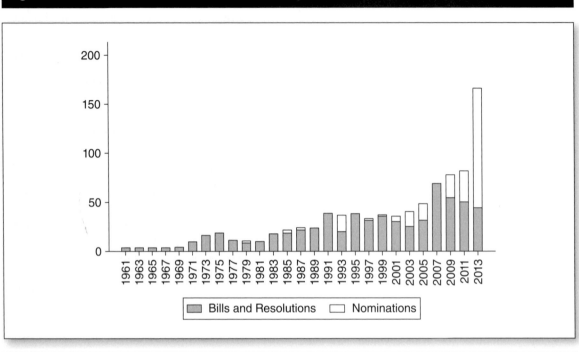

Source: www.senate.gov.

Note: Figures for the 113th Congress are through August 31, 2014.

shows the number of cloture petitions filed to end or prevent filibusters in Congresses since the mid-20th century. Plainly, the record of filibustering since the late 1980s is very different from previous decades. Minority obstructionism has become the norm on important measures and has extended from a wide variety of presidential nominations to executive and judicial positions.

Partisan polarization contributes to filibustering in powerful ways. A minority party leader finds it much easier to employ obstructionist tactics when no one from his or her party objects. Moreover, the obstructionism is more likely to succeed in blocking majority party legislation—forcing compromise or killing legislation—when the minority party is united and can prevent cloture. In response, the majority party leader attempts cloture more frequently, often

several times on the same bill. The majority party members complain about minority obstructionism, and minority party members complain that the majority is too quick to attempt to shut off debate and minority amendments.

Do filibusters matter? They do. In the polarized Congress of the past two decades, filibusters have made the Senate the primary burial ground of legislation. Political scientist Barbara Sinclair has demonstrated that in Congresses since the early 1990s, 33 of 80 major bills that died at some stage had passed the House but died in the Senate; only 3 died in the House after passing the Senate (others passed neither house or were vetoed). In contrast, in the 1970s and 1980s, only 12 of 42 major bills that died at some stage had passed the House but died in the Senate; 8 died in the House after passing the Senate.

The problems associated with the filibuster continue to intensify. In March 2009, Senate Republicans—all 41 of them—signed a letter to President Barack Obama to encourage him to renominate President George W. Bush's nominees for the federal courts. They warned, "Regretfully, if we are not consulted on, and approve of, a nominee from our states, the Republican Conference will be unable to support moving forward on that nominee. And we will act to preserve this principle and the rights of our colleagues if it is not." That is, before President Obama nominated a single person to the federal courts, the Republican minority demanded that the president defer to them under threat of blocking his nominees by filibuster. In his 2012 State of the Union Address before a joint session of Congress, President Obama complained of minority party obstruction on his executive and judicial branch nominations.

Figure 2 shows that the minority obstruction expanded from legislative measures (bills and resolutions) to nominations. In 1993, Democratic President Bill Clinton's first year in office, Republicans began to obstruct action on nominations with some frequency. Democrats followed suit in the middle years of the Republican Bush administration (2001–2008), but Republicans have made obstruction of presidential nominations a regular practice under Democratic President Obama since 2009. In response, the Democratic Senate majority in the fall of 2013 forced a rules change on nominations to require only a simple majority for cloture on all nominations except those for the Supreme Court. The huge number of cloture motions on nominations shown in Figure 2 reflects the Republican response, which was to force Democrats to go through the cloture process on even more nominations. The number of legislative measures subject to cloture slipped a little as Democrats simply gave up trying to push some measures.

In the polarized Congress, conference committees have fallen into disuse. Because conference committees approve compromise legislation with the majority support of conferees from each house, the like-minded majority party conferees do not need the support of minority party members and can largely ignore them. As a result, majority party members consult with one another without any minority legislators or staff present and appear to announce outcomes. In recent Congresses, this went so far as to circumvent conference committees altogether by having majority party and committee leaders of the two houses negotiate compromises without appointing conference committees and then having the agreements incorporated as amendments between the houses. Even the formality of minority party participation is avoided.

These patterns have intensified and even personalized partisan conflict. Legislators who value a meaningful voice in policymaking are either frustrated for being excluded (the House minority party) or for having a majority but not the supermajority required to pass legislation (the Senate majority party). Tolerance of the other party has become very thin. Distrust of the other side is so widespread that opportunities for real cross-party deliberation are ignored.

Largely because of the Senate (and often with the contribution of divided party control of the House, Senate, and presidency), polarized parties create a strong bias against passing legislation. In fact, more major legislation has been killed since the parties became so polarized in the late 1980s than in the previous two decades. A polarized Senate gets hung up on filibusters, while a House, Senate, and presidency controlled by different and polarized parties cannot agree on legislation.

Aggressive Presidents and a Weakened Congress

Over the past decade, the power of Congress has been challenged on several fronts. A series of crises—terrorism, the war in Iraq, and the economic crisis—led the president to seek and receive broad powers with little detailed direction in the legislation from Congress. The president also has asserted broad powers without any participation by Congress and has acted through executive orders or other means. And President George W. Bush and his top advisers claimed a general theory of presidential power, now called *the theory of the unitary executive*, which posits that the president can control the actions of all executive branch agencies, even when the law gives authority directly to department and agency officials.

This is a large and complex subject; so I can only introduce the major ways Congress has yielded power to the president in recent years. Congress, under the basic constitutional framework, must delegate some power to the executive branch to implement policies it deems desirable. Unless the president has constitutional power of his own, Congress can detail how the delegated power is to be used. Failure to provide the detail, or at least to limit the delegation to a short period or carefully control spending for the purpose, grants the president power that Congress could reserve for itself.

Emergencies and National Security

Incentives to delegate broad power to the president are greatest in emergencies. A president argues that the national interest requires that he quickly be given authority to act with the flexibility required to meet unknown contingencies. Legislators can hope that their institution's control over spending and oversight activities will keep the executive in check, but, in practice, the president's advantage in public relations, control over information, and partisan considerations may limit Congress's ability to check the use of power once it is delegated to the president. In a Congress highly polarized by party, the tendency to grant unfettered power to the executive is exceptionally great when the same party controls the houses of Congress and the White House.

During 2001 to 2006, the 6 years of Republican majorities in Congress and a Republican president, the fight against terrorism and the wars in Iraq and Afghanistan led Congress to grant sweeping powers to President Bush. By historical standards, Congress held very few hearings on the broad sweep of issues during the period—prewar intelligence, the conduct of the war in Iraq, the National Security Agency's

surveillance program, the treatment of detainees, and reform of the intelligence apparatus. The use of federal dollars and constitutionality of executive actions were frequently questioned by legislators and the media but seldom in congressional hearings or investigations. Once the Department of Homeland Security was created in 2003 from 22 agencies, Congress did not seriously scrutinize the functioning of the new department until one of its units, the Federal Emergency Management Agency, mismanaged the response to Hurricane Katrina. In the intensely partisan atmosphere of Washington, serious oversight of a Republican administration by a Republican Congress could only give the opposition opportunities to score points. Partisan convenience, rather than a commitment to check the use of power, seemed to drive the congressional oversight agenda.

In the meantime, President Bush took existing trends in presidential assertions of unilateral power to a much greater extreme. The administration broadened its interpretation of executive privilege to deny information to Congress. President Bush used executive orders more broadly to direct executive agencies, sometimes in contravention of statute. He used signing statements liberally when signing legislation into law to assert that he would not implement features of the law that he considered unconstitutional infringements on his power.

President Obama promised to end wars and give greater consideration to civil liberties in his administration, but Congress found itself responding ineffectually to initiatives taken by the executive branch. Disclosures about the extent to which the National Security Agency gathered data on Americans' electronic communications made clear that members of Congress, even members of the intelligence committees, were unaware of the reach of the agency. The president's decision to use military force against the Islamic State forces in Iraq and Syria was met with no immediate congressional action to endorse or object to his actions. At this writing (November 2014), it is uncertain whether Congress will bother to consider a "use of force" resolution. The president argues that he does not need one, and the top leaders of both parties have said nothing to the contrary.

The Bush Theory of a Unitary Executive

President Bush and key figures in his administration subscribed to the theory of a unitary executive. The theory holds that the president has direct authority over all parts of the executive branch. Bush administration officials used the logic of the argument to justify presidential signing statements and other intrusions into statutory governance of executive agencies. To be sure, there is a compelling argument that the commander-in-chief role assigned to the president by the Constitution gives the president strong authority over the use of the armed forces. But it is reasonable to argue and seems historically accurate to say that Congress is free to direct or constrain other executive agencies by law, which the president is obligated to observe.

Democrats, once again in the majority after the 2006 elections, objected to Bush's view of his powers but were able to do little about it before the end of Bush's second term. They did step up oversight activities, forced dozens of administration officials to testify, and attempted to impose a timetable for withdrawal from Iraq, but the president proved to have a strategic advantage in most of these confrontations with Congress. Once his policy was in place, he could rely on Senate Republicans to obstruct votes on unfriendly legislation and, if need be, veto legislation to block it. And he could delay or assert executive privilege when unfriendly congressional committees attempted to investigate executive actions—and the approaching end of his second term meant that he did not have to delay for long. President Obama, of course dealing with a friendly Congress, ordered executive agencies to ignore President Bush's signing statements unless they first consult the Department of Justice.

Obama did not endorse the unitary executive perspective but, like all modern presidents, interpreted his inherent or implicit powers under the Constitution very broadly. With a Democrat in the White House, it became congressional Republicans' turn to criticize presidential overreach in the treatment of illegal immigrants, targeting of U.S. citizens abroad who are engaged in terrorist activities, implementation of health care reform, and even raising of the minimum wage for federal contractors. After they regained a House majority in the 2010 elections, Republicans occasionally sought to check the use of presidential power, but the Democratic Senate stood in the way.

Emergencies and the Economy

Emergencies can motivate even an opposition Congress to grant sweeping authority to a president, as the Democrats did in 2008 in response to the economic crisis. As Wall Street investment banks were about to collapse in late 2008, the Bush administration asked for and received a $700 billion authorization for the Troubled Asset Relief Program (TARP) to "restore liquidity and stability to the financial system," primarily by purchasing soured assets (mainly mortgage-backed securities) and stabilizing the banking system. The fear, widely shared by economists and administration officials, was that the economy would suffer badly if major financial institutions failed. While some Republicans opposed the bill, most Republicans and nearly all Democrats supported the legislation. To the surprise of many members of Congress, the administration used most of the first half of the TARP funds to buy ownership stakes in banks and insurance companies to shore up their balance sheets.

Congress appeared nervous about a broad delegation of power to the Treasury and so imposed multiple mechanisms overlapping oversight and reporting responsibilities. A Congressional Oversight Panel, soon chaired by a Harvard professor, was created to review the work of the Treasury and report to Congress every 30 days. The comptroller general of the General Accountability Office, an arm of Congress, was required to monitor the program and report every 60 days. The Treasury office itself was required to file reports with Congress, a special inspector general was created, and a board comprising executive officials was established to oversee implementation of the bill and report to Congress quarterly.

The oversight was likely to be taken seriously, but the delegation of power nevertheless represented one of the vaguest delegations of power for an authorization of such a large sum of money. Moreover, the administration moved so quickly in dedicating the funds that congressional oversight would long postdate irreversible executive branch action. Later reports indicated that the executive branch had a difficult time accounting for the way the banks used federal funds.

The Continuing Battle Over Appointments

The tension between Congress and the president persists, and Congress often suffers when the president can act unilaterally on a matter on which the public appears to side with him. During his first term, President Obama was regularly frustrated by Senate Republicans who refused to allow the Senate to vote on his nominees to executive and judicial positions. The president normally has the opportunity to make appointments on his own when Congress is in recess, appointments that last for the remainder of the next session of Congress. To block President Obama from making recess appointments, the Republican-controlled House refused to allow the Senate to recess. The House was able to do this by exploiting the constitutional provisions that "neither house . . . shall, without the consent of the other, adjourn for more than three days" (Article I, Section 5). Lacking authority to adjourn, the Senate agreed with the House to hold a pro forma legislative session every 3 days, which, in a long-accepted interpretation, meant that the Senate was not in recess and the president was not authorized to make recess appointments.

In early 2012, President Obama decided to proceed with recess appointments while the Senate was holding pro forma sessions once every 3 days. In the most noteworthy case, the confirmation of a director for the Consumer Financial Protection Bureau had been held up in the Senate since July 2011. Republicans in Congress complained bitterly about the president's move, but the new director took

office. Backed by an opinion from his Justice Department, President Obama argued that the periodic pro forma sessions at which no legislative business was conducted were not sufficient to deny the president his constitutional power to make recess appointments. The dispute was settled in court in mid-2014—and the president lost. It did not matter much for Obama, at least not at first. By then the Senate had adopted the practice of closing debate on nominations by a simple majority, which meant that Republicans could no longer block Senate action on Obama's nominees. When Obama or another president faces an opposing majority in the Senate, however, the court ruling will deeply limit the president's options in dealing with an unfriendly Senate.

The Unpopular Congress

The popularity of Congress ebbs and flows with the public's confidence in government. When the president's ratings and trust in government improved after the tragic events of September 11, 2001, Congress's approval ratings improved, too (Figure 3). Nevertheless, Congress's performance ratings are almost always below those of the president and the Supreme Court. When President George W. Bush earned approval ratings in the 20s, Congress managed to fall into the teens. And in the past few years, when President Obama's approval rating sometimes dipped to the low 40s, Congress dropped to all-time lows—reaching 9, 10, and 11 percent at times in 2011 to 2013—and managed to reach 20 percent only a couple of times since early 2011.

The legislative process is easy to dislike—it often generates political posturing and grandstanding, it necessarily involves bargaining, and it often leaves broken promises in its trail. Members of Congress often appear self-serving as they pursue their political careers and represent interests and reflect values that are controversial. And the intense partisanship that Congress has exhibited in the past two decades is quite distasteful to many Americans. The public relations efforts of the congressional parties probably make matters worse by emphasizing such partisan

Figure 3 Public Job Approval for Congress, 1974–2014

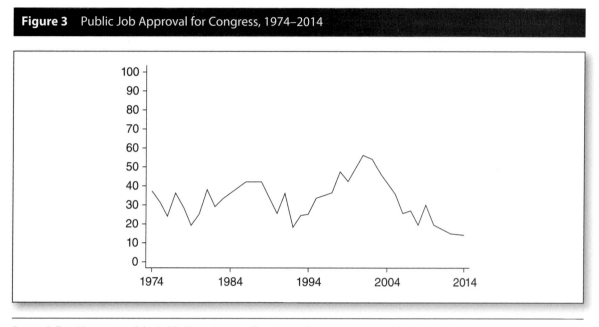

Source: Gallup, "Congress and the Public," http://www.gallup.com/poll/1600/congress-public.aspx.

and derisive messages. In contrast, the Supreme Court is cloaked in ritual and is seldom seen or heard by the general public. The president is represented by a single, large, professional public relations machine.

A few scandals surely contribute to Congress's low standing. In fact, Congress seems to be a never-ending source of comic relief, like the joke about the legislator who kept referring to the presiding officer as "Your Honor." There is no doubt that a large majority of today's members behave ethically. In fact, the ethical standards applied by the public, the media, and Congress itself are likely higher today than at any other time. Yet there is no denying that the seemingly regular flow of scandals harms Congress's standing with the American people.

Incumbents and candidates for Congress contribute to the generally low esteem of their colleagues in another way. Many of them, maybe most, complain about Congress—they run for Congress by running against Congress. This is an old art form in American campaigns. Candidates promise to end "business as usual" in Washington and to push through reforms to "fix" Congress—to end partisanship, reform the system of congressional perks and earmarks, stop the influence of money and special interests, and so on. While Congress languishes with mediocre approval ratings, individual members of Congress continue to do quite well. Typically, Gallup finds that about 70 percent of the public approve of the way their own U.S. representative is handling his or her job. Most incumbents, typically more than 90 percent, successfully gain reelection when they seek it.

Congressional campaigns have become personal and often very ugly. In the polarized environment of the recent past, candidates win their parties' primaries to get on the general election ballot by demonstrating their commitment to party principles. In the general election campaign, the candidates demonize their opponents. The winning candidates emerging from these campaigns have acquired a partisan style that they carry with them into Congress, reinforcing the partisan polarization.

HIGHLIGHTS OF RECENT CONGRESSIONAL ETHICS SCANDALS

- In 1989, House Speaker James Wright (D-TX) resigned after Republicans charged him with ethics violations for receiving extraordinarily large royalties on a book.

- In 1991, Senator David Durenberger (R-MI) was condemned in a unanimously approved Senate resolution for a book deal and for seeking reimbursement for expenses for staying in a condo that he owned.

- In 1991, the Senate Ethics Committee found that three senators had substantially and improperly interfered with a federal investigation of Lincoln Savings and Loan Association. Two others were found to have exercised poor judgment in the affair. The five senators came to be known at the "Keating Five," named after the chair of Lincoln.

- In 1992, the disclosure that many House members had repeatedly overdrawn their accounts at the House disbursement office led people to believe that members enjoyed special privileges.

- In 1995, a long investigation of sexual harassment charges against Senator Robert Packwood (R-OR) led to his forced resignation from office.

- In 1995, Representative Dan Rostenkowski (D-IL), former chair of the House Ways and Means Committee, was found guilty of illegally receiving cash for personal use from the House post office. He later served a prison term.

- In 1995, Representative Enid Waldholtz (R-UT) retired after her husband was charged with felonies in conjunction with raising funds for her campaign.

- In 1997, Speaker Newt Gingrich (R-GA) agreed to pay $300,000 in fines based on charges that he used nonprofit organizations for political purposes and misled the House Committee on Standards of Official Conduct.

- In 1998, Representative Jay Kim (R-CA) pleaded guilty to charges involving more than $250,000 in illegal campaign contributions.

- In 2002, Representative James A. Traficant, Jr. (D-OH) was convicted of receiving bribes in exchange for helping businesses get government contracts and of engaging in a pattern of racketeering since taking office in 1985.

- In 2004, House Majority Leader Tom Delay (R-TX) was issued letters of admonition by the House ethics committee for improperly promising to endorse the son of Representative Nick Smith (R-MI) in exchange for Smith's vote on a bill and for attending a fundraising event with lobbyists for a company that was lobbying him on pending legislation.

- In 2005, Representative Duke Cunningham (R-CA) resigned and pleaded guilty to taking more than $2.4 million in bribes and related tax evasion and fraud, the largest financial sum involving an individual member.

- In 2006, Representative Tom Delay (R-TX) resigned after being indicted in Texas for laundering money through a national party committee in his effort to redraw Texas congressional districts.

- In 2006, Representative William Jefferson (D-LA) won reelection to the House but was denied a Ways and Means Committee assignment after FBI agents videotaped him appearing to solicit a bribe and later found $90,000 of the marked cash in his freezer—making this "the cold cash scandal." Jefferson was defeated for reelection in 2008 and convicted for bribery a year later.

- In 2006, Representative Mark Foley (R-FL) resigned after it was disclosed that he sent sexually explicit e-mail messages to underage House pages.

- In 2006, Representative Bob Ney (R-OH) pleaded guilty to making false statements and conspiracy in relation to receiving thousands of dollars in gifts from lobbyist Jack Abramoff. A Ney aide also pleaded guilty for receiving gifts. Separately, Abramoff pleaded guilty to charges of conspiracy, fraud, and tax evasion.

- In 2008, Senator Ted Stevens (R-AK) was convicted of seven counts of failing to include on his Senate financial disclosure forms gifts related to the renovation of his Alaska home. Stevens was defeated for reelection in November 2008.

- In 2008, Representative Tim Mahoney (D-FL) confessed that he had had an extramarital affair with a staff member. Shortly after news reports indicated that Mahoney attempted to buy the staff member's silence, his wife filed for divorce and he was defeated for reelection.

- In 2010, Representative Charles Rangel (D-NY) was censured for violating House rules in using his office to raise money for a college building named after him, failing to disclose financial assets, and violating New York City rules by housing his campaign committees in rent-controlled apartments.

- In 2011, Senator John Ensign (R-NV) resigned his seat before a Senate investigation into his activities following an extramarital affair with a staff member. The activities included payments to the staff member's family and arranging for the staff member's father to be hired as a lobbyist.

- In 2011, Representative Anthony Weiner (D-NY) resigned from Congress after the public disclosure of his Twitter message to a woman with a link to a sexually suggestive photo of himself. Weiner admitted to having "exchanged messages and photos of an explicit nature with about six women."

- In 2012, Congresswoman Laura Richardson (D-CA) was fined by the House for breaking federal law and House rules in pressuring her staff to campaign for her and destroy evidence. After her reprimand by the House, she was defeated for reelection by a fellow Democrat.

- In 2013, Congressman Jesse Jackson Jr. (D-IL) pled guilty to using campaign money to buy personal items.

- In 2013, Congressman Trey Radel (R-FL) was arrested for buying cocaine from an undercover officer. He resigned from office in early 2014.

- In 2013, former Congressman Rick Renzi (R-AZ) was convicted of using his office for personal financial gain and stealing from a family insurance business to pay for his 2002 campaign. Renzi did not run for reelection in 2008.

Directions for Reform

Partisanship, mean and ugly campaigns, congressional gridlock, and the low esteem of Congress feed on one another. They have produced a dysfunctional Congress that alienates the public, discourages qualified people from running for seats in the House and Senate, and far too often fails to act on serious problems. Presidents fill the voids created by a handcuffed Congress when they can, weakening congressional participation in important policy arenas and undermining the representational basis for policymaking.

What can be done? First, it is important to keep in mind that the partisan polarization behind much of Congress's problems is not readily remedied by Congress. We have a right to expect more civil and tolerant behavior by legislators and their leaders, but we cannot expect legislators to move far from the policy positions that got them elected. Thus, in the short run, the burden is on American voters to

elect more moderate candidates who, as legislators, will demand less partisan behavior from their leaders and insist on the compromises necessary to address the policy challenges facing the country. I am not hopeful.

Nevertheless, legislators should take steps to improve their institution. In both houses, policymaking and interpersonal relations would be improved with fewer 3- and 4-day weeks and more 5-day weeks, having less conflict between floor and committee sessions, and perhaps keeping legislators in Washington for more weekends. We cannot expect legislators to keep their partisanship in check when they spend little time with one another except to rush from place to place and cast votes. Moreover, we cannot expect Congress to engage in creative legislative activity and meaningful oversight on the part-time schedule that Congress has maintained in recent decades. Unfortunately, I would not expect legislators to happily give up time in their districts and states to make this possible.

In the House, the majority party must work much harder to protect the minority party's ability to participate in policymaking in a meaningful way. The standing committees should be used whenever possible as forums for the exchange of ideas, layover rules guaranteeing the passage of time before action is taken should be observed, and amending opportunities in committee and on the floor should be preserved. The majority party cannot be expected to tolerate a minority that repeatedly fails to propose serious amendments and uses nearly all its opportunities to participate to score political points. So again, we would be asking legislators to set aside their real differences to reduce partisanship and find a way to compromise across a wide partisan divide.

In the Senate, no reform could be more important than filibuster reform. The practice is long-standing, but it is justified by neither the Constitution nor early Senate rules. It developed quite accidentally when the Senate failed to include the motion of the previous question, used in the House to limit debate, in a codification of its rules. The practice has come to be a regular means of obstructionism for the minority, effectively raising the threshold for passing legislation from 51 to 60 for nearly all legislation of greater than the most modest importance. I am not optimistic about the Senate minority party endorsing filibuster reform anytime soon.

6-2 The Politics of Legislative Stalemate

Sarah A. Binder

Political scientists have disagreed about the importance of divided party control of Congress and the presidency for policymaking. One point of view, articulated by David Mayhew, argues that both parties respond to public pressure for policy change. Consequently, we get major policy changes under both divided and unified party control of the major policymaking institutions. In this essay, Sarah A. Binder takes an opposing view. She argues that divided party control of Congress and the presidency has significant consequences for our politics and policy outcomes.

Most of the imbalances I have analyzed . . . have not been major, permanent, systemic problems. More precisely, at least during recent generations, many alleged problems have proven to be nonexistent, short-term, limited, tolerable, or correctable.

—Mayhew (2011, p. 190)

We hope that Mayhew is right and that this difficult patch will prove to be routine, short term and self-correcting. . . . But we doubt it. These are perilous times and the political responses to them are qualitatively different from what we have seen before.

—Mann and Ornstein (2012, p. 111)

In October 2013, Congress and the president hit an impasse over funding the government and increasing the nation's borrowing limit. Lawmakers' inability to reach common ground shut down the government and brought the country perilously close to defaulting on its debt. Such legislative drama—coupled with Congress's paltry legislative records since 2011—has fueled debate over whether the U.S. national political system is irreparably dysfunctional. Thomas Mann and Norman Ornstein, in *It's Even Worse Than It Looks* (2012), offer the most pungent critique, arguing that transformation of the Republican Party into an "insurgent outlier" has paralyzed our governing institutions. In contrast, David Mayhew in *Partisan Balance* (2011) urges caution, arguing that antimajoritarian biases in American

politics are rarely permanent. In short, Mayhew says that our political system is self-correcting; Mann and Ornstein suggest instead that the Republican Party has forced our legislative machinery off the rails.

In this piece, I tackle the debate between Mayhew and his critics and offer new data to evaluate the problem-solving capacity of Congress and the president in recent, polarized times. I admit that it can be hard to see the forest through the trees: A better assessment might be made a decade hence. Still, the evidence points us toward middle ground. On one hand, my earlier work on legislative stalemate that explained patterns in legislative performance in the second half of the 20th century still accounts fairly well for Congress's legislative performance in recent years (see Binder 2003). In other

Source: This piece is an original essay commissioned for this volume.

words, recent congressional deadlock may be different in *degree* from past deadlock but not necessarily in *kind*. On the other hand, we see a marked increase in the frequency of legislative deadlock over the past decade, with the 112th Congress in 2011 and 2012 ranking as the most gridlocked during the postwar era (albeit tied with the final 2 years of the Clinton administration in the late 1990s). Moreover, even when Congress and the president manage to reach agreement on the big issues of the day, these deals are often half-measures and second-bests. In short, whether our political system will self-correct in the coming years remains an open question.

Setting the Scene

At the close of the 112th Congress in early January 2013, numerous Washington observers charged that the 112th Congress was the most dysfunctional Congress ever. Brinkmanship and last-minute deals prevailed. With a newly elected Republican majority in the House and a small Democratic majority returning in the Senate, lawmakers' disagreements nearly caused a governmental shutdown in April of 2011 and came close to forcing the government to default on its obligations that summer. In the following Congress in October 2013, lawmakers actually went over the brink, failing to pass a bill to fund government operations and bumping right up against the Treasury's debt limit. Beyond fiscal policy deadlock, legislators' efforts in both Congresses to reach long-term solutions on perennial issues of transportation, agriculture, education, environment, and more often ended in stalemate. As Senator Joe Manchin (D-WV) summed up Congress's performance early in 2013, "Something has gone terribly wrong when the biggest threat to our American economy is the American Congress" (as cited in Steinhauer 2012). Judging by the public's reaction, Congress's performance was abysmal: At times only 10 percent of the public would admit to pollsters that they approved of Congress's on-the-job performance.

It is tempting to pin the entire blame for inaction on heightened partisan polarization. The first 2 years of the Obama administration, however, complicate the finger-pointing. In the 111th Congress, under unified Democratic Party control with a short-lived filibuster-proof Senate, Congress and the president produced a legislative record deemed to rival Lyndon Johnson's accomplishments in the 1960s Great Society. With GOP support ranging from some to none, the Democratic Congress enacted a mammoth economic stimulus bill, adopted landmark health care reform, revamped the financial regulatory system, abandoned the military's "Don't Ask, Don't Tell" policy, ratified a new arms control treaty, temporarily extended Bush-era tax cuts, and more.

The divergent records of the 111th and 112th Congresses pose a challenge for judging Congress's recent legislative performance. Two questions arise. First, how well do journalists' descriptions capture Congress's legislative performance across the 4 years? One approach counts the number of accomplishments that meet a threshold of landmark significance, as ably executed by Mayhew in his now-classic work *Divided We Govern* (1991). In his recent work, Mayhew implies that a denominator might be useful: He analyzes the fate of key presidential proposals over the past 60 years. Once we account for the demand for legislation as well as its supply, are the 111th and 112th Congresses still rivals for the best and worst Congresses, respectively, of the postwar period? Below, I update a time series on legislative gridlock to provide a better metric for judging the records of recent Congresses.

Second, with a longer time series on legislative deadlock, how well do our models of legislative gridlock perform? I use my model from *Stalemate* (originally tested with data from 1947 to 2000) to generate predicted levels of legislative deadlock over the past decade. If the model consistently underestimates the level of legislative gridlock in recent years, then we need to seriously consider why legislative stalemate has increased. If instead the model yields relatively accurate predictions, then we might hesitate to conclude that the system is no longer self-correcting. To be sure, this is an easier judgment after significant passage of time. Still, such analysis should help us put recent Congresses' collective capacity for identifying and resolving problems into perspective. I conclude by suggesting that some caution may be in order when drawing firm conclusions about the ability of our political system to self-correct in the near term, given its recent off-road travel.

The Landscape of Congressional Deadlock

The contemporary study of legislative performance began with publication of Mayhew's *Divided We Govern* in 1991, the first book to bring systematic, quantitative evidence to bear in testing claims about the impact of divided party control on the production of landmark laws. To be sure, *Divided We Govern* came on the heels of a series of works by presidential and legislative scholars perplexed and frustrated by the frequent periods of divided party government that prevailed after World War II. Between 1897 and 1954, divided party control of government occurred 14 percent of the time; between 1955 and 1990, two thirds of the time. And scholars observed in the 1960s, unified party control of the executive and the legislature does not guarantee a productive Congress, but divided control tends to undermine it. Decades later, scholars were still calling for a new theory of coalitional government to explain how Congress and the president could secure major policy change in the presence of divided government.

In *Divided We Govern*, Mayhew returned us to this matter by asking a simple and accessible question about Congress's performance in the postwar era: "Were many important laws passed?" Mayhew's empirical goal was to set up a test of the effect of divided party control on the level of lawmaking. Toward that end, he identified landmark laws in a two-stage process that combined contemporary judgments about the significance of Congress's work each session with policy specialists' retrospective judgments about the importance of legislation. Based on these data, Mayhew generated a comprehensive list of landmark laws enacted in each Congress between 1946 and 1990 (subsequently updated through 2012). Mayhew then tested whether the presence of divided government reduced the number of major laws enacted each Congress.

The key contribution of *Divided We Govern* was the null result for the impact of divided government on lawmaking. Unified party control of Congress and the White House fails to yield significantly higher levels of lawmaking. It matters little whether a single party controls both the White House and Congress: Not much more gets done than under divided party control. Having absolved divided government as a cause of legislative inaction, Mayhew disentangled several other influences on Congress's performance. Some of those forces—including legislators' electoral incentives—point toward constancy in the record of lawmaking. But other forces, Mayhew demonstrated, appear to be important alternative sources of variation in explaining congressional productivity, including shifting public moods, presidential cycles, and issue coalitions that cut across the left–right divide.

Mayhew's work provoked theoretical and methodological debates about how to explain and measure variation in Congress's legislative performance over the postwar period. Much of the methodological debate centered on whether a measure of Congress's legislative capacity requires a denominator—a baseline against which to compare Congress's output. Mayhew's concerns about the difficulty of defining and identifying a relevant and measurable denominator were well taken. Still, I offered in *Stalemate* a measure that captures the degree of legislative deadlock by isolating the set of salient issues on the agenda and then determining the fate of those issues in each Congress. The result is a ratio of failed measures to all issues on the agenda for each Congress. My sense is that this measure of gridlock is up to the task, largely because it meets key benchmarks we might impose to judge a measure's construct validity. The measure identified Johnson's Great Society Congress as the most productive of the postwar period and determined that Clinton's second-session Congresses were the most deadlocked. Both assessments comport with historical and contemporary coverage of Congress's postwar performance.

As I explained in detail in Appendix A to *Stalemate*, I devised a method for identifying every policy issue on the legislative agenda, based on the issues discussed in the unsigned editorials in *The New York Times*. Using the level of *Times* attention to an issue in any given Congress as an indicator of issue salience, I identified for each Congress between the 80th (1947–1948) and the 106th (1999–2000) the most salient issues on the legislative agenda.[1] I then turned to news coverage and congressional documents to determine whether or not Congress and the president took legislative action in that Congress to address each salient issue. The measurement strategy produced a denominator of every major legislative issue raised by elite observers of Capitol Hill and a numerator that captured Congress's record in acting on those issues. The resulting gridlock score captures the percentage of agenda items left in limbo at the close of the Congress.

Figures 1a and 1b display the size of the policy agenda from 1947 to 2012, coupled with the number of failed legislative issues for each Congress. All

Figure 1a Size of the Legislative Agenda (All Issues), 1947–2012

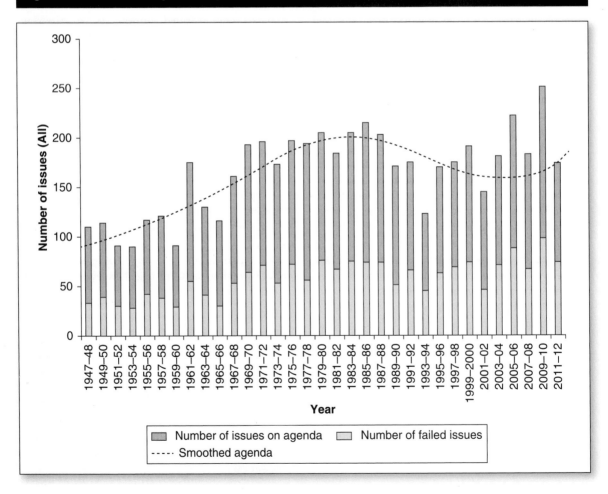

Figure 1b Size of the Legislative Agenda (Salient Issues), 1947–2012

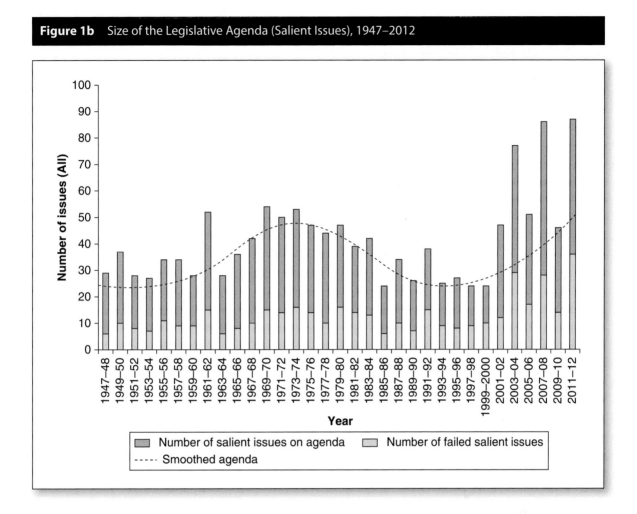

issues are included in the top panel; salient issues in the bottom. Looking first at the smoothed trend line in the total number of legislative issues mentioned each Congress in the *Times* editorials, the size of the overall agenda increases as expected with the return of large liberal majorities during the mid-1960s and stays at this expanded level through the advent of the civil rights, environmental, and women's movements of the 1970s. Only in recent years do we see a slight increase in the size of the agenda, no doubt reflecting both later efforts to renew the spate of landmark laws of the earlier, activist period and

newer issues brought to the fore by the war on terror, global climate change, and so on.

The trend in the number of salient issues in the bottom panel is more eye-catching. The overall size of the agenda increases only incrementally over the most recent decade, but the number of salient issues rises markedly in the 108th (2003–2004), 110th (2005–2006), and 112th (2011–2012) Congresses. The data suggest a marked increase in the number of big-ticket legislative issues attracting the attention of the *Times*' editorial board. It is also possible that the increased gridlock in recent years has indirectly fueled the size of the salient agenda, as the big issues of the day remain unresolved and thus recur on the nation's agenda. Failure to address reform of immigration law, entitlement programs, and the tax code, for example, likely helped fuel the size of the salient agenda in recent years. It also appears that a spate of new issues in the past decade caught the attention of the *Times'* editorial writers, including homeland security, global warming, cybersecurity, the return of deficits after the 1990s, the U.S. wars in Iraq and Afghanistan, the onset of financial crisis, and the worst economy since the Great Depression.

The updated time series of the degree of legislative deadlock on salient issues each Congress between 1947 and 2012 appears in Figure 2. Four features of the time series stand out. First, the frequency of deadlock shows a secular increase over time. Second, the direst claims about the 112th Congress are essentially true. By this measure, the 112th Congress can claim to be the "worst Congress ever" over the postwar period, although the title is shared with the last Congress of the Clinton administration in 1999–2000. In both Congresses, almost three quarters of the most salient issues remained unresolved at the end of the Congress. Coming on the heels of the 1998 GOP effort to impeach President Clinton and in the run-up to a fiercely competitive contest for the White House, we probably shouldn't be surprised about the essentially dead heat between the Congresses to claim the honor of most dysfunctional.

Still, caution is in order when comparing the two Congresses. Some of the issues considered "successfully" addressed in the 112th Congress might never have been deemed acceptable outcomes in previous Congresses. For example, Congress and the president have traditionally authorized and funded federal highway programs in multiyear reauthorization bills. But following expiration of highway programs in 2009, Congress and the president passed a series of temporary reauthorizations to keep federal programs running. Even when the parties were finally able to agree to a multiyear bill in 2012, that agreement reauthorized only 2 years of highway programs;

conflict over raising the federal gas tax stymied efforts to finance a traditional 6-year bill. I code the highway bill as a successful legislative response, even though the 2-year bill avoided making any decisions about how to ensure the solvency of federal highway trust funds after the end of the 2 years. Another problem—how to raise the federal debt ceiling in the summer of 2011—was resolved in part by establishing the "supercommittee" to come up with more than a trillion dollars in federal savings. The 2011 deficit reduction package is scored a success, even though the supercommittee that resulted from the agreement eventually failed. In other words, the 71 percent deadlock score for the 112th Congress likely underestimates the true level of legislative stalemate.

Third, although the 111th Congress was relatively productive compared with Congress's performances over the past decade (with the exception of the 9/11 Congress), the 111th fell far shy of the records of the Great Society Congresses. To be sure, the 111th Congress was nearly 30 points more productive than the 112th was. But even the widely heralded 111th Congress left a lengthy list of major issues in legislative limbo, including proposals to address education, campaign finance, global warming, immigration, and gun control. In short, even with the 111th Congress's unified party control and its short-lived, filibuster-proof majority, lawmakers struggled to surmount significant barriers to major policy change.

Finally, a brief look at the 107th Congress, spanning before and after the attacks of September 11, 2001, is instructive. Overall, the Congress (with unified Republican control of both branches for just a few months early in 2001) was fairly productive, leaving just 34 percent of the policy agenda in 2001 and 2002 in stalemate. Indeed, the 107th Congress outperformed the 111th—somewhat unexpectedly given the accolades earned by Congress at the end of Obama's first 2 years in office. But the 107th Congress's performance was shaped by the events of September 11. Eight of the thirty-five salient issues in that Congress stemmed directly from the attacks

Figure 2   Frequency of Legislative Gridlock, 1947–2012

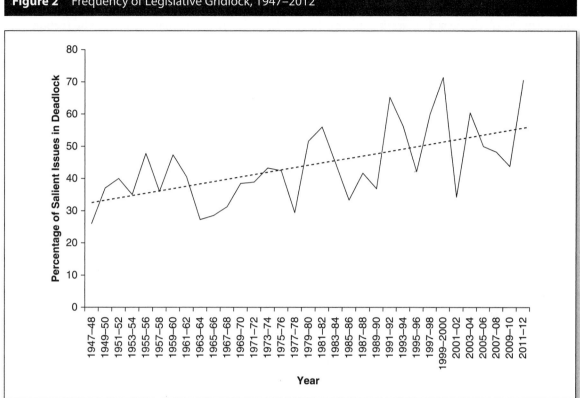

of September 11. And on those eight issues, Congress and the president mustered a perfect record—enacting the Patriot Act, writing the Authorization for the Use of Military Force, addressing the needs of 9/11 victims, and more. Even on less salient issues stemming from September 11, congressional deadlock stood at barely 10 percent, with just a single issue left in legislative limbo.[2] But any cooperative spirit and unity of purpose did not extend to the rest of the policy agenda. If we exclude the issues related to September 11, Congress and the president deadlocked on just under half of the salient policy matters. Congress does appear to retain the capacity to act swiftly when a true crisis occurs—as evidenced further in Congress's 2008 bailout of Wall Street

after the Federal Reserve and Treasury allowed Lehman Brothers to go under. However, as we might expect, legislative unity dissipates when Congress turns its attention back to the regular policy agenda.

Explaining Patterns of Gridlock

The longer time series allows me to repose the question that motivated *Stalemate*: How do we account for Congress's uneven legislative performance over time? In that work, I used the measure of the frequency of legislative gridlock to test alternative institutional and electoral explanations for variation in congressional stalemate. I found that unified party control of Congress and the White House reduced the frequency of deadlock. Divided government—aided by parties' influence over the content of the floor agenda—empowers the opposition party to block agenda issues it opposes. But party control alone, I argued, was insufficient to explain variation in Congress's performance.

I pointed instead to two other factors that shape Congress's record. First, the smaller the ideological center, the tougher the time Congress has securing policy agreement. The rise of polarized political parties—even before the Bush and Obama presidencies—complicated the challenge of building coalitions of sufficient size to overcome the multiple veto points institutionalized on Capitol Hill. Second, bicameral policy differences interfere with the crafting of policy coalitions, even in periods of unified party control. Although electoral and policy differences between the branches tend to garner the most attention in Washington, policy differences between the House and Senate also seem to complicate lawmakers' capacity to find common ground acceptable to both chambers. The results of the 2010 and 2012 congressional elections—delivering control of the House to Republicans while keeping the Senate in Democratic hands—make plain the barriers imposed by bicameral differences.

How does this basic model hold up when we incorporate the records of the Congresses between 2001 and 2012? The new results deliver a reasonably similar story to my earlier work: Congress still struggles to legislate when partisan polarization rises and when the two chambers diverge in their policy views. Moreover, when I use the original model to estimate predicted levels of deadlock for the most recent decade, the original model does a decent job of predicting the number of failed legislative issues in three of the past six Congresses (running from 2007–2010). In the remaining Congresses, the model misses the mark. The model overestimates failure in the 107th Congress (2001–2002), which is not surprising given Congress's legislative responsiveness in the wake of September 11. Interestingly, the model underestimates legislative failure in the 108th Congress, likely reflecting in part Democrats' willingness to filibuster GOP initiatives in a period of unified party control. And the model underestimates legislative deadlock in the 112th Congress (2011–2012), confirming the common observation that legislative dysfunction reigned in the 112th Congress once Republicans regained control of the House. That said, the model's average error over the past decade is roughly a single failed legislative issue, suggesting that the original model continues to help explain patterns in legislative deadlock even in more polarized times.

What broader conclusions can we draw from the updated analysis? First, the results confirm the media's recent focus on the impact of polarized parties on Congress's ability to legislate. That said, because we typically use lawmakers' floor voting records, it is difficult to disentangle the extent to which partisan polarization captures ideological differences across lawmakers' or members' partisan "team-play" behavior. Regardless of whether we deem polarization a function of ideological differences, strategic disagreement by partisans seeking electoral advantage, or a mix of the two, the results are clear: When ideological and electoral incentives propel the parties to the wings, abandoning the political center, lawmakers struggle to find broadly palatable solutions to the range of problems they face.

Second, the results confirm my earlier conclusion about the impact of bicameral differences on the difficulty of legislating. Even after controlling for the level of polarization and party control of the two branches, policy differences between the two chambers matter to Congress's ability to legislate. As the centers of the House and Senate chambers diverge in their policy views—regardless of whether party control is unified or split between the chambers—legislative deadlock grows.

Third, the effect of party control appears attenuated. *Stalemate* identified an independent effect of party control on legislative performance: The frequency of deadlock was higher in periods of divided, rather than unified, party control. In his recent work, Mayhew also identified a party effect: Unified party control increases the chances that presidential proposals will be enacted. Still, in the longer time series presented here, divided party government shows only limited impact on lawmakers' capacity to govern. Looking more closely at the level of gridlock over the past decade, the record of the 108th Congress (under unified Republican control in 2003–2004) seems to diminish the effect of party control. In 2003–2004, 60 percent of the agenda was left in limbo at the end of the Congress; in comparison, deadlock in periods of unified party control over the longer postwar period averaged 40 percent. If we drop the 108th Congress from the analysis, we find that divided government drives up the frequency of gridlock.

I suspect that the recent, rising proclivity of opposition party senators to filibuster the majority's agenda—by insisting on 60 votes for adoption of most amendments and measures—has undermined the legislative power of majority parties, even in periods of unified party control. Increased minority party exploitation of its parliamentary rights would help explain the litany of legislative measures left in limbo after Democrats lost their filibuster-proof majority in winter 2010, as well as the heavy load of measures left undone at the close of the Republican-led 108th Congress. As electoral incentives increase for the minority party to play a more confrontational role in the Senate and as the costs of filibustering decline, unified party control might prove a less powerful tool for driving the legislative process.

Discussion and Conclusions

Stepping back from the data, the analysis suggests that there is a good deal of truth both to Mayhew's sanguine view and to Mann and Ornstein's more dire analysis of the state of Congress and its legislative capacity. To be sure, in many ways Congress's recent legislative performance fits the well-established pattern from *Stalemate*: When elections yield more polarized parties and chambers, bargaining is more difficult and compromise is more often out of reach. To the extent that recent Congresses fit the broader pattern established in the postwar period, we might be on safe ground concurring with Mayhew that the recent "imbalances" during the Obama

administration are not likely to be "permanent, systemic problems." Still, that is a hypothesis that can be tested only over time.

Still, three reservations temper such a conclusion. First, levels of legislative deadlock have steadily risen over the past half-century: Stalemate at times now reaches nearly three quarters of the salient issues on Washington's agenda. Granted, legislators differ over what issues and conditions constitute "problems." That might increasingly be the case as the parties polarize: Lawmakers today disagree even about basic scientific facts (such as the evidence on whether or not the earth is actually warming). But the absolute level of deadlock does raise eyebrows. Moreover, issues left in limbo on the agenda rarely disappear from the policy agendas. Although a larger agenda in itself might account for Congress's sluggish record, pushing issues off to the future sometimes makes problems worse.

Second, even when Congress and the president muster agreement on a policy solution, such agreements sometimes manage to create new problems. For example, some economists argued that fiscal policy brinkmanship in the 112th Congress—last-minute decision making that increased uncertainty about future policy—harmed the economy and set back the economic recovery. Moreover, markets' dismay over Congress's dysfunction that summer led to the first-ever downgrade of the U.S. sovereign credit rating. If both congressional inaction and action make problems worse, then it's hard to see how quickly the political system will rebound from its current partisan impasse. The system no doubt is corrigible, but it might take a long time to right itself.

Third, it is not clear whether current levels of polarization are going to subside anytime soon. On two dimensions—both the degree of polarization and the parties' relative contribution to polarization—Nolan McCarty, Keith Poole, and Howard Rosenthal (2006) concur with critics about the unprecedented nature of recent polarization. The distance between the parties ideologically has all but returned to heights not seen since the end of the 19th century. Partisan polarization appears to be on the verge of passing historical levels in the Senate and has surpassed House records stemming from the turn of the century. In addition, such polarization might be deemed "asymmetric": Many argue that Republicans (particularly in the House) have moved further to the right than Democrats have moved to the left. One might wonder whether the asymmetric pattern stems in part from Republicans' minority status: Having lost the White House in 2008, the GOP is unleashed to shoot for the conservative moon (in part pulled by its Tea Party voters). So long as some degree of polarization is driven by sheer partisan team play—in which the opposition party is more likely to object to proposals endorsed by the president—then extreme levels of polarization will continue to lead to unprecedented levels of deadlock. As President Obama put it, Republicans seem to need a "permission structure" that allows them to engage in the business of crafting legislative compromise that could lead to agreements with Obama and the Democrats. This is, in a word, an *unorthodox* barrier to getting both parties back to the business of negotiating. Whether both House and Senate wings of the Republican Party can self-correct and how long it might take to do so remain to be seen.

Fourth, changes in the structure of electoral competition in recent decades likely alter lawmakers' calculations about coming to the bargaining table. As Frances Lee (2013) observes in recent work, margins of party control in the House and Senate since 1980 have been half the size (on average) of margins between 1933 and the 1980s. Presidential elections have also been close, with the last landslide Electoral College win in 1984. Close party competition for control of Congress and the White House appears to affect party politics in Congress. Fierce electoral competition brings control of national institutions within reach for both parties, limiting lawmakers' incentives to compromise with the other party. Why settle on half a loaf of policy when a full loaf will be delivered to the party base upon winning unified party control? Electioneering rivals governance in the contemporary Congress, harming the institution's legislative capacity.

Ultimately, Mayhew may well be correct that our political system will weather this rough patch with little harm done. Even so, we are left in the meantime with a national legislature plagued by low legislative capacity. Half-measures, second-bests, and just-in-time legislating are the new norm: Electoral, partisan, and institutional barriers limit Congress's capacity for more than lowest-common-denominator deals. Even if lawmakers ultimately find a way to get their institution back on track, Congress's recent difficulties have been costly—both to the fiscal health of the country and to its citizens' trust in government. The economy will eventually regain footing. Regenerating the standing of Congress in the public's eye will be much harder.

Notes

1. I consider salient issues those matters on which *The New York Times* editorialized four or more times in a given Congress. This salience filter brought the number of major issues successfully addressed roughly in line with Mayhew's number of landmark laws enacted in each Congress.

2. There were eight issues related to September 11 that attracted fewer than four *Times* editorials.

References

Binder, Sarah A. 2003. *Stalemate: Causes and Consequences of Legislative Gridlock*. Washington, DC: Brookings Institution Press.

Lee, Frances E. 2013. Presidents and Party Teams: Debt Limits and Executive Oversight, 2001–2013. *Presidential Studies Quarterly* 43 (4): 775–791.

McCarty, Nolan, Keith T. Poole, and Howard Rosenthal. 2006. *Polarized America: The Dance of Ideology and Unequal Riches*. Cambridge: MIT Press.

Mann, Thomas E., and Norman J. Ornstein. 2012. *It's Even Worse Than It Looks*. New York: Basic Books.

Mayhew, David. 1991. *Divided We Govern*. Newhaven, CT: Yale University Press, 2005.

Mayhew, David. 2011. *Partisan Balance*. Princeton, NJ: Princeton University Press.

Steinhauer, Jennifer. 2012. A Showdown Long Foreseen. *New York Times*, December 30. http://www.nytimes.com/2012/12/31/us/politics/fiscal-crisis-impasse-long-in-the-making.html (accessed May 11, 2014).

6-3 Congressional Committees in a Continuing Partisan Era

John H. Aldrich and David W. Rohde

In the essay below, John Aldrich and David Rohde describe the theory of conditional party government. This theory posits that a cohesive party, one in which the party members agree on most issues, will empower its leadership to play a central role in policymaking. With cohesive majority parties over the last three decades, majority party leaders have directed the actions of standing committees and assumed a direct role in designing legislation.

The two principal organizing structures of Congress are the political parties and the committee system. During the history of the institution, the relative influence of the two has shifted back and forth. From 1890 to 1910, the majority party dominated the House of Representatives, with the Speaker empowered to appoint committees and their chairs and to control the legislative agenda. After the revolt against Speaker Joe Cannon in 1910, power shifted to committees, whose leaders were selected based on seniority. From the 1920s through the 1970s party influence was relatively weak, and that period became known as the era of committee government. Then, beginning with the reform period in the 1970s, institutional changes were adopted that strengthened parties and weakened the sway of committees and their chairs. Moreover, the extent and intensity of partisan conflict in Congress increased. Of course, even in strong party eras Congress members did not abandon the committee system. Speaker Cannon's powers, for example, were exercised in large part through the committee system. This shifting balance of power therefore reflects the degree of autonomy of the committees and their chairs from their legislative party organizations, as well as any additional, independent powers granted the party.

In this chapter we discuss the transformation of the party-committee balance from the 1970s to the present, focusing mainly on the House but also considering the Senate. We begin by considering the Democratic Party reforms of the 1970s that launched the transformation and how the Democrats applied the party leadership's new powers. Then we consider further developments after the Republicans won control of both houses in the 1994 elections. We also discuss additional institutional changes that the GOP made and the ways in which the Republican Party leadership interacted with the committee system to achieve its legislative goals. The return of the Democratic majority after the 2006 elections gives us a single but important session to examine the party-committee balance under new party (and committee) leadership. We will also briefly discuss Senate committees and then offer some conclusions.

The Committee System and the Era of Committee Government

The most important thing to recognize about the House and Senate committee systems is that they are designed institutions. That is, they are created by the membership to serve the interests of the chamber and its members. Committees, through division of

Source: John H. Aldrich and David W. Rohde, "The Congressional Committees in a Continuing Partisan Era," in *Congress Reconsidered*, 9th ed., ed. Lawrence C. Dodd and Bruce I. Oppenheimer (Washington, D.C.: CQ Press, 2009), 217–229, 232–240. Some notes appearing in the original have been deleted.

labor, permit the chamber to stretch its capabilities by having only a subset of members consider each issue and piece of legislation in detail. Furthermore, committees encourage the development of expertise through members' specialization in the issue areas covered by their committees' jurisdictions.[1] In addition to these benefits to the chamber, committees also provide benefits to individual members. Richard Fenno has argued that members of Congress pursue one or more of three goals: reelection, power within the chamber, and good public policy.[2] The achievement of each of these goals is potentially influenced by committee membership. Members can use committee service to identify themselves with issues that are important to constituents and to secure benefits for their districts, thus enhancing their chances for reelection.[3] Committee and subcommittee chairmanships also provide members with positions of power in the chamber. And committee members are in the best position to influence public policy within their committees' jurisdictions.[4]

Congress used committees to conduct business from the beginning of the institution, although it took most of a century for the system to develop into the form we know today.[5] Standing committees (that is, permanent committees with recognized substantive jurisdictions) were widely used by the 1820s. They included members from both the majority and minority parties, and as the committees developed expertise their parent chambers began to defer to their judgments on legislative policy. Throughout the 1800s, the influence of the majority party leadership over committees grew. Speakers had the right to appoint committee members and chairs, and they chaired the Rules Committee, which set the terms of debate for bills on the House floor. The Speaker lost these powers in the revolt against Speaker Cannon in 1910. After that the Speaker could no longer appoint committees, and each party developed its own procedures for that purpose. Seniority in committee service became the almost inviolable basis for choosing committee chairs. Moreover, the Rules Committee was autonomous and the Speaker barred from serving on it.

As a result of these developments, committees became largely independent from party influence. Because committee chairs were chosen and maintained in power by seniority, they had no particular incentive to be responsive to the wishes of their party or its leaders in producing legislation. The chairs shaped their committees' agendas, appointed subcommittees (and usually chose their chairs), and decided when hearings would be held and how bills would be handled. These developments might have been less consequential if the committee leaders were ideologically representative of their party, but that was not the case. From 1930 on, the Democrats were usually in the majority, and because southern Democrats were more likely to accumulate seniority than their northern counterparts, they were disproportionately represented among committee leaders. Conservative southerners often allied with Republicans to block or alter Democratic legislation, a situation that greatly frustrated northerners. Although that pattern had begun in the 1930s, their frustration became particularly pronounced in the 1950s and 1960s.

Party Reform: Gateway to the Partisan Era

Initial attempts at reform of committee government included a successful effort in 1961 to expand the Rules Committee to reduce the influence of southern conservatives on the panel. Then in 1970 Congress passed the Legislative Reorganization Act. It contained a number of important features, such as the requirement that committees make public roll call votes, and it generally required committees to permit the public to attend their meetings. The act also made it much easier to obtain recorded votes on amendments on the House floor and set the stage for electronic voting, which markedly sped up floor voting. These changes started to shift the locus of legislative decision making from the committees to the floor. The reorganization act, however, took no action to revise the seniority system or to reduce the powers of committee chairs.[6] The conservative coalition was able to block any such actions that would have undermined their institutional position.

However, the makeup of the House (and Senate) membership was changing. The Voting Rights Act of 1965 had enfranchised black voters in the South, and their strong tilt to the Democratic Party was liberalizing the party's voter base there. Reinforcing that effect was the gradual departure from the party of conservative voters who no longer saw the Democrats as standing for their interests. As a consequence of these developments, new southern Democrats were becoming more like their northern colleagues, and the Democratic membership in Congress was becoming less divided and more homogeneous.[7] This set the stage for efforts to strengthen the majority party leadership relative to the committee system. Since the revolt against Cannon, the diverse memberships of the congressional parties had been reluctant to enhance party power because their very diversity meant that there would be great uncertainty about the ends for which that power would be used. That is, members could not be sure what policies leaders would seek, and so individual members feared that powerful leaders would seek policies far different from their own preferred outcome. If, on the other hand, the preferences of party members were to become more similar, members would not have to be as concerned that leaders with preferences different from theirs would be chosen, and it would be safer to grant leaders stronger powers.

This relationship is the essence of the theoretical perspective that we have labeled *conditional party government,* or CPG for short.[8] If the legislators in a party have very heterogeneous policy preferences, they will not be likely to grant strong powers to their leadership. As policy preferences become more homogeneous, members will be progressively more likely to empower their party leaders because they will have less reason to fear the use of those powers. This tendency will be further reinforced as the positions of the two parties become more different because the consequences to each party's members of the other party's winning the competition to control policy will become more and more negative.

By the early 1970s, liberal Democrats were a clear majority of the House Democratic caucus, but not of the entire House membership. Because they could not muster a majority on the floor for the kinds of reforms they favored, the liberals targeted the rules of the Democratic caucus instead. Only Democrats could vote on these efforts, which combined strategies dealing both with committees and with the party and its leadership. First they sought to undermine the independence and power of committee leaders, so that the remaining conservatives would be less able to impede passage of their desired legislation. This strategy followed two tracks. First, the liberals wanted to end the automatic nature of the seniority system. To this end the caucus adopted rules providing for a secret ballot vote on all committee chairs at the beginning of every Congress. If the prospective chair (usually still the most senior Democrat on the committee) was voted down, there would be a competitive election of the chair in the caucus. This change was shown to have real consequences in 1975 when three southern Democrats were removed from committee chairmanships and replaced by more loyal northerners. Chairs were put on notice that they could not buck their party's policy wishes with impunity.

The second track of the strategy involved adopting rules that restricted the powers of those chosen as chairs. The principal vehicle was a set of rules known as the Subcommittee Bill of Rights, which required that committee members bid for the chairs of subcommittees in order of seniority, ending the ability of full committee chairs simply to appoint those positions. Subcommittees had to receive specific jurisdictions, and committee legislation had to be referred to subcommittees accordingly. In addition, subcommittee chairs would control their own budgets and staffs, rather than the chair of the full committee doing so.

The other strategy of the reformers was to give more powers to the party leadership. The Speaker received the right to appoint the chair and the Democratic members of the Rules Committee. That meant that the leadership could again control the flow of legislation and strategically shape the terms of floor consideration. In addition, the power to assign Democrats to other committees was vested in a new Steering and Policy Committee, most of whose members were party leaders or appointed by the Speaker. The reformers wanted the leadership to have more influence over the allocation of prized assignments, to make members more responsive to the leaders. Finally, the Speaker was given the authority to refer bills to more than one committee and to set deadlines for reporting, further reducing the ability of committees to act as roadblocks.

Partisanship Takes Hold: 1983–1994

The reforms were adopted by the mid-1970s and some of their consequences were quickly apparent, but divisions remained in the Democratic caucus, preventing the full effects of the changes from being visible. Indeed, many observers complained that the reforms had merely made Congress less efficient by further decentralizing power to subcommittees. This viewpoint was reinforced by Ronald Reagan's success in 1981 at splitting off southern Democrats to support his budget and tax proposals. The recession of 1982, however, helped bring fifty-seven Democrats to the House, including many moderate-to-liberal southerners. Consequently the conservative coalition was no longer a majority of the House. The newcomers made up over one-fifth of the Democratic caucus, and they provided support for stronger use of the leadership's powers to advance the party agenda and to compete with the priorities of the Reagan administration.

As we noted earlier, one reform strategy sought to induce committee chairs to refrain from blocking party bills and to support the Democratic Party's legislative program. After the removal of the three southern chairs in 1975, committee chairs recognized that their continued hold on their positions depended to a degree on their party support, and their behavior changed accordingly. Research shows that members who occupied, or were close in seniority to, committee chairs dramatically increased their levels of party support between 1971 and 1982.[9] For example, in 1973–1974 the party unity score of Rep. Jamie Whitten, D-Miss., was thirty-eight points below the party average and eighteen points below the average for southern Democrats. Anticipating a liberal challenge when the chairmanship of the Appropriations Committee (where he ranked second) became vacant, Whitten began to change his behavior. By 1988, Whitten's party unity score was not only higher than the average southern Democrat's, it was two points higher than the average Democrat's.[10] Moreover, the Democratic caucus continued to use the mechanism for voting on chair candidates to pressure or remove committee leaders whose performance was deemed unsatisfactory.

The other reform strategy was to strengthen the party leadership, and it had a substantial impact on the relationship between the leadership and committees. As Barbara Sinclair has said, "Party and committee leaders must work together . . . since both are agents of and ultimately responsible to the Democratic Caucus."[11] In the changed environment, most committee leaders came to think of themselves as part of a team with the majority leadership. Committee chairs realized that they could not act independently of party priorities in drafting legislation. In turn, they expected party leaders to provide adequate staff support and assistance in moving bills to passage on the floor.[12]

One of the most important tools available to the party leadership was control of the Rules Committee. During the 1980s, the Democrats increasingly used the resolutions (called "special rules") that set the terms for floor consideration of legislation to structure the agenda to the advantage of the party.[13] For example, special rules could bar amendments completely, giving members a take-it-or-leave-it choice between the bill the leadership favored and nothing. Or the rule could permit just those amendments that the leadership wanted to consider, barring others that the Republican minority wanted but that would cause policy or electoral difficulties for some Democrats. Moreover, if the reporting committee had not adequately taken the majority party's wishes into account, special rules could be used to alter the bill as reported to bring the policy closer to the preference of the majority. This was done multiple times on defense authorization bills reported from the Armed Services Committee.

Not surprisingly, the majority party's use of its powers provoked anger and frustration among Republicans. One response from the GOP was to change its party rules to mimic those of the Democrats, so as to make its own leadership more able to compete. For example, the Republicans gave the minority leader the right to make Republican appointments to the Rules Committee and created a new committee assignment system in which the leadership had more voting power. The party leader was also empowered to designate "leadership issues," and on those bills all members of the party leadership were obliged to support the positions of the Republican Conference.

The Republicans also adopted progressively more confrontational tactics to protest their treatment and to undermine the Democratic majority. Some complaints came from GOP leaders and mainline conservatives, but most active were members of a group of populist conservatives known as the Conservative Opportunity Society (COS), led by Newt Gingrich of Georgia, then a backbencher. Gingrich and COS believed that the Republicans would be a perpetual minority unless they stopped going along with the Democrats as a means of attempting to have some influence on legislation. Instead, they argued that the GOP had to draw contrasts with the Democrats and let the public make a choice. The COS organized protests against the Democrats' management of the chamber and fought against the use of special rules to control the agenda and limit Republican influence. These efforts culminated in late 1988, when Gingrich filed a formal complaint with the House Ethics Committee against Speaker Jim Wright, D-Texas. The ensuing investigation led to Wright's resignation from the House.

Republican Rule and Its Consequences: 1994–2000

Republican confrontations with the Democratic majority continued into the 1990s, especially after President Bill Clinton was elected in 1992, restoring unified government. The GOP was able to take advantage of the political context in 1994, successfully exploiting negative public feelings about government performance, the condition of the nation, and Clinton personally.[14] The Republicans won majority control of both houses of Congress for the first time since the election of 1952. The new majority in the House chose Newt Gingrich as their Speaker, and the party set out to transform the operation of the chamber to set the stage for major changes in government policy.

Republican Procedural Changes

Gingrich's transforming efforts commenced almost immediately.[15] Little more than a week after election day he made clear his intent to depart from the seniority system in selecting committee chairs to a greater extent than the Democrats ever did, announcing that he had chosen Bob Livingston, La., as the new chair of the Appropriations Committee. Livingston ranked fifth in committee seniority but was considered more ideologically dependable and more effective than the more senior committee members. A few days later, Gingrich again bypassed seniority to select more dependable chairs for Judiciary and Commerce. Gingrich was asserting the right to name the new chairs before the newly elected majority had yet arrived in Washington, and the Republican Conference members tacitly ratified his decisions by their acquiescence.

The powers of committees and their chairs were also changed significantly. Three committees were abolished outright, and most remaining committees were limited to five subcommittees. These actions eliminated twenty-five subcommittees and 12 percent of full committee slots. As one COS member said, "Our system will prevent members from getting locked into the status quo."[16]

The Republican leadership gave its chairs the right to appoint subcommittee chairs and control over committee staff. This reflected Gingrich's view that chairs should control their committees, but he also believed that the party should control the chairs. He required committee chairs to consult with him before choosing subcommittee heads, and he pressured one chair to name two freshman representatives to head subcommittees. Gingrich also required each member of the Appropriations Committee to sign a "letter of fidelity," pledging to cut the budget as much as the Speaker wanted. To further weaken the capacities of committee leaders to build an independent power base, the Republicans adopted a six-year term limit for all committee and subcommittee chairmen.

Gingrich also announced a new Republican committee assignment process, and it was adopted by the Republican Conference in December. It gave the Speaker control over a much larger fraction of votes on the Committee on Committees. Republican House members also confirmed their leader's right to appoint the members and chair of the Rules Committee. Overall, under the new GOP majority, committees had less independent power and the party leadership had more.

It is worth noting one thing that the GOP did not do. It didn't adopt a wholesale realignment of committee jurisdictions, as some reformers had wanted. The existing pattern of jurisdictions had too many implications for the reelection, policy, and power goals of members, and most of them were unwilling to accept the risks involved in major change.[17] When the GOP took over the majority, Gingrich authorized Rep. David Dreier of California (vice chair of a joint committee on congressional reform in the previous Congress) to draft four plans of varying comprehensiveness for revamping the committee system. After it became apparent that there would be significant resistance from the chairs and members of affected committees, Gingrich opted for a version of the least-extensive plan. Thus we see that although Republican members were willing to support strengthening their leadership's influence over committees, they were not willing to sacrifice their other interests that were served by the committee system.

Party Leaders and Committees

The rules changes that the new Republican majority adopted thus set the stage for greater influence by party leaders over the activities and legislative products of committees. Because of limited space we can only present a few examples, mostly drawn from the 104th Congress (1995–1997), which we can then compare with the first session under the Democratic majority in the 110th.

Influencing Bill Creation in Committees. Majority leadership involvement in the crafting of bills in committee did not originate with the 104th Congress. As Sinclair shows,[18] such activity had become more

frequent as committee autonomy decreased in the postreform era. It was, however, still infrequent in the Democrat-controlled Congresses, as most leader activity involved stages of the process after initial drafting. The 104th marked a major increase in this role for majority leadership.

The most extensive instance of leadership influence on bill creation was the drafting and revision of the legislation designed to implement the Contract with America.[19] Although there was substantial initial consultation on general matters during the crafting of the contract, the top GOP leaders determined which issues would be included and many of the particulars. For example, it was Gingrich who decided that school prayer would not be included. Committee consideration of these predrafted bills was largely pro forma, a necessary consequence of the leadership's pledge to pass them in the Congress's first hundred days.

The contract was of central importance, but the leadership's involvement in committees' initial consideration of bills was not limited to that legislation. Another example involves the major reform of agriculture subsidy policy that became known as the Freedom to Farm Act. In September 1995, the GOP leadership sent a letter to the Agriculture Committee chair, Pat Roberts of Kansas. They wrote, "We give the committee leave" to write major budget-cutting farm legislation. They indicated that they hoped the committee would support Roberts's bill, but if not "we will feel compelled" to bring the bill to the floor allowing unlimited amendments, or to replace the committee's bill with true reforms.[20] Moreover, during the consideration of the bill in committee, John Boehner of Ohio (a member, who was also GOP Conference chair) went so far as to say, "If this committee can't do it [make $13 billion in cuts called for in the budget plan], the future of this committee is seriously in doubt."[21] Rarely in congressional history has the majority leadership sought to dictate to and threaten a committee in so direct a fashion.

Bypassing Committees and Postcommittee Adjustments. In some instances, the Republican leadership simply bypassed committees altogether to achieve its policy and political goals. Gingrich had personally picked the chair of the Judiciary Committee, the independent-minded Henry Hyde of Illinois. Hyde was suitably responsive to the leadership and the Republican Conference during the speedy processing of a large number of bills from the Contract with America. However, the bill to repeal the 1994 ban on assault weapons, which Hyde opposed, went to the floor without committee consideration. When asked why Judiciary was not given the opportunity to consider the bill, the chairman said: "We have a reputation of being deliberative."[22]

Another device for bypassing committees was the use of leader-appointed party task forces.[23] Often, but not always, task forces had the assent of committees (or at least of their leaders), and they usually contained some members of the appropriate committees. A key difference, however, was that they contained only Republicans, and at times they were used to secure a different policy outcome than the committee of jurisdiction preferred. For example, in 1995 the Government Reform and Oversight Committee approved a bill to abolish the Commerce Department that was insufficiently radical to satisfy many of the GOP freshmen. The dissenters expressed their displeasure, and in response the leadership chose a different, more radical bill to accomplish the goal. The source of the bill was a GOP task force set up by Gingrich and chaired by a freshman. The bill had no hearings and no committee markup.[24]

The leadership could also use its control over the Rules Committee to make adjustments in the content of legislation after the committees had made their decisions. Barbara Sinclair's research shows that under the Republicans this kind of action was most frequent in the "revolutionary" 104th Congress, occurring on nearly half the major bills. But postcommittee adjustments continued to occur in later Congresses, for example, on more than one-third of the major bills in the 105th Congress.[25] One instance was the 1997 budget resolution, when Gingrich supervised adjustments to placate dissident Republicans and the White House. Another occurred in 1999, when moderate Republicans threatened to oppose the GOP tax bill because it was not sufficiently concerned with deficit reduction. Speaker Hastert brokered a change that made the tax rate cut dependent on a declining national debt.[26]

Special Rules and Control of the Floor. As we noted earlier, leaders of the majority can use their powers to support and defend the decisions of committees or to undermine them if the committees have not produced a result the party wanted. One way is through their general control of the floor agenda.

We saw that when they were in the minority, GOP members frequently attacked the Democrats for writing rules that barred them from offering amendments. As the majority in the 104th, however, they demonstrated that they were quite prepared to do the same thing. In one instance, on the recissions bill (legislation to make cuts in previously appropriated funds) taken up in March 1995, the Rules Committee wrote a rule that had the effect of blocking cutting defense spending to increase social spending. The rule prompted strong objections from a number of GOP moderates.[27]

In another example, a group of conservative Democrats wanted to offer a substitute amendment for the Republican Medicare reform plan, but the Rules Committee barred their amendment. Gene Taylor, D-Miss., said, "I am furious. . . . The Republicans came to power promising change, open rules." He charged, "They are no more fair than the Democrats."[28]

Not Everything Is Partisan

To this point we have focused our attention on the increased partisanship in Congress and on the strengthening of the influence of the party structure relative to committees. In this section we want to emphasize that one should not overinterpret these patterns. Specifically, it is important to recognize that much of Congress's business does not involve party conflict, as the data displayed in Table 1 demonstrate.[29] The table shows data from three Congresses on the proportion of bills over which there was some conflict, either in committee or on the floor. The standard for conflict was very minimal: Was there even one roll call on the bill on which

Table 1 Conflict on Legislation in the 96th, 100th, and 104th Congresses

	96th Congress (1979–1980)	100th Congress (1987–1988)	104th Congress (1995–1996)
Prestige committees	51.3% (150)	65.7% (67)	76.3% (93)
Policy committees	40.7% (317)	28.7% (394)	34.3% (376)
Constituency committees	20.8% (438)	17.8% (499)	23.8% (315)
All committees	32.8% (905)	25.6% (960)	35.1% (784)

Note: Given above are the percentages of bills considered by those committees that exhibited some conflict, either in committee or on the floor (the number of bills in each category is in parentheses). See endnote 29.

there was a minority larger than 10 percent? Despite this low threshold, however, only about one-third of the bills saw any conflict at all.

Why was there so seldom conflict on legislation, if Congress has become ever more partisan over the period covered by these data? The reason is that the agenda that Congress deals with is multifaceted and diverse, and only a portion of it deals with the types of issues that provoke interparty disagreement. The parties care intensely about bills that relate to divisions among their members, their activists, and their electoral coalitions—things such as tax policy, the scope of government, regulation of business, and social issues such as abortion and gay rights. Most legislation, however, does not tap into these divisive subjects. Much legislation involves renewal of, or funding for, existing programs with wide support in the country or Congress, or proposals for new policies with many perceived benefits. This type of bill provides all members the chance to (in David Mayhew's words) "claim credit" or "take positions" and thereby enhance their chances for reelection.[30] Because members do not run directly against one another, there is not a zero-sum relationship among them, and all members can potentially benefit from the adoption of legislation.

This relationship is readily apparent in Table 1 when we consider different types of committees.[31] The prestige committees—those most important to the party leadership—deal with more conflictual legislation in every Congress and also exhibit a systematic increase in conflict over time. The policy committees, which process most of Congress's substantive legislation, reveal an intermediate level of conflict and no systematic increase. Finally, the constituency committees—those most involved with providing electoral benefits to members—show the least amount of conflict on legislation.

Not only does the propensity for partisan disagreement vary across types of committees and from bill to bill, but it also varies within a single piece of legislation. Consider the Freedom to Farm Act that we mentioned earlier, which in 1996 sought to reform federal farm policy. Table 2 shows the results of two roll calls on that bill.[32] The first vote involved an effort to cut the peanut price support program, a typical "distributive" policy issue that had offered electorally important benefits to some members from agricultural districts. In this instance, within both the Democratic and Republican parties, the members from the agriculture committees responded quite differently from other members, being much less inclined to support the abolition of peanut supports. Differences between the parties are small, and differences within them are large.

The second vote was on the Democrats' substitute proposal, which sought to keep farm policy closer to the status quo. Here the interparty differences are great. Only one Republican supported the Democrats'

Table 2	Votes on the 1996 Freedom to Farm Act	
	Phase out peanut supports	**Democratic substitute**
Republicans		
Agriculture committees	8.8% (34)	0.0% (34)
Others	61.3% (199)	0.5% (200)
All members	53.6% (233)	0.4% (234)
Democrats		
Agriculture committees	20.0% (25)	100.0% (23)
Others	48.5% (163)	84.8% (164)
All members	44.6% (188)	86.6% (187)
All members		
Agriculture committees	13.6% (59)	40.4% (57)
Others	55.5% (362)	38.5% (364)
All members	49.6% (421)	38.7% (421)

Note: Given above are the percentages of members voting "aye" on the two votes (the number of members is in parentheses). "Agriculture committees" means representatives who are on either the Committee on Agriculture or on the Appropriations Subcommittee on Agriculture and Rural Development. "Others" includes all other members.

proposal, but 86 percent of the Democrats did. Moreover, the voting of committee members is virtually the same as that of members not on the committees. Thus some issues can provoke partisan responses while others do not, even within a single bill.

Senate Contrasts

Committees are less central to the work of the Senate than of the House because of a number of institutional differences between the two chambers.

First, the Senate must deal with essentially the same legislative jurisdiction with less than one-fourth the number of members. Senators are therefore spread more thinly and are less specialized. For example, in 2001 senators served on an average of 3.3 standing committees and 8.9 subcommittees; the corresponding numbers for representatives were 1.9 and 3.9. On the other hand, only about half of House members are the chair or ranking minority member of a committee or subcommittee, whereas most senators are, giving them an institutional power base on which to focus.[33]

The Senate's rules and traditions also vest more power in individuals and small groups than those of the House. The most familiar manifestation of this is the ability of a minority to block passage of legislation through filibuster, but there are many other aspects of the institution that reinforce individual power to delay or block Senate action. The House is a "majoritarian" institution, in which the majority can work its will with even one more vote than the minority, but in the Senate the majority must usually pay attention to at least some minority views to achieve any results.

Another major difference is the role of the House Rules Committee that we discussed earlier. Through special rules, the majority party can decide which amendments, if any, may be considered on the floor. Moreover, regular House rules require that amendments be germane. In the Senate, neither of these conditions holds. Usually the only way to limit amendments is if senators *unanimously* consent to do so, and amendments need not be germane. Thus the Senate floor plays a much larger role in shaping the content of legislative outcomes than does the House floor, and it is much easier for senators who do not serve on the committee with jurisdiction to have an impact.

As a result of these differences, both Senate committees and Senate parties have been institutionally weaker than their House counterparts, and individual senators have been more consequential. Furthermore, because the majority party leadership usually has had to deal with some members of the minority, partisan conflict in the Senate has tended to be less frequent and less vitriolic. Nevertheless, over the last couple of decades party conflict has intensified in the Senate as well.[34] We have already considered some of the similarities and differences between the House and Senate over appropriations. As another example, in 1995 the new GOP majority adopted some rules to enhance party influence in the Senate. As in the House, six-year term limits were imposed on committee chairs. Chairs were to be chosen by successive, secret ballot votes, first among Republican committee members, then in the whole GOP Conference. Moreover, on some aspects of the Senate's business partisan conflict was as vigorous as any seen in the House. The prime example was confirmation of judicial nominations, in which only the Senate has a role. Democrats used the power of the filibuster to block nominations by President George W. Bush that they regarded as unacceptable, while frustrated Republicans railed against their actions. . . .

The House Under Speakers Hastert and Pelosi

We developed the theory of conditional party government to explain the ebb and flow of party influence in Congress over time. We have argued that as the policy preferences of party members become more homogeneous, and as the ideological centers of gravity of the two parties become more divergent, rank-and-file members will be progressively more willing to delegate strong powers to their leaders to advance the party's program and to benefit it electorally. In this chapter we described how the relationship between the party organizations in Congress and the committee systems changed, arguing that the changes were in accord with the expectations of CPG, especially after the Republican takeover in 1994. Although most observers found the arguments and evidence persuasive with respect to the Gingrich Congresses, some also raised the reasonable question of whether CPG would continue to account for congressional organization and policy making.[35] In this concluding section, we

address that issue by discussing developments in Congress in the last decade, during the speakerships of Dennis Hastert and Nancy Pelosi.

CPG theory has a number of key features that we have to account for to demonstrate continued applicability: (1) Have intraparty homogeneity and interparty divergence remained high? (2) If so, has the majority party in particular continued to delegate strong powers to its leadership? and (3) Has the majority leadership continued to exercise its powers to facilitate achievement of the party's legislative and electoral goals?

With regard to the first question, the data are unequivocal. All research on the subject shows that the polarization of the parties continues.[36] The median positions of the parties on roll call measures have even been a bit farther apart during the last ten years than they were in the 104th Congress. Moreover, the proportion of Congress that takes positions in the middle of the ideological spectrum is smaller than ever. This evidence indicates that the underlying "condition" for CPG is still well satisfied. We will now consider the other two features of the argument separately for the periods of Gingrich's two successors, as each provides a separate opportunity to test the predictions of CPG against data based on new members, leaders, and circumstances.

Hastert's Speakership

The selection of Dennis Hastert, R-Ill., as Speaker provided a strong challenge for CPG theory because on taking office he promised that regular procedures would be restored. However, with regard to the willingness of members to delegate power to party leaders, none of the significant authority granted to the Republican House leadership was rescinded. To the contrary, Hastert sought and was granted additional power. For example, in late 2002 Hastert asked the GOP conference to give him and the party even more influence over the Appropriations Committee by requiring that the chairs of its subcommittees be approved by the party Steering Committee.[37] In addition the Speaker arranged to give the Steering Committee the right to approve full committee chairs. In 2001 and 2003, under Hastert's leadership, the committee bypassed a number of more senior and more moderate members to pick more junior and more conservative candidates for chairmanships. For example, Chris Shays of Connecticut, who had joined with Democrats against his party leaders in the successful fight for campaign finance reform legislation, was passed over for chair of the Government Reform Committee (where he was most senior) in favor of Tom Davis of Virginia, who had served on the committee only half as long. And in 2005, in perhaps the strongest use of leadership power against a committee chairman in a century, Chris Smith of New Jersey was removed from the top spot on Veterans Affairs because of his persistent efforts to increase spending on veterans programs. The leadership had warned Smith to be more compliant with their priorities or risk punishment.[38] When he continued, the threats were fulfilled.

Moreover, regarding the continued exercise of leadership powers, Hastert and his colleagues showed that they were more than willing to manipulate the legislative process for majority party advantage. For example, Hastert and then-Senate majority leader Bill Frist, R-Tenn., presented a compromise that they had negotiated on the Medicare bill in late 2003, and Hastert pressured Ways and Means Committee chair Bill Thomas of California to accept it against his will.[39] Around the same time, majority leader Tom DeLay of Texas gave the Armed Services Committee chair an ultimatum to pass the defense authorization bill within two days, or else the leadership would strip out a popular provision and send it to the floor alone.[40]

Thus the Republican leadership continued to pressure and influence committees' actions. They also continued to use the tools at their disposal to structure the floor agenda and actions taken after bills are passed. Despite Hastert's promise to restore the use of regular procedures, the GOP continued to use restrictive special rules to block the Democrats from offering many of their preferred amendments. David Dreier, R-Calif., noted as chair of the Rules Committee that he used to complain about Democrats' use of special rules but that he learned "pretty quickly" that the majority party needed to use that device. "'I had not known what it took to govern,' he acknowledged. Now 'our number one priority is to move our agenda.'"[41] Indeed, Don Wolfensberger, former head of the Republican staff on the Rules Committee, concluded, "By the 107th Congress (2001–2003) . . . the Republicans had far exceeded the Democrats' worst excesses in restricting floor amendments."[42]

The GOP leadership in both chambers at times restricted minority members from participation in the deliberations of conference committees. (These are temporary panels set up to resolve differences in legislation after bills have been passed by both houses.) For example, in 2003 only two moderate Democratic senators and no House Democrats were permitted to participate in the conference on the Medicare bill, and on the energy bill no Democrats at all were permitted in conference meetings. In using all of these techniques, the Republicans denied that they were being unfair to the Democrats. They contended that they were just doing what was necessary to enact their legislative agenda. As Speaker Hastert said in an interview in late 2003, "While a Speaker should strive to be fair, he is also judged by how he gets the job done. The job of the Speaker is to rule fairly, but ultimately to carry out the will of the majority."[43]

Pelosi's Speakership

The transition to Democratic rule after the elections of 2006 offered another opportunity to assess the predictions of CPG theory, especially the expectation that while polarization continued, the House Democrats could be expected to delegate strong powers to their leadership. The rules package for the 110th Congress that Speaker Nancy Pelosi, Calif., and her allies drafted and submitted confirmed the accuracy of that expectation. The package included all the main leadership powers that the Democrats exercised the last time they were the majority, plus some new ones from the era of Republican control. The most striking of these was Pelosi's decision to retain the six-year term limit for committee chairs. Moreover, she did not even inform senior Democrats of this decision until shortly before the vote on the new rules. Many of them objected (including John Dingell, the incoming chair of the Energy and Commerce Committee, who said, "I think it's dumb"), but all party members including Dingell voted for the provisions.

CPG theory would also lead us to expect the vigorous exercise of leadership powers on behalf of the party's program in the new Congress, with the support of the vast majority of Democratic representatives. This expectation is also borne out. Pelosi selected six bills—all high priorities for the party—to be considered in the first one hundred hours of legislative business. These bills bypassed committee consideration and were put together without GOP input. All were considered under closed or restrictive rules, so that Republicans were blocked from offering amendments. The Democrats successfully completed consideration of all six well before the hundred-hour deadline.

Of course the Democratic Party is not so homogeneous that it lacks any recalcitrant members. John Dingell was one, and his committee had jurisdiction over one of the Democrats' priority issues for the new Congress: the energy bill. Seeking to return processes to the regular order of the past, Dingell proceeded to construct a bill according to his own lights, and his committee's draft included two significant provisions that were at odds with leadership priorities: They were an attempt to preempt states from regulating greenhouse gases from automobiles and a provision to override a recent Supreme Court decision confirming the authority of the Environmental Protection Agency to act to combat global warming.[44]

Pelosi called Dingell and some other members of the Energy Committee to a meeting in her office with the leadership. There she demanded that Dingell remove the two provisions from the draft bill. After some negotiations, Dingell agreed to comply.[45] Rep. Henry Waxman, D-Calif., chairman of the Energy Committee's Oversight Subcommittee, who attended the meeting, later said, "I have never seen a speaker take such an active and forceful role on policy. . . . [Former Speakers] Tip O'Neill or Tom Foley would not have told John Dingell or Dan Rostenkowski [a former Ways and Means chair] not to report out a bill, or what kind of bill to report out of committee. . . . [Dingell] was shocked by her action."[46] Pelosi also succeeded in other conflicts with Dingell, including the creation of a select committee on global warming and pushing through a floor amendment to the energy bill on renewable energy standards, over the chairman's objections.[47]

Despite these conflicts, it should be clear from our earlier discussion that CPG theory does not anticipate that the general relationship between the leadership and the committee chairs would necessarily be confrontational. Just as the Speaker is the top agent of the party caucus, chairs are agents too in the current era, of both the party and the leadership. Party leaders would prefer that they be faithful agents who can be trusted to pursue shared goals on their own. Leaders must also, however, be able to monitor activity and constrain chairs if they stray. That occurred in the 2007 interactions over energy policy. As majority leader Steny Hoyer, D-Md., put it, "There is a necessity for a unity of voice and purpose in the Democratic Party . . . and the only way you're going to do that was to have a central management to create consensus, not simply individual discrete committee agendas."[48] But as Barney Frank, D-Mass., chairman of the Financial Services Committee, said, "This is not a zero-sum game. . . . It's a mutually supportive relationship."[49]

Pelosi also repeatedly demonstrated her willingness to employ control of the floor agenda through special rules to give preference to party priorities. As was the case with the six bills with which the Democrats opened the Congress, special rules that restricted or prohibited amendments were applied to the overwhelming majority of bills that came to the floor during 2007. These rules were drafted at the direction of the Democratic leadership, and partisan conflict over procedural arrangements reached unprecedented levels. In the 100th Congress, when there were substantial efforts at procedural manipulation under the direction of Speaker Wright, 90 percent of the Democrats opposed 90 percent of the Republicans on only 18 percent of the floor votes on special rules. In the 104th Congress, the first with Newt Gingrich as Speaker, that proportion increased to 58 percent. In the first session of the 110th Congress, however, fully 99 percent of the special rules votes saw this degree of party conflict![50]

Another development in this Congress regarding the Rules Committee is a remarkable and telling indicator of how much the relationship between parties and committees has changed since the prereform era. Before 1974, when the Speaker regained the right to appoint the majority members and the chair of the Rules Committee, the committee was an independent center of power, and many members desired appointment to it so that they could exercise influence within the House. Virtually all appointees to Rules had to serve a number of terms in office before they could secure a place. Moreover, the committee was deemed so important and desirable that it was designated an "exclusive" committee—a member of it could serve on no other standing committee. In 2007, however, when the Democrats had to appoint five new members because they had regained majority status, four of the five were freshmen. The exclusive designation was removed, and Rules Committee members were given additional committee assignments as well. Having lost its independent power, Rules was no longer as important or desirable a post. It was merely an extension of the majority party leadership.

Control over special rules is not the only procedural advantage the majority leadership can bring to bear on behalf of its party. For example, in April 2008 President Bush sought approval for a trade agreement that his administration had negotiated with Colombia. He expected that a vote would take place within sixty legislative days because of the stipulation in congressional rules known as "fast-track,"

giving such measures priority.[51] Bush knew that there was opposition to the agreement among some Democrats, but he judged that the short time frame and the oncoming election would exert pressure on Congress to comply with his wishes. Democrats, on the other hand, had been trying to persuade the administration to take some additional action to help economically distressed Americans before they addressed the trade deal. Speaker Pelosi responded to the Bush stratagem by bringing to the House floor a rules change that stripped fast-track procedures from this trade agreement. The change, which puts off a vote until the Speaker decides the time is right, secured the support of all but ten Democrats.

Moreover, the new Republican minority has sought to use its limited capabilities to encourage solidarity among its members and to compete with the majority. For example, Rep. Walter Jones, R-N.C., a generally conservative member who nonetheless had become a vigorous opponent of the war in Iraq, was passed over twice during the 110th Congress for the top minority position on a subcommittee of the Armed Services Committee because of his deviation from party orthodoxy.[52] Also, Jeff Flake, R-Ariz., another conservative who frequently disagreed with his party leaders in the previous Congress about their support for too much spending, was removed from his place on the Judiciary Committee. The minority leader, John Boehner, R-Ohio, later informed him that the action was taken because of Flake's verbal attacks on party leaders.[53]

Thus all indications are that the theoretical account offered by CPG is as applicable in 2008 as it was in 1995. Partisan policy disagreement is at least as strong and partisan conflict just as intense. Indeed, these conditions continue to be reinforced by the close division of the two chambers. In every election since 1994, members of both parties have believed that they had a good chance to win majority control. That perception makes every decision on policy and legislative strategy potentially a high-stakes choice, giving the majority party strong incentive to use its institutional powers to the maximum. Therefore, as long as the legislative parties remain ideologically homogeneous and the ideological divergence between the two parties remains great, and as long as the partisan division of the chambers is close, we expect conditional party government theory to continue to provide a good explanation for congressional organization and activity.

Notes

1. This interest in developing and sharing expertise is the central focus in the "informational" theory of legislative organization presented by Keith Krehbiel in *Information and Legislative Organization* (Chicago: University of Chicago Press, 1991).
2. Richard F. Fenno Jr., *Congressmen in Committees* (Boston: Little Brown, 1973), chap. 1.
3. Indeed, David Mayhew contended that the institutional structure of the Congress was principally designed to foster members' reelection. See David R. Mayhew, *Congress: The Electoral Connection* (New Haven: Yale University Press, 1974). Also see E. Scott Adler, *Why Congressional Reforms Fail: Reelection and the House Committee System* (Chicago: University of Chicago Press, 2002).
4. See Richard C. Hall, *Participation in Congress* (New Haven: Yale University Press, 1996); and C. Lawrence Evans, *Leadership in Committee* (Ann Arbor: University of Michigan Press, 2001).
5. For more information on the history of the committee system, see Joseph Cooper, *The Origins of the Standing Committees and the Development of the Modern House* (Houston: Rice University Studies, 1970); and Christopher J. Deering and Steven S. Smith, *Committees in Congress,* 3rd ed. (Washington, D.C.: CQ Press, 1997).
6. For a detailed analysis of the growth of amending activity on the floors of both chambers see Steven S. Smith, *Call to Order: Floor Politics in the House and Senate* (Washington, D.C.: Brookings Institution Press, 1989).
7. For more details, see David W. Rohde, *Parties and Leaders in the Postreform House* (Chicago: University of Chicago Press, 1991), chap. 3.
8. See Rohde, *Parties and Leaders,* chap. 2; and John H. Aldrich, *Why Parties? The Origin and Transformation of Political Parties in America* (Chicago: University of Chicago Press, 1995), chaps. 6 and 7. An alternative (but compatible) theory of partisan organization of Congress is offered by Gary W. Cox and Mathew D. McCubbins, *Legislative Leviathan* (Berkeley: University of California Press, 1993).
9. Sara Brandes Crook and John R. Hibbing, "Congressional Reform and Party Discipline: The Effects of Changes in the Seniority System on Party Loyalty in the House of Representatives," *British Journal of Political Science* 15 (1985): 207–226. See also Fiona M. Wright, "The Caucus Reelection Requirement and the Transformation of Committee Chairs," *Legislative Studies Quarterly* 25 (2000): 469–480.
10. See Rohde, *Parties and Leaders,* 75–76.
11. Barbara Sinclair, *Legislators, Leaders, and Lawmaking: The U.S. House of Representatives in the Postreform Era* (Baltimore: Johns Hopkins University Press, 1995), 164.
12. For more details on this transformed relationship see Sinclair, *Legislators, Leaders, and Lawmaking,* chap. 9; and Rohde, *Parties and Leaders,* chap. 4.
13. Much has been written about the new role of the Rules Committee. See, for example, Bruce I. Oppenheimer, "The Rules Committee: New Arm of Leadership in a Decentralized House," in *Congress Reconsidered,* ed. Lawrence C. Dodd and Bruce I. Oppenheimer (New York: Praeger, 1977), 96–116; Stanley Bach and Steven S. Smith, *Managing Uncertainty in the House of Representatives* (Washington, D.C.: Brookings Institution Press, 1988); Sinclair, *Legislators, Leaders, and Lawmaking,* chap. 8; and Rohde, *Parties and Leaders,* 98–118.
14. See Gary C. Jacobson, *The Politics of Congressional Elections,* 5th ed. (New York: Longman, 2001), 178–185.
15. The discussion in this section is drawn from John H. Aldrich and David W. Rohde, "The Transition to Republican Rule in the House: Implications for Theories of Congressional Politics," *Political Science Quarterly* 112 (1997–1998): 541–567; and C. Lawrence Evans and Walter J. Oleszek, *Congress under Fire: Reform Politics and the Republican Majority* (Boston: Houghton Mifflin, 1997).

16. Quoted in Guy Gugliotta, "In New House, Barons Yield to the Boss," *Washington Post,* December 1, 1994, 1.

17. See Adler, *Why Congressional Reforms Fail.*

18. Sinclair, *Legislators, Leaders, and Lawmaking,* 163–197.

19. For more detail on the contract and Congress's actions on it, see James G. Gimpel, *Fulfilling the Contract: The First 100 Days* (Boston: Allyn and Bacon, 1996).

20. *Washington Post,* October 8, 1995, A5.

21. *Roll Call,* October 2, 1995, 20.

22. *Washington Post,* March 26, 1996, A9.

23. Task forces had been used before the GOP majority took over. See Sinclair, *Legislators, Leaders, and Lawmaking.* For more recent details on task force use, see Barbara Sinclair, *Unorthodox Lawmaking: New Legislative Processes in the U.S. Congress,* 2nd ed. (Washington, D.C.: CQ Press, 2000).

24. See *CQ Weekly,* September 23, 1995, 2886; *Roll Call,* October 12, 1995, 3. For more systematic analysis of bypassing committees, see Charles J. Finocchiaro, "Setting the Stage: Party and Procedure in the Pre-Floor Agenda Setting of the U.S. House," PhD diss., Michigan State University, 2003; and Sinclair, *Unorthodox Lawmaking.*

25. Sinclair, *Unorthodox Lawmaking,* 94.

26. Ibid., 211 and 20, respectively.

27. *Roll Call,* March 20, 1995, 18.

28. *Congressional Quarterly Weekly Report,* October 21, 1995, 3207.

29. The data are adapted from Tables 1–4 in Jamie L. Carson, Charles J. Finocchiaro, and David W. Rohde, "Consensus and Conflict in House Decision Making: A Bill-Level Examination of Committee and Floor Behavior," paper delivered at the annual meeting of the Midwest Political Science Association, Chicago, April 2001. The data include all public bills and joint resolutions referred to a committee and either reported by the committee or debated on the floor.

30. See Mayhew, *Congress: The Electoral Connection,* 52–73.

31. The classification was developed by Deering and Smith, *Committees in Congress,* 3rd ed., chap. 3. The prestige committees are Appropriations and Ways and Means; the policy committees are Banking, Commerce, Education, Foreign Affairs, Government Operations, and Judiciary; the constituency committees are Agriculture, Armed Services, Interior, Merchant Marine, Science, Transportation, and Veterans Affairs. (Committee names change over time. These are the names for the 96th Congress.) The committees that the authors term "unrequested" are omitted, as are Rules and Budget because they consider few bills. Note that bills referred to more than one committee are counted for each committee to which they were referred.

32. These data are taken from Mark S. Hurwitz, Roger J. Moiles, and David W. Rohde, "Distributive and Partisan Issues in Agriculture Policy in the 104th House," *American Political Science Review* 95 (2001): 915.

33. The dominant role of Senate subcommittee chairs is discussed in C. Lawrence Evans, *Leadership in Committee: A Comparative Analysis of Leadership Behavior in the U.S. Senate* (Ann Arbor: University of Michigan Press, 2001).

34. For discussions of various ways in which parties can be consequential in the Senate, see *Why Not Parties? Party Effects in the United States Senate,* ed. Nathan W. Monroe, Jason M. Roberts, and David W. Rohde (Chicago: University of Chicago Press, 2008).

35. See, for example, Lawrence C. Dodd and Bruce I. Oppenheimer, "Congress and the Emerging Order: Conditional Party Government or Constructive Partisanship?" in *Congress Reconsidered,* 6th ed., ed. Lawrence C. Dodd and Bruce I. Oppenheimer (Washington, D.C.: CQ Press, 1997), 390–413.

36. See, for example, Richard Fleisher and Jon R. Bond, "The Shrinking Middle in the U.S. Congress," *British Journal of Political Science* 34 (July 2004): 429–451; and Sean Theriault, "The Case of the Vanishing Moderates: Party Polarization in the Modern Congress," manuscript, University of Texas, 2004.

37. Remember that the Steering Committee is weighted toward leadership influence. See *Roll Call,* November 18, 2002, 1.

38. *CQ Weekly,* July 26, 2003, 1910.

39. *Washington Post,* November 30, 2003, A8.

40. *CQ Weekly,* November 8, 2003, 2785.

41. Jim VandeHei, "Using the Rules Committee to Block Democrats," *Washington Post,* June 16, 2003, A21.

42. Don Wolfensberger, "The Motion to Recommit in the House: The Creation, Evisceration, and Restoration of a Minority Right," paper prepared for the Conference on the History of Congress, Stanford University, December 5–6, 2003, 31.

43. *Roll Call,* November 17, 2003, 4.

44. See Richard E. Cohen, "Power Surge," *National Journal,* July 21, 2007, 23.

45. *The Hill,* June 19, 2007, 3.

46. Quoted in Cohen, "Power Surge," 22.

47. *The Hill,* February 6, 2007, 1. Pelosi did, however, agree to Dingell's request that the select committee would not have any legislative jurisdiction.

48. Quoted in *Washington Post,* July 9, 2007, A4.

49. Quoted in *Roll Call,* November 5, 2007, 22.

50. The data on the 100th and 104th Congresses come from the PIPC House roll call database ("Roll Call Voting Data for the United States House of Representatives, 1953–2004," compiled by the Political Institutions and Public Choice Program, Michigan State University). The data are available from Michael Crespin's Web site, http://crespin .myweb.uga.edu. The data on the 110th Congress were compiled for this essay.

51. Fast-track legislation had expired in July 2007, but since the Colombia agreement was negotiated before expiration, the rules continued to apply to it.

52. See *The Hill,* October 16, 2007, 3.

53. See Robert D. Novak, "Bad Behavior?" January 13, 2007, at http://townhall.com.

Chapter 7

The Presidency

7-1 From *Presidential Power*

Richard E. Neustadt

In his classic treatise Presidential Power, *Richard E. Neustadt presents a problem that confronts every occupant of the White House: His authority does not match the expectations for his performance. We expect our presidents to be leaders, Neustadt tells us, but the office guarantees no more than that they will be clerks. In the following excerpt, Neustadt explains that the key to presidential success lies in persuasion and shows how the ability to persuade depends on bargaining.*

The limits on command suggest the structure of our government. The Constitutional Convention of 1787 is supposed to have created a government of "separated powers." It did nothing of the sort. Rather, it created a government of separated institutions *sharing* powers.[1] "I am part of the legislative process," Eisenhower often said in 1959 as a reminder of his veto.[2] Congress, the dispenser of authority and funds, is no less part of the administrative process. Federalism adds another set of separated institutions. The Bill of Rights adds others. Many public purposes can only be achieved by voluntary acts of private institutions; the press, for one, in Douglass Cater's phrase, is a "fourth branch of government."[3] And with the coming of alliances abroad, the separate institutions of a London, or a Bonn, share in the making of American public policy.

What the Constitution separates our political parties do not combine. The parties are themselves composed of separated organizations sharing public authority. The authority consists of nominating powers. Our national parties are confederations of state and local party institutions, with a headquarters that represents the White House, more or less, if the party has a President in office. These confederacies manage presidential nominations. All other public offices depend upon electorates confined within the states.[4] All other nominations are controlled within the states. The President and congressmen who bear one party's label are divided by dependence upon different sets of voters. The differences are sharpest at the stage of nomination. The White House has too small a share in nominating congressmen, and Congress has too little weight in nominating presidents for party to erase their constitutional separation. Party links are stronger than is frequently supposed, but nominating processes assure the separation.[5]

The separateness of institutions and the sharing of authority prescribe the terms on which a President persuades. When one man shares authority with another, but does not gain or lose his job upon the other's whim, his willingness to act upon the urging of the other turns on whether he conceives the action right for him. The essence of a President's persuasive

Source: Reprinted with the permission of Simon & Schuster Publishing Group from the Free Press edition of *Presidential Power and the Modern Presidents: The Politics of Leadership from Roosevelt to Reagan* by Richard E. Neustadt. Copyright © 1990 by Richard E. Neustadt. All Rights Reserved.

task is to convince such men that what the White House wants of them is what they ought to do for their sake and on their authority. (Sex matters not at all; for *man* read *woman*.)

Persuasive power, thus defined, amounts to more than charm or reasoned argument. These have their uses for a President, but these are not the whole of his resources. For the individuals he would induce to do what he wants done on their own responsibility will need or fear some acts by him on his responsibility. If they share his authority, he has some share in theirs. Presidential "powers" may be inconclusive when a President commands, but always remain relevant as he persuades. The status and authority inherent in his office reinforce his logic and his charm.

Status adds something to persuasiveness; authority adds still more. When Truman urged wage changes on his secretary of commerce [Charles Sawyer] while the latter was administering the [recently seized] steel mills, he and Secretary Sawyer were not just two men reasoning with one another. Had they been so, Sawyer probably would never have agreed to act. Truman's status gave him special claims to Sawyer's loyalty or at least attention. In Walter Bagehot's charming phrase, "no man can *argue* on his knees." Although there is no kneeling in this country, few men—and exceedingly few cabinet officers—are immune to the impulse to say "yes" to the President of the United States. It grows harder to say "no" when they are seated in his Oval Office at the White House, or in his study on the second floor, where almost tangibly he partakes of the aura of his physical surroundings. In Sawyer's case, moreover, the President possessed formal authority to intervene in many matters of concern to the secretary of commerce. These matters ranged from jurisdictional disputes among the defense agencies to legislation pending before Congress and, ultimately, to the tenure of the secretary, himself. There is nothing in the record to suggest that Truman voiced specific threats when they negotiated over wage increases. But given his formal powers and their relevance to Sawyer's other interests, it is safe to assume that Truman's very advocacy of wage action conveyed an implicit threat.

A President's authority and status give him great advantages in dealing with the men he would persuade. Each "power" is a vantage point for him in the degree that other men have use for his authority. From the veto to appointments, from publicity to budgeting, and so down a long list, the White House now controls the most encompassing array of vantage points in the American political system. With hardly an exception, those who share in governing this country are aware that at some time, in some degree, the doing of *their* jobs, the furthering of *their* ambitions, may depend upon the President of the United States. Their need for presidential action, or their fear of it, is bound to be recurrent if not actually continuous. Their need or fear is his advantage.

A President's advantages are greater than mere listing of his "powers" might suggest. Those with whom he deals must deal with him until the last day of his term. Because they have continuing relationships with him, his future, while it lasts, supports his present influence. Even though there is no need or fear of him today, what he could do tomorrow may supply today's advantage. Continuing relationships may convert any "power," any aspect of his status, into vantage points in almost any case. When he induces other people to do what he wants done, a President can trade on their dependence now and later.

The President's advantages are checked by the advantages of others. Continuing relationships will pull in both directions. These are relationships of mutual dependence. A President depends upon the persons whom he would persuade; he has to reckon with his need or fear of them. They too will possess status or authority, or both, else they would be of little use to him. Their vantage points confront his own; their power tempers his.

Persuasion is a two-way street. Sawyer, it will be recalled, did not respond at once to Truman's plan for wage increases at the steel mills. On the contrary, the secretary hesitated and delayed and only acquiesced when he was satisfied that publicly he would not bear the onus of decision. Sawyer had some points of vantage all his own from which to resist presidential pressure. If he had to reckon with coercive implications in the President's "situations of strength," so had Truman to be mindful of the implications underlying Sawyer's place as a department head, as steel administrator, and as a cabinet spokesman for business. Loyalty is reciprocal. Having taken on a dirty job in the steel crisis, Sawyer had strong claims to loyal support. Besides, he had authority to do some things that the White House could ill afford. . . . [H]e might have resigned in a huff (the removal power also works two ways). Or . . . he might have declined to sign necessary orders. Or he might have let it be known publicly that he deplored what he was told to do and protested its doing. By following any of these courses Sawyer almost surely would have strengthened the position of management, weakened the position of the White House, and embittered the union. But the whole purpose of a wage increase was to enhance White House persuasiveness in urging settlement upon union and companies alike. Although Sawyer's status and authority did not give him the power to prevent an increase outright, they gave him capability to undermine its purpose. If his authority over wage rates had been vested by a statute, not by revocable presidential order, his power of prevention might have been complete. So Harold Ickes [Sr.] demonstrated in the famous case of helium sales to Germany before the Second World War.[6]

The power to persuade is the power to bargain. Status and authority yield bargaining advantages. But in a government of "separated institutions sharing power," they yield them to all sides. With the array of vantage points at his disposal, a President may be far more persuasive than his logic or his charm could make him. But outcomes are not guaranteed by his advantages. There remain the counter pressures those whom he would influence can bring to bear on him from vantage points at their disposal. Command has limited utility; persuasion becomes give-and-take. It is well that the White House holds the vantage points it does. In such a business any President may need them all—and more.

This View of Power as akin to bargaining is one we commonly accept in the sphere of congressional relations. Every textbook states and every legislative session demonstrates that save in times like the extraordinary Hundred Days of 1933—times virtually ruled out by definition at mid-century—a President will often be unable to obtain congressional action on his terms or even to halt action he opposes. The reverse is equally accepted: Congress often is frustrated by the President. Their formal powers are so intertwined that neither will accomplish very much, for very long, without the acquiescence of the other. By the same token, though, what one demands the other can resist. The stage is set for that great game, much like collective bargaining, in which each seeks to profit from the other's needs and fears. It is a game played catch-as-catch-can, case by case. And everybody knows the game, observers and participants alike.

The concept of real power as a give-and-take is equally familiar when applied to presidential influence outside the formal structure of the federal government. . . . When he deals with [governors, union officials, company executives and even citizens or workers] a President draws bargaining advantage from his status or authority. By virtue of their public places or their private rights they have some capability to reply in kind.

In spheres of party politics the same thing follows, necessarily, from the confederal nature of our party organizations. Even in the case of national nominations a President's advantages are checked by those of others. In 1944 it is by no means clear that Roosevelt got his first choice as his running mate. In 1948 Truman, then the President, faced serious revolts against his nomination. In 1952 his intervention from the White House helped assure the choice of Adlai Stevenson, but it is far from clear that Truman could have done as much for any other candidate acceptable to him.[7] In 1956 when Eisenhower was President, the record leaves obscure just who backed Harold Stassen's efforts to block Richard Nixon from renomination as vice president. But evidently everything did not go quite as Eisenhower wanted, whatever his intentions may have been.[8] The outcomes in these instances bear all the marks of limits on command and of power checked by power that characterize congressional relations. Both in and out of politics these checks and limits seem to be quite widely understood.

Influence becomes still more a matter of give-and-take when Presidents attempt to deal with allied governments. A classic illustration is the long unhappy wrangle over Suez policy in 1956. In dealing with the British and the French before their military intervention, Eisenhower had his share of bargaining advantages but no effective power of command. His allies had their share of counterpressures, and they finally tried the most extreme of all: action despite him. His pressure then was instrumental in reversing them. But had the British government been on safe ground at home, Eisenhower's wishes might have made as little difference after intervention as before. Behind the decorum of diplomacy—which was not very decorous in the Suez affair—relationships among allies are not unlike relationships among state delegations at a national convention. Power is persuasion, and persuasion becomes bargaining. The concept is familiar to everyone who watches foreign policy.

In only one sphere is the concept unfamiliar: the sphere of executive relations. Perhaps because of civics textbooks and teaching in our schools, Americans instinctively resist the view that power in this sphere resembles power in all others. Even Washington reporters, White House aides, and congressmen are not immune to the illusion that administrative agencies comprise a single structure, "the" executive branch, where presidential word is law, or ought to be. Yet . . . when a President seeks something from executive officials his persuasiveness is subject to the same sorts of limitations as in the case of congressmen, or governors, or national committeemen, or private citizens, or foreign governments. There are no generic differences, no differences in kind and only sometimes in degree. The incidents preceding the dismissal of [General Douglas] MacArthur and the incidents surrounding seizure of the steel mills make it plain that here as elsewhere influence derives from bargaining advantages; power is a give-and-take.

Like our governmental structure as a whole, the executive establishment consists of separated institutions sharing powers. The President heads one of these; cabinet officers, agency administrators, and military commanders head others. Below the departmental level, virtually independent bureau chiefs head many more. Under mid-century conditions, federal operations spill across dividing lines on organization charts; almost every policy entangles many agencies; almost every program calls for interagency collaboration. Everything somehow involves the President. But operating agencies owe their existence least of all to one another—and only in some part to him. Each has a separate statutory base; each has its statutes to administer; each deals with a different set of subcommittees at the Capitol. Each has its own peculiar set of clients, friends, and enemies outside the formal government. Each has a different set of specialized careerists inside its own bailiwick. Our Constitution gives the President the "take-care" clause and the appointive power. Our statutes give him central budgeting and a degree of personnel control. All agency administrators are responsible to him. But they also are responsible to Congress, to their clients, to their staffs, and to themselves. In short, they have five masters. Only after all of those do they owe any loyalty to each other.

"The members of the cabinet," Charles G. Dawes used to remark, "are a president's natural enemies." Dawes had been Harding's budget director, Coolidge's vice president, and Hoover's ambassador to London; he also had been General Pershing's chief assistant for supply in World War I. The words are highly colored, but Dawes knew whereof he spoke. The men who have to serve so many masters cannot help but be somewhat the "enemy" of any one of them. By the same token, any master wanting service is in some degree the "enemy" of such a servant. A President is likely to want loyal support but not to relish trouble on his doorstep. Yet the more his cabinet members cleave to him, the more they may need help from him in fending off the wrath of rival masters.

Help, though, is synonymous with trouble. Many a cabinet officer, with loyalty ill rewarded by his lights and help withheld, has come to view the White House as innately hostile to department heads. Dawes's dictum can be turned around.

A senior presidential aide remarked to me in Eisenhower's time: "If some of these cabinet members would just take time out to stop and ask themselves, 'What would I want if I were President?' they wouldn't give him all the trouble he's been having." But even if they asked themselves the question, such officials often could not act upon the answer. Their personal attachment to the President is all too often overwhelmed by duty to their other masters.

Executive officials are not equally advantaged in their dealings with a President. Nor are the same officials equally advantaged all the time. Not every officeholder can resist like a MacArthur or Sawyer. . . . The vantage points conferred upon officials by their own authority and status vary enormously. The variance is heightened by particulars of time and circumstance. In mid-October 1950, Truman, at a press conference, remarked of the man he had considered firing in August and would fire the next April for intolerable insubordination:

> Let me tell you something that will be good for your souls. It's a pity that you . . . can't understand the ideas of two intellectually honest men when they meet. General MacArthur . . . is a member of the Government of the United States. He is loyal to that Government. He is loyal to the President. He is loyal to the President in his foreign policy. . . . There is no disagreement between General MacArthur and myself.[9]

MacArthur's status in and out of government was never higher than when Truman spoke those words. The words, once spoken, added to the general's credibility thereafter when he sought to use the press in his campaign against the President. And what had happened between August and October? Near victory had happened, together with that premature conference on postwar plans, the meeting at Wake Island.

If the bargaining advantages of a MacArthur fluctuate with changing circumstances, this is bound to be so with subordinates who have at their disposal fewer powers, lesser status, to fall back on. And when officials have no powers in their own right, or depend upon the President for status, their counterpressure may be limited indeed. White House aides, who fit both categories, are among the most responsive men of all, and for good reason. As a director of the budget once remarked to me, "Thank God I'm here and not across the street. If the President doesn't call me, I've got plenty I can do right here and plenty coming up to me, by rights, to justify my calling him. But those poor fellows over there, if the boss doesn't call them, doesn't ask them to do something, what *can* they do but sit?" Authority and status so conditional are frail reliances in resisting a President's own wants. Within the White House precincts, lifted eyebrows may suffice to set an aide in motion; command, coercion, even charm aside. But even in the White House a President does not monopolize effective power. Even there persuasion is akin to bargaining. A former Roosevelt aide once wrote of cabinet officers:

> Half of a President's suggestions, which theoretically carry the weight of orders, can be safely forgotten by a Cabinet member. And if the President asks about a suggestion a second time, he can be told that it is being investigated. If he asks a third time, a wise Cabinet officer will give him at least part of what he suggests. But only occasionally, except about the most important matters, do Presidents ever get around to asking three times.[10]

The rule applies to staff as well as to the cabinet, and certainly has been applied *by* staff in Truman's time and Eisenhower's.

Some aides will have more vantage points than a selective memory. Sherman Adams, for example, as the assistant to the President under Eisenhower, scarcely deserved the appellation "White House aide" in the meaning of the term before his time or as applied to other members of the Eisenhower entourage. Although Adams was by no means "chief of staff" in any sense so sweeping—or so simple—as press commentaries often took for granted, he apparently became no more dependent on the President than Eisenhower on him. "I need him," said the President when Adams turned out to have been remarkably imprudent in the Goldfine case, and delegated to him, at least nominally, the decision on his own departure.[11] This instance is extreme, but the tendency it illustrates is common enough. Any aide who demonstrates to others that he has the President's consistent confidence and a consistent part in presidential business will acquire so much business on his own account that he becomes in some sense independent of his chief. Nothing in the Constitution keeps a well-placed aide from converting status into power of his own, usable in some degree even against the President—an outcome not unknown in Truman's regime or, by all accounts, in Eisenhower's.

The more an officeholder's status and his powers stem from sources independent of the President, the stronger will be his potential pressure on the President. Department heads in general have more bargaining power than do most members of the White House staff; but bureau chiefs may have still more, and specialists at upper levels of established career services may have almost unlimited reserves of the enormous power which consists of sitting still. As Franklin Roosevelt once remarked:

> The Treasury is so large and far-flung and ingrained in its practices that I find it almost impossible to get the action and results I want—even with Henry [Morgenthau] there. But the Treasury is not to be compared with the State Department. You should go through the experience of trying to get any changes in the thinking, policy, and action of the career diplomats and then you'd know what a real problem was. But the Treasury and the State

Department put together are nothing compared with the Na-a-vy. The admirals are really something to cope with—and I should know. To change anything in the Na-a-vy is like punching a feather bed. You punch it with your right and you punch it with your left until you are finally exhausted, and then you find the damn bed just as it was before you started punching.[12]

In the right circumstances, of course, a President can have his way with any of these people. . . . [But] as between a President and his "subordinates," no less than others on whom he depends, real power is reciprocal and varies markedly with organization, subject matter, personality and situation. The mere fact that persuasion is directed at executive officials signifies no necessary easing of his way. Any new congressman of the Administration's party, especially if narrowly elected, may turn out more amenable (though less useful) to the President than any seasoned bureau chief "downtown." *The probabilities of power do not derive from the literary theory of the Constitution.*

There IS a widely held belief in the United States that were it not for folly or for knavery, a reasonable President would need no power other than the logic of his argument. No less a personage than Eisenhower has subscribed to that belief in many a campaign speech and press-conference remark. But faulty reasoning and bad intentions do not cause all quarrels with Presidents. The best of reasoning and of intent cannot compose them all. For in the first place, what the President wants will rarely seem a trifle to the people he wants it from. And in the second place, they will be bound to judge it by the standard of their own responsibilities, not his. However logical his argument according to his lights, their judgment may not bring them to his view.

Those who share in governing this country frequently appear to act as though they were in business for themselves. So, in a real though not entire sense, they are and have to be. When Truman and MacArthur fell to quarreling, for example, the stakes were no less than the substance of American foreign policy, the risks of greater war or military stalemate, the prerogatives of Presidents and field commanders, the pride of a proconsul and his place in history. Intertwined, inevitably, were other stakes as well: political stakes for men and factions of both parties; power stakes for interest groups with which they were or wished to be affiliated. And every stake was raised by the apparent discontent in the American public mood. There is no reason to suppose that in such circumstances men of large but differing responsibilities will see all things through the same glasses. On the contrary, it is to be expected that their views of what ought to be done and what they then should do will vary with the differing perspectives their particular responsibilities evoke. Since their duties are not vested in a "team" or a "collegium" but in themselves, as individuals, one must expect that they will see things for themselves. Moreover, when they are responsible to many masters and when an event or policy turns loyalty against loyalty—a day-by-day occurrence in the nature of the case—one must assume that those who have the duties to perform will choose the terms of reconciliation. This is the essence of their personal responsibility. When their own duties pull in opposite directions, who else but they can choose what they will do?

When Truman dismissed MacArthur, the latter lost three posts: the American command in the Far East, the Allied command for the occupation of Japan, and the United Nations command in Korea. He also lost his status as the senior officer on active duty in the United States armed forces. So long as he held those positions and that status, though, he had a duty to his troops, to his profession, to himself (the last is hard for any man to disentangle from the rest). As a public figure and a focus for men's hopes he had a duty to constituents at home, and in Korea and Japan. He owed a duty also to those other constituents, the UN governments contributing to his field forces. As a patriot he had a duty to his country. As an accountable official and an expert guide he stood at the call of Congress. As a military officer he had, besides, a duty to the President, his constitutional

commander. Some of these duties may have manifested themselves in terms more tangible or more direct than others. But it would be nonsense to argue that the last negated all the rest, however much it might be claimed to override them. And it makes no more sense to think that anybody but MacArthur was effectively empowered to decide how he himself would reconcile the competing demands his duties made upon him.

. . . Reasonable men, it is so often said, *ought* to be able to agree on the requirements of given situations. But when the outlook varies with the placement of each man, and the response required in his place is for each to decide, their reasoning may lead to disagreement quite as well—and quite as reasonably. Vanity, or vice, may weaken reason, to be sure, but it is idle to assign these as the cause of . . . MacArthur's defiance. Secretary Sawyer's hesitations, cited earlier, are in the same category. One need not denigrate such men to explain their conduct. For the responsibilities they felt, the "facts" they saw, simply were not the same as those of their superiors; yet they, not the superiors, had to decide what they would do.

Outside the executive branch the situation is the same, except that loyalty to the President may often matter *less*. There is no need to spell out the comparison with governors of Arkansas, steel company executives, trade union leaders, and the like. And when one comes to congressmen who can do nothing for themselves (or their constituents) save as they are elected, term by term, in districts and through party structures differing from those on which a President depends, the case is very clear. An able Eisenhower aide with long congressional experience remarked to me in 1958: "The people on the Hill don't do what they might *like* to do, they do what they think they *have* to do in their own interest as *they* see it." This states the case precisely.

The essence of a President's persuasive task, with congressmen and everybody else, is to induce them to believe that what he wants of them is what their own appraisal of their own responsibilities requires them to do in their interest, not his. Because men may differ in their views on public policy, because differences in outlook stem from differences in duty—duty to one's office, one's constituents, one-self—that task is bound to be more like collective bargaining than like a reasoned argument among philosopher kings. Overtly or implicitly, hard bargaining has characterized all illustrations offered up to now. This is the reason why: Persuasion deals in the coin of self-interest with men who have some freedom to reject what they find counterfeit.

A President draws influence from bargaining advantages. But does he always need them? . . . [S]uppose most players of the governmental game see policy objectives much alike, then can he not rely on logic (or on charm) to get him what he wants? The answer is that even then most outcomes turn on bargaining. The reason for this answer is a simple one: Most who share in governing have interests of their own beyond the realm of policy objectives. The sponsorship of policy, the form it takes, the conduct of it, and the credit for it separate their interest from the President's despite agreement on the end in view. In political government the means can matter quite as much as ends; they often matter more. And there are always differences of interest in the means.

Let me introduce a case externally the opposite of my previous examples: the European Recovery Program of 1948, the so-called Marshall Plan. This is perhaps the greatest exercise in policy agreement since the Cold War began. When the then secretary of state, George Catlett Marshall, spoke at the Harvard commencement in June 1947, he launched one of the most creative, most imaginative ventures in the history of American foreign relations. What makes this policy most notable for present purposes, however, is that it became effective upon action by the Eightieth Congress, at the behest of Harry Truman, in the election year 1948.[13]

Eight months before Marshall spoke at Harvard, the Democrats had lost control of both houses of Congress for the first time in fourteen years. Truman, whom the secretary represented, had just finished his second troubled year as President-by-succession.

Truman was regarded with so little warmth in his own party that in 1946 he had been urged not to participate in the congressional campaign. At the opening of Congress in January 1947, Senator Robert A. Taft, "Mr. Republican," had somewhat the attitude of a President-elect. This was a vision widely shared in Washington, with Truman relegated thereby to the role of caretaker-on-term. Moreover, within just two weeks of Marshall's commencement address, Truman was to veto two prized accomplishments of Taft's congressional majority: the Taft-Hartley Act and tax reduction.[14] Yet scarcely ten months later the Marshall Plan was under way on terms to satisfy its sponsors, its authorization completed, its first-year funds in sight, its administering agency in being: all managed by as thorough a display of executive-congressional cooperation as any we have seen since the Second World War. For any President at any time this would have been a great accomplishment. In years before mid-century it would have been enough to make the future reputation of his term. And for a Truman, at this time, enactment of the Marshall Plan appears almost miraculous.

How was the miracle accomplished? How did a President so situated bring it off? In answer, the first thing to note is that he did not do it by himself. Truman had help of a sort no less extraordinary than the outcome. Although each stands for something more complex, the names of Marshall, Vandenberg, Patterson, Bevin, Stalin tell the story of that help.

In 1947, two years after V-J Day, General Marshall was something more than secretary of state. He was a man venerated by the President as "the greatest living American," literally an embodiment of Truman's ideals. He was honored at the Pentagon as an architect of victory. He was thoroughly respected by the secretary of the Navy, James V. Forrestal, who that year became the first secretary of defense. On Capitol Hill, Marshall had an enormous fund of respect stemming from his war record as Army chief of staff, and in the country generally no officer had come out of the war with a higher reputation for judgment, intellect, and probity. Besides, as secretary of state, he had behind him the first generation of matured foreign service officers produced by the reforms of the 1920s, and mingled with them, in the departmental service, were some of the ablest of the men drawn by the war from private life to Washington. In terms both of staff talent and staff use, Marshall's years began a State Department "golden age" that lasted until the era of McCarthy. Moreover, as his undersecretary, Marshall had, successively, Dean Acheson and Robert Lovett, men who commanded the respect of the professionals and the regard of congressmen. (Acheson had been brilliantly successful at congressional relations as assistant secretary in the war and postwar years.) Finally, as a special undersecretary Marshall had Will Clayton, a man highly regarded, for good reason, at both ends of Pennsylvania Avenue.

Taken together, these are exceptional resources for a secretary of state. In the circumstances, they were quite as necessary as they obviously are relevant. The Marshall Plan was launched by a lame-duck Administration "scheduled" to leave office in eighteen months. Marshall's program faced a congressional leadership traditionally isolationist and currently intent upon economy. European aid was viewed with envy by a Pentagon distressed and virtually disarmed through budget cuts, and by domestic agencies intent on enlarged welfare programs. It was not viewed with liking by a Treasury intent on budget surpluses. The plan had need of every asset that could be extracted from the personal position of its nominal author and from the skills of his assistants.

Without the equally remarkable position of the senior senator from Michigan, Arthur H. Vandenberg, it is hard to see how Marshall's assets could have been enough. Vandenberg was chairman of the Senate Foreign Relations Committee. Actually, he was much more than that. Twenty years a senator, he was the senior member of his party in the chamber. Assiduously cultivated by FDR and Truman, he was a chief Republican proponent of bipartisanship in foreign policy and consciously conceived himself its living symbol to his party, to the country, and abroad. Moreover, by informal but entirely operative agreement with his colleague Taft, Vandenberg

held the acknowledged lead among Senate Republicans in the whole field of international affairs. This acknowledgment meant more in 1947 than it might have meant at any other time. With confidence in the advent of a Republican administration two years hence, most of the gentlemen were in a mood to be responsive and responsible. The war was over, Roosevelt dead, Truman a caretaker, theirs the trust. That the senator from Michigan saw matters in this light his diaries make clear.[15] And this was not the outlook from the Senate side alone; the attitudes of House Republicans associated with the Herter Committee and its tours abroad suggest the same mood of responsibility. Vandenberg was not the only source of help on Capitol Hill. But relatively speaking his position there was as exceptional as Marshall's was downtown.

Help of another sort was furnished by a group of dedicated private citizens who organized one of the most effective instruments for public information seen since the Second World War: the Committee for the Marshall Plan, headed by the eminent Republicans whom FDR in 1940 had brought to the Department of War: Henry L. Stimson as honorary chairman and Robert P. Patterson as active spokesman. The remarkable array of bankers, lawyers, trade unionists, and editors, who had drawn together in defense of "internationalism" before Pearl Harbor and had joined their talents in the war itself, combined again to spark the work of this committee. Their efforts generated a great deal of vocal public support to buttress Marshall's arguments, and Vandenberg's, in Congress.

But before public support could be rallied, there had to be a purpose tangible enough, concrete enough, to provide a rallying ground. At Harvard, Marshall had voiced an idea in general terms. That this was turned into a hard program susceptible of presentation and support is due, in major part, to Ernest Bevin, the British foreign secretary. He well deserves the credit he has sometimes been assigned as, in effect, coauthor of the Marshall Plan. For Bevin seized on Marshall's Harvard speech and organized a European response with promptness and concreteness beyond the State Department's expectations. What had been virtually a trial balloon to test reactions on both sides of the Atlantic was hailed in London as an invitation to the Europeans to send Washington a bill of particulars. This they promptly organized to do, and the American Administration then organized in turn for its reception without further argument internally about the pros and cons of issuing the "invitation" in the first place. But for Bevin there might have been trouble from the secretary of the treasury and others besides.[16]

If Bevin's help was useful at that early stage, Stalin's was vital from first to last. In a mood of self-deprecation Truman once remarked that without Moscow's "crazy" moves "we would never have had our foreign policy . . . we never could have got a thing from Congress."[17] George Kennan, among others, had deplored the anti-Soviet overtone of the case made for the Marshall Plan in Congress and the country, but there is no doubt that this clinched the argument for many segments of American opinion. There also is no doubt that Moscow made the crucial contributions to the case.

By 1947 events, far more than governmental prescience or open action, had given a variety of publics an impression of inimical Soviet intentions (and of Europe's weakness) and a growing urge to "do something about it." Three months before Marshall spoke at Harvard, Greek-Turkish aid and promulgation of the Truman Doctrine had seemed rather to crystallize than to create a public mood and a congressional response. The Marshall planners, be it said, were poorly placed to capitalize on that mood, nor had the secretary wished to do so. Their object, indeed, was to cut across it, striking at the cause of European weakness rather than at Soviet aggressiveness, per se. A strong economy in Western Europe called, ideally, for restorative measures of continental scope. American assistance proffered in an anti-Soviet context would have been contradictory in theory and unacceptable in fact to several of the governments that Washington was anxious to assist. As Marshall, himself, saw it, the logic of his purpose forbade him to play his strongest congressional card. The Russians

then proceeded to play it for him. When the Europeans met in Paris, Molotov walked out. After the Czechs had shown continued interest in American aid, a Communist coup overthrew their government while Soviet forces stood along their borders within easy reach of Prague. Molotov transformed the Marshall Plan's initial presentation; Czechoslovakia assured its final passage, which followed by a month the takeover in Prague.

Such was the help accorded Truman in obtaining action on the Marshall Plan. Considering his politically straitened circumstances he scarcely could have done with less. Conceivably some part of Moscow's contribution might have been dispensable, but not Marshall's or Vandenberg's or Bevin's or Patterson's or that of the great many other men whose work is represented by their names in my account. Their aid was not extended to the President for his own sake. He was not favored in this fashion just because they liked him personally or were spellbound by his intellect or charm. They might have been as helpful had all held him in disdain, which some of them certainly did. The Londoners who seized the ball, Vandenberg and Taft and the congressional majority, Marshall and his planners, the officials of other agencies who actively supported them or "went along," the host of influential private citizens who rallied to the cause—all these played the parts they did because they thought they had to, in their interest, given their responsibilities, not Truman's. Yet they hardly would have found it in their interest to collaborate with one another or with him had he not furnished them precisely what they needed from the White House. Truman could not do without their help, but he could not have had it without unremitting effort on his part.

The crucial thing to note about this case is that despite compatibility of views on public policy, Truman got no help he did not pay for (except Stalin's). Bevin scarcely could have seized on Marshall's words had Marshall not been plainly backed by Truman. Marshall's interest would not have comported with the exploitation of his prestige by a president who undercut him openly or subtly or even inadvertently at any point. Vandenberg, presumably, could not have backed proposals by a White House that begrudged him deference and access gratifying to his fellow partisans (and satisfying to himself). Prominent Republicans in private life would not have found it easy to promote a cause identified with Truman's claims on 1948—and neither would the prominent New Dealers then engaged in searching for a substitute.

Truman paid the price required for their services. So far as the record shows, the White House did not falter once in firm support for Marshall and the Marshall Plan. Truman backed his secretary's gamble on an invitation to all Europe. He made the plan his own in a well-timed address to the Canadians. He lost no opportunity to widen the involvements of his own official family in the cause. Averell Harriman, the secretary of commerce; Julius Krug, the secretary of the interior; Edwin Nourse, the Economic Council chairman; James Webb, the director of the budget—all were made responsible for studies and reports contributing directly to the legislative presentation. Thus these men were committed in advance. Besides, the President continually emphasized to everyone in reach that he did not have doubts, did not desire complications and would foreclose all he could. Reportedly his emphasis was felt at the Treasury, with good effect. And Truman was at special pains to smooth the way for Vandenberg. The senator insisted on "no politics" from the Administration side; there was none. He thought a survey of American resources and capacity essential; he got it in the Krug and Harriman reports. Vandenberg expected advance consultation; he received it, step by step, in frequent meetings with the President and weekly conferences with Marshall. He asked for an effective liaison between Congress and agencies concerned; Lovett and others gave him what he wanted. When the senator decided on the need to change financing and administrative features of the legislation, Truman disregarded Budget Bureau grumbling and acquiesced with grace. When, finally, Vandenberg desired a Republican to head the new administering agency, his candidate, Paul Hoffman, was appointed despite the President's own preference for another. In all these ways Truman employed the sparse advantages his "powers" and his status then accorded him to gain the sort of help he had to have.

Truman helped himself in still another way. Traditionally and practically, no one was placed as well as he to call public attention to the task of Congress (and its Republican leadership). Throughout the fall and winter of 1947 and on into the spring of 1948, he made repeated use of presidential "powers" to remind the country that congressional action was required. Messages, speeches, and an extra session were employed to make the point. Here, too, he drew advantage from his place. However, in his circumstances, Truman's public advocacy might have hurt, not helped, had his words seemed directed toward the forthcoming election. Truman gained advantage for his program only as his own endorsement of it stayed on the right side of that fine line between the "caretaker" in office and the would-be candidate. In public statements dealing with the Marshall Plan he seems to have risked blurring this distinction only once, when he called Congress into session in November 1947 asking both for interim aid to Europe and for peacetime price controls. The second request linked the then inflation with the current Congress (and with Taft), becoming a first step toward one of Truman's major themes in 1948. By calling for both measures at the extra session he could have been accused—and was—of mixing home-front politics with foreign aid. In the event no harm was done the European program (or his politics). But in advance a number of his own advisers feared that such a double call would jeopardize the Marshall Plan. Their fears are testimony to the narrowness of his advantage in employing his own "powers" for its benefit.[18]

It is symptomatic of Truman's situation that bipartisan accommodation by the White House then was thought to mean congressional consultation and conciliation on a scale unmatched in Eisenhower's time. Yet Eisenhower did about as well with opposition congresses as Truman did, in terms of requests granted for defense and foreign aid. It may be said that Truman asked for more extraordinary measures. But it also may be said that Eisenhower never lacked for the prestige his predecessor had to borrow. It often was remarked, in Truman's time, that he seemed a split personality, so sharply did his conduct differentiate domestic politics from national security. But personality aside, how else could he, in his first term, gain ground for an evolving foreign policy? The plain fact is that Truman had to play bipartisanship as he did or lose the game.

Had Truman lacked the personal advantages his "powers" and his status gave him, or if he had been maladroit in using them, there probably would not have been a massive European aid program in 1948. Something of the sort, perhaps quite different in its emphasis, would almost certainly have come to pass before the end of 1949. Some American response to European weakness and to Soviet expansion was as certain as such things can be. But in 1948 temptations to await a Taft plan or a Dewey plan might well have caused at least a year's postponement of response had the outgoing Administration bungled its congressional or public or allied or executive relations. Quite aside from the specific virtues of their plan, Truman and his helpers gained that year, at least, in timing the American response. As European time was measured then, this was a precious gain. The President's own share in this accomplishment was vital. He made his contribution by exploiting his advantages. Truman, in effect, lent Marshall and the rest the perquisites and status of his office. In return they lent him their prestige and their own influence. The transfer multiplied his influence despite his limited authority in form and lack of strength politically. Without the wherewithal to make this bargain, Truman could not have contributed to European aid.

Bargaining advantages convey no guarantees. Influence remains a two-way street. In the fortunate instance of the Marshall Plan, what Truman needed was actually in the hands of men who were prepared to "trade" with him. He personally could deliver what they wanted in return. Marshall, Vandenberg, Harriman, et al., possessed the prestige, energy, associations, staffs essential to the legislative effort.

Truman himself had a sufficient hold on presidential messages and speeches, on budget policy, on high-level appointments, and on his own time and temper to carry through all aspects of his necessary part. But it takes two to make a bargain. It takes those who have prestige to lend it on whatever terms. Suppose that Marshall had declined the secretaryship of state in January 1947; Truman might not have found a substitute so well equipped to furnish what he needed in the months ahead. Or suppose that Vandenberg had fallen victim to a cancer two years before he actually did; Senator Wiley of Wisconsin would not have seemed to Taft a man with whom the world need be divided. Or suppose that the secretary of the treasury had been possessed of stature, force, and charm commensurate with that of his successor in Eisenhower's time, the redoubtable George M. Humphrey. And what if Truman then had seemed to the Republicans what he turned out to be in 1948, a formidable candidate for President? It is unlikely that a single one of these "supposes" would have changed the final outcome; two or three, however, might have altered it entirely. Truman was not guaranteed more power than his "powers" just because he had continuing relationships with cabinet secretaries and with senior senators. Here, as everywhere, the outcome was conditional on who they were and what he was and how each viewed events, and on their actual performance in response.

Granting that persuasion has no guarantee attached, how can a President reduce the risks of failing to persuade? How can he maximize his prospects for effectiveness by minimizing chances that his power will elude him? The Marshall Plan suggests an answer: He guards his power prospects in the course of making choices. Marshall himself, and Forrestal and Harriman, and others of the sort held office on the President's appointment. Vandenberg had vast symbolic value partly because FDR and Truman had done everything they could, since 1944, to build him up. The Treasury Department and the Budget Bureau—which together might have jeopardized the plans these others made—were headed by officials whose prestige depended wholly on their jobs. What

Truman needed from those "givers" he received, in part, because of his past choice of men and measures. What they received in turn were actions taken or withheld by him, himself. The things they needed from him mostly involved his own conduct where his current choices ruled. The President's own actions in the past had cleared the way for current bargaining. His actions in the present were his trading stock. Behind each action lay a personal choice, and these together comprised his control over the give-and-take that gained him what he wanted. In the degree that Truman, personally, affected the advantages he drew from his relationships with other men in government, his power was protected by his choices.

By "choice" I mean no more than what is commonly referred to as "decision": a President's own act of doing or not doing. Decision is so often indecisive, and indecision is so frequently conclusive, that *choice* becomes the preferable term. "Choice" has its share of undesired connotations. In common usage it implies a black-and-white alternative. Presidential choices are rarely of that character. It also may imply that the alternatives are set before the choice maker by someone else. A President is often left to figure out his options for himself. . . .

If Presidents could count upon past choices to enhance their current influence, as Truman's choice of men had done for him, persuasion would pose fewer difficulties than it does. But Presidents can count on no such thing. Depending on the circumstances, prior choices can be as embarrassing as they were helpful in the instance of the Marshall Plan. . . . Truman's hold upon MacArthur was weakened by his deference toward him in the past.

Assuming that past choices have protected influence, not harmed it, present choices still may be inadequate. If Presidents could count on their own conduct to provide them enough bargaining advantages, as Truman's conduct did where Vandenberg and Marshall were concerned, effective bargaining might be much easier to manage than it often is. In the steel crisis, for instance, Truman's own persuasiveness with companies and union, both, was burdened by the conduct of an independent wage board and of

government attorneys in the courts, to say nothing of Wilson, Arnall, Sawyer, and the like. Yet in practice, if not theory, many of *their* crucial choices never were the President's to make. Decisions that are legally in others' hands, or delegated past recall, have an unhappy way of proving just the trading stock most needed when the White House wants to trade. One reason why Truman was consistently more influential in the instance of the Marshall Plan than in the steel case or the MacArthur case is that the Marshall Plan directly involved Congress. In congressional relations there are some things that no one but the President can do. His chance to choose is higher when a message must be sent, or a nomination submitted, or a bill signed into law, than when the sphere of action is confined to the executive, where all decisive tasks may have been delegated past recall.

But adequate or not, a President's choices are the only means in his own hands of guarding his own prospects for effective influence. He can draw power from continuing relationships in the degree that he can capitalize upon the needs of others for the Presidency's status and authority. He helps himself to do so, though, by nothing save ability to recognize the preconditions and the chance advantages and to proceed accordingly in the course of the choice making that comes his way. To ask how he can guard prospective influence is thus to raise a further question: What helps him guard his power stakes in his own acts of choice?

Notes

1. The reader will want to keep in mind the distinction between two senses in which the word *power* is employed. When I have used the word (or its plural) to refer to formal constitutional, statutory, or customary authority, it is either qualified by the adjective "formal" or placed in quotation marks as "power(s)." Where I have used it in the sense of effective influence on the conduct of others, it appears without quotation marks (and always in the singular). Where clarity and convenience permit, *authority* is substituted for "power" in the first sense and *influence* for power in the second.

2. See, for example, his press conference of July 22, 1959, as reported in the *New York Times,* July 23, 1959.

3. See Douglass Cater, *The Fourth Branch of Government* (Boston: Houghton Mifflin, 1959).

4. With the exception of the vice presidency, of course.

5. See David B. Truman's illuminating study of party relationships in the Eighty-first Congress, *The Congressional Party* (New York: Wiley, 1959), especially chaps. 4, 6, 8.

6. As secretary of the interior in 1939, Harold Ickes refused to approve the sale of helium to Germany despite the insistence of the State Department and the urging of President Roosevelt. Without the secretary's approval, such sales were forbidden by statute. See *The Secret Diaries of Harold L. Ickes* (New York: Simon & Schuster, 1954), vol. 2, especially pp. 391–93, 396–99.

   In this instance the statutory authority ran to the secretary as a matter of his discretion. A President is unlikely to fire cabinet officers for the conscientious exercise of such authority. If the President did so, their successors might well be embarrassed both publicly and at the Capitol were they to reverse decisions previously taken. As for a President's authority to set aside discretionary determinations of this sort, it rests, if it exists at all, on shaky legal ground not likely to be trod save in the gravest of situations.

7. Truman's *Memoirs* indicate that having tried and failed to make Stevenson an avowed candidate in the spring of 1952, the President decided to support the candidacy of Vice President Barkley. But Barkley withdrew early in the convention for lack of key northern support. Though Truman is silent on the matter, Barkley's active candidacy nearly was revived during the balloting, but the forces then aligning to revive it were led by opponents of Truman's Fair Deal, principally Southerners. As a practical matter, the President could not have lent his weight to their endeavors and could back no one but Stevenson to counter them. The latter's strength could not be shifted, then, to Harriman or Kefauver. Instead the other Northerners had to be withdrawn. Truman helped withdraw them. But he had no other option. See Harry S Truman, *Memoirs,* vol. 2, *Years of Trial and Hope* (Garden City, N.Y.: Doubleday, Time Inc., 1956), pp. 495–96.

8. The reference is to Stassen's public statement of July 23, 1956, calling for Nixon's replacement on the Republican ticket by Governor Herter of Massachusetts, the later secretary of state. Stassen's statement was issued after a conference with the President. Eisenhower's public statements on the vice-presidential nomination, both before and after Stassen's call, permit of alternative inferences: either that the President would have preferred another candidate, provided this could be arranged without a showing of White House dictation, or that he wanted Nixon on condition that the latter could show popular appeal. In the event, neither result was achieved. Eisenhower's own remarks lent strength to rapid party moves that smothered Stassen's effort. Nixon's nomination thus was guaranteed too quickly to appear the consequence of popular demand. For the public record on this matter see reported statements by Eisenhower, Nixon, Stassen, Herter, and Leonard Hall (the National Republican Chairman) in the *New York Times* for March 1, 8, 15, 16; April 27; July 15, 16, 25–31; August 3, 4, 17, 23, 1956. See also the account from private sources by Earl Mazo in *Richard Nixon: A Personal and Political Portrait* (New York: Harper, 1959), pp. 158–87

9. Stenographic transcript of presidential press conference, October 19, 1950, on file in the Truman Library at Independence, Missouri.

10. Jonathan Daniels, *Frontier on the Potomac* (New York: Macmillan, 1946), pp. 31–32.

11. Transcript of presidential press conference, June 18, 1958, in *Public Papers of the Presidents Dwight D. Eisenhower, 1958* (Washington, D.C.: National Archives, 1959), p. 479. In the summer of 1958, a congressional investigation into the affairs of a New England textile manufacturer, Bernard Goldfine, revealed that Sherman Adams had accepted various gifts and favors from him (the most notoriety attached to a vicuna coat). Adams also had made inquiries about the status of a Federal Communications Commission proceeding in which Goldfine was involved. In September 1958 Adams was allowed to resign. The episode was highly publicized and much discussed in that year's congressional campaigns.

12. As reported in Marriner S. Eccles (*Beckoning Frontiers,* New York: Knopf, 1951), p. 336.

13. In drawing together these observations on the Marshall Plan, I have relied on the record of personal participation by Joseph M. Jones, *The Fifteen Weeks* (New York: Viking, 1955), especially pp. 89–256; on the recent study by Harry Bayard Price, *The Marshall Plan and Its Meaning* (Ithaca: Cornell University Press, 1955), especially pp. 1–86; on the Truman *Memoirs,* vol. 2, chaps. 7–9; on Arthur H. Vandenberg Jr., ed., *The Private Papers of Senator Vandenberg* (Boston: Houghton Mifflin, 1952), especially pp. 373 ff.; and on notes of my own made at the time. This is an instance of policy development not covered, to my knowledge, by any of the university programs engaged in the production of case studies.

14. Secretary Marshall's speech, formally suggesting what became known as the Marshall Plan, was made at Harvard on June 5, 1947. On June 20 the President vetoed the Taft-Hartley Act; his veto was overridden three days later. On June 16 he vetoed the first of two tax reduction bills (HR 1) passed at the first session of the Eightieth Congress; the second of these (HR 3950), a replacement for the other, he also disapproved on July 18. In both instances his veto was narrowly sustained.

15. *Private Papers of Senator Vandenberg,* pp. 378–79, 446.

16. The initial reluctance of the Secretary of the Treasury, John Snyder, to support large-scale spending overseas became a matter of public knowledge on June 25, 1947. At a press conference on that day he interpreted Marshall's Harvard speech as a call on Europeans to help themselves, by themselves. At another press conference the same day, Marshall for his own part had indicated that the United States would consider helping programs on which Europeans agreed. The next day Truman held a press conference and was asked the inevitable question. He replied, "General Marshall and I are in complete agreement." When pressed further, Truman remarked sharply, "The secretary of the treasury and the secretary of state and the President are in complete agreement." Thus the President cut Snyder off, but had programming gathered less momentum overseas, no doubt he would have been heard from again as time passed and opportunity offered.

The foregoing quotations are from the stenographic transcript of the presidential press conference June 26, 1947, on file in the Truman Library at Independence, Missouri.

17. A remark made in December 1955, three years after he left office, but not unrepresentative of views he expressed, on occasion, while he was President.

18. This might also be taken as testimony to the political timidity of officials in the State Department and the Budget Bureau where that fear seems to have been strongest. However, conversations at the time with White House aides incline me to believe that there, too, interjection of the price issue was thought a gamble and a risk. For further comment see my "Congress and the Fair Deal: A Legislative Balance Sheet," *Public Policy,* vol. 5 (Cambridge: Harvard University Press, 1954), pp. 362–64.

7-2 From *Going Public*

Samuel Kernell

> *Richard Neustadt, writing in 1960, judged that the president's ability to lead depended on skill at the bargaining table in cutting deals with other politicians. In the following essay Samuel Kernell examines how the leadership strategy of modern presidents has evolved. He finds that, rather than limiting their leadership to quiet diplomacy with fellow Washingtonians, modern presidents often "go public," a set of activities borrowed from presidential election campaigns and directed toward persuading other politicians to adopt their policy preferences. Some examples of going public are a televised press conference, a special prime-time address to the nation, traveling outside Washington to deliver a speech to a business or professional convention, and a visit to a day care center with network cameras trailing behind.*

Introduction: Going Public in Theory and Practice

When President George H. W. Bush delivered his State of the Union address to the joint assembly of the mostly Democratic Congress on January 28, 1992, he assumed what was becoming a familiar stance:

> I pride myself that I am a prudent man, and I believe that patience is a virtue. But I understand that politics is for some a game. . . . I submit my plan tomorrow. And I am asking you to pass it by March 20. And I ask the American people to let you know they want this action by March 20. From the day after that, if it must be: The battle is joined. And you know when principle is at stake, I relish a good fair fight.

Once upon a time, these might have been fighting words, but by the 1990s presidents had so routinely come to appeal for public support in their dealings with Congress that Bush's rhetoric scarcely caused a stir among his Washington audience. Presidential appeals for public support had, in fact, become commonplace. Two years later Bill Clinton would use the same forum to launch a six-month public relations campaign to persuade Congress to expand coverage of federal health care beyond Medicare to include everyone not covered by employer insurance. What raised eyebrows was not the announcement or even the scope of the plan. Rather it was the bravado— some would say hubris—with which Clinton warned the assembled legislators that if they failed to give him a fully comprehensive program "I will take this pen and veto it." Two days after his 2004 reelection George W. Bush held a press conference in which he outlined an ambitious policy agenda headed by overhaul of the Social Security system. He matter-of-factly told reporters, "I earned capital in the campaign, political capital, and now I intend to spend it. It is my style."[1] Six weeks later he unveiled in his State of the Union address his partial privatization scheme for Social Security and announced a "sixty cities in sixty days" campaign to push it through Congress.

I call the approach to presidential leadership that has come into vogue at the White House "going public." It is a strategy whereby a president promotes himself and his policies in Washington by appealing directly to the American public for support. Forcing compliance from fellow Washingtonians by going over their heads to enlist constituents' pressure is a

Source: Samuel Kernell, *Going Public: New Strategies of Presidential Leadership,* 3d ed. (Washington, D.C.: CQ Press, 1997), 1–12, 17–26, 34–38, 57–64; and Samuel Kernell, *Going Public: New Strategies of Presidential Leadership,* 4th ed. (Washington, D.C.: CQ Press, 2006), 40–57.

tactic that was known but seldom attempted during the first half of the century. Theodore Roosevelt probably first enunciated the strategic principle of going public when he described the presidency as the "bully pulpit." Moreover, he occasionally put theory into practice with public appeals for his Progressive Party reforms. During the next thirty years, other presidents also periodically summoned public support to help them in their dealings with Congress. Perhaps the most famous such instance is Woodrow Wilson's ill-fated whistle-stop tour of the country on behalf of his League of Nations treaty. Equally noteworthy, historically, is Franklin D. Roosevelt's series of radio "fireside chats," which were designed less to subdue congressional opposition than to remind politicians of his continuing national mandate for the New Deal.

These historical instances are significant in large part because they are rare. Unlike Richard Nixon, who thought it important "to spread the White House around" by traveling and speaking extensively,[2] these earlier presidents were largely confined to Washington and obliged to address the country through the nation's newspapers. The concept and legitimizing precedents of going public may have been established during these years, but the emergence of presidents who *routinely* did so to promote their policies outside Washington awaited the development of modern systems of transportation and mass communications. Going public should be appreciated as a strategic adaptation to the information age.

The regularity with which recent presidents have sought public backing for their Washington dealings has altered the way politicians both inside and outside the White House regard the office. The following chapters present numerous instances of presidents preoccupied with public relations, as if these activities chiefly determined their success. Cases are recounted of other Washington politicians intently monitoring the president's popularity ratings and his addresses on television, as if his performance in these realms governed their own behavior. We shall also examine various testimonials of central institutional figures, including several Speakers of the House of Representatives, citing the president's prestige and rhetoric as they explain Congress's actions. If the public ruminations of politicians are to be believed, the president's effectiveness in rallying public support has become a primary consideration for those who do business with him.

Presidential Theory

Going public has become routine. This was not always the case. After World War I Congress refused to support President Wilson's League of Nations, a peace treaty the president himself had helped negotiate. In this instance Congress determined to amend the treaty and a president equally determined to finalize the agreement the other countries had ratified left him with little choice but to go public to try to marshal public opinion to force the Senate's agreement. Today our information-age presidents opt to go public regardless of the political climate in Washington.

There is another reason to systematically study this leadership strategy. Compared with many other aspects of the modern presidency, scholarship has only recently directed its attention toward this feature of the president's repertoire. Although going public had not become a keystone of presidential leadership in the 1950s and 1960s, when much of the influential scholarship on the subject was written, sufficient precedents were available for scholars to consider its potential for presidential leadership in the future.

Probably the main reason traditional presidential scholarship shortchanged going public is its fundamental incompatibility with bargaining. Presidential power is the "power to bargain," Richard E. Neustadt taught a generation of students of the presidency.[3] When Neustadt published his definitive study of presidential leadership in 1960, the "bargaining president" had already become a centerpiece of pluralist theories of American politics. Nearly a decade earlier, Robert A. Dahl and Charles

E. Lindblom had described the politician in America generically as "the human embodiment of a bargaining society." They made a special point to include the president in writing that despite his possessing "more hierarchical controls than any other single figure in the government . . . like everyone else . . . the President must bargain constantly."[4] Since Neustadt's landmark treatise, other major works on the presidency have reinforced and elaborated this theme.[5]

Going public violates bargaining in several ways. First, it rarely includes the kinds of exchanges necessary, in pluralist theory, for the American political system to function properly. At times, going public will be merely superfluous—fluff compared with the substance of traditional political exchange. Practiced in a dedicated way, however, it may displace bargaining.

Second, going public fails to extend benefits for compliance, but freely imposes costs for noncompliance. In appealing to the public to "tell your senators and representatives by phone, wire, and Mailgram that the future hangs in balance," the president seeks the aid of a third party—the public—to force other politicians to accept his preferences.[6] If targeted representatives are lucky, the president's success may cost them no more than an opportunity at the bargaining table to shape policy or to extract compensation. If unlucky, they may find themselves both capitulating to the president's wishes and suffering the reproach of constituents for having resisted him in the first place. By imposing costs and failing to offer benefits, going public is more akin to force than to bargaining. Nelson W. Polsby makes this point when he says that members of Congress may "find themselves ill disposed toward a president who prefers to deal indirectly with them [by going public] through what they may interpret as coercion rather than face-to-face in the spirit of mutual accommodation."[7] This senator may echo the sentiments, if not the actions, of those on Capitol Hill who find themselves repeatedly pressured by the president's public appeals: "A lot of Democrats, even if they like the President's proposal, will vote against him because of his radio address on Saturday."[8]

Third, going public entails public posturing. To the extent that it fixes the president's bargaining position, posturing makes subsequent compromise with other politicians more difficult. Because negotiators must be prepared to yield some of their clients' preferences to make a deal, bargaining proverbially proceeds best behind closed doors. Consider the difficulty Ronald Reagan's widely publicized challenge "My tax proposal is a line drawn in dirt" posed for subsequent budget negotiations in Washington.[9] Similarly, during his nationally televised State of the Union address in 1994, President Bill Clinton sought to repair his reputation as someone too willing to compromise away his principles by declaring to the assembled joint session of Congress, "If you send me [health care] legislation that does not guarantee every American private health insurance that can never be taken away, you will force me to take this pen, veto the legislation, and we'll come right back here and start all over again."[10] Not only did these declarations threaten to cut away any middle ground on which a compromise might be constructed, they probably stiffened the resolve of the president's adversaries, some of whom would later be needed to pass the administration's legislative program.

Finally, and possibly most injurious to bargaining, going public undermines the legitimacy of other politicians. It usurps their prerogatives of office, denies their role as representatives, and questions their claim to reflect the interests of their constituents. For a traditional bargaining stance with the president to be restored, these politicians would first have to reestablish parity, probably at a cost of conflict with the White House.[11]

Given these fundamental incompatibilities, one may further speculate that by spoiling the bargaining environment, going public renders the president's future influence ever more dependent upon his ability to generate popular support for himself and his policies. The degree to which a president draws upon public opinion determines the kind of leader he will be.

Presidential Practice

Bargaining and going public have never been particularly compatible styles of leadership. In the early twentieth century, when technology limited presidents' capacity to engage in public relations, they did so sparingly. On rare occasions, presidents might enlist public support as their contribution to bargains with politicians for whom their position was potentially risky. But generally, these two leadership strategies coexisted in a quiet tension. In modern times, though, going public is likely to take the form of an election campaign. George W. Bush's "sixty cities in sixty days" Social Security reform tour in 2005 is a recent example to which we shall later return. When presidents adopt intensive public relations as their leadership strategy they render bargaining increasingly difficult. The decision to go public at one juncture may preclude and undermine the opportunity to bargain at another, and vice versa. All this means that the decision to bargain or to go public must be carefully weighed.

The two case studies below reveal that modern presidents and their advisers carefully attend to this strategic issue. We compare instances of presidential success and failure in order to understand the potential gains and losses embedded in presidents' choices.

Ronald Reagan Enlists Public Opinion as a Lever

No president has enlisted public strategies to better advantage than did Ronald Reagan. Throughout his tenure, he exhibited a full appreciation of bargaining and going public as the modern office's principal strategic alternatives. The following examples from a six-month survey of White House news coverage show how entrenched this bifurcated view of presidential strategy has become. The survey begins in late November 1984, when some members of the administration were pondering how the president might exploit his landslide victory and others were preparing a new round of budget cuts and a tax reform bill for the next Congress.

November 29, 1984. Washington Post columnist Lou Cannon reported the following prediction from a White House official: "We're going to have confrontation on spending and consultation on tax reform." The aide explained, "We have somebody to negotiate with us on tax reform, but may not on budget cuts."[12] By "confrontation" he was referring to the president's success in appealing to the public on national television, that is, in going public. By "consultation" he meant bargaining.

January 25, 1985. The above prediction proved accurate two months later, when another staffer offered as pristine an evocation of going public as one is likely to find: "We have to look at it, in many ways, like a campaign. He [Reagan] wants to take his case to the people. You have a constituency of 535 legislators as opposed to 100 million voters. But the goal is the same—to get the majority of voters to support your position."[13]

February 10, 1985. In a nationally broadcast radio address, President Reagan extended an olive branch, inviting members of Congress to "work with us in the spirit of cooperation and compromise" on the budget. This public statement probably did little to allay the frequently voiced suspicion of House Democratic leaders that such overtures were mainly intended for public consumption. One Reagan aide insisted, however, that the president simply sought to reassure legislators that "he would not 'go over their heads' and campaign across the country for his budget without trying first to reach a compromise."[14] In this statement the aide implicitly concedes the harm public pressure can create for bargaining but seeks to incorporate it advantageously into the strategic thinking of the politicians with whom the administration must deal by not forswearing its use.

March 9, 1985. After some public sparring, the administration eventually settled down to intensive budget negotiations with the Republican-led Senate Finance Committee. Failing to do as well as he would like, however, Reagan sent a message to his party's senators through repeated unattributed statements to the press that, if necessary, he would "go to the people to carry our message forward." * Again, public appeals, though held in reserve, were threatened.

March 11, 1985. In an interview with a *New York Times* correspondent, a senior Reagan aide sized up his president: "He's liberated, he wants to get into a fight, he feels strongly and wants to push his program through himself. . . . Reagan never quite believed his popularity before the election, never believed the polls. Now he has it, and he's going to push . . . ahead with our agenda."[15]

May 16, 1985. To avoid entangling tax reform with budget deliberations in Congress, Reagan, at the request of Republican leaders, delayed unveiling his tax reform proposal until late May. A couple of weeks before Reagan's national television address on the subject, White House aides began priming the press with leaks on the proposal's content and promises that the president would follow it with a public relations blitz. In the words of one White House official, the plan was to force Congress to make a "binary choice between tax reform or no tax reform."[16] The administration rejected bargaining, as predicted nearly six months earlier by a White House aide, apparently for two strategic reasons. First, Reagan feared that in a quietly negotiated process, the tax reform package would unravel under the concerted pressure of the special interests. Second, by taking the high-profile approach of "standing up for the people against the special interests," in the words of one adviser, tax reform might do for Republicans what

Social Security did for Democrats—make them the majority party.[17]

During these six months, when bargaining held out promise—as it had during negotiations with the Senate Finance Committee—public appeals were held in reserve. The White House occasionally, however, threatened an appeal in trying to gain more favorable consideration. On other occasions, when opponents of the president's policies appeared capable of extracting major concessions—House Democrats on the budget and interest groups on tax reform, for example—the White House disengaged from negotiations and tried through public relations to force Congress to accept the president's policies. Although by 1985 news items such as the preceding excerpts seemed unexceptional as daily news, they are a recent phenomenon. One does not routinely find such stories in White House reporting twenty years earlier when, for example, John Kennedy's legislative agenda was stalled in Congress.

President Clinton Snares Himself by Bargaining

Shortly after assuming office, Bill Clinton received some bad news. The Bush administration had underestimated the size of the next year's deficit by $50 billion. The president's campaign promises of new domestic programs and a middle-class tax cut would have to be put on hold in favor of fulfilling his third, now urgent pledge to trim $500 billion from the deficit over the next five years. On February 17, 1993, President Clinton appeared before a joint session of Congress and a national television audience to unveil his deficit reduction package. The president's deficit-cutting options were constrained by two considerations: he wanted to include minimal stimulus spending to honor his campaign promise, and he faced a Congress controlled by fellow Democrats who were committed to many of the programs under the budget ax. Even with proposed cuts

---

*Jonathan Fuerbringer, "Reagan Critical of Budget View of Senate Panel," New York Times, March 9, 1985. Senate Majority Leader Bob Dole told reporters that if the president liked the Senate's final budget package he would campaign for it "very vigorously . . . going to television, whatever he needs to reduce federal spending." Karen Tumulty, "Reagan May Get Draft of Budget Accord Today," Los Angeles Times, April 4, 1985, 1.

in defense spending, the only way the budget could accommodate these constraints was through a tax increase. The package raised taxes on the highest-income groups and introduced a broad energy consumption tax. During the following weeks, the president and his congressional liaison team quietly lobbied Congress. He would not again issue a public appeal until the eve of the final vote in August.

The president soon learned that Republicans in both chambers had united in opposition to the administration proposal. Led by Newt Gingrich in the House of Representatives and Bob Dole in the Senate, Republicans retreated to the sidelines and assumed the role of Greek chorus, ominously chanting "tax and spend liberals." This meant that the administration needed virtually every Democratic vote to win. Democratic members appreciated this, and many began exploiting the rising value of their votes to extract concessions that would make the legislation more favorable to their constituents.

By June the president's bargaining efforts had won him a watered-down bill that even he had difficulty being enthusiastic about. Meanwhile, the Republicans' public relations campaign had met with success: the American public had come to regard President Clinton as a "tax and spend liberal." Whereas shortly after the February speech, the *Los Angeles Times* had found half of its polling respondents willing to describe the president's initiative as "bold and innovative" and only 35 percent of them willing to describe it as "tax and spend," by June these numbers had reversed. Now, 53 percent labeled it "tax and spend" and only 28 percent still regarded it as "bold and innovative."[18] Given this turnaround in the public's assessment of the initiative, it was not surprising that the public also downgraded its evaluation of the initiative's sponsor. During the previous five months, President Clinton's approval rating had plunged from 58 to 41 percent.

This was the situation when several of Clinton's senior campaign consultants sounded the alarm in a memo: in only six months the president had virtually exhausted his capacity for leadership. If he did not turn back the current tide of public opinion, he would be weakened beyond repair. In response, the president assembled his senior advisers to evaluate current strategy. This set the stage for a confrontation between those advisers who represented the president in bargaining with other Washingtonians and those staffers who manned the White House public relations machinery. The argument that erupted between these advisers should disabuse anyone of the notion that bargaining and cultivating public support are separate, self-contained spheres of action that do not encroach on one another.[19]

The president's chief pollster, Stanley Greenberg, opened the discussion by stating his and his fellow consultants' position: "We do not exaggerate when we say that our current course, advanced by our economic team and Congressional leaders, threatens to sink your popularity further and weaken your presidency. . . . The immediate problem," he explained, "is that thanks to the Republican effort no one views your economic package as anything other than a tax scheme. You must exercise a 'bold zero option,' which is consultant talk for 'rid your policy of any taxes that affect the middle class.'" (In fact, the only tax still in the bill was a 4.3-cent-per-gallon gasoline tax that would raise a modest $20 billion.) Greenberg then unveiled polling data that found broad public support for such a move. He closed by warning everyone in the room, "We have a very short period of time. And if we don't communicate something serious and focused in the period, we're going to be left with what our detractors used to characterize our plan. . . . Don't assume we can fix it in August." This concluded the case for going public. And in order to use this strategy, Clinton had to change course on taxes.

According to those present, the economic and congressional advisers had listened to this argument "with a slow burn." Finally, the president's chief lobbyist, Howard Paster, blurted out, "This isn't an election! The Senate breaks its ass to get a 4.3-cent-a-gallon tax passed, and we can't just abandon it." Besides, they needed the $20 billion provided by the tax to offset other concessions that would be necessary to get the bill passed. "I need all the chips that are available," Paster pleaded. "Don't bargain them away here. Let me have maximum latitude."

From here, the discussion deteriorated into name calling and blame assigning that stopped only when Clinton started screaming at everyone—"a purple fit" is how one participant described it. In the end the president decided that he had to stay the course but that he would begin traveling around the country to explain to the public that his economic package was the "best" that could be enacted. In mid-August, after a concerted public relations campaign that concluded with a nationally televised address, the legislation barely passed. (In the Senate, Vice President Al Gore cast the tie-breaking vote.) The new administration's first legislative initiative had drained its resources both in Congress and across the nation. From here, the Clinton administration limped toward even more difficult initiatives represented by the North American Free Trade Agreement (NAFTA) and health care reform.

Clearly, as both case studies show, going public appears to foster political relations that are quite at odds with those traditionally cultivated through bargaining. One may begin to examine this phenomenon by asking, what is it about modern politics that would inspire presidents to go public in the first place?

How Washington and Presidents Have Changed

The incompatibility of bargaining and going public presents some pressing theoretical questions. Why should presidents come to favor a strategy of leadership that appears so incompatible with the principles of pluralist theory? Why, if other Washington elites legitimately and correctly represent the interests of their clients and constituents, would anything be gained by going over their heads? The answers to these questions are complex, reflecting changes in the capital and in presidents. In this chapter we consider the changes within Washington, the locale of presidential activity. . . .

Some would account for the rise of going public by resorting to the imperative of technology. Certainly, advances in transportation and communications have been indispensable to this process, but they have not been sufficient in themselves to alter political relations in such a contradictory way. . . .

There are more fundamental reasons for the discrepancy between theory and current practice. Politics in Washington may no longer be as tractable to bargaining as it once was. Presidents prefer to go public because the strategy offers a better prospect of success than it did in the past. Perhaps the most consequential development in the modern era is the regularity of divided party control of government. Every president since Jimmy Carter has at some time had to deal with a Congress in which the opposition party controlled one or both chambers. On such occasions, each side frequently finds political advantage in frustrating the other and playing a blame game. Posturing in preparation for the next election takes precedence over bargaining and passing new policy.

Moreover, beginning in the 1970s close observers of American politics detected a pervasive decoupling of traditional allegiances. The most prominent of these trends saw voters abandoning their political party affiliations. From the 1960s to the 1980s the proportion of survey respondents who classified themselves as Independent (or some other noncommittal category) grew from 24 to 41 percent; twenty-five years later, despite a resurgent partisanship among both voters and politicians on a number of dimensions, this basic, defining fact has not changed. Entering the 2006 midterm election period, most surveys show Independent to be the single most popular choice when respondents are asked their party identification.[20] And voters continue to split their ballots, if not quite at the record rates of the 1980s, still to a degree unknown in the 1950s and 1960s.* Consequently, political relations among politicians in Washington remain loose and individualistic. In part ballot splitting reflects the dramatic

---

*During the 1990s, the American National Election Surveys found 30 percent of respondent voters reporting that they had split their ballot between the presidential and House candidates. This compares to 18 percent in 2004 and the 1960s and 14 percent during the 1950s. The author wishes to thank Martin B. Wattenberg for supplying these figures in a personal communication, March 10, 2006.

growth of incumbency advantage, especially in House elections, during the 1980s. From 1976 until 1992 at least 90 percent of these incumbents who sought reelection won both their primary and general elections. Some years the figure reached a 98 percent success rate. If this success better insulated these politicians from party and institutional leaders, it served paradoxically to make many of them more sensitive to public opinion from their constituencies. After all, they were winning, in their view, by dint of heroic effort to respond to their constituents.[21]

As politicians in Washington became more sensitive (and perhaps responsive) to public pressure, presidents learned that mobilizing these pressures worked. For exposition I classify the earlier era up to the 1970s as "institutionalized pluralism" and the latter era as "individualized pluralism." Since the 1994 midterm congressional elections, when an ideologically infused resurgent Republican Party surprisingly took over control of the House of Representatives and the Senate for the first time in a generation, politics in Washington has in one important respect shifted away from those relations described by individualized pluralism. Specifically, a series of vigorous Republican Party leaders in Congress have restored a level of discipline and policy coherence unseen since the 1960s. Nonetheless, given the recentness and limited scope of this development and continuing, unabated expectations of presidential leadership via public relations, I have retained this bifurcated classification of the modern evolution of Washington politics from predominantly private elite transactions to the mobilization of interested publics. We will consider how recently strengthened partisanship in Congress may temper presidents' incentives to go public....

The President's Place in Institutionalized Pluralism

Constructing coalitions across the broad institutional landscape of Congress, the bureaucracy, interest groups, courts, and state governments requires a politician who possesses a panoramic view and commands the resources necessary to engage the disparate, parochial interests of Washington's political elites. Only the president enjoys such vantage and resources. Traditional presidential scholarship leaves little doubt as to how they should be employed. Nowhere has Dahl and Lindblom's framework of the bargaining society been more forcefully employed than in Richard E. Neustadt's classic *Presidential Power*, published in 1960. Neustadt observes:

Status and authority yield bargaining advantages. But in a government of "separated institutions sharing powers," they yield them to all sides. With the array of vantage points at his disposal, a President may be far more persuasive than his logic or his charm could make him. But outcomes are not guaranteed by his advantages. There remain the counter pressures those whom he would influence can bring to bear on him from vantage points at their disposal. Command has limited utility; persuasion becomes give-and-take....

The President's advantages are checked by the advantages of others. Continuing relationships will pull in both directions. These are relationships of mutual dependence. A President depends upon the men he would persuade; he has to reckon with his need or fear of them. They too will possess status, or authority, or both, else they would be of little use to him. Their vantage points confront his own; their power tempers his.*

Bargaining is thus the essence of presidential leadership, and pluralist theory explicitly rejects unilateral forms of influence as usually insufficient and ultimately costly. The ideal president is one who seizes the center of the Washington bazaar and actively barters with fellow politicians to build winning coalitions. He must do so, according to this theory, or he will forfeit any claim to leadership....

---

*Richard E. Neustadt, Presidential Power, 28–29. Copyright 1980. Reprinted by permission of John Wiley and Sons, Inc. Compare with Dahl and Lindblom's earlier observation: "The President possesses more hierarchical controls than any other single figure in the government; indeed, he is often described somewhat romantically and certainly ambiguously as the most powerful democratic executive in the world. Yet like everyone else in the American policy process, the President must bargain constantly—with Congressional leaders, individual Congressmen, his department heads, bureau chiefs, and leaders of nongovernmental organizations" (Dahl and Lindblom, Politics, Economics, and Welfare, 333).

The Calculus of Those Who Deal with the President

Those Washingtonians who conduct business with the president observe his behavior carefully. Their judgment about his leadership guides them in their dealings with him. Traditionally, the professional president watchers have asked themselves the following questions: What are his priorities? How much does he care whether he wins or loses on a particular issue? How will he weigh his options? Is he capable of winning?

Each person will answer these questions about the president's will and skill somewhat differently, of course, depending upon his or her institutional vantage. The chief lobbyist for the United Auto Workers, a network White House correspondent, and the mayor of New York City may size up the president differently depending upon what they need from him. Nonetheless, they arrive at their judgments about the president in similar ways. Each observes the same behavior, inspects the same personal qualities, evaluates the views of the same recognized opinion leaders—columnists and commentators, among others—and tests his or her own tentative opinions with those of fellow community members. Local opinion leaders promote a general agreement among Washingtonians in their assessments of the president. Their agreement is his reputation.[22]

A president with a strong reputation does better in his dealings largely because others expect fewer concessions from him. Accordingly, he finds them more compliant; an orderly marketplace prevails. Saddled with a weak reputation, conversely, a president must work harder. Because others expect him to be less effective, they press him harder in expectation of greater gain. Comity at the bargaining table may give way to contention as other politicians form unreasonable expectations of gain. Through such expectations, the president's reputation regulates community relations in ways that either facilitate or impede his success. In a world of institutionalized pluralism, bargaining presidents seldom actively traded upon their prestige, leaving it to influence Washington political elites only through their anticipation of the electorate's behavior. As a consequence, prestige remained largely irrelevant to other politicians' assessments of the president.* Once presidents began going public and interjecting prestige directly into their relations with fellow politicians, and once these politicians found their resistance to this pressure diminished because of their own altered circumstances, the president's ability to marshal public opinion soon became an important ingredient of his reputation. New questions were added to traditional ones: Does the president feel strongly enough about an issue to go public? Will he follow through on his threats to do so? Does his standing in the country run so deep that it will likely be converted into mail to members of Congress, or is it so shallow that it will expire as he attempts to use it?

In today's Washington, the answers to these questions contribute to the president's reputation. Consequently, his prestige and reputation have lost much of their separateness. The community's estimates of Carter and Reagan rose and fell with the polls. Through reputation, prestige has begun to play a larger role in regulating the president's day-to-day transactions with other community members. Grappling with the unclear causes of Carter's failure in Washington, Neustadt arrived at the same conclusion:

A President's capacity to draw and stir a television audience seems every bit as interesting to current Washingtonians as his ability to wield his formal powers. This interest is his opportunity. While national party organizations fall away, while congressional party discipline relaxes, while interest groups proliferate and issue networks rise, a President who wishes to compete for leadership in framing policy and shaping coalitions has to make the most he can out of his popular connection. Anticipating home reactions, Washingtonians ... are vulnerable

---

* Neustadt observed that President Truman's television appeal for tighter price controls in 1951 had little visible effect on how Washington politicians viewed the issue. This is the only mention of a president going public in the original eight chapters of the book. Neustadt, Presidential Power, 45.

to any breeze from home that presidential words and sights can stir. If he is deemed effective on the tube they will anticipate. That is the essence of professional reputation.[23]

The record supports Neustadt's speculation. In late 1978 and early 1979, with his monthly approval rating dropping to less than 50 percent, President Carter complained that it was difficult to gain Congress's attention for his legislative proposals. As one congressional liaison official stated, "When you go up to the Hill and the latest polls show Carter isn't doing well, then there isn't much reason for a member to go along with him."[24] A member of Congress concurred: "The relationship between the President and Congress is partly the result of how well the President is doing politically. Congress is better behaved when he does well. . . . Right now, it's almost as if Congress is paying no attention to him."[25]

The President's Calculus

The limited goods and services available for barter to the bargaining president would be quickly exhausted in a leaderless setting where every coalition partner must be dealt with individually. When politicians are more subject to environmental forces, however, other avenues of presidential influence open up. No politician within Washington is better positioned than the president to go outside the community and draw popular support. With members more sensitive to influences beyond Washington, the president's hand in mobilizing public opinion has been strengthened. For the new Congress—indeed, for the new Washington generally—going public may at times be the most effective course available.

Under these circumstances, the president's prestige becomes his political capital. It is something to be spent when the coffers are full, to be conserved when they are low, and to be replenished when they are empty. Early in 1997, when asked by campaign-weary news reporters why President Clinton maintained such a heavy travel schedule after his election victory, press secretary Michael D. McCurry lectured them on modern political science: "Campaigns are about

framing a choice for the American people. . . .When you are responsible for governing you have to use the same tools of public persuasion to advance your program, to build public support for the direction you are attempting to lead."[26]

If public relations are to be productive the message must be tailored to a correctly targeted audience. For this, presidents require accurate, precisely measured readings of public opinion. Modern presidents must be attentive to the polls, but they need not crave the affection of the public. Their relationship with it may be purely instrumental. However gratifying public approval may be, popular support is a resource the expenditure of which must be coolly calculated. As another Clinton aide explained, "Clinton has come to believe that if he keeps his approval ratings up and sells his message as he did during the campaign, there will be greater acceptability for his program. . . . The idea is that you have to sell it as if in a campaign."[27]

Bargaining presidents require the sage advice of politicians familiar with the bargaining game; presidents who go public need pollsters. Compare the relish with which President Nixon reportedly approached the polls with the disdain Truman expressed. "Nixon had all kinds of polls all the time," recalled one of his consultants. "He sometimes had a couple of pollsters doing the same kind of survey at the same time. He really studied them. He wanted to find the thing that would give him an advantage."[28] The confidant went on to observe that the president wanted poll data "on just about anything and everything" throughout his administration.

Indicative of current fashion, presidents from Carter through Bush have all had in-house pollsters taking continuous—weekly, even daily—readings of public opinion.[29] When George H. W. Bush reportedly spent $216,000 of Republican National Committee (RNC) money on in-house polling in one year, many Washington politicians probably viewed it as an excessive indulgence, reflecting the RNC's largesse more than any practical need for data. But this figure soon looked modest after Clinton spent nearly ten times that amount in

1993, when he averaged three or four polls and an equal number of focus groups each month.[30]

Pollsters vigilantly monitor the pulse of opinion to warn of slippage and to identify opportunities for gain. Before recommending a policy course, they assess its costs in public support. Sometimes, as was the case with Clinton's pollsters, they go so far as to ask the public whether the president should bargain with congressional leaders or challenge them by mobilizing public opinion. These advisers' regular and frequently unsolicited denials that they affected policy belie their self-effacement.

To see how the strategic prescriptions of going public differ from those of bargaining, consider the hypothetical case of a president requiring additional votes if he is to prevail in Congress. If a large number of votes is needed, the most obvious and direct course is to go on prime-time television to solicit the public's active support. Employed at the right moment by a popular president, the effect may be dramatic. This tactic, however, has considerable costs and risks. A real debit of lost public support may occur when a president takes a forthright position. There is also the possibility that the public will not respond, which damages the president's future credibility. Given this, a president understandably finds the *threat* to go public frequently more attractive than the *act*. To the degree that such a threat is credible, the anticipated responses of some representatives and senators may suffice to achieve victory.

A more focused application of influence via public relations becomes available as an election nears. Fence-sitting representatives and senators may be plied with promises of reelection support. This may be done privately and selectively, or it may be tendered openly to all who may vote on the president's program. Presidential support can be much more substantial than endorsement. Presidents at least as far back as 1938, when Franklin Roosevelt failed to purge anti–New Deal Democrats in the midterm elections, have at times actively sought to improve their own fortunes in the next Congress by influencing the current election. During the 1970 midterm congressional election campaigns, President Nixon raced around the country "in a white heat," trying desperately to secure a Republican Congress that would not convene for another generation.[31] In the 1999–2000 election cycle outgoing President Clinton pushed the modern president's efforts to serve his party's candidates to what would seem to be an individual's physical limits. By one count he participated in 295 congressional fund-raising events garnering more than $160 million for his party's candidates. Were it not for the tragic events of 9/11 and the subsequent invasion of Afghanistan, President Bush might have matched his predecessor. After getting off to a slow start in the next election cycle, the president made up ground rapidly. By the 2002 election he had attended seventy-four fund-raisers, an impressive number except when compared to Clinton, but he garnered significantly more money for Republican congressional candidates than had his Democratic counterpart. . . .

The variety of methods for generating publicity notwithstanding, going public offers fewer and simpler stratagems than does its pluralist alternative. At the heart of the latter lies bargaining, which must involve choice: choice among alternative coalitions, choice of specific partners, and choice of the goods and services to be bartered. Above all, it requires empathy, the ability of one politician to discern what his or her counterpart minimally needs in return for cooperation. The number, variety, and subtlety of choices place great demands upon strategic calculation, so much so that pluralist leadership must be understood as an art. In Neustadt's schema, the president's success ultimately reduces to intuition an ability to sense "right choices."[32]

Going public also requires choice, and it leaves ample room for the play of talent. If anyone doubts it, consider the obviously staged town meetings that President Bush's advance team assembled during his [2005] "sixty cities in sixty days" promotion of Social Security reform. Public relations is a less obscure matter than bargaining with fellow politicians, every one of them a professional bent on extracting as much from the president while surrendering as little as possible. Going public promises a more straightforward presidency than its pluralist counterpart—its options fewer, its strategy simpler, and consequently, its practitioner's actions both more predictable and easily observed.

Notes

1. Dan Froomkin, "Bush Agenda: Bold but Blurry," *Washington Post*, November 5, 2004.
2. Robert B. Semple Jr., "Nixon Eludes Newsmen on Coast Trip," *New York Times*, August 3, 1970, 16.
3. Richard E. Neustadt, *Presidential Power* (New York: John Wiley and Sons, 1980).
4. Robert A. Dahl and Charles E. Lindblom, *Politics, Economics, and Welfare* (New York: Harper and Row, 1953), 333.
5. Among them are Aaron Wildavsky, *The Politics of the Budgetary Process* (Boston: Little, Brown, 1964); Graham T. Allison, *The Essence of Decision: Explaining the Cuban Missile Crisis* (New York: HarperCollins, 1987); Hugh Heclo, *The Government of Strangers* (Washington, D.C.: Brookings Institution, 1977); and Nelson W. Polsby, *Consequences of Party Reform* (New York: Oxford University Press, 1983).
6. From Ronald Reagan's address to the nation on his 1986 budget. Jack Nelson, "Reagan Calls for Public Support of Deficit Cuts," *Los Angeles Times*, April 25, 1985, 1.
7. Nelson W. Polsby, "Interest Groups and the Presidency: Trends in Political Intermediation in America," in *American Politics and Public Policy*, ed. Walter Dean Burnham and Martha Wagner Weinbey (Cambridge: MIT Press, 1978), 52.
8. Hedrick Smith, "Bitterness on Capitol Hill," *New York Times*, April 24, 1985, 14.
9. Ed Magnuson, "A Line Drawn in Dirt," *Time*, February 22, 1982, 12–13.
10. William J. Clinton, *Public Papers of the Presidents of the United States: William J. Clinton, 1994*, vol. 1 (Washington, D.C.: Government Printing Office, 1995), 126–135.
11. See David S. Broder, "Diary of a Mad Majority Leader," *Washington Post*, December 13, 1981, C1, C5; David S. Broder, "Rostenkowski Knows It's His Turn," *Washington Post National Weekly Edition*, June 10, 1985, 13.
12. Lou Cannon, "Big Spending-Cut Bill Studied," *Washington Post*, November 29, 1984, A8.
13. Bernard Weinraub, "Reagan Sets Tour of Nation to Seek Economic Victory," *New York Times*, January 25, 1985, 43.
14. Bernard Weinraub, "Reagan Calls for 'Spirit of Cooperation' on Budget and Taxes," *New York Times*, February 10, 1985, 32. On Democratic suspicions of Reagan's motives see Hedrick Smith, "O'Neill Reflects Democratic Strategy on Budget Cuts and Tax Revisions," *New York Times*, December 6, 1984, B20; and Margaret Shapiro, "O'Neill's New Honeymoon with Reagan," *Washington Post National Weekly Edition*, February 11, 1985, 12.
15. Bernard Weinraub, "In His 2nd Term, He Is Reagan the Liberated," *New York Times*, March 11, 1985, 10.
16. David E. Rosenbaum, "Reagan Approves Primary Elements of Tax Overhaul," *New York Times*, May 16, 1985, 1.
17. Robert W. Merry and David Shribman, "G.O.P. Hopes Tax Bill Will Help It Become Majority Party Again," *Wall Street Journal*, May 23, 1985. See also Rosenbaum, "Reagan Approves Primary Elements of Tax Overhaul," 14. Instances such as those reported here continued into summer. See, for example, Jonathan Fuerbringer, "Key Issues Impede Compromise on Cutting Deficit," *New York Times*, June 23, 1985, 22.
18. These figures are reported in Richard E. Cohen, *Changing Course in Washington* (New York: Macmillan, 1994), 180.
19. The account of this meeting comes from Bob Woodward, *The Agenda* (New York: Simon and Schuster, 1994).
20. An excellent source for monitoring these trends is www.pollingreport.com.
21. Gary C. Jacobson, *The Politics of Congressional Elections*, 5th ed. (New York: Longman, 2001), 21–34.

22. This discussion of reputation follows closely that of Neustadt in *Presidential Power*, chap. 4.

23. Neustadt, *Presidential Power*, 238.

24. Cited in Gary C. Jacobson, *The Politics of Congressional Elections*, 4th ed. (New York: Longman, 1997), 193–194.

25. Statement by Rep. Richard B. Cheney cited in Charles O. Jones, "Congress and the Presidency," in *The New Congress*, eds. Thomas E. Mann and Norman J. Ornstein (Washington, D.C.: American Enterprise Institute, 1981), 241.

26. Alison Mitchell, "Clinton Seems to Keep Running Though the Race Is Run and Won," *New York Times*, February 12, 1997, A1, A12.

27. Ibid., A12.

28. Cited in George C. Edwards III, *The Public Presidency* (New York: St. Martin's Press, 1983), 14.

29. B. Drummond Ayres Jr., "G.O.P. Keeps Tabs on Nation's Mood," *New York Times*, November 16, 1981, 20.

30. These figures are cited in George C. Edwards III, "Frustration and Folly: Bill Clinton and the Public Presidency," in *The Clinton Presidency: First Appraisals*, eds. Colin Campbell and Bert A. Rockman (Chatham, N.J.: Chatham House, 1996), 234.

31. Rowland Evans and Robert Novak, *Nixon in the White House: The Frustration of Power*, (New York: Random House, 1971).

32. Neustadt, *Presidential Power*, especially chap. 8.

Chapter 8

The Bureaucracy

8-1 The Politics of Bureaucratic Structure

Terry M. Moe

Legislators, presidents, and other political players care about the content and implementation of policy. They also care about the way executive agencies are structured: Where in the executive branch are new agencies placed? What kind of bureaucrat will be motivated to aggressively pursue, or to resist the pursuit of, certain policy goals? Who should report to whom? What rules should govern bureaucrats' behavior? In the following essay, Terry M. Moe observes that these questions are anticipated and answered by politicians as they set policy. They are the subjects of "structural" politics. The federal bureaucracy is not structured on the basis of a theory of public administration, Moe argues, but should instead be viewed as the product of politics.

American Public Bureaucracy is not designed to be effective. The bureaucracy arises out of politics, and its design reflects the interests, strategies, and compromises of those who exercise political power.

This politicized notion of bureaucracy has never appealed to most academics or reformers. They accept it—indeed, they adamantly argue its truth—and the social science of public bureaucracy is a decidedly political body of work as a result. Yet, for the most part, those who study and practice public administration have a thinly veiled disdain for politics, and they want it kept out of bureaucracy as much as possible. They want presidents to stop politicizing the departments and bureaus. They want Congress to stop its incessant meddling in bureaucratic affairs. They want all politicians to respect bureaucratic autonomy, expertise, and professionalism.[1]

The bureaucracy's defenders are not apologists. Problems of capture, inertia, parochialism, fragmentation, and imperialism are familiar grounds for criticism. And there is lots of criticism. But once the subversive influence of politics is mentally factored out, these bureaucratic problems are understood to have bureaucratic solutions—new mandates, new rules and procedures, new personnel systems, better training and management, better people. These are the quintessential reforms that politicians are urged to adopt to bring about effective bureaucracy. The goal at all times is the greater good: "In designing any political structure, whether it be the Congress, the executive branch, or the judiciary, it is important to

Source: Can the government govern? By Chubb, John E. ; Peterson, Paul E. eds; Brookings Institution. Reproduced with permission of Brookings Institution Press in the format Republish in a book via Copyright Clearance Center. Some notes appearing in the original have been deleted.

build arrangements that weigh the scale in favor of those advocating the national interest." [2]

The hitch is that those in positions of power are not necessarily motivated by the national interest. They have their own interests to pursue in politics—the interests of southwest Pennsylvania or cotton farmers or the maritime industry—and they exercise their power in ways conducive to those interests. Moreover, choices about bureaucratic structure are not matters that can be separated off from all this, to be guided by technical criteria of efficiency and effectiveness. Structural choices have important consequences for the content and direction of policy, and political actors know it. When they make choices about structure, they are implicitly making choices about policy. And precisely because this is so, issues of structure are inevitably caught up in the larger political struggle. Any notion that political actors might confine their attention to policymaking and turn organizational design over to neutral criteria or efficiency experts denies the realities of politics.

This essay is an effort to understand bureaucracy by understanding its foundation in political choice and self-interest. The central question boils down to this: what sorts of structures do the various political actors—interest groups, presidents, members of Congress, bureaucrats—find conducive to their own interests, and what kind of bureaucracy is therefore likely to emerge from their efforts to exercise political power? In other words, why do they build the bureaucracy they do? . . .

A Perspective on Structural Politics

Most citizens do not get terribly excited about the arcane details of public administration. When they choose among candidates in elections, they pay attention to such things as party or image or stands on policy. If pressed, the candidates would probably have views or even voting records on structural issues—for example, whether the Occupational Safety and Health Administration should be required to carry out cost-benefit analysis before proposing a formal rule or whether the Consumer Product Safety Commission should be moved into the Commerce Department—but this is hardly the stuff that political campaigns are made of. People just do not know or care much about these sorts of things.

Organized interest groups are another matter. They are active, informed participants in their specialized issue areas, and they know that their policy goals are crucially dependent on precisely those fine details of administrative structure that cause voters' eyes to glaze over. Structure is valuable to them, and they have every incentive to mobilize their political resources to get what they want. As a result, they are normally the only source of political pressure when structural issues are at stake. Structural politics is interest group politics.

Interest Groups: The Technical Problem of Structural Choice

Most accounts of structural politics pay attention to interest groups, but their analytical focus is on the politicians who exercise public authority and make the final choices. This tends to be misleading. It is well known that politicians, even legislators from safe districts, are extraordinarily concerned about their electoral popularity and, for that reason, are highly responsive to their constituencies. To the extent this holds true, their positions on issues are not really their own, but are induced by the positions of others. If one seeks to understand why structural choices turn out as they do, then, it does not make much sense to start with politicians. The more fundamental questions have to do with how interest groups decide what kinds of structures they want politicians to provide. This is the place to start.

In approaching these questions about interest groups, it is useful to begin with an extreme case. Suppose that, in a given issue area, there is a single dominant group (or coalition) with a reasonably complex problem—pollution, poverty, job safety, health—it seeks to address through governmental action, and that the group is so powerful that politicians will enact virtually any proposal the group offers, subject to reasonable budget constraints. In effect, the group is able to exercise public authority on its own by writing legislation that is binding on everyone and enforceable in the courts.

The dominant group is an instructive case because, as it makes choices about structure, it faces no political problems. It need not worry about losing its grip on public authority or about the influence of its political opponents—considerations which would otherwise weigh heavily in its calculations. Without the usual uncertainties and constraints of politics, the group has the luxury of concerning itself entirely with the technical requirements of effective organization. Its job is to identify those structural arrangements that best realize its policy goals.

It is perhaps natural to think that, since a dominant group can have anything it wants, it would proceed by figuring out what types of behaviors are called for by what types of people under what types of conditions and by writing legislation spelling all this out in the minutest detail. If an administrative agency were necessary to perform services, process applications, or inspect business operations, the jobs of bureaucrats could be specified with such precision that they would have little choice but to do the group's bidding.

For simple policy goals—requiring, say, little more than transfer payments—these strategies would be attractive. But they are quite unsuited to policy problems of any complexity. The reason is that, although the group has the political power to impose its will on everyone, it almost surely lacks the knowledge to do it well. It does not know what to tell people to do.

In part, this is an expertise problem. Society as a whole simply has not developed sufficient knowledge to determine the causes of or solutions for most social problems; and the group typically knows much less than society does, even when it hires experts of its own. These knowledge problems are compounded by uncertainty about the future. The world is subject to unpredictable changes over time, and some will call on specific policy adjustments if the group's interests are to be pursued effectively. The group could attempt to specify all future contingencies in the current legislation and, through continuous monitoring and intervention, update it over time. But the knowledge requirements of a halfway decent job would prove enormously costly, cumbersome, and time-consuming.

A group with the political power to tell everyone what to do, then, will typically not find it worthwhile to try. A more attractive option is to write legislation in general terms, put experts on the public payroll, and grant them the authority to "fill in the details" and make whatever adjustments are necessary over time. This compensates nicely for the group's formidable knowledge problems, allowing it to pursue its own interests without knowing exactly how to implement its policies and without having to grapple with future contingencies. The experts do what the group is unable to do for itself. And because they are public officials on the public payroll, the arrangement economizes greatly on the group's resources and time.

It does, however, raise a new worry: there is no guarantee the experts will always act in the group's best interests. Experts have their own interests—in career, in autonomy—that may conflict with those of the group. And, due largely to experts' specialized knowledge and the often intangible nature of their outputs, the group cannot know exactly what its expert agents are doing or why. These are problems of conflict of interest and asymmetric information, and they are unavoidable. Because of them, control will be imperfect.

When the group's political power is assured, as we assume it is here, these control problems are at the heart of structural choice. The most direct approach is for the group to impose a set of rules to constrain bureaucratic behavior. Among other things, these rules might specify the criteria and procedures bureaucrats are to use in making decisions; shape incentives by specifying how bureaucrats are to be evaluated, rewarded, and sanctioned; require them to collect and report certain kinds of information on their internal operations, and set up oversight procedures by which their activities can be monitored. These are basic components of bureaucratic structure.

But some slippage will remain. The group's knowledge problems, combined with the experts' will and capacity to resist (at least at the margins), make perfect control impossible. Fortunately, though, the group can do more than impose a set of rules on its agents. It also has the power to choose who its agents will be—and wise use of this power could make the extensive use of rules unnecessary.

The key here is reputation. Most individuals in the expert market come with reputations that speak to their job-relevant traits: expertise, intelligence, honesty, loyalty, policy preferences, ideology. "Good" reputations provide reliable information. The reason is that individuals value good reputations, they invest in them—by behaving honestly, for instance, even when they could realize short-term gains through cheating—and, having built up reputations, they have strong incentives to maintain them through consistent behavior. To the group, therefore, reputation is of enormous value because it allows predictability in an uncertain world. And predictability facilitates control.

To see more concretely how this works, consider an important reputational syndrome: professionalism. If individuals are known to be accountants or securities lawyers or highway engineers, the group will immediately know a great deal about their "type." They will be experts in certain issues. They will have specialized educations and occupational experiences. They will analyze issues, collect data, and propose solutions in characteristic ways. They will hew to the norms of their professional communities. Particularly when professionalism is combined with reputational information of a more personal nature, the behavior of these experts will be highly predictable.

The link between predictability and control would seem especially troublesome in this case, since professionals are widely known to demand autonomy in their work. And, as far as restrictive rules and hierarchical directives are concerned, their demand for autonomy does indeed pose problems. But the group is forced to grant experts discretion anyway, owing to its knowledge problems. What professionalism does—via reputation—is allow the group to anticipate how expert discretion will be exercised under various conditions; it can then plan accordingly as it designs a structure that takes best advantage of their expertise. In the extreme, one might think of professionals as automatons, programmed to behave in specific ways. Knowing how they are programmed, the group can select those with the desired programs, place them in a structure designed to accommodate them, and turn them loose to exercise free choice. The professionals would see themselves as independent decision makers. The group would see them as under control. And both would be right.

The purpose of this illustration is not to emphasize professionalism per se, but to clarify a general point about the technical requirements of organizational design. A politically powerful group, acting under uncertainty and concerned with solving a complex policy problem, is normally best off if it resists using its power to tell bureaucrats exactly what to do. It can use its power more productively by selecting the right types of bureaucrats and designing a structure that affords them reasonable autonomy. Through the judicious allocation of bureaucratic roles and responsibilities, incentive systems, and structural checks on bureaucratic choice, a select set of bureaucrats can be unleashed to follow their expert judgment, free from detailed formal instructions.

Interest Groups: The Political Problem of Structural Choice

Political dominance is an extreme case for purposes of illustration. In the real world of democratic politics, interest groups cannot lay claim to unchallenged legal authority. Because this is so, they face two fundamental problems that a dominant group does not. The first I will call political uncertainty, the second political compromise. Both have enormous consequences for the strategic design of public bureaucracy—consequences that entail substantial departures from effective organization.

Political uncertainty is inherent in democratic government. No one has a perpetual hold on public authority nor, therefore, a perpetual right to control public agencies. An interest group may be powerful enough to exercise public authority today, but tomorrow its power may ebb, and its right to exercise public authority may then be usurped by its political opponents. Should this occur, they would become the new "owners" of whatever the group had created, and they could use their authority to destroy—quite legitimately—everything the group had worked so hard to achieve.

A group that is currently advantaged, then, must anticipate all this. Precisely because its own authority is not guaranteed, it cannot afford to focus entirely on technical issues of effective organization. It must also design its creations so that they have the capacity to pursue its policy goals in a world in which its enemies may achieve the right to govern. The group's task in the current period, then, is to build agencies that are difficult for its opponents to gain control over later. Given the way authority is allocated and exercised in a democracy, this will often mean building agencies that are insulated from public authority in general—and thus insulated from formal control by the group itself.

There are various structural means by which the group can try to protect and nurture its bureaucratic agents. They include the following:

- It can write detailed legislation that imposes rigid constraints on the agency's mandate and decision procedures. While these constraints will tend to be flawed, cumbersome, and costly, they serve to remove important types of decisions from future political control. The reason they are so attractive is rooted in the American separation-of-powers system, which sets up obstacles that make formal legislation extremely difficult to achieve—and, if achieved, extremely difficult to overturn. Should the group's opponents gain in political power, there is a good chance they would still not be able to pass corrective legislation of their own.
- It can place even greater emphasis on professionalism than is technically justified, since professionals will generally act to protect their own autonomy and resist political interference. For similar reasons, the group can be a strong supporter of the career civil service and other personnel systems that insulate bureaucratic jobs, promotion, and pay from political intervention. And it can try to minimize the power and number of political appointees, since these too are routes by which opponents may exercise influence.
- It can oppose formal provisions that enhance political oversight and involvement. The legislative veto, for example, is bad because it gives opponents a direct mechanism for reversing agency decisions. Sunset provisions, which require reauthorization of the agency after some period of time, are also dangerous because they give opponents opportunities to overturn the group's legislative achievements.
- It can see that the agency is given a safe location in the scheme of government. Most obviously, it might try to place the agency in a friendly executive department, where it can be sheltered by the group's allies. Or it may favor formal independence, which provides special protection from presidential removal and managerial powers.
- It can favor judicialization of agency decision making as a way of insulating policy choices from outside interference. It can also favor making various types of agency actions—or inactions—appealable to the courts. It must take care to design these procedures and checks, however, so that they disproportionately favor the group over its opponents.

The driving force of political uncertainty, then, causes the winning group to favor structural designs it would never favor on technical grounds alone: designs that place detailed formal restrictions on bureaucratic discretion, impose complex procedures for agency decision making, minimize opportunities for oversight, and otherwise insulate the agency from politics. The group has to protect itself and its agency from the dangers of democracy, and it does so by imposing structures that appear strange and incongruous indeed when judged by almost any reasonable standards of what an effective organization ought to look like.

But this is only part of the story. The departure from technical rationality is still greater because of a second basic feature of American democratic politics: legislative victory of any consequence almost always requires compromise. This means that opposing groups will have a direct say in how the agency and its mandate are constructed. One form that this can take, of course, is the classic compromise over policy that is written about endlessly in textbooks and newspapers. But there is no real disjunction between policy and structure, and many of the opponents' interests will also be pursued through demands for structural concessions. What sorts of arrangements should they tend to favor?

- Opponents want structures that work against effective performance. They fear strong, coherent, centralized organization. They like fragmented authority, decentralization, federalism, checks and balances, and other structural means of promoting weakness, confusion, and delay.
- They want structures that allow politicians to get at the agency. They do not want to see the agency placed within a friendly department, nor do they favor formal independence. They are enthusiastic supporters of legislative veto and reauthorization provisions. They favor onerous requirements for the collection and reporting of information, the monitoring of agency operations, and the review of agency decisions—thus laying the basis for active, interventionist oversight by politicians.
- They want appointment and personnel arrangements that allow for political direction of the agency. They also want more active and influential roles for political appointees and less extensive reliance on professionalism and the civil service.
- They favor agency decision making procedures that allow them to participate, to present evidence and arguments, to appeal adverse agency decisions, to delay, and, in general, to protect their own interests and inhibit effective agency

action through formal, legally sanctioned rules. This means that they will tend to push for cumbersome, heavily judicialized decision processes, and that they will favor an active, easily triggered role for the courts in reviewing agency decisions.
- They want agency decisions to be accompanied by, and partially justified in terms of, "objective" assessments of their consequences: environmental impact statements, inflation impact statements, cost-benefit analysis. These are costly, time-consuming, and disruptive. Even better, their methods and conclusions can be challenged in the courts, providing new opportunities for delaying or quashing agency decisions.

Political compromise ushers the fox into the chicken coop. Opposing groups are dedicated to crippling the bureaucracy and gaining control over its decisions, and they will pressure for fragmented authority, labyrinthine procedures, mechanisms of political intervention, and other structures that subvert the bureaucracy's performance and open it up to attack. In the politics of structural choice, the inevitability of compromise means that agencies will be burdened with structures fully intended to cause their failure.

In short, democratic government gives rise to two major forces that cause the structure of public bureaucracy to depart from technical rationality. First, those currently in a position to exercise public authority will often face uncertainty about their own grip on political power in the years ahead, and this will prompt them to favor structures that insulate their achievements from politics. Second, opponents will also tend to have a say in structural design, and, to the degree they do, they will impose structures that subvert effective performance and politicize agency decisions.

Legislators and Structural Choice

If politicians were nothing more than conduits for political pressures, structural choice could be understood without paying much attention to them. But politicians, especially presidents, do sometimes have preferences about the structure of government that are not simple reflections of what the groups want. And when this is so, they can use their control of public authority to make their preferences felt in structural outcomes.

The conduit notion is not so wide of the mark for legislators, owing to their almost paranoid concern for reelection. In structural politics, well informed interest groups make demands, observe legislators' responses, and accurately assign credit and blame as decisions are made and consequences realized. Legislators therefore have strong incentives to do what groups want—and, even in the absence of explicit demands, to take entrepreneurial action in actively representing group interests. They cannot satisfy groups with empty position taking. Nor can they costlessly "shift the responsibility" by delegating tough decisions to the bureaucracy. Interest groups, unlike voters, are not easily fooled.

This does not mean that legislators always do what groups demand of them. Autonomous behavior can arise even among legislators who are motivated by nothing other than reelection. This happens because politicians, like groups, recognize that their current choices are not just means of responding to current pressures, but are also means of imposing structure on their political lives. This will sometimes lead them to make unpopular choices today in order to reap political rewards later on.

It is not quite right, moreover, to suggest that legislators have no interest of their own in controlling the bureaucracy. The more control legislators are able to exercise, the more groups will depend on them to get what they want; and this, in itself, makes control electorally attractive. But the attractiveness of control is diluted by other factors. First, the winning group—the more powerful side—will pressure to have its victories removed from political influence. Second, the capacity for control can be a curse for legislators in later conflict, since both sides will descend on them repeatedly. Third, oversight for purposes of serious policy control is time-consuming, costly, and difficult to do well; legislators typically have much more productive ways to spend their scarce resources.

The result is that legislators tend not to invest in general policy control. Instead, they value "particularized" control: they want to be able to intervene quickly, inexpensively, and in ad hoc ways to protect or advance the interests of particular clients in particular matters. This sort of control can be managed by an individual legislator without collective action; it has direct payoffs; it will generally be carried out behind the scenes; and it does not involve or provoke conflict. It generates political benefits without political costs. Moreover, it fits in quite nicely with a bureaucratic structure designed for conflict avoidance: an agency that is highly autonomous in the realm of policy yet highly constrained by complex procedural requirements will offer all sorts of opportunities for particularistic interventions.

The more general point is that legislators, by and large, can be expected either to respond to group demands in structural politics or to take entrepreneurial action in trying to please them. They will not be given to flights of autonomous action or statesmanship.

Presidents and Structural Choice

Presidents are motivated differently. Governance is the driving force behind the modern presidency. All presidents, regardless of party, are expected to govern effectively and are held responsible for taking action on virtually the full range of problems facing society. To be judged successful in the eyes of history—arguably the single most important motivator for presidents—they must appear to be strong leaders. They need to achieve their policy initiatives, their initiatives must be regarded as socially valuable, and the structures for attaining them must appear to work.

This raises two basic problems for interest groups. The first is that presidents are not very susceptible to the appeals of special interests. They want to make groups happy, to be sure, and sometimes responding to group demands will contribute nicely to governance. But this is often not so. In general, presidents have incentives to think in grander terms about what is best for society as a whole, or at least broad chunks of it, and they have their own agendas that may depart substantially from what even their more prominent group supporters might want. Even when they are simply responding to group pressures—which is more likely, of course, during their first term—the size and heterogeneity of their support coalitions tend to promote moderation, compromise, opposition to capture, and concern for social efficiency.

The second problem is that presidents want to control the bureaucracy. While legislators eagerly delegate their powers to administrative agencies, presidents are driven to take charge. They do not care about all agencies equally, of course. Some agencies are especially important because their programs are priority items on the presidential agenda. Others are important because they deal with sensitive issues that can become political bombshells if something goes wrong. But most all agencies impinge in one way or another on larger presidential responsibilities—for the budget, for the economy, for national defense—and presidents must have the capacity to direct and constrain agency behavior in basic respects if these larger responsibilities are to be handled successfully. They may often choose not to use their capacity for administrative control; they may even let favored groups use it when it suits their purposes. But the capacity must be there when they need it.

Presidents therefore have a unique role to play in the politics of structural choice. They are the only participants who are directly concerned with how the bureaucracy as a whole should be organized. And they are the only ones who actually want to run it through hands-on management and control. Their ideal is a rational, coherent, centrally directed bureaucracy that strongly resembles popular textbook notions of what an effective bureaucracy, public or private, ought to look like.

In general, presidents favor placing agencies within executive departments and subordinating them to hierarchical authority. They want to see important oversight, budget, and policy coordination functions given to department superiors—and, above them, to the Office of Management and Budget and other presidential management agencies—so that the bureaucracy can be brought under unified direction. While they value professionalism and civil service for their contributions to expertise, continuity, and impartiality, they want authority in the hands of their own political appointees—and they want to choose appointees whose types appear most conducive to presidential leadership.

This is just what the winning group and its legislative allies do not want. They want to protect their agencies and policy achievements by insulating them from politics, and presidents threaten to ruin everything by trying to control these agencies from above. The opposing groups are delighted with this, but they cannot always take comfort in the presidential approach to bureaucracy either. For presidents will tend to resist complex procedural protections, excessive judicial review, legislative veto provisions, and many other means by which the losers try to protect themselves and cripple bureaucratic performance. Presidents want agencies to have discretion, flexibility, and the capacity to take direction. They do not want agencies to be hamstrung by rules and regulations—unless, of course, they are presidential rules and regulations designed to enhance presidential control.

Legislators, Presidents, and Interest Groups

Obviously, presidents and legislators have very different orientations to the politics of structural choice. Interest groups can be expected to anticipate these differences from the outset and devise their own strategies accordingly.

Generally speaking, groups on both sides will find Congress a comfortable place in which to do business. Legislators are not bound by any overarching notion of what the bureaucracy as a whole ought to look like. They are not intrinsically motivated by effectiveness or efficiency or coordination or management or any other design criteria that might limit the kind of bureaucracy they are willing to create. They do not even want to retain political control for themselves.

The key thing about Congress is that it is open and responsive to what the groups want. It willingly builds, piece by piece—however grotesque the pieces, however inconsistent with one another—the kind of bureaucracy interest groups incrementally demand in their structural battles over time. This "congressional bureaucracy" is not supposed to function as a coherent whole, nor even to constitute one. Only the pieces are important. That is the way groups want it.

Presidents, of course, do not want it that way. Interest groups may find them attractive allies on occasion, especially when their interests and the presidential agenda coincide. But, in general, presidents are a fearsome presence on the political scene. Their broad support coalitions, their grand perspective on public policy, and their fundamental concern for a coherent, centrally controlled bureaucracy combine to make them maverick players in the game of structural politics. They want a "presidential bureaucracy" that is fundamentally at odds with the congressional bureaucracy everyone else is busily trying to create.

To the winning group, presidents are a major source of political uncertainty over and above the risks associated with the future power of the group's opponents. This gives it even greater incentives to pressure for structures that are insulated from politics—and, when possible, disproportionately insulated from presidential politics. Because of the seriousness of the presidency's threat, the winning group will place special emphasis on limiting the powers and numbers of political appointees, locating effective authority in the agency and its career personnel, and opposing new hierarchical powers—of review, coordination, veto—for units in the Executive Office or even the departments.

The losing side is much more pragmatic. Presidents offer important opportunities for expanding the scope of conflict, imposing new procedural constraints on agency action, and appealing unfavorable decisions. Especially if presidents are not entirely sympathetic to the agency and its mission, the losing side may actively support all the trappings of presidential bureaucracy—but only, of course, for the particular case at hand. Thus, while presidents may oppose group efforts to cripple the agency through congressional bureaucracy, groups may be able to achieve much the same end through presidential bureaucracy. The risk, however, is that the next president could turn out to be an avid supporter of the agency, in which case presidential bureaucracy might be targeted to quite different ends indeed. If there is a choice, sinking formal restrictions into legislative concrete offers a much more secure and permanent fix.

Bureaucracy

Bureaucratic structure emerges as a jerry-built fusion of congressional and presidential forms, their relative roles and particular features determined by the powers, priorities, and strategies of the various designers. The result is that each agency cannot help but begin life as a unique structural reflection of its own politics.

Once an agency is created, the political world becomes a different place. Agency bureaucrats are now political actors in their own right. They have career and institutional interests that may not be entirely congruent with their formal missions, and they have powerful resources—expertise and delegated authority—that might be employed toward these selfish ends. They are new players whose interests and resources alter the political game.

It is useful to think in terms of two basic types of bureaucratic players: political appointees and careerists. Careerists are the pure bureaucrats. As they carry out their jobs, they will be concerned with the technical requirements of effective organization, but they will also face the same problem that all other political actors face: political uncertainty. Changes in group power, committee composition, and presidential administration represent serious threats to things that bureaucrats hold dear. Their mandates could be restricted, their budgets cut, their discretion curtailed, their reputations blemished. Like groups and politicians, bureaucrats cannot afford to concern themselves solely with technical matters. They must take action to reduce their political uncertainty.

One attractive strategy is to nurture mutually beneficial relationships with groups and politicians whose political support the agency needs. If these are to provide real security, they must be more than isolated quid pro quos; they must be part of an ongoing stream of exchanges that give all participants expectations of future gain and thus incentives to resist short-term opportunities to profit at one another's expense. This is most easily done with the agency's initial supporters. Over time, however, the agency will be driven to broaden its support base, and it may move away from some of its creators—as regulatory agencies sometimes have, for example, in currying favor with the business interests they are supposed to be regulating. All agencies will have a tendency to move away from presidents, who, as temporary players, are inherently unsuited to participation in stable, long-term relationships.

Political appointees are also unattractive allies. They are not long-term participants, and no one will treat them as though they are. They have no concrete basis for participating in the exchange relationships of benefit to careerists. Indeed, they may not want to, for they have incentives to pay special attention to White House policy, and they will try to forge alliances that further those ends. Their focus is on short-term presidential victories, and relationships that stabilize politics for the agency may get in the way and have to be challenged.

As this begins to suggest, the strategy of building supportive relationships is inherently limited. In the end, much of the environment remains out of control. This prompts careerists to rely on a second, complementary strategy of uncertainty avoidance: insulation. If they cannot control the environment, they can try to shut themselves off from it in various ways. They can promote further professionalization and more extensive reliance on civil service. They can formalize and judicialize their decision procedures. They can base decisions on technical expertise, operational experience, and precedent, thus making them "objective" and agency-centered. They can try to monopolize the information necessary for effective political oversight. These insulating strategies

are designed, moreover, not simply to shield the agency from its political environment, but also to shield it from the very appointees who are formally in charge.

All of this raises an obvious question: why can't groups and politicians anticipate the agency's alliance and insulationist strategies and design a structure ex ante that adjusts for them? The answer, of course, is that they can. Presidents may push for stronger hierarchical controls and greater formal power for appointees than they otherwise would. Group opponents may place even greater emphasis on opening the agency up to political oversight. And so on. The agency's design, therefore, should from the beginning incorporate everyone's anticipations about its incentives to form alliances and promote its own autonomy.

Thus, however active the agency is in forming alliances, insulating itself from politics, and otherwise shaping political outcomes, it would be a mistake to regard the agency as a truly independent force. It is literally manufactured by the other players as a vehicle for advancing and protecting their own interests, and their structural designs are premised on anticipations about the roles the agency and its bureaucrats will play in future politics. The whole point of structural choice is to anticipate, program, and engineer bureaucratic behavior. Although groups and politicians cannot do this perfectly, the agency is fundamentally a product of their designs, and so is the way it plays the political game. That is why, in our attempt to understand the structure and politics of bureaucracy, we turn to bureaucrats last rather than first.

Structural Choice as a Perpetual Process

The game of structural politics never ends. An agency is created and given a mandate, but, in principle at least, all of the choices that have been made in the formative round of decision making can be reversed or modified later.

As the politics of structural choice unfolds over time, three basic forces supply its dynamics. First, group opponents will constantly be on the lookout for opportunities to impose structures of their own that will inhibit the agency's performance and open it up to external control. Second, the winning group must constantly be ready to defend its agency from attack—but it may also have attacks of its own to launch. The prime reason is poor performance: because the agency is burdened from the beginning with a structure unsuited to the lofty goals it is supposed to achieve, the supporting group is likely to be dissatisfied and to push for more productive structural arrangements. Third, the president will try to ensure that agency behavior is consistent with broader presidential priorities, and he will take action to impose his own structures on top of those already put in place by Congress. He may also act to impose structures on purely political grounds in response to the interests of either the winning or opposing group.

All of this is going on all the time, generating pressures for structural change that find expression in both the legislative and executive processes. These are potentially of great importance for bureaucracy and policy, and all the relevant participants are intensely aware of it. However, the choices about structure that are made in the first period, when the agency is designed and empowered with a mandate, are normally far more enduring and consequential than those that will be made later. They constitute an institutional base that is protected by all the impediments to new legislation inherent in separation of powers, as well as by the political clout of the agency's supporters. Most of the pushing and hauling in subsequent years is likely to produce only incremental change. This, obviously, is very much on everyone's minds in the first period.

Notes

1. Harold Seidman and Robert Gilmour, *Politics, Position, and Power: From the Positive to the Regulatory State,* 4th ed. (Oxford University Press, 1986); and Frederick C. Mosher, *Democracy and the Public Service,* 2d ed. (Oxford University Press, 1982).

2. Seidman and Gilmour, *Politics, Position, and Power,* p. 330.

8-2 From *The Politics of Presidential Appointments*

David E. Lewis

In this essay, political scientist David Lewis outlines the remarkable history of presidential efforts to control the federal bureaucracy through personnel appointments. Presidents have replaced merit-based positions with presidential appointments, created new layers of political appointees over civil servants, added staff aides to top offices, laid off civil servants, and reorganized departments to accommodate more presidential appointees. As a result, the merit-based civil service today comprises a smaller portion of the federal workforce than it did in the mid-twentieth century.

Few people have heard of Schedule C appointments to the federal service. If queried most would connect a discussion of "Schedule C" to Internal Revenue Service tax forms, but in 1953 the creation of the Schedule C by President Eisenhower was a watershed event in the history of federal personnel management. Eisenhower created this new category of appointments after his inauguration not only in response to pressure from Republican partisans to create more jobs for party members, but also to help rein in the sprawling New Deal bureaucracy created and staffed by presidents Roosevelt and Truman for the previous twenty years. The creation of this new category of federal personnel gave the administration the authority to add over one thousand new appointees to the executive branch and immediately gain substantial influence in important public-policy areas like conservation and the environment.

Prior to Eisenhower's order, important bureaucratic jobs—like director and assistant director of the U.S. Fish and Wildlife Service, director of the National Park Service, and chief and deputy chief of the Soil Conservation Service—had to be filled by career employees who had worked their way up through the agency according to nonpolitical criteria. After Eisenhower's order, these jobs could and were filled by political appointees reviewed by the Republican National Committee and named by the White House. Future presidential administrations expanded the number of jobs included in Schedule C, both managerial positions and other confidential positions like staff, counsel, and special assistant positions.

It is hard to understand the details or importance of President Eisenhower's order without an understanding of the history and details of the civil service system in the United States. Very important and practical choices about the number and location of appointees occur in the context of a unique history and sometimes complex set of civil service laws and rules.

This chapter . . . begins with a brief history of the federal personnel system. It then describes the contours of the modern personnel system, including an explanation of the different types of appointed positions and how they get created. The chapter then describes the presidential personnel operation and how it responds to pressures to fill existing positions and satisfy demands for patronage. The next section

Source: David E. Lewis, *The Politics of Presidential Appointments: Political Control and Bureaucratic Performance,* by David E. Lewis (Princeton, N.J.: Princeton University Press, 2008), 11–25, 27–37, 39–43, 49–50. © 2008 Princeton University Press. Reprinted by permission of Princeton university Press. Notes appearing in the original have been deleted.

describes the most common politicization techniques and the tools Congress has used to rein them in. The chapter concludes with a case study of the reorganization of the Civil Service Commission to illustrate the different politicization techniques and demonstrate how politicization is used to change public policy.

A Brief History of the Federal Personnel System

One of the unique features of the Constitution is that it makes virtually no mention of the bureaucracy; its few limited references to departments or officers give virtually no detail apart from the fact that principal officers are to be nominated by the president and confirmed by the Senate. Congress is empowered to determine the means of appointing inferior officers, and the president is granted the ability to request information from principal officers in writing. Apart from these few details the Constitution is silent about the design, function, and administration of the bureaucratic state.

The Constitution's silence leaves responsibility for the creation, nurturing, and maintenance of the continuing government to elected officials, who are divided by different constituencies, institutional responsibilities, and political temperaments. It is the decisions of these persons in the context of a shifting electoral, partisan, and historical landscape that shapes the nature and history of the modern personnel system.

The Personnel System before Merit

The personnel system that presided from 1789 to 1829 was selected and populated by and with persons from the same social class, who were defined by enfranchisement, property, common upbringing, and shared values. They were drawn from what Leonard White calls "a broad class of gentlemen." The selection of federal personnel was dictated in large part by "fitness for public office," but fitness for office was itself defined by standing, wealth, or public reputation rather than relevant experience, expertise, or demonstrated competence.

Long tenure and expectations of continued service were the norm, reinforced by the long dominance of one party in power from 1800 to 1829, the absence of a national party system, and, apparently, the personal conviction of early presidents that persons should not be removed from office because of their political beliefs. Presidents did fill vacancies and newly created offices in the expanding federal government with their partisans, but outright removals of Federalists by Republicans were rare. Regular rotation only occurred at the level of department heads.

The increasingly permanent and class-based federal service did have its detractors. There was a growing sentiment, particularly with expanded franchise, that more positive action needed to be taken to democratize the public service itself. Of particular concern to many were instances where sons inherited the jobs of their fathers, accentuating fears that federal jobs were becoming a type of property or privilege. In 1820 Congress enacted the Tenure of Office Act, requiring the explicit reappointment of all federal officials every four years as a way of contravening the establishment of a professional class.

The old system was not overturned fully until the presidency of Andrew Jackson. Upon assuming office in 1829 Jackson said, "The duties of all public officers are, or at least admit of being made, so plain and simple that men of intelligence may readily qualify themselves for their performance; I can not but believe that more is lost by the long continuance of men in office than is generally to be gained by their experience." Jackson believed that public office was not reserved for a particular class or incumbents in government. Rather, it should be opened to the broader public. The political benefits of such an action were not lost on Jackson.

While his actions to democratize the federal service only led to the turnover of 10 percent of the federal workforce, his actions set in motion a full-fledged patronage system in the United States. Undergirded by the development of national parties hungry for federal office as a way of securing funds and votes, the regular rotation of a large percentage of federal offices became the norm. The national parties, loose confederations of state and local parties, gave out offices and expected activity for the party and political assessments in return. Office holders would return 1 to 6 percent of their salaries to the party. . . .

The vast majority of federal jobs were located outside of Washington, D.C. They were an important political resource and were viewed proprietarily by congressmen who sought to distribute patronage to local and state machines that brought them to power. Presidents were expected to consult with the senators and, to a lesser extent, representatives in the states where appointments were made. The power of this norm was reinforced by the practice of senatorial courtesy whereby the Senate would refuse to confirm a nomination if an objection was raised by the senator from the state where the appointment was being made. While some strong presidents, such as Jackson or Polk, resisted this norm in principle, all usually followed it in practice.

The deleterious consequences of the spoils system for bureaucratic performance were somewhat mitigated by several factors. First, Andrew Jackson was partly right that many federal jobs did not require a tremendous amount of expertise or special training. . . . Most of the work in the civil service was still clerical and very little authority or discretion was delegated to subcabinet officials. In addition, many of the persons turned out of office with electoral turnover would return once their party returned to power.

Second, jobs requiring more expertise were sometimes filled by persons who did not turn over with each administration. Certain auditors, comptrollers, clerks, and personnel in the scientific offices stayed from administration to administration to conduct the business of government. . . . Indeed, some employees of long tenure moved up to key positions because of their expertise. Their competence and expertise in public work outweighed party patronage considerations in their selection.

This dual personnel system persisted during a period when the size and activities of government were limited. As the federal government grew in size and complexity, however, the weaknesses of the spoils system became increasingly apparent. The quality of the federal service suffered. Rotation in office did lead to the dismissal of many qualified federal officials, such as those who kept the accounts and records, made it difficult to sustain reforms, and prevented the development of consistent, purposeful management practices. Rotation-induced instability prevented functional specialization and the development of managerial and policy-specific expertise. These factors, coupled with low pay, decreased the prestige of federal jobs and their reliability as long-term careers. Day-to-day performance was also hindered by the low quality of patronage appointees who were only competent in their jobs by happy accident or the limited requirements of their occupations. Many appointees spent a portion of their time in other jobs, in work for the party, or in leisure.

. . . The challenges of the Civil War, economic and territorial expansion, periodic monetary crises, massive immigration, and technological change meant the federal government would need to take on new responsibilities and expand to fit its new roles; and public pressure for greater federal government involvement meant the administration of government would have to change. It would have to specialize, organize, and stabilize in order to provide the expertise and services demanded by agricultural interests, businesses, pensioners, consumers, and voters of all types through their elected officials. Congress and the president faced increasing pressure to build a professional bureaucracy by enacting civil service reforms.

The Creation and Extension of Merit

A number of different groups were involved in the nascent push for civil service reform. Included among these groups were urban merchants, bankers, and brokers, often motivated by their own frustrating experience with corrupt and inefficient postal offices and customs houses. A larger class of professionals including lawyers, academics, journalists, and clergy were also supportive of reform, partly as a moral crusade against the corruptions of the spoils system but also as a means of confronting a political system not responsive enough to their interests.

Agency officials were also supportive of reform as a means of improving the performance of offices they were supposed to manage.

Efforts to alter the system usually engendered hostility from the parties and their sympathizers in Congress. As public pressure to change the personnel system mounted, however, the national parties acquiesced reluctantly, fearful of giving up the patronage they held or hoped to gain in the next election. They became more supportive when they needed to cultivate reform-oriented voters. They were also more supportive when they were out of power or expected to lose power since civil service would limit the opposition party's control over spoils. . . .

The first serious government-wide attempt at reform came in the 1870s during the Grant Administration. The reform was motivated more by a desire to heal divisions in the Republican Party than that for substantive reform. Republicans had experienced significant losses in the 1870 elections and a split emerged among reformers within the party and Grant-aligned machine elements, particularly in the Senate. To appease reformers, Grant requested a law authorizing the president to issue regulations governing the admission of persons to the civil service, to hire employees to assess the fitness of persons for the civil service, and to establish regulations governing the conduct of civil servants appointed under the new regulations. In response, the Republican majority delegated to the president sweeping authority to create a civil service system with the hope of bridging the rift before the 1872 elections.

When the commission recommended its first set of rules in 1872, Republicans in Congress said little. After the 1872 elections, however, their tone changed. When the first civil service examinations came online in the Treasury Department in 1873, members of Congress were openly hostile. They responded by refusing appropriations for the commission in 1874. Since Grant's primary interest in the commission was to hold together the different factions in the party, he did little to defend it. When Congress refused to appropriate funds again in 1875, Grant revoked the commission's rules and closed its offices.

Rutherford B. Hayes pledged to support civil service reform during his candidacy in 1876. When he assumed office in 1877 he requested appropriations from Congress to reactivate the Grant Civil Service Commission. Congress turned down his request, but Hayes took a number of other actions to further the cause of civil service. He appointed noted civil service reformer Carl Schurz as Secretary of the Interior, where Schurz installed a vigorous merit system. Hayes also instituted competitive examinations in the New York City customhouse and post office after a public investigation of the customhouse and a bitter feud with Senator Conkling from New York over patronage.

Hayes's actions coincided with the formation of a number of civil service reform associations. These organizations appeared earliest in the northeast where Hayes's controversy over appointments to the New York customhouse drew the most attention. By 1881 the number of groups had grown substantially and societies existed from San Francisco to New York.

The assassination of Hayes's successor, James Garfield, by a disappointed office seeker in the summer of 1881 galvanized popular support for a more concrete and permanent merit system. One month after Garfield's assassination, the local civil service reform associations that started during the Hayes administration coalesced into the National Civil Service Reform League. In December 1881, Democratic Senator George Pendleton introduced reform legislation drafted by the league. The bill was reported from committee in May 1882 but had little support in the Republican Congress. The league, however, pressured for the legislation with a poster campaign and the publication of lists of opponents to civil service reform. With Garfield's assassination reformers had their crystallizing event and leading journals and newspapers aided their efforts.

Enthusiasm for reform increased after the elections in the fall of 1882. Republicans fared poorly and reform was clearly an issue. President Chester Arthur expressed his support for the legislation, and debate on the Pendleton bill began as soon as Congress convened on December 12, 1882. Debate lasted through December 27 and on January 16, 1883, President Arthur signed the Pendleton Act into law. The law created—for the first time in the United States—a merit-based federal civil service.

The law provided for the creation of a three-person bipartisan Civil Service Commission (CSC) that would administer exams and promulgate rules under the act. Under the provisions of the Pendleton Act only 10.5 percent of all federal workers were included in the merit system, and these were primarily employees in large post offices or customs houses. Some employees from the departmental service in Washington, D.C.[,] were also included. At this time being under the merit system meant only that persons had to do well on competitive examinations to be appointed. There were no effective protections against adverse job actions or firing after appointment. Job tenure was only protected by the requirement that new persons appointed to the job had to have done well on the same competitive examination. Formal job tenure and protection from partisan dismissal were not established until the late 1890s. Rigorous prohibition on political activity by civil servants was not enacted until Congress passed the Hatch Act in 1939.

The Pendleton Act delegated to the president authority to add the remaining unclassified federal jobs into the merit system with the exception of positions requiring Senate confirmation and common laborers. Presidents added significantly to the civil service through presidential action; 65 percent of the growth in civil service coverage between 1884 and 1903 was through executive order. Once positions were added, it was difficult for Congress to remove them since they would presumably have to do so over the president's veto. They were unlikely to override a president's veto given that one party was sure to prefer to have these positions under civil service at any given time. . . .

Presidents, with a few exceptions, resisted pressures to remove positions once they had been included in the merit system. Presidents were bolstered by the interests that had pushed for the enactment of civil service reform in the first place. Notably, civil service reform leagues continued to push for the preservation and expansion of the federal merit system while also pressuring states and localities to adopt reforms of their own. Efforts to roll back merit system gains were met with howls of protest . . . .

Nascent government unions also pushed for the expansion of the merit system. The passage of the Pendleton Act provided an environment in which federal employees could organize more easily since the act weakened the ties of federal employees to political patrons. Workers in several occupations, such as mail carriers and postal clerks, organized in the late 1880s and early 1890s. Postal unions were particularly effective at lobbying for pay increases and tenure protections. . . .

These unions were instrumental in the passage of the Lloyd-Lafollette Act in 1912 that formally allowed the unionization of government workers (provided they joined unions that would not strike). The act also prohibited dismissal for reasons other than efficiency, and gave employees the right to be notified of possible firing in writing and respond.

The Lloyd-Lafollette [A]ct spurred a period of more aggressive unionization and the National Federation of Federal Employees organized in 1917 under the auspices of the American Federation of Labor (AFL). This was followed by the American Federation of Government Employees (AFGE) in 1932 and the United Federal Workers of America (under the Congress of Industrial Organizations [CIO]) in 1937. These unions, along with the occupation-specific unions like the postal unions, were instrumental in securing higher salaries and benefits for federal workers. They helped secure the enactment of the Civil Service Retirement Act of 1920 and the Classification Acts of 1923 and 1949. The former provided retirement and survivor benefits as well as improved tenure protections for civil service workers. The latter two acts created a job classification and pay system on the principle of equal pay for equal work and outlined detailed grievance procedures that strengthened worker protections against adverse personnel actions. . . .

The merit system continued to expand as all nineteenth-century and most twentieth-century presidents through Franklin Delano Roosevelt used executive orders to include new classes of employees in the merit system. Presidents frequently blanketed positions into the civil service just prior to leaving office. It was not unusual for Congress to allow new agencies to be created outside the merit system originally, only to add them into the system later. For example, many agencies created to mobilize for war or to combat the Great Depression were originally created outside the merit system. In some cases, the creation of new agencies and new programs provided patronage opportunities that excited either the president or Congress. In fact, in the 1930s Congress on occasion specifically prohibited the president from placing agencies in the merit system. Once these agencies were populated according to the dictates of the politicians in power, they moved to blanket them into the civil service system. This protected their partisans from removal and ensured a degree of long-term loyalty to the programmatic mission of the agencies or to the patrons themselves.

The percentage of federal jobs in the traditional merit system has varied substantially over time (Figure 1). By 1897, the advent of the McKinley presidency, close to 50 percent of the federal civilian workforce was under the merit system, and by 1932 close to 80 percent of federal workers held merit positions, a proportion that dipped during the New Deal but reached its peak of almost 88 percent in 1951. This figure underestimates the actual extension of the merit system because many employees not covered by the traditional merit system were employed under other agency-specific personnel systems, like the Tennessee Valley Authority (TVA) or the Foreign Service, which included merit-like provisions. In addition, many of the excluded employees were employed overseas and were unlikely to be consequential for patronage.

While the percentage of jobs included in the merit system peaked at midcentury, it is now decreasing as the federal government shifts its strategy away from a one-size-fits-all personnel system to an agency-specific

Figure 1   Percentage of Federal Civilian Jobs in the Traditional Merit System, 1883–2004

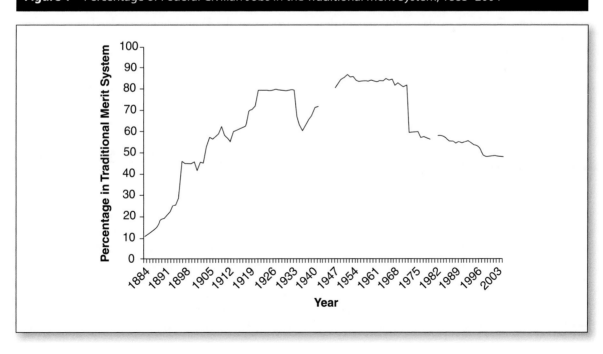

model. This trend has accelerated at the start of the twenty-first century, since Congress enacted legislation providing both the Department of Homeland Security and the Department of Defense with authority to create their own personnel systems. If these new systems are implemented effectively, the number of federal employees under the traditional merit system will dip below 30 percent of the federal civilian workforce.

The Modern Personnel System

Today the federal government employs 2.5 million civilians in full-time positions (and 1.4 million uniformed military personnel). Each civilian job is defined by a pay category and an appointment authority. To ensure equal pay for equal work, an elaborate pay system, including three primary classification schemes for blue-collar, white-collar, and top-level management positions, has been developed. The Federal Wage System (FWS) covers trade, craft, skilled, and unskilled laborers. The General Schedule (GS) defines the pay rates for administrative, technical, and professional jobs, while the Senior Level and Scientific and Professional (SL/ST) system does the same for high-level, but nonmanagerial, positions. Top-level management and professional jobs are covered under the Senior Executive Service (SES) pay schedule or the Executive Schedule (EX). The EX, with a few exceptions, is reserved for positions requiring presidential nomination and Senate confirmation. In each pay system there is a series of numerical pay categories that in the GS system are called *grades*. There are currently fifteen grades in the GS system. These pay categories define a pay range for jobs with equivalent levels of responsibility, qualifications, or experience. Each pay category allows for some flexibility in differentiating between employees who hold similar positions but have different levels of experience or backgrounds. In the GS system these are called *steps*. . . .

Of the 2.5 million full-time civilian employees, about 1.32 million are included in the traditional merit system. At the heart of the civil service system is a series of rules and regulations governing how people can obtain federal jobs and what their rights are with regard to promotion, removal, and other personnel actions. Merit system principles demand that persons be hired, promoted, and fired only on the basis of merit rather than on other factors, such as party membership, gender, or race. Persons initially establish their merit through competitive examination or, in some cases, appropriate background qualifications. Once a person's qualifications have been established, a determination is made about his or her eligibility for both position and pay grade. Persons employed under the merit system have a series of rights formerly defined in the *Federal Personnel Manual*, most notably rights to notification and appeal in cases of adverse personnel actions such as demotion or removal. These rights are now defined in the *Code of Federal Regulations* and various Office of Personnel Management (OPM) handbooks.

Excepted Positions

As suggested above, more than half of all federal jobs are now "excepted" from the traditional merit system described above (Figure 2). The excepted service is a residual category, catching all jobs that are not subject to the appointment provisions of Title 5 of the United States Code. There are four categories of excepted jobs: positions requiring presidential nomination and Senate confirmation (PAS); jobs filled by persons in the SES; positions in what are known as Schedules A, B, and C; and positions in agency-specific personnel systems.

The most visible positions outside the traditional merit system are those that require presidential nomination and Senate confirmation. These positions are at the top of the federal personnel hierarchy. The United States Constitution (Article II, sec. 2, cl. 2) requires that all "ambassadors, other public ministers and consuls, judges of the Supreme Court, and all other officers of the United States" be appointed in this manner. The manner of appointing "inferior" officers is up to Congress (and the president) as the result of legislative determinations. Where one draws the line between "principal" and "inferior" officers, however, is unclear. In 2004 there were 1,137 PAS positions in the executive branch,

Figure 2   Federal Civilian Personnel System Appointment Authorities

Note: Excludes job-specific excepted positions. PAS excludes part-time, advisory, U.S. Attorneys, U.S. Marshals, and ambassadorial positions. The "excepted service" includes PAS, SES, Schedules A, B, C, and personnel in agency-specific personnel systems.

about 945 of which were policymaking positions. The remainder is comprised of appointments to minor advisory or committee-supervisory roles often requiring only part-time employment, paid on a per diem basis. Of the 945 positions, about 186 were U.S. attorneys or U.S. marshals and 154 were ambassadors, leaving 550–600 key executive PAS positions in the cabinet departments and major independent agencies. The average cabinet department dealing with domestic affairs has fifteen to thirty PAS positions, including a secretary, a deputy secretary, a handful of under- and assistant secretaries, an inspector general, and a chief financial officer.

Between PAS positions and the competitive civil service in the federal hierarchy is a space filled by a mixture of career employees from the Senior Executive Service (SES) and political appointees who will be designated noncareer members of this service. The SES was created by the Civil Service Reform Act of 1978 and is comprised of a cadre of approximately 7,000 senior management officials. The OPM, based on its own assessment and the requests of agencies, allocates a certain number of SES positions to each department or agency, and the administration chooses which of the jobs in the agency will be SES jobs. Presidents or their subordinates can choose either an existing member of the SES (a career civil servant who applied to be a part of the SES) or a political appointee from outside who will fill an SES job. By law political appointees cannot exceed 10 percent of the entire SES or 25 percent of the allocated SES positions in a specific agency. In 2004 there were 6,811 persons in the SES, 674 of whom were appointees. Some examples of appointed SES positions include Chief of Staff at the U.S Agency for International Development, Director of Intergovernmental Affairs for the Department of Defense, Deputy Assistant Secretary for Special Education and Rehabilitative Services, and Deputy General Counsel in the Department of Health and Human Services.

A key motivation in creating the SES was to give presidents more flexibility in controlling policy and programmatic positions pivotal for implementing the administration's program. One way in which it did this was to provide more appointees at this level; another was to increase the ease with which presidents could reassign career senior management officials. Under the law the president can reassign a career SES executive to any other position, provided the president and the new agency head have been in office for at least 120 days and the executive has been given 15 days notice (60 if the reassignment includes a geographical change).

Since the creation of the merit system it has been clear that there are some positions for which it is not feasible to hold exams, even in agencies where the merit system is otherwise entirely appropriate. There are three classes of such positions, designated as Schedules A, B, and C. There are no examinations at all for Schedule A positions, which historically have included lawyers, military chaplains, or positions in isolated localities. Schedule B positions have examinations attached to them but they establish a threshold level of acceptability and do not utilize comparisons among applicants. This schedule has included positions in new agencies or programs for which there are no established directions or guidelines, federal work-study positions, and positions set aside for those with certain types of disabilities.

The third schedule, Schedule C, is reserved for positions of a confidential or policy-determining nature. As the start of the chapter suggested, the schedule was created by President Eisenhower in 1953. Schedule C originally included both management positions below the PAS level and the assorted staff assigned to appointees (confidential assistants, drivers, and so forth). As such, the pay range for Schedule C appointees varied dramatically according to position. Top-level management positions in Schedule C were eventually converted to NEA [National Education Association] positions in 1966 and SES positions in 1978. Lower-paying Schedule C positions remain (GS 15 and below). In 2004 there were 1,596 persons appointed to Schedule C positions in the federal government.

These constitute an important subtype of political appointment and, while technically selected by agency officials, presidents since Reagan have exercised substantial control over them. . . . Typical Schedule C posts include special or confidential assistants to PAS appointees, directors of communications, press, or outreach offices, and officials in legislative liaison offices. Some current examples include the White House liaison in the Department of Interior, the confidential assistant to the Assistant Secretary of Education for Vocational and Adult Education, and the Director of Media Affairs in the Department of Labor.

The last, and by far the largest, set of positions are excepted because they are located in agencies that have authority to govern their own personnel systems (Table 1). They can be low- or high-paying jobs of varying levels of responsibility and character. Calling them "excepted" is something of a misnomer, however, since the rights of employees in these personnel systems are usually very similar to those in the Title 5 civil service system. There has been a dramatic increase in the number of "excepted" jobs because recent congressional decisions give certain agencies authority to create their own personnel systems outside the merit system defined by Title 5. The most significant actions in this regard have been the reorganization in 1970 of the postal service into a government corporation, with its own personnel system (800,000 employees); the creation of the Department of Homeland Security in 2002, with authority to create its own personnel system (170,000 civilian employees); and Congress's decision in 2003 to grant the Department of Defense authority to create its own personnel system (660,000 civilian employees). Agencies, bolstered by outside critiques of the federal

Table 1	Examples of Agencies with Broad Exceptions from the Traditional Merit Personnel System

Department of Defense

Department of Homeland Security

Federal Aviation Agency

United States Postal Service

Postal Rates Commission

Central Intelligence Agency

National Security Agency

Tennessee Valley Authority

Federal Bureau of Investigation

General Accounting Office

Panama Canal Commission

Board of Governors, Federal Reserve System

Peace Corps

Railroad Retirement Board

Overseas Private Investment Corporation

Nuclear Regulatory Commission

Federal Election Commission

Source: U.S. General Accounting Office 1997a; U.S. Senate 2000.

personnel system, have long clamored for more control over their own personnel systems, claiming that they need more flexibility in hiring, promoting, and firing in order to improve performance. Flexible personnel systems allow them to respond more quickly to changes in the job market, agency personnel needs, and new programmatic responsibilities. Increased flexibility, however, can also lead to fewer protections against abuses in hiring, firing, and promotion, as well as inequities in pay, benefits, and treatment for comparable work.

In sum, politicization, when it does occur, is, at the top levels, defined both by pay and by appointment authority. It involves an increase in the number of PAS, SES, Schedule C, and similarly excepted agency-specific appointees.

The Modern Presidential Personnel Process

Given these different types of appointments, it is worth reviewing how presidents and their staffs go about filling PAS positions and determining where to place SES and Schedule C appointees. Both policy and patronage concerns shape modern personnel politics. On the policy side, presidents are confronted with a need to fill hundreds of executive-level PAS positions across the government requiring specific skills, experience, and expertise. These jobs range from the Secretary of Defense to the Assistant Secretary of Labor for Occupational Safety and Health to the Under Secretary of Commerce for Intellectual Property. The success of the administration in controlling the bureaucracy depends upon their success in filling these slots. . . .

There is almost uniform concern articulated voluntarily by persons involved in presidential personnel about how important it is to find loyal people with the right skills and background to fill these jobs. . . . Personnel is policy and White House officials recognize that in order to get control of policy, you need people who are loyal to the president and qualified for the job to which they have been appointed. In practice, evaluations of competence can be colored by ideology and the immediate need to fill literally thousands of jobs. Reagan aide Lyn Nofziger, for example, stated, "As far as I'm concerned, anyone who supported Reagan is competent." That said, and importantly, most senior personnel officials define their job as finding the most competent people for senior administration posts.

Starting with President Nixon, many presidents have employed professional recruiters to help identify qualified persons for top executive posts. The most important personnel task at the start of each administration is that of identifying candidates to fill these positions. Each administration has produced lists of positions to be filled first. These include positions important for public safety but also usually positions that need to be filled early to advance the president's policy agenda. Transition advice to

President Kennedy focused on the "pressure points" in government. In the Reagan administration the transition focused first on the "Key 87" positions, which included executive posts necessary for implementation of Reagan's economic program. These priority positions naturally receive the most attention throughout the president's term whenever vacancies occur. In some cases, the existing number of positions is sufficient to gain control and advance the president's agenda; in others, it is not.

On the patronage side, presidents and their personnel operations are besieged by office seekers who have a connection to the campaign, to the party, interest groups, or patrons in Congress important to the administration. Recent administrations have received tens of thousands of resumes, and even more recommendations and communications dealing with specific candidates or jobs. . . . Overall, the Clinton administration received over 100,000 resumes. . . .

Dealing with requests for jobs involves evaluating the skills and backgrounds of priority job seekers and locating appropriate or defensible jobs in levels of pay and responsibility. In many cases, priority placements are young, inexperienced, or primarily qualified through political work. This makes them unqualified for top executive posts. The less background experience, the harder it is to find them jobs. Such applicants are usually given staff, liaison, advance, and public affairs jobs for which they are best qualified given their campaign experience. In other cases, people connected to the candidates either through personal relationships or contributions are too senior to take such jobs but are either not qualified for or not interested in top executive posts. Personnel officials often recommend these persons for ambassadorships, positions on commissions, or advisory posts. . . .

In practice, presidents and their subordinates in presidential personnel (PPO) determine the number and location of political appointees by starting with where their predecessor had appointees and then making incremental adjustments. Each administration learns what jobs were filled by appointees in the last administration through a variety of sources, including transition reports produced by teams sent to the different agencies in the executive branch prior to the inauguration, contacts with the previous administration, and government publications. Subsequent adjustments to the number and location of appointees are made based upon concerns about policy and the need to satisfy concerns for patronage.

The distinction drawn between policy and patronage activities in presidential personnel is not to suggest that policy-driven personnel practices have no patronage component or that efforts to reward campaign supporters cannot influence policy. On the contrary, patronage concerns invariably influence appointments, and appointees of all types can influence policy outputs. Rather, the point is that one process revolves primarily around filling *positions* and the other process revolves primarily around placing *persons*. These two fundamentally different goals are managed differently and have different effects on the number and penetration of political appointments in the bureaucracy.

Common Politicization Techniques

One factor that can influence the number and penetration of appointees in specific cases is the extent to which presidents and their appointees confront career personnel in management positions that do not share their ideology or priorities. Conflict between the president and agencies can emerge for a number of reasons. Sometimes the disagreement stems from what agencies do. Some agencies are designed with a specific policy goal in mind. For example, the Office of Economic Opportunity was the hallmark of Lyndon Johnson's Great Society. It was anathema to Richard Nixon, and he set about politicizing (and dismantling) it in the early 1970s.

In other cases the political biases of a particular agency have less to do with the mission of the agency embedded in law or executive decree than with issues of personnel. Career managers can be unresponsive because they are known to be partisans from the other party. For example, surveys of top executives from the Nixon and Ford administrations showed that many top managers, particularly executives in social service agencies, were unsympathetic to the policy goals of the Nixon administration. More recent surveys confirm that top careerists in defense agencies are more likely to be Republican and conservative, whereas top careerists in social welfare agencies are likely to be Democrats and liberal.

Career managers also often feel bound by legal, moral, or professional norms to certain courses of action and these courses of action may be at variance with the president's agenda. Agencies act to implement policy directives spelled out in statutes, executive decrees, or informal directions from Congress. They are legally bound to implement the laws enacted, and the amount of discretion administrators possess to alter policy is not always clear. Differences of opinion arise about both managers' power and their responsibilities given this power. This is starkly illustrated in cases where career employees are asked to implement administrative policies they believe to be of questionable legality. For instance, career employees make administrative changes in the level and type of civil rights enforcement that might or

might not include affirmative action as a remedy. Directions from political appointees can also bump up against professional norms. The ranger in the Forest Service, the statistician in the Bureau of Labor Statistics, and the lawyer in the Justice Department has a point beyond which they cannot go and still maintain their professional integrity. . . .

A number of different techniques for politicizing agencies address the perceived lack of responsiveness from career officials. These techniques are often used concurrently with other strategies for gaining control of the bureaucracy, such as budgeting, public statements, and administrative actions. To help visualize what this problem looks like, consider Figure 3, an organizational chart from a hypothetical department in which the top three levels are filled by presidential appointments with Senate confirmation. Below this is a level of career managers who direct the operating programs and bureaus. Assume that one of these career managers is unresponsive or problematic to the administration in power for one of the reasons listed above.

Figure 3   Hypothetical Agency Problem

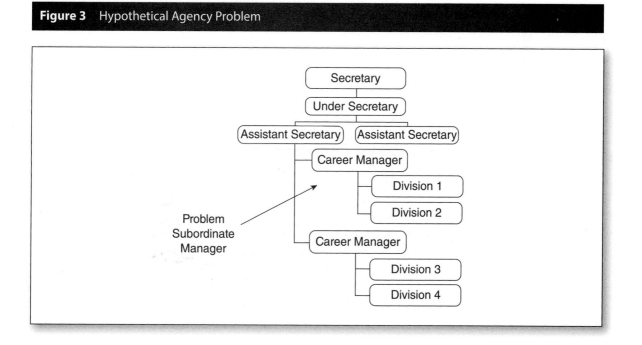

Replacement

The first and most obvious solution to this dilemma is to remove the resistant career manager and replace this person with an appointee or more acceptable career person. If the position is a general SES position the president can replace the career SES manager with an appointee after a period of time, provided doing so will not put the agency over the statutory limit for the number of appointees in the SES or agency.

The president can also try to change the appointment authority of the position in question (Figure 4). For example, a presidential administration could change a GS 15 career management position to a Schedule C position or a general SES position. Changes in appointment authority can sometimes be performed internally, as in the case of deciding which jobs are SES jobs. In other cases changes are performed with a request to the Office of Personnel Management (or earlier, the CSC). Most experienced personnel officers know how to use the appropriate terms of art to ensure their applications are approved.

The OPM director and many of her subordinates serve at the pleasure of the president, easing the way for the White House to get its way. . . .

There are . . . three techniques well known in bureaucratic lore for getting unwanted employees to leave their current jobs. The first and most obvious strategy for convincing a careerist to leave is the *frontal assault*. Political appointees meet privately with the career manager in question and tell the manager that her services are no longer needed. Career managers are offered help finding another job, a going-away party, and even a departmental award. The career manager is informed that if she refuses to leave, her employment record and references will suffer.

The career manager can also be *transferred* within the agency to a position she is unlikely to accept. The transfer offer is usually accompanied by a raise and perhaps a promotion to a newly created position. In such cases, appointees know ahead of time the types of jobs the career employee is likely or unlikely to accept. For example, the career manager known to

Figure 4　Replacement

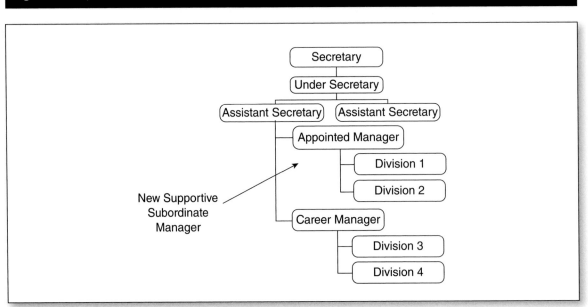

have strong ties to the East Coast may be offered a job in Dallas or St. Louis. Appointees inform the career employee that if she does not want the new job, she can resign without prejudice from the agency and stay on in their current position for a limited amount of time until she finds another position.

With a change in administration, careerists identified with the past administration's policies worry about being transferred to "turkey farms"—jobs with few responsibilities, limited staff, and no access to policymaking. . . . As noted above, by law SES careerists cannot be removed without consent for 120 days by the new administration, but many waive these rights if the new administration requests it. If career employees do not waive this right, the new administration can transfer them after 120 days, provided they have been given appropriate written notice.

A related strategy is the *new-activity* technique. Political appointees hatch plans for a new agency initiative, and the career employee in question is selected for the job ostensibly on the basis of his past performance and unique qualifications. The career manager is even promoted and given an increase in pay. The new initiative appears to be meaningful, but the real purpose behind it is to move the career manager out of his current position. . . .

Layering

Political appointees' difficulty in getting what they want through attempting to remove career employees and reclassifying their jobs often leads them to adopt other strategies. One of the most prominent is *layering,* the practice of adding politically appointed managers on top of career managers as a means of enhancing political control. . . . These new appointees can more carefully monitor the career managers and assume some of their policy-determining responsibilities through their influence in budget preparation, personnel decisions, and other administrative responsibilities. . . .

Add Appointed Ministerial Staff

A similar strategy is to *add appointed ministerial staff.* For instance, the Senate-confirmed assistant secretary adds two special assistants. Titled positions like assistant secretaries often acquire title-riding appointees like chiefs of staff, special assistants, counsels, and public affairs personnel to help them perform their job. The strategy of adding ministerial staff is different from layering in that the appointees added have little formal authority. While they have little formal authority, such appointees can acquire substantial informal authority as experts, gatekeepers, and public spokespeople.

Ministerial staff of this type usually comprises Schedule C appointees. Schedule C positions are created specifically for persons attached to the incoming appointees. Schedule C appointees gain power from being the primary advisors to higher-level appointees and from speaking with the implied authority of the appointee. In other contexts ministerial staff is given special projects, review budgets and legal documents, and help in personnel and administrative decisions. Schedule C positions can be training grounds for other appointed positions. Persons working for higher-level appointees often gain valuable experience and exposure and move from these positions into managerial positions with more formal responsibility.

Reorganization

A fourth common politicization technique is *reorganization*. Reorganization has been used strategically by managers to diminish the influence of problematic career managers and enhance political control. . . . The nominal purpose of the reorganization can be to align organizational structure to better meet the bureau's stated goals or to increase efficiency but have the real or dual purpose of getting better control of the bureau. In large, modern agencies with complicated organizational structures, reorganizations can be subtle and effective means of getting political appointees in charge of important administrative responsibilities. In reorganizations, positions are created and disbanded, upgraded and downgraded, and these decisions are informed by the political needs of administration officials.

For example, in the 1980s enforcement activities within the Environmental Protection Agency (EPA) were reorganized at least three times. In 1981 the Office of Enforcement was disbanded and the legal staff was parsed out to various other offices within the agency. EPA director Anne Burford assembled a new Office of Legal and Enforcement Counsel not long after, but key positions remained vacant into 1982. In 1983 a distinct Office of Enforcement Counsel was created under an assistant administrator. The effect of Burford's reorganizations, however, was to diminish the influence of inherited personnel partly through a decline in morale and high turnover among attorneys who had served in the old Office of Enforcement.

Reorganization can also be used to create parallel bureaucratic structures or processes to circumvent existing structures. This form of politicization takes two common forms. In the first, a new manager who is sympathetic to the goals of the administration is added to the management structure with staff and resources. . . . In this case, however, it is not the problematic career manager who is given this post; rather, it is the trusted, sympathetic manager with closer ties to the administration. This manager duplicates or explicitly assumes tasks performed by the division headed by the less-responsive career manager. The administration then cuts the disfavored manager out of decision making and downgrades the manager's division. . . .

Reductions-in-Force (RIF)

The final prominent technique for politicizing is the *reduction-in-force (RIF)*. While RIFs are a normal part of organizational life in both the private and public sectors, they can also be used strategically to transform an unresponsive agency. Through RIFs federal officials cut employment as a way of getting control of the bureau. According to a general rule of "save grade, save pay," those career employees with the least experience lose their jobs first during RIFs, but those who stay with more seniority are bumped down in position and often assume tasks that are new or are different from what they were doing before. They often have to do more work for the same amount of pay, and the new tasks they assume are frequently jobs not performed by people in their pay scale. These ripple effects increase attrition beyond

that caused by the initial RIF. For example, reducing the employment of Division 1 and Division 2 will lead to attrition in both divisions. The career manager in charge of these divisions and her subordinates will have to do more work with fewer employees and manage through declining morale for an administration with whom they likely disagree ideologically.

The Reagan administration's treatment of the Council on Environmental Quality (CEQ) is a good example of this approach. In 1982 the CEQ's staff had been reduced from forty-nine, under President Carter, to fifteen. The administration fired all of the immediate council staff, some of whom had served since the Nixon and Ford administrations. Appointees from the campaign staff replaced those removed.

Informal Aids to Politicization

There are also a number of ways to augment politicization efforts informally. One common technique for politicizing administration is to leave career positions vacant for significant periods of time and have appointees take over these responsibilities in an acting role. For example, during the second George W. Bush administration, when Sandra Bates, a career manager within the General Services Administration (GSA), decided to leave her position as Commissioner of the Federal Technology Service (FTS), Barbara Shelton was selected to fill that job in an acting role until a replacement was found. Although career managers generally assume acting roles when appointees leave, Shelton was an appointee. She was the politically appointed regional administrator of the GSA's Mid-Atlantic region. No immediate plans were announced to select a permanent replacement in the agency. GSA was pursuing an internal reorganization wherein the FTS would be merged with the Federal Supply Service.

With lax oversight and informal norms, different presidential administrations have also been successful in influencing personnel choices inside the *civil service* without changing the appointment authority of the jobs themselves. Technically, personnel chosen for positions under the merit system are to be chosen outside the influence of politics. In reality, both

Congress and the president can strongly influence the hiring of careerists at higher levels in the permanent federal service. The most formal and blatant attempt to do this was the Eisenhower administration's "Willis Directive." Charles Willis, an assistant to Eisenhower chief-of-staff Sherman Adams, wrote and circulated an elaborate personnel plan for the new administration. The plan invited officials from the Republican National Committee (RNC), Republican congressmen, or other prominent state Republicans to recommend personnel for jobs both *inside* and outside the civil service. All jobs at GS 14 and above were called "controlled" positions. Federal agencies were to announce vacancies on forms supplied by the RNC and make regular reports to the RNC on how vacancies were filled. Both the spirit and contents of the plan violated Civil Service Rule 4, which state[s] that career positions are to be filled "without regard to political or religious affiliation." . . .

In total, the numbers and percentages of appointees vary from administration to administration because of replacement, layering, reorganization, and RIFs. These politicization techniques can be augmented by less formal techniques, such as strategic vacancies, political influence in the hiring of careerists, and bending of the rules in administrative determinations and rulings.

Congressional Responses

Of course, politicization choices happen with an eye toward Congress since the legislative branch has both the means of learning about politicization and a variety of ways to respond. . . . Civil servants in the affected agencies complain to the press or friendly members of Congress. As one personnel official explained to me, "the *Washington Post* is their inspector general." Others confirmed that the possibility that their actions might appear on the front page of the *Washington Post* constrained personnel actions. Personnel officials also suggested that members of Congress were attentive to appointee head-counts, and the existence of congressional reports including such counts confirms their claim.

Personnel officials recognize that their missteps can lead to problems for the president and adjust their behavior accordingly. At minimum, an influential member of Congress can informally communicate his displeasure with the agency or the White House. Members can also publicize the president's action, creating an embarrassing situation for the White House. For example, in 1987 several Democratic members of Congress accused the Reagan administration of "packing" the top ranks of government with appointees to the detriment of the federal service. Backed by a GAO report tracking appointments, these members denounced an increase in appointees to the SES, particularly in the agencies that manage the government such as the OPM (personnel), the GSA (facilities), and the OMB (finances). During the Clinton administration, Republicans publicly complained about the politicization of the Commerce Department, and they requested that the GAO investigate the burrowing of Democratic appointees and staff into civil service positions. In the second George W. Bush administration, the Democratic minority used charges of cronyism coupled with data on appointee increases to score political points.

More concretely, Congress can refuse presidential requests to create new Senate-confirmed positions or use their appropriations power to limit these and other types of appointed positions. For example, efforts to elevate the EPA to a cabinet department in the George H. W. Bush administration were derailed partly due to Congress's refusal to accede to the president's requests for additional appointees. Congress has also enacted limits on the number of positions that could be paid at appointee-level salaries as a means of limiting the number of appointees. They occasionally include specific language in appropriations bills mandating that none of the appropriations be used to pay the salaries of more than a set number of appointees. For example, the Department of Transportation and Related Agencies Appropriations Act, enacted in the late 1980s, includes the following language, "None of the funds in this Act shall be available for salaries and expenses of more than [insert number] political and Presidential appointees in the Department of Transportation." The number of appointees allowed has varied in other bills from a low of 88 to a high of 138.

These instances are rare but this should not be taken as evidence that presidents can act with a free hand. On the contrary, White House officials anticipate the likely response of Congress and adjust their behavior accordingly. They are less likely to politicize if they expect Congress to overturn their action or impose serious political costs on the president. . . .

Conclusion

To understand politicization decisions from administration to administration one has to understand the context of both the history of the merit system and the details defining the different strategies and techniques employed. The professional merit-based civil service system was a late arrival in the United States. The United States federal government operated for almost one hundred years without a formal professional civil service, yet the importance of ensuring both loyalty and competence in the federal service was already evident. During the height of the spoils system, a dual personnel system existed with a continuing body of professionals working side by side with patronage appointees. The dual system presaged numerous attempts to institute merit systems in the period leading up to the formal creation of the merit system.

The 1883 reforms embodied in the Pendleton Act were focused on the task of eliminating spoils. Reformers sought to end assessments, political activity by public employees, and patronage hiring and firing through the expansion of merit protection and the merit system. The U.S. personnel system's narrow focus on spoils had a lasting effect on public personnel management. The United States was slow to focus on positive human resource management activities like recruitment, training, morale, and benefits. Instead, the personnel system was defined by rules designed to protect workers from the evil of spoils. Part of Congress's recent motivation for allowing individual agencies to develop personnel systems outside the traditional merit-based civil service system is to allow them to escape the cumbersome and antiquated federal personnel system. Isolated exceptions to Title 5 have now become a landslide, with less than one-half of all federal personnel under the traditional merit system. The Merit Systems Protection Board, the appellate body that hears employee complaints, is cutting its budget and closing regional offices.

While the federal personnel system continues to change dramatically, the politicization calculus remains much the same. Political actors are making decisions about the numbers of Senate-confirmed, noncareer SES, and Schedule C appointees in an effort to make the bureaucracy responsive to them and satisfy demands for patronage. In the same way they feared turning over competent, long-tenured professionals in the Jacksonian era, so, too, they fear politicizing too much now. . . .

Chapter 9

The Judiciary

9-1 From *A Matter of Interpretation: Federal Courts and the Law*

Antonin Scalia

Supreme Court judges and indeed—as we learn in the essay by Carp, Manning, and Stidham, later in this section—judges at every level of the federal judiciary decide cases in close accord with the political views of those who appointed them. Years of Democratic control of the White House and Congress created the activist federal judiciary of the 1960s and 1970s that advanced federal protections of civil rights and civil liberties. With the resurgence of the Republican Party in national politics, the federal judiciary has gradually, with turnover in members, become more conservative. Some observers note these trends and conclude that judges are little more than partisan politicians disguised in robes. Unsurprisingly, judges do not view themselves this way. Instead, they account for their sometimes sharply differing opinions on criteria that do not fit neatly on the familiar partisan or ideological dimensions that are used to classify elected officeholders. In the next two essays, two current Supreme Court justices—one conservative and appointed by a Republican president, the other a moderate, appointed by a Democrat—explain how they approach decisions, decisions on which they frequently disagree. As you read and weigh these alternative views, note that both judges begin with the same assumption—that as the unelected branch the judiciary should, when possible, defer to the decisions of democratically elected officeholders.

In the following essay, excerpted from his highly regarded series of lectures to Princeton law students, Justice Antonin Scalia explains how he approaches decisions. Some call this style "literalist" or "originalist," in that Scalia weighs decisions against a close reading of the texts of laws and the Constitution. He reminds us that in a constitutional democracy judges are not charged with deciding what fair and just policy should be. This responsibility belongs with elected officials, who better reflect their citizenry's views on such matters. Nor should judges try to read the minds of those who make the law. A judge's role begins and ends with applying the law (including the Constitution) to the particular circumstances of a legal disagreement. Scalia's critics have complained that the application of law is frequently not so simple. Laws conflict or fail to consider the many contingencies that reach the Supreme Court.

Source: Antonin Scalia. *A Matter of Interpretation: Federal Courts and the Law.* Edited by Amy Gutmann. © 1997 Princeton University Press. Reprinted by permission of Princeton University Press. Some notes appearing in the original have been deleted.

The following essay attempts to explain the current neglected state of the science of construing legal texts, and offers a few suggestions for improvement. It is addressed not just to lawyers but to all thoughtful Americans who share our national obsession with the law.

The Common Law

The first year of law school makes an enormous impact upon the mind. Many students remark upon the phenomenon. They experience a sort of intellectual rebirth, the acquisition of a whole new mode of perceiving and thinking. Thereafter, even if they do not yet know much law, they do—as the expression goes—"think like a lawyer."

The overwhelming majority of the courses taught in that first year, and surely the ones that have the most profound effect, teach the substance, and the methodology, of the common law—torts, for example; contracts; property; criminal law. American lawyers cut their teeth upon the common law. To understand what an effect that must have, you must appreciate that the common law is not really common law, except insofar as judges can be regarded as common. That is to say, it is not "customary law," or a reflection of the people's practices, but is rather law developed by the judges. Perhaps in the very infancy of Anglo-Saxon law it could have been thought that the courts were mere expositors of generally accepted social practices; and certainly, even in the full maturity of the common law, a well-established commercial or social practice could form the basis for a court's decision. But from an early time—as early as the Year Books, which record English judicial decisions from the end of the thirteenth century to the beginning of the sixteenth—any equivalence between custom and common law had ceased to exist, except in the sense that the doctrine of *stare decisis* rendered prior judicial decisions "custom." The issues coming before the courts involved, more and more, refined questions to which customary practice provided no answer.

Oliver Wendell Holmes's influential book *The Common Law*[1]—which is still suggested reading for entering law students—talks a little bit about Germanic and early English custom. . . . This is the image of the law—the common law—to which an aspiring American lawyer is first exposed, even if he has not read Holmes over the previous summer as he was supposed to. He learns the law, not by reading statutes that promulgate it or treatises that summarize it, but rather by studying the judicial opinions that invented it. This is the famous case-law method, pioneered by Harvard Law School in the last century, and brought to movies and TV by the redoubtable Professor Kingsfield of *Love Story* and *The Paper Chase*. The student is directed to read a series of cases, set forth in a text called a "casebook," designed to show how the law developed. . . . Famous old cases are famous, you see, not because they came out right, but because the rule of law they announced was the intelligent one. Common-law courts performed two functions: One was to apply the law to the facts. All adjudicators—French judges, arbitrators, even baseball umpires and football referees—do that. But the second function, and the more important one, was to *make* the law.

If you were sitting in on Professor Kingsfield's class when *Hadley* v. *Baxendale* was the assigned reading, you would find that the class discussion would not end with the mere description and dissection of the opinion. [This case, a familiar example of 19th century English common law, involves liability in failing to perform a contracted obligation.-Ed.] Various "hypotheticals" would be proposed by the crusty (yet, under it all, good-hearted) old professor, testing the validity and the sufficiency of the "foreseeability" rule. What if, for example, you are a blacksmith, and a young knight rides up on a horse that has thrown a shoe. He tells you he is returning to his ancestral estate, Blackacre, which he must reach that very evening to claim his inheritance, or else it will go to his wicked, no-good cousin, the sheriff of Nottingham. You contract to put on a new shoe, for the going rate of three farthings. The shoe is defective, or is badly shod, the horse goes lame, and the knight reaches Blackacre too late. Are you really liable for the full amount of his inheritance? Is it reasonable to impose that degree of liability for three farthings? Would not the parties have set a different price if liability of that amount had been contemplated? Ought there not to be, in other words, some limiting principle to damages beyond mere foreseeability? Indeed, might not that principle—call it presumed assumption of risk—explain why *Hadley* v. *Baxendale* reached the right result after all, though not for the precise reason it assigned?

What intellectual fun all of this is! It explains why first-year law school is so exhilarating: because it consists of playing common-law judge, which in turn consists of playing king—devising, out of the brilliance of one's own mind, those laws that ought to govern mankind. How exciting! And no wonder so many law students, having drunk at this intoxicating well, aspire for the rest of their lives to be judges!

Besides the ability to think about, and devise, the "best" legal rule, there is another skill imparted in the first year of law school that is essential to the making of a good common-law judge. It is the technique of what is called "distinguishing" cases. That is a necessary skill, because an absolute prerequisite to common-law lawmaking is the doctrine of *stare decisis*—that is, the principle that a decision made in one case will be followed in the next. Quite obviously, without such a principle common-law courts would not be making any "law"; they would just be resolving the particular dispute before them. It is the requirement that future courts adhere to the principle underlying a judicial decision which causes that decision to be a legal rule. (There is no such requirement in the civil-law system, where it is the text of the law rather than any prior judicial interpretation of that text which is authoritative. Prior judicial opinions are consulted for their persuasive effect, much as academic commentary would be; but they are not *binding*.)

Within such a precedent-bound common-law system, it is critical for the lawyer, or the judge, to establish whether the case at hand falls within a principle that has already been decided. Hence the technique—or the art, or the game—of "distinguishing" earlier cases. It is an art or a game, rather than a science, because what constitutes the "holding" of an earlier case is not well defined and can be adjusted to suit the occasion. . . .

It should be apparent that by reason of the doctrine of *stare decisis*, as limited by the principle I have just described, the common law grew in a peculiar fashion—rather like a Scrabble board. No rule of decision previously announced could be *erased*, but qualifications could be *added* to it. The first case lays on the board: "No liability for breach of contractual duty without privity"; the next player adds "unless injured party is member of household." And the game continues.

As I have described, this system of making law by judicial opinion, and making law by distinguishing earlier cases, is what every American law student, every newborn American lawyer, first sees when he opens his eyes. And the impression remains for life. His image of the great judge—the Holmes, the Cardozo—is the man (or woman) who has the intelligence to discern the best rule of law for the case at hand and then the skill to perform the broken-field running through earlier cases that leaves him free to impose that rule: distinguishing one prior case on the left, straight-arming another one on the right, high-stepping away from another precedent about to tackle him from the rear, until (bravo!) he reaches the goal—good law. That image of the great judge remains with the former law student when he himself becomes a judge, and thus the common-law tradition is passed on.

Democratic Legislation

All of this would be an unqualified good, were it not for a trend in government that has developed in recent centuries, called democracy. In most countries, judges are no longer agents of the king, for there are no kings. . . . [O]nce we have taken this realistic view of what common-law courts do, the uncomfortable relationship of common-law lawmaking to democracy (if not to the technical doctrine of the separation of powers) becomes apparent. Indeed, that was evident to many even before legal realism carried the day. It was one of the principal motivations behind the law-codification movement of the nineteenth century. . . .

The nineteenth-century codification movement ... was generally opposed by the bar, and hence did not achieve substantial success, except in one field: civil procedure, the law governing the trial of civil cases.[2] (I have always found it curious, by the way, that the only field in which lawyers and judges were willing to abandon judicial lawmaking was a field important to nobody except litigants, lawyers, and judges. Civil procedure used to be the *only* statutory course taught in first-year law school.) Today, generally speaking, the old private-law fields—contracts, torts, property, trusts and estates, family law—remain firmly within the control of state common-law courts.[3] Indeed, it is probably true that in these fields judicial lawmaking can be more freewheeling than ever, since the doctrine of *stare decisis* has appreciably eroded. Prior decisions that even the cleverest mind cannot distinguish can nowadays simply be overruled.

My point in all of this is not that the common law should be scraped away as a barnacle on the hull of democracy. I am content to leave the common law, and the process of developing the common law, where it is. It has proven to be a good method of developing the law in many fields—and perhaps the very best method. An argument can be made that development of the bulk of private law by judges (a natural aristocracy, as Madison accurately portrayed them)[4] is a desirable limitation upon popular democracy. ...

But though I have no quarrel with the common law and its process, I do question whether the *attitude* of the common-law judge—the mind-set that asks, "What is the most desirable resolution of this case, and how can any impediments to the achievement of that result be evaded?"—is appropriate for most of the work that I do, and much of the work that state judges do. We live in an age of legislation, and most new law is statutory law. ... Every issue of law resolved by a federal judge involves interpretation of text—the text of a regulation, or of a statute, or of the Constitution. Let me put the Constitution to one side for the time being, since many believe that document is in effect a charter for judges to develop an evolving common law of freedom of speech, of privacy rights, and the like. I think that is wrong—indeed, as I shall discuss below, I think it frustrates the whole purpose of a written constitution. But we need not pause to debate that point now, since a very small proportion of judges' work is constitutional interpretation in any event. (Even in the Supreme Court, I would estimate that well less than a fifth of the issues we confront are constitutional issues—and probably less than a twentieth if you exclude criminal-law cases.) By far the greatest part of what I and all federal judges do is to interpret the meaning of federal statutes and federal agency regulations. Thus the subject of statutory interpretation deserves study and attention in its own right, as the principal business of judges and (hence) lawyers. It will not do to treat the enterprise as simply an inconvenient modern add-on to the judge's primary role of common-law lawmaker. Indeed, attacking the enterprise with the Mr. Fix-it mentality of the common-law judge is a sure recipe for incompetence and usurpation.

The Science of Statutory Interpretation

The state of the science of statutory interpretation in American law is accurately described by a prominent treatise on the legal process as follows:

> Do not expect anybody's theory of statutory interpretation, whether it is your own or somebody else's, to be an accurate statement of what courts actually do with statutes. The hard truth of the matter is that American courts have no intelligible, generally accepted, and consistently applied theory of statutory interpretation.[5]

Surely this is a sad commentary: We American judges have no intelligible theory of what we do most.

Even sadder, however, is the fact that the American bar and American legal education, by and large, are unconcerned with the fact that we have no intelligible theory. Whereas legal scholarship has been at pains to rationalize the common law—to devise the *best* rules governing contracts, torts, and so forth—it has been seemingly agnostic as to whether there is even any such thing as good or bad rules of statutory interpretation. There are few law-school courses on the subject, and certainly no required ones; the science of interpretation (if it is a science) is left to be picked up piecemeal, through the reading of cases (good and bad) in substantive fields of law that happen to involve statutes, such as securities law, natural resources law, and employment law. . . .

"Intent of the Legislature"

Statutory interpretation is such a broad subject that the substance of it cannot be discussed comprehensively here. It is worth examining a few aspects, however, if only to demonstrate the great degree of confusion that prevails. We can begin at the most fundamental possible level. So utterly unformed is the American law of statutory interpretation that not only is its methodology unclear, but even its very *objective* is. Consider the basic question: What are we looking for when we construe a statute?

You will find it frequently said in judicial opinions of my court and others that the judge's objective in interpreting a statute is to give effect to "the intent of the legislature." This principle, in one form or another, goes back at least as far as Blackstone.[6] Unfortunately, it does not square with some of the (few) generally accepted concrete rules of statutory construction. One is the rule that when the text of a statute is clear, that is the end of the matter. Why should that be so, if what the legislature *intended*, rather than what it *said*, is the object of our inquiry? In selecting the words of the statute, the legislature might have misspoken. Why not permit that to be demonstrated from the floor debates? Or indeed, why not accept, as proper material for the court to consider, later explanations by the legislators—a sworn affidavit signed by the majority of each house, for example, as to what they *really* meant?

Another accepted rule of construction is that ambiguities in a newly enacted statute are to be resolved in such fashion as to make the statute, not only internally consistent, but also compatible with previously enacted laws. We simply assume, for purposes of our search for "intent," that the enacting legislature was aware of all those other laws. Well of course that is a fiction, and if we were really looking for the subjective intent of the enacting legislature we would more likely find it by paying attention to the text (and legislative history) of the new statute in isolation.

The evidence suggests that, despite frequent statements to the contrary, we do not really look for subjective legislative intent. We look for a sort of "objectified" intent—the intent that a reasonable person would gather from the text of the law, placed alongside the remainder of the *corpus juris*. As Bishop's old treatise nicely put it, elaborating upon the usual formulation: "[T]he primary object of all rules for interpreting statutes is to ascertain the legislative intent; *or, exactly, the meaning which the subject is authorized to understand the legislature intended.*"[7] And the reason we adopt this objectified version is, I think, that it is simply incompatible with democratic government, or indeed, even with fair government, to have the meaning of a law determined by what the lawgiver meant, rather than by what the lawgiver promulgated. That seems to me one step worse than the trick the emperor Nero was said to engage in: posting edicts high up on the pillars, so that they could not easily be read. Government by unexpressed intent is similarly tyrannical. It is the *law* that governs, not the intent of the lawgiver. That seems to me the essence of the famous American ideal set forth in the Massachusetts constitution: A government of laws, not of men. Men may intend what they will; but it is only the laws that they enact which bind us.

In reality, however, if one accepts the principle that the object of judicial interpretation is to determine the intent of the legislature, being bound by genuine but unexpressed legislative intent rather than the law is only the *theoretical* threat. The *practical* threat is that, under the guise or even the self-delusion of pursuing unexpressed legislative intents, common-law judges will in fact pursue their own objectives and desires, extending their lawmaking proclivities from the common law to the statutory field. When you are told to decide, not on the basis of what the legislature said, but on the basis of what it *meant*, and are assured that there is no necessary connection between the two, your best shot at figuring out what the legislature meant is to ask yourself what a wise and intelligent person *should* have meant; and that will surely bring you to the conclusion that the law means what you think it *ought* to mean—which is precisely how judges decide things under the common law. As Dean Landis of Harvard Law School (a believer in the search for legislative intent) put it in a 1930 article:

> [T]he gravest sins are perpetrated in the name of the intent of the legislature. Judges are rarely willing to admit their role as actual lawgivers, and such admissions as are wrung from their unwilling lips lie in the field of common and not statute law. To condone in these instances the practice of talking in terms of the intent of the legislature, as if the legislature had attributed a particular meaning to certain words, when it is apparent that the intent is that of the judge, is to condone atavistic practices too reminiscent of the medicine man.[8] . . .

The text is the law, and it is the text that must be observed. I agree with Justice Holmes's remark, quoted approvingly by Justice Frankfurter in his article on the construction of statutes: "Only a day or two ago—when counsel talked of the intention of a legislature, I was indiscreet enough to say I don't care what their intention was. I only want to know what the words mean." [9] And I agree with Holmes's other remark, quoted approvingly by Justice Jackson: "We do not inquire what the legislature meant; we ask only what the statute means." [10]

Textualism

The philosophy of interpretation I have described above is known as textualism. In some sophisticated circles, it is considered simpleminded—"wooden," "unimaginative," "pedestrian." It is none of that. To be a textualist in good standing, one need not be too dull to perceive the broader social purposes that a statute is designed, or could be designed, to serve; or too hidebound to realize that new times require new laws. One need only hold the belief that judges have no authority to pursue those broader purposes or write those new laws.

Textualism should not be confused with so-called strict constructionism, a degraded form of textualism that brings the whole philosophy into disrepute. I am not a strict constructionist, and no one ought to be—though better that, I suppose, than a nontextualist. A text should not be construed strictly, and it should not be construed leniently; it should be construed reasonably, to contain all that it fairly means. The difference between textualism and strict constructionism can be seen in a case my Court decided four terms ago.[11] The statute at issue provided for an increased jail term if, "during and in relation to . . . [a] drug trafficking crime," the defendant "uses . . . a firearm." The defendant in this case had sought to purchase a quantity of cocaine; and what he had offered to give in exchange for the cocaine was an unloaded firearm, which he showed to the drug-seller. The Court held, I regret to say, that the defendant was subject to the increased penalty, because he had "used a firearm during and in relation to a drug trafficking crime." The vote was not even close (6–3). I dissented. Now I cannot say whether my colleagues in the majority voted the way they did because they are strict-construction textualists, or because they are not textualists at all. But a proper textualist, which is to say my kind of textualist, would surely have voted to acquit. The phrase "uses a gun" fairly connoted use of a gun for what guns are normally used for, that is, as a weapon. As I put the point in my dissent, when you ask someone, "Do you use a cane?" you are not inquiring whether he has hung his grandfather's antique cane as a decoration in the hallway.

But while the good textualist is not a literalist, neither is he a nihilist. Words do have a limited range of meaning, and no interpretation that goes beyond that range is permissible. My favorite example of a departure from text—and certainly the departure that has enabled judges to do more freewheeling law-making than any other—pertains to the Due Process Clause found in the Fifth and Fourteenth Amendments of the United States Constitution, which says that no person shall "be deprived of life, liberty, or property without due process of law." It has been interpreted to prevent the government from taking away certain liberties *beyond* those, such as freedom of speech and of religion, that are specifically named in the Constitution. (The first Supreme Court case to use the Due Process Clause in this fashion was, by the way, *Dred Scott*[12]—not a desirable parentage.) Well, it may or may not be a good thing to guarantee additional liberties, but the Due Process Clause quite obviously does not bear that interpretation. By its inescapable terms, it guarantees only process. Property can be taken by the state; liberty can be taken; even life can be taken; but not without the *process* that our traditions require—notably, a validly enacted law and a fair trial. To say otherwise is to abandon textualism, and to render democratically adopted texts mere springboards for judicial lawmaking.

Of all the criticisms leveled against textualism, the most mindless is that it is "formalistic." The answer to that is, *of course it's formalistic!* The rule of law is *about* form. If, for example, a citizen performs an act—let us say the sale of certain technology to a foreign country—which is prohibited by a widely publicized bill proposed by the administration and passed by both houses of Congress, *but not yet signed by the President*, that sale is lawful. It is of no consequence that everyone knows both houses of Congress and the President wish to prevent that sale. Before the wish becomes a binding law, it must be embodied in a bill that passes both houses and is signed by the President. Is that not formalism? A murderer has been caught with blood on his hands, bending over the body of his victim; a neighbor with a video camera has filmed the crime; and the murderer has confessed in writing and on videotape. We nonetheless insist that before the state can punish this miscreant, it must conduct a full-dress criminal trial that results in a verdict of guilty. Is that not formalism? Long live formalism. It is what makes a government a government of laws and not of men. . . .

Legislative History

Let me turn now . . . to an interpretive device whose widespread use is relatively new: legislative history, by which I mean the statements made in the floor debates, committee reports, and even committee testimony, leading up to the enactment of the legislation. My view that the objective indication of the words, rather than the intent of the legislature, is what constitutes the law leads me, of course, to the conclusion that legislative history should not be used as an authoritative indication of a statute's meaning. This was the traditional English, and the traditional American, practice. Chief Justice Taney wrote:

> In expounding this law, the judgment of the court cannot, in any degree, be influenced by the construction placed upon it by individual members of Congress in the debate which took place on its passage, nor by the motives or reasons assigned by them for supporting or opposing amendments that were offered. The law as it passed is the will of the majority of both houses, *and the only mode in which that will is spoken is in the act itself*; and we must gather their intention from the language there used, comparing it, when any ambiguity exists, with the laws upon the same subject, and looking, if necessary, to the public history of the times in which it was passed.[13]

That uncompromising view generally prevailed in this country until the present century. The movement to change it gained momentum in the late 1920s and 1930s, driven, believe it or not, by frustration with common-law judges' use of "legislative intent" and phonied-up canons to impose their own views—in those days views opposed to progressive social legislation. I quoted earlier an article by Dean Landis inveighing against such judicial usurpation. The solution he proposed was not the banishment of legislative intent as an interpretive criterion, but rather the use of legislative history to place that intent beyond manipulation.[14]

Extensive use of legislative history in this country dates only from about the 1940s. . . . In the past few decades, however, we have developed a legal culture in which lawyers routinely—and I do mean routinely—make no distinction between words in the text of a statute and words in its legislative history. My Court is frequently told, in briefs and in oral argument, that "Congress said thus-and-so"—when in fact what is being quoted is not the law promulgated by Congress, nor even any text endorsed by a single house of Congress, but rather the statement of a single committee of a single house, set forth in a committee report. Resort to legislative history has become so common that lawyerly wags have popularized a humorous quip inverting the oft-recited (and oft-ignored) rule as to when its use is appropriate: "One should consult the text of the statute," the joke goes, "only when the legislative history is ambiguous." Alas, that is no longer funny. Reality has overtaken parody. A few terms ago, I read a brief that *began* the legal argument with a discussion of legislative history and then continued (I am quoting it verbatim): "Unfortunately, the legislative debates are not helpful. Thus, we turn to the other guidepost in this difficult area, statutory language."[15]

As I have said, I object to the use of legislative history on principle, since I reject intent of the legislature as the proper criterion of the law. What is most exasperating about the use of legislative history, however, is that it does not even make sense for those who *accept* legislative intent as the criterion. It is much more likely to produce a false or contrived legislative intent than a genuine one. . . .

Ironically, but quite understandably, the more courts have relied upon legislative history, the less worthy of reliance it has become. In earlier days, it was at least genuine and not contrived—a real part of the legislation's *history*, in the sense that it was part of the *development* of the bill, part of the attempt to inform and persuade those who voted.

Nowadays, however, when it is universally known and expected that judges will resort to floor debates and (especially) committee reports as authoritative expressions of "legislative intent," affecting the courts rather than informing the Congress has become the primary purpose of the exercise. It is less that the courts refer to legislative history because it exists than that legislative history exists because the courts refer to it. One of the routine tasks of the Washington lawyer-lobbyist is to draft language that sympathetic legislators can recite in a prewritten "floor debate"—or, even better, insert into a committee report. . . .

I think that Dean Landis, and those who joined him in the prescription of legislative history as a cure for what he called "willful judges," would be aghast at the results a half century later. On balance, it has facilitated rather than deterred decisions that are based upon the courts' policy preferences, rather than neutral principles of law. Since there are no rules as to how much weight an element of legislative history is entitled to, it can usually be either relied upon or dismissed with equal plausibility. If the willful judge does not like the committee report, he will not follow it; he will call the statute not ambiguous enough, the committee report too ambiguous, or the legislative history (this is a favorite phrase) "as a whole, inconclusive." . . .

Interpreting Constitutional Texts

Without pretending to have exhausted the vast topic of textual interpretation, I wish to address a final subject: the distinctive problem of constitutional interpretation. The problem is distinctive, not because special principles of interpretation apply, but because the usual principles are being applied to an unusual text. Chief Justice Marshall put the point as well as it can be put in *McCulloch* v. *Maryland*:

A constitution, to contain an accurate detail of all the subdivisions of which its great powers will admit, and of all the means by which they may be carried into execution, would partake of the prolixity of a legal code, and could scarcely be embraced by the human mind. It would probably never be understood by the public. Its nature, therefore, requires, that only its great outlines should be marked, its important objects designated, and the minor ingredients which compose those objects be deduced from the nature of the objects themselves.[16]

In textual interpretation, context is everything, and the context of the Constitution tells us not to expect nit-picking detail, and to give words and phrases an expansive rather than narrow interpretation—though not an interpretation that the language will not bear.

Take, for example, the provision of the First Amendment that forbids abridgment of "the freedom of speech, or of the press." That phrase does not list the full range of communicative expression. Handwritten letters, for example, are neither speech nor press. Yet surely there is no doubt they cannot be censored. In this constitutional context, speech and press, the two most common forms of communication, stand as a sort of synecdoche for the whole. That is not strict construction, but it is reasonable construction.

It is curious that most of those who insist that the drafter's intent gives meaning to a statute reject the drafter's intent as the criterion for interpretation of the Constitution. I reject it for both. . . . [T]he Great Divide with regard to constitutional interpretation is not that between Framers' intent and objective meaning, but rather that between *original* meaning (whether derived from Framers' intent or not) and *current* meaning. The ascendant school of constitutional interpretation affirms the existence of what is called The Living Constitution, a body of law that (unlike normal statutes) grows and changes from age to age, in order to meet the needs of a changing society. And it is the judges who determine those needs and "find" that changing law. Seems familiar, doesn't it? Yes, it is the common law returned, but infinitely more powerful than what the old common law ever pretended to be, for now it trumps even the statutes of democratic legislatures. . . .

If you go into a constitutional law class, or study a constitutional law casebook, or read a brief filed in a constitutional law case, you will rarely find the discussion addressed to the text of the constitutional provision that is at issue, or to the question of what was the originally understood or even the originally intended meaning of that text. The starting point of the analysis will be Supreme Court cases, and the new issue will presumptively be decided according to the logic that those cases expressed, with no regard for how far that logic, thus extended, has distanced us from the original text and understanding. Worse still, however, it is known and understood that if that logic fails to produce what in the view of the current Supreme Court is the *desirable* result for the case at hand, then, like good common-law judges, the Court will distinguish its precedents, or narrow them, or if all else fails overrule them, in order that the Constitution might mean what it *ought* to mean. Should there be—to take one of the less controversial examples—a constitutional right to die? If so, there is.[17] Should there be a constitutional right to reclaim a biological child put out for adoption by the other parent? Again, if so, there is.[18] If it is good, it is so. Never mind the text that we are supposedly construing; we will smuggle these new rights in, if all else fails, under the Due Process Clause (which, as I have described, is textually incapable of containing them). Moreover, what the Constitution meant yesterday it does not necessarily mean today. As our opinions say in the context of our Eighth Amendment jurisprudence (the Cruel and Unusual Punishments Clause), its meaning changes to reflect "the evolving standards of decency that mark the progress of a maturing society."[19]

This is preeminently a common-law way of making law, and not the way of construing a democratically adopted text. . . . Proposals for "dynamic statutory construction," such as those of Judge Calabresi . . . are concededly avant-garde. The Constitution, however, even though a democratically adopted text, we formally treat like the common law. What, it is fair to ask, is the justification for doing so?

One would suppose that the rule that a text does not change would apply *a fortiori* to a constitution. If courts felt too much bound by the democratic process to tinker with statutes, when their tinkering could be adjusted by the legislature, how much more should they feel bound not to tinker with a constitution, when their tinkering is virtually irreparable. It certainly cannot be said that a constitution naturally suggests changeability; to the contrary, its whole purpose is to prevent change—to embed certain rights in such a manner that future generations cannot readily take them away. A society that adopts a bill of rights is skeptical that "evolving standards of decency" always "mark progress," and that societies always "mature," as opposed to rot. Neither the text of such a document nor the intent of its framers (whichever you choose) can possibly lead to the conclusion that its only effect is to take the power of changing rights away from the legislature and give it to the courts.

Flexibility and Liberality of the Living Constitution

The argument most frequently made in favor of the Living Constitution is a pragmatic one: Such an evolutionary approach is necessary in order to provide the "flexibility" that a changing society requires; the Constitution would have snapped if it had not been permitted to bend and grow. This might be a persuasive argument if most of the "growing" that the proponents of this approach have brought upon us in the past, and are determined to bring upon us in the future, were the *elimination* of restrictions upon democratic government. But just the opposite is true. Historically, and particularly in the past thirty-five years, the "evolving" Constitution has imposed a vast array of new constraints—new inflexibilities—upon administrative, judicial, and legislative action. To mention only a few things that formerly could be done or not done, as the society desired, but now cannot be done:

- admitting in a state criminal trial evidence of guilt that was obtained by an unlawful search;[20]
- permitting invocation of God at public-school graduations;[21]

- electing one of the two houses of a state legislature the way the United States Senate is elected, i.e., on a basis that does not give all voters numerically equal representation;[22]
- terminating welfare payments as soon as evidence of fraud is received, subject to restoration after hearing if the evidence is satisfactorily refuted;[23]
- imposing property requirements as a condition of voting;[24]
- prohibiting anonymous campaign literature;[25]
- prohibiting pornography.[26]

And the future agenda of constitutional evolutionists is mostly more of the same—the creation of *new* restrictions upon democratic government, rather than the elimination of old ones. *Less* flexibility in government, not *more*. As things now stand, the state and federal governments may either apply capital punishment or abolish it, permit suicide or forbid it—all as the changing times and the changing sentiments of society may demand. But when capital punishment is held to violate the Eighth Amendment, and suicide is held to be protected by the Fourteenth Amendment, all flexibility with regard to those matters will be gone. No, the reality of the matter is that, generally speaking, devotees of The Living Constitution do not seek to facilitate social change but to prevent it.

There are, I must admit, a few exceptions to that—a few instances in which, historically, greater flexibility has been the result of the process. But those exceptions serve only to refute another argument of the proponents of an evolving Constitution, that evolution will always be in the direction of greater personal liberty. (They consider that a great advantage, for reasons that I do not entirely understand. All government represents a balance between individual freedom and social order, and it is not true that every alteration of that balance in the direction of greater individual freedom is necessarily good.) But in any case, the record of history refutes the proposition that the evolving Constitution will invariably enlarge individual rights. The most obvious refutation is the modern Court's limitation of the constitutional protections afforded to property. The provision prohibiting impairment of the obligation of contracts, for example, has been gutted.[27] I am sure that We the People agree with that development; we value property rights less than the Founders did. So also, we value the right to bear arms less than did the Founders (who thought the right of self-defense to be absolutely fundamental), and there will be few tears shed if and when the Second Amendment is held to guarantee nothing more than the state National Guard. But this just shows that the Founders were right when they feared that some (in their view misguided) future generation might wish to abandon liberties that they considered essential, and so sought to protect those liberties in a Bill of Rights. We may *like* the abridgment of property rights and *like* the elimination of the right to bear arms; but let us not pretend that these are not *reductions* of *rights*.

Or if property rights are too cold to arouse enthusiasm, and the right to bear arms too dangerous, let me give another example: Several terms ago a case came before the Supreme Court involving a prosecution for sexual abuse of a young child. The trial court found that the child would be too frightened to testify in the presence of the (presumed) abuser, and so, pursuant to state law, she was permitted to testify with only the prosecutor and defense counsel present, with the defendant, the judge, and the jury watching over closed-circuit television. A reasonable enough procedure, and it was held to be constitutional by my Court.[28] I dissented, because the Sixth Amendment provides that "[i]n *all* criminal prosecutions the accused shall enjoy the right . . . to be confronted with the witnesses against him" (emphasis added). There is no doubt what confrontation meant—or indeed means today. It means face-to-face, not watching from another room. And there is no doubt what one of the major purposes of that provision was: to induce *precisely* that pressure upon the witness which the little girl found it difficult to endure. It is difficult to accuse someone to his face, particularly when you are lying. Now no extrinsic factors have changed since that provision

was adopted in 1791. Sexual abuse existed then, as it does now; little children were more easily upset than adults, then as now; a means of placing the defendant out of sight of the witness existed then as now (a screen could easily have been erected that would enable the defendant to see the witness, but not the witness the defendant). But the Sixth Amendment nonetheless gave *all* criminal defendants the right to *confront* the witnesses against them, because that was thought to be an important protection. The only significant things that *have* changed, I think, are the society's sensitivity to so-called psychic trauma (which is what we are told the child witness in such a situation suffers) and the society's assessment of where the proper balance ought to be struck between the two extremes of a procedure that assures convicting 100 percent of all child abusers, and a procedure that assures acquitting 100 percent of those falsely accused of child abuse. I have no doubt that the society is, as a whole, happy and pleased with what my Court decided. But we should not pretend that the decision did not *eliminate* a liberty that previously existed. . . .

It seems to me that that is where we are heading, or perhaps even where we have arrived. Seventy-five years ago, we believed firmly enough in a rock-solid, unchanging Constitution that we felt it necessary to adopt the Nineteenth Amendment to give women the vote. The battle was not fought in the courts, and few thought that it could be, despite the constitutional guarantee of Equal Protection of the Laws; that provision did not, when it was adopted, and hence did not in 1920, guarantee equal access to the ballot but permitted distinctions on the basis not only of age but of property and of sex. Who can doubt that if the issue had been deferred until today, the Constitution would be (formally) unamended, and the courts would be the chosen instrumentality of change? The American people have been converted to belief in The Living Constitution, a "morphing" document that means, from age to age, what it ought to mean. And with that conversion has inevitably come the new phenomenon of selecting and confirming federal judges, at all levels, on the basis of their views regarding a whole series of proposals for constitutional evolution. If the courts are free to write the Constitution anew, they will, by God, write it the way the majority wants; the appointment and confirmation process will see to that. This, of course, is the end of the Bill of Rights, whose meaning will be committed to the very body it was meant to protect against: the majority. By trying to make the Constitution do everything that needs doing from age to age, we shall have caused it to do nothing at all.

Notes

I am grateful for technical and research assistance by Matthew P. Previn, and for substantive suggestions by Eugene Scalia.

1. Oliver Wendell Holmes, Jr., *The Common Law* (1881).
2. The country's first major code of civil procedure, known as the Field Code (after David Dudley Field, who played a major role in its enactment), was passed in New York in 1848. By the end of the nineteenth century, similar codes had been adopted in many states. *See* Lawrence M. Friedman, *A History of American Law* 340–47 (1973).
3. The principal exception to this statement consists of so-called Uniform Laws, statutes enacted in virtually identical form by all or a large majority of state legislatures, in an effort to achieve nationwide uniformity with respect to certain aspects of some common-law fields. *See, e.g.*, Uniform Commercial Code, 1 U.L.A. 5 (1989); Uniform Marriage and Divorce Act 9A U.L.A. 156 (1987); Uniform Consumer Credit Code, 7A U.L.A. 17 (1985).
4. "The [members of the judiciary department], by the mode of their appointment, as well as by the nature and permanency of it, are too far removed from the people to share much in their prepossessions." *The Federalist* No. 49, at 341 (Jacob E. Cooke ed., 1961).
5. Henry M. Hart, Jr. & Albert M. Sacks, *The Legal Process* 1169 (William N. Eskridge, Jr. & Philip P. Frickey eds., 1994).
6. *See* 1 William Blackstone, *Commentaries on the Laws of England* 59–62, 91 (photo reprint 1979) (1765).
7. Joel Prentiss Bishop, *Commentaries on the Written Laws and Their Interpretation* 57–58 (Boston: Little, Brown, & Co. 1882) (emphasis added) (citation omitted).

8. James M. Landis, *A Note on "Statutory Interpretation,"* 43 Harv. L. Rev. 886, 891 (1930).
9. Felix Frankfurter, *Some Reflections on the Reading of Statutes*, 47 Colum. L. Rev. 527, 538 (1947).
10. Oliver Wendell Holmes, *Collected Legal Papers* 207 (1920), *quoted in* Schwegmann Bros. v. Calvert Distillers Corp., 341 U.S. 384, 397 (1951) (Jackson, J., concurring).
11. Smith v. United States, 508 U.S. 223 (1993).
12. Dred Scott v. Sandford, 60 U.S. (19 How.) 393, 450 (1857).
13. Aldridge v. Williams, 44 U.S. (3 How.) 9, 24 (1845) (emphasis added).
14. *See* Landis, *supra* note 17, at 891–92.
15. Brief for Petitioner at 21, Jett v. Dallas Indep. Sch. Dist., 491 U.S. 701 (1989), *quoted in* Green v. Bock Laundry Machine Co., 490 U.S. 504, 530 (1989) (Scalia, J., concurring).
16. McCulloch v. Maryland, 17 U.S. (4 Wheat.) 316, 407 (1819).
17. *See* Cruzan v. Director, Mo. Dep't of Health, 497 U.S. 261, 279 (1990).
18. *See In re* Kirchner, 649 N.E.2d 324, 333 (Ill.), *cert. denied*, 115 S. Ct. 2599 (1995).
19. Rhodes v. Chapman, 452 U.S. 337, 346 (1981), quoting from Trop v. Dulles, 356 U.S. 86, 101 (1958) (plurality opinion).
20. *See* Mapp v. Ohio, 367 U.S. 643 (1961).
21. *See* Lee v. Weisman, 505 U.S. 577 (1992).
22. *See* Reynolds v. Sims, 377 U.S. 533 (1964).
23. *See* Goldberg v. Kelly, 397 U.S. 254 (1970).
24. *See* Kramer v. Union Free Sch. Dist., 395 U.S. 621 (1969).
25. *See* McIntyre v. Ohio Elections Comm'n, 115 S. Ct. 1511 (1995).
26. Under current doctrine, pornography may be banned only if it is "obscene," *see* Miller v. California, 413 U.S. 15 (1973), a judicially crafted term of art that does not embrace material that excites "normal, healthy sexual desires," Brocket v. Spokane Arcades, Inc., 472 U.S. 491, 498 (1985).
27. *See* Home Building & Loan Ass'n v. Blaisdell, 290 U.S. 398 (1934).
28. *See* Maryland v. Craig, 497 U.S. 836 (1990).

9-2 From *Active Liberty*

Stephen Breyer

Justice Stephen Breyer's book Active Liberty, *from which this essay is excerpted, has been widely viewed as an activist judge's response to Justice Scalia's paean to judicial restraint. Yet Breyer does not envision a broadly activist role for judges in shaping social policy. For one thing, he agrees fundamentally with Scalia that unelected, life-tenured judges should subordinate their personal views on policy to those who are elected to make these decisions. Reflecting this, Breyer's decisions show his reluctance to overrule acts of Congress and executive decisions. For Breyer, the primacy of democracy requires that judges play a special role as guardians of citizens' rights and opportunities to influence government. On a variety of issues, this hierarchy of values leads Breyer to decide cases in ways that Scalia believes overstep judges' mandate. Breyer accepts broad regulation of campaign finance as advancing the performance of democracy, whereas Scalia argues that such laws affront First Amendment protections of free speech.*

The theme as I here consider it falls within an interpretive tradition. . . . That tradition sees texts as driven by *purposes*. The judge should try to find and "honestly . . . say what was the underlying purpose expressed" in a statute. The judge should read constitutional language "as the revelation of the great purposes which were intended to be achieved by the Constitution" itself, a "framework for" and a "continuing instrument of government." The judge should recognize that the Constitution will apply to "new subject matter . . . with which the framers were not familiar." Thus, the judge, whether applying statute or Constitution, should "reconstruct the past solution imaginatively in its setting and project the purposes which inspired it upon the concrete occasions which arise for their decision." Since law is connected to life, judges, in applying a text in light of its purpose, should look to *consequences*, including "contemporary conditions, social, industrial, and political, of the community to be affected." And since "the purpose of construction is the ascertainment of meaning, nothing that is logically relevant should be excluded."[1]

That tradition does not expect highly general instructions themselves to determine the outcome of difficult concrete cases where language is open-ended and precisely defined purpose is difficult to ascertain. Certain constitutional language, for example, reflects "fundamental aspirations and . . . 'moods,' embodied in provisions like the due process and equal protection clauses, which were designed not to be precise and positive directions for rules of action." A judge, when interpreting such open-ended provisions, must avoid being "willful, in the sense of enforcing individual views." A judge cannot "enforce whatever he thinks best." "In the exercise of" the "high power" of judicial review, says Justice Louis Brandeis, "we must be ever on our guard, lest we erect our prejudices into legal principles." At the same time, a judge must avoid being "wooden, in uncritically resting on formulas, in assuming the familiar to be the necessary, in not realizing that any problem can be solved if only one principle is involved but that unfortunately all controversies of importance involve if not a conflict at least an interplay of principles."[2]

How, then, is the judge to act between the bounds of the "willful" and the "wooden"? The tradition answers with an *attitude*, an attitude that hesitates to rely upon any single theory or grand view of law, of interpretation, or of the Constitution. It champions the need to search for purposes; it calls for restraint, asking judges to "speak . . . humbly as the voice of the law." And it finds in the democratic nature of our system more than simply a justification for judicial restraint. Holmes reminds the judge as a general matter to allow "[c]onsiderable latitude . . . for differences of view." . . .

[O]ne can reasonably view the Constitution as focusing upon active liberty, both as important in itself and as a partial means to help secure individual (modern) freedom. The Framers included elements designed to "control and mitigate" the ill effects of more direct forms of democratic government, but in doing so, the Framers "did not see themselves as repudiating either the Revolution or popular government." Rather, they were "saving both from their excesses." The act of ratifying the Constitution, by means of special state elections with broad voter eligibility rules, signaled the democratic character of the document itself.[3]

As history has made clear, the original Constitution was insufficient. It did not include a majority of the nation within its "democratic community." It took a civil war and eighty years of racial segregation before the slaves and their descendants could begin to think of the Constitution as theirs. Nor did women receive the right to vote until 1920. The "people" had to amend the Constitution, not only to extend its democratic base but also to expand and more fully to secure basic individual (negative) liberty.

But the original document sowed the democratic seed. Madison described something fundamental about American government, then and now, when he said the Constitution is a "charter . . . of power . . . granted by liberty," not (as in Europe) a "charter of liberty . . . granted by power."[4] . . .

In sum, our constitutional history has been a quest for workable government, workable democratic government, workable democratic government protective of individual personal liberty. Our central commitment has been to "government of the people, by the people, for the people." And the applications following illustrate how this constitutional understanding helps interpret the Constitution—in a way that helps to resolve problems related to *modern* government. . . .

Statutory Interpretation

The [first] example concerns statutory interpretation. It contrasts a literal text-based approach with an approach that places more emphasis on statutory purpose and congressional intent. It illustrates why judges should pay primary attention to a statute's purpose in difficult cases of interpretation in which language is not clear. It shows how overemphasis on text can lead courts astray, divorcing law from life—indeed, creating law that harms those whom Congress meant to help. And it explains why a purposive approach is more consistent with the framework for a "delegated democracy" that the Constitution creates.[5]

The interpretive problem arises when statutory language does not clearly answer the question of what the statute means or how it applies. Why does a statute contain such language? Perhaps Congress used inappropriate language. Perhaps it failed to use its own drafting expertise or failed to have committee hearings, writing legislation on the floor instead. Perhaps it chose politically symbolic language or ambiguous language over more precise language—possibilities that modern, highly partisan, interest-group-based politics (responding to overly simplified media accounts) make realistic. Perhaps no one in Congress thought about how the statute would apply in certain circumstances. Perhaps it is impossible to use language that foresees how a statute should apply in all relevant circumstances.

The founding generation of Americans understood these or similar possibilities. They realized that judges, though mere "fallible men," would have to exercise judgment and discretion in applying newly codified law. But they expected that judges, when doing so, would remain faithful to the legislators' will. The problem of statutory interpretation is how to meet that expectation.

Most judges start in the same way. They look first to the statute's language, its structure, and its history in an effort to determine the statute's purpose. They then use that purpose (along with the language, structure, and history) to determine the proper interpretation. Thus far, there is agreement. But when the problem is truly difficult, these factors without more may simply limit the universe of possible answers without clearly identifying a final choice. What then?

At this point judges tend to divide in their approach. Some look primarily to text, i.e., to language and text-related circumstances, for further enlightenment. They may try to tease further meaning from the language and structure of the statute itself. They may look to language-based canons of interpretation in the search for an "objective" key to the statute's proper interpretation, say a canon like *noscitur a sociis*, which tells a judge to interpret a word so that it has the same kind of meaning as its neighbors. Textualism, it has been argued, searches for "meaning . . . in structure." It means "preferring the language and structure of the law whenever possible over its legislative history and imputed values." It asks judges to avoid invocation of vague or broad statutory purposes and instead to consider such purposes at "lower levels of generality." It hopes thereby to reduce the risk that judges will interpret statutes subjectively, substituting their own ideas of what is good for those of Congress.[6]

Other judges look primarily to the statute's purposes for enlightenment. They avoid the use of interpretive canons. They allow context to determine the level of generality at which they will describe a statute's purpose—in the way that context tells us not to answer the lost driver's request for directions, "Where am I?" with the words "In a car." They speak in terms of congressional "intent," while understanding that legal conventions govern the use of that term to describe, not the intent of any, or every, individual legislator, but the intent of the group—in the way that linguistic conventions allow us to speak of the intentions of an army or a team, even when they differ from those of any, or every, soldier or member. And they examine legislative history, often closely, in the hope that the history will help them better understand the context, the enacting legislators' objectives, and ultimately the statute's purposes. At the heart of a purpose-based approach stands the "reasonable member of Congress"—a legal fiction that applies, for example, even when Congress did not in fact consider a particular problem. The judge will ask how this person (real or fictional), aware of the statute's language, structure, and general objectives (actually or hypothetically), *would have wanted* a court to interpret the statute in light of present circumstances in the particular case.

[A] recent case illustrate[s] the difference between the two approaches. In [it] the majority followed a more textual approach; the dissent, a more purposive approach. . . . The federal habeas corpus statute is ambiguous in respect to the time limits that apply when a state prisoner seeks access to federal habeas corpus. It says that a state prisoner (ordinarily) must file a federal petition within one year after his state court conviction becomes final. But the statute tolls that one-year period during the time that "a properly filed application for State post-conviction *or other collateral review*" is pending. Do the words "other collateral review" include an earlier application for a federal habeas corpus petition? Should the one-year period be tolled, for example, when a state prisoner mistakenly files a habeas petition in federal court before he exhausts all his state collateral remedies?

It is unlikely that anyone in Congress thought about this question, for it is highly technical. Yet it is important. More than half of all federal habeas corpus petitions fall into the relevant category—i.e., state prisoners file them prematurely before the prisoner has tried to take advantage of available state remedies. In those cases, the federal court often dismisses the petition and the state prisoner must return to state court to exhaust available state remedies before he can once again file his federal habeas petition in federal court. If the one-year statute of limitations is not tolled while the first federal habeas petition was pending, that state prisoner will likely find that the one year has run—and his federal petition is time-barred—before he can return to federal court.[7]

A literal reading of the statute suggests that this is just what Congress had in mind. It suggests that the one-year time limit is tolled only during the time that *state* collateral review (or similar) proceedings are in process. And that reading is supported by various linguistic canons of construction.[8]

Nonetheless, the language does not foreclose an alternative interpretation—an interpretation under which such petitions would fall within the scope of the phrase "other collateral review." The word "State" could be read to modify the phrase "post-conviction . . . review," permitting "*other* collateral review" to refer to federal proceedings. The phrase "properly filed" could be interpreted to refer to purely formal filing requirements rather than calling into play more important remedial questions such as the presence or absence of "exhaustion." A purposive approach favors this latter linguistic interpretation.[9]

Why? [Consider] our hypothetical legislator, the reasonable member of Congress. Which interpretation would that member favor (if he had thought of the problem, which he likely had not)? Consider the consequences of the more literal interpretation. That interpretation would close the doors of federal habeas courts to many or most state prisoners who mistakenly filed a federal habeas petition too soon, but not to all such prisoners. Whether the one-year window was still open would depend in large part on how long the federal court considering the premature federal petition took to dismiss it. In cases in which the court ruled quickly, the short time the federal petition was (wrongly) present in the federal court might not matter. But if a premature federal petition languishes on the federal court's docket while the one year runs, the petitioner would likely lose his one meaningful chance to seek federal habeas relief. By way of contrast, state court delay in considering a prisoner petition in state court would not matter. Whenever *state* proceedings are at issue, the statute tolls the one-year limitations period.

Now ask *why* our reasonable legislator would want to bring about these consequences. He might believe that state prisoners have too often abused the federal writ by filing too many petitions. But the distinction that a literal interpretation would make between those allowed to file and those not allowed to file—a distinction that in essence rests upon federal court processing delay—is a *random* distinction, bearing no logical relation to any abuse-related purpose. Would our reasonable legislator, even if concerned about abuse of the writ, choose to deny access to the Great Writ on a *random* basis? Given our traditions, including those the Constitution grants through its habeas corpus guarantees, the answer to this question is likely no. Would those using a more literal text-based approach answer this question differently? I do not think so. But my real objection to the text-based approach is that it would prevent them from posing the question at all.[10]

[This] example suggest[s] the danger that lurks where judges rely too heavily upon just text and textual aids when interpreting a statute. . . . [W]hen difficult statutory questions are at issue, courts do better to focus foremost upon statutory purpose, ruling out neither legislative history nor any other form of help in order to locate the role that Congress intended the statutory words in question to play.

For one thing, near-exclusive reliance upon canons and other linguistic interpretive aids in close cases can undermine the Constitution's democratic objective. Legislation in a delegated democracy is meant to embody the people's will, either directly (insofar as legislators see themselves as translating how their constituents feel about each proposed law) or indirectly (insofar as legislators see themselves as exercising delegated authority to vote in accordance with what they see as the public interest). Either way, an interpretation of a statute that tends to implement the legislator's will helps to implement the public's will and is therefore consistent with the Constitution's democratic purpose. For similar reasons an interpretation that undercuts the statute's objectives tends to undercut that constitutional objective. . . .

Use of a "reasonable legislator" fiction also facilitates legislative accountability. Ordinary citizens think in terms of general purposes. They readily understand their elected legislators' thinking similarly. It is not impossible to ask an ordinary citizen to determine whether a particular law is consistent with a general purpose the ordinary citizen might support.

It is not impossible to ask an ordinary citizen to determine what general purpose a legislator sought to achieve in enacting a particular statute. And it is not impossible for the ordinary citizen to judge the legislator accordingly. But it *is* impossible to ask an ordinary citizen (or an ordinary legislator) to understand the operation of linguistic canons of interpretation. And it *is* impossible to ask an ordinary citizen to draw any relevant electoral conclusion from consequences that might flow when courts reach a purpose-thwarting interpretation of the statute based upon their near-exclusive use of interpretive canons. Were a segment of the public unhappy about application of the Arbitration Act to ordinary employment contracts, whom should it blame?

For another thing, that approach means that laws will work better for the people they are presently meant to affect. Law is tied to life, and a failure to understand how a statute is so tied can undermine the very human activity that the law seeks to benefit. The more literal text-based, canon-based interpretation of the Foreign Sovereign Immunities jurisdictional statute, for example, means that foreign nations, those using tiered corporate ownership, will find their access to federal courts cut off, undermining the statute's basic jurisdictional objectives. The textual approach to the habeas corpus statute randomly closes courthouse doors in a way that runs contrary to our commitment to basic individual liberty. And it does so because it tends to stop judges from asking a relevant purpose-based question: Why would Congress have wanted a statute that produces those consequences?[11]

In sum, a "reasonable legislator" approach is a workable method of implementing the Constitution's democratic objective. It permits ready translation of the general desire of the public for certain ends, through the legislator's efforts to embody those ends in legislation, into a set of statutory words that will carry out those general objectives. I have argued that the Framers created the Constitution's complex governmental mechanism in order better to translate public will, determined through collective deliberation, into sound public policy. The courts constitute part of that mechanism. And judicial use of the "will

of the reasonable legislator"—even if at times it is a fiction—helps statutes match their means to their overall public policy objectives, a match that helps translate the popular will into sound policy. An overly literal reading of a text can too often stand in the way.

Constitutional Interpretation: Speech

The [next] example focuses on the First Amendment and how it . . . show[s] the importance of reading the First Amendment not in isolation but as seeking to maintain a system of free expression designed to further a basic constitutional purpose: creating and maintaining democratic decision-making institutions.

The example begins where courts normally begin in First Amendment cases. They try to classify the speech at issue, distinguishing among different speech-related activities for the purpose of applying a strict, moderately strict, or totally relaxed presumption of unconstitutionality. Is the speech "political speech," calling for a strong pro-speech presumption, "commercial speech," calling for a mid-range presumption, or simply a form of economic regulation presumed constitutional?

Should courts begin in this way? Some argue that making these kinds of categorical distinctions is a misplaced enterprise. The Constitution's language makes no such distinction. It simply protects "the freedom of speech" from government restriction. "Speech is speech and that is the end of the matter." But to limit distinctions to the point at which First Amendment law embodies the slogan "speech is speech" cannot work. And the fact that the First Amendment seeks to protect active liberty as well as modern liberty helps to explain why.[12]

The democratic government that the Constitution creates now regulates a host of activities that inevitably take place through the medium of speech. Today's workers manipulate information, not wood or metal. And the modern information-based workplace, no less than its more materially based predecessors, requires the application of community standards seeking to assure, for example, the absence of anti-competitive restraints; the accuracy of information; the absence of discrimination; the protection of health, safety, the environment, the consumer; and so forth.

Laws that embody these standards obviously affect speech. Warranty laws require private firms to include on labels statements of a specified content. Securities laws and consumer protection laws insist upon the disclosure of information that businesses might prefer to keep private. Health laws forbid tobacco advertising, say, to children. Anti-discrimination laws insist that employers prevent employees from making certain kinds of statements. Communications laws require cable broadcasters to provide network access. Campaign finance laws restrict citizen contributions to candidates.

To treat all these instances alike, to scrutinize them all as if they all represented a similar kind of legislative effort to restrain a citizen's "modern liberty" to speak, would lump together too many different kinds of activities under the aegis of a single standard, thereby creating a dilemma. On the one hand, if strong First Amendment standards were to apply across the board, they would prevent a democratically elected government from creating necessary regulation. The strong free speech guarantees needed to protect the structural democratic governing process, if applied without distinction to all governmental efforts to control speech, would unreasonably limit the public's substantive economic (or social) regulatory choices. The limits on substantive choice would likely exceed what any liberty-protecting framework for democratic government could require, depriving the people of the democratically necessary room to make decisions, including the leeway to make regulatory mistakes. . . . Most scholars, including "speech is speech" advocates, consequently see a need for distinctions. The question is, Which ones? Applied where?

At this point, reference to the Constitution's more general objectives helps. First, active liberty is particularly at risk when law restricts speech directly related to the shaping of public opinion, for example, speech that takes place in areas related to politics and policy-making by elected officials. That special risk justifies especially strong pro-speech judicial presumptions. It also justifies careful review whenever the speech in question seeks to shape public opinion, particularly if that opinion in turn will affect the political process and the kind of society in which we live.

Second, whenever ordinary commercial or economic regulation is at issue, this special risk normally is absent. Moreover, strong pro-speech presumptions risk imposing what is, from the perspective of active liberty, too severe a restriction upon the legislature—a restriction that would dramatically limit the size of the legislative arena that the Constitution opens for public deliberation and action. The presence of this second risk warns against use of special, strong pro-speech judicial presumptions or special regulation-skeptical judicial review.

The upshot is that reference to constitutional purposes in general and active liberty in particular helps to justify the category of review that the Court applies to a given type of law. But those same considerations argue, among other things, against category boundaries that are too rigid or fixed and against too mechanical an application of those categories. Rather, reference to active liberty will help courts define and apply the categories case by case.

Consider campaign finance reform. The campaign finance problem arises out of the explosion of campaign costs, particularly those related to television advertising, together with the vast disparity in ability to make a campaign contribution. In the year 2000, for example, election expenditures amounted to $1.4 billion, and the two presidential candidates spent about $310 million. In 2002, an off-year without a presidential contest, campaign expenditures still amounted to more than $1 billion. A typical House election cost $900,000, with an open seat costing $1.2 million; a typical Senate seat cost about $4.8 million, with an open contested seat costing about $7.1 million.[13] . . .

A small number of individuals and groups underwrite a very large share of these costs. In 2000, about half the money the parties spent, roughly $500 million, was soft money, i.e., money not subject to regulation under the then current campaign finance laws. Two-thirds of that money—almost $300 million—came from just 800 donors, each contributing a minimum of $120,000. Of these donors, 435 were corporations or unions (whose *direct* contributions the law forbids). The rest, 365, were individual citizens. At the same time, 99 percent of the 200 million or so citizens eligible to vote gave less than $200. Ninety-six percent gave nothing at all.[14]

The upshot is a concern, reflected in campaign finance laws, that the few who give in large amounts may have special access to, and therefore influence over, their elected representatives or, at least, create the appearance of undue influence. (One study found, for example, that 55 percent of Americans believe that large contributions have a "great deal" of impact on how decisions are made in Washington; fewer than 1 percent believed they had no impact.) These contributions (particularly if applied to television) may eliminate the need for, and in that sense crowd out, smaller individual contributions. In either case, the public may lose confidence in the political system and become less willing to participate in the political process. That, in important part, is why legislatures have tried to regulate the size of campaign contributions.[15]

Our Court in 1976 considered the constitutionality of the congressional legislation that initially regulated campaign contributions, and in 2003 we considered more recent legislation that tried to close what Congress considered a loophole—the ability to make contributions in the form of unregulated soft money. The basic constitutional question does not concern the desirability or wisdom of the legislation but whether, how, and the extent to which the First Amendment permits the legislature to impose limits on the amounts that individuals or organizations or parties can contribute to a campaign. Here it is possible to sketch an approach to decision-making that draws upon the Constitution's democratic objective.[16]

It is difficult to find an easy answer to this basic constitutional question in language, in history, or in tradition. The First Amendment's language says that Congress shall not abridge "the freedom of speech." But it does not define "the freedom of speech" in any detail. The nation's Founders did not speak directly about campaign contributions. . .

Neither can we find the answer through the use of purely conceptual arguments. Some claim, for example, that "money is speech." Others say, "money is not speech." But neither contention helps. Money is not speech, it is money. But the expenditure of money enables speech, and that expenditure is often necessary to communicate a message, particularly in a political context. A law that forbade the expenditure of money to communicate could effectively suppress the message.

Nor does it resolve the problem simply to point out that campaign contribution limits inhibit the political "speech opportunities" of those who wish to contribute more. Indeed, that is so. But the question is whether, in context, such a limitation is prohibited as an abridgment of "the freedom of speech." To announce that the harm imposed by a contribution limit is under no circumstances justified is simply to state an ultimate constitutional conclusion; it is not to explain the underlying reasons.[17]

Once we remove our blinders, however, paying increased attention to the Constitution's general democratic objective, it becomes easier to reach a solution. To understand the First Amendment as seeking in significant part to protect active liberty, "participatory self-government," is to understand it as protecting more than the individual's modern freedom. It is to understand the amendment as seeking to facilitate a conversation among ordinary citizens that will encourage their informed participation in the electoral process. It is to suggest a constitutional purpose that goes beyond protecting the individual from government restriction of information about matters that the Constitution commits to individual, not collective, decision-making. It is to understand the First Amendment as seeking primarily to encourage the exchange of information and ideas necessary for citizens themselves to shape that "public opinion which is the final source of government in a democratic state." In these ways the Amendment helps to maintain a form of government open to participation (in Constant's words) by "all the citizens, without exception."[18]

To focus upon the First Amendment's relation to the Constitution's democratic objective is helpful because the campaign laws seek to further a similar objective. They seek to democratize the influence that money can bring to bear upon the electoral process, thereby building public confidence in that process, broadening the base of a candidate's meaningful financial support, and encouraging greater public participation. Ultimately, they seek thereby to maintain the integrity of the political process—a process that itself translates political speech into governmental action. Insofar as they achieve these objectives, those laws, despite the limits they impose, will help to further the kind of open public political discussion that the First Amendment seeks to sustain, both as an end and as a means of achieving a workable democracy.

To emphasize the First Amendment's protection of active liberty is not to find the campaign finance laws automatically constitutional. Rather, it is to recognize that basic democratic objectives, including some of a kind that the First Amendment seeks to further, lie on both sides of the constitutional equation. Seen in terms of modern liberty, they include protection of the citizen's speech from government interference; seen in terms of active liberty, they include promotion of a democratic conversation. That, I believe, is why our Court has refused to apply a strong First Amendment presumption that would almost automatically find the laws unconstitutional. Rather the Court has consistently rejected "strict scrutiny" as the proper test, instead examining a campaign finance law "close[ly]" while applying what it calls "heightened scrutiny." In doing so, the Court has emphasized the power of large campaign contributions to "erod[e] public confidence in the electoral process." It has noted that contribution limits are "aimed at protecting the integrity of the process"; pointed out that in doing so they "tangibly benefit public participation in political debate"; and concluded that that is why "there is no place for the strong presumption against constitutionality, of the sort often thought to accompany the words 'strict scrutiny.'" In this statement it recognizes the possibility that, just as a restraint of trade is sometimes lawful because it furthers, rather than restricts, competition, so a restriction on speech, even when political speech is at issue, will sometimes prove reasonable, hence lawful. Consequently the Court has tried to look realistically both at a campaign finance law's *negative* impact upon those primarily wealthier citizens who wish to engage in more electoral communication and

its *positive* impact upon the public's confidence in, and ability to communicate through, the electoral process. And it has applied a constitutional test that I would describe as one of proportionality. Does the statute strike a reasonable balance between electoral speech-restricting and speech-enhancing consequences? Or does it instead impose restrictions on speech that are disproportionate when measured against their electoral and speech-related benefits, taking into account the kind, the importance, and the extent of those benefits, as well as the need for the restriction in order to secure them?[19]

In trying to answer these questions, courts need not totally abandon what I have referred to as judicial modesty. Courts can defer to the legislature's own judgment insofar as that judgment concerns matters (particularly empirical matters) about which the legislature is comparatively expert, such as the extent of the campaign finance problem, a matter that directly concerns the realities of political life. But courts should not defer when they evaluate the risk that reform legislation will defeat the participatory self-government objective itself. That risk is present, for example, when laws set contribution limits so low that they elevate the reputation-related or media-related advantages of incumbency to the point of insulating incumbent officeholders from effective challenge.[20]

A focus upon the Constitution's democratic objective does not offer easy answers to the difficult questions that campaign finance laws pose. But it does clarify the First Amendment's role in promoting active liberty and suggests an approach for addressing those and other vexing questions. In turn, such a focus can help the Court arrive at answers faithful to the Constitution, its language, and its parts, read together as a consistent whole. Modesty suggests when, and how, courts should defer to the legislature in doing so. . . .

My argument is that, in applying First Amendment presumptions, we must distinguish among areas, contexts, and forms of speech. Reference . . . back to at least one general purpose, active liberty, helps both to generate proper distinctions and also properly to apply the distinctions generated. The active liberty reference helps us to preserve speech that is essential to our democratic form of government, while simultaneously permitting the law to deal effectively with such modern regulatory problems as campaign finance. . . .

Notes

1. Hand, *supra* note I, at 109; *United States v. Classic*, 313 U.S. 299, 316 (1941) (Stone, J.); Hand, *id.*, at 157; Aharon Barak, *A Judge on Judging: The Role of a Supreme Court in a Democracy*, 116 Harv. L. Rev. 16, 28 (2002) ("The law regulates relationships between people. It prescribes patterns of behavior. It reflects the values of society. The role of the judge is to understand the purpose of law in society and to help the law achieve its purpose."); Goldman, *supra* note I, at 115; Felix Frankfurter, *Some Reflections on the Reading of Statutes*, 47 Colum. L. Rev. 527, 541 (1947).

2. Felix Frankfurter, *The Supreme Court in the Mirror of Justices*, in *Of Law and Life & Other Things That Matter* 94 (Philip B. Kurland ed., 1965); *id.* at 95; Hand, *supra* note I, at 109; *New State Ice Co. v. Liebmann*, 285 U.S. 262, 311 (1932) (Brandeis, J., dissenting); Frankfurter, *supra* note 3, at 95.

3. *Id.* at 517.

4. Bailyn, *supra* note I, at 55 (quoting James Madison).

5. Aharon Barak, *A Judge on Judging: The Role of a Supreme Court in a Democracy*, 116 Harv. L. Rev. 28–29 (2002).

6. See, e.g., Antonin Scalia, *Common-Law Courts in a Civil-Law System: The Role of United States Federal Courts in Interpreting the Constitution and Laws*, in *A Matter of Interpretation: Federal Courts and the Law* 26–27 (Amy Gutmann ed., 1997); see William N. Eskridge Jr., Philip P. Frickey, & Elizabeth Garrett, *Cases and Materials on Legislation-Statutes and the Creation of Public Policy* 822 (3d ed. 2001); Frank H. Easterbrook, *Text, History, and Structure in Statutory Interpretation*, 17 Harv. J. L. & Pub. Pol'y 61, 64 (1994).

7. *Duncan*, 533 U.S. 167 at 185 (Breyer, J. dissenting) (citing U.S. Dept. of Justice, Office of Justice Programs, Bureau of Justice Statistics, *Federal Habeas Corpus Review: Challenging State Court Criminal Convictions* 17 [1995]).

8. See *id.* at 172–75.

9. *Id.* at 190–93 (Breyer, J., dissenting).

10. *Id.* at 190 (Breyer, J., dissenting).

11. Barak, *supra* note I, at 28–29.

12. See, e.g., Alex Kozinski & Stuart Banner, *Who's Afraid of Commercial Speech?* 76 Va. L. Rev. 627, 631 (1990); Martin H. Redish, *The First Amendment in the Marketplace: Commercial Speech and the Values of Free Expression*, 39 Geo. Wash. L. Rev. 429, 452–48 (1971); cf. 44 *Liquormart, Inc. v. Rhode Island*, 517 U.S. 484, 522 (1996) (Thomas, J., concurring in part and concurring in the judgment); U.S. Const. art. I.

13. Ctr. for Responsive Politics, *Election Overview, 2000 Cycle: Stats at a Glance*, at http://www.opensecrets.org/overview/index.asp?Cycle=2000 accessed Mar. 8, 2002 (aggregating totals using Federal Election Commission data); Ctr. for Responsive Politics, *Election Overview*, at http://www.opensecrets.org/overview/stats.asp accessed Nov. 21, 2003 (based on FEC data).

14. Taken from the record developed in *McConnell v. Federal Election Comm'n*, No. 02-1674 et al., Joint Appendix 1558. In the 2002 midterm election, less than one-tenth of one percent of the population gave 83 percent of all (hard and soft) itemized campaign contributions. Ctr. for Responsive Politics, see *supra* note 2.

15. Taken from the record developed in *McConnell*, No. 02-1674 et al., Joint Appendix 1564.

16. *Buckley v. Valeo*, 424 U.S. I (1976); *McConnell v. FEC*, 540 U.S. 93 (2003).

17. U.S. Const. amend. I.

18. *Masses Publishing Co. v. Patten*, 244 F.535, 540 (S.D.N.Y. 1917 Hand, J.) Benjamin Constant, *The Liberty of the Ancients Compared with That of the Moderns* (1819), in *Political Writings*, at 327 (Biancamaria Fontana trans. & ed., 1988).

19. *McConnell*, 540 U.S. at 136, 231; see also *Nixon v. Shrink Mo. Gov't PAC*, 528 U.S. 377, 399–402 (2000) (Breyer, J., concurring); *id.* at 136 (internal quotation marks omitted); *id.* at 137 (internal quotation marks omitted); see *Board of Trade of Chicago v. United States*, 246 U.S. 231 (1918); see *McConnell*, 540 U.S. at 134–42.

20. *McConnell*, 540 U.S. at 137.

9-3 *Federalist* No. 78

Alexander Hamilton

May 28, 1788

Of the several branches laid out in the Constitution, the judiciary is the least demo-cratic—that is, the least responsive to the expressed preferences of the citizenry. Indeed, it is hard to imagine an institution designed to be less responsive to the public than the Supreme Court, whose unelected judges enjoy lifetime appointments. During the Constitution's ratification, this fact exposed the judiciary to all sorts of wild speculation from opponents about the dire consequences the judiciary would have for the new repub-lic. In one of the most famous passages of The Federalist, *Alexander Hamilton seeks to calm fears by declaring the judiciary to be "the least dangerous branch." Unlike the president, the Court does not control a military force, and unlike Congress, it cannot confiscate citizens' property through taxation. At the same time, Hamilton does not shrink from assigning the judiciary a critical role in safeguarding the Constitution against congressional and presidential encroachments he sees as bound to occur from time to time. By assigning it this role, he assumed that the Supreme Court has the authority of "judicial review" even though there was no provision for it in the Constitution.*

We proceed now to an examination of the judiciary department of the proposed government. In unfolding the defects of the existing Confederation, the utility and necessity of a federal judicature have been clearly pointed out. It is the less necessary to recapitulate the considerations there urged, as the propriety of the institution in the abstract is not disputed; the only questions which have been raised being relative to the manner of constituting it, and to its extent. To these points, therefore, our observations shall be confined.

The manner of constituting it seems to embrace these several objects: 1st. The mode of appointing the judges. 2d. The tenure by which they are to hold their places. 3d. The partition of the judiciary authority between different courts, and their relations to each other.

First.

As to the mode of appointing the judges; this is the same with that of appointing the officers of the Union in general, and has been so fully discussed . . . that nothing can be said here which would not be useless repetition.

Second.

As to the tenure by which the judges are to hold their places; this chiefly concerns their duration in office; the provisions for their support; the precautions for their responsibility.

According to the plan of the convention, all judges who may be appointed by the United States are to hold their offices during good behavior. . . . The standard of good behavior for the continuance in office of the judicial magistracy, is certainly one of the most valuable of the modern improvements in the practice of government. In a monarchy it is an excellent barrier to the despotism of the prince; in a republic it is a no less excellent barrier to the encroachments and oppressions of the representative body. And it is the best expedient which can be devised in any government, to secure a steady, upright, and impartial administration of the laws.

Whoever attentively considers the different departments of power must perceive, that, in a government in which they are separated from each other, the judiciary, from the nature of its functions, will always be the least dangerous to the political rights of the

Constitution; because it will be least in a capacity to annoy or injure them. The Executive not only dispenses the honors, but holds the sword of the community. The legislature not only commands the purse, but prescribes the rules by which the duties and rights of every citizen are to be regulated. The judiciary, on the contrary, has no influence over either the sword or the purse; no direction either of the strength or of the wealth of the society; and can take no active resolution whatever. It may truly be said to have neither FORCE nor WILL, but merely judgment; and must ultimately depend upon the aid of the executive arm even for the efficacy of its judgments.

This simple view of the matter suggests several important consequences. It proves incontestably, that the judiciary is beyond comparison the weakest of the three departments of power[1]; that it can never attack with success either of the other two; and that all possible care is requisite to enable it to defend itself against their attacks. It equally proves, that though individual oppression may now and then proceed from the courts of justice, the general liberty of the people can never be endangered from that quarter; I mean so long as the judiciary remains truly distinct from both the legislature and the Executive. For I agree, that "there is no liberty, if the power of judging be not separated from the legislative and executive powers."[2] And it proves, in the last place, that as liberty can have nothing to fear from the judiciary alone, but would have every thing to fear from its union with either of the other departments; that as all the effects of such a union must ensue from a dependence of the former on the latter, notwithstanding a nominal and apparent separation; that as, from the natural feebleness of the judiciary, it is in continual jeopardy of being overpowered, awed, or influenced by its co-ordinate branches; and that as nothing can contribute so much to its firmness and independence as permanency in office, this quality may therefore be justly regarded as an indispensable ingredient in its constitution, and, in a great measure, as the citadel of the public justice and the public security.

The complete independence of the courts of justice is peculiarly essential in a limited Constitution.

By a limited Constitution, I understand one which contains certain specified exceptions to the legislative authority; such, for instance, as that it shall pass no bills of attainder, no ex post facto laws, and the like. Limitations of this kind can be preserved in practice no other way than through the medium of courts of justice, whose duty it must be to declare all acts contrary to the manifest tenor of the Constitution void. Without this, all the reservations of particular rights or privileges would amount to nothing.

Some perplexity respecting the rights of the courts to pronounce legislative acts void, because contrary to the Constitution, has arisen from an imagination that the doctrine would imply a superiority of the judiciary to the legislative power. It is urged that the authority which can declare the acts of another void, must necessarily be superior to the one whose acts may be declared void. As this doctrine is of great importance in all the American constitutions, a brief discussion of the ground on which it rests cannot be unacceptable.

There is no position which depends on clearer principles, than that every act of a delegated authority, contrary to the tenor of the commission under which it is exercised, is void. No legislative act, therefore, contrary to the Constitution, can be valid. To deny this, would be to affirm, that the deputy is greater than his principal; that the servant is above his master; that the representatives of the people are superior to the people themselves; that men acting by virtue of powers, may do not only what their powers do not authorize, but what they forbid.

If it be said that the legislative body are themselves the constitutional judges of their own powers, and that the construction they put upon them is conclusive upon the other departments, it may be answered, that this cannot be the natural presumption, where it is not to be collected from any particular provisions in the Constitution. It is not otherwise to be supposed, that the Constitution could intend to enable the representatives of the people to substitute their will to that of their constituents. It is far more rational to suppose, that the courts were designed to be an intermediate body between the people and the legislature, in order, among other things, to keep the latter within the limits assigned to their authority. The interpretation of the laws is the proper and peculiar province of the courts. A constitution is, in fact, and must be regarded by the judges, as a fundamental law. It therefore belongs to them to ascertain its meaning, as well as the meaning of any particular act proceeding from the legislative body. If there should happen to be an irreconcilable variance between the two, that which has the superior obligation and validity ought, of course, to be preferred; or, in other words, the Constitution ought to be preferred to the statute, the intention of the people to the intention of their agents.

Nor does this conclusion by any means suppose a superiority of the judicial to the legislative power. It only supposes that the power of the people is superior to both; and that where the will of the legislature, declared in its statutes, stands in opposition to that of the people, declared in the Constitution, the judges ought to be governed by the latter rather than the former. They ought to regulate their decisions by the fundamental laws, rather than by those which are not fundamental.

This exercise of judicial discretion, in determining between two contradictory laws, is exemplified in a familiar instance. It not uncommonly happens, that there are two statutes existing at one time, clashing in whole or in part with each other, and neither of them containing any repealing clause or expression. In such a case, it is the province of the courts to liquidate and fix their meaning and operation. So far as they can, by any fair construction, be reconciled to each other, reason and law conspire to dictate that this should be done; where this is impracticable, it becomes a matter of necessity to give effect to one, in exclusion of the other. The rule which has obtained in the courts for determining their relative validity is, that the last in order of time shall be preferred to the first. But this is a mere rule of construction, not derived from any positive law, but from the nature and reason of the thing. It is a rule not enjoined upon the courts by legislative provision, but adopted by themselves, as consonant to truth and propriety, for the direction of their conduct as interpreters of the law. They thought it reasonable, that between the interfering acts of an EQUAL authority, that which was the last indication of its will should have the preference.

But in regard to the interfering acts of a superior and subordinate authority, of an original and derivative power, the nature and reason of the thing indicate the converse of that rule as proper to be followed. They teach us that the prior act of a superior ought to be preferred to the subsequent act of an inferior and subordinate authority; and that accordingly, whenever a particular statute contravenes the Constitution, it will be the duty of the judicial tribunals to adhere to the latter and disregard the former.

It can be of no weight to say that the courts, on the pretense of a repugnancy, may substitute their own pleasure to the constitutional intentions of the legislature. This might as well happen in the case of two contradictory statutes; or it might as well happen in every adjudication upon any single statute. The courts must declare the sense of the law; and if they should be disposed to exercise WILL instead of JUDGMENT, the consequence would equally be the substitution of their pleasure to that of the legislative body. The observation, if it prove any thing, would prove that there ought to be no judges distinct from that body.

If, then, the courts of justice are to be considered as the bulwarks of a limited Constitution against legislative encroachments, this consideration will afford a strong argument for the permanent tenure of judicial offices, since nothing will contribute so much as this to that independent spirit in the judges which must be essential to the faithful performance of so arduous a duty.

This independence of the judges is equally requisite to guard the Constitution and the rights of individuals from the effects of those ill humors, which the arts of designing men, or the influence of particular conjunctures, sometimes disseminate among the people themselves, and which, though they speedily give place to better information, and more deliberate reflection, have a tendency, in the meantime, to occasion dangerous innovations in the government, and serious oppressions of the minor party in the community. . . . Until the people have, by some solemn and authoritative act, annulled or changed the established form, it is binding upon themselves collectively, as well as individually; and no presumption, or even knowledge, of their sentiments, can warrant their representatives in a departure from it, prior to such an act. But it is easy to see, that it would require an uncommon portion of fortitude in the judges to do their duty as faithful guardians of the Constitution, where legislative invasions of it had been instigated by the major voice of the community.

But it is not with a view to infractions of the Constitution only, that the independence of the judges may be an essential safeguard against the effects of occasional ill humors in the society. These sometimes extend no farther than to the injury of the private rights of particular classes of citizens, by unjust and partial laws. Here also the firmness of the judicial magistracy is of vast importance in mitigating the severity and confining the operation of such laws. It not only serves to moderate the immediate mischiefs of those which may have been passed, but it operates as a check upon the legislative body in passing them; who, perceiving that obstacles to the success of iniquitous intention are to be expected from the scruples of the courts, are in a manner compelled, by the very motives of the injustice they meditate, to qualify their attempts. . . .

That inflexible and uniform adherence to the rights of the Constitution, and of individuals, which we perceive to be indispensable in the courts of justice, can certainly not be expected from judges who hold their offices by a temporary commission. Periodical appointments, however regulated, or by whomsoever made, would, in some way or other, be fatal to their necessary independence. If the power of making them was committed either to the Executive or legislature, there would be danger of an improper complaisance to the branch which possessed it; if to

both, there would be an unwillingness to hazard the displeasure of either; if to the people, or to persons chosen by them for the special purpose, there would be too great a disposition to consult popularity, to justify a reliance that nothing would be consulted but the Constitution and the laws.

There is yet a further and a weightier reason for the permanency of the judicial offices, which is deducible from the nature of the qualifications they require. It has been frequently remarked, with great propriety, that a voluminous code of laws is one of the inconveniences necessarily connected with the advantages of a free government. To avoid an arbitrary discretion in the courts, it is indispensable that they should be bound down by strict rules and precedents, which serve to define and point out their duty in every particular case that comes before them; and it will readily be conceived from the variety of controversies which grow out of the folly and wickedness of mankind, that the records of those precedents must unavoidably swell to a very considerable bulk, and must demand long and laborious study to acquire a competent knowledge of them. Hence it is, that there can be but few men in the society who will have sufficient skill in the laws to qualify them for the stations of judges. And making the proper deductions for the ordinary depravity of human nature, the number must be still smaller of those who unite the requisite integrity with the requisite knowledge. . . .

Notes

1. The celebrated Montesquieu, speaking of them, says: "Of the three powers above mentioned, the judiciary is next to nothing." "Spirit of Laws." vol. i., page 186. [See Charles de Secondat, Baron de Montesquieu, *The Spirit of Laws*, trans. Thomas Nugent, rev. J. V. Pritchard (London: G. Bell & Sons Ltd., 1914).]
2. Idem, page 181.

9-4 Selecting Justice: The Ideology of Federal Judges Appointed by President Barack Obama

Robert A. Carp and Kenneth L. Manning

Authority to appoint federal judges gives presidents an opportunity to continue to influence national policy long after they have left office. Presidents naturally prefer to select men and women who they believe will decide cases the same way they would if they were on the bench. But no president's appointees are mere clones. Once in office, these lifetime appointees may prove to be more liberal or conservative than their president. Some differ because presidents select them for reasons other than their ideological compatibility. These "other" considerations include ethnicity and gender, sponsorship by a key constituency, and political deals with key senators. For this essay, Robert A. Carp and Kenneth L. Manning offer an early appraisal of the ideology of the federal district judges that President Barack Obama appointed.

On December 19, 2013, President Barack Obama nominated Michael P. Boggs to fill a vacancy on the U.S. district court in northern Georgia. A judge on the Georgia Court of Appeals, Boggs had previously served in the state legislature. Boggs's background was hardly that of the stereotypical progressive Democrat. During his stint as a Georgia lawmaker, Boggs had sponsored legislation that sought to restrict access to abortion rights and he had voted to retain the state flag that contained the Confederate battle emblem.

Liberal interests howled in protest to the Boggs judicial nomination. "It breaks my heart that this is the first African-American president who is doing something like this," said U.S. Representative David Scott (D-GA).[1] More than two dozen liberal interest groups also registered their disapproval of the Boggs pick, as did a liberal Democratic U.S. senator from Connecticut, Richard Blumenthal, who warned, "I am strongly considering whether he should be withdrawn because I have very serious concerns about

some of the really unwise and inappropriate views he has stated."[2] The Boggs nomination, which upset so many progressive activists, was reportedly part of a bipartisan deal brokered between the White House and Republican Senators as a means of moving forward on a group of stalled judicial nominations.[3] Despite the liberal angst, the White House appeared to view this deal making as a necessary part of the ideological give and take of Washington. Defending the move, White House counsel Kathryn Ruemmler asked rhetorically, "Do we work with Republican senators to find a compromise, or should we leave the seats vacant?"[4]

On the other hand, some critics of the president have suggested that Obama's judicial appointees are left-leaning extremists and that the president is trying to "pack the courts with liberals."[5] "These [liberal] groups are scrambling for a new way to pack the courts," said Andrew Kloster of the Heritage Foundation, a conservative think tank. "Just having diversity of skin color or gender isn't enough to get

Source: This piece is an original essay commissioned for this volume.

what these liberal groups are really after, which is a certain type of political agenda."[6] At the same time, conservatives have blasted some senators for their "rubber-stamping of Obama's left-wing judicial nominees" and their votes for "Obama's liberal activist judges."[7] Ramesh Ponnuru, a senior editor for the influential conservative magazine *National Review*, urged that "Republicans shouldn't let Obama pack the courts."[8]

So which side is correct—conservatives who contend that Obama's appointees are left-wing extremists or others who suggest that Obama has worked in a bipartisan fashion to nominate qualified, mainstream (though liberal) judges? This article seeks to shed light on this matter by addressing two basic questions: What should we anticipate of the Obama administration's motivation and potential to make an ideological imprint on the federal courts? What do the empirical data tell us about the way the Obama judges have been deciding cases during their time on the bench?[9]

Judicial scholars have identified four general factors that determine whether chief executives can obtain a judiciary that is sympathetic to their political values and attitudes: the degree of the president's commitment to making ideologically based appointments; the number of vacancies to be filled; the level of the chief executive's political clout; and the ideological climate into which the new judicial appointees enter.[10]

Presidential Support for Ideologically Based Appointments

One key aspect of the success of chief executives in appointing a federal judiciary that mirrors their own political beliefs is the depth of their commitment to doing so. Some presidents may be content merely to fill the federal bench with party loyalists and pay little attention to their nominees' specific ideologies. Some may consider ideological factors when appointing Supreme Court justices but may not regard those same factors as important for trial and appellate judges. Other presidents may discount ideologically based appointments; they tend to be

nonideological. Still others may place factors such as past political loyalty ahead of ideology in selecting judges.

For example, Harry Truman had strong political views, but when selecting judges, he placed a candidate's loyalty to the president ahead of the candidate's overall political orientation. On the other hand, Ronald Reagan, Lyndon Johnson, and George W. Bush are examples of presidents who took great pains to select judges who shared their ideological beliefs. What do we know about Obama's resolve in making ideologically based judicial appointments?

When Obama first campaigned for the presidency, he placed a lot of emphasis on the word *change*, although he was short on the specifics of that vague term. Change might suggest that the new president would seek to chart a very different course than his predecessor and that Obama would wish to appoint an unabashedly liberal judiciary to counterbalance George W. Bush's staunchly conservative approach. However, President Obama's nominees have not generated universal antipathy from all persons of a right-leaning persuasion. Consider, for example, the aforementioned nomination of Boggs. What's more, the circumstances surrounding the Boggs nomination were not unprecedented. Robert E. Bacharach, a U.S. trial judge from Oklahoma, was selected in 2012 by Obama for a seat on the 10th Circuit Court of Appeals. Both of Bacharach's home-state senators, Republicans James Inhofe and Tom Coburn, supported him. "I like the guy," Inhofe told a local reporter. "I told him that it's not very often the White House and I agree on anything."[11] (Still, Senate Republicans filibustered the nomination, giving no specific reason other than a vow to block all Obama's appellate court nominees because 2012 was a presidential election year.)

With regard to his two Supreme Court nominations so far, Obama also appears to have attempted to avoid bruising political battles. Sonia Sotomayor, who was chosen in 2009 to fill the vacancy that occurred when Justice David Souter announced he would retire, was initially selected for a federal judgeship by President George H. W. Bush. The first

Hispanic woman nominated to the U.S. Supreme Court, Sotomayor was widely recognized as a loyal Democrat. However, a review of her judicial and legal record turned up no real instances of liberal ideological extremism. Some Republicans criticized Sotomayor for comments she had made in past speeches about a "wise Latina" being better able to reach a conclusion "than a white male who hadn't lived that life."[12] However, these attacks yielded little political fruit for the GOP. Given Sotomayor's solid qualifications and her ethically irreproachable background, Republicans were unable to mount a serious challenge to her nomination and she was confirmed easily.[13]

About 9 months later, President Obama was presented with a second Supreme Court opening with the retirement of Justice John Paul Stevens. And again the president chose to downplay ideology and nominated a noncontroversial candidate. As one seasoned commentator quipped, "President Obama's announcement of Elena Kagan was perfectly boring—and that's what makes her such a bold choice."[14] This commentator then added:

Nominating Kagan . . . required some courage. Obama defied those populists who said he should reach beyond the Eastern elite for somebody with more "real world" experience. He defied liberal interest groups—his own base—that favored a more ideological liberal. . . . Instead, he chose brain over bio, sending to the Senate neither a compelling American story nor a liberal warrior but a superbly skilled, non-ideological builder of bridges.[15]

On August 5, 2010, the Senate confirmed Kagan's appointment by a vote of 63 to 37.

Some liberals have been disappointed by the general lack of emphasis the Obama administration seems to place on judicial nominations, and this dismay by some on the left suggests that Obama does not appear to put a priority on furthering an ideological agenda. *Washington Post* reporter Philip Rucker noted that, "during Obama's first term,

judicial nominations often fell by the wayside in the face of the economic crisis and other policy priorities at the White House. Many liberal allies complained that the president did little to champion nominees once they were named."[16] Noted court watcher Jeffrey Toobin observed,

The President's lethargy on the matter of judicial nominations is inexplicable. So is his silence on the subject. . . . George W. Bush complained loudly when he felt Democrats in the Senate had delayed or obstructed his judicial nominees. Obama has said little. . . . As a former president of the Harvard Law Review and long-time lecturer at the University of Chicago Law School, Obama has a great deal of familiarity with legal issues but hardly ever talks about them.[17]

Toobin has not been alone in his criticism. Others also "blame Obama for his unconcern with the judicial nomination process. . . . Obama could have been much more diligent about making nominations to fill the large and growing number of vacancies on the lower courts."[18] Even Democrats in Congress have grumbled about Obama's apparent lack of interest in the nomination process. *The New York Times* reported that after Senate Majority Leader Harry Reid complained to the president that Senate Republicans were blocking dozens of Obama's nominees to serve as ambassadors, Obama indifferently said to Reid, "You and [Republican leader] Mitch [McConnell] work it out." Senator Reid reportedly "seethed" at Obama after "the impression the president left with Mr. Reid was clear: Capitol Hill is not my problem. . . . Reid told other senators and his staff members that he was astonished by how disengaged the president seemed."[19]

Let's return to the original question: Does the evidence suggest that President Obama is trying to move the judicial center of gravity in a liberal direction? To be sure, Obama's judges have exhibited clear tendencies to be more liberal than those appointed by Republican presidents, and in that way the answer appears to be yes. However, the backgrounds of Obama's judges have been well within the mainstream of U.S. political thought. What's more, President Obama has clearly sought to avoid acrimonious political battles by cutting deals with Republicans at times and by selecting a number of nominees who have not had especially controversial pasts and have been unlikely to incite a lot of controversy. Additionally, the lack of emphasis that the Obama administration seems to have placed on judicial nominations in general suggests, too, that the White House has not approached the judicial selection process as a means of forcefully pushing an ideological agenda. In sum, there is little evidence for the proposition that Obama has sought to aggressively further an ideological agenda by appointing rigid ideologues to the bench.

The Number of Vacancies to Be Filled

A second element affecting the capacity of chief executives to establish a policy link between themselves and the judiciary is the number of appointments available to them. The more judges a president can select, the greater the potential for the White House to put its stamp on the judicial branch. For example, George Washington's influence on the Supreme Court was significant because he was able to nominate 10 individuals to the high court; Jimmy Carter's was nil because no vacancies occurred during his term as president.

The number of appointment opportunities depends on several factors: how many judicial vacancies are inherited from the previous administration, how many judges and justices die or resign during the president's term, how long the president serves, and whether Congress passes legislation that significantly increases the number of judgeships. Historically, the last factor seems to have been the most important in influencing the number of judgeships available, and politics in its most basic form permeates this process. Research has shown that federal judicial posts tend to be created during periods when one political party exercises outsized control in Washington, D.C.[20] Thus the number of vacancies a president can fill—which is a function

of politics, fate, and the size of judicial workloads—is another variable that helps determine a chief executive's impact on the composition of the federal judiciary.

The Clinton administration provides a good case in point. President George H. W. Bush left his successor, President Bill Clinton, with a whopping 100 lower-court vacancies—14 percent of the total. However, although Clinton inherited a large number of unfilled judicial slots, his Republican Congresses were loath to enact any type of omnibus judgeship bill that would have enhanced his capacity to pack the judiciary. As a result, Clinton was given an average number of vacancies to fill during the entire course of his two terms in office. When George W. Bush took the reins of power in early 2001, he was presented with 29 court of appeals and 62 district court vacancies.

In contrast, when President Obama assumed office in 2009, he inherited 49 judicial vacancies—44 at the district-court level and 15 in the courts of appeals. This number was not as large as those provided to his two predecessors, but 49 open judicial positions did give Obama the opportunity to make a good start in filling the bench with judges who shared his philosophy.

Despite this initial opportunity for the president, the Obama White House was slow to fill many judicial vacancies and, as previously noted, has been subjected to criticism for this lack of enthusiasm and activity. Two court watchers at *The Washington Post* noted in 2011,

> Federal judges have been retiring at a rate of one per week this year, driving up vacancies that have nearly doubled since President Obama took office. The departures are increasing workloads dramatically and delaying trials in some of the nation's federal courts.[21]

They observed, "Since Obama took office, federal judicial vacancies have risen steadily as dozens of judges have left without being replaced by the president's nominees."[22] What's more, the languid pace of selecting judges could not all be blamed on the hectic, early days of a new administration facing many daunting challenges. The slow rate of nominations continued into Obama's second term. On April 10, 2013, *The New York Times* observed that "Mr. Obama has been slow to nominate judges to fill the vacancies on the [D.C. Court of Appeals]."[23] The newspaper noted that, at that time, the D.C. Court of Appeals held 4 vacant judicial positions out of a total of 11, and that Obama had only nominated two people since 2009 to fill the seats.

As of September 1, 2014, there were 58 vacant seats out of 874 authorized active judgeships on the federal district and appellate courts, continuing one of the longest periods of high-vacancy rates in modern times. The Obama administration had nominees pending for only 29 (50%) of these judgeships. Between extraordinary Republican delaying tactics, relatively slow White House nominations, and a dysfunctional Senate confirmation system, there seems now to be a "perfect storm" with regard to delay in filling judicial vacancies.[24]

What about the possibility of Congress's passing a new omnibus judge bill that would give the president the opportunity to fill the judiciary with men and women of like-minded values—a phenomenon that greatly enhanced President Kennedy's and President Carter's ideological impact on the judiciary? Given the deeply polarized nature of contemporary Washington, D.C., the odds these days of Republicans' giving President Obama the opportunity to appoint a number of new judges to the bench are virtually nil. Republicans in the Senate have been loath to approve Obama's nominees to fill existing judicial positions; the idea that the president would be given a significant number of additional new judicial slots to fill is, at this point, inconceivable. Measures were introduced in Congress between 2009 and early 2013 to create a few new emergency judicial positions, but these efforts stalled. Between the budget-cutting mentality that prevailed in Congress and the bitter political divisions that characterized the times, Congress has shown no indication that it might offer the president an omnibus judges bill that would serve to increase his impact on the federal judiciary.[25]

So what are we to conclude about this second predictor of whether President Obama will have a substantial impact on the ideological direction of the federal judiciary—the number of vacancies he can fill? The data suggest that in terms of pure numbers, the president is having an average set of opportunities to make an ideological impact on the federal bench. However, due to extraordinary obstructionism by Republicans in the Senate and a slow nomination process by the president's team, the Obama administration has been on pace to install a below-average number of judges. *The New York Times* stated it succinctly when it noted in August 2012,

> President Obama is set to end his [first] term with dozens fewer lower court appointments than both Presidents Bill Clinton and George W. Bush achieved in their first four years, and probably with less of a lasting ideological imprint on the judiciary than many liberals had hoped for and conservatives had feared.[26]

Indeed, through his first term, Obama appointed 172 Article III judges (i.e., jurists on the U.S. Supreme Court, U.S. courts of appeals, and U.S. district courts). This number is not small, but it is significantly below the 204 judges appointed by his predecessor, George W. Bush, during his first term in office and also behind the 201 jurists selected by Clinton during his first 4 years. We can see, therefore, that Obama's pace of filling judgeships is about 15% below that of the previous two presidents.

Of course, since Obama won a second term, his ultimate influence will undoubtedly be large. As of September 1, 2014, Obama had filled 274 of the 813 federal judgeships active at that time, representing 33.7% of the total.[27] Thus, around one third of active federal judges currently bear the Obama stamp—a factor of real significance. Still, at this point the data suggest that at least in terms of sheer numbers Obama's ultimate imprint on the federal bench may turn out to be slightly more limited than that of other recent two-term presidents. It is clear that much of Obama's judicial legacy depends on how successful he will be in filling judicial vacancies during his final years in office.

The President's Political Clout

Another factor determining whether the president can get a sympathetic federal judiciary is the scope and degree of presidential skill in overcoming any political obstacles. The key stumbling block is often the U.S. Senate. If the Senate is controlled by the president's political party, the White House will find it much easier to secure confirmation than if opposition forces are in control, but this is hardly a given: Even though the Republicans were firmly in control of the Senate in 2006, the George W. Bush White House was obliged to negotiate a three-judge nomination deal with the two Democratic senators from Michigan to obtain confirmation of some of Bush's judges.[28] More expected is the case in which the opposition is in the majority in the Senate and presidents have little choice but to engage in a sort of political horse-trading to get their nominees approved. For example, in the summer of 1999, President Clinton found it expedient to make a deal with Republican senator Orrin Hatch of Utah to nominate Ted Stewart, a conservative Republican from that state who was backed by Hatch but vigorously opposed by liberals and environmental groups, to ensure smooth sailing for at least 10 of Clinton's judicial nominations that had been blocked in the Senate.[29]

What about President Obama's political influence? Although the president was elected by a clear electoral majority in 2008—and reelected by a decisive margin in 2012—his "glory days" have been limited. The high approval numbers given to the president during his early days in office are long gone, and during his second term in office President Obama's net approval rating has topped 50 percent only for a few brief months. As of September 1, 2014, the president's approval rating as measured by Gallup stood at 42 percent, with 51 percent disapproving of the way Obama is handling his job.[30]

And while it's true that the president was able to get a number of pieces of legislation passed during his first 2 years in office, including his landmark health care reform law, the Obama legislative agenda ground to a virtual halt after the 2010 elections, when Republicans recaptured control of the House of Representatives and a series of bitter budgetary battles subsequently dominated relations between Capitol Hill and the White House.

In terms of Obama's success vis-à-vis the Senate judicial confirmation process, there is little question that the process has become delay-filled and bitterly acrimonious. Russ Wheeler of the Brookings Institution noted, "It used to be more collegial. Minority senators realized elections had consequences and the federal system needs judges. [Now] all those rules are out the window. It's fighting tooth and nail every day."[31] In this struggle so far the Obama administration has encountered quite a bit of success, some notable failures, and plenty of continual obstructionism.

During the early months of the Obama administration, scholars observed that "the [Senate Judiciary] Committee did its job, with the greatest obstruction and delay of Obama nominees occurring at the floor stages of confirmation. Behind such a generalization are layers of nuance that shaped both committee and floor activity and, at times, the lack thereof."[32] These experts further noted that this "surface cooperation" was somewhat deceptive:

> It would be a vast overstatement to suggest that the minority members of the committee simply "went along" with the administration's picks. To the contrary, there was a pattern of regularized and systematic opposition that had an impact on the processing of virtually all Obama nominees, but that impact could be seen, in most instances, in processing delay, not definitive and resolute obstruction save for a handful of . . . nominees.[33]

This "delaying action" on the part of opponents to Obama's judicial appointees did not abate over time. Considering Obama's first full term, two respected judicial researchers observed that the president's judicial nominations "faced nearly historic delays in reaching the Senate floor, and confirmation rates for the nation's federal trial and appellate courts remained depressed."[34] The average length of the confirmation process for Obama's successful appellate court nominees during his first term was around 220 days; it was about 190 days for district court positions. By historical standards, these numbers are very high, even compared with the Clinton and George W. Bush administrations.[35] As recently as the early 1990s, the average length of the confirmation process for a successful judicial nomination was around 100 days, and during much of the 1970s it was well under 50 days. With regard to Obama's political influence, these data clearly indicate that the administration was unable to spur prompt Senate action on the president's judicial nominations.

However, though the process was long and drawn out, Obama nominees in the 111th (2009–2010) and 112th (2011–2012) Congresses were confirmed at higher rates than were George W. Bush's nominees: The Senate confirmed roughly 60 percent of Obama's appellate court nominations but only 50 percent of Bush's nominees. The confirmation rate for Obama's district court nominees during his first term was around 65%, slightly better than for George W. Bush's nominees. These numbers do not approach those seen prior to the 1980s, when nearly 90% of judicial nominees gained Senate approval.[36] Still, in terms of the sheer percentage of nominees approved, the data indicate that a majority of Obama's nominees have been confirmed.

Perhaps the most notable shift in the power struggle over judges between the Senate and the White House came in November 2013, when Democrats changed the Senate rules and eliminated the possibility of a filibuster for lower-court nominees. The rule change was precipitated by increasing frustration among Democrats toward Republicans' refusals to allow votes on numerous presidential nominations, particularly three nominees to the D.C.

Circuit Court of Appeals.[37] The judicial candidates in question at the time were well-regarded, highly qualified individuals with strong credentials. Still, Republicans filibustered their nominations and refused to allow a vote on their approval, arguing that the D.C. court was underworked and did not need the judges. Most legal experts considered this argument unfounded, and reports indicated that Democrats increasingly came to feel that the GOP was altering the balance of power between the executive and legislative branches by refusing to allow the duly elected president to fulfill his constitutional authority to appoint jurists and other governmental officials. Senator Elizabeth Warren, a Democrat from Massachusetts, asserted that "[Republicans] have filibustered people [President Obama] has nominated to fill out his administration, and they are now filibustering judges to block him from filling any of the vacancies with highly qualified people: We need to call out these filibusters for what they are: Naked attempts to nullify the results of the last election."[38]

The filibuster rule change did pave the way for some judicial nominees to be approved, including the three individuals tapped for the key D.C. Circuit court. But attention has increasingly turned to the use of another tactic—the "blue-slip" process—as a means of delaying or blocking judicial nominations. The blue-slip tradition dictates that when a judge is nominated by the president, the chair of the Senate Judiciary Committee sends a form (printed on aqua-hued paper) to home-state senators seeking their approval of a judicial nominee. If the Senators approve, the committee may move forward with the nomination. However, if one or both of the Senators withhold the blue slip or signal their disapproval, the nomination typically stalls. The blue-slip process is not mandated by law or by Senate rules; it is, rather, an institutional norm.[39]

There is growing evidence that the blue-slip process is increasingly being used as a means of preventing President Obama from filling judicial vacancies. For example, in June 2013, President Obama nominated Jennifer May-Parker to a U.S. district court

position in North Carolina after she had been recommended for the position by Republican senator
Richard Burr from that state. However, after she was
selected, Senator Burr reversed his position and
withheld his blue-slip support for May-Parker. As of
September 1, 2014, May-Parker's nomination
remained blocked by Senator Burr and the judgeship
was still vacant. In Texas a number of federal judicial positions remain unfilled and lack nominees,
reportedly due in large part to the blue-slip process.
One news report indicated that the White House has
sought informal preclearance of any nominees from
John Cornyn and Ted Cruz, the two Republicans
senators from the Lone Star State, before any names
are formally put forward by the administration. This
is because the White House realizes that the senators
could use the blue-slip process to block any nominations.[40] So far, the Texas senators have not cooper-
ated, and as of September 1, 2014, the state had nine
vacant district court judgeships, with three nominees
pending. Two of the judgeships had been vacant
since 2011, and one position had been empty for
nearly 6 years—since November 2008.

Other Republican delaying tactics have included
frequent refusals of unanimous consent to floor
votes on nominations and extensive use of holds on
nominees by individual senators.[41] And there is little
question that these delays and obstructions are
deeply tinted by partisanship. In April 2013, Senate
Judiciary Committee chairman Patrick Leahy, a
Democrat from Vermont, noted that, "of the 35 judicial emergency vacancies, 24 are in states with
Republican senators. In fact, close to half of all judicial emergency vacancies are in just three states, each
of which is represented by two Republican senators."[42]

The Obama administration has also had some
high-profile judicial nominees blocked outright by
Republicans. Goodwin Liu, who was tapped in 2010
for a seat on the Ninth Circuit Court of Appeals,
withdrew his name after Senate Republicans blocked
a vote on his confirmation via a filibuster in 2011.[43]
In 2013, a similar parliamentary fate befell Caitlin
Halligan, who was selected by President Obama to
fill a vacancy on the D.C. Court of Appeals. Halligan
withdrew her name from consideration after the
Senate GOP twice blocked her nomination from
coming up for a vote in the Senate. Both Liu and
Halligan were considered to be very accomplished
and qualified nominees but were staunchly opposed
by Republicans who argued that the nominees were
too ideological. In a post-filibuster Senate, these
nominees presumably could have been approved.
Still, they were two high-profile defeats for the
Obama administration in the ongoing judicial confirmation battles.

So what is one to conclude about the impact of
the president's political clout in terms of his success
in shaping the judiciary with his court appointments? Though the president has seen a somewhat
weak but stable level of support by the American
public, he has been able to appoint a significant
number of lower-court judges, along with two well-
regarded Supreme Court justices, though this has
come at the expense of significant delay. Thus, if the
Obama cohort is deciding cases in a generally liberal
direction on most issues, this third variable—the
president's political clout—should lend some weight
to the president's capacity to make an ideological
impact on the judiciary.

The Judicial Climate the New Judges Enter

A final matter affects the capacity of chief executives to secure a federal judiciary that reflects their
own political values: the philosophical orientations of
the current sitting district and appellate court judges
with whom the new appointees would interact.
Because federal judges serve lifetime appointments
during good behavior, presidents must accept the
composition and value structure of the judiciary as it
exists when they take office. If the existing judiciary
already reflects the president's political and legal orientations, the impact of the new judicial appointees
will be immediate and substantial. However, if the
new chief executive faces a trial and appellate judiciary whose values are radically different from his
own, the impact of the president's subsequent judicial

appointments will be weaker and slower to materialize. New judges must respect the controlling legal precedents and the constitutional interpretations that prevail in the judiciary at the time they enter it or risk being overruled by a higher court. That reality may limit the capacity of a new set of judges to go their own way—at least in the short term.

Consider, for example, President Reagan's impact on the judicial branch. By the end of his second term, he had appointed an unprecedented 368 lifetime lower-court federal judges to courts of general jurisdiction, 50 percent of those on the bench. When he entered the White House, the Supreme Court was already teetering to the right because of Richard Nixon's and Gerald R. Ford's conservative appointments. Although Jimmy Carter's liberal appointees were still serving on trial and appellate court benches, Reagan found a good many conservative judges from Nixon and Ford on the bench when he took office. Thus, he had a major role in shaping the entire federal judiciary in his own conservative image for some time to come. George H. W. Bush's judges had a much easier time making their impact felt because they entered a judicial realm wherein well over half the judges already possessed conservative Republican values.

On the other hand, President Clinton's impact on the judiciary was slower in manifesting itself; his judicial nominees entered an arena in which appointees of GOP presidents with strong conservative orientations held more than 75 percent of the trial and appellate court judgeships. When George W. Bush entered the White House, Democratic presidents had appointed 51 percent of the federal judges. At the end of his 8 years in office, roughly 60 percent of lower federal judges bore the Republican label. Thus, when Obama assumed office, the judiciary was clearly dominated by those who did not share his mainstream Democratic values.

When George W. Bush turned over the Oval Office to Obama in January 2009, around 59 percent of the federal trial court judiciary had been selected by Republican presidents—a decisive majority.[44] What was the scorecard in the fall of 2014 as Obama approached completion of the sixth year of his presidency? Of the 813 active judges sitting on the bench as of September 1, 2014, Democrats had appointed 437 compared with the 376 appointed by Republicans.[45] This gave a slight edge to the Democrats, though the overall partisan makeup of the lower federal bench was split quite evenly between the two parties. Still, it also meant that nearly 54% of the federal bench at that time had been appointed by Democrats, a significant shift since George W. Bush left office. If Obama holds with past practice and continues to appoint judges who are selected overwhelmingly from the ranks of Democrats, by the time he concludes his second term in office, we anticipate that a substantial majority (though not an overwhelming one) of the judges on the federal bench will have been appointed by Democrats. This is a fact of significant consequence; it means that the climate the Obama judges are entering is one that is receptive to them and that they stand to have a modest but real ideological impact.

Sources and Definitions

Let us now turn to a quantitative analysis of the decision making by Obama judges. Before we examine the data we have collected, we need to say a word about the data's source and offer working definitions of the terms *conservative* and *liberal*. The data on trial courts were taken from a database consisting of more than 112,000 opinions published in the Federal Supplement from 1933 through 2013. Included in this overall data set were 763 decisions handed down by 113 judges appointed by President Obama.[46] Only cases that easily fit into one of 31 case types and that contained a clear, underlying liberal–conservative dimension were used. This included cases such as state and federal habeas corpus pleas, labor-management disputes, questions involving the right to privacy, and environmental protection cases. Excluded were cases involving matters that do not exhibit a clear ideological dimension, such as patent cases, admiralty disputes, and land condemnation hearings. The number of cases not selected was about the same as the number included.

In the realm of civil rights and civil liberties, liberal judges tended to take a broadening position; that is, they sought to extend those freedoms in their rulings. By contrast, conservative judges preferred to limit such rights. For example, in a case in which a governmental agency wanted to prevent a controversial person from speaking in a public park or at a state university, liberal judges would be more inclined than would their conservative counterparts to uphold the right of the would-be speaker. Or in a case concerning affirmative action in public higher education, a liberal judge would be more likely to take the side favoring special admissions for minority petitioners.

In the area of government regulation of the economy, liberal judges would probably uphold legislation that benefited working people or the economic underdog. Thus, if the secretary of labor sought an injunction against an employer for paying less than the minimum wage, a liberal judge would be more disposed to endorse the labor secretary's arguments, whereas a conservative judge would tend to side with business—especially big business.

Another broad category of cases often studied by judicial scholars is criminal justice. In general, liberal judges are more sympathetic to the motions made by criminal defendants. For instance, in a case in which the accused claimed to have been coerced by the government to make an illegal confession, liberal judges would be more likely than would their conservative counterparts to agree that the government had acted improperly.

Figure 1 Percentage of Liberal Decisions by District Court Judges Appointed by the 10 Most Recent Presidents

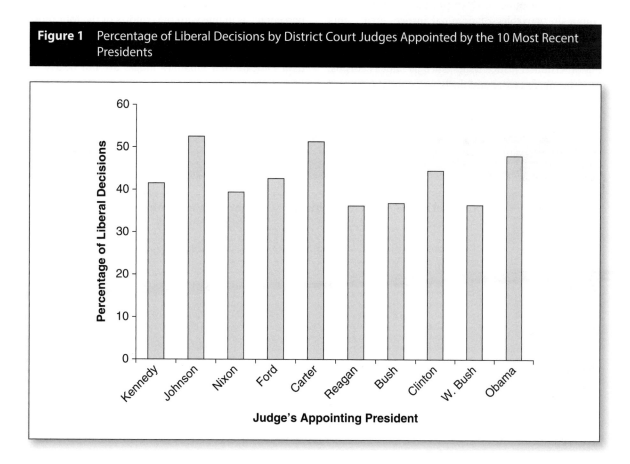

Figure 1 compares the total liberalism scores of the judicial cohorts appointed by 10 of the most recent presidents—five Democrats and five Republicans. The data indicate that 48 percent of the decisions of the Obama jurists have been decided in a liberal direction. These numbers indicate that Obama's cohort is roughly in the middle of those appointees of Democratic presidents Kennedy, Johnson, Carter, and Clinton, which were respectively 42, 53, 51, and 45 percent. The data also tell us that the Obama contingent is distinctly more liberal than the appointees of the five most recent GOP administrations of Nixon, Ford, Reagan, George H. W. Bush, and George W. Bush, which were respectively 39, 43, 36, 37, and 36 percent.

Let us turn up our examining microscope a notch and compare the voting patterns of Obama's jurists with those of other modern presidents on the three composite variables of criminal justice, civil rights and liberties, and labor and economic regulation. The first column in Table 1 provides data on judges' voting on criminal justice issues, such as habeas corpus, motions made before and during a criminal trial, and forfeiture of property in a criminal case. In this realm, the voting record of the Obama team, at 31 percent liberal, puts him about midway between the 25 percent score of the Kennedy cohort and the nearly 38 percent score of the Clinton appointees. The data also demonstrate that on this variable the Obama judges are somewhat more liberal than any of the appointees of the five most recent Republican presidents, who varied from a high of 33 percent (Ford) to a low of 25 percent (Reagan). The second column in Table 1 contains data on the dimension of civil rights and liberties; that is, it examines judges' decisions on issues such as abortion, freedom of speech, the right to privacy, discrimination against racial minorities, and so on. In this realm, almost 42 percent of the Obama cohort's decisions have been liberal in nature. As with criminal justice cases, this percentage is in line with the cohorts of the four most recent Democratic presidents: Kennedy (43), Johnson (58), Carter (50), and Clinton (41). Interestingly, the data indicate that Obama's judges are not nearly as liberal on these issues as were previous Democrats.

Table 1 Percentage of Liberal Decisions in Three Case Types by Judges Appointed by the 10 Most Recent Presidents

Appointing President	Criminal Justice Cases	Civil Rights and Liberties Cases	Labor and Economic Regulation Cases	All Cases
Kennedy	24.9	42.9	62.4	41.5
Johnson	36.9	57.5	63.4	52.5
Nixon	26.8	37.6	51.1	39.4
Ford	32.9	38.6	52.7	42.6
Carter	37.6	50.0	61.9	51.3
Reagan	25.2	32.6	49.7	36.2
Bush	26.6	33.3	50.0	36.8
Clinton	37.8	41.3	55.5	44.5
W. Bush	29.5	31.7	50.7	36.4
Obama	31.1	41.9	64.9	48.0

In our third column in Table 1, we present data on the judges' decisional patterns in the area of labor and economic regulation. (A typical case might be a dispute between a labor union and a company—a worker alleging a violation of the Fair Labor Standards Act or a petitioner challenging the right of a government regulator to circumscribe his activity.) On this composite variable, nearly 65 percent of the decisions of the Obama appointees have been on the liberal side—slightly more liberal than any recent president. The numbers for Kennedy, Johnson, Carter, and Clinton are 62, 63, 62, and 56 percent, respectively. As we would anticipate, these scores are much lower than the GOP presidents' numbers: Nixon (51), Ford (53), Reagan (50), Bush (50), and W. Bush (51).

This somewhat high liberalism score for the Obama cohort in labor and economic regulation is noteworthy. In 2008 the United States was plunged into the greatest economic crisis the nation had faced in more than 70 years. To address the crisis, Washington, D.C., engaged in a variety of government-led efforts—economic stimulus spending, liberalized central banking policies, tightened banking regulations, and federal financial bailouts. Could the results we identify in this study be a reflection to some extent of these economic times, a period during which governmental actors engaged in an active interventionist role in economic matters? Or could the data simply provide evidence of a concerted effort on the part of Obama's appointment team to select judges who are particularly inclined to support the interests of consumers, employees, and labor unions? At this point, we can only note the phenomenon, not provide a cogent explanation for it. In any case, these numbers may mute some suggestions by the political left that Obama is too cozy with wealthy business interests.[47] He may or may not be, but our data suggest that, at least at this point, his judges are not. We should keep in mind, however, that the Obama jurists are still in their early years. The judges selected by President Obama will leave an imprint on the judiciary that will last for decades. As time progresses and the economy recovers, the data could shift. Still, this is a finding of real interest.

Traditional Versus Nontraditional

In previous research, we have compared the decisional patterns of presidents' so-called "nontraditional" appointees (i.e., women and minorities) with those of his white, male judges. Such analyses seemed warranted for two reasons. First, conventional wisdom suggested that women and minorities might be somewhat more liberal in their voting patterns than their white male counterparts (although evidence for this tends to be inconclusive).[48] This is because members of historically underrepresented groups often have been subjected to racial and gender discrimination by law and also in the workplace in terms of equal pay for equal work and promotions. Second, we investigated this pattern because recent presidents have appointed nontraditional judges in record numbers, thus making the presence of these jurists worthy of heightened analysis.

This past research on the differences between traditional and nontraditional judges appointed by Clinton and George W. Bush did not find statistically significant distinctions. There were scant differences between Bush's traditional and nontraditional cohorts: 32 percent of his traditional judges handed down liberal decisions, while 33 percent of his nontraditional jurists did so.[49] Among Clinton jurists, the data indicated a liberalism rate of 46 percent by women and minority judges versus 42 percent for his white male appointees.[50] This difference was not, however, statistically significant.

As others have recognized, President Obama has clearly made gender and racial diversity a high priority in terms of selecting judicial candidates. Obama is on track to be the first president in U.S. history to have a majority of his judicial nominees be either women or persons of color. This marks a significant change, especially when one considers that only a generation ago Reagan appointed a judicial cohort that was 15% nontraditional.

So what do the data show about the ideology of Obama's traditional and nontraditional judges? The facts are, in some ways, quite remarkable. As shown in Table 2, during the period of observation, Obama's white male appointees rendered liberal decisions 47.9 percent of the time, while 48.0 percent of his female or minority judges did so. One would be hard-pressed to analyze 763 cases and identify a more precisely even balance! Not only is the difference not statistically significant at the 0.05 level, there is simply no difference to speak of. The jurists appointed by President Obama have exhibited no ideological distinctions with regard to gender and/or race in their decision making.

Table 2 Percentage of Liberal Decisions by Traditional and Nontraditional Judges Appointed by Obama

	Percentage Liberal Decisions (*n*)	Percentage Conservative Decisions (n)
Traditional	47.9 (151)	52.1 (164)
Nontraditional	48.0 (215)	52.0 (233)

Odds ratio (α) = .998; chi square = < .001 (p = .988)

Note: *"Nontraditional" judges are women and/or members of a racial or ethnic minority group; "traditional" jurists are white males.

Conclusions

This article has explored the ideological influence that President Obama is having on the decision-making patterns of the federal trial courts. Our estimation is that despite the delays and slowdowns in the appointment process itself, the president is still having a significant impact on the ideological orientation of the federal judiciary, particularly in the realm of labor and economic regulation. As one would expect, the Obama team is clearly more liberal than the judges selected by any of the five most recent Republican presidents. Obama's overall liberalism score of 48.0 percent indicates that his appointees appear to be mainstream Democrats—not as liberal as Johnson's cohort at 52.5 percent

but slightly more to the left than Clinton's cohort at 44.5 percent.

However, the data on the Obama judges do not support the contention that his jurists are ideological extremists. It is true that in the realm of labor and economic regulation we find data to indicate that the Obama judges are more liberal than those of other recent presidents, but the difference here is quite modest—only 1.5 percentage points more liberal than Johnson's judges. And even then we should hesitate before jumping to a definitive conclusion on this matter since the Obama jurists are still in their early years on the bench. Overall, the data suggest that Obama's judges are not shaping up to be for the left what the George W. Bush judges were for the right. The jurists appointed by Bush were among the most conservative since 1932. One cannot make a similar claim about the ideological disposition of Obama's judges on the left side of the political spectrum. The Obama appointees are liberal, but they are not setting a new ideological record. As such, the judges appointed by President Obama are well within the mainstream of American political ideology. As Obama serves out the remainder of his second term and fills more vacancies on the federal bench, there is every reason to believe that this trend will continue.

Notes

1. Quoted in Carl Hulse, "Post-Filibuster, Obama Faces New Anger Over Judicial Choices," *New York Times*, February 27, 2014, http://www.nytimes.com/2014/02/28/us/politics/post-filibuster-obama-faces-new-anger-over-judicial-choices.html.
2. Quoted in ibid.
3. Ibid.
4. Quoted in Jennifer Bendery, "House Democrat Unleashes on Obama Judicial Nominees, White House Pushes Back Hard," *Huffington Post*, February 26, 2014, http://www.huffingtonpost.com/2014/02/26/david-scott-obama-judicial-nominee_n_4861043.html.
5. Jonathan S. Tobin, "Can Obama Pack the Courts With Liberals?" *Commentary*, May 28, 2013, http://www.commentarymagazine.com/2013/05/28/can-obama-pack-the-courts-with-liberals/.

6. Quoted in Dave Boyer, "Unions Pressing for Judges Friendly to Labor," *Washington Times*, February 11, 2014, http://www.washingtontimes.com/news/2014/feb/11/alliance-sees-more-lack-of-diversity-on-bench/?utm_source=RSS_Feed&utm_medium=RSS.

7. Alex Roarty, "The Latest Conservative Attack Against Mark Pryor: Group Goes Up With Ad Attacking Vulnerable Democrat's Record On Judges," *National Journal*, November 8, 2013, http://www.nationaljournal.com/hotline-on-call/the-latest-conservative-attack-against-mark-pryor-20131108. The advertisement referenced in the article and quoted here is available at www.youtube.com/watch?v=M-GYxLKSYwM.

8. Ramesh Ponnuru, "Republicans Shouldn't Let Obama Pack the Courts," *Bloomberg View,* November 11, 2013, http://www.bloombergview.com/articles/2013-11-11/republicans-shouldn-t-let-obama-pack-the-courts.

9. This research study was initially presented at the 2014 annual meeting of the Southwestern Political Science Association meeting. It is a significant update, including new data, of a previous study: Robert A. Carp, Kenneth L. Manning, and Ronald Stidham, "A First Term Assessment: The Ideology of Barack Obama's District Court Appointees," *Judicature* 97 (2013): 128.

10. For a summary of this literature, see Robert A. Carp, Ronald Stidham, and Kenneth L. Manning, "Policy Links Between the Citizenry, the President, and the Federal Judiciary," in *Judicial Process in America*, 9th ed. (Washington, DC: CQ Press, 2014), 158–180.

11. Philip Rucker, "Obama Pushing to Diversify Federal Judiciary Amid GOP Delays," *Washington Post*, March 3, 2013, http://www.washingtonpost.com/politics/obama-pushing-to-diversify-federal-judiciaryamid-gop-delays/2013/03/03/16f7d206-7aab-11e2-9a75-dab0201670da_print.html.

12. Carolina A. Miranda, "Just What Is a 'Wise Latina,' Anyway?" *Time*, July 14, 2009, http://content.time.com/time/politics/article/0,8599,1910403,00.html.

13. "Senate Confirms Sotomayor to U.S. Supreme Court," *Fox News*, August 6, 2009, http://www.foxnews.com.

14. Dana Milbank, "In Kagan, Obama Picks a Nominee, Not a Fight," *Washington Post*, May 11, 2010, http://www.washingtonpost.com/wp-dyn/content/article/2010/05/10/AR2010051003402.html.

15. Ibid.

16. Philip Rucker, "Obama Pushing to Diversify Federal Judiciary Amid GOP Delays," *Washington Post*, March 3, 2013, http://www.washingtonpost.com/politics/obama-pushing-to-diversify-federal-judiciaryamid-gop-delays/2013/03/03/16f7d206-7aab-11e2-9a75-dab0201670da_print.html.

17. Jeffrey Toobin, "Obama's Unfinished Judicial Legacy," *New Yorker*, July 31, 2012, http://www.newyorker.com/online/blogs/comment/2012/07/why-judges-matter.html.

18. Jamelle Bouie, "A Bad Deal for Judicial Nominees," *American Prospect*, December 13, 2010, http://prospect.org/article/bad-deal-judicial-nominees.

19. Carl Hulse, Jeremy W. Peters, and Michael D. Shearaug, "Obama Is Seen as Frustrating His Own Party," *New York Times*, August 18, 2014, http://www.nytimes.com/2014/08/19/us/aloof-obama-is-frustrating-his-own-party.html.

20. Jon R. Bond, "The Politics of Court Structure: The Addition of New Federal Judges," *Law and Policy Quarterly* 2 (1980): 182, 183, 187.

21. Jerry Markon and Shailagh Murray, "Federal Judicial Vacancies Reaching Crisis Point," *Washington Post,* February 8, 2011, http://www.washingtonpost.com/wp-dyn/content/article/2011/02/07/AR2011020706034.html.

22. Ibid.

23. Jeremy W. Peters, "Easy Hearing for Obama's Choice for Court," *New York Times*, April 11, 2013, http://www.nytimes.com/2013/04/11/us/politics/sri-srinivasan-nominee-for-federal-court-has-easy-senate-hearing.html.

24. Markon and Murray, "Federal Judicial Vacancies."

25. Gary Martin, "Vacancies, Backlogs Plague Federal Judiciary," *Houston Chronicle*, March 3, 2013, A33.

26. Charlie Savage, "Obama Lags on Judicial Picks, Limiting His Mark on Courts," *New York Times*, August 17, 2012, http://www.nytimes.com/2012/08/18/us/politics/obama-lags-on-filling-seats-in-the-judiciary.html.

27. These figures do not include the 560 judges on senior status as of September 1, 2014.

28. Sam Hananel, "Judicial Nomination Held Up Over Same-Sex Ceremony," *Detroit Free Press*, October 6, 2006, http://www.freep.com.

29. Neil A. Lewis, "Clinton Critic Is Key to Deal to End Tie-Up on Judgeships," *New York Times*, July 3, 1999, http://www.nytimes.com/1999/07/03/us/clinton-critic-is-key-to-deal-to-end-tie-up-on-judgeships.html.

30. See "Gallup Daily: Obama Job Approval," http://www.gallup.com/poll/113980/gallup-daily-obama-job-approval.aspx.

31. Matt Viser, "Senators Can Still Block Nominations Without Filibuster," *Boston Globe*, November 29, 2013, http://www.bostonglobe.com/news/politics/2013/11/29/with-filibuster-gone-senate-attention-will-shift-alternative-means-thwart-obama-court-nominees/7Xo7mLycJLokNlnOuraHQN/story.html.

32. Sheldon Goldman, Elliot Slotnick, and Sara Schiavoni, "Obama's Judiciary at Midterm: The Confirmation Drama Continues," *Judicature* 94 (2011): 280.

33. Ibid.

34. Sarah Binder and Forrest Maltzman, "New Wars of Advice and Consent," *Judicature* 97 (2013): 48.

35. Matt Viser, "As Obama, Senate Collide, Courts Caught Short," *Boston Globe*, March 10, 2013, http://www.bostonglobe.com/news/nation/2013/03/10/obama-senate-collide-gridlock-hits-federal-courts/zQVtUmOSol9sHre7OuX3MP/story.html.

36. Ibid.

37. Jeremy W. Peters, "In Landmark Vote, Senate Limits Use of the Filibuster," *New York Times*, November 21, 2013, http://www.nytimes.com/2013/11/22/us/politics/reid-sets-in-motion-steps-to-limit-use-of-filibuster.html.

38. Quoted in Burgess Everett, "Elizabeth Warren Calls for Filibuster Changes," *Politico*, November 13, 2013, http://www.politico.com/story/2013/11/elizabeth-warren-filibuster-99799.html

39. Viser, "Senators Can Still Block Nominations."

40. Jeffrey Toobin, "Blue-Slip Battle: The Senate Obstructionists' Secret Weapon," *New Yorker*, November 26, 2013, http://www.newyorker.com/online/blogs/comment/2013/11/blue-slip-battle-senate-obstructionists-secret-weapon.html.

41. Hananel, "Judicial Nomination Held Up."

42. Quoted in Amanda Terkel, "Mitch McConnell: Senate GOP Has Treated Obama's Judicial Nominees 'Very Fairly,'" *Huffington Post*, April 17, 2013, http://www.huffingtonpost.com/2013/04/09/ obamas-judicial-nominees_n_3046778.html.

43. Denied a place on the federal bench, Liu was subsequently named by Governor Jerry Brown to fill a position on the California State Supreme Court.

44. Robert A. Carp, Kenneth L. Manning, and Ronald Stidham, "Right On: The Decision-Making Behavior of George W. Bush's Judicial Appointees," *Judicature* 92 (2009): 312.

45. Of the active appellate court judges on that date, 94 had been selected by Democrats and 78 were chosen by Republicans; at the district court level, 336 were tapped by Democrats and 289 had been appointed by the GOP.

46. These rulings were handed down in three key issue areas: civil liberties and rights, criminal justice, and labor and economic regulation. Though we coded only district court rulings, prior research suggests that the behavior of jurists at this level is comparable to that of judges appointed by the same president to the courts of appeals. See Ronald Stidham, Robert A. Carp, and Donald R. Songer, "The Voting Behavior of President Clinton's Judicial Appointees," *Judicature* 80 (1996): 16–20; and Robert A. Carp, Donald Songer, C. K. Rowland, and Lisa Richey-Tracy, "The Voting Behavior of Judges Appointed by President Bush," *Judicature* 76 (1993): 298–302.

47. Peter Baker, "On the Left, Seeing Obama Giving Away Too Much, Again," *New York Times*, January 1, 2013, http://www.nytimes.com/2013/01/02/us/politics/some-liberals-say-obama-squandered-his-tax-leverage.html.

48. See Robert A. Carp, Kenneth L. Manning, and Ronald Stidham, "President Clinton's District Judges: 'Extreme Liberals' or Just Plain Moderates?" *Judicature* 84 (2001): 284.

49. Carp et al., "Right On."

50. Ibid.

Chapter 10

Public Opinion

10-1 Analyzing and Interpreting Polls

Herbert Asher

Public opinion polls have gained a prominent place in modern American politics. Polls themselves often are newsworthy, particularly during campaigns and times of political crisis. Unfortunately, as Herbert Asher shows in the following essay, polls are open to misinterpretation and misuse. The wording of questions, the construction of a sample, the choice of items to analyze and report, the use of surveys to measure trends, and the examination of subsets of respondents all pose problems of interpretation. Every consumer of polling information must understand these issues to properly use the information polls provide.

Interpreting a poll is more an art than a science, even though statistical analysis of poll data is central to the enterprise. An investigator examining poll results has tremendous leeway in deciding which items to analyze, which sample subsets or breakdowns to present, and how to interpret the statistical results. Take as an example a poll with three items that measure attitudes toward arms control negotiations. The investigator may construct an index from these three items. . . . Or the investigator may emphasize the results from one question, perhaps because of space and time constraints and the desire to keep matters simple, or because those particular results best support the analyst's own policy preferences. The investigator may examine results from the entire sample and ignore subgroups whose responses deviate from the overall pattern. Again time and space limitations or the investigator's own preferences may influence these choices. Finally, two investigators may interpret identical poll results in sharply different ways depending on the perspectives and values they bring to their data analysis; the glass may indeed be half full or half empty.

As the preceding example suggests, the analysis and interpretation of data entail a high degree of subjectivity and judgment. Subjectivity in this context does not mean deliberate bias or distortion, but simply professional judgments about the importance and relevance of information. Certainly, news organizations' interpretations of their polls are generally done in the least subjective and unbiased fashion. But biases can slip in—sometimes unintentionally, sometimes deliberately—when, for example, an organization has sponsored a poll to promote a particular position. Because this final phase of polling is likely to have the most direct influence on public opinion, this chapter includes several case studies to illustrate the judgmental aspects of analyzing and interpreting poll results.

Source: Herbert Asher, *Polling and the Public: What Every Citizen Should Know,* 4th ed. (Washington, D.C.: CQ Press, 1998), 141–169.

Choosing Items to Analyze

Many public opinion surveys deal with multifaceted, complex issues. For example, a researcher querying Americans about their attitudes toward tax reform might find initially that they overwhelmingly favor a fairer tax system. But if respondents are asked about specific aspects of tax reform, their answers may reflect high levels of confusion, indifference, or opposition. And depending upon which items the researcher chooses to emphasize, the report might convey support, indifference, or opposition toward tax reform. American foreign policy in the Middle East is another highly complex subject that can elicit divergent reactions from Americans depending on which aspects of the policy they are questioned about.

Some surveys go into great depth on a topic through multiple items constructed to measure its various facets. The problem for an investigator in this case becomes one of deciding which results to report. Moreover, even though an extensive analysis is conducted, the media might publicize only an abbreviated version of it. In such a case the consumer of the poll results is at the mercy of the media to portray accurately the overall study. Groups or organizations that sponsor polls to demonstrate support for a particular position or policy option often disseminate results in a selective fashion which enables them to put the organization and its policies in a favorable light.

In contrast with in-depth surveys on a topic, *omnibus surveys* are superficial in their treatment of particular topics because of the need to cover many subjects in the same survey. Here the problem for an investigator becomes one of ensuring that the few questions employed to study a specific topic really do justice to the substance and complexity of that topic. It is left to the consumer of both kinds of polls to judge whether they receive the central information on a topic or whether other items might legitimately yield different substantive results.

The issue of prayer in public schools is a good example of how public opinion polling on a topic can be incomplete and potentially misleading. Typically, pollsters ask Americans whether they support a constitutional amendment that would permit voluntary prayer in public schools, and more than three-fourths of Americans respond that they would favor such an amendment. This question misses the mark. Voluntary prayer by individuals is in no way prohibited; the real issue is whether there will be *organized* voluntary prayer. But many pollsters do not include items that tap this aspect of the voluntary prayer issue. Will there be a common prayer? If so, who will compose it? Will someone lead the class in prayer? If so, who? Under what circumstances and when will the prayer be uttered? What about students who do not wish to participate or who prefer a different prayer?

The difficulty with both the in-depth poll and the omnibus survey is that the full set of items used to study a particular topic is usually not reported and thus the consumer cannot make informed judgments about whether the conclusions of the survey are valid. Recognizing this, individuals should take a skeptical view of claims by a corporate executive or an elected officeholder or even a friend that the polls demonstrate public support for or opposition to a particular position. The first question to ask is: What is the evidence cited to support the claim? From there one might examine the question wording, the response alternatives, the screening for nonattitudes, and the treatment of "don't know" responses. Then one might attempt the more difficult task of assessing whether the questions used to study the topic at hand were really optimal. Might other questions have been used? What aspects of the topic were not addressed? Finally, one might ponder whether different interpretations could be imposed on the data and whether alternative explanations could account for the reported patterns.

In evaluating poll results, there is always the temptation to seize upon those that support one's position and ignore those that do not. The problem is that one or two items cannot capture the full complexity of most issues. For example, a *Newsweek* poll conducted by the Gallup Organization in July 1986 asked a number of questions about sex laws and lifestyles. The poll included the following three items (Alpern 1986, 38):

Do you approve or disapprove of the Supreme Court decision upholding a state law against certain sexual practices engaged in privately by consenting adult homosexuals? [This question was asked of the 73 percent who knew about the Supreme Court decision.]

Disapprove	47%
Approve	41%

In general, do you think that states should have the right to prohibit particular sexual practices conducted in private between consenting adult homosexuals?

No	57%
Yes	34%

Do you think homosexuality has become an accepted alternative lifestyle or not?

Yes	32%
No	61%
Don't know	7%

Note that the first two items tap citizens' attitudes toward the legal treatment of homosexuals, while the third addresses citizens' views of homosexuality as a lifestyle. Although differently focused, all three questions deal with aspects of gay life. It would not be surprising to see gay rights advocates cite the results of the first two questions as indicating support for their position. Opponents of gay rights would emphasize the results of the third question.

An Eyewitness News/*Daily News* poll of New York City residents conducted in February 1986 further illustrates how the selective use and analysis of survey questions can generate very different impressions of popular opinion on an issue. This poll asked a number of gay rights questions:

On another matter, would you say that New York City needs a gay rights law or not?

Yes, need gay rights law	39%
No, do not need gay rights law	54%
Don't know/no opinion	8%

On another matter, do you think it should be against the law for landlords or private employers to deny housing or a job to someone because that person is homosexual or do you think landlords and employers should be allowed to do that if they want to?

Yes, should be against law	49%
No, should not be against law	47%

Volunteered responses

Should be law only for landlord	1%
Should be law only for employers	8%
Don't know/no opinion	3%

Although a definite majority of the respondents oppose a gay rights law in response to the first question, a plurality also believe that it should be illegal for landlords and employers to deny housing and jobs to persons because they are homosexual. Here the two questions both address the legal status of homosexuals, and it is clear which question gay rights activists and gay rights opponents would cite in support of their respective policy positions. It is not clear, however, which question is the better measure of public opinion. The first question is unsatisfactory because one does not know how respondents interpreted the scope of a gay rights law. Did they think it referred only to housing and job discrimination, or did they think it would go substantially beyond that? The second question is inadequate if it is viewed as equivalent to a gay rights law. Lumping housing and jobs together constitutes another flaw since citizens might have divergent views on these two aspects of gay rights.

Additional examples of the importance of item selection are based on polls of Americans' attitudes about the Iraqi invasion of Kuwait in 1990. Early in the Persian Gulf crisis, various survey organizations asked Americans, using different questions, how they felt about taking military action against Iraq. Not surprisingly, the organizations obtained different results.

Do you favor or oppose direct U.S. military action against Iraq at this time? (Gallup, August 3–4, 1990)

Favor	23%
Oppose	68%
Don't know/refused	9%

Do you agree or disagree that the U.S. should take all actions necessary, including the use of military force, to make sure that Iraq withdraws its forces from Kuwait? (ABC News/ *Washington Post,* August 8, 1990)

Agree	66%
Disagree	33%
Don't know	1%

Would you approve or disapprove of using U.S. troops to force the Iraqis to leave Kuwait? (Gallup, August 9–12, 1990, taken from *Public Perspective,* September/October 1990, 13)

Approve	64%
Disapprove	36%

(I'm going to mention some things that may or may not happen in the Middle East and for each one, please tell me whether the U.S. should or should not take military action in connection with it). . . . If Iraq refuses to withdraw from Kuwait? (NBC News/*Wall Street Journal,* August 18–19, 1990, taken from *Public Perspective,* September/October 1990, 13)

No military action	51%
Military action	49%

Note that the responses to these questions indicate varying levels of support for military action even though most of the questions were asked within two weeks of each other. The first question shows the most opposition to military action. This is easily explained: the question concerns military action *at this time,* an alternative that many Americans may have seen as premature until other means had been tried. The other three questions all indicate majority support for military action, although that support ranges from a bare majority to about two-thirds of all Americans. It is clear which question proponents and opponents of military action would cite to support their arguments.

Throughout the Persian Gulf crisis, public opinion was highly supportive of President Bush's policies; only in the period between October and December 1990 did support for the president's handling of the situation drop below 60 percent. For example, a November 1990 CBS News/*New York Times* poll showed the following patterns of response:

Do you approve or disapprove of the way George Bush is handling Iraq's invasion of Kuwait?

Approve	50%
Disapprove	41%
Don't know/NA	8%

Likewise, an ABC News/*Washington Post* poll in mid-November reported:

Do you approve or disapprove of the way George Bush is handling the situation caused by Iraq's invasion of Kuwait?

Approve	59%
Disapprove	36%
Don't know/NA	5%

Some opponents of the military buildup tried to use these and similar polls to demonstrate that support for the president's policies was decreasing, since earlier polls had indicated support levels in the 60–70 percent range. Fortunately, the *Washington Post* poll cited above asked respondents who disapproved of Bush's policy whether the president was moving too slowly or too quickly. It turned out that 44 percent of the disapprovers said "too slowly" and 37 percent "too quickly." Thus, a plurality of the disapprovers preferred more rapid action against Iraq—a result that provided little support for those critics of the president's policies who were arguing against a military solution.

Shortly before the outbreak of the war, the *Washington Post* conducted a survey of American attitudes about going to war with Iraq. To assess the effects of question wording, the *Post* split its sample in half and used two different versions of the same question followed by the identical follow-up question to each item.

Version 1

As you may know, the U.N. Security Council has authorized the use of force against Iraq if it doesn't withdraw from Kuwait by January 15. If Iraq does not withdraw from Kuwait, should the United States go to war against Iraq to force it out of Kuwait at some point after January 15 or not?

Go to war sometime after January 15	62%
No, do not go to war	32%

How long after January 15 should the United States wait for Iraq to withdraw from Kuwait before going to war to force it out?

Do not favor war at any point	32%
Immediately	18%
Less than one month	28%
1–3 months	8%
4 months or longer	2%

Version 2

The United Nations has passed a resolution authorizing the use of military force against Iraq if they do not withdraw their troops from Kuwait by January 15. If Iraq does not withdraw from Kuwait by then, do you think the United States should start military actions against Iraq, or should the United States wait longer to see if the trade embargo and economic sanctions work?

U.S. should start military actions	49%
U.S. should wait longer to see if sanctions work	47%

How long after January 15 should the United States wait for Iraq to withdraw from Kuwait before going to war to force it out?

U.S. should start military actions	49%

For those who would wait:

Less than a month	15%
1–3 months	17%
4 months or longer	9%

Morin (1991) points out how very different portraits of the American public can be painted by examining the two versions with and without the follow-up question. For example, version 1 shows 62 percent of Americans supporting war against Iraq, while version 2 shows only 49 percent. These different results stem from inclusion of the embargo and sanctions option in the second version. Thus it appears that version 2 gives a less militaristic depiction of the American public. Responses to the follow-up question, however, provide a different picture of the public. For example, the first version shows that 54 percent of Americans (18 + 28 + 8) favor going to war within three months. But the second version shows that 81 percent of Americans (49 + 15 + 17) favor war within three months. The point, of course, is that the availability of different items on a survey can generate differing descriptions of the public's preferences.

The importance of item selection is illustrated in a final example on the Gulf War from an April 3, 1991, ABC News/*Washington Post* poll conducted just after the conflict. It included the following three questions:

Do you approve or disapprove of the way that George Bush is handling the situation involving Iraqi rebels who are trying to overthrow Saddam Hussein?

Approve	69%
Disapprove	24%
Don't know	7%

Please tell me if you agree or disagree with this statement: The United States should not have ended the war with Iraqi President Saddam Hussein still in power.

Agree	55%
Disagree	40%
Don't know	5%

Do you think the United States should try to help rebels overthrow Hussein or not?

Yes	45%
No	51%
Don't know	4%

Note that the responses to the first item indicate overwhelming approval for the president. But if one analyzed the second question in isolation, one might conclude that a majority of Americans did not support the president and indeed wanted to restart the war against Saddam Hussein. But the third item shows that a majority of Americans oppose helping the rebels. The lesson of this and the previous examples is clear.

Constructing an interpretation around any single survey item can generate a very inaccurate description of public opinion. Unfortunately, advocates of particular positions have many opportunities to use survey results selectively and misleadingly to advance their cause.

The health care debate in 1993 and 1994 also provides examples of how the selection of items for analysis can influence one's view of American public opinion. *Washington Post* polls asked Americans whether they thought the Clinton health plan was better or worse than the present system (Morin 1994). In one version of the question, the sample was given the response options "better" or "worse," while in the other version respondents could choose among "better," "worse," or "don't know enough about the plan to say." The following responses were obtained:

Version 1		Version 2	
better	52%	better	21%
worse	34%	worse	27%
don't know (volunteered)	14%	don't know enough	52%

Clearly, very different portrayals of American public opinion are presented by the two versions of the question. The first version suggests that a majority of Americans believed that the Clinton plan was better than the status quo, while the second version suggests that a plurality of citizens with opinions on the issue felt that the Clinton plan was worse. It is obvious which version of the question supporters and opponents of the Clinton health plan would be more likely to cite.

Another example from the health care reform area deals with Americans' feelings about the seriousness of the health care problem. Certainly, the more seriously the problem was viewed, the greater the impetus for changing the health care system. Different polling organizations asked a variety of questions designed to tap the importance of the health care issue (questions taken from the September/October 1994 issue of *Public Perspective*, 23, 26):

Louis Harris and Associates (April 1994): Which of the following statements comes closest to expressing your overall view of the health care system in this country? . . . There are some good things in our health care system, but fundamental changes are needed to make it better. . . . Our health care system has so much wrong with it that we need to completely rebuild it. . . . On the whole, the health care system works pretty well and only minor changes are necessary to make it work.

Fundamental changes needed	54%
Completely rebuild it	31%
Only minor changes needed	14%

NBC/*Wall Street Journal* (March 1994): Which of the following comes closest to your belief about the American health care system—the system is in crisis; the system has major problems, but is not in crisis; the system has problems, but they are not major; or the system has no problems?

Crisis	22%
Major problems	50%
Minor problems	26%

Gallup (June 1994): Which of these statements do you agree with more: The country has health care problems, but no health care crisis, or, the country has a health care crisis?

Crisis	55%
Problems but no crisis	41%
Don't know	4%

Gallup (June 1994): Which of these statements do you agree with more: The country has a health care crisis, or the country has health care problems, but no health care crisis?

Crisis	35%
Problems but no crisis	61%
Don't know	4%

Certainly if one were trying to make the case that health care reform was an absolute priority, one would cite the first version of the Gallup question in which 55 percent of the respondents labeled health care a crisis. But if one wanted to move more slowly and incrementally on the health care issue, one would likely cite the NBC News/*Wall Street Journal* poll in which only 22 percent of Americans said there was a crisis. Health care reform is the kind of controversial public policy issue that invites political leaders to seize upon those poll results to advance their positions. In such situations, citizens should be sensitive to how politicians are selectively using the polls.

Schneider (1996) has provided an excellent example of how examination of a single trial heat question may give a misleading impression of the electoral strength of presidential candidates. A better sense of the candidates' true electoral strength is achieved by adding to the analysis information about the incumbent's job approval rating. For example, in a trial heat question in May 1980 incumbent president Jimmy Carter led challenger Ronald Reagan by 40 to 32 percent, yet at the time Carter's job rating was quite negative: 38 percent approval and 51 percent disapproval. Thus Carter's lead in the trial heat item was much more fragile than it appeared; indeed, Reagan went on to win the election. Four years later, in May of 1984, President Reagan led challenger Walter Mondale by 10 percentage points in the trial heat question. But Reagan's job rating was very positive: 54 percent approval compared with 38 percent disapproval. Thus Reagan's 10-point lead looked quite solid in view of his strong job ratings, and he won overwhelmingly in November. Finally, in April 1992, incumbent president George Bush led challenger Bill Clinton by 50 to 34 percent in the trial heat question, a huge margin. But Bush's overall job rating was negative—42 percent approval versus

48 percent disapproval. Bush's lead over Clinton, then, was not as strong as it appeared, and Clinton ultimately won the election.

By collecting information on multiple aspects of a topic, pollsters are better able to understand citizens' attitudes (Morin and Berry 1996). One of the anomalies of 1996 was the substantial number of Americans who were worried about the health of the economy at a time when by most objective indicators the economy was performing very well. Part of the answer to this puzzle was Americans' ignorance and misinformation about the country's economic health. For example, even though unemployment was substantially lower in 1996 than in 1991, 33 percent of Americans said it was higher in 1996 and 28 percent said the same. The average estimate of the unemployment rate was 20.6 percent when in reality it was just over 5 percent. Americans' perceptions of inflation and the deficit were similar; in both cases Americans thought that the reality was much worse than it actually was. It is no wonder that many Americans expressed economic insecurity during good economic times; they were not aware of how strongly the economy was performing.

The final example in this section focuses on how the media selects what we learn about a poll even when the complete poll and analyses are available to the citizenry. The example concerns a book entitled *Sex in America: A Definitive Survey* by Robert T. Michael et al., published in 1994, along with a more specialized and comprehensive volume, *The Social Organization of Sexuality: Sexual Practices in the United States* by Edward O. Laumann et al. Both books are based on an extensive questionnaire administered by the National Opinion Research Center to 3,432 scientifically selected respondents. . . .

Because of the importance of the subject matter and because sex sells, media coverage of the survey was widespread. How various media reported the story indicates how much leeway the media have and how influential they are in determining what citizens learn about a given topic. For example, the *New York Times* ran a front-page story on October 7, 1994, entitled "Sex in America: Faithfulness in

Marriage Thrives After All." Less prominent stories appeared in subsequent issues, including one on October 18, 1994, inaccurately entitled "Gay Survey Raises a New Question."

Two of the three major news magazines featured the sex survey on the covers of their October 17, 1994, issues. The *Time* cover simply read "Sex in America: Surprising News from the Most Important Survey since the Kinsey Report." The *U.S. News & World Report* cover was more risqué, showing a partially clad man and woman in bed; it read "Sex in America: A Massive New Survey, the Most Authoritative Ever, Reveals What We Do Behind the Bedroom Door." In contrast, *Newsweek* simply ran a two-page story with the lead "Not Frenzied, But Fulfilled. Sex: Relax. If you do it—with your mate—around twice a week, according to a major new study, you basically wrote the book of love."

Other magazines and newspapers also reported on the survey in ways geared to their readership. The November issue of *Glamour* featured the survey on its cover with the teaser "Who's doing it? And how? MAJOR U.S. SEX SURVEY." The story that followed was written by the authors of the book. While the cover of the November 15, 1994, *Advocate* read "What That Sex Survey Really Means," the story focused largely on what the survey had to say about the number of gays and lesbians in the population. The lead stated "10%: Reality or Myth? There's little authoritative information about gays and lesbians in the landmark study *Sex in America*—but what there is will cause big trouble." Finally, the *Chronicle of Higher Education*, a weekly newspaper geared to college and university personnel, in its October 17, 1994, issue headlined its story "The Sex Lives of Americans. Survey that had been target of conservative attacks produces few startling results."

Both books about the survey contain a vast amount of information and a large number of results and findings. But most of the media reported on such topics as marital fidelity, how often Americans have sex, how many sex partners people have, how often people experience orgasm, what percentages of the population are gay and lesbian, how long sex takes, and the time elapsed between a couple's first meeting and their first sexual involvement. Many of the reports also presented results for married vs. singles, men vs. women, and other analytical groupings. While most of the media coverage cited above was accurate in reporting the actual survey results, it also was selective in focusing on the more titillating parts of the survey, an unsurprising outcome given the need to satisfy their readerships.

Examining Trends with Polling Data

Researchers often use polling data to describe and analyze trends. To isolate trend data, a researcher must ensure that items relating to the topic under investigation are included in multiple surveys conducted at different points in time. Ideally, the items should be identically worded. But even when they are, serious problems of comparability can make trend analysis difficult. Identically worded items may not mean the same thing or provide the same stimulus to respondents over time because social and political changes in society have altered the meaning of the questions. For example, consider this question:

Some say that the civil rights people have been trying to push [have been pushed] too fast. Others feel they haven't pushed fast enough. How about you? Do you think that civil rights leaders are trying to push too fast, are going too slowly, or are they moving at about the right speed?

The responses to this item can be greatly influenced by the goals and agenda of the civil rights leadership at the time of the survey. A finding that more Americans think that the civil rights leaders are moving too fast or too slowly may reflect not a change in attitude from past views about civil rights activism but a change in the civil rights agenda itself. In this case, follow-up questions designed to measure specific components of the civil rights agenda are needed to help define the trend.

There are other difficulties in achieving comparability over time. For example, even if the wording of

an item were to remain the same, its placement within the questionnaire could change, which in turn could alter the meaning of a question. Likewise, the definition of the sampling frame and the procedures used to achieve completed interviews could change. In short, comparability entails much more than simply wording questions identically. Unfortunately, consumers of poll results seldom receive the information that enables them to judge whether items are truly comparable over time.

Two studies demonstrate the advantages and disadvantages of using identical items over time. Abramson, Silver, and Anderson (1990) complained that the biennial National Election Studies (NES) conducted by the Survey Research Center at the University of Michigan, Ann Arbor, were losing their longitudinal comparability as new questions were added to the surveys and old ones removed. Baumgartner and Walker (1988), in contrast, complained that the use of the same standard question over time to assess the level of group membership in the United States had systematically underestimated the extent of such activity. They argued that new measures of group membership should be employed, which, of course, would make comparisons between past and present surveys more problematic. Although both the old and the new measures can be included in a survey, this becomes very costly if the survey must cover many other topics.

Two other studies show how variations in question wording can make the assessment of attitude change over time difficult. Borrelli and colleagues (1987) found that polls measuring Americans' political party loyalties in 1980 and in 1984 varied widely in their results. They attributed the different results in these polls to three factors: whether the poll sampled voters only; whether the poll emphasized "today" or the present in inquiring about citizens' partisanship; and whether the poll was conducted close to election day, which would tend to give the advantage to the party ahead in the presidential contest. The implications of this research for assessing change in party identification over time are evident—that is, to conclude that genuine partisan change occurred in either of the two polls, other possible sources of observed differences, such as modifications in the wording of questions, must be ruled out. In a study of support for aid to the Nicaraguan contras between 1983 and 1986, Lockerbie and Borrelli (1990) argue that much of the observed change in American public opinion was not genuine. Instead, it was attributable to changes in the wording of the questions used to measure support for the contras. Again, the point is that one must be able to eliminate other potential explanations for observed change before one can conclude that observed change is genuine change.

Smith's (1993) critique of three major national studies of anti-Semitism conducted in 1964, 1981, and 1992 is an informative case study of how longitudinal comparisons may be undermined by methodological differences across surveys. The 1981 and 1992 studies were ostensibly designed to build upon the 1964 effort, thereby facilitating an analysis of trends in anti-Semitism. But, as Smith notes, longitudinal comparisons among the three studies were problematic because of differences in sample definition and interview mode, changes in question order and question wording, and insufficient information to evaluate the quality of the sample and the design execution. In examining an eleven-item anti-Semitism scale, he did find six items highly comparable over time that indicated a decline in anti-Semitic attitudes.

Despite the problems of sorting out true opinion change from change attributable to methodological factors, there are times when public opinion changes markedly and suddenly in response to a dramatic occurrence and the observed change is indeed genuine. Two examples from CBS News/*New York Times* polls in 1991 about the Persian Gulf war illustrate dramatic and extensive attitude change. The first example concerns military action against Iraq. Just before the January 15 deadline imposed by the UN for the withdrawal of Iraq from Kuwait, a poll found that 47 percent of Americans favored beginning military action against Iraq if it did not withdraw; 46 percent were opposed. Two days after the deadline and after the beginning of the allied air campaign against Iraq, a poll found 79 percent of Americans saying the United States had done the right thing in beginning military action against Iraq. The second example focuses on people's attitudes toward a ground war in the Middle East. Before the allied ground offensive began, only 11 percent of Americans said the United States should begin fighting the ground war soon; 79 percent said bombing from the air should continue. But after the ground war began, the numbers shifted dramatically: 75 percent of Americans said the United States was right to begin the ground war, and only 19 percent said the nation should have waited longer. Clearly, the Persian Gulf crisis was a case in which American public opinion moved dramatically in the direction of supporting the president at each new stage.

Examining Subsets of Respondents

Although it is natural to want to know the results from an entire sample, often the most interesting information in a poll comes from examining the response patterns of subsets of respondents defined according to certain theoretically or substantively relevant characteristics. For example, a January 1986 CBS News/*New York Times* poll showed President Reagan enjoying unprecedented popularity for a six-year incumbent: 65 percent approved of the president's performance, and only 24 percent disapproved. But these overall figures mask some analytically interesting variations. For example, among blacks only 37 percent approved of the president's performance; 49 percent disapproved. The sexes also differed in their views of the president, with men expressing a 72 percent approval rate compared with 58 percent for women. (As expected among categories of party loyalists, 89 percent of the Republicans, 66 percent of the independents, and only 47 percent of the Democrats approved of the president's performance.) Why did blacks and whites—and men and women—differ in their views of the president?

There is no necessary reason for public opinion on an issue to be uniform across subgroups. Indeed, on many issues there are reasons to expect just the opposite. That is why a fuller understanding of American public opinion is gained by taking a closer look at the views of relevant subgroups of the sample. In doing so, however, one should note that dividing the sample into subsets increases the sampling error and lowers the reliability of the sample estimates. For example, a sample of 1,600 Americans might be queried about their attitudes on abortion. After the overall pattern is observed, the researcher might wish to break down the sample by religion—yielding 1,150 Protestant, 400 Catholic, and 50 Jewish respondents—to determine whether religious affiliation is associated with specific attitudes toward abortion. The analyst might observe that Catholics on the whole are the most opposed to abortion. To find out which Catholics are most likely to oppose abortion, she might further divide the 400 Catholics into young and old Catholics or regular church attenders and nonregular attenders, or into four categories of young Catholic churchgoers, old Catholic churchgoers, young Catholic nonattenders, and old Catholic nonattenders. The more breakdowns done at the same time, the quicker the sample size in any particular category plummets, perhaps leaving insufficient cases in some categories to make solid conclusions.

Innumerable examples can be cited to demonstrate the advantages of delving more deeply into poll data on subsets of respondents. An ABC News/*Washington Post* poll conducted in February 1986 showed major differences in the attitudes of men and women toward pornography; an examination of only the total sample would have missed these important divergences. For example, in response to the question "Do you think laws against pornography in this country are too strict, not strict enough, or just about right?" 10 percent of the men said the laws were too strict, 41 percent said not strict enough, and 47 percent said about right. Among women, only 2 percent said the laws were too strict, a sizable 72 percent said they were not strict enough, and 23 percent thought they were about right (Sussman 1986b, 37).

A CBS News/*New York Times* poll of Americans conducted in April 1986 found widespread approval of the American bombing of Libya; 77 percent of the sample approved of the action, and only 14 percent disapproved. Despite the overall approval, differences among various subgroups are noteworthy. For example, 83 percent of the men approved of the bombing compared with 71 percent of the women. Of the white respondents, 80 percent approved in contrast to only 53 percent of the blacks (Clymer 1986). Even though all of these demographically defined groups gave at least majority support to the bombing, the differences in levels of support are both statistically and substantively significant.

Polls showed dramatic differences by race in the O. J. Simpson case, with blacks more convinced of Simpson's innocence and more likely to believe that he could not get a fair trial. For example, a field poll of Californians (*U.S. News & World Report*, August 1, 1994) showed that only 35 percent of blacks believed that Simpson could get a fair trial compared with 55 percent of whites. Also, 62 percent of whites thought Simpson was "very likely or somewhat likely" to be guilty of murder compared with only 38 percent for blacks. Comparable results were found in a national *Time*/CNN poll (*Time*, August 1, 1994): 66 percent of whites thought Simpson got a fair preliminary hearing compared with only 31 percent of black respondents, while 77 percent of the white respondents thought the case against Simpson was "very strong" or "fairly strong" compared with 45 percent for blacks. A *Newsweek* poll (August 1, 1994) revealed that 60 percent of blacks believed that Simpson was set up (20 percent attributing the setup to the police); only 23 percent of whites believed in a setup conspiracy. When asked whether Simpson had been treated better or worse than the average white murder suspect, whites said better by an overwhelming 52 to 5 percent margin, while blacks said worse by a 30 to 19 percent margin. These reactions to the Simpson case startled many Americans who could not understand how their compatriots of another race could see the situation so differently.

School busing to achieve racial integration has consistently been opposed by substantial majorities in national public opinion polls. A Harris poll commissioned by *Newsweek* in 1978 found that 85 percent of whites opposed busing (Williams 1979, 48). An ABC News/*Washington Post* poll conducted in February 1986 showed 60 percent of whites against busing (Sussman 1986a). The difference between the two polls might reflect genuine attitude change about busing in that eight-year period, or it might be a function of different question wording or different placement within the questionnaire. Whatever the reason, additional analysis of both these polls shows that whites are not monolithic in their opposition to busing. For example, the 1978 poll showed that 56 percent of white parents whose children had been bused viewed the experience as "very satisfactory." The 1986 poll revealed sharp differences in busing attitudes among younger and older whites. Among whites age thirty and under, 47 percent supported busing and 50 percent opposed it, while among whites over age thirty, 32 percent supported busing and 65 percent opposed it. Moreover, among younger whites whose families had experienced busing firsthand, 54 percent approved of busing and 46 percent opposed it. (Of course, staunch opponents of busing may have moved to escape busing, thereby guaranteeing that the remaining population would be relatively more supportive of busing.)

Another example of the usefulness of examining poll results within age categories is provided by an ABC News/*Washington Post* poll conducted in May 1985 on citizens' views of how the federal budget deficit might be cut. One item read, "Do you think the government should give people a smaller Social Security cost-of-living increase than they are now scheduled to get as a way of reducing the budget deficit, or not?" Among the overall sample, 19 percent favored granting a smaller cost-of-living increase and 78 percent opposed. To test the widespread view that young workers lack confidence in the Social Security system and doubt they will ever get out of the system what they paid in, Sussman (1985c) investigated how different age groups responded to the preceding question. Basically, he found that all age groups strongly

opposed a reduction in cost-of-living increases. Unlike the busing issue, this question showed no difference among age groups—an important substantive finding, particularly in light of the expectation that there would be divergent views among the old and young. Too often people mistakenly dismiss null (no difference) results as uninteresting and unexciting; a finding of no difference can be just as substantively significant as a finding of a major difference.

An example where age does make a difference in people's opinions is the topic of physician-assisted suicide. A *Washington Post* poll conducted in 1996 asked a national sample of Americans, "Should it be legal or illegal for a doctor to help a terminally ill patient commit suicide?" (Rosenbaum 1997). The attitudes of older citizens and younger citizens were markedly different on this question—the older the age group, the greater the opposition to doctor-assisted suicide. For example, 52 percent of respondents between ages eighteen and twenty-nine thought doctor-assisted suicide should be legal; 41 percent said it should be illegal. But for citizens over age seventy, the comparable figures were 35 and 58 percent. Even more striking were some of the racial and income differences on this question. Whites thought physician involvement in suicide should be legal by a 55 to 35 percent margin; blacks opposed it 70 to 20 percent. At the lowest income levels, doctor-assisted suicide was opposed by a 54 to 37 percent margin; at the highest income level it was supported by a 58 to 30 percent margin.

In many instances the categories used for creating subgroups are already established or self-evident. For example, if one is interested in gender or racial differences, the categories of male and female or white and black are straightforward candidates for investigation. Other breakdowns require more thought. For example, what divisions might one use to examine the effects of age? Should they be young, middle-aged, and old? If so, what actual ages correspond to these categories? Is middle age thirty-five to sixty-five, forty to sixty, or what? Or should more than three categories of age be defined? In samples selected to study the effects of religion, the typical breakdown is Protestant,

Catholic, and Jewish. But this simple threefold division might overlook some interesting variations; that is, some Protestants are evangelical, some are fundamentalist, and others are considered mainline denominations. Moreover, since most blacks are Protestants, comparisons of Catholics and Protestants that do not also control for race may be misleading.

Establishing categories is much more subjective and judgmental in other situations. For example, religious categories can be defined relatively easily by denominational affiliation, as mentioned earlier, but classifying respondents as evangelicals or fundamentalists is more complicated. Those who actually belong to denominations normally characterized as evangelical or fundamentalist could be so categorized. Or an investigator might identify some evangelical or fundamentalist beliefs, construct some polling questions around them, and then classify respondents according to their responses to the questions. Obviously, this would require some common core of agreement about the definition of an evangelical or fundamentalist. Wilcox (1984, 6) argues:

> Fundamentalists and evangelicals have a very similar set of religious beliefs, including the literal interpretation of the Bible, the need for a religious conversion known as being "born-again," and the need to convert sinners to the faith. The evangelicals, however, are less anti-intellectual and more involved in the secular world, while the fundamentalists criticize the evangelicals for failing to keep themselves "pure from the world."

Creating subsets by ideology is another common approach to analyzing public opinion. The most-often-used categories of ideology are liberal, moderate, and conservative, and the typical way of obtaining this information is to ask respondents a question in the following form: "Generally speaking, do you think of yourself as a liberal, moderate, or conservative?" However, one can raise many objections to this procedure, including whether people really assign common

meanings to these terms. Indeed, the levels of ideological sophistication and awareness have been an ongoing topic of research in political science.

Journalist Kevin Phillips (1981) has cited the work of political scientists Stuart A. Lilie and William S. Maddox, who argue that the traditional liberal-moderate-conservative breakdown is inadequate for analytical purposes. Instead, they propose a fourfold classification of liberal, conservative, populist, and libertarian, based on two underlying dimensions: whether one supports or opposes governmental intervention in the economy and whether one supports or opposes expansion of individual behavioral liberties and sexual equality. They define liberals as those who support both governmental intervention in the economy and expansion of personal liberties, conservatives as those who oppose both, libertarians as citizens who favor expanding personal liberties but oppose governmental intervention in the economy, and populists as persons who favor governmental economic intervention but oppose the expansion of personal liberties. According to one poll, populists made up 24 percent of the electorate, conservatives 18 percent, liberals 16 percent, and libertarians 13 percent, with the rest of the electorate not readily classifiable or unfamiliar with ideological terminology.

This more elaborate breakdown of ideology may help us to better understand public opinion, but the traditional categories still dominate political discourse. Thus, when one encounters citizens who oppose government programs that affect the marketplace but support pro-choice court decisions on abortion, proposed gay rights statutes, and the Equal Rights Amendment, one feels uncomfortable calling them liberals or conservatives since they appear to be conservative on economic issues and liberal on lifestyle issues. One might feel more confident in classifying them as libertarians.

Additional examples of how an examination of subsets of respondents can provide useful insights into the public's attitudes are provided by two CBS News/*New York Times* surveys conducted in 1991, one dealing with the Persian Gulf crisis and the other with attitudes toward police. Although the rapid and successful conclusion of the ground war against Iraq resulted in widespread approval of the enterprise, before the land assault began there were differences of opinion among Americans about a ground war. For example, in the February 12–13 CBS News/*New York Times* poll, Americans were asked: "Suppose several thousand American troops would lose their lives in a ground war against Iraq. Do you think a ground war against Iraq would be worth the cost or not?" By examining the percentage saying it would be worth the cost, one finds the following results for different groups of Americans:

All respondents	45%
Independents	46%
Men	56%
Republicans	54%
Women	35%
Eighteen to twenty-nine year-olds	50%
Whites	47%
Thirty to forty-four year-olds	44%
Blacks	30%
Forty-five to sixty-four year-olds	51%
Democrats	36%
Sixty-five years and older	26%

Note that the youngest age group, the one most likely to suffer the casualties, is among the most supportive of a ground war. Note also the sizable differences between men and women, whites and blacks, and Democrats and Republicans.

Substantial racial differences in opinion also were expressed in an April 1–3, 1991, CBS News/*New York Times* poll on attitudes toward local police. Overall, 55 percent of the sample said they had substantial confidence in the local police, and 44 percent said little confidence. But among whites the comparable percentages were 59 percent and 39 percent, while for blacks only 30 percent had substantial confidence and fully 70 percent expressed little confidence in the police. Even on issues in which the

direction of white and black opinion was the same, there were still substantial racial differences in the responses. For example, 69 percent of whites said that the police in their own community treat blacks and whites the same, and only 16 percent said the police were tougher on blacks than on whites. Although a plurality—45 percent—of blacks agreed that the police treat blacks and whites equally, fully 42 percent of black respondents felt that the police were tougher on blacks. Certainly if one were conducting a study to ascertain citizens' attitudes about police performance, it would be foolish not to examine the opinions of relevant subgroups.

Another example of the importance of examining subsets of respondents is provided by a January 1985 ABC News/*Washington Post* poll that queried Americans about their attitudes on a variety of issues and presented results not only for the entire sample but also for subsets of respondents defined by their attentiveness to public affairs (Sussman 1985b). Attentiveness to public affairs was measured by whether the respondents were aware of four news events: the subway shooting in New York City of four alleged assailants by their intended victim; the switch in jobs by two key Reagan administration officials, Donald Regan and James Baker; the Treasury Department's proposal to simplify the tax system; and protests against South African apartheid held in the United States. Respondents then were divided into four levels of awareness, with 27 percent in the highest category, 26 percent in the next highest, 25 percent in the next category, and 22 percent falling in the lowest. The next step in the analysis was to compare the policy preferences of the highest and lowest awareness subsets.

There were some marked differences between these two groups. For example, on the issue of support for the president's military buildup, 59 percent of the lowest awareness respondents opposed any major cuts in military spending to lessen the budget deficit. In contrast, 57 percent of the highest awareness group said that military spending should be limited to help with the budget deficit. On the issue of tax rates, a majority of both groups agreed with the president that taxes were too high, but there was a difference in the size of the majority. Among the lowest awareness respondents, 72 percent said taxes were too high and 24 percent said they were not, while among the highest awareness respondents, 52 percent said taxes were too high and 45 percent said they were not (Sussman 1985b).

Opinions about the future of Social Security and Medicare also are affected by citizens' knowledge about the two programs (Pianin and Brossard 1997). In one poll, the more people knew about Social Security and Medicare, the more likely they were to believe that these programs were in crisis and that major governmental action was needed. For example, among highly knowledgeable respondents, 88 percent believed that Social Security either was in crisis or had major problems; only 70 percent of respondents with little knowledge agreed. Likewise, 89 percent of the highly knowledgeable respondents believed Social Security would go bankrupt if Congress did nothing compared to only 61 percent for the less-informed respondents.

All these findings raise some interesting normative issues about public opinion polls. . . . [T]he methodology of public opinion polls is very democratic. All citizens have a nearly equal chance to be selected in a sample and have their views counted; all respondents are weighted equally (or nearly so) in the typical data analysis. Yet except at the polls all citizens do not have equal influence in shaping public policy. The distribution of political resources, whether financial or informational, is not uniform across the population. Polls themselves become a means to influence public policy, as various decision makers cite poll results to legitimize their policies. But should the views of all poll respondents be counted equally? An elitist critic would argue that the most informed segments of the population should be given the greatest weight. Therefore, in the preceding example of defense spending, more attention should be given to the views of the highest awareness subset (assuming the validity of the levels of awareness), which was more supportive of reducing military spending. An egalitarian argument would assert that all respondents should be counted equally. . . .

Interpreting Poll Results

An August 1986 Gallup poll on education showed that 67 percent of Americans would allow their children to attend class with a child suffering from AIDS, while 24 percent would not. What reaction might there be to this finding? Some people might be shocked and depressed to discover that almost one-fourth of Americans could be so mean-spirited toward AIDS victims when the scientific evidence shows that AIDS is not a disease transmitted by casual contact. Others might be reassured and relieved that two-thirds of Americans are sufficiently enlightened or tolerant to allow their children to attend school with children who have AIDS. Some people might feel dismay: How could 67 percent of Americans foolishly allow their children to go to school with a child who has AIDS when there is no absolute guarantee that AIDS cannot be transmitted casually?

Consider this example from a 1983 poll by the National Opinion Research Center (NORC): "If your party nominated a black [man] for President, would you vote for him if he were qualified for the job?" Eighty-five percent of the white respondents said yes. How might this response be interpreted? One might feel positive about how much racial attitudes have changed in the United States. A different perspective would decry the fact that in this supposedly tolerant and enlightened era, 15 percent of white survey respondents could not bring themselves to say they would vote for a qualified black candidate.

In neither example can we assign a single correct meaning to the data. Instead, the interpretation one chooses will be a function of individual values and beliefs, and purposes in analyzing the survey. This is demonstrated in an analysis of two national surveys on gun control, one sponsored by the National Rifle Association (NRA) and conducted by Decision/Making/Information, Inc., and the other sponsored by the Center for the Study and Prevention of Handgun Violence and conducted by Cambridge Reports, Inc. (pollster Patrick Caddell's firm). Although the statistical results from both surveys were comparable, the two reports arrived at substantially different conclusions. The NRA's analysis concluded:

Majorities of American voters believe that we do *not* need more laws governing the possession and use of firearms and that more firearms laws would *not* result in a decrease in the crime rate. (Wright 1981, 25)

In contrast, the center's report stated:

It is clear that the vast majority of the public (both those who live with handguns and those who do not) want handgun licensing and registration. . . . The American public wants some form of handgun control legislation. (Wright 1981, 25)

Wright carefully analyzed the evidence cited in support of each conclusion and found that

the major difference between the two reports is not in the findings, but in what is said about or concluded about the findings: what aspects of the evidence are emphasized or de-emphasized, what interpretation is given to a finding, and what implications are drawn from the findings about the need, or lack thereof, for stricter weapons controls. (Wright 1981, 38)

In essence, it was the interpretation of the data that generated the difference in the recommendations.

Two polls on tax reform provide another example of how poll data can be selectively interpreted and reported (Sussman 1985a). The first poll, sponsored by the insurance industry, was conducted by pollster Burns Roper. Its main conclusion, reported in a press conference announcing the poll results, was that 77 percent of the American public "said that workers should not be taxed on employee benefits" and that only 15 percent supported such a tax, a conclusion very reassuring to the insurance industry. However, Roper included other items in the poll that the insurance industry chose not to emphasize. As Sussman points out, the 77 percent opposed to the taxing of fringe benefits were then asked, "Would you still oppose counting the value of employee benefits as taxable income for employees if the additional tax revenues went directly to the reduction of federal budget deficits and not into new spending?" Twenty-six percent were no longer opposed to taxing fringe benefits under this condition, bringing the overall opposition down to 51 percent of the sample.

A second follow-up question asked, "Would you still oppose counting the value of employee benefits as taxable income for employees if the additional tax revenues permitted an overall reduction of tax rates for individuals?" (a feature that was part of the Treasury Department's initial tax proposals). Now only 33 percent of the sample was opposed to taxing fringes, 50 percent supported it, and 17 percent were undecided. Thus, depending upon which results one used, one could show a majority of citizens supportive of or opposed to taxing fringe benefits.

The other poll that Sussman analyzed also tapped people's reactions to the Treasury Department's tax proposal. A number of questions in the survey demonstrated public hostility to the Treasury proposal. One item read:

The Treasury Department has proposed changing the tax system. Three tax brackets would be created, but most current deductions from income would be eliminated. Non-federal income taxes and property taxes would not be deductible, and many deductions would be limited. Do you favor or oppose this proposal? (Sussman 1985a)

Not surprisingly, 57 percent opposed the Treasury plan, and only 27 percent supported it. But as Sussman points out, the question is highly selective and leading since it focuses on changes in the tax system that hurt the taxpayer. For example, nowhere does it inform the respondent that a key part of the Treasury plan was to reduce existing tax rates so that 80 percent of Americans would be paying either the same amount or less in taxes than they were paying before. Clearly, this survey was designed to obtain a set of results compatible with the sponsor's policy objectives.

Morin (1995) describes a situation in which polling data were misinterpreted and misreported in the *Washington Post* because of faulty communication between a *Post* reporter and a local polling firm that was conducting an omnibus survey in the Washington, D.C., area. Interested in how worried federal employees were about their jobs given the budgetary battles between the Clinton White House and the Republican Congress in 1995, the reporter commissioned the polling firm to include the following questions in its survey: "Do you think your agency or company will probably be affected by federal budget cutbacks? Do you think your own job will be affected?" The poll discovered that 40 percent of the federal workers interviewed believed their own jobs might be affected. Unfortunately, when the polling outfit prepared a report for its client, the reporter, the report concluded that these federal workers felt their jobs were jeopardized. And then the reporter's story stated, "Four out of every 10 federal employees fear losing their jobs because of budget reductions." As Morin points out, this conclusion does not follow from the polling questions asked. The belief that one's job will likely be affected is not equivalent to the fear of losing one's job. Instead, the effects might be lower salary increases, decreased job mobility, increased job responsibilities, and the like. A correction quickly appeared in the *Post* clarifying what the polling data actually had said. One lesson of this example is the responsibility that pollsters have to clients to communicate carefully and accurately what poll results mean. Another lesson is that one should not try to read too much into the responses to any single survey item. In this case, if the reporter wanted to know exactly how federal workers thought their jobs would be affected, a specific question eliciting this information should have been included in the survey.

Weighting the Sample

Samples are selected to be representative of the population from which they are drawn. Sometimes adjustments must be made to a sample before analyzing and reporting results. These adjustments may be made for substantive reasons or because of biases in the characteristics of the selected sample. An example of adjustments made for substantive reasons is pollsters' attempts to determine who the likely voters will be and to base their election predictions not on the entire sample but on a subset of likely voters.

To correct for biases, weights can be used so that the sample's demographic characteristics more accurately reflect the population's overall properties. Because sampling and interviewing involve statistics and probability theory as well as logistical problems of contacting respondents, the sample may contain too few blacks, or too few men, or too few people in the youngest age category. Assuming that one knows the true population proportions for sex, race, and age, one can adjust the sample by the use of weights to bring its numbers into line with the overall population values. For example, if females constitute 60 percent of the sample but 50 percent of the overall population, one might weight each female respondent by five-sixths, thereby reducing the percentage of females in the sample to 50 percent (five-sixths times 60 percent).

A 1986 *Columbus Dispatch* preelection poll on the gubernatorial preferences of Ohioans illustrates the consequences of weighting. In August 1986 the *Dispatch* sent a mail questionnaire to a sample of Ohioans selected from the statewide list of registered voters. The poll showed that incumbent Democratic governor Richard Celeste was leading former GOP governor James Rhodes, 48 percent to 43 percent, with Independent candidate and former Democratic mayor of Cleveland Dennis Kucinich receiving 9 percent; an undecided alternative was not provided to respondents (Curtin 1986a). Fortunately, the *Dispatch* report of its poll included the sample size for each category (unlike the practice of the national media). One table presented to the reader showed the following relationship between political party affiliation and gubernatorial vote preference (Curtin 1986b):

Gubernatorial preference	Democrat	Republican	Independent
Celeste	82%	14%	33%
Rhodes	9	81	50
Kucinich	9	5	17
Total %	100	100	100
(N)	(253)	(245)	(138)

Given the thrust of the news story that Celeste was ahead, 48 to 43 percent, the numbers in the table were surprising because Rhodes was running almost as well among Republicans as Celeste was among Democrats, and Rhodes had a substantial lead among Independents. Because the N's were provided, one could calculate the actual number of Celeste, Rhodes, and Kucinich votes in the sample as follows:

Celeste votes = .82(253) + .14(245) + .33(138) = 287

Rhodes votes = .09(253) + .81(245) + .50(138) = 291

Kucinich votes = .09(253) + .05(245) + .17(138) = 58

The percentages calculated from these totals show Rhodes slightly *ahead*, 46 to 45 percent, rather than trailing. At first I thought there was a mistake in the poll or in the party affiliation and gubernatorial vote preference. In rereading the news story, however, I learned that the sample had been weighted. The reporter wrote, "Results were adjusted, or weighted, slightly to compensate for demographic differences between poll respondents and the Ohio electorate as a whole" (Curtin 1986b). The reporter did inform the reader that the data were weighted, but nowhere did he say that the adjustment affected who was ahead in the poll.

The adjustment probably was statistically valid since the poll respondents did not seem to include sufficient numbers of women and blacks, two groups that were more supportive of the Democratic gubernatorial candidate. However, nowhere in the news story was any specific information provided on how the weighting was done. This example illustrates that weighting can be consequential, and it is probably typical in terms of the scant information provided to citizens about weighting procedures.

When Polls Conflict: A Concluding Example

A variety of factors can influence poll results and their subsequent interpretation. Useful vehicles for a review of these factors are the polls that led up to the 1980, 1984, 1988, 1992, and 1996 presidential elections—polls that were often highly inconsistent. For example, in the 1984 election, polls conducted at comparable times yielded highly dissimilar results. A Harris poll had Reagan leading Mondale by 9 percentage points, an ABC News/*Washington Post* poll had Reagan ahead by 12 points, a CBS News/*New York Times* survey had Reagan leading by 13 points, a *Los Angeles Times* poll gave Reagan a 17-point lead, and an NBC News poll had the president ahead by 25 points (Oreskes 1984). In September 1988 seven different polls on presidential preference were released within a three-day period with results ranging from Bush ahead by 8 points to a Dukakis lead of 6 points (Morin 1988). In 1992 ten national polls conducted in the latter part of August showed Clinton with leads over Bush ranging from 5 to 19 percentage points (Elving 1992). And in 1996, the final preelection polls showed Clinton leading Dole by margins ranging from 7 to 18 percentage points. How can polls on an ostensibly straightforward topic such as presidential vote preference differ so widely? Many reasons can be cited, some obvious and others more subtle in their effects.

Among the more subtle reasons are the method of interviewing and the number of callbacks that a pollster uses to contact respondents who initially were unavailable. According to Lewis and Schneider (1982, 43), Patrick Caddell and George Gallup in their 1980 polls found that President Reagan received less support from respondents interviewed personally than from those queried over the telephone. Their speculation about this finding was that weak Democrats who were going to desert Carter found it easier to admit this in a telephone interview than in a face-to-face situation.

With respect to callbacks, Dolnick (1984) reports that one reason a Harris poll was closer than others in predicting Reagan's sizable victory in 1980 was that it made repeated callbacks, which at each stage "turned up increasing numbers of well-paid, well-educated Republican-leaning voters." A similar situation occurred in 1984. Traugott (1987) found that persistence in callbacks resulted in a more Republican sample, speculating that Republicans were less likely to have been at home or available initially.

Some of the more obvious factors that help account for differences among compared polls are question wording and question placement. Some survey items mention the presidential and vice-presidential candidates, while others mention only the presidential challengers. Some pollsters ask follow-up questions of undecided voters to ascertain whether they lean toward one candidate or another; others do not. Question order can influence responses. Normally, incumbents and better known candidates do better when the question on vote intention is asked at the beginning of the survey rather than later. If vote intention is measured after a series of issue and problem questions have been asked, respondents may have been reminded of shortcomings in the incumbent's record and may therefore be less willing to express support for the incumbent.

Comparable polls also can differ in how the sample is selected and how it is treated for analytical purposes. Some polls sample registered voters; others query adult Americans. There are differences as well in the methods used to identify likely voters. As Lipset (1980) points out, the greater the number of respondents who are screened out of the sample because they do not seem to be likely voters, the more probable it is that the remaining respondents will be relatively more Republican in their vote preferences.

Some samples are weighted to guarantee demographic representativeness; others are not.

It is also possible that discrepancies among polls are not due to any of the above factors, but may simply reflect statistical fluctuations. For example, if one poll with a 4 percent sampling error shows Clinton ahead of Dole, 52 to 43 percent, this result is statistically congruent with other polls that might have a very narrow Clinton lead of 48 to 47 percent or other polls that show a landslide Clinton lead of 56 to 39 percent.

Voss et al. (1995) summarized and compared many of the methodological differences among polls conducted by eight polling organizations for the 1988 and 1992 presidential elections. Even though all eight organizations were studying the same phenomenon, there were enough differences in their approaches that polls conducted at the same time using identical questions might still get somewhat different results for reasons beyond sampling error. One feature Voss et al. examined was the sampling method—how each organization generated a list of telephone numbers from which to sample. Once the sample was selected, polling organizations conducting telephone interviews still had to make choices about how to handle "busy signals, refusals, and calls answered by electronic devices, how to decide which household members are eligible to be interviewed, and how to select the respondent from among those eligible" (Voss et al. 1995). The investigators also examined the various weighting schemes used by each survey operation to ensure a representative sample. Much of this methodological information is not readily available to the consumer of public opinion polls, and if it were many consumers would be overwhelmed by the volume of methodological detail. Yet these factors can make a difference. For example, the eight polling organizations analyzed by Voss et al. treated refusals quite differently. Some of the outfits did not call back after receiving a refusal from a potential respondent; other organizations did make callbacks. One organization generally tried to call back but with a different interviewer, but then gave up if a second refusal was obtained.

Just as different methodological features can affect election polls, they also can influence other surveys. One prominent example dealt with the widely divergent estimates of rape obtained from two different national surveys. Much of this discrepancy stemmed from the methodological differences between the two surveys (Lynch 1996). Because the poll consumer is unaware of many of the design features of a survey, he or she must assume the survey design was appropriate for the topic at hand. Then the consumer can ask whether the information collected by the survey was analyzed and interpreted correctly.

References

Abramson, Paul R., Brian Silver, and Barbara Anderson. 1990. "The Decline of Overtime Comparability in the National Election Studies." *Public Opinion Quarterly* 54 (summer): 177–190.

Alpern, David M. 1986. "A *Newsweek* Poll: Sex Laws." *Newsweek*, 14 July, 38.

Baumgartner, Frank R., and Jack L. Walker. 1988. "Survey Research and Membership in Voluntary Associations." *American Journal of Political Science* 32 (November): 908–928.

Borrelli, Stephen, Brad Lockerbie, and Richard G. Niemi. 1987. "Why the Democrat-Republican Partisan Gap Varies from Poll to Poll." *Public Opinion Quarterly* 51 (spring): 115–119.

Clymer, Adam. 1986. "A Poll Finds 77% in U.S. Approve Raid on Libya." *New York Times*, 17 April, A-23.

Curtin, Michael. 1986a. "Celeste Leading Rhodes 48% to 43%, with Kucinich Trailing." *Columbus Dispatch*, 10 August, 1-A.

———. 1986b. "Here Is How Poll Was Taken." *Columbus Dispatch*, 10 August, 8-E.

Dolnick, Edward. 1984. "Pollsters Are Asking: What's Wrong." *Columbus Dispatch*, 19 August, C-1.

Elving, Ronald D. 1992. "Polls Confound and Confuse in This Topsy-Turvy Year." *Congressional Quarterly Weekly Report*, 12 September, 2725–2727.

Laumann, Edward O., et al. 1994. *The Social Organization of Sexuality*. Chicago: University of Chicago Press.

Lewis, I. A., and William Schneider. 1982. "Is the Public Lying to the Pollsters?" *Public Opinion* 5 (April/May): 42–47.

Lipset, Seymour Martin. 1980. "Different Polls, Different Results in 1980 Politics." *Public Opinion* 3 (August/September): 19–20, 60.

Lockerbie, Brad, and Stephen A. Borrelli. 1990. "Question Wording and Public Support for Contra Aid, 1983–1986." *Public Opinion Quarterly* 54 (summer): 195–208.

Lynch, James P. 1996. "Clarifying Divergent Estimates of Rape from Two National Surveys." *Public Opinion Quarterly* 60 (winter): 558–619.

Michael, Robert T., John H. Gagnon, Edward O. Laumann, and Gina Kolata. 1994. *Sex in America: A Definitive Survey*. Boston: Little, Brown.

Morin, Richard. 1988. "Behind the Numbers: Confessions of a Pollster." *Washington Post*, 16 October, C-1, C-4.

———. 1991. "2 Ways of Reading the Public's Lips on Gulf Policy." *Washington Post*, 14 January, A-9.

———. 1994. "Don't Know Much About Health Care Reform." *Washington Post* National Weekly Edition, 14–20 March, 37.

———. 1995. "Reading between the Numbers." *Washington Post* National Weekly Edition, 4–10 September, 30.

Morin, Richard, and John M. Berry. 1996. "Economic Anxieties." *Washington Post* National Weekly Edition, 4–10 November, 6–7.

Oreskes, Michael. 1984. "Pollsters Offer Reasons for Disparity in Results." *New York Times*, 20 October, A-8.

Phillips, Kevin P. 1981. "Polls Are Too Broad in Analysis Divisions." *Columbus Dispatch*, 8 September, B-3.

Pianin, Eric, and Mario Brossard. 1997. "Hands Off Social Security and Medicare." *Washington Post* National Weekly Edition, 7 April, 35.

Rosenbaum, David E. 1997. "Americans Want a Right to Die. Or So They Think." *New York Times*, 8 June, E3.

Schneider, William. 1996. "How to Read a Trial Heat Poll." Transcript, CNN "Inside Politics Extra," 12 May (see AllPolitics Web site).

Smith, Tom W. 1993. "Actual Trends or Measurement Artifacts? A Review of Three Studies of

Anti-Semitism." *Public Opinion Quarterly* 57 (fall): 380–393.

Sussman, Barry. 1985a. "To Understand These Polls, You Have to Read the Fine Print." *Washington Post* National Weekly Edition, 4 March, 37.

_____. 1985b. "Reagan's Support on Issues Relies Heavily on the Uninformed." *Washington Post* National Weekly Edition, 1 April, 37.

_____. 1985c. "Social Security and the Young." *Washington Post* National Weekly Edition, 27 May, 37.

_____. 1986a. "It's Wrong to Assume that School Busing Is Wildly Unpopular." *Washington Post* National Weekly Edition, 10 March, 37.

_____. 1986b. "With Pornography, It All Depends on Who's Doing the Looking." *Washington Post* National Weekly Edition, 24 March, 37.

Traugott, Michael W. 1987. "The Importance of Persistence in Respondent Selection for Preelection Surveys." *Public Opinion Quarterly* 51 (spring): 48–57.

Voss, D. Stephen, Andrew Gelman, and Gary King. 1995. "Preelection Survey Methodology: Details from Eight Polling Organizations, 1988 and 1992." *Public Opinion Quarterly* 59 (spring): 98–132.

Wilcox, William Clyde. 1984. "The New Christian Right and the White Fundamentalists: An Analysis of a Potential Political Movement." Ph.D. diss., Ohio State University.

Williams, Dennis A. 1979. "A New Racial Poll." *Newsweek*, 26 February, 48, 53.

Wright, James D. 1981. "Public Opinion and Gun Control: A Comparison of Results from Two Recent National Surveys." *Annals of the American Academy of Political and Social Science* 455 (May): 24–39.

10-2 A Simple Theory of the Survey Response: Answering Questions Versus Revealing Preferences

John Zaller and Stanley Feldman

> *Political scientists frequently use surveys to measure public opinion, but the meaning of the responses they receive is open to question. In this paper, political scientists John Zaller and Stanley Feldman argue that people do not hold strong or stable attitudes about most issues and political phenomena. The opinions that people express in polls and surveys often reflect the considerations that are "at the top of their heads" at the moment they answer the survey questions, considerations that can be influenced by circumstances.*

. . . Virtually all public opinion research proceeds on the assumption that citizens possess reasonably well formed attitudes on major political issues and that surveys are passive measures of these attitudes. The standard view is that when survey respondents say they favor X they are simply describing a preexisting state of feeling favorably toward X.

Accumulating evidence on the vagaries of mass political attitudes, however, has made this view increasingly dubious. If, as is well known, people are asked the same question in a series of interviews, their attitude reports are highly changeable. Many, as much evidence also shows, react strongly to the context in which questions are asked, to the order in which options are presented, and to wholly nonsubstantive changes in question wording. These phenomena are more than methodological curiosities; they raise serious doubts about what public opinion surveys measure.

In view of this, we propose a new understanding of the mass survey response. Most citizens, we argue, simply do not possess preformed attitudes at the level of specificity demanded in surveys. Rather, they carry around in their heads a mix of only partially consistent ideas and considerations. When questioned, they call to mind a sample of these ideas, including an oversample of ideas made salient by the questionnaire and other recent events, and use them to choose among the options offered. But their choices do not, in most cases, reflect anything that can be described as true attitudes; rather, they reflect the thoughts that are most accessible in memory at the moment of response.

A model based on these claims can, as we show, provide a far better account of the existing evidence on political attitudes, including such related matters as attitude consistency and the effects of political awareness, than can currently dominant models of the survey response.

. . .

Limits of Existing Theories

Response Instability

One of the most unsettling findings of opinion research has been the discovery of a large component of randomness in most people's answers to survey questions. If the same people are asked the same question in repeated interviews, only about half give the same answers. The data in Table 1,

Source: A Simple Theory of the Survey Response: Answering Questions versus Revealing Preferences, John Zaller and Stanley Feldman. Copyright © 1992 *American Journal of Political Science* 36, no. 3 (August 1992): 579-616. Reproduced with permission of Blackwell Publishing Ltd.

based on interviews of the same persons six months apart, illustrate the problem. As can be seen from the entries on the main diagonals, only 45% to 55% gave the same answer both times, even though about 30% could have done so by chance alone. The amount of response instability differs from one issue to another, but the cases shown in Table 1 are fairly typical.

In his famous paper "The Nature of Belief Systems in Mass Publics," Converse . . . argued that response instability is due mainly to individuals who lack

meaningful attitudes but nevertheless indulge interviewers by politely choosing between the response options put in front of them—but choosing in an almost random fashion. "Large portions of an electorate," he suggested, "simply do not have meaningful beliefs, even on issues that have formed the basis for intense political controversy among elites for substantial periods of time." . . .

This conclusion has been strongly challenged by scholars who contend that, although people's "survey responses" fluctuate greatly, citizens have underlying

Table 1   Response Stability over Repeated Interviews: Two Examples

American Relations with Russia
(Corner Percentaging)

	Attitudes in January 1980			
June 1980:	**Cooperate**	**Middle**	**Tougher**	**Unsure**
Cooperate	25%	8	8	2
Middle	7	4	5	1
Tougher	5	5	17	2
Unsure	4	2	3	4
N=	(338)	(153)	(266)	(74)

Level of Government Services
(Corner Percentaging)

	Attitudes in January 1980			
June 1980:	**Cut**	**Middle**	**Keep Same**	**Unsure**
Cut	24%	6	5	6
Middle	8	4	2	2
Keep Same	5	4	15	3
Unsure	8	2	3	6
N=	(362)	(122)	(208)	(138)

Source: National Election Studies, 1980 Panel Survey.

"true attitudes" that are overwhelmingly stable. . . . The fluctuations that appear in people's overt survey responses are attributed to "measurement error," where such error is said to stem from the inherent difficulty of mapping one's attitudes onto the unavoidably vague language of survey questions.

Both approaches to response instability have critical deficiencies. Converse's thesis, which takes any instability as evidence of a "nonattitude," was an extreme claim intended to characterize attitudes only on highly abstract issues. On more typical issues . . . people's attitudes may be more or less "crystallized" and are, as a result of this, more or less stable. But this only raises the question of how crystallization can be measured apart from its supposed effect on response stability. Since no one has ever said, attitude crystallization remains . . . more a metaphor than a testable theory of attitude stability.

. . .

What Needs to Be Done

. . .

The challenge . . . is to devise a theory that accommodates both response instability and response effects and that is crafted to the kinds of problems and data facing analysts of public opinion. This is what we attempt to do in this paper. The theory we propose is, we admit, simpler than would be necessary to explain all of the findings that psychologists have now documented. But a theory sufficiently complex to do this would have little value to most political scientists, and our aim is, above all, to reach this group—convincing it that the conventional understanding of public opinion is unworkable and that a practical alternative is available.

An Alternative Model of the Survey Response

According to conventional attitude theory, individuals choose whichever prespecified option comes closest to their own position. But if, as we contend, people typically do not have fixed positions on issues, how do they make their choices?

Since most survey research takes the "true attitude" as its primitive unit of analysis, little attention has been devoted to this question. If, however, one turns to studies that employ depth interviews, one finds much useful evidence. Among the best of these is Hochschild's study of attitudes toward equality, *What's Fair?* From her interviews with 28 persons, Hochschild found that people would, if asked to do so, readily answer fixed-choice questions, but that given the opportunity to talk, "people do not make simple statements; they shade, modulate, deny, retract, or just grind to a halt in frustration. These manifestations of uncertainty are just as meaningful and interesting as the definitive statements of a belief system." . . .

Hochschild particularly emphasizes the ambivalence of many of her respondents. This ambivalence frequently leads them to contradict themselves—which is to say, *to give temporally unstable responses in the course of a single conversation.*

. . .

It is easy to object to the limitations on rigor inherent [within] in depth interviews such as Hochschild's. Nonetheless, we are persuaded that the basic point about ambivalence—*that individuals possess multiple and often conflicting opinions toward important issues*—represents an important insight. Much psychological research reinforces this view. Memory researchers, for example, have shown that people store huge amounts of information in their long-term memories, but can retrieve and use only a fraction of it at one time. The particular material they do recall depends on a combination of chance and recency of activation. Hence, people make quite different judgments and belief statements, depending on the information they happen to recall from long-term memory. . . .

Another research tradition, mainly concerned with social cognition, focuses on the organization of ideas in the mind. A central concept in much of this research is the "schema," a term that has been adapted from cognitive psychology. A schema is a cognitive structure that organizes prior information and experience around a central value or idea and that guides the interpretation of new information and experience.

A critical point about schemas is that people typically have several of them available for understanding any given phenomena. For example, an individual being introduced to a "professor" would react quite differently if the new person were instead described as "a mother of four." That is, different associations would come to mind, different qualities of the person would be noticed, different conclusions would be drawn from the person's mannerisms, and so forth. In short, the perceiver's attitude toward the person would be different. . . .

. . . Our model will follow Hochschild in assuming that people carry around in their heads a mix of more or less consistent "considerations," where a consideration is defined as a *reason for favoring one side of an issue rather than another.* (E.g., a person who thinks about "Pentagon waste" while deciding a question about defense spending has raised a consideration that may well control her decision on that issue.)

The first axiom of our model may now be stated as:

AXIOM 1: The ambivalence axiom. Most people possess opposing considerations on most issues, that is, considerations that might lead them to decide the issue either way.

We emphasize that the concept of consideration, as used in this axiom, is not just another word for schema. First, it is cast in the language of everyday political discourse . . . , as befits a term intended for political rather than psychological analysis. Second, it makes no reference to mental structures or operations, such as the interpretation of raw sensory input, that are central to the concept of schema.

Our next problem is to decide how individuals transform the diverse considerations in their heads into closed-ended responses. One possibility, as Taylor and Fiske . . . suggest, is that individuals make choices "off the top of the head" on the basis of the first idea that comes to mind. Thus, people may make social judgments by seizing on "a single, sufficient and salient explanation . . . often the first satisfactory

one that comes along. . . . [I]nstead of employing base rate or consensus information logically, people are more often influenced by a single, colorful piece of case history evidence. . . . Instead of reviewing all the evidence that bears upon a particular problem, people frequently use the information which is most salient or available to them, that is, that which is most easily brought to mind." . . . Tversky and Kahneman's . . . well-known work on framing effects reinforces the view that individuals often are overly influenced by a single, dominant consideration.

At the same time, much data in both political science . . . and cognitive psychology . . . indicate that on other occasions, individuals reach decisions by averaging across a range of competing ideas. Thus, Kelley . . . shows that voters seem to decide which presidential candidate to support by summing up all of their "likes" and "dislikes" about each party and presidential candidate and choosing the one with the highest net total.

The axioms we propose allow individuals to respond to survey questions on the basis of either one or many considerations, depending on how many happen to be readily accessible in memory at the moment the question is posed:

AXIOM 2: The response axiom. Individuals answer survey questions by averaging across the considerations that happen to be salient at the moment of response, where saliency is determined by the *accessibility* axiom.

AXIOM 3: The accessibility axiom. The accessibility of any given consideration depends on a stochastic sampling process, where considerations that have been recently thought about are somewhat more likely to be sampled.

For the case in which a person devotes great thought and attention to an issue, Axiom 3 implies that there may be multiple considerations salient in memory at the moment of answering questions about the issue and hence many considerations to be averaged across. But a person who rarely thinks about an issue and who is confronted by an interview situation that requires a succession of quick answers . . . may have only one consideration immediately available in memory, in which case the averaging rule reduces to answering on the basis of a single "top-of-the-head" consideration. . . .

These three axioms, although spare and informal, can be used both to organize much existing research and to generate testable new hypotheses about the nature of the mass survey response, as we shall now begin to show.

Data

Since we base much of our analysis on data from the 1987 Pilot Study of the National Election Studies (NES), it is worth pausing briefly to describe this study. The survey attempted to measure, inter alia, the "considerations" that underlie people's responses to standard closed-ended survey items. The study was conducted in two waves a month apart; 457 persons were interviewed in the May wave and 360 in the June wave. All had previously participated in the 1986 National Election Study. Other technical details of the study are available through the NES at the University of Michigan.

The basic method was to ask people a closed-ended policy item and then to ask them to talk in their own words about the issues it raised. The closed-ended items were telephone versions of the standard NES items on job guarantees, aid to blacks, and government services and spending. In form A, respondents were asked the open-ended probes immediately after answering the given closed-ended policy item. The exact form of the "retrospective" open-ended probes was:

Still thinking about the question you just answered, I'd like you to tell me what ideas came to mind as you were answering that question. Exactly what things went through your mind. (Any others?)

This probe was designed to elicit a "memory dump" of the considerations immediately salient in people's

minds. Prior work by Ericsson and Simon . . . shows that such probes can work effectively if asked immediately after a given task has been carried out.

In form B, interviewers read the items in the usual way, but, without waiting for an answer, they asked respondents to give their reactions to the principal idea elements in the question. For the job guarantees question, the probes were as follows:

Before telling me how you feel about this, could you tell me what kinds of things come to mind when you think about *government making sure that every person has a good standard of living?* (Any others?)

Now, what comes to mind when you think about *letting each person get ahead on their own?* (Any others?)

Immediately following these probes, the interviewer reread the original closed-ended question and took the person's reply to it. . . .

The two types of probes are clearly not equivalent. The "retrospective" probes, which were posed after people had answered the question in the normal way, were designed to find out what exactly was on people's minds at the moment of response. The "prospective" or "stop-and-think" probes, on the other hand, were designed to induce people to search their memories more carefully than they ordinarily would for pertinent considerations. Note that the stop-and-think probes do not raise new ideas or push the respondent in a particular direction; they simply require the respondent to say explicitly what meaning he or she attaches to the defining phrases of the question.

Respondents were randomly assigned to question form and answered the same type of the question in each wave of the study. The three test items and associated open-ended probes appeared near the end of each wave of the survey. Interviewers wrote down as faithfully as possible all responses to the open-ended probes, including incidental side comments (e.g., "This is a tough one"). The transcribed comments were subjected to an elaborate classification scheme, with as many as four comments coded for each probe. Respondents on the stop-and-think side averaged about 3.7 codable comments per policy item, with almost all respondents offering at least one codable comment. The average on the retrospective side was 2.9.

All comments, including side comments, were rated on several variables by staff coders at the Institute for Social Research at the University of Michigan. . . . The most important variable was "directional thrust of comment," which indicated which side of the issue, if any, the remark favored. Although this variable noted ambivalence, confusion, and nonissue concerns, 75% of comments had a clear directional thrust. The other key coding classification was "frame of reference," a variable that included more than 140 categories and tried to capture the substantive content of each remark. The frame codes referred to general principles (e.g., equality, the role of government), individualism and the work ethic, the fairness of the economic system, particular groups (e.g., blacks, the elderly), personal experience, and particular government programs. . . .

. . .

Tests of the Model

Preliminary Check of the Ambivalence Axiom

We begin assessment of the model by making a plausibility check of the axiom that claims that most individuals hold multiple, conflicting ideas on most issues. Our data give us three ways to measure the extent of ambivalence in the public, as follows:

1. A count of the number of opposing remarks by each person that can be paired against one another. If, for example, a respondent makes two comments with a liberal thrust and two with a conservative thrust, his score on the conflict scale is two. If he makes three (or more) on one side of the issue and only two on the other, the conflict score is still two, since the number of opposing comments that can be paired remains two.

2. A count of the times people spontaneously express ambivalence or difficulty in making up their minds. A special code was created to capture such remarks; it reads as follows: "Mention indicates ambivalence, conflict (e.g., 'I see merit in both sides'; 'That's a tough question'; 'Depends'; 'Both are valid points')."

3. A count of the number of times people make "two-sided comments." Included in the frame of reference codes are special "star codes" that indicate a directional thrust to the comment but also ambivalence with respect to that direction. Star codes apply to cases in which respondents had a preference but were clearly paying some attention to the other side of the issue. Instructions to coders for use of star codes read as follows:

> A star code is used only for cases in which there is a single thought or comment that encompasses two opposing elements (e.g., "Although I think X, I nevertheless favor Y" Star codes are used for comments in which R sees two sides to an issue.

Examples of star codes are "people should try to get ahead on their own, but government should help when necessary" and respondent "admits problem(s) with any program or type of program, but insists it is worthwhile anyway." A count of the star-coded remarks may thus be considered a measure of ambivalence.

From these three measures we created a fourth: a summary of the indices on which a person scored + 1 or higher. Because conflict and ambivalence are equally consequential whether they occur within the course of one interview or across separate interviews, all indices are calculated across both waves of the survey.

Frequency distributions on these four measures are shown in Table 2. As can be seen, each measure captures substantial amounts of ambivalence, a result that is consistent with the first axiom. Even on the more conservative evidence of the retrospective probes, which involve only one query in each wave, the summary measure indicates that 36% to 48% of respondents are to some degree ambivalent on these three issues. And this is surely an understatement. What the retrospective probes capture, as explained, is the reason the person has answered the item as he just has; they cannot capture anything like the full range of ideas in the person's head. However, the prospective probes were designed to tap a wider range of the ideas in people's minds; on evidence from them, roughly 75% of respondents are at least somewhat conflicted on the three issues.

These results provide clear initial support for the model's first axiom, the ambivalence axiom. Since the other two axioms cannot be tested directly, we turn now to an examination of the deductive implications of the three axioms taken all together.

First Deductions from the Model

We begin with deductions from the model that are entirely straightforward and perhaps uninteresting and proceed to more useful and important ones. If,

Table 2 Expressions of Conflict and Ambivalence on Political Issues

	Retrospective Probes			Stop-and-Think Probes		
	Conflicting Considerations			Conflicting Considerations		
	Jobs	Services	Aid to Blacks	Jobs	Services	Aid to Blacks
Count						
0	73.9%	57.8	73.4	36.9%	30.7	29.0
1	22.6	33.6	22.6	27.3	29.0	21.6
2	3.5	5.2	4.0	22.2	21.6	25.0
3+	0.0	3.4	0.0	13.1	18.7	24.4
	Expressions of Ambivalence			Expressions of Ambivalence		
0	76.9	83.5	78.8	63.2	72.2	71.1
1+	23.1	15.5	27.8	36.8	27.8	28.9
	Two-Sided Remarks (Star Codes)			Two-Sided Remarks (Star Codes)		
0	75.0	91.7	81.4	64.9	85.2	72.3
1+	25.0	8.3	18.6	35.1	14.8	27.7
	Total Indications			Total Indications		
0	60.2	51.4	63.6	25.9	24.3	24.7
1	15.7	37.6	16.9	39.1	50.9	44.0
2	18.5	7.3	12.7	9.8	14.8	12.0
3	5.6	3.7	6.8	25.3	10.1	19.3

Source: 1987 NES Pilot Study.

as the accessibility axiom claims, the accessibility of a given consideration depends on the amount of thought devoted to an issue, we should find that people who are, in general, more politically involved have more considerations at the top of their heads and available for use in answering survey questions. This is the first of 18 deductions from the model that we make and test (Deduction 1). (To keep track of the deductions, each will be numbered in parentheses, as here.) Despite some indication of nonmonotonicity in the data, Table 3 essentially confirms this expectation.

Similarly, we would expect persons who have greater interest in an issue to have, all else equal, more thoughts about that issue readily accessible in memory than other persons (Deduction 2). Since the Pilot Study did not directly ask respondents how important or interesting each of the policy issues was to them, our ability to test this expectation is limited. We did, however, find that blacks raised more considerations than whites in connection with the aid to minorities item (p < .01). Government employees also had slightly more to say than other

persons about the government services item (p = .07). Unemployed persons, however, were not more likely to raise considerations pertinent to the job guarantees item.

Axioms 2 and 3 claim people answer survey questions by averaging across whatever considerations are salient in memory. If this is so, we should find strong correlations between measures of people's thoughts as they answer a survey item and the direction of decision on the item itself (Deduction 3). Thus if, for example, a person makes two remarks that favor the liberal side of the issue and one that favors the conservative side, we would expect that the person would, on average, take the liberal side of the issue. Although this inference may seem hardly worth testing, it is by no means obvious that it can be confirmed. Social psychologists, working in the domain of social cognition, have turned up cases in which the direction of people's open-ended thoughts is uncorrelated, or even negatively correlated, with evaluations of the given issue.

. . . The surprising noncorrelations occur because people typically do not *construct* attitude statements from ideas they can retrieve from memory as they are questioned. Instead, people *recall* attitudes formed at an earlier time. Thus, they maintain, there is no necessary correlation between top-of-the-head ideas and attitude statements. . . .

Notwithstanding this, our data indicate substantial correlations between the ideas most accessible to individuals at the moment of response and the response given. To show this, we created additive indices of people's open-ended remarks, coded for directional thrust. We then correlated these indices with responses to the closed-ended items, as shown in Table 4. On the stop-and-think side, correlations between the indices and their associated dichotomous item in each wave of the survey averaged about .40. When an index of all remarks over both waves of the survey is correlated with a scale that consists of responses to the closed-ended items from the two waves, the correlations average about .50. In the other half of the study, the correlations between individuals' retrospective

| Table 3 | Effect of Political Awareness on Volume of Open-Ended Comments |

	Level of Political Awareness				
	Low		**Medium**		**High**
Standard of living	2.3	2.9	3.5	3.5	3.2
Government services	2.3	3.2	4.3	4.6	4.7
Aid to blacks	3.3	3.9	4.4	5.2	4.4
N =	44	53	54	38	46

Source: 1987 NES Pilot Study.

Note: Cell entries are the average number of discrete substantive remarks in the given cell. These data are derived from stop-and-think probes, but results from retrospective probes show the same pattern.

remarks and their closed-ended responses in the same wave of the survey averaged .70. When retrospective remarks and items were summed and correlated across waves of the survey, the correlations averaged .80. . . .

Table 4	Relationship between Available Thoughts and Closed-Ended Items

	Wave 1	**Wave 2**	**Combined**
	Correlations with Remarks Made Just *before* Answering Closed-Ended Question		
Job guarantees	.39	.39	.50
	(212)	(161)	(173)
Government services	.31	.36	.41
	(187)	(153)	(165)
Aid to blacks	.57	.48	.63
	(220)	(165)	(166)
	Correlations with Remarks Made Just *after* Answering Closed-Ended Question		
Job guarantees	.79	.70	.79
	(126)	(123)	(105)
Government services	.79	.70	.78
	(137)	(105)	(106)
Aid to blacks	.67	.83	.83
	(144)	(114)	(112)

Source: 1987 NES Pilot Study.

Note: Cell entry is Pearson correlation between open-ended remarks made just before (or just after) answering closed item and scores on the closed item. First column shows correlations from first wave of survey; second column shows correlations from second wave; third column shows correlations between remarks from both waves and combined item scores on both waves.

We should add that the findings of correlations between top-of-the-head thoughts and attitude reports are not, taken alone, clinching evidence that the former have caused the latter. Rather, the correlations—which, as we have indicated, could not be taken for granted in light of past research—simply represent one of more than a dozen cases in which we have been able to develop evidence that is consistent with the three-axiom model.

Explaining Response Instability

Response instability over repeated interviews is, as we have indicated, one of the most important and disturbing empirical regularities associated with the mass survey response. In this section, we attempt to use our model to explain this instability. We begin with simple illustrations of our approach and then proceed to more systematic analysis.

When asked in the May interview about the proper level of government services, one respondent, identified as a teacher, emphatically favored higher levels of services and spending. The country was facing an educational crisis, the teacher said, and more expenditures for education were drastically needed. Any cuts in federal services or spending would inevitably reduce the already inadequate funds available for education. Just a month later, however, the same individual favored cuts in government spending. Government was too big and had to be cut back. There was no reference to the educational crisis that had preoccupied this individual just a few weeks earlier.

Researchers have long known that different people can answer identical questions as if they concerned different topics. What the vignette of the vacillating teacher shows is that *the same person can answer the same question at different times as if it involved different topics.* This can happen, according to the model, because the considerations that determine people's survey answers vary across interviews. Thus, people can give strongly felt, contradictory survey responses without either changing their mix of feelings on the issue or consciously experiencing any ambivalence or conflict—if the particular considerations that determine their survey responses have shifted.

. . .

If, as the model claims, individuals possess competing considerations on most issues, and if they answer on the basis of whatever ideas happen to be at the top of their minds at the moment of response, one would expect a fair amount of over-time instability in people's attitude reports (Deduction 4). The reason is that the consideration(s) that are . . . accessible at one interview might not be so prominent at the next. This inference is strongly supported by a mass of existing evidence (e.g., Table 1).

The model not only anticipates response instability, but also expects it to have a definite structure. Suppose that 80% of the considerations in one person's head induce her toward a liberal response on a given issue, while 20% induce her toward a conservative response; and suppose that for a second person, these proportions are reversed. If each based her survey responses on a one-element sample from the distribution of considerations in her head, each would exhibit response instability over time, but over the long run, the first person would be liberal 80% of the time and the second would be conservative 80% of the time. Thus, citizens would have central tendencies that are stable over time, but their attitude statements would fluctuate greatly around these central tendencies (Deduction 5). . . .

If, as shown in Table 3, more politically aware persons have a larger number of considerations at the top of their head and accessible for use in answering questions, they should, all else being equal, exhibit greater stability in their closed-ended responses. The reason is that attitude reports formed from an average of many considerations will be a more reliable indicator of the underlying population of considerations than an average based on just one or two considerations (Deduction 6).

Although initial research failed to confirm this expectation, Feldman . . . and Zaller . . . have more recently shown in separate data sets that political awareness is, in fact, associated with a reduction in the chance variation associated with people's attitude reports. (The difference between the initial and later tests of this expectation is that the recent work uses tests of political information as the measure of political awareness.)

By parallel logic, people should be more stable in their responses to close-ended policy items concerning doorstep issues—that is, issues so close to everyday concerns that most people routinely give some thought to them (Deduction 7). . . .

Another implication of our model is that greater ambivalence ought to be associated with higher levels of response instability (Deduction 8). Since, as we just saw, some individuals who exhibit no apparent ambivalence within a single interview may nonetheless be quite conflicted, it is essential that, in testing this implication of the model, we employ a measure of ambivalence that spans both interviews. Accordingly, we have built a measure of the extent to which an individual's considerations consistently favor one or the other side of a given issue across both waves of the survey. We constructed this measure by means of the following formula:

$$\frac{\Sigma(\text{liberal remarks}) - \Sigma(\text{conservative remarks})}{\Sigma(\text{liberal}) + \Sigma(\text{conservative}) + \Sigma(\text{ambivalent})}$$

A score of one on this measure would indicate that the person's remarks were either all liberal in their thrust or all conservative, while a score of zero would indicate that the person had made an equal number of liberal and conservative remarks. We expect higher stability on the closed-ended items for cases in which all of the person's remarks run in the same direction. The data in Table 5 support this expectation. In five of six trials, this measure was associated with a statistically significant increase in response stability; in the sixth case, the relationship achieves marginal statistical significance ($p = .07$).

. . .

Explaining the Effects of Extra Thought

Survey responses, as conceived here, are not "attitudes" per se; they are unreliable indicators of the mix of considerations in the person's mind—unreliable

Table 5 Response Stability and Consistency of Considerations

Consistency of considerations:	Job Guarantees	Government Services	Aid to Blacks
	Retrospective Considerations		
	N	N	N
.00	.50 (7)	.59 (11)	.57 (7)
.01 to .50	.80 (20)	.70 (25)	.71 (19)
.51 to .99	.77 (15)	.78 (16)	.80 (15)
1.00	.91 (63)	.87 (54)	.96 (71)
	($\rho < .01$)	($\rho < .02$)	($\rho < .01$)
	Stop-and-Think Considerations		
Consistency of considerations:	N	N	N
.00	.63 (16)	.54 (14)	.57 (14)
.01 to .50	.68 (74)	.77 (63)	.83 (66)
.51 to .99	.73 (37)	.80 (50)	.84 (44)
1.00	.88 (45)	.73 (37)	.88 (41)
	($\rho < .02$)	($\rho < .07$)	($\rho < .01$)

Source: 1987 NES Pilot Study.

Note: Cell entries are proportion stable in their responses to closed-ended items from wave 1 to wave 2. Measure of consistency is described in text. P-values are based on uncollapsed measure.

because, among other things, people normally answer without retrieving from memory all relevant considerations. If, however, people could be artificially induced to retrieve a larger than normal number of considerations, it should improve the reliability of their responses to closed-ended items.

Our intent in designing the stop-and-think probes was to create such an inducement. By requiring individuals to discuss the elements of a question before answering it, we were inducing them to call to mind and take account of a wider range of ideas than they normally would. We therefore expected that responses following the stop-and-think treatment would be, all else equal, more reliable indicators of the set of underlying considerations than

responses made in the standard way, that is, in the retrospective condition (Deduction [9]).

Unfortunately, our ability to test this expectation is compromised by an artifact. Because of the use of an explicit "no interest" option in the retrospective condition but not in the stop-and-think condition, more respondents failed in the retrospective condition to respond to the issue item. Low-awareness persons were most affected by this question difference; their no opinion rate averaged 38% in the retrospective condition but only 4% in the stop-and-think condition. This means that retrospective respondents, especially less-aware ones, are a more *selected* group and would, for this reason alone, be expected to be more ideologically consistent than their stop-and-think counterparts. This artifact runs against the grain of the anticipated stop-and-think effect, making it more difficult to demonstrate the effect, particularly for less-aware respondents.

We developed two tests of the expectation of increased response reliability in the stop-and-think condition. In the first test, we expected a measure of social welfare ideology to be more strongly correlated with the target items (jobs, government services, and aid to blacks) in the stop-and-think condition than in the retrospective condition. We used the following interactive regression model to test this expectation, where Form refers to question form:

$$Item = b_0 + b_1 \times Form + b_2 \times Ideo. + b_3 \times Form \times Ideo.$$

When we estimated this model for respondents who scored in the upper 40% of our measure of political awareness, we found that the critical coefficient, b_3, ran in the expected direction for all three items, but achieved statistical significance in only one case. To increase the statistical power of the interaction test in our small sample—the number of cases in each test averaged about 140—we reestimated the model under the constraint that all coefficients be equal across the three items. The results, shown in the top panel of Table 6, confirmed expectations: the effect of ideology is twice as large in the stop-and-think condition, a difference that is statistically significant.

We also estimated the model, under the same constraints, for respondents scoring in the bottom 40% of the awareness measure. Here we found that, as also shown in Table 6, the stop-and-think test not only failed to increase consistency, but might actually have reduced it. We shall return to this apparent reversal in a moment. But first, we have a second test of Deduction [9]. If extra thought induces more reliable attitude reports, it should enhance not only correlations with ideology but also the over-time stability of these responses. As can be seen in Table 7, however, the data completely fail to support this expectation. In fact, less-aware people exhibit *less* consistency in the stop-and-think condition, while more-aware ones show no effect.

It is essential to evaluate these results in light of the selection artifact we have described. The gain in reliability among highly informed persons in Table 6 runs against the grain of the artifact and so is especially likely to be real. The null findings and apparent reversals, because they might have been caused by the artifact, are more suspect. But might not the reversals also represent real effects of the stop-and-

Table 6	The Effect of Stop-and-Think on Ideological Consistency	

	Low Awareness	High Awareness
Intercept	0.01	−.20
Ideology	0.89	0.62
	(.21)	(.14)
Form	−0.36	0.00
	(.21)	(0.20)
Ideology × Form	−0.24	0.62
	(.27)	(.26)
N =	434	437

Source: 1987 NES Pilot Study.

think treatment? Indeed, they might. In an impressive series of experiments, Tim Wilson and colleagues . . . have shown that, contrary to our model, asking people to articulate the reasons for their attitudes consistently *reduces* the predictive reliability of attitude reports, especially for persons less knowledgeable about the given attitude object.

The explanation for the disruptive effects of thought, as Wilson et al. maintain, is that asking people to think about the *reasons* for their attitudes causes them to sample ideas that are too heavily weighted in the direction of cognitive reactions to the attitude object rather than affective ones. Attitude reports that are based on this unrepresentative sample are, as they conclude, less reliable than reports based on the ideas that are otherwise most accessible in memory.

Table 7 The Effect of Stop-and-Think on Test-Retest Correlations

	Retrospective	Stop-and-Think
Low Awareness		
Job guarantees	.68	.45
	(40)	(62)
Government services	.56	.43
	(41)	(58)
Minority aid	.79	.53
	(53)	(57)
Middle Awareness		
Job guarantees	.64	.41
	(29)	(60)
Government services	.48	.38
	(31)	(51)
Minority aid	.81	.51
	(33)	(58)
High Awareness		
Job guarantees	.70	.55
	(39)	(51)
Government services	.61	.58
	(37)	(48)
Minority aid	.70	.86
	(32)	(45)

Source: 1987 NES Pilot Study.

Note: Cell entries are test-retest Pearson correlations. Numbers are in parentheses.

Note that this argument accepts the central assertion of our model, which is that people's attitude reports (and also, as the Wilson et al. studies show, behaviors) reflect the ideas that are at the top of the head at the moment of decision rather than any deeper type of "true attitude." In fact, it is precisely because attitude reports depend on immediately salient ideas that extra thought, in bringing a biased sample of ideas to the top of the head, proves disruptive.

. . .

Summary

The model we have proposed is, like all models, a simplification of what actually occurs. In addition, it has less formal precision than conventional measurement error models . . . and pays less attention to mental processes than do the attitude models of psychologists. But, despite its limitations, the simple three-axiom model is, we believe, uniquely sensitive to the wide range of empirical regularities associated with the mass survey response. Our hope, therefore, is that as others criticize our model and propose alternatives, they keep their theorizing on a sufficiently broad plane that it can accommodate the range of empirical regularities we have examined.

The empirical phenomena for which our model offers an explanation . . . may be grouped under three general headings:

1. Dependence of attitude reports on probabilistic memory search. Because attitude reports are based on memory searches that are both probabilistic and incomplete, attitude reports tend to be (1) unstable over time; (2) centered on the mean of the underlying considerations; and (3) correlated with the outcomes of memory searches (Deductions 3-5). This is also why people who are more conflicted in their underlying considerations are more unstable in their closed-ended survey responses (Deduction 8).

2. Effects of ideas recently made salient. The notion that individuals' survey responses can be deflected in the direction of ideas made recently salient has been used to explain question order effects, endorsement effects, race-of-interviewer effects, reference group effects, question framing effects, and TV news priming effects (Deductions 9-16).

3. Effects of thought on attitude reports. The notion that thinking about an issue, as gauged by general levels of political awareness, enables people to recall a larger number of considerations and hence to make more reliable responses has been used to explain why more politically aware persons exhibit greater response stability and why the public as a whole is more stable on "doorstep" issues (Deductions 6, 7). It also explains why more politically aware persons, and persons especially concerned about an issue, are able to recall more thoughts relevant to it (Deductions 1, 2). Finally, the notion that greater thought makes attitude reports more reliable has been invoked, with only limited success, to explain the effects of extra thought at the moment of responding to an issue (Deduction [9]).

. . .

Normative Implications of the Model

The normative implications of Converse's nonattitudes thesis are extremely bleak. In the limiting case of a public without attitudes—a claim that Converse did not actually make—self-government makes little sense. As Achen . . . put it, "Democratic theory loses its starting point." In contrast, the implication of Achen's empirical investigation was relatively optimistic: most members of the public have true attitudes that are almost perfectly stable. The disturbingly high levels of response change discovered by Converse, Achen argued, are due to the vague questions of survey researchers rather than to the vague minds of citizen respondents.

Our position falls somewhere between the Converse and Achen positions. We agree with Converse that there is a great deal of uncertainty, tentativeness, and incomprehension in the typical mass survey response. The problem, we further agree, is much deeper than vague questions. And yet,

with Achen, we reject the premise of Converse's black-and-white model, which is that most response fluctuation is due to essentially random guessing by people who have no meaningful opinions.

Our claim is that even when people exhibit high levels of response instability, the opinions they express may still be based on real considerations. Even when these considerations turn out to be transitory, the opinion statements they generate are not, for that reason, necessarily lacking in authenticity.

This argument extends to the interpretation of aggregate survey results. Thus, if 55% of Americans report that they approve of the way George Bush is doing his job as president, it should not be taken as evidence that a majority of the public is unequivocally supportive of the president. Rather, it should be taken to mean that 55% of Americans are *on balance* positive toward Bush's job performance—even though the particular 55% who express approval will naturally change from one survey to the next, depending on the cross-cutting accidents of many different people's memory searches. . . .

There is, then, no inconsistency between our assertions of individual-level ambivalence and instability, on the one hand, and belief in the meaningfulness of aggregate-level poll results, on the other—provided one reads polls as revealing a *balance of considerations* rather than as counts of people's "true attitudes."

This conception of an ambivalent public may fall short of our ideal of what public opinion ought to be like, as this ideal is expressed in political oratory and democratic mythology. But if democracy is possible in a country that both glorifies economic individualism and demands the welfare state; that professes to cherish equality and practices racial discrimination; that insists on both higher levels of government services and lower taxes; and that hates Congress but reelects congressional incumbents at extremely high rates—then it is also possible under our understanding of mass public opinion.

10-3 From *Culture War? The Myth of a Polarized America*

Morris P. Fiorina

Many observers of politics have asserted that Americans are increasingly polarized, particularly over cultural or social issues. That polarization, it is claimed, has intensified partisanship in the electorate and in Washington. In the following essay, Morris Fiorina challenges the assumption that Americans have become more deeply divided on cultural issues. He argues, rather, that political elites, particularly candidates for office, have become more polarized along party and ideological lines, thus changing the choices available to the voters. That, in turn, has produced a sorting of the electorate and the deceptive appearance of polarization in the mass public.

[MANY OBSERVERS OF American politics in recent years refer] to "the 50:50 nation." During the late 1990s and early 2000s this phrase began to appear in popular discussions of American politics, as did a similar phrase, "the 49 percent nation." Such phraseology referred to the closely divided national elections of the late 1990s, when the winning party's popular vote share repeatedly came in right around 49 percent of the total vote:

- 1996 Clinton Vote   49.2%
- 1996 Republican House Vote   48.9
- 1998 Republican House Vote   48.9
- 2000 Gore Vote   48.4
- 2000 Republican House Vote   48.3
- 2002 Republican House Vote   50.9

If we consider only the two-party vote, the parties are almost exactly evenly matched nationally—50:50—or at least they were until the 2002 House elections, when the Republicans broke through that ceiling and got to 52.9 percent. Clearly, recent national elections have been exceedingly close. No presidential candidate has won a majority of the popular vote since 1988, the past three elections constituting the longest

such streak since the so-called "era of indecision," when no presidential candidate won a majority of the popular vote in the four elections from 1880 to 1892.

The question is what to make of these recent close elections? For most commentators, the answer is obvious: the American electorate is polarized. In the previously quoted words of the *Economist*, the close recent U.S. elections " . . . *reflect deep demographic divisions. . . . The 50-50 nation appears to be made up of two big, separate voting blocks, with only a small number of swing voters in the middle.*" The top panel of Figure 1 depicts this claim graphically. The electorate is highly polarized: a large number of "progressives" on the left support the Democrats, a large number of "orthodox" on the right support the Republicans, and very few people occupy the middle ground. With a polarized electorate like this, elections will be very close, half the voters will cheer, and half the voters will seethe, as *USA Today* asserts.

But the U-shaped distribution in the top panel of the figure is not the only electoral configuration that will produce close elections. Most obviously, consider the bell-shaped distribution in the bottom panel of Figure 1, which is the inverse of the U-shaped distribution in the top. In the lower figure most

Source: Fiorina, Morris P.; Abrams, Samuel J.; Pope, Jeremy C., *Culture War? The Myth of a Polarized America,* 3rd Edition, © 2011, pp.11-26. Reprinted by permission of Pearson Education, Inc. Upper Saddle River, NJ.

people hold moderate or centrist positions and relatively few are extreme partisans. But if the Democratic and Republican parties position themselves equidistant from the center on opposite sides, then the bottom configuration too produces close elections. In both examples the electorate is *closely* divided, but only in the top panel of the figure would we say that the voters are *deeply* divided. In the top panel it would be accurate to say that voters are polarized, but in the bottom panel we would more accurately call most voters ambivalent or indifferent.

When an election results in a near 50:50 outcome, the standard interpretation seems to be that the electorate is polarized as in the top panel of Figure 1. Why should that be the default interpretation? When an individual voter reports that he or she is on the fence (50:50) about whom to vote for, everyone understands that there are a number of plausible interpretations;

the individual likes both candidates equally, dislikes both candidates equally, or really doesn't give a damn. No one suggests that the individual is polarized. But the aggregate and individual situations are analogous. In each case a continuous variable (percent of the vote/ probability of voting for a given candidate) is compressed into a dichotomous variable (Republican or Democratic victory/Republican or Democratic vote), with enormous loss of information.

In sum, close elections may reflect equal numbers of voters who hate one candidate and love the other, voters who like both, voters who do not care much at all about either candidate, or various combinations of these conditions. Without taking a detailed look at voter attitudes, we cannot determine whether close elections reflect a polarized electorate that is deeply divided, or an ambivalent electorate that is closely divided between the choices it is offered. So, let us

Figure 1   Two Very Different Close Election Scenarios

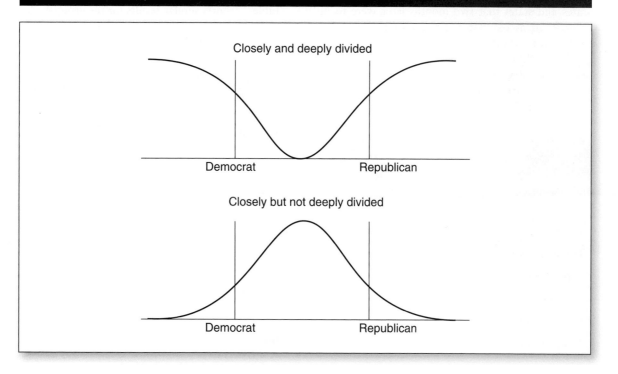

take a closer look at the public opinion that underlies the knife-edge elections of the past few years. Is it as divided as election outcomes seem to suggest?

Is the Country Polarized?

You've got 80% to 90% of the country that look at each other like they are on separate planets. (Bush reelection strategist Matthew Dowd).

Is America polarized? Strictly speaking the question should be "has America become *more* polarized?" for that is the claim. But if the country is not polarized to begin with, the question of whether it has become more polarized is moot. Barely two months before the supposed "values chasm separating the blue states from the red ones" emerged in the 2000 election, the Pew Research Center for the People & the Press conducted an extensive national survey that included a wide sampling of issues, a number of those which figure prominently in discussions of the culture war. We have divided the Pew survey respondents into those who resided in states that two months later were to be categorized as blue states and states that two months later were to be categorized as red states. The question is whether there is any indication in these data that the election results would leave one half the country "seething" and one half "cheering," as *USA Today* reports.

Table 1 indicates that the residents of blue and red states certainly intended to vote differently: the

percentage expressing an intention to vote for George Bush was ten points higher in the red states. Reminiscent of our discussion of dichotomous choices, however, the partisan and ideological predispositions underlying these voting differences were less distinct. The difference between the proportions of red and blue state respondents who consider themselves Democrats is not statistically significant, and the difference in the proportions who consider themselves Republicans is barely so—in both red and blue states self-identified independents are the largest group. Similarly, about a fifth of the respondents in both red and blue states consider themselves liberals (the four point difference is not statistically significant), and while there are more conservatives in the red states, there are more conservatives than liberals even in the blue states. In both the red and blue states the largest group of people classified themselves as moderates. In sum, while the aggregate voting patterns of red and blue states would turn out to be quite distinct in November, the underlying patterns of political identification were much less so.

Table 2 reports similar results for the group evaluations reported by residents of red and blue states. Unsurprisingly, red state residents regard the

Table 1	Red Versus Blue States: Political Inclinations	
	Blue	**Red**
Vote intention: Bush	34%	44%
Democratic self-ID	36	32
Republican self-ID	25	31
Liberal self-ID	22	18
Conservative self-ID	33	41
Moderate self-ID	45	41

Table 2	Red Versus Blue States: Group Evaluations (Percent very/mostly favorable toward . . .)	
	Blue	**Red**
Republican Party	50%	58%
Democratic Party	64	55
Evangelical Christians	60	63
Jews	79	77
Catholics	77	79
Muslims	56	47
Atheists	37	27

Republican Party more favorably than the Democrats, but 55 percent of them regard the Democratic Party favorably. Conversely, blue state residents regard the Democratic Party more favorably than the Republicans, but 50 percent report favorable evaluations of the Republican Party. Evangelical Christians are evaluated equally positively by solid majorities in both red and blue states, as are Jews and Catholics. Muslims fare less well overall and red state residents regard them lower still, but one wonders how much experience many people have with actual Muslims—especially in many of the red states—as opposed to the abstract concept of a Muslim. Finally, in a standard finding, neither red nor blue state residents like atheists: Americans do not care very much what or how people believe, but they are generally negative toward people who don't believe in anything.

Table 3	Red Versus Blue States: Beliefs and Perceptions (Percent strongly supporting statement)	
Gov't almost always wasteful and inefficient	39%	44%
Discrimination main reason blacks cannot get ahead	25	21
Immigrants strengthen our country	44	32
Fight for country right or wrong	35	43
Too much power concentrated in large companies	64	62
Corporations make too much profit	44	43
Al Gore is more liberal than he lets on	55	59
George Bush is more conservative than he lets on	59	57
Wish Clinton could run again (strongly disagree)	51	61

Across a range of other matters, blue and red state residents differ little, if at all. Figures in Table 3 indicate that similar proportions regard the government as *almost always* wasteful and inefficient—relative to the red states, the blue states clearly are not wellsprings of support for big government. Only small minorities in either category regard discrimination as the main reason that African Americans can't get ahead—the blue states are not hotbeds of racial liberalism. Immigrants receive a warmer reception among blue state residents, but multiculturalism remains a minority position even in the blue states. Blue state residents are less likely to endorse unqualified patriotism.

On the other hand, red state residents are just as likely as blue state residents to believe that large companies have too much power and to think that corporations make too much profit—the red states are not the running dogs of corporate America. Amusingly, majorities in both red and blue states agree that Al Gore is more of a liberal than he lets on, and that George Bush is more of a conservative than he lets on—they were not fooled by all the talk about "progressives" and "compassionate conservatives." And finally—and counter to suggestions of numerous Democrats after the election—majorities in both red and blue states *strongly* disagree with the proposition that they wish Bill Clinton could run again. Clinton was more favorably regarded in the blue states, but Clinton fatigue by no means was limited to the red states.

When it comes to issue sentiments, Table 4 shows that in many cases the small differences we have seen so far become even smaller. Contrary to Republican dogma, red state citizens are equally as unenthusiastic about using the surplus (har!) to cut taxes as blue state citizens. Nearly equal numbers of blue and red state residents think the surplus should be used to pay off the national debt, increase domestic spending, and bolster Social Security and Medicare. Contrary to Democratic dogma, blue state citizens are equally as enthusiastic as red state citizens about abolishing the inheritance tax, giving government grants to religious organizations, adopting school vouchers, and partially privatizing Social Security.

Table 4 Red Versus Blue States: Issue Sentiments	Blue	Red
Should use the surplus to cut taxes	14%	14%
. . . pay off the national debt	21	23
. . . increase domestic spending	28	24
. . . bolster SS and Medicare	35	38
Favor abolition of inheritance tax	70	72
. . . gov't grants to religious organizations	67	66
. . . school vouchers for low and middle income parents	54	50
. . . partial privatization of SS	69	71
. . . Medicare coverage of prescription drugs	91	92
. . . increasing defense spending	30	37
Do whatever it takes to protect the environment	70	64

Table 5 Red Versus Blue States: Religion and Morals	Blue	Red
Protestant	50%	69%
"Born again" or Evangelical Christian	28	45
Very involved in church activities	21	29
Religion is very important in my life	62	74
Churches should keep out of politics	46	43
Ever right for clergy to discuss candidates or issues from the pulpit? (yes)	35	33
Ban dangerous books from school libraries (yes)	37	42
Homosexuality should be accepted by society		
Agree strongly	41	31
Agree not strongly	16	14

Overwhelming majorities in both red and blue states favor providing prescription drugs through Medicare, and solid majorities endorse protecting the environment, whatever it takes. Neither red nor blue state residents attach high priority to increasing defense spending. Looking at this series of issue items, one wonders why anyone would bother separating respondents into red and blue categories—the differences are insignificant.

But, we have not considered the specific issues that define the culture war. Table 5 brings us to the heart of the matter—questions of religion, morality, and sexuality. The proportion of Protestants is significantly higher in the red states, of course, as is the proportion of respondents who report having a

"born again" experience. There is a real difference here between the heartland and the coasts. But the significance of this difference fades when we dig deeper. Only a minority of red state respondents reports being very involved in church activities—only marginally more than those blue state respondents who report heavy involvement. A higher proportion of red state respondents report that religion is very important in their lives, but a healthy 62 percent majority of blue state respondents feel similarly. Very similar proportions think churches should stay out of politics, and the minority of red state residents who approve of the clergy talking politics from the pulpit is slightly smaller than the minority in the blue states. Book-burners are only slightly more common in the red states. Finally, there is a clear difference in one of the major issues of the culture war, homosexuality, but probably less of a difference than many would have expected. The level of support for societal acceptance of homosexuality is ten percentage points higher in the blue states (twelve points if we add those who waffle to those who fully accept homosexuality). The difference is statistically significant, but it hardly conjures up an image of two coalitions of deeply opposed states engaged in a culture war. Opinion is almost as divided within the red and the blue states as it is between them. Significantly, this ten- to twelve-point difference on the issue of homosexual acceptance is about as large a difference as we found between red and blue state respondents in the survey. Readers can judge for themselves whether differences of this magnitude justify the military metaphors usually used to describe them.

A legitimate objection to the preceding comparisons is that they include all citizens rather than just voters. Only about half of the age-eligible electorate goes to the polls in contemporary presidential elections, and far fewer vote in lower-level elections. It is well known that partisanship and ideology are strong correlates of who votes: more intense partisans and more extreme ideologues are more likely to vote. Thus, it is possible that the *voters* in red states differ more from the *voters* in blue states than the residents do. To consider this possibility we turn to the 2000 National Election Study which—after the election—asks individuals whether and how they voted. In 2000, the NES reported a vote distribution reasonably close to the actual national division: 50.6 percent of the respondents reported voting for Gore, 45.5 percent for Bush, and the remainder for minor candidates.

Tables 6 and 7 report differences among reported voters in the NES that are only marginally larger than those reported among all respondents in the Pew Survey. Again, the largest difference is for the vote itself. To reiterate, even if an individual feels 55:45 between the two candidates, she has to vote one way or the other. The reported vote for Bush is 54 percent in the red states

Table 6   Red Versus Blue States: Political Inclinations

	Blue	Red
Bush vote	37%	54%
Democratic self-ID*	40	32
Republican self-ID	25	34
Liberal self-ID	20	11
Conservative self-ID	24	31
Clinton job approval**	71	57
Clinton foreign policy job approval	70	63
Clinton economic job approval	81	74
Democrats better able to handle economy	35	27
Republicans better able to handle economy	24	29
Prefer unified control	24	24

*Party identifiers include strong and weak identifiers, not independent leaners.

Liberal identifiers are scale postions 1–2, conservative identifiers 6–7.

**Unless otherwise noted approval figures in the table combine "strongly approve" and "approve."

versus 37 percent in the blue states—a seventeen-point gap, which is larger than the ten-point gap in vote *intention* in the earlier Pew Survey. Self-identified Democrats were significantly more common among blue state voters and self-identified Republicans significantly more common among red state voters, but in neither case does the difference reach double digits; independents and minor party affiliates were a third of the actual electorate in both categories. Self-identified liberals are more common in the blue states, but self-identified conservatives were at least as numerous as liberals in blue states. Again, moderates or centrists were the majority in both categories. An overwhelming majority of blue state voters approved of Bill Clinton's general job performance as well as his foreign policy job performance and his economic job performance, but so did a heavy, if smaller, majority of red state voters. Only minorities of both blue state and red state voters thought that one party could better handle the economy. Finally, rather than blue state residents favoring Democratic control of the Presidency and Congress and red state residents favoring Republican control, nearly identical majorities of both prefer divided control.

Table 7 indicates that issue preferences in the two categories of states are surprisingly similar in many instances. Four in ten voters in both red and blue states agree that immigration should decrease, and seven in ten believe that English should be the official language of the United States (the proportion is actually slightly higher in the blue states). Four in ten voters in both categories put environmental considerations above employment considerations, a surprising similarity in light of the image of red states as hotbeds of clear-cutters and blue states as strongholds of tree-huggers. Narrow majorities of voters in both categories support school vouchers, and large majorities support the death penalty. In neither blue nor red states are people wildly in favor of government intervention to ensure fair treatment of African Americans in employment, and virtually identical (small) proportions support racial preferences in hiring.

Again, when we turn to the specific issues that define the culture war, larger differences emerge, but there also are numerous surprises. A solid majority of blue state voters support stricter gun control laws, but so does a narrow majority of red state voters. Support for women's equality is overwhelming and identical among voters in both categories of states. Although regular church attenders are significantly more common in the red states, similar proportions in both red and blue states believe the moral climate of the country has deteriorated since 1992, and identical proportions believe that others' moral views should be tolerated. Support for unrestricted abortion is eleven points higher among blue state voters, but such

Table 7 Red Versus Blue States: Issue Preferences

	Blue	Red
Immigration should decrease*	41%	43%
Make English official language	70	66
Environment over jobs	43	42
Favor school vouchers	51	54
Favor death penalty	70	77
Government should ensure fair treatment of blacks in employment	57	51
Blacks should get preferences in hiring	13	14
Stricter gun control	64	52
Equal women's role**	83	82
Attend church regularly	50	65
Moral climate: much worse	26	30
somewhat worse	25	25
Tolerate others' moral views	62	62
Abortion—always legal	48	37
Allow homosexual adoption	52	40
No gay job discrimination	73	62
Favor gays in military (strongly)	60	44

*Unless otherwise noted, the figures in the table combine "strongly" or "completely agree" responses with "mostly" or "somewhat agree" responses.

**Scale positions 1–2

unqualified support falls short of a majority, and more than a third of red state voters offer similarly unqualified support. The 2000 NES is particularly rich in items tapping people's views about matters related to sexual orientation. Here we find differences between blue and red state voters that are statistically significant, though smaller in magnitude than regular consumers of the news might have expected. A narrow majority of blue state voters would allow homosexuals to adopt children, but so would four in ten red state voters. Solid majorities of voters in both categories support laws that would ban employment discrimination against gays. Sixty percent of blue state voters fully support gays in the military, contrasted with 44 percent of red state voters. This 16 percent difference is the single largest disparity we

found between the issue preferences of red and blue state voters. Perhaps Bill Clinton picked the one issue in the realm of sexual orientation that was most likely to create controversy. But the evidence supports the alternative hypothesis that Clinton's executive order polarized the electorate: according to Gallup data, popular support for gays in the military rose through the 1980s and had reached 60 percent in 1989 before plummeting in the wake of Clinton's executive order.

All in all, the comparison of blue and red state residents who claim to have voted in 2000 seems consistent with the picture reflecting comparisons of all residents of blue and red states. There are numerous similarities between red and blue state voters, some differences, and a few notable differences, but little that calls to mind the portrait of a culture war between the states.

10-4 The Polarized Electorate

Alan I. Abramowitz

> *The partisan polarization among American policymakers and the electorate reflects a polity that is deeply divided along racial, ideological, and cultural lines. Taking a view that contrasts with the arguments of Morris P. Fiorina in the previous selection, political scientist Alan I. Abramowitz argues that the polarization is real and affects the competitiveness of elections. The forces that produced this polarization remain strong and, if anything, appear to be growing in strength.*

In the first two decades of the 21st century, the United States has entered a new era of electoral competition between the two major political parties. This new era of party competition has three main characteristics that distinguish it from the patterns of electoral competition that were evident for half a century following the end of World War II. First, there is a close balance of support for the two major political parties at the national level that has resulted in intense competition for control of Congress and the White House. Second, despite the close balance of support between the parties at the national level, there is widespread one-party dominance at the state and local level. Third, there is a very high degree of consistency in the outcomes of elections over time and across different types of elections. These three characteristics are closely related. All of them reflect the central underlying reality of American electoral politics in the current era: an electorate that is strongly partisan and deeply divided along racial, ideological, and cultural lines.

Competitive Elections

Recent national elections in the United States have been highly competitive. Shifts in party control of both chambers of Congress and the White House have been fairly regular, and popular vote margins in presidential elections have been relatively close. Democrats controlled both chambers of Congress for 34 of the 40 years between 1954 and 1994. Since then, however, the House has changed hands three times—in 1994, 2006, and 2010—and the Senate has changed hands four times—in 1994, 2001 (as a result of a party switch by one Republican senator), 2002, and 2006. Moreover, majorities in both chambers have generally been smaller than they were in many of the Congresses during the years when Democrats enjoyed uninterrupted control of the legislative branch.

While swings in party control of the White House occurred frequently between the 1950s and 1990s, many of the elections during those years were decided by very large popular vote margins. In contrast, the popular vote margins in recent presidential elections have been fairly small. During most of the 20th century, landslide elections were the rule and not the exception. Of the 17 presidential elections between 1920 and 1984, 10 were won by a double-digit margin. But there hasn't been a landslide election since Ronald Reagan's drubbing of Walter Mondale in 1984.

Not only have the results of recent presidential elections been considerably closer on average than were earlier ones, they have also been much more stable. It was not unusual in the earlier elections of

Source: This piece is an original essay commissioned for this volume.

the postwar era for the margin between the Democratic and Republican candidates to fluctuate widely from one election to the next. For example, the five elections between 1956 and 1972 included Republican landslides in 1956 and 1972, a Democratic landslide in 1964, and two closely contested elections in 1960 and 1968. In contrast, the four most recent presidential elections had the closest popular vote margins and the least election-to-election variability in Democratic margin of any set of four consecutive presidential elections in the past century. To find a series of presidential elections with outcomes as close and as stable as these, one has to go back to the last quarter of the 19th century.

One-Party Dominance of State and Local Elections

Despite the competitiveness of recent presidential and congressional elections at the national level, there has been a marked decline in the competitiveness of elections at the state and local levels in many parts of the United States over the past several decades. There are far fewer swing states and congressional districts and far more strongly Democratic and Republican states and districts now than there were in the 1960s and 1970s. What is striking about the results of the 2012 presidential election at the state level is that despite the closeness of the national popular vote, there were very few closely contested states.

The 2012 results continued the recent pattern of presidential elections that are decided by a narrow margin at the national level but by a landslide or near-landslide margin in many states. And that included some of the most populous and electoral-vote–rich states in the country. Thus, President Obama carried California with its 55 electoral votes by a margin of 23 points, New York with its 29 electoral votes by 28 points, and Illinois with its 20 electoral votes by 17 points. Meanwhile, Mitt Romney won Texas's 38 electoral votes by a margin of 16 points.

This pattern of many deep-red and deep-blue states, including several of the nation's most populous states, represents a dramatic change from the pattern of electoral competition seen in close presidential elections during the 1960s and 1970s. In 1960 and 1976, when John F. Kennedy and Jimmy Carter won close, hard-fought battles for the White House, 20 states were decided by a margin of less than 5 percentage points. Moreover, in those elections every one of the nation's most populous states was closely contested, including California, New York, Illinois, and Texas.

The decline in the number of competitive states since the 1960s and 1970s has been paralleled by a similar trend at the congressional district level. Far more districts today are dominated by one party, and far fewer are closely divided. In 1976, only 26 out of 435 House districts were won by a margin of at least 20 percentage points in the presidential election, while 187 districts were won by a margin of less than 5 percentage points. In contrast, in 2012, 232 out of 435 House districts were won by a margin of at least 20 percentage points in the presidential election, and only 47 were won by a margin of less than 5 percentage points.

Some political observers have attributed the recent decline in the number of competitive House districts to partisan gerrymandering. But most of the decline in district competitiveness actually occurred between redistricting cycles. Moreover, as we have seen, the same trend of declining competitiveness has occurred over this time period at the state level. These trends clearly cannot be explained by clever line drawing to protect incumbents. To explain declining party competition in states and congressional districts, one has to look to deeper trends in American society.

Consistency of Election Results

The third major feature of the recent era of electoral competition in the United States has been a very high degree of consistency in the preferences of voters and, therefore, in the outcomes of elections at the state and local levels as well as the national level. Not only have the election-to-election swings in the national popular vote been much smaller than in earlier time periods, but the outcomes at the local and state levels have been exceptionally stable. Thus, only two states, Indiana and North Carolina, switched sides between the 2008 and 2012 presidential elections. This was the smallest number of states switching sides in two consecutive presidential elections since the end of World War II. Moreover, the correlation between Democratic share of the vote in 2008 and Democratic share of the vote in 2012 across all 50 states and the District of Columbia was a remarkable .98. This was the strongest correlation between two consecutive elections in the postwar era. The Democratic share of the vote in 2008 almost perfectly predicted the Democratic share of the vote in 2012.

Recent elections have also been marked by an extraordinary degree of consistency in the outcomes of elections at different levels. Thus, the correlation between the Democratic share of the presidential vote and the Democratic share of the vote for U.S. House of Representatives across all districts with contested House races in 2012 was .95. This was the highest correlation between presidential and U.S. House election results in the entire post–World War II era. As a result, only 25 out of 435 House districts were won by a candidate from the opposite party from the presidential candidate who carried that district. In the 113th Congress, only 16 Republicans represented a district carried by Barack Obama and only nine Democrats represented a district carried by Romney. This was the smallest number of districts represented by a member from the presidential minority party in any Congress since the end of World War II. And while results of Senate elections have not been as consistent with presidential voting as the results of House elections, there has been a marked increase in recent years in the relationship between presidential and Senate election outcomes. As a result, the vast majority of U.S. senators now come from the same party as the winner of the most recent presidential election in their state.

The growing consistency of election results in recent years extends all the way from the presidential contest at the top of the ticket down to state legislative races. Thus, the party composition of state legislatures in the United States is now strongly related to the results of presidential elections. The correlation between the Democratic share of the presidential vote in 2012 and the Democratic share of state legislative seats in 2012 was an impressive .85. Altogether, more than 80 percent of state legislative chambers in 2013 were controlled by the party whose candidate carried the state in the 2012 presidential election.

A Strongly Partisan Electorate

The remarkable consistency in the results of recent presidential elections and among the results of presidential, congressional, and state legislative elections, as well as the large number of deep-blue and deep-red states and districts, can be explained by the fact that the American electorate today is sharply divided along party lines. The results of all these elections closely reflected the underlying strength of the parties in the states and districts, and the fact that, while the nation as a whole is closely divided between supporters of the two parties, the large majority of states and congressional districts now clearly favor one party or the other.

The partisan divide was clearly evident in the results of the 2012 election, at the individual level as well as at the state and district levels. Thus, according to the national exit poll, 93 percent of Republican identifiers voted for Romney, while 92 percent of Democratic identifiers voted for Obama. This was the highest level of party loyalty in any presidential election since the beginning of exit polls in 1972, and it continued a pattern of strong partisan voting by Democratic and Republican identifiers in recent presidential elections. Data from the 2012 American National Election Study (ANES) confirm this pattern: 91 percent of party identifiers, including leaning independents, voted for their own party's presidential candidate, while only 7 percent defected to the opposing party's candidate. This was the highest level of party loyalty in any presidential election since the ANES began asking the party identification question in 1952.

Independents made up 29 percent of the electorate according to the national exit poll, and they divided their votes relatively evenly—50 percent for Romney and 45 percent for Obama. However, based on data from the ANES and other surveys, we know that the large majority of self-identified independents lean toward a party and that these leaning independents vote very similarly to regular partisans. In fact, in recent elections, leaning independents have been more loyal to their party than have weak party identifiers. In the 2012 ANES, only 9 percent of leaning independents defected to the opposing party's presidential candidate, compared with 14 percent of weak party identifiers.

Another sign of the strength of party loyalties in the American electorate can be seen in the extraordinarily high level of straight-ticket voting in 2012. According to the national exit poll, 92 percent of Obama voters supported a Democratic House candidate, while 92 percent of Romney voters supported a Republican House candidate. Similarly, data from state exit polls showed that in most states with competitive Senate races, close to 90 percent of voters supported presidential and Senate candidates from the same party.

Both increased party loyalty and increased partisan consistency in voting reflect that, over the past several decades, the party divide has become increasingly associated with other, deeper divisions in American society: a racial divide between a declining white majority and a rapidly growing nonwhite minority, an ideological divide over the proper role and size of government, and a cultural divide over values, morality, and lifestyles.

The Racial Divide

Perhaps the most important of these three divides for the contemporary American party system is the racial divide. It is so important because despite dramatic progress in race relations in recent decades, race and ethnicity continue to powerfully influence many aspects of American society, from housing patterns and educational opportunities to jobs and health care. And over the past 30 years, the impact of the racial divide on the American party system and elections has been increasing due to the growing racial and ethnic diversity of American society and the response to this trend among racially conservative white voters.

The nonwhite share of the American population has increased steadily since the 1980s as a result of higher birthrates among nonwhites and high levels of immigration from Latin America and Asia. This demographic shift has altered the racial composition of the American electorate as well, although at a slower rate due to lower levels of citizenship, voter registration, and turnout among nonwhites. Nevertheless, between 1992 and 2012, the nonwhite share of the electorate more than doubled, going from 13 percent to 28 percent according to data from national exit polls.

As the nonwhite share of the American electorate has grown in recent decades, the racial divide between the Democratic and Republican electoral coalitions has steadily widened. According to national exit poll data, between 1992 and 2012, the nonwhite share of Republican voters increased from 6 percent to 11 percent, while the nonwhite share of Democratic voters increased from 21 percent to 45 percent. And this deep racial divide between the party coalitions was not confined to presidential voters; it was just as large among voters in the 2012 U.S. House elections.

The growing dependence of the Democratic Party on nonwhite voters has contributed to the flight of racially and economically conservative white voters to the GOP, thereby further increasing the size of the racial divide between the party coalitions. The effects of this trend were clearly evident in voting patterns in 2012. Among white voters, according to data from the national exit poll, the 2012 presidential election was a Romney landslide: Obama lost the white vote by a margin of 20 percentage points, 59 percent to 39 percent. No Democratic candidate before Obama had ever won the presidency while losing the white vote by anything close to this large a margin. Yet despite this enormous deficit among white voters, Obama won the national popular vote by a margin of almost 4 percentage points. He did this by winning 80 percent of the nonwhite vote, compared with only 18 percent for Romney. According to the exit poll, Obama defeated Romney by 93 percent to 6 percent among African American voters, 71 percent to 27 percent among Hispanic voters, and 73 percent to 26 percent among Asian American voters.

The Ideological Divide

The growing dependence of the Democratic Party on nonwhite voters and the resulting flight of conservative whites to the Republican Party have also contributed to a growing ideological divide between the parties. Since at least the New Deal era, Democrats and Republicans have differed on the question of the proper role and size of government. In recent years, however, that ideological divide has widened due mainly to the rightward drift of the GOP.

The sharp divide between the parties over the proper role and size of government was clearly evident during the 2012 campaign, with Republicans—including the party's presidential nominee, Romney—advocating cuts in taxes on upper-income households and corporations; sharp reductions in spending on a variety of social programs; elimination of many health, safety, and environmental regulations; and repeal of the health care reform law passed by Congress in 2010. On the other side, Democrats, including President Obama, were calling for tougher regulation of financial institutions and corporate polluters, increases in taxes on upper-income Americans to ensure adequate funding of federal programs, and full implementation of the health care reform law.

The sharp partisan divide over the proper role and size of government was evident in the 2012 electorate, as can be seen in the data from the national exit poll displayed in Table 1. For example, 74 percent of Obama voters favored a more active role for the government in solving societal problems, while 84 percent of Romney voters felt that the government was already doing too many things that should be the responsibility of private individuals or businesses. Along the same lines, 84 percent of Obama

voters wanted the recently passed health care law to be preserved or expanded, while 89 percent of Romney voters wanted it to be partially or completely repealed. Finally, 83 percent of Obama voters favored increasing taxes on households with incomes of greater than $250,000, compared with only 42 percent of Romney voters.

Table 1 Liberalism of Obama and Romney Voters on Issues

Issue	Obama Voters	Romney Voters	Difference
Role of government	74%	16%	58%
Health care law	84%	11%	73%
Taxes	83%	42%	41%
Abortion	84%	40%	44%
Same-sex marriage	76%	26%	50%
Average liberalism	80%	27%	53%

Source: 2012 national exit poll.

The Cultural Divide

Economic issues weren't the only ones that divided Democrats and Republicans in 2012. Since the 1970s, a new set of issues have emerged in American politics alongside the older issues of spending, taxation, and regulation—issues such as gay marriage and abortion that reflect deeply felt moral and religious beliefs and lifestyle choices. Building on a growing alliance with religious conservatives of all faiths and evangelical Protestants in particular, the Republican Party has become increasingly associated with policies supportive of traditional values and lifestyles, including restrictions on access to abortion and opposition to same-sex marriage and other legal rights for homosexuals. Meanwhile, the Democratic Party has gradually shifted to the left on these issues, with President Obama himself finally announcing his support for legalization of same-sex marriage in 2012.

Today, the vast majority of Democratic candidates and elected officials, including President Obama, support a woman's fundamental right to choose whether to terminate a pregnancy, as well as her right to have access to contraceptives under the new health care law. And an increasing number of prominent Democrats, along with the president, now support the right of same-sex couples to marry, as well as protection from job discrimination and other legal rights for gays and lesbians. Certainly one of the most dramatic actions taken by President Obama during his first term was his decision to end the U.S. military's "Don't Ask, Don't Tell" policy and allow gays and lesbians to serve openly in the armed forces. It was a decision that was strongly opposed by most Republican leaders, including the party's 2008 presidential candidate, John McCain, and its 2012 standard-bearer, Romney.

The 2012 election was supposed to be all about jobs and the economy. And those certainly were the top issues on the minds of voters as they went to the polls. Nevertheless, cultural issues played a significant role in the 2012 elections. According to the national exit poll, white born-again or evangelical Christians made up 26 percent of the electorate, and despite any reservations they may have had about supporting a Mormon, they voted for Romney over Obama by an overwhelming 78 percent to 21 percent margin. On the other hand, those who described their religious affiliation as "something else" or "none" made up 19 percent of the electorate, and they voted for Obama over Romney by an almost equally overwhelming margin of 72 percent to 25 percent. And voters who identified themselves as gay, lesbian, or bisexual made up 5 percent of the electorate, and they supported Obama over Romney by 76 percent to 22 percent.

The results in Table 1 show that on cultural issues, just as on economic issues, there was a sharp divide between Obama and Romney voters. Fully 84 percent of Obama voters wanted abortion to remain legal under all or most conditions, while 60 percent of Romney voters wanted abortion to be illegal under all or most conditions. Similarly, 76 percent of Obama voters favored legalizing same-sex marriage in their own state, compared with only 26 percent of Romney voters.

Diverging Electoral Coalitions

Evidence examined thus far indicates that over the past several decades, growing racial, ideological, and cultural divisions within American society have resulted in a growing divide between the electoral coalitions supporting the two major political parties. This can be seen in Table 2, which compares the racial and ideological composition of the Democratic and Republican electoral coalitions in 1972 and 2012 based on data from the ANES. The results in this table show very clearly that in terms of race and ideology, the Democratic and Republican electoral coalitions are much more distinctive today than they were in 1972—and the contrast would undoubtedly be even greater if we could go back

Table 2 Diverging Electoral Coalitions, 1972–2012

	Democratic Voters		Republican Voters	
	1972	2012	1972	2012
Nonwhites	17%	42%	3%	12%
White liberals	22%	32%	10%	2%
White moderates	43%	21%	42%	18%
White conservatives	18%	6%	45%	68%

Source: ANES surveys.

Note: Respondents who opted out of ideology question coded as moderates.

further in time. Unfortunately, we cannot because the ideology question was not added to the ANES survey instrument until 1972.

In 1972, while conservative whites made up the largest single Republican voting bloc, they were less than half of all Republican voters and they barely outnumbered moderate whites. In 1972, moderate plus liberal whites actually outnumbered conservative whites among Republican voters. In contrast, in 2012, conservative whites made up more than two thirds of Republican voters, greatly outnumbering moderate and liberal whites combined. In terms of its electoral base, the Republican Party is much more conservative today than it was in 1972. And while nonwhites account for a slightly larger proportion of GOP voters today than they did in 1972, they remain a very small minority of Republican voters despite the dramatic increase in the minority share of the overall electorate during these four decades.

The Democratic electoral coalition has also undergone a makeover since 1972. In the case of the Democrats, however, the result has been to increase the influence of nonwhites and white liberals at the expense of moderate-to-conservative whites. In 1972, moderate-to-conservative whites made up about three fifths of Democratic voters. In contrast, in 2012, moderate-to-conservative whites made up only about one fourth of Democratic voters. Today's Democratic electoral coalition is dominated by nonwhites and white liberals. These two groups together made up only about two fifths of Democratic voters in 1972. In 2012, they made up about three fourths of Democratic voters. As a result of these changes, the center of gravity of the Democratic Party in the electorate has shifted considerably to the left of where it was in the 1970s.

Growing Affective Polarization: Evidence From Candidate Feeling Thermometers

The rise of partisan polarization within the American electorate over the past four decades has involved voters' feelings about the parties and candidates as well as their ideological and issue positions.

In fact, the increase in affective polarization in recent years has been even greater than the increases in issue or ideological polarization. This can be seen in Table 3, which displays the trends in relative feeling thermometer evaluations of the Democratic and Republican presidential candidates between 1968, the first time the feeling thermometer scales were included in the ANES survey, and 2012. The feeling thermometer scale goes from a low of 0 degrees to a high of 100 degrees. A rating of 50 degrees is labeled as neutral.

The statistics shown in this table are the average difference between the feeling thermometer ratings of the candidates by Democratic and Republican voters and the standard deviation of the feeling thermometer difference scores for all voters. The former statistic measures the size of the divide between the parties, while the latter measures the

Table 3 The Rise of Affective Polarization: Feeling Thermometer Ratings of Presidential Candidates, 1972–2012		
Year	**Party Difference**	**Standard Deviation**
1968	46.8	38.6
1972	54.5	47.9
1976	47.9	40.1
1980	55.5	43.7
1984	71.8	49.0
1988	67.6	46.6
1992	63.6	44.3
1996	69.0	47.1
2000	63.8	44.0
2004	91.4	56.7
2008	72.3	48.9
2012	105.2	62.3

Source: ANES.

overall divide in evaluations of the candidates within the electorate.

The results in Table 3 show that both the average difference between the relative thermometer ratings of Democrats and Republicans and the overall dispersion of these ratings by voters have increased substantially over this time period and especially since 2000, with the 2012 election setting new records for both measures. Moreover, the increase in affective polarization in recent years has been fairly symmetrical. Both Democrats and Republicans now favor their own party's presidential candidate over the opposing party's candidate much more strongly than in the past, especially in elections involving an incumbent. Thus, both the 2004 Bush–Kerry contest and the 2008 Obama–Romney contest produced very strong preferences by partisans for their own party's standard-bearer. In 2004, Republicans rated George W. Bush an average of 50 degrees higher than John Kerry, while Democrats rated Kerry an average of 41 degrees higher than Bush. Similarly, in 2012, Democrats rated Obama an average of 55 degrees higher than Romney, while Republicans rated Romney an average of 50 degrees higher than Obama.

The increase in affective polarization in recent years is a direct result of the increase in polarization over issues and ideology during the same time period. Democratic and Republican voters prefer their own party's candidates more intensely than in the past because they prefer their own party's ideology and policy positions more intensely than in the past. Thus, the correlation between ideology and relative feeling thermometer ratings increased from .47 in 1984 to .66 in 2012. Over the same time period, the correlation between location on the social welfare issues scale and relative feeling thermometer ratings increased from .53 to .72. In terms of shared variance, the relationship between ideology and relative feeling thermometer ratings nearly doubled in strength over these 28 years, while the relationship between social welfare attitudes and relative feeling thermometer ratings was about 1.8 times stronger in 2012 than in 1984.

These results contradict the claim by Morris Fiorina and his coauthors that more divided voter

evaluations of political leaders today reflect more polarized choices, not more polarized voter positions. In fact, the difference in affective polarization between 1984 and 2012 can be explained only by a growing divide between Democratic and Republican voters on ideology and policy issues. Presenting polarized candidate choices to an overwhelmingly centrist electorate would be expected to produce mainly indifferent evaluations among voters. Only voters who are clearly on one side or the other of the ideological divide would be expected to have strong preferences between two candidates on opposite sides of that divide. Polarized evaluations of candidates or political leaders such as those seen in 2012 require both polarized candidate choices and polarized voter positions on issues and ideology.

Discussion and Conclusions

America today is a polarized nation. Polarized politics in Washington and in many state capitols around the United States is based on deep divisions in American society. There is no "disconnect" between political elites and activists on the one hand and the American public on the other hand. Democratic and Republican leaders reflect the diverging characteristics, priorities, and values of the constituents who elected them. Today's Democratic electoral base is dominated by nonwhites and secular white liberals who view Republican politicians and voters as religious extremists, racial bigots, and defenders of multinational corporations and the wealthiest 1 percent of the population. It is pro-government, pro-choice on abortion, and pro–gay marriage. In contrast, today's Republican electoral base is dominated by socially and economically conservative white voters who view the current Democratic president as an extreme liberal or socialist and his supporters as unpatriotic moochers who would rather live off government handouts than work. It is anti-government, anti-choice on abortion, and anti–gay marriage.

Because partisanship is now rooted in racial, cultural, and ideological divisions in American society, and because the two party bases are roughly equal in size and loyalty, elections tend to be highly competitive at the national level, which further fuels the intensity of partisan conflict. Every election is a battle for control of the White House and/or both chambers of Congress. Deeply rooted partisanship also explains the growing one-party domination of many states and congressional districts, and the remarkable consistency in the results of elections over time and across different elected offices. The late House Speaker Tip O'Neill's famous remark that "all politics is local" has been turned on its head. Today, it is more accurate to say that all politics is national.

Deeply rooted partisanship and the close balance in support for the two major parties at the national level have also contributed to the frequency of divided party control of national government. This situation is made even more likely by the distinct advantages that each party has in different types of elections—Democrats appear to have a growing advantage in presidential elections due to the movement of several swing states into the Democratic column in recent years, while Republicans have an advantage in congressional elections due to the concentration of Democratic voters in urban House districts and the overrepresentation of sparsely populated Republican-leaning states in the Senate. As a result, we have had divided party government in Washington in one way or another for 25 of the past 33 years.

Divided party control was a fairly regular occurrence in American politics in the decades following World War II, even before the current era of polarized politics. But divided party government today has very different consequences. During the 1950s, 1960s, and 1970s, divided government could work fairly well because it was much easier to build bipartisan coalitions to pass legislation. There were enough moderate-to-liberal Republicans and moderate-to-conservative Democrats that it was possible to build cross-party coalitions on at least some major issues. Today, however, there are almost no members in the middle in either chamber. As a result, divided party control almost inevitably leads to a politics of confrontation and gridlock. And with control of both chambers at stake every 2 years, leaders of both parties in Congress often appear to be more concerned with posturing and positioning for the next election than with legislating and addressing pressing national problems.

The forces producing rising polarization in the American electorate appear far from spent. These include, most important, the growing racial and ethnic diversity of American society, growing secularism and the decline of traditional religion, and the growing influence of partisan media. Over the short term, and perhaps over the medium term, polarization within the electorate and among political leaders is more likely to increase than decrease. If this diagnosis is correct and polarization is grounded in deep divisions in American society, rather than trying to reduce polarization by tinkering with electoral rules and procedures, which is unlikely to prove effective, political scientists and others concerned about the future of American democracy should focus on finding ways to help the political system function in an age of polarization.

Chapter 11

Voting, Campaigns, and Elections

11-1 From *The Reasoning Voter*

Samuel L. Popkin

Voters confront difficult choices with incomplete and usually biased information. Many voters are not strongly motivated to learn more. Even if they want to learn more, the information they need is often not available in a convenient form. In the following essay, Samuel L. Popkin argues that this predicament does not necessarily lead voters to make irrational decisions. Voters instead rely on low-cost shortcuts to obtain information and make decisions. Popkin's analysis can help us to better understand the role of campaigns in voters' decision-making processes as well as other features of American politics.

In recent decades, journalists and reformers have complained with increasing force about the lack of content in voting and the consequent opportunities for manipulating the electorate. And yet over the same period academic studies of voting have begun to expose more and more about the substance of voting decisions and the limits to manipulation of voters. The more we learn about what voters know, the more we see how campaigns matter in a democracy. And the more we see, the clearer it becomes that we must change both our critiques of campaigns and our suggestions for reforming them.

In this [essay] I summarize my findings about how voters reason and show how some modest changes which follow from my theory could ameliorate some defects of the campaign process.

I have argued . . . that the term *low-information rationality*, or "gut" rationality, best describes the kind of practical reasoning about government and

politics in which people actually engage. . . . [L]ow-information reasoning is by no means devoid of substantive content, and is instead a process that economically incorporates learning and information from past experiences, daily life, the media, and political campaigns. . . .

Gut rationality draws on the information short-cuts and rules of thumb that voters use to obtain and evaluate information and to choose among candidates. These information shortcuts and rules of thumb must be considered when evaluating an electorate and considering changes in the electoral system.

How Voters Reason

It is easy to demonstrate that Americans have limited knowledge of basic textbook facts about their government and the political debates of the day. But evaluating citizens only in terms of such factual knowledge is a misleading way to assess their competence as voters.

Because voters use shortcuts to obtain and evaluate information, they are able to store far more data about politics than measurements of their textbook knowledge would suggest. Shortcuts for obtaining information at low cost are numerous. People learn about specific government programs as a by-product of ordinary activities, such as planning for retirement, managing a business, or choosing a college. They obtain economic information from their activities as consumers, from their workplace, and from their friends. They also obtain all sorts of information from the media. Thus they do not need to know which party controls Congress, or the names of their senators, in order to know something about the state of the economy or proposed cuts in Social Security or the controversies over abortion. And they do not need to know where Nicaragua is, or how to describe the Politburo, in order to get information about changes in international tensions which they can relate to proposals for cutting the defense budget.

When direct information is hard to obtain, people will find a proxy for it. They will use a candidate's past political positions to estimate his or her future positions. When they are uncertain about those past positions, they will accept as a proxy information about the candidate's personal demographic characteristics and the groups with which he or she has associated. And since voters find it difficult to gather information about the past competence of politicians who have performed outside their district or state, they will accept campaign competence as a proxy for competence in elected office—as an indication of the political skills needed to handle the issues and problems confronting the government.

Voters use evaluations of personal character as a substitute for information about past demonstrations of political character. They are concerned about personal character and integrity because they generally cannot infer the candidate's true commitments from his past votes, most of which are based on a hard-to-decipher mixture of compromises between ideal positions and practical realities. Evaluating any sort of information for its relevance to politics is a reasoning process, not a reflex projection directly from pocketbook or personal problems to votes. But in making such evaluations, voters use the shortcut of relying on the opinions of others whom they trust and with whom they discuss the news. These opinions can serve as fire alarms that alert them to news deserving more than their minimal attention. As media communities have developed, voters have the additional shortcut of validating their opinions by comparing them with the opinions of political leaders whose positions and reputations people grow to know over time.

People will use simplifying assumptions to evaluate complex information. A common simplifying assumption is that a politician had significant control over an observable result, such as a loss of jobs in the auto industry. This saves people the trouble of finding out which specific actions really caused the result. Another example of a simplifying assumption is the notion that "My enemy's enemy is my friend."

People use party identification as running tallies of past information and shortcuts to storing and encoding their past experiences with political parties. They are able to encode information about social groups prominent in the party, the priorities of the party, and the performance of the party and its president in various policy areas. This generalized information about parties provides "default values" from which voters can assess candidates about whom they have no other information. In keeping generalized tallies by issue area, they avoid the need to know the specifics of every legislative bill.

As a shortcut in assessing a candidate's future performance, without collecting more data, people assemble what data they have about the candidate into a causal narrative or story. Because a story needs a main character, they can create one from their knowledge of people who have traits or characteristics like those of the candidate. This allows them to go beyond the incomplete information they have about a candidate, and to hold together and remember more information than they otherwise could. Because these stories are causal narratives, they allow voters to think about government in causal terms and to evaluate what it will do. Narratives thus help people incorporate their reasoning about government into their projections about candidates; their assumptions "confer political significance on some facts and withhold it from others." They offer people a way to connect personal and political information, to project that information into the future, and to make a complete picture from limited information.

Finally, people use shortcuts when choosing between candidates. When faced with an array of candidates in which some are known well and some are known poorly, and all are known in different and incomparable ways, voters will seek a clear and accessible criterion for comparing them. This usually means looking for the sharpest differences between the candidates which can be related to government performance. Incorporating these differences into narratives allows them to compare the candidates without spending the calculation time and the energy needed to make independent evaluations of each candidate.

Working Attitudes

People do not and cannot use all the information they have at one time. What they use will depend in part on the point of view or frame with which they view the world; attitudes and information are brought to bear if they fit the frame. Of the attitudes and bits of information available, people tend to use those they consider important or those they have used recently. As the changes in voter attitudes entailed by the emergence of new candidates in primaries suggest, attitudes and information will also be brought to the foreground when they fit with what is *expected* in a situation. Our realizations, the thoughts that come clearly to mind, depend in part on what others say about their own thoughts and perceptions.

Thus, as options change, expectations change. If a Democrat were asked in early 1984 what he or she thought of Walter Mondale as a presidential candidate, and the reply was "He'll be all right," that response could be interpreted as coming from a nonthinking voter who was passively following a media report about the thinking of others. But the same response could also be interpreted as an indication of a complex ability to come to grips with the available choices, with issue concerns that cannot be

satisfied simultaneously, and with the compromises considered necessary to reach consensus with other people. Similarly, if the same voter were asked a few weeks later what he or she thought about Gary Hart and the reply was "He's just what we need," the response could be interpreted to mean that this voter was simply following the media-reported bandwagon. On the other hand, it could be interpreted to mean that reported changes in public expectations had brought other attitudes and concerns forward in the voter's mind. As this example suggests, the information voters use depends on the reasoning they do, and the reasoning they do depends in part on their expectations. It also indicates that the way in which the content of a voter's response is interpreted depends on a theory about how voters use information and make choices. And I am convinced that any such theory must account for the "working attitudes" of voters—the combinations of feeling, thought, and information they bring to bear when they make their choices at the polls.

Why Campaigns Matter

Changes in government, in society, and in the role of the mass media in politics have made campaigns more important today than they were fifty years ago, when modern studies of them began. Campaign communications make connections between politics and benefits that are of concern to the voter; they offer cognitive focal points, symbolic "smoking guns," and thus make voters more aware of the costs of misperception. Campaigns attempt to achieve a common focus, to make one question and one cleavage paramount in voters' minds. They try to develop a message for a general audience, a call that will reach beyond the "disinterested interest" of the highly attentive, on one hand, and the narrow interests of issue publics, on the other. Each campaign attempts to organize the many cleavages within the electorate by setting the political agenda in the way most favorable to its own candidates. . . .

The spread of education has both broadened and segmented the electorate. Educated voters pay more attention to national and international issues and they are now connected in many more electronic communities—groups of people who have important identifications maintained through media rather than direct, personal contact. There are also today more government programs—Medicare, Social Security, welfare, and farm supports are obvious examples—that have a direct impact on certain groups, which become issue publics. Other issue publics include coalitions organized around policies toward specific countries, such as Israel or Cuba; various conservation and environmental groups; and groups concerned with social issues, such as abortion and gun control. Furthermore, there are now a great many more communications channels with which these people can keep in touch with those outside their immediate neighborhoods or communities. Such extended groups are not new, and modern communications technology is not necessary to mobilize them, as the abolitionist and temperance movements remind us; but the channels to mobilize such groups are more available today, and I believe that the groups they have nurtured are more numerous. When the national political conventions were first telecast in 1952, all three networks showed the same picture at the same time because there was only one national microwave relay; today, with the proliferation of cable systems and satellite relays, television can now show ... hundred[s of] channels. Furthermore, as channels and options have proliferated, and as commuting time has increased and two-career families become more common, the proportion of people watching mainstream networks and network news is also dropping.

Over the past fifty years, as surveys have become increasingly available to study public opinion, there have been many gains in knowledge about voting and elections. There have also been losses, as national surveys have replaced the detailed community orientation of the original Columbia studies. We know much more about individuals and much less about extended networks, and we have not adequately examined the implications for society and campaigning of the transitions from face-to-face to electronic communities.

Both primaries and the growth of media communication have increased the amount of exposure people get to individual candidates, particularly the quantity of personal information they get about the candidates. This increases the importance of campaigns because it gives voters more opportunities to abandon views based on party default values in favor of views based on candidate information, and also more opportunities to shift from views based on a candidate's record to views based on his or her campaign image. Moreover, as primaries have expanded, parties have had to deal with the additional task of closing ranks after the campaign has pitted factions within the party against each other. Primaries have also changed the meaning of political party conventions. Conventions no longer deliberate and choose candidates; instead, they present the electorate with important cues about the social composition of the candidate's coalition and about the candidate's political history and relations with the rest of the party. The more primaries divide parties, the more cues are needed to reunite parties and remind supporters of losing candidates about their differences with the other party.

The Implications of Shortcuts

Recognizing the role of low-information rationality in voting behavior has important implications for how we measure and study attitudes, how we evaluate the effects of education, and how we evaluate electoral reforms. To begin with, we must acknowledge that the ambivalence, inconsistency, and changes in preference that can be observed among voters are not the result of limited information. They exist because as human beings we can never use all of what we know at any one time. We can be as ambivalent when we have a lot of information and concern as when we have little information and limited concern. Nor do inconsistency, ambivalence, and change result from a lack of education (especially civic education) or a lack of political interest. Ambivalence is simply an immutable fact of life. Economists and psychologists have had to deal with the inconsistencies people demonstrate in cognitive experiments on framing and choice: preference reversals and attitude changes can no longer be attributed to a lack of information, a lack of concern, a lack of attention, low stakes, or the existence of "non-attitudes."

The use of information shortcuts is likewise an inescapable fact of life, and will occur no matter how educated we are, how much information we have, and how much thinking we do. Professionals weighing résumés and past accomplishments against personal interviews, or choosing from an array of diverse objects, have the same problems and use the same shortcuts as voters choosing presidents. What we have called Gresham's law of information—that new and personal information, being easier to use, tends to drive old and impersonal political information out of circulation—applies not only to the inattentive and the uneducated but to all of us. We must therefore stop considering shortcuts pejoratively, as the last refuge of citizens who are uneducated, lacking in the political experience and expertise of their "betters," or cynically content to be freeloaders in our democracy.

Drunkard's Searches and information shortcuts provide an invaluable part of our knowledge and must therefore be considered along with textbook knowledge in evaluating any decision-making process. As Abraham Kaplan has noted, the Drunkard's Search—metaphorically, looking for the lost keys under the nearest streetlight—seems bothersome because of the assumption that we should begin any search rationally, in the most likely places rather than in those that are the best lit and nearest to hand. He adds, "But the joke may be on us. It may be sensible to look first in an unlikely place just *because* 'it's lighter there.' . . . The optimal pattern of search does not simply mirror the pattern of probability density of what we seek. We accept the hypothesis that a thing sought is in a certain place because we remember having seen it there, or because it is usually in places of that kind, or for like reasons. But . . . we look in a certain place for additional reasons: we happen to be in the place already, others are looking elsewhere." At least when people look under the streetlight, they will almost certainly find their keys if they are there; if they look by the car, in

the dark, they are far less likely to find them even if they are there.

. . . [W]e should keep in mind the main features about how voters obtain information and reason about their political choices. The Drunkard's Search is an aid to calculation as well as an information shortcut. By telling us where to look, it also tells us how to choose, how to use easily obtained information in making comparisons and choices. As long as this is how we search and choose, people will neither have nor desire all the information about their government that theorists and reformers want them to have.

The faith that increased education would lead to higher levels of textbook knowledge about government, and that this knowledge in turn would enable the electorate to measure up to its role in democratic theory, was misplaced. Education doesn't change *how* we think. Education broadens the voter, because educated voters pay attention to more problems and are more sensitive to connections between their lives and national and international events. However, educated voters still *sample* the news, and they still rely on shortcuts and calculation aids in assessing information, assembling scenarios, and making their choices. Further, an educated, broadened electorate is a more diffuse electorate, an electorate segmented by the very abundance of its concerns. Such an electorate will be harder to form into coalitions. The more divided an electorate, the more time and communication it takes to assemble people around a single cleavage.

Since all citizens sample the news and use shortcuts, they must be judged in part by the quality of the "fire alarms" to which they respond. They must be judged in part by *who* they know and respond to, not simply by *what* they know. Furthermore, this use of fire alarms has an important implication. Since people can only respond to the fire alarms they hear, it matters how the fire alarms to which they are exposed are chosen. If it matters whether the responses to a policy or crisis are mediated electronically by Jesse Jackson and Jesse Helms, or by Bill Bradley and Robert Dole, then attention must be given to how the mediators are chosen by the networks.

11-2 No Compromise: The Electoral Origins of Legislative Gridlock

Gary C. Jacobson

> *Political scientist Gary C. Jacobson argues that the polarization of the parties in Congress, and the gridlock it has produced, is a product of elections—that is, of who gets elected and by whom. In recent decades, party realignment in the South and intensified party loyalty throughout the nation have made the coalitions of voters supporting Democrats and Republicans more different. Serving those coalitions has reinforced the polarization of parties in Congress and generated gridlock when party control of the House, Senate, and presidency becomes divided.*

During the summer of 2011, congressional Republicans played chicken with the Barack Obama administration over the United States' fiscal future. The Republican strategy, a brainchild of the party's radically conservative Tea Party faction, was to force Obama's Democrats to accept massive cuts in federal spending by refusing to raise the legal debt ceiling if they did not comply. Without a higher debt limit, the government would be unable to borrow enough money to pay all its bills, threatening national and global economic turmoil. The administration was agreeable to some cuts but insisted on raising revenues—mainly by rescinding tax breaks enjoyed by wealthy individuals and corporations—as part of any deficit reduction package. Republicans adamantly refused to consider any revenue increases.

In the end, both sides blinked, kicking the metaphorical can down the road. The final agreement raised the debt ceiling enough to ensure the government's borrowing capacity until 2013, made much more modest spending cuts than Republicans had initially demanded, and raised no new revenues. It did nothing to address the long-term fiscal challenge posed by the major entitlement programs, Social Security, Medicare, and Medicaid. That chore was handed off to a new bipartisan, bicameral committee of 12 that was supposed to come up with a comprehensive deficit reduction plan and submit it to

Congress by November 23; its failure would trigger $1.2 trillion in spending cuts starting January 2013 and extending over the next decade, half from defense, half from domestic programs (excluding the major entitlements). The committee, too, failed to break the fiscal gridlock, as Republicans rejected any tax increases and Democrats refused to attack the deficit through cuts alone.

With the axe not scheduled to fall until 2013, it was left to the 2012 electorate to resolve the stalemate. It did not, instead reinstating the status quo, with Obama back in the White House, Democrats in control of the Senate, and Republicans in control of the House. The automatic spending cuts triggered by Congress's failure to act before the January 2013 deadline—cuts designed to be so unappealing that Congress would act to avoid them—instead became the basis for negotiations on the fiscal 2014 budget. This time, Republicans sought to use the October 1, 2013, deadline for funding the government in the coming year to eviscerate Obama's signature Affordable Care Act (aka Obamacare) by defunding or delaying its implementation in the continuing resolution needed to keep the government going. Obama and Democratic Senate leaders refused even to discuss the possibility. The stalemate led to an expensive and unpopular partial government shutdown that lasted from October 1 to October 16,

---

Source: This piece is an original essay commissioned for this volume.

when the House Republicans, badly losing the battle for public opinion, finally capitulated and allowed a clean continuing resolution to pass, mainly with Democratic votes. Again, fundamental fiscal issues remained unresolved.

Although rarely as dramatic as in the 112th and 113th Congresses, legislative gridlock is nothing new. The governing institutions set up by the U.S. Constitution are inherently prone to stalemate and, according to James Madison's famous account in *Federalist* Number 51, designedly so. The bicameral legislature, presidential veto, and the distinct electoral bases and calendars of representatives, senators, and presidents were meant to thwart simple majority rule, and they always have. In abstract terms, the framers imposed high transaction costs (the time, effort, and resources needed to build cross-institutional coalitions to enact laws) in return for low-conformity costs (living under new laws passed over one's objection).[1] The Senate's requirement of a supermajority of (at present) 60 votes to overcome filibusters on most types of legislation added yet another barrier to action. As one astute analyst of the American political process has observed, "it is perhaps more surprising that we get policy innovation at all at regular intervals, instead of unremitting stalemate."[2]

Both formal and informal studies of legislative gridlock agree on its institutional foundations, but they also find that its actual prevalence depends on the distribution of preferences within and across institutions: The wider the ideological distance between chambers, between partisans within each chamber, or between the president and the median representative or the 41st most distant opposition senator (the so-called "veto pivot"), the smaller the set of mutually agreeable changes in the status quo and thus the higher the likelihood of gridlock. In abstract terms, the greater the distance between participants capable of blocking action on any policy dimension, the wider the range of alternatives to the status quo that fall between their ideal positions and thus cannot pass, because any change within this range represents a move away from one side's ideal point, which it will therefore block.[3]

Ideological distances in turn reflect the preferences of the disparate electoral coalitions responsible for electing the president and each chamber's Democratic and Republican delegations. Institutionally, the potential for gridlock is a constant (barring a rare change in institutional rules); the extent to which that potential is fulfilled depends ultimately on electoral politics. In this essay, I first document the increasing partisan divergence—and thus propensity toward legislative gridlock—in national politics since the 1970s. I then examine and confirm the sturdy electoral underpinnings of this trend. Finally, I focus on politics and policy during the first 5 years of the Obama administration to illustrate how electoral and congressional politics interact in an era when the conditions for legislative gridlock are at their maximum.

Partisan Polarization in Congress

The propensity for legislative gridlock varies with the ideological distance between the congressional parties, and by every measure, the parties have become increasingly distant from each other since the mid-1970s. One widely used measure of polarization is the distance between the House and Senate parties' average first-dimension DW-NOMINATE scores (Figure 1). DW-NOMINATE scores are calculated from all nonunanimous roll-call votes cast during each Congress and locate each member for each Congress on a liberal–conservative scale that ranges from –1.0 to 1.0; the higher the score, the more conservative the member.[4] Since the 1970s, the Republican means have moved sharply to the right on this scale and Democratic means rather less sharply to the left, leaving the parties in the 112th and 113th (1st Session) Congresses more distant from each other, ideologically, than at any previous time in American history.

The potential for more frequent gridlock inherent in these trends is evident in Figures 2a through 2d. Figures 2a and 2b show the distribution of DW-NOMINATE scores for each House party's

Figure 1   Mean DW-NOMINATE Scores of the Congressional Parties, 92nd to 113th Congresses

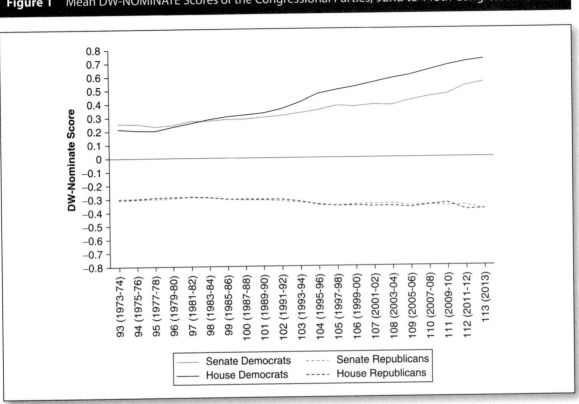

Source: Keith T. Poole, "The Polarization of the Congressional Parties," updated January 19, 2014, http://voteview.com/political_polarization.asp.

members for the two full Congresses bracketing this period, the 93rd (1973–1974) and the 112th (2011–2012); Figures 2c and 2d display the comparable Senate data. In the 1970s, the distribution of ideological locations of the congressional parties, while clearly distinct, overlapped in the middle. By the second Congress of the Obama administration, every Republican was to the right of every Democrat in both chambers, and the parties' modal positions were much further apart than they had been earlier.[5] As the parties drew apart, the proportion of moderates in each party and chamber—defined here as members near the ideological center, with DW-NOMINATE scores between –0.2 and 0.2—also

declined sharply (Figure 3). The change was particularly notable in the House, in which, by this standard, only one moderate Republican has served at any time during the past decade. The proportion of moderate House Democrats increased somewhat after the 2006 and 2008 elections, when the party took several dozen seats in Republican-leaning districts, where any hope of electoral survival required moderation, but 29 of the 41 Democrats with DW-NOMINATE scores greater than –0.2 were replaced by Republicans in 2010. The 112th (2011–2012) and 113th (2013–2014) Congresses contained fewer moderates than any other Congress in at least the past century.

Figure 2a   Ideological Positions on Roll-Call Votes, House of Representatives, 93rd Congress (1973–1974)

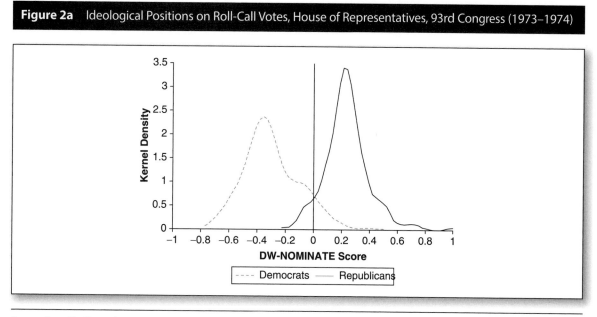

Source: Compiled by author.

Figure 2b   Ideological Positions on Roll-Call Votes, House of Representatives, 112th Congress (2011–2012)

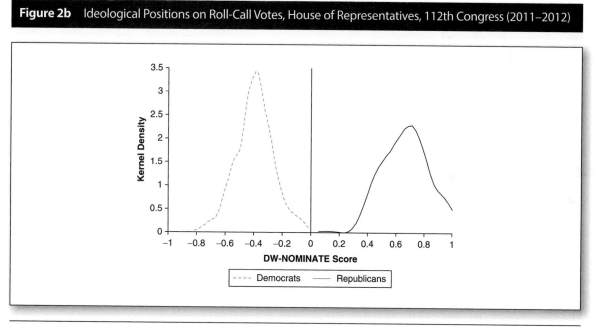

Source: Compiled by author.

Figure 2c   Ideological Positions on Roll-Call Votes, Senate, 93rd Congress (1973–1974)

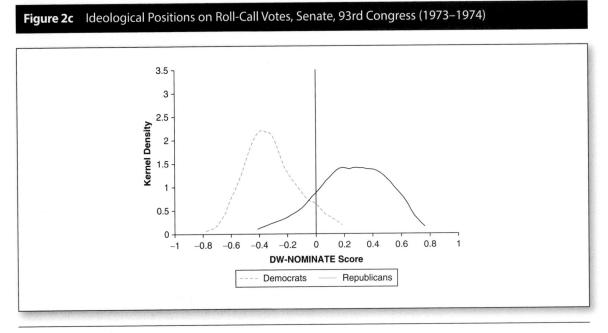

Source: Compiled by author.

Figure 2d   Ideological Positions on Roll-Call Votes, Senate, 112th Congress (2011–2012)

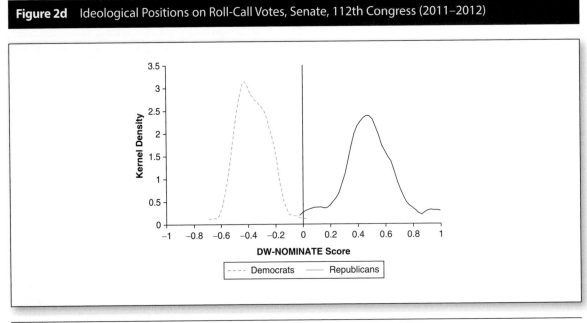

Source: Compiled by author.

Another common measure of roll-call voting in Congress—the frequency with which partisans have supported the president's initiatives—reiterates the polarizing trend observed in the DW-NOMINATE data (Figure 4). Since the 1970s, the president's partisans have become much more consistently supportive of his policies and the other party's much less so, with the partisan gap growing from about 30 percentage points to about 70. Party unity in the House and Senate on divisive votes has also risen steadily, reaching its highest point in at least five decades during the Obama administration.[6]

All these trends point to a heightened propensity for partisan disagreement and a diminished range of politically attainable changes in the direction of national policy when neither party has the votes to impose its will unilaterally—which is almost always the case. Congressional polarization also encourages the unrestrained use of procedural devices to obstruct or circumvent obstruction that make legislative politics so frustrating and embittering to participants and so ugly to the public.[7]

The Electoral Origins of Congressional Polarization

The congressional parties have been driven apart by a diverse array of interacting internal and external forces. A full account of this complex story is beyond the scope of this essay,[8] but one essential component has clearly been the corresponding

Figure 3   The Disappearance of Moderates

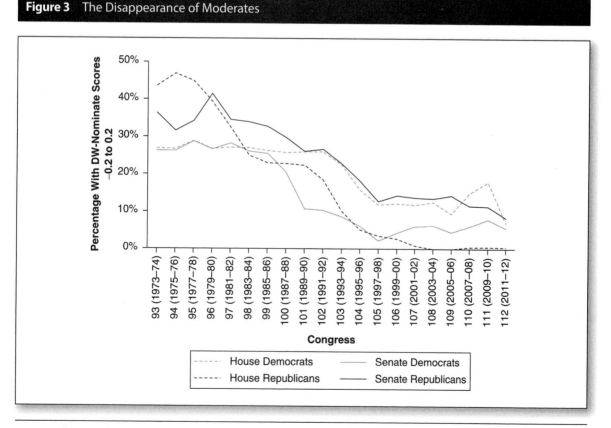

Source: Compiled by author.

Figure 4   Presidential Support in Congress, 93rd to 112th Congresses

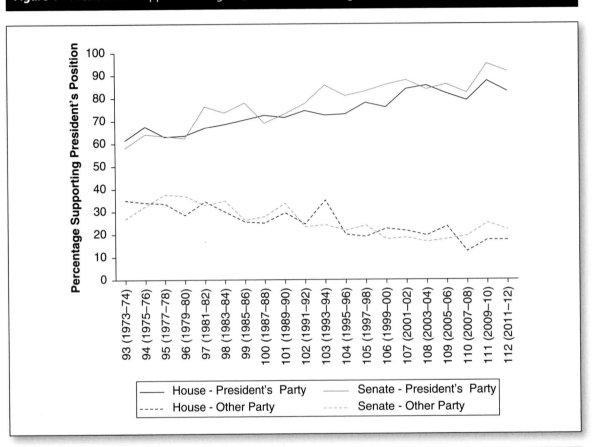

Source: Compiled by George C. Edwards III and posted at http://presdata.tamu.edu; annual scores are averaged for each 2-year Congress.

polarization of the congressional parties' respective electoral constituencies. Two major trends have given the congressional parties increasingly divergent electoral coalitions. First, the partisan, ideological, and policy views of voters have grown more internally consistent, more distinctive between parties, and more predictive of voting in national elections.[9] Second, electoral units into which voters are sorted have become more homogeneously partisan.[10] That is, over the past several decades, changes in the preferences, behavior, and distribution of

congressional voters have given the congressional parties more internally homogenous, divergent, and polarized electoral bases.

A principal source of this electoral transformation was the historic partisan realignment of the South.[11] The civil rights revolution, and particularly the Voting Rights Act of 1965, brought southern blacks into the electorate as Democrats while moving conservative whites to abandon their ancestral allegiance to the Democratic Party in favor of the ideologically and racially more compatible Republicans. In-migration also contributed to an increasingly Republican electorate, which gradually replaced conservative Democrats with conservative Republicans in southern House and Senate seats. Conservative whites outside the South also moved toward the Republican Party, while liberals became overwhelmingly Democratic. The level of consistency between party identification and ideology thus grew across the board; in 1972, self-identified liberals and conservatives identified with the "appropriate" party 71 percent of the time; in 2012, they did so 88 percent of the time.[12]

Party loyalty among congressional voters also increased over this period;[13] so the relationship between ideology and voting became much stronger. Figure 5 displays the growing proportion of self-identified liberals and diminishing proportion of self-identified conservatives voting for Democratic candidates for House and Senate in elections since 1972. The shift among conservatives is particularly notable, as is the pivotal role of the 1994 election in solidifying support for Republican candidates among conservatives. In 2012, according to the American National Election Study (ANES), 90 percent of self-identified liberals voted for Democrats in the House elections, while nearly 86 percent of conservatives voted for Republicans.

Figure 5   Ideology and Voting in Congressional Elections, 1972–2012

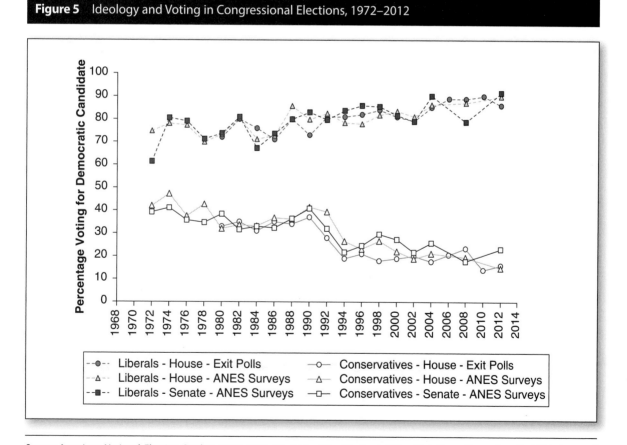

Source: American National Election Studies, 1972–2012; "Portrait of the Electorate," *New York Times*, November 13, 1994, A15; and National Exit Polls, 1996–2012.

As a consequence of these trends, the ideological leanings of the parties' respective electoral constituencies—defined as those voters who reported voting for the winning Republican and Democratic House and Senate candidates—have become increasingly divergent (Figure 6). In the 1970s, average ideological differences between the parties' electoral constituencies were modest, about 0.5 points on the ANES's 7-point liberal–conservative scale.[14] By 2012, the ideological gap had more than tripled in both chambers.[15]

The divergence of electoral constituencies is equally striking in aggregate voting data. The presidential vote in a state or district offers a serviceable measure of its relative political leanings.[16] Figure 7 displays the average difference in the share of the major party presidential vote between districts won by House Democrats and those won by Republicans in elections since 1972 (the midterm data are from the presidential election 2 years prior). Back in the early 1970s, House districts won by Democrats and Republicans differed in their average presidential vote by only about 7 percentage points, which was a low point for the postwar period. Since then, the gap has more than tripled, with most of the increase occurring since 1992. In 2012, Obama's share of the vote in districts won by Democrats was on average 26 percentage points higher than in districts won by Republicans (66 percent compared with 40 percent). A similar though less pronounced trend appears in comparable

Figure 6   Ideological Divergence of Electoral Constituencies of House and Senate Parties, 1972–2012

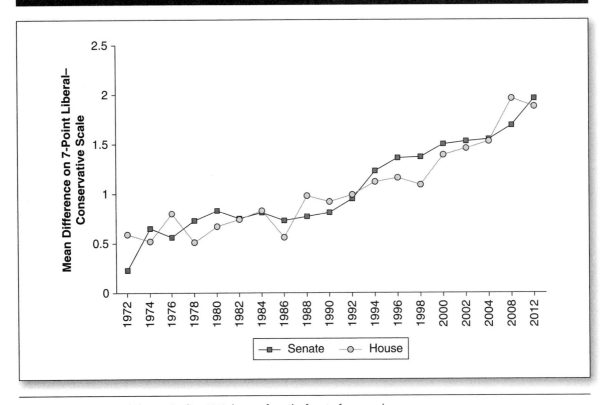

Figure 7   Difference in the Democratic Presidential Vote Between Districts Won by Democratic and Republican Representatives, 1972–2012

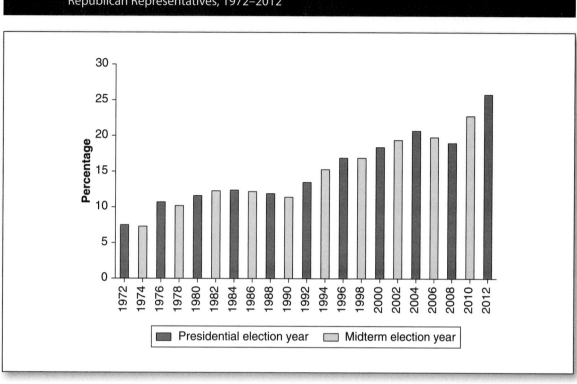

Source: Compiled by author.

Senate data (Figure 8); the divergence is smaller because states tend to be more heterogeneous, politically and otherwise, than House districts. But in both chambers, the congressional party coalitions now represent constituencies that are far more dissimilar, politically, than they were in the 1970s.

Figures 9a and 9b offer an additional perspective on this development that echoes the patterns depicted in Figures 2a and 2b. Figure 9a displays the distribution of the 1972 presidential vote (normalized as a deviation from the major-party vote for the Democrat) in the House districts won by Democrats and Republicans in the 1972 election. Figure 9b does the same for the districts won by each party's candidates in 2012. After 1972, each party's delegation represented a set of districts that were largely similar in their political leanings, although some Democrats did represent lopsidedly Democratic (largely urban and minority) districts. The Republicans and Democrats elected in 2012 represent much more politically dissimilar sets of districts. After 1972, 38 percent of House members represented districts where their party's presidential candidate's vote was below its national average; after 2012, only 6 percent did so. Comparable data from the Senate elections of 1974 and 2012 (not shown) reveal the same pattern of change toward more polarized electorates.

Figure 8 Difference in the Democratic Presidential Vote Between States Won by Democratic and Republican Senators, 1972–2012

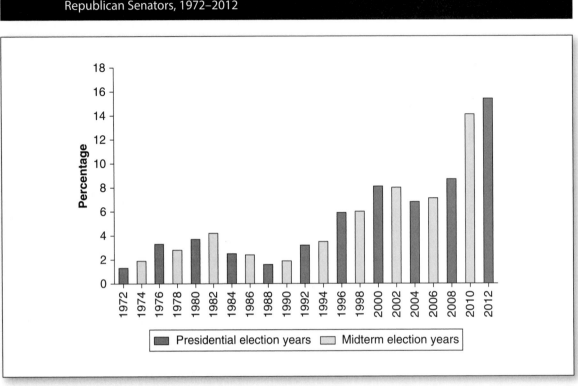

Source: Compiled by author.

Viewed together, these figures suggest a close relationship between the increasing divergence of partisans in Congress and the electorate, and the correlation coefficients listed in Table 1 provide strong support for this interpretation. The correlations over the past four decades between the two measures of House and Senate divergence (differences in average DW-NOMINATE and presidential support scores calculated from the data in Figures 1 and 4) and the two measures of constituency divergence (the ideological differences in Figure 6 and the district and state presidential vote gaps in Figures 7 and 8) are all very high, averaging 0.90.

These measures are silent about the direction of causation, but both logic and evidence point to an interactive process: Voters have sorted themselves into political camps by responding to the more sharply differentiated alternatives presented by the national parties and their candidates, while changes in roll-call voting have reflected the parties' increasingly divergent electoral coalitions.[17] Through this inherently interactive process, electoral and congressional politics have coevolved in a way that has made gridlock and stalemate increasingly likely, with consequences fully on display during the first 3 years of the Obama administration.

Figure 9a   Distribution of Democratic Presidential Vote by Party of the House Winner, 1972

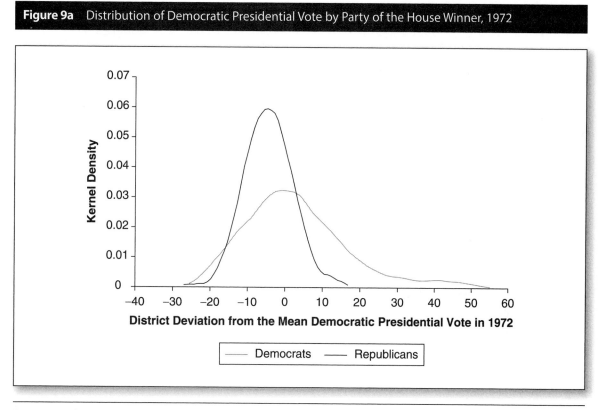

Source: Compiled by author.

Action and Gridlock During the Obama Administration

The Obama administration illustrates gridlocked politics but also the conditions under which gridlock can be broken even when partisan polarization is at a peak. During the 111th Congress, Obama pushed through a $787 billion economic stimulus package targeting the deep recession he had inherited, initiated comprehensive reforms of the nation's health care system, and signed a major redesign of financial regulation aimed at preventing a repeat of the financial meltdown that had made the recession so severe.[18] Not every major initiative

was successful—an ambitious clean energy bill died in the Senate—but these legislative achievements made the 111th Congress among the most productive in many years. What happened to gridlock?

The government managed to avoid gridlock despite the extreme partisan divisions in the House and Senate, because Democratic victories in the 2006 and 2008 elections had left them with a 257-to-178 House margin and, between July 2009 and January 2010, a 60-to-40 majority in the Senate,[19] and because a handful of moderate Republicans remained in the Senate. The Democratic House majority was large enough to pass the stimulus,

Figure 9b   Distribution of Democratic Presidential Vote by Party of the House Winner, 2012

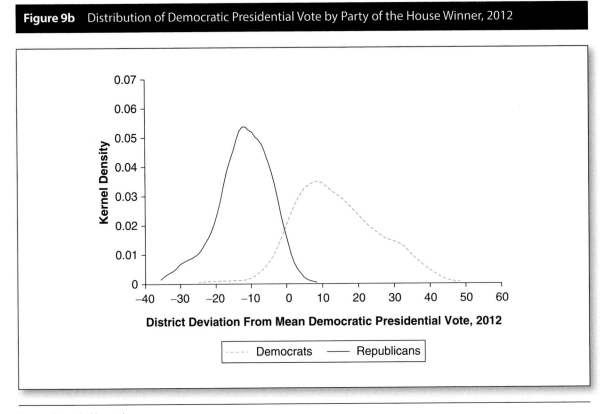

Source: Compiled by author.

health care reform, and financial regulation bills over nearly unanimous Republican opposition (no Republicans voted for the first two bills, only three for the third) despite some Democratic defections (of 7, 34, and 19 members, respectively, on the three bills).

In the Senate, the stimulus bill needed three Republican votes to overcome a filibuster because two Democratic senators were unavailable.[20] The three votes came from Arlen Specter, who left the Republican Party in April to become an independent voting organizationally with the Democrats, and the Senate's two most moderate Republicans, both from Maine: Olympia Snowe (DW-NOMINATE, 0.048) and Susan Collins (DW-NOMINATE, 0.035). The filibuster-breaking vote on health care reform in December 2009, in contrast, was a strictly party-line vote, with all 60 Democrats in favor and all 40 Republicans opposed. Democrats lost their 60th Senate vote when Republican Scott Brown won the special election for the late Ted Kennedy's Massachusetts seat in January 2010, and final enactment of health care reform in March 2010 depended on the use of a special budget reconciliation procedure that disallows filibusters.[21] Again, no Republicans voted for the bill; with three Democratic defectors, the final vote was 56 to 43. Finally, financial reform, like the stimulus bill, needed three Republican votes to reach the 60 needed for cloture (Snowe and Collins again, plus Brown).

Table 1	Electoral and Congressional Polarization, 1972–2012	

Correlations Between Congressional Party Differences in	House	Senate
DW-NOMINATE scores and local presidential vote	.96	.85
Presidential support scores and local presidential vote	.94	.75
DW-NOMINATE scores and electoral constituents' ideology	.95	.95
Presidential support scores and electoral constituents' ideology	.89	.87

The Democratic president and congressional majorities were able to act, then, not because they managed to bridge the partisan divide but because they had, for a time, sufficient votes to proceed in the face of intense Republican opposition (with a little help from the few remaining moderate Senate Republicans). And the Republican opposition was extraordinarily intense. The Obama administration made a concerted effort to win Republican votes on all these bills, especially the health care legislation, but with the few exceptions noted, completely failed. Failure was ensured by the strategy of all-out opposition to Obama that Republican congressional leaders had adopted as their ticket back to majority status. The appeal of that strategy, and its success, is a direct result of electoral realities. Republicans went with the conservatives who dominate their electoral constituencies and whose disdain for Obama preceded his presidency.[22] Any hesitation they may have

had about pursuing a deliberate gridlock strategy ended with the emergence of the raucous Tea Party movement, largely an expression of the Republican Party's extreme right wing,[23] whose members' anger and energy convinced Republican leaders that they had nothing to gain by compromise and potentially much to gain from unbending opposition.

The electoral logic and effect of this strategy can be discerned in survey data from the 2008 and 2010 Cooperative Congressional Election Studies (CCES), which provide national samples large enough to permit analyses at the House district level.[24] Regarding health care reform, the 2008 CCES asked, "Do you favor or oppose the U.S. government guaranteeing health insurance for all citizens, even if it means raising taxes?" About 62 percent of respondents said they supported the idea, and 38 percent opposed it; so it was generally popular at the time. Partisan divisions were substantial, however, with 88 percent of Democrats, 61 percent of independents, and only 23 percent of Republicans supporting such a plan. More important, the distribution of opinion across House voters and districts provided little reason for congressional Republicans to support such a policy. Figure 10 displays the distribution of district-level opinion on the health care question among four sets of respondents: The dotted lines show the distribution of opinion among all constituents across the set of districts won in 2008 by Republicans (black) or Democrats (gray). The solid lines show the distributions for those respondents who said they voted for the Republican or Democratic winner—that is, the voters who formed the electoral constituencies of each party's House delegation. Taken as a whole, the two parties' constituencies differed only modestly on this question; in the median Democratic district, 65 percent of respondents supported this kind of health care reform; in the median Republican district, it was 58 percent. The parties' electoral constituencies, in contrast, were thoroughly polarized on the issue; a large majority of House Democrats' electoral constituencies strongly favored the idea, while few of the Republicans' electoral constituencies gave it more

Figure 10   Distribution of Opinions on Health Care Reform Across U.S. House Districts, 2008

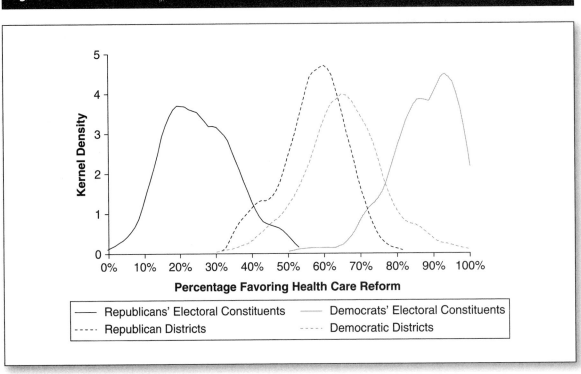

Source: 2008 Cooperation Congressional Election Study.

than minimal support. Partisan divisions that emerged in Congress on the health care issue were thus firmly rooted in the opinions of those constituents whose opinions matter most to reelection-oriented representatives.

The fierce partisan debate over the health care bill in the months leading up to final passage in 2010 left the public thoroughly divided on its virtues. Ordinary Republicans remained as opposed to the idea as they had been in 2008, while its support dropped a few points among Democrats and quite substantially among independents, which proved costly to Democrats on Election Day.[25] Obamacare was a prime target of the Republicans' 2010 campaigns, which won a 242-to-193 Republican House majority and reduced the

Democrats' Senate majority by 6, to 53 to 47, for the 112th Congress. The election left the House parties' bases even further apart on health care than they had been in 2008 (Figure 11). The average difference between Republican and Democratic districts grew from 8 points to 14 points; the difference between electoral constituencies, from 62 points to 75 points. It is thus no surprise that the first bill the House Republican leadership introduced in the 112th Congress was to repeal the health care reform law; nor is it a surprise that it passed the House but was not even taken up by the Senate. Republicans subsequently made more than 50 equally futile attempts to repeal or dismantle Obamacare during the 112th and 113th Congresses. Even after the rocky roll-out of the health insurance

Figure 11   Distribution of Support for Obama's Health Care Reform Legislation Across House Districts, 2010

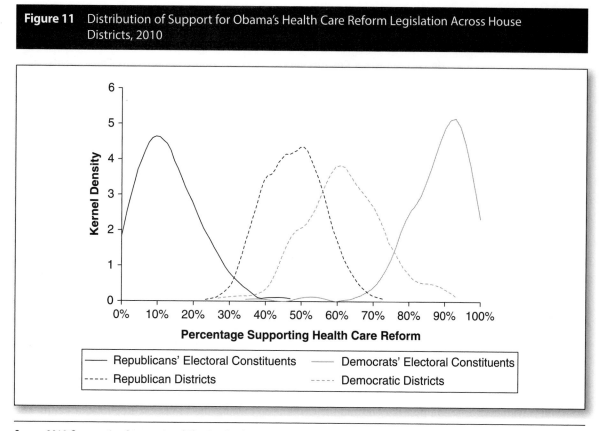

Source: 2010 Cooperative Congressional Election Study.

exchanges in late 2013, Senate Democrats blocked any changes opposed by the administration, and Obama would certainly have vetoed any that might have passed. Gridlock prevailed, preserving the new status quo. At this writing, it remains to be seen whether the new Republican majority in the Senate following the 2014 elections will be able to circumvent Democratic obstruction to its plans to repeal the health care reform law.

Health care reform generated the widest differences of opinion among the congressional parties' constituencies, but they were also sharply divided on most other items on Obama's legislative agenda. Table 2 lists the distribution of responses to 2010 CCES questions concerning support for seven of his

major initiatives that were subject to roll-call votes in the House.[26] The table distinguishes not only electoral constituents from all constituents but also, within electoral constituencies, the respective parties' primary constituencies, defined as those who voted for the winning candidate and who had also said they participated in the winner's party's primary in 2010. The threat of primary challenges to members who stray too far from party orthodoxy is thought to be one source of partisan intransigence in Congress, because primaries are low-turnout affairs that attract a disproportionate share of strong partisans and ideologues.[27] This view is supported by the CCES data, particularly for Republicans. On average across these agenda items, the House parties' full

Table 2   Constituents' Support for Obama's Agenda (in Percentages)

	House Democrats' Constituents			House Republicans' Constituents		
	Primary	**Electoral**	**All**	**All**	**Electoral**	**Primary**
Health care reform	91	88	61	48	13	7
Economic stimulus	87	85	60	48	14	8
Clean energy	89	86	66	56	25	17
Repeal "Don't Ask, Don't Tell"	86	84	67	59	35	28
Financial reform	96	95	75	68	44	36
Stem cell research	90	87	69	48	43	35
Children's health insurance	95	94	77	71	47	40
Average	91	88	68	57	32	24
Average number supported	6.4	6.2	4.7	4.1	2.2	1.7

Source: 2010 Cooperative Congressional Election Study; weighted Ns range from 3,972 to 20,593.

constituencies are only 9 points apart, while their electoral constituencies are 56 points apart and their primary constituencies 67 points apart.

The message in these data is that insofar as members of Congress faithfully represent the views of the people who put and keep them in office, sharp partisan divisions on roll-call votes will be the norm. The intransigence that produces gridlock is evidence of individual responsiveness and collective responsibility—to the people and parties who actually elect members, if not to their broader constituencies or to the nation as a whole. It is thus no surprise that the 2010 elections, which resulted in House and Senate majorities with unusually disparate electoral bases and thus disparate locations on the ideological spectrum, ushered in a period of spectacular gridlock on budgets, deficits, and other issues regarding the scope of government, for these are issues that fundamentally divide the parties' electoral coalitions.

The 2010 election reinstituted divided government, putting the House in Republican hands and leaving the Democratic Senate majority well short of the 60 votes needed to overcome a filibuster; the 2012 election left that configuration unchanged. The resulting sharp increase in the prospects for legislative gridlock after 2010 is illustrated by the data in Table 3 and Figure 12. The table lists the DW-NOMINATE scores for key locations in the legislative process in the 111th and 112th Congresses: President Obama,[28] the median members of the House and Senate, the Senate Republican filibuster pivot (the one 41st from the most conservative end of the spectrum), and the chambers' veto pivots (the Democrats ranked 34th and 190th from the liberal end of the spectrum in, respectively, the Senate and House, who would presumably vote to sustain a veto of any legislation to their ideological right). The list also includes the median member of the majority party in the House, another key participant according

Table 3 Ideological Location of the Parties in the 111th and 112th Congresses

DW-NOMINATE Score	111th Congress	112th Congress
Barack Obama	−0.363	−0.363
House median	−0.198	0.446
House majority party median	−0.370	0.661
House veto pivot	−0.347	−0.329
Senate median	−0.263	−0.186
Senate Republican filibuster pivot	−0.021	0.294
Senate Democratic filibuster pivot	−0.309	−0.276
Senate veto pivot	−0.380	−0.315

Source: Compiled by author.

to the "party cartel" theory, which posits that the House majority uses agenda control to keep any bill off the floor if it is not supported by a majority of the majority members.[29] Figure 12 displays the differences in the ideological locations of the key participants in each of the two Congresses.

The election brought a huge increase in the ideological distance between the House and Senate medians; the gap is even larger under the party cartel scenario, where the House majority-party median is supposed to be decisive. The distances between both the House floor and majority-party medians and the opposite-party Senate filibuster pivot also grew dramatically, as did the distance between the two Senate filibuster pivots. Clearly, the range of changes in the status quo that would be blocked by one chamber or the other and within the Senate greatly increased after 2010. The same is true for Obama and the

House, particularly under the party cartel scenario. The ideological distance between the president and the median Senator grew only modestly, but the gap between the president and the Republican filibuster pivot became much wider. The ideological location at which the president's veto would be overridden moved a bit rightward but remained well to the left of center; even if Republicans had taken the Senate as well as the House in 2010 or 2012, they would have found it impossible to repeal the health care or financial regulation bills over Obama's objection. The gaps between the House and Senate medians, the Senate parties' filibuster pivots, and the president and the House floor and party medians were all the widest since at least the 93rd Congress.

These dramatically enlarged gridlock intervals severely reduced range of possible agreements on departures from the status quo. Only where the failure to agree would result not in continuation of the status quo but in an outcome completely unacceptable to large majorities on both sides—for example, no budget and hence no money to keep the government running, or no increase in the debt ceiling and hence a default on government bonds and chaos in the financial markets—could important legislation pass during the 112th and 113th Congresses. And even in these cases, the process was unusually ugly. Thus, the partisan disputes over taxes, spending, and deficits that brought the U.S. government to the brink of paper insolvency in the summer of 2011, for example, unified the public on at least one thing: disdain for Congress. Public comments on the process were scathing, with "ridiculous," "disgusting," and "stupid" topping the list of one-word descriptions reported in a July 2011 Pew survey.[30] In surveys taken through the rest of the year, disapproval of Congress's performance averaged 83 percent and approval 12 percent. Minority leader Nancy Pelosi remarked on *The Daily Show*, "You wonder who are these people who approve of Congress?"[31] Disapproval of Congress was even higher (85 percent) after the government shutdown in October of 2013, and the sentiment was thoroughly bipartisan.[32] It was also predictable; Americans invariably say they detest the kind of partisan bickering and

Figure 12   Ideological Distances Between Key Participants, 111th and 112th Congresses

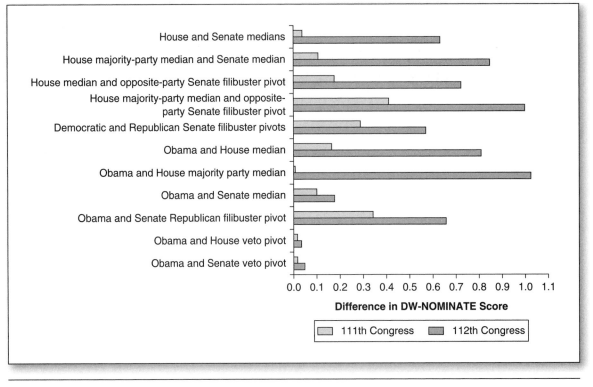

Source: Compiled by author.

stalemate epitomized by the showdowns and stop-gap measures arising in the 112th and 113th Congresses from unresolved fights over the nation's finances.[33] The irony is that the divisive politics and partisan gridlock they condemn are largely the products of their own electoral decisions and of the winners' fidelity to the people who put them in Congress.

Notes

1. Samuel Kernell, Gary C. Jacobson, and Thad Kousser, *The Logic of American Politics*, 5th ed. (Washington, DC: CQ Press, 2012), 22–26.

2. Charles Stewart III, *Analyzing Congress* (New York: Norton), 80.

3. Ibid.; Keith Krehbiel, *Pivotal Politics: A Theory of U.S. Lawmaking* (Chicago: University of Chicago Press, 1998); Sarah H. Binder, *Stalemate: Causes and Consequences of Legislative Gridlock* (Washington, DC: Brookings Institution, 2003); and David W. Brady and Craig Volden, *Revolving Gridlock: Politics and Policy From Jimmy Carter to George W. Bush*, 2nd ed. (Boulder, CO: Westview Press, 2006).

4. For an explanation of the methodology for computing these scores and justification for their interpretation as measures of liberal–conservative ideology, see Nolan M. McCarty, Keith T. Poole, and Howard Rosenthal, *Income Redistribution and the Realignment of American Politics* (Washington, DC: American Enterprise Institute Press, 1997); and Keith

T. Poole and Howard Rosenthal, *Congress: A Political History of Roll Call Voting* (New York: Oxford University Press, 1997), Chapters 3 and 11. The data used here are from Keith T. Poole, "The Polarization of the Congressional Parties," updated January 19, 2014, http://voteview.com/political_polarization.asp (accessed July 12, 2011).

5. The apparent overlap in Figure 2d is an artifact of the kernel density estimator; the most conservative Senate Democrat had a DW-NOMINATE score of −0.014, the most liberal Republican, 0.035.

6. Gary C. Jacobson, *The Politics of Congressional Elections*, 8th ed. (New York: Pearson, 2012), 261–262.

7. Barbara Sinclair, *Unorthodox Lawmaking: New Legislative Processes in the U.S. Congress*, 4th ed. (Washington, DC: CQ Press, 2012), 141–165.

8. For a lucid and thorough account, see Barbara Sinclair, *Party Wars: Polarization and the Politics of National Policy Making* (Norman: University of Oklahoma Press, 2006).

9. Gary C. Jacobson, "The Electoral Basis of Partisan Polarization in Congress," presented at the Annual Meeting of the American Political Science Association, Washington, DC, August 31–September 3, 2000; Larry M. Bartels, "Partisanship and Voting Behavior, 1952–1996," *American Journal of Political Science* 44 (January 2000): 35–50.

10. Jeffrey M. Stonecash, Mark D. Brewer, and Mach D. Mariani, *Diverging Parties: Social Change, Realignment, and Party Polarization* (Boulder, CO: Westview Press, 2003); Gary C. Jacobson, *The Politics of Congressional Elections*, 6th ed. (New York: Longman, 2004), 236–243; Matthew Levendusky, *The Partisan Sort: How Liberals Became Democrats and Conservatives Became Republicans* (Chicago: University of Chicago Press, 2009), 38–77; and Alan I. Abramowitz, *The Disappearing Center: Engaged Citizens, Polarization, and American Democracy* (New Haven, CT: Yale University Press, 2010), 34–61.

11. Earle Black and Merle Black, *Politics and Society in the South* (Cambridge, MA: Harvard University Press, 1987); Paul Frymer, "The 1994 Aftershock: Dealignment or Realignment in the South," in *Midterm: The Elections of 1994 in Context*, ed. Philip A. Klinkner (Boulder, CO: Westview Press, 1995), 99–113; Richard Nadeau and Harold W. Stanley, "Class Polarization Among Native Southern Whites, 1952–90," *American Journal of Political Science* 37 (August 1993): 900–919; M. V. Hood III, Quentin Kidd, and Irwin L. Morris, "Of Byrd[s] and Bumpers: Using Democratic Senators to Analyze Political Change in the South, 1960–1995," *American Journal of Political Science* 43 (April 1999): 465–487; Martin P. Wattenberg, "The Building of a Republican Regional Base in the South: The Elephant Crosses the Mason-Dixon Line," *Public Opinion Quarterly* 55 (1991): 424–431; and Charles S. Bullock III, Donna R. Hoffman, and Ronald Keith Gaddie, "The Consolidation of the White Southern Congressional Vote," *Political Research Quarterly* 58 (June 2005): 231–243.

12. Based on analysis of data in the American National Election Study Cumulative Data File and the 2012 American National Election Study (face-to-face component).

13. Jacobson, *Politics of Congressional Elections*, 19–120.

14. The scale points are as follows: extremely liberal, liberal, slightly liberal, middle-of-the-road, slightly conservative, conservative, and extremely conservative.

15. Realignment in the South explains only part of this change, since the gap between Republican and Democratic constituencies outside the South also grew (from 0.7 to 1.6 points in the House, from 0.6 to 1.4 in the Senate).

16. Relative because the large differences between election years produced by the ups and downs of party fortunes in presidential elections have to be factored out of the measurement.

17. Gary C. Jacobson, "Polarization in National Politics: The Electoral Connection," in *Polarized Politics: Congress and the President in a Partisan Era*, ed. Jon R. Bond and Richard Fleisher (Washington, DC: CQ Press, 2000), 25–28. Statistical analysis also indicates reciprocal causation; Granger causation tests find significant effects in both directions for three of the four House pairings; in the four Senate pairings, one or the other causal direction is significant (at p < .10 or better), but the direction varies.

18. The specific bills were the American Recovery and Reinvestment Act of 2009, signed into law on February 17, 2009; the Patient Protection and Affordable Care Act, signed on March 22, 2010; and

the Dodd–Frank Wall Street Reform and Consumer Protection Act, signed on July 21, 2010.

19. The Democratic total includes two independents who voted to organize with the Democrats.

20. Ted Kennedy of Massachusetts because of illness, Al Franken of Minnesota because his disputed election kept him from taking his seat until July 7.

21. Sinclair, *Unorthodox Lawmaking*, 210–230.

22. Gary C. Jacobson, "Obama and the Polarized Public," in *Obama in Office: the First Two Years*, ed. James A. Thurber (Boulder, CO: Paradigm, 2011), 19–40.

23. Gary C. Jacobson, "The President, the Tea Party, and the Voting Behavior in 2010: Insights From the Cooperative Congressional Election Study," presented at the Annual Meeting of the American Political Science Association, Seattle, Washington, September 1–4, 2011.

24. The 2008 CCES included 32,800 respondents, and the 2010 CCES, 55,399 respondents; for details on these surveys, see Stephen Ansolabehere, "Guide to the 2008 Cooperative Congressional Elections Survey," Harvard University, 2009; Stephen Ansolabehere, *Cooperative Congressional Election Study, 2010: Common Content* [computer file], Release 1, May 17, 2011, Cambridge, MA, Harvard University, http://projects.iq.harvard.edu/cces.

25. Jacobson, "Obama and the Polarized Public," 31.

26. Except for the stem cell bill, which was never brought to a vote.

27. Levendusky, *Partisan Sort*, 135–136.

28. The president's DW-NOMINATE score is calculated from his stated positions, if any, on bills before Congress.

29. Gary W. Cox and Mathew D. McCubbins, *Setting the Agenda: Responsible Party Government in the U.S. House of Representatives* (New York: Cambridge University Press, 2005), 37–49; and "Agenda Power in the House of Representatives, 1877–1986," in *Party, Process, and Political Change in Congress: New Perspectives on the History of Congress*, ed. David W. Brady and Mathew D. McCubbins (Stanford, CA: Stanford University Press, 2002), 113–118.

30. Pew Research Center for the People and the Press, "Pew Research Center/*Washington Post* July 28–31, 2011 Omnibus: Final Topline," http://people-press.org/files/legacy-questionnaires/08-1-11%20Topline%20For%20Release.pdf.

31. *The Daily Show With Jon Stewart*, broadcast November 9, 2011, http://www.thedailyshow.com/watch/wed-november-9-2011/nancy-pelosi.

32. The question was asked in 21 surveys between August and December 2011 and in 10 surveys between October and November 2013; see "Congress—Job Rating," *PollingReport.com*, http://www.pollingreport.com/CongJob.htm (accessed April 10, 2014); Frank Newport, "Congressional Approval Sinks to Record Low," *Gallup*, November 12, 2013, http://www.gallup.com/poll/165809/congressional-approval-sinks-record-low.aspx (accessed April 10, 2013).

33. John R. Hibbing and Elizabeth Theiss-Morse, *Congress as Public Enemy: Public Attitudes Toward American Political Institutions* (New York: Cambridge University Press, 1995), 16–20.

11-3 America's Ignorant Voters

Michael Schudson

The meagerness of the average American's political knowledge has dismayed observers for decades. But Michael Schudson asks whether the informed citizen—meaning one who knows basic facts about government and politics—is truly the foundation of effective democracy. Reviewing the evidence, Schudson argues, contrary to conventional wisdom, that the problem is not growing worse. Moreover, voters may not recall many facts but still be able to vote in a way that reflects reasonable evaluations of candidates and parties.

Every week, the *Tonight Show's* Jay Leno takes to the streets of Los Angeles to quiz innocent passersby with some simple questions: On what bay is San Francisco located? Who was president of the United States during World War II? The audience roars as Leno's hapless victims fumble for answers. Was it Lincoln? Carter?

No pollster, let alone a college or high school history teacher, would be surprised by the poor showing of Leno's sample citizens. In a national assessment test in the late 1980s, only a third of American 17-year-olds could correctly locate the Civil War in the period 1850–1900; more than a quarter placed it in the 18th century. Two-thirds knew that Abraham Lincoln wrote the Emancipation Proclamation, which seems a respectable showing, but what about the 14 percent who said that Lincoln wrote the Bill of Rights, the 10 percent who checked the Missouri Compromise, and the nine percent who awarded Lincoln royalties for *Uncle Tom's Cabin?*

Asking questions about contemporary affairs doesn't yield any more encouraging results. In a 1996 national public opinion poll, only 10 percent of American adults could identify William Rehnquist as the chief justice of the Supreme Court. In the same survey, conducted at the height of Newt Gingrich's celebrity as Speaker of the House, only 59 percent could identify the job he held. Americans sometimes demonstrate deeper knowledge about a major issue before the nation, such as the Vietnam War, but most could not describe the thrust of the Clinton health care plan or tell whether the Reagan administration supported the Sandinistas or the contras during the conflict in Nicaragua (and only a third could place that country in Central America).

It can be misleading to make direct comparisons with other countries, but the general level of political awareness in leading liberal democracies overseas does seem to be much higher. While 58 percent of the Germans surveyed, 32 percent of the French, and 22 percent of the British were able to identify Boutros Boutros-Ghali as secretary general of the United Nations in 1994, only 13 percent of Americans could do so. Nearly all Germans polled could name Boris Yeltsin as Russia's leader, as could 63 percent of the British, 61 percent of the French, but only 50 percent of the Americans.

How can the United States claim to be [a] model democracy if its citizens know so little about political life? That question has aroused political reformers and preoccupied many political scientists since the early 20th century. It can't be answered without some historical perspective.

Source: Michael Schudson, "America's Ignorant Voters", originally published in *The Wilson Quarterly*, Vol. 24, No. 2, Spring, 2000.

Today's mantra that the "informed citizen" is the foundation of effective democracy was not a central part of the nation's founding vision. It is largely the creation of late-19th-century Mugwump and Progressive reformers, who recoiled from the spectacle of powerful political parties using government as a job bank for their friends and a cornucopia of contracts for their relatives. (In those days before the National Endowment for the Arts, Nathaniel Hawthorne, Herman Melville, and Walt Whitman all subsidized their writing by holding down federal patronage appointments.) Voter turnout in the late 19th century was extraordinarily high by today's standards, routinely over 70 percent in presidential elections, and there is no doubt that parades, free whiskey, free-floating money, patronage jobs, and the pleasures of fraternity all played a big part in the political enthusiasm of ordinary Americans.

The reformers saw this kind of politics as a betrayal of democratic ideals. A democratic public, they believed, must reason together. That ideal was threatened by mindless enthusiasm, the wily maneuvers of political machines, and the vulnerability of the new immigrant masses in the nation's big cities, woefully ignorant of Anglo-Saxon traditions, to manipulation by party hacks. E. L. Godkin, founding editor of the *Nation* and a leading reformer, argued that "there is no corner of our system in which the hastily made and ignorant foreign voter may not be found eating away the political structure, like a white ant, with a group of natives standing over him and encouraging him."

This was in 1893, by which point a whole set of reforms had been put in place. Civil service reform reduced patronage. Ballot reform irrevocably altered the act of voting itself. For most of the 19th century, parties distributed at the polls their own "tickets," listing only their own candidates for office. A voter simply took a ticket from a party worker and deposited it in the ballot box, without needing to read it or mark it in any way. Voting was thus a public act of party affiliation. Beginning in 1888, however, and spreading across the country by 1896, this system was replaced with government-printed ballots that listed all the candidates from each eligible party. The voter marked the ballot in secret, as we do today, in an act that affirmed voting as an individual choice rather than a social act of party loyalty. Political parades and other public spectacles increasingly gave way to pamphlets in what reformers dubbed "educational" political campaigns. Leading newspapers, once little more than organs of the political parties, began to declare their independence and to portray themselves as nonpartisan commercial institutions of public enlightenment and public-minded criticism. Public secondary education began to spread.

These and other reforms enshrined the informed citizen as the foundation of democracy, but at a tremendous cost: Voter turnout plummeted. In the presidential election of 1920, it dropped to 49 percent, its lowest point in the 20th century—until it was matched in 1996. Ever since, political scientists and others have been plumbing the mystery created by the new model of an informed citizenry: How can so many, knowing so little, and voting in such small numbers, build a democracy that appears to be (relatively) successful?

There are several responses to that question. The first is that a certain amount of political ignorance is an inevitable byproduct of America's unique political environment. One reason Americans have so much difficulty grasping the political facts of life is that their political system is the world's most complex. Ask the next political science Ph.D. you meet to explain what government agencies at what level—federal, state, county, or city—take responsibility for the homeless. Or whom he or she voted for in the last election for municipal judge. The answers might make Jay Leno's victims seem less ridiculous. No European country has as many elections, as many elected offices, as complex a maze of overlapping governmental jurisdictions, as the American system. It is simply harder to "read" U.S. politics than the politics of most nations.

The hurdle of political comprehension is raised a notch higher by the ideological inconsistencies of American political parties. In Britain, a voter can confidently cast a vote without knowing a great deal about the particular candidates on the ballot. The Labor candidate generally can be counted on to follow the Labor line, the Conservative to follow the Tory line. An American voter casting a ballot for a Democrat or Republican has no such assurance. Citizens in other countries need only dog paddle to be in the political swim; in the United States they need the skills of a scuba diver.

If the complexity of U.S. political institutions helps explain American ignorance of domestic politics, geopolitical factors help explain American backwardness in foreign affairs. There is a kind of ecology of political ignorance at work. The United States is far from Europe and borders only two other countries. With a vast domestic market, most of its producers have relatively few dealings with customers in other countries, globalization notwithstanding. Americans, lacking the parliamentary form of government that prevails in most other democracies, are also likely to find much of what they read or hear about the wider world politically opaque. And the simple fact of America's political and cultural superpower status naturally limits citizens' political awareness. Just as employees gossip more about the boss than the boss gossips about them, so Italians and Brazilians know more about the United States than Americans know about their countries.

Consider a thought experiment. Imagine what would happen if you transported those relatively well-informed Germans or Britons to the United States with their cultural heritage, schools, and news media intact. If you checked on them again about a generation later, after long exposure to the distinctive American political environment—its geographic isolation, superpower status, complex political system, and weak parties—would they have the political knowledge levels of Europeans or Americans? Most likely, I think, they would have developed typically American levels of political ignorance.

Lending support to this notion of an ecology of political knowledge is the stability of American political ignorance over time. Since the 1940s, when social scientists began measuring it, political

ignorance has remained virtually unchanged. It is hard to gauge the extent of political knowledge before that time, but there is little to suggest that there is some lost golden age in U.S. history. The storied 1858 debates between Senator Stephen Douglas and Abraham Lincoln, for example, though undoubtedly a high point in the nation's public discourse, were also an anomaly. Public debates were rare in 19th-century political campaigns, and campaign rhetoric was generally overblown and aggressively partisan.

Modern measurements of Americans' historical and political knowledge go back at least to 1943, when the *New York Times* surveyed college freshmen and found "a striking ignorance of even the most elementary aspects of United States history." Reviewing nearly a half-century of data (1945–89) in *What Americans Know about Politics and Why It Matters* (1996), political scientists Michael Delli Carpini and Scott Keeter conclude that, on balance, there has been a slight gain in Americans' political knowledge, but one so modest that it makes more sense to speak of a remarkable stability. In 1945, for example, 43 percent of a national sample could name neither of their U.S. senators; in 1989, the figure was essentially unchanged at 45 percent. In 1952, 67 percent could name the vice president; in 1989, 74 percent could do so. In 1945, 92 percent of Gallup poll respondents knew that the term of the president is four years, compared with 96 percent in 1989. Whatever the explanations for dwindling voter turnout since 1960 may be, rising ignorance is not one of them.

As Delli Carpini and Keeter suggest, there are two ways to view their findings. The optimist's view is that political ignorance has grown no worse despite the spread of television and video games, the decline of political parties, and a variety of other negative developments. The pessimist asks why so little has improved despite the vast increase in formal education during those years. But the main conclusion remains: no notable change over as long a period as data are available.

Low as American levels of political knowledge may be, a generally tolerable, sometimes admirable, political democracy survives. How? One explanation is provided by a school of political science that goes under the banner of "political heuristics." Public opinion polls and paper-and-pencil tests of political knowledge, argue researchers such as Arthur Lupia, Samuel Popkin, Paul Sniderman, and Philip Tetlock, presume that citizens require more knowledge than they actually need in order to cast votes that accurately reflect their preferences. People can and do get by with relatively little political information. What Popkin calls "low-information rationality" is sufficient for citizens to vote intelligently.

This works in two ways. First, people can use cognitive cues, or "heuristics." Instead of learning each of a candidate's issue positions, the voter may simply rely on the candidate's party affiliation as a cue. This works better in Europe than in America, but it still works reasonably well. Endorsements are another useful shortcut. A thumbs-up for a candidate from the Christian Coalition or Ralph Nader or the National Association for the Advancement of Colored People or the American Association of Retired Persons frequently provides enough information to enable one to cast a reasonable vote.

Second, as political scientist Milton Lodge points out, people often process information on the fly, without retaining details in memory. If you watch a debate on TV—and 46 million did watch the first presidential debate between President Bill Clinton and Robert Dole in 1996—you may learn enough about the candidates' ideas and personal styles to come to a judgment about each one. A month later, on election day, you may not be able to answer a pollster's detailed questions about where they stood on the issues, but you will remember which one you liked best—and that is enough information to let you vote intelligently.

The realism of the political heuristics school is an indispensable corrective to unwarranted bashing of the general public. Americans are not the political dolts they sometimes seem to be. Still, the political heuristics approach has a potentially fatal flaw: It subtly substitutes voting for citizenship. Cognitive shortcuts have their place, but what if a citizen wants to persuade someone else to vote for his or her chosen candidate? What may be sufficient in the voting booth is inadequate in the wider world of the democratic process: discussion, deliberation, and persuasion. It is possible to vote and still be disenfranchised.

Yet another response to the riddle of voter ignorance takes its cue from the Founders and other 18th-century political thinkers who emphasized the importance of a morally virtuous citizenry. Effective democracy, in this view, depends more on the "democratic character" of citizens than on their aptitude for quiz show knowledge of political facts. Character, in this sense, is demonstrated all the time in everyday life, not in the voting booth every two years. From Amitai Etzioni, William Galston, and Michael Sandel on the liberal side of the political spectrum to William J. Bennett and James Q. Wilson on the conservative side, these writers emphasize the importance of what Alexis de Tocqueville called "habits of the heart." These theorists, along with politicians of every stripe, point to the importance of civil society as a foundation of democracy. They emphasize instilling moral virtue through families and civic participation through churches and other voluntary associations; they stress the necessity for civility and democratic behavior in daily life. They would not deny that it is important for citizens to be informed, but neither would they put information at the center of their vision of what makes democracy tick.

Brown University's Nancy Rosenblum, for example, lists two essential traits of democratic character. "Easy spontaneity" is the disposition to treat others identically, without deference, and with an easy grace. This capacity to act as if many social differences are of no account in public settings is one of the things that make[s] democracy happen on the streets. This is the disposition that foreign visitors have regularly labeled "American" for 200 years, at least since 1818, when the British reformer and journalist William Cobbett remarked upon Americans' "universal civility." Tocqueville observed in 1840 that strangers in America who meet "find neither danger nor advantage in telling each other freely what they think. Meeting by chance, they neither seek nor avoid each other. Their manner is therefore natural, frank, and open."

Rosenblum's second trait is "speaking up," which she describes as "a willingness to respond at least minimally to ordinary injustice." This does not involve anything so impressive as organizing a demonstration, but something more like objecting when an adult cuts ahead of a kid in a line at a movie theater, or politely rebuking a coworker who slurs a racial or religious group. It is hard to define "speaking up" precisely, but we all recognize it, without necessarily giving it the honor it deserves as an element of self-government. . . .

The Founding Fathers were certainly more concerned about instilling moral virtues than disseminating information about candidates and issues. Although they valued civic engagement more than their contemporaries in Europe did, and cared enough about promoting the wide circulation of ideas to establish a post office and adopt the First Amendment, they were ambivalent about, even suspicious of, a politically savvy populace. They did not urge voters to "know the issues"; at most they hoped that voters would choose wise and prudent legislators to consider issues on their behalf. On the one hand, they agreed that "the diffusion of knowledge is productive of virtue, and the best security for our civil rights," as a North Carolina congressman put it in 1792. On the other hand, as George Washington cautioned, "however necessary it may be to keep a watchful eye over public servants and public measures, yet there ought to be limits to it, for suspicions unfounded and jealousies too lively are irritating to honest feelings, and oftentimes are productive of more evil than good."

If men were angels, well and good—but they were not, and few of the Founders were as extravagant as Benjamin Rush in his rather scary vision of an education that would "convert men into republican machines." In theory, many shared Rush's emphasis on education; in practice, the states made little provision for public schooling in the early years of the Republic. Where schools did develop, they were defended more as tutors of obedience and organs of national unity than as means to create a watchful citizenry. The Founders placed trust less in education than in a political system designed to insulate decision making in the legislatures from the direct influence of the emotional, fractious, and too easily swayed electorate.

All of these arguments—about America's political environment, the value of political heuristics, and civil society—do not add up to a prescription for resignation or complacency about civic education. Nothing I have said suggests that the League of Women Voters should shut its doors or that newspaper editors should stop putting politics on page one. People may be able to vote intelligently with very little information—even well educated people do exactly that on most of the ballot issues they face—but democratic citizenship means more than voting. It means discussing and debating the questions before the political community—and sometimes raising new questions. Without a framework of information in which to place them, it is hard to understand even the simple slogans and catchwords of the day. People with scant political knowledge, as research by political scientists Samuel Popkin and Michael Dimock suggests, have more difficulty than others in perceiving differences between candidates and parties. Ignorance also tends to breed more ignorance; it inhibits people from venturing into situations that make them feel uncomfortable or inadequate, from the voting booth to the community forum to the town hall.

What is to be done? First, it is important to put the problem in perspective. American political ignorance is not growing worse. There is even an "up" side to Americans' relative indifference to political and historical facts: their characteristic openness to experiment, their pragmatic willingness to judge ideas and practices by their results rather than their pedigree.

Second, it pays to examine more closely the ways in which people do get measurably more knowledgeable. One of the greatest changes Delli Carpini and Keeter found in their study, for example, was in the percentage of Americans who could identify the first 10 amendments to the Constitution as the Bill of Rights. In 1954, the year the U.S. Supreme Court declared school segregation unconstitutional in *Brown v. Board of Education,* only 31 percent of Americans could do so. In 1989, the number had moved up to 46 percent.

Why the change? I think the answer is clear: The civil rights movement, along with the rights-oriented Warren Court, helped bring rights to the forefront of the American political agenda and thus to public consciousness. Because they dominated the political agenda, rights became a familiar topic in the press and on TV dramas, sitcoms, and talk shows, also finding their way into school curricula and textbooks. Political change, this experience shows, can influence public knowledge.

This is not to say that only a social revolution can bring about such an improvement. A lot of revolutions are small, one person at a time, one classroom at a time. But it does mean that there is no magic bullet. Indeed, imparting political knowledge has only become more difficult as the dimensions of what is considered political have expanded into what were once nonpolitical domains (such as gender relations and tobacco use), as one historical narrative has become many, each of them contentious, and as the relatively simple framework of world politics (the Cold War) has disappeared.

In this world, the ability to name the three branches of government or describe the New Deal does not make a citizen, but it is at least a token of membership in a society dedicated to the ideal of self-government. Civic education is an imperative we must pursue with the full recognition that a high level of ignorance is likely to prevail—even if that fact does not flatter our faith in rationalism, our pleasure in moralizing, or our confidence in reform.

11-4 U.S. Presidential Election Forecasting: Want a Better Forecast? Measure the Campaign, Not Just the Economy

Lynn Vavreck

Explaining election outcomes is a major industry for pollsters and political scientists. Presidential outcomes draw the most attention. More often than not, explanations place heavy emphasis on the state of the economy. In 2012, the Republican candidate for president, Mitt Romney, campaigned in a manner that seemed to fit the pattern— he emphasized that the economic recovery was too slow under incumbent Democrat Barack Obama. In this essay, political scientist Lynn Vavreck argues that Romney miscalculated. As the economy gradually improved after the Great Recession of 2008 and 2009, pivotal voters saw the economy as improving and blamed any weakness on Obama's predecessor. The result was that Romney failed to find a way to voters who would determine the outcome, and Obama won. Romney's campaign mattered to the outcome—in this case, with negative consequences for Romney.

On February 4, 2012, at a victory rally in Las Vegas, Nevada, Mitt Romney foreshadowed the future of the 2012 general election campaign:

> Three years ago, a newly elected President Obama told America that if Congress approved his plan to borrow nearly a trillion dollars, he would hold unemployment below 8%. It hasn't been below 8% since. This week he's been trying to take a bow for 8.3% unemployment. Not so fast, Mr. President . . . if you take into account all the people who are struggling for work or who have just stopped looking, the real unemployment rate is over 15%. (Romney 2012)

By almost any measure, the topic most discussed by the candidates in the 2012 presidential election was jobs. From the lack of jobs, to the creation of jobs, to the number of jobs shipped overseas, both candidates spent a good deal of time telling voters about the state of the nation's economy vis-à-vis the number of jobs in America. But as Romney focused on what he defined as the "real" unemployment rate, just a few weeks later at the United Auto Worker's Convention, President Obama talked about something else:

> Today, GM is back on top as the number one automaker in the world . . . Chrysler is growing faster in America than any other car company. Ford is investing billions in American plants and factories, and plans to bring thousands of jobs back home. All told, the entire industry has added more than 200,000 new jobs over the past two and a half years. 200,000 new jobs. (Obama 2012)

Obama's discussion of jobs was not about the *rate* of unemployment—whether real or unreal— it was about the *change* in unemployment; and as we

Source: Lynn Vavreck, "Want a Better Forecast? Measure the Campaign, Not Just the Economy," *Political Science and Politics,* Volume 47/Issue 02/April 2014, pp 345-347. Copyright © American Political Science Association 2014. Reproduced with permission.

entered 2012 and closed in on Election Day, the unemployment rate was trending downward.

These competing characterizations of the US economy help to illustrate two important elements of election forecasting. First, the change in an economic indicator, relative to its level, better predicts the incumbent party's share of the two-party vote. And second, presidential candidates make important campaign decisions, like whether to enter the race or what to talk about if they do, based on the state of the nation's economy at the start of election year.

As scholars of elections we have paid a good deal of attention to the relationship between economic indicators and vote share, but we have paid less attention to how candidates use information about the nation's economy to make decisions about messaging or about running at all. We have spilt gallons of ink debating and refining models that forecast election outcomes with little more than a cursory nod to the fact that these predictions are made by evaluating elections in which competing candidates typically wage hard-fought campaigns. In reality then, our economic forecasting models tell us what to expect given the typical level and quality of campaigning in presidential races over the last several decades.

Just as variations in the state of the economy can shift forecasts, so too can variations in the level and quality of campaigning, but we know much less about how this translation works. This gap is mainly because data on campaign effort and intensity are difficult to come by. But when we collect these data and use them to model election outcomes alongside economic indicators, we see that what candidates do and what they say, given the state of the economy, plays a significant role in whether economic forecasts prove correct and in how close they come to the eventual two-party vote (Vavreck 2009, 109).

There is almost no better pair of campaigns with which to illustrate the importance of variations in candidate behavior to predicting election outcomes than the campaigns run in 2012 by Barack Obama and Mitt Romney. A simple economic forecast done months before the election predicted an Obama victory by about 2.4 points (Sides and Vavreck 2013, 177–78). If we knew in April 2012 that Mitt Romney would get the nomination and talk mainly about the fact that the economy was not growing fast enough, would we have more or less confidence in the 2.4-point victory the model delivered? Or is this information irrelevant to that prediction entirely? In *The Message Matters* (2009, 109), I explain why and demonstrate how this knowledge boosts our confidence in our estimate of the outcome. Here are the stylized facts.

In nearly every presidential election since 1948 at least one candidate has focused his campaign predominantly on the state of the nation's economy (see Vavreck 2009, 61). Typically, the candidate who focuses a campaign on the nation's economy is the candidate predicted to win based on a simple economic forecast (of the last 16 candidates in this position, 11 of them did so). But sometimes candidates who are not predicted to win highlight the economy, too (George McGovern, Bob Dole, John McCain, and Mitt Romney). Clearly, candidates understand the powerful role that the state of the nation's economy plays in American presidential elections and craft their messaging strategies in light of it.

Leading up to 2012, Mitt Romney surely took stock of the national economy and determined that despite high levels of unemployment and low levels of growth, the *changes* in these indicators leading up to 2012 were moving in directions that benefited the incumbent party (see Sides and Vavreck 2013, 178, for the simple scatter plot showing this relationship). Yet, he and his team decided to focus their campaign on jobs and unemployment—a squarely economic message. The decision by Romney to focus his messaging on the economy increases our confidence in the economic model's prediction because since 1948 no candidate predicted to lose based on the economy, who made the economy the central message of his campaign, has ever won.[1] It was unlikely that Romney would be the first.

Having said that, however, data on people's perceptions of the nation's economy and changes to it over the course of 2012 illustrate why Romney may have deemed this strategy a viable one. In partnership with YouGov, Inc., John Sides and I were able to analyze data from a three-wave rolling panel study each week in 2012. YouGov interviewed 45,000 people representative of the population in December of 2011 and then for the Cooperative Campaign Analysis Project (CCAP) and our work on *The Gamble* (2013), we re-interviewed 1,000 of this initial set each week of 2012. We then interviewed everyone again after the election. Over the course of the year, the unemployment rate in the country shifted by a half a percentage point from the high to the low (roughly 6 percentage points of change) and the change in gross domestic product (GDP) was just above 1 percentage point. Each week of the survey, including the baseline survey in 2011, we asked people whether the nation's economy had gotten better, stayed the same, or gotten worse over the last year.

Thus, despite what the Romney campaign may have thought was a favorable distribution of opinions about the state of the nation's economy, tying those mainly negative opinions to Obama's presidency was not going to be straightforward. They had found an issue on which public opinion was lopsided, they just made the wrong inference about what that meant for their campaign.

In December of 2011, only 20% of the population thought the economy had improved over the last year. The remainder split nearly evenly between thinking it got worse or stayed the same. Given this distribution of opinion it is not hard to see why Romney thought a campaign focused on Obama's failure to turn the economy around could win him votes. The problem for Romney was the slippage between people's perceptions of the economy and the actual economy (Bartels 2002; Campbell et al. 1960, 133) and the fact that voters were not blaming Obama for the slow recovery—they were blaming George Bush (see Duch and Stevenson 2008 for a discussion of attribution effects and economic evaluations).

In an April 2012 YouGov poll, we asked how much blame Obama and Bush each deserved for

"the poor economic conditions of the past few years." Slightly more than half (56%) of respondents gave Bush a great deal or a lot of the blame, while only 41% gave Obama that much blame. A similar gap existed among independents with no leaning toward a political party: 58% blamed Bush, but only 42% blamed Obama. Altogether, 47% of respondents blamed Bush more than Obama, 21% blamed them equally, and 32% blamed Obama more than Bush (Sides and Vavreck 2013, 26). Thus, despite what the Romney campaign may have thought was a favorable distribution of opinions about the state of the nation's economy, tying those mainly negative opinions to Obama's presidency was not going to be straightforward. They had found an issue on which public opinion was lopsided, they just made the wrong inference about what that meant for their campaign.

Using our panel data we can illustrate how successful Romney was at convincing voters the economy had not improved fast enough during 2012. All told, 30% of the electorate changed their opinion of national economic trends between December 2011 and Election Day 2012—a share that does not vary significantly by party. Although there is roughly equal movement among Democrats, Republicans, and independents, shifts among Democrats were more likely to be in the "got better" direction (22% of Democrats moved in this way) while among Republicans only 13% shifted in this way (and 16% moved in the "got worse" direction). Independents are between the partisans, with 17% improving their evaluations of the nation's economy over the year. Still, 11% of Democrats and 13% of independents updated their impressions of the nation's economy in the way that Romney wanted them to during 2012. Where is the slippage between that movement and Romney's vote share?

Consider registered independents who eventually shifted their assessment of the economy in a negative direction (of the 45,000 respondents, there are 987 of them in the CCAP data). Their initial distribution of vote choice in December of 2011 was predominantly slanted toward Romney, 59% to

36%. This pro-Romney split is going to significantly limit the benefit, in terms of votes, Romney can get when these people change their assessments of the nation's economy in his favor because most of them were supporting Romney from the beginning. But among the registered independents who were initially supporting Obama and whose evaluations of the economy moved Romney's way, how many also reported changing their vote choice and casting a ballot for Romney? Only 4.2%.[2] Doing a little math suggests that Romney could have gained almost .4% of the vote from changing the views of independents on the economy.[3] Four tenths of a point is not nothing by any stretch of the imagination, and by comparing this to some of the work in *The Gamble* about electioneering effectiveness (2013, 220), this shift is worth a little more than having two Romney field offices in a county, on average and all else equal. But the flip side of this is that Obama picks up about .36% of the vote among the independents in this group who initially preferred Romney (although their economic assessments are becoming more negative). Romney is gaining some votes by convincing independents the economy has gotten worse, but Obama is gaining some votes as well—presumably for other reasons. The shifts are in nearly equal and opposite directions. This is another common pattern that John Sides and I illustrate across multiple dimensions of campaigning in *The Gamble* (2013).

And here is the critical piece of evidence: the objective change in GDP over the first half of the election year correlates with incumbent party vote share at .75. Even if a candidate is successful at changing people's minds about the state of the nation's economy, it's not clear the payoff is there.

In the last 60 years of presidential campaigns, all of the candidates challenged by national economic tides, who tried to *reshape* voters' assessments of the economy, lost their elections. Surely part of the explanation for this is that people's opinions are hard to move, but perhaps a larger part of the story is that election outcomes are more highly correlated with objective economic conditions than with people's retrospective assessments of the economy—something that is counterintuitive for most political analysts and difficult for candidates and strategists to believe. The data on this point, however, are clear. Since the American National Election Study started asking its traditional retrospective economic assessment question (1980), the percentage of people who describe the economy as "getting better" over the last year is correlated with incumbent party vote share at .46. But, the percentage saying the economy got better over the year correlates with the *actual* half-year growth rate at just .57. And here is the critical piece of evidence: the objective change in GDP over the first half of the election year correlates with incumbent party vote share at .75. *Even if a candidate is successful at changing people's minds about the state of the nation's economy, it's not clear the payoff is there.*

Would knowing, nine months before the election, that Romney planned to center his campaign on the too-slow pace of the economic recovery have affected the forecasts of the 2012 election? Yes. Among candidates disadvantaged by national economic conditions, who tried to refocus the election off of the economy and on to something else, nearly a third went on to win. But among those who tried to reframe the objective economy to benefit their candidacies—none went on to win.

If Romney had tried to reset the 2012 election off of a discussion of the economy and on to something else—something on which he was closer to most voters than Obama and on which Obama was constrained to his unpopular position (Vavreck 2009, 33)—he would have had a better shot at beating a sitting incumbent president in a slowly growing economy. The effect of the quality of campaigns is "baked in" to our forecasting models, but we must try to systematize and appreciate how campaign effort and quality shape outcomes and, therefore, forecasts. With 2016 right around the corner, we have our work cut out for us.

Notes

1. To be clear, some candidates who were predicted to lose based on the economy who talked about things other than the economy were able to win these elections. So being disadvantaged alone is not enough to guarantee a loss.

2. This number is less of an advantage than it seems since Romney loses 3.8% of his initial vote to Obama (among registered independent supporters whose views of the economy change in Romney's direction). And since Romney had more initial supporters among this group, his losses are actually greater than Obama's as a percent of the electorate. This is the best evidence illustrating the slippage between changing opinions about the economy and vote choice. Some people change their views of the economy Romney's way but change their vote the other way.

3. To get .0039 multiply the 4.2% switch rate by the 36% who are initial Obama supporters among the 26% of the electorate who are registered independents with declining views of the economy in December of 2011.

References

Bartels, Larry M. 2002. "Beyond the Running Tally: Partisan Bias in Political Perceptions," *Political Behavior* 24 (2): 117–50.

Campbell, Angus, and Converse, Philip E., Miller, Warren E., and Stokes, Donald E. 1960. *The American Voter.* New York: John Wiley.

Duch, Raymond M., and Stevenson, Randolph T. 2008. *The Economic Vote: How Political and Economic Institutions Condition Election Results.* New York: Cambridge University Press.

Obama, Barack. 2012. "Remarks by the President to UAW Conference." Washington Marriott Wardman Park, Washington, DC. www.Whitehouse.gov. February 28.

Romney, Mitt. 2012. "Remarks in Las Vegas Following the Nevada Caucuses" on The American Presidency Project website, http://www.presidency.ucsb.edu/ws/?pid=99395 February 4.

Sides, John, and Vavreck, Lynn. 2013. *The Gamble: Choice and Chance in the 2012 Presidential Election.* Princeton, NJ: Princeton University Press.

Vavreck, Lynn. 2009. *The Message Matters: The Economy and Presidential Campaigns.* Princeton, NJ: Princeton University Press.

Chapter 12

Political Parties

12-1 From *Why Parties?*

John H. Aldrich

American political parties were created by politicians and committed citizens who sought to win elections and control legislatures, executives, and even the courts. The parties exist at local, state, and national levels—wherever elections are held for coveted offices. The system of political parties that has evolved over time is fragmented and multilayered. In the following essay, John H. Aldrich describes the nature of the political problems that parties solve for candidates and voters. As much as we may dislike partisanship, modern democracies could not, Aldrich explains, function without it.

Is the Contemporary Political Party Strong or in Decline?

The Case for the Importance of Political Parties

The path to office for nearly every major politician begins today, as it has for over 150 years, with the party. Many candidates emerge initially from the ranks of party activists, all serious candidates seek their party's nomination, and they become serious candidates in the general election only because they have won their party's endorsement. Today most partisan nominations are decided in primary elections—that is, based on votes cast by self-designated partisans in the mass electorate. Successful nominees count on the continued support of these partisans in the general election, and for good reason. At least since surveys have provided firm evidence, all presidential nominees have won the support of no less than a majority of their party in the electorate, no matter how overwhelming their defeat may have been.

This is an age of so-called partisan dealignment in the electorate. Even so, a substantial majority today consider themselves partisans. The lowest percentage of self-professed (i.e., "strong" and "weak") partisans yet recorded in National Election Studies (NES) surveys was 61 percent in 1974, and another 22 percent expressed partisan leanings that year. Evidence from panel surveys demonstrates that partisanship has remained as stable and enduring for most adults after dealignment as it did before it, and it is often the single strongest predictor of candidate choice in the public.

If parties have declined recently, the decline has not occurred in their formal organizations. Party organizations are if anything stronger, better financed, and more professional at all levels now. Although its importance to candidates may be less than in the past, the party provides more support— more money, workers, and resources of all kinds— than any other organization for all but a very few candidates for national and state offices.

Once elected, officeholders remain partisans. Congress is organized by parties. Party-line votes elect its leadership, determine what its committees will be, assign members to them, and select their chairs. Party caucuses remain a staple of congressional life, and they and other forms of party organizations in Congress have become stronger in recent years. Party voting in committee and on the floor of both houses, though far less common in the United States than in many democracies, nonetheless remains the first and most important standard for understanding congressional voting behavior, and it too has grown stronger, in this case much stronger, in recent years.

Relationships among the elected branches of government are also heavily partisan. Conference committees to resolve discrepancies between House and Senate versions of legislation reflect partisan as well as interchamber rivalries. The president is the party's leader, and his agenda is introduced, fought for, and supported on the floor by his congressional party. His agenda becomes his party's congressional agenda, and much of it finds its way into law.

The Case for Weak and Weakening Parties

As impressive as the scenario above may be, not all agree that parties lie at the heart of American politics, at least not anymore. The literature on parties over the past two decades is replete with accounts of the decline of the political party. Even the choice of titles clearly reflects the arguments. David Broder perhaps began this stream of literature with *The Party's Over* (1972). Since then, political scientists have written extensively on this theme: for example, Crotty's *American Political Parties in Decline* (1984), Kirkpatrick's *Dismantling the Parties* (1978), Polsby's *Consequences of Party Reform* (1983) . . . , Ranney's thoughtful *Curing the Mischiefs of Faction* (1975), and Wattenberg's *The Decline of American Political Parties* (1990).

Those who see larger ills in the contemporary political scene often attribute them to the failure of parties to be stronger and more effective. In "The Decline of Collective Responsibility" (1980), Fiorina argued that such responsibility was possible only through the agency of the political party. Jacobson

concluded his study of congressional elections (1992) by arguing that contemporary elections induce "responsiveness" of individual incumbents to their districts but do so "without [inducing] responsibility" in incumbents for what Congress does. As a result, the electorate can find no one to hold accountable for congressional failings. He too looked to a revitalized party for redress. These themes reflect the responsible party thesis, if not in being a call for such parties, at least in using that as the standard for measuring how short the contemporary party falls.

The literature on the presidency is not immune to this concern for decaying parties. Kernell's account of the strategy of "going public" (1986)—that is, generating power by marshaling public opinion—is that it became more common as the older strategy of striking bargains with a small set of congressional (and partisan) power brokers grew increasingly futile. The earlier use of the president's power to persuade (Neustadt 1960, 1990) failed as power centers became more diverse and fragmented and brokers could no longer deliver. Lowi argued this case even more strongly in *The Personal President* (1985). America, he claimed, has come to invest too much power in the office of the president, with the result that the promise of the presidency and the promises of individual presidents go unfulfilled. Why? Because the rest of government has become too unwieldy, complicated, and fragmented for the president to use that power effectively. His solution? Revitalize political parties.

Divided partisan control over government, once an occasional aberration, has become the ordinary course of affairs. Many of the same themes in this literature are those sounded above—fragmented, decentralized power, lack of coordination and control over what the government does, and absence of collective responsibility. Strong political parties are, among other things, those that can deliver the vote for most or all of their candidates. Thus another symptom of weakened parties is regularized divided government, in the states as well as in the nation.

If divided government is due to weakened parties, that condition must be due in turn to weakened partisan loyalties in the electorate. Here the evidence is clear. The proportions and strength of party attachments in the electorate declined in the mid-1960s. There was a resurgence in affiliation twenty years later, but to a lower level than before 1966. The behavioral consequences of these changes are if anything even clearer. Defection from party lines and split-ticket voting are far more common for all major offices at national, state, and local levels today than before the mid-1960s. Elections are more candidate centered and less party centered, and those who come to office have played a greater role in shaping their own more highly personalized electoral coalitions. Incumbents, less dependent on the party for winning office, are less disposed to vote the party line in Congress or to follow the wishes of their party's president. Power becomes decentralized toward the individual incumbent and, as Jacobson argues, individual incumbents respond to their constituents. If that means defecting from the party, so be it.

Is the Debate Genuine?

Some believe that parties have actually grown stronger over the past few decades. This position has been put most starkly by Schlesinger: "It should be clear by now that the grab bag of assumptions, inferences, and half-truths that have fed the decline-of-parties thesis is simply wrong" (1985, p. 1152). Rather, he maintains, "Thanks to increasing levels of competition between the parties, then, American political parties are stronger than before" (p. 1168). More common is the claim that parties were weakened in the 1960s but have been revitalized since then. Rohde pointed out that "in the last decade, however, the decline of partisanship in the House has been reversed. Party voting, which had been as low as 27 percent in 1972, peaked at 64 percent in 1987" (1989, p. 1). Changes in party voting in the Senate have been only slightly less dramatic, and Rohde has also demonstrated that party institutions in the House strengthened substantially in the same period (1991). If, as Rohde says, parties in the government are stronger, and if . . . others are correct that party organizations are stronger, a thesis of

decline with resurgence must be taken seriously. The electorate's partisan affiliations may be a lagging rather than a leading indicator, and even they have rebounded slightly.

A Theory of Political Parties

As diverse as are the conclusions reached by these and other astute observers, all agree that the political party is—or should be—central to the American political system. Parties are—or should be—integral parts of all political life, from structuring the reasoning and choice of the electorate, through all facets of campaigns and seemingly all facets of the government, to the very possibility of effective governance in a democracy.

How is it that such astute observers of American politics and parties, writing at virtually the same time and looking at much the same evidence, come to such diametrically opposed conclusions about the strength of parties? Eldersveld . . . wrote that "political parties are complex institutions and processes, and as such they are difficult to understand and evaluate" (1982, p. 407). As proof, he went on to consider the decline of parties thesis. At one point he wrote, "The decline in our parties, therefore, is difficult to demonstrate, empirically or in terms of historical perspective" (p. 417). And yet he then turned to signs of party decline and concluded his book with the statement: "Despite their defects they continue today to be the major instruments for democratic government in this nation. With necessary reforms we can make them even more central to the governmental process and to the lives of American citizens. Eighty years ago, Lord James Bryce, after studying our party system, said, 'In America the great moving forces are the parties. The government counts for less than in Europe, the parties count for more. . . .' If our citizens and their leaders wish it, American parties will still be the 'great moving forces' of our system" (1982, pp. 432–33).

The "Fundamental Equation" of the New Institutionalism Applied to Parties

That parties are complex does not mean they are incomprehensible. Indeed complexity is, if not an intentional outcome, at least an anticipated result of those who shape the political parties. Moreover, they are so deeply woven into the fabric of American politics that they cannot be understood apart from either their own historical context and dynamics or those of the political system as a whole. Parties, that is, can be understood only in relation to the polity, to the government and its institutions, and to the historical context of the times.

The study of political parties, second, is necessarily a study of a major pair of political *institutions*. Indeed, the institutions that define the political party are unique, and as it happens they are unique in ways that make an institutional account especially useful. Their establishment and nature are fundamentally extralegal; they are nongovernmental political institutions. Instead of statute, their basis lies in the actions of ambitious politicians that created and maintain them. They are, in the parlance of the new institutionalism, *endogenous institutions*—in fact, the most highly endogenous institutions of any substantial and sustained political importance in American history.

By endogenous, I mean it was the actions of political actors that created political parties in the first place, and it is the actions of political actors that have shaped and altered them over time. And political actors have chosen to alter their parties dramatically at several times in our history, reformed them often, and tinkered with them constantly. Of all major political bodies in the United States, the political party is the most variable in its rules, regulations, and procedures—that is to say, in its formal organization—and in its informal methods and traditions. It is often the same set of actors who write the party's rules and then choose the party's outcomes, sometimes at nearly the same time and by the same method. Thus, for example, one night national party conventions debate, consider any proposed amendments, and then adopt their rules by a majority vote of credentialed delegates. The next night these same delegates debate, consider any proposed amendments, and then adopt their platform by majority vote, and they choose their presidential nominee by majority vote the following night.

Who, then, are these critical political actors? Many see the party-in-the-electorate as comprising major actors. To be sure, mobilizing the electorate to capture office is a central task of the political party. But America is a republican democracy. All power flows directly or indirectly from the great body of the people, to paraphrase Madison's definition. The public elects its political leaders, but it is that leadership that legislates, executes, and adjudicates policy. The parties are defined in relation to this republican democracy. Thus it is political leaders, those Schlesinger (1975) has called "office-seekers"—*those who seek and those who hold elective office*—who are the central actors in the party.

Ambitious office seekers and holders are thus the first and most important actors in the political party. A second set of important figures in party politics comprises those who hold, or have access to, critical resources that office seekers need to realize their ambitions. It is expensive to build and maintain the party and campaign organizations necessary to compete effectively in the electoral arena. Thomas Ferguson, for example, has made an extended argument for the "primary and constitutive role large investors play in American politics" (1983, p. 3). Much of his research emphasizes this primary and constitutive role in party politics in particular, such as in partisan realignments. The study of the role of money in congressional elections has also focused in part on concentrations of such sources of funding, such as from political action committees which political parties are coming to take advantage of. Elections are also fought over the flow of information to the public. The electoral arm of political parties in the eighteenth century was made up of "committees of correspondence," which were primarily lines of communication among political elites and between them and potential voters, and one of the first signs of organizing of the Jeffersonian Republican party was the hiring of a newspaper editor. The press was first a partisan press, and editors and publishers from Thomas Ritchie to Horace Greeley long were critical players in party politics. Today those with specialized knowledge relevant to communication, such as pollsters, media and advertising experts, and computerized fund-raising specialists, enjoy influence in party, campaign, and even government councils that greatly exceeds their mere technical expertise.

In more theoretical terms, this second set of party actors include those Schlesinger (1975) has called "benefit seekers," those for whom realization of their goals depends on the party's success in capturing office. Party activists shade from those powerful figures with concentrations of, or access to, money and information described above to the legions of volunteer campaign activists who ring doorbells and stuff envelopes and are, individually and collectively, critical to the first level of the party—its office seekers. All are critical because they command the resources, whether money, expertise, and information or merely time and labor, that office seekers need to realize their ambitions. As a result, activists' motivations shape and constrain the behavior of office seekers, as their own roles are, in turn, shaped and constrained by the office seekers. The changed incentives of party activists have played a significant role in the fundamentally altered nature of the contemporary party, but the impact of benefit seekers will be seen scattered throughout this account.

Voters, however, are neither office seekers nor benefit seekers and thus are not a part of the political party at all, even if they identify strongly with a party and consistently support its candidates. Voters are indeed critical, but they are critical as the targets of party activities. Parties "produce" candidates, platforms, and policies. Voters "consume" by exchanging their votes for the party's product (see Popkin et al. 1976). Some voters, of course, become partisans by becoming activists, whether as occasional volunteers, as sustained contributors, or even as candidates. But until they do so, they may be faithful consumers, "brand name" loyalists as it were, but they are still only the targets of partisans' efforts to sell their wares in the political marketplace.

Why, then, do politicians create and recreate the party, exploit its features, or ignore its dictates? The simple answer is that it has been in their interests to do so. That is, this is a *rational choice* account of the party, an account that presumes that rational, elective office seekers and holders use the party to achieve their ends.

I do not assume that politicians are invariably self-interested in a narrow sense. This is not a theory in which elective office seekers simply maximize their chances of election or reelection, at least not for its own sake. They may well have fundamental values and principles, and they may have preferences over policies as means to those ends. They also care about office, both for its own sake and for the opportunities to achieve other ends that election and reelection make possible. . . . Just as winning elections is a means to other ends for politicians (whether career or policy ends), so too is the political party a means to these other ends.

Why, then, do politicians turn to create or reform, to use or abuse, partisan institutions? The answer is that parties are designed as attempts to solve problems that current institutional arrangements do not solve and that politicians have come to believe they cannot solve. These problems fall into three general and recurring categories.

The Problem of Ambition and Elective Office Seeking

Elective office seekers, as that label says, want to win election to office. Parties regulate access to those offices. If elective office is indeed valuable, there will be more aspirants than offices, and the political party and the two-party system are means of regulating that competition and channeling those ambitions. Major party nomination is necessary for election, and partisan institutions have been developed—and have been reformed and re-reformed—for regulating competition. Intra-institutional leadership positions are also highly valued and therefore potentially competitive. There is, for example, a fairly well institutionalized path to the office of Speaker of the House. It is, however, a Democratic party institution. Elective politicians, of course, ordinarily desire election more than once. They are typically careerists who want a long and productive career in politics. Schlesinger's ambition theory (1966) ... is precisely about this general problem. Underlying this theory, though typically not fully developed, is a problem. The problem is that if office is desirable, there will be more, usually many more, aspirants than there are offices to go around. When stated in rigorous form, it can be proved that in fact there is no permanent solution to this problem. And it is a problem that can adversely affect the fortunes of a party. In 1912 the Republican vote was split between William Howard Taft and Theodore Roosevelt. This split enabled Woodrow Wilson to win with 42 percent of the popular vote. Not only was Wilson the only break in Republican hegemony of the White House in this period, but in that year Democrats increased their House majority by sixty-five additional seats and captured majority control of the Senate. Thus failure to regulate intraparty competition cost Republicans dearly.

For elective office seekers, regulating conflict over who holds those offices is clearly of major concern. It is ever present. And it is not just a problem of access to government offices but is also a problem internal to each party as soon as the party becomes an important gateway to office.

The Problem of Making Decisions for the Party and for the Polity

Once in office, partisans determine outcomes for the polity. They propose alternatives, shape the agenda, pass (or reject) legislation, and implement what they enact. The policy formation and execution process, that is, is highly partisan. The parties-in-government are more than mere coalitions of like-minded individuals, however; they are enduring institutions. Very few incumbents change their partisan affiliations. Most retain their partisanship throughout their career, even though they often disagree (i.e., are not uniformly like-minded) with some of their partisan peers. When the rare incumbent does change parties, it is invariably to join the party more consonant with that switcher's policy interests. This implies that there are differences between the two parties at some fundamental and enduring level on policy positions, values, and beliefs. Thus, parties

are institutions designed to promote the achievement of collective choices—choices on which the parties differ and choices reached by majority rule. As with access to office and ambition theory, there is a well-developed theory for this problem: *social choice theory*. Underlying this theory is the well-known problem that no method of choice can solve the elective officeholders' problem of combining the interests, concerns, or values of a polity that remains faithful to democratic values, as shown by the consequences flowing from Arrow's theorem (Arrow 1951). Thus, in a republican democracy politicians may turn to partisan institutions to solve the problem of collective choice. In the language of politics, parties may help achieve the goal of attaining policy majorities in the first place, as well as the often more difficult goal of maintaining such majorities.

The Problem of Collective Action

The third problem is the most pervasive and thus the furthest-ranging in substantive content. The clearest example, however, is also the most important. To win office, candidates need more than a party's nomination. Election requires persuading members of the public to support that candidacy and mobilizing as many of those supporters as possible. This is a problem of collective action. How do candidates get supporters to vote for them—at least in greater numbers than vote for the opposition—as well as get them to provide the cadre of workers and contribute the resources needed to win election? The political party has long been the solution.

As important as wooing and mobilizing supporters are, collective action problems arise in a wide range of circumstances facing elective office seekers. Party action invariably requires the concerted action of many partisans to achieve collectively desirable outcomes. Jimmy Carter was the only president in the 1970s and 1980s to enjoy unified party control of government. Democrats in Congress, it might well be argued, shared an interest in achieving policy outcomes. And yet Carter was all too often unable to get them to act in their shared collective interests. In 1980 not only he but the Democratic congressional parties paid a heavy price for failed cooperation. The theory here, of course, is the *theory of public goods* and its consequence, the *theory of collective action.*

The Elective Office Seekers' and Holders' Interests Are to Win

Why should this crucial set of actors, the elective office seekers and officeholders, care about these three classes of problems? The short answer is that these concerns become practical problems to politicians when they adversely affect their chances of winning. Put differently, politicians turn to their political party—that is, use its powers, resources, and institutional forms—when they believe doing so increases their prospects for winning desired outcomes, and they turn from it if it does not.

Ambition theory is about winning per se. The breakdown of orderly access to office risks unfettered and unregulated competition. The inability of a party to develop effective means of nomination and support for election therefore directly influences the chances of victory for the candidates and thus for their parties. The standard example of the problem of social choice theory, the "paradox of voting," is paradoxical precisely because all are voting to win desired outcomes, and yet there is no majority-preferred outcome. Even if there happens to be a majority-preferred policy, the conditions under which it is truly a stable equilibrium are extremely fragile and thus all too amenable to defeat. In other words, majorities in Congress are hard to attain and at least as hard to maintain. And the only reason to employ scarce campaign resources to mobilize supporters is that such mobilization increases the odds of victory. Its opposite, the failure to act when there are broadly shared interests—the problem of collective action—reduces the prospects of victory, whether at the ballot box or in government. Scholars may recognize these as manifestations of theoretical problems and call them "impossibility results" to emphasize their generic importance. Politicians recognize the consequences of these impossibility results by their adverse effects on their chances of winning—of securing what it is in their interests to secure.

So why have politicians so often turned to political parties for solutions to these problems? Their existence creates incentives for their use. It is, for example, incredibly difficult to win election to major office without the backing of a major party. It is only a little less certain that legislators who seek to lead a policy proposal through the congressional labyrinth will first turn to their party for assistance. But such incentives tell us only that an ongoing political institution is used when it is useful. Why form political parties in the first place? . . .

First, parties are institutions. This means, among other things, that they have some durability. They may be endogenous institutions, yet party reforms are meant not as short-term fixes but as alterations to last for years, even decades. Thus, for example, legislators might create a party rather than a temporary majority coalition to increase their chances of winning not just today but into the future. Similarly, a long and successful political career means winning office today, but it also requires winning elections throughout that career. A standing, enduring organization makes that goal more likely.

Second, American democracy chooses by plurality or majority rule. Election to office therefore requires broad-based support wherever and from whomever it can be found. So strong are the resulting incentives for a two-party system to emerge that the effect is called Duverger's law (Duverger 1954). It is in part the need to win vast and diverse support that has led politicians to create political parties.

Third, parties may help officeholders win more, and more often, than alternatives. Consider the usual stylized model of pork barrel politics. All winners get a piece of the pork for their districts. All funded projects are paid for by tax revenues, so each district pays an equal share of the costs of each project adopted, whether or not that district receives a project. Several writers have argued that this kind of legislation leads to "universalism," that is, adoption of a "norm" that every such bill yields a project to every district and thus passes with a "universal" or unanimous coalition. Thus everyone "wins." . . . As a result, expecting to win only a bit more than half the time and lose the rest of the time, all legislators prefer consistent use of the norm of universalism. But consider an alternative. Suppose some majority agree to form a more permanent coalition, to control outcomes now and into the future, and develop institutional means to encourage fealty to this agreement. If they successfully accomplish this, they will win regularly. Members of this institutionalized coalition would prefer it to universalism, since they always win a project in either case, but they get their projects at lower cost under the institutionalized majority coalition, which passes fewer projects. Thus, even in this case with no shared substantive interests at all, there are nonetheless incentives to form an enduring voting coalition—to form a political party. And those in the excluded minority have incentives to counterorganize. United, they may be more able to woo defectors to their side. If not, they can campaign to throw those rascals in the majority party out of office.

In sum, these theoretical problems affect elective office seekers and officeholders by reducing their chances of winning. Politicians therefore may turn to political parties as institutions designed to ameliorate them. In solving these theoretical problems, however, from the politicians' perspective parties are affecting who wins and loses and what is won or lost. And it is to parties that politicians often turn, because of their durability as institutionalized solutions, because of the need to orchestrate large and diverse groups of people to form winning majorities, and because often more can be won through parties. Note that this argument rests on the implicit assumption that winning and losing hang in the balance. Politicians may be expected to give up some of their personal autonomy only when they face an imminent threat of defeat without doing so or only when doing so can block opponents' ability to build the strength necessary to win.

This is, of course, the positive case for parties, for it specifies conditions under which politicians find them useful. Not all problems are best solved, perhaps even solved at all, by political parties. Other arrangements, perhaps interest groups, issue networks, or personal electoral coalitions, may be superior at different times and under different conditions. The party may even be part of the problem. In such cases politicians turn elsewhere to seek the means to win. Thus this theory is at base a theory of ambitious politicians seeking to achieve their goals. Often they have done so through the agency of the party, but sometimes, this theory implies, they will seek to realize their goals in other ways.

The political party has regularly proved useful. Their permanence suggests that the appropriate question is not When parties? but How much parties and how much other means? That parties are endogenous implies that there is no single, consistent account of the political party—nor should we expect one. Instead, parties are but a (major) part of the institutional context in which current historical conditions—the problems—are set, and solutions are sought with permanence only by changing that web of institutional arrangements. Of these the political party is by design the most malleable, and thus it is intended to change in important ways and with relatively great frequency. But it changes in ways that have, for most of American history, retained major political parties and, indeed, retained two major parties.

References

Arrow, Kenneth J. 1951. *Social Choice and Individual Values*. New York: Wiley.

Broder, David S. 1972. *The Party's Over: The Failure of Politics in America*. New York: Harper and Row.

Crotty, William. 1984. *American Political Parties in Decline*. 2d ed. Boston: Little, Brown.

Duverger, Maurice. 1954. *Political Parties: Their Organization and Activities in the Modern State*. New York: Wiley.

Eldersveld, Samuel J. 1982. *Political Parties in American Society*. New York: Basic Books.

Ferguson, Thomas. 1983. "Party Realignment and American Industrial Structures: The Investment Theory of Political Parties in Historical Perspective". In *Research in Political Economy*, vol. 6, ed. Paul Zarembka, pp. 1–82. Greenwich, Conn.: JAI Press.

Fiorina, Morris P. 1980. "The Decline of Collective Responsibility in American Politics". *Daedalus* 109 (summer): 25–45.

Jacobson, Gary C. 1992. *The Politics of Congressional Elections.* 3d ed. New York: Harper-Collins.

Kernell, Samuel. 1986. *Going Public: New Strategies of Presidential Leadership.* Washington, D.C.: CQ Press.

Kirkpatrick, Jeane J. 1978. *Dismantling the Parties: Reflections on Party Reform and Party Decomposition.* Washington, D.C.: American Enterprise Institute of Public Policy Research.

Lowi, Theodore. 1985. *The Personal President: Power Invested, Promise Unfulfilled.* Ithaca, N.Y.: Cornell University Press.

Neustadt, Richard E. 1960. *Presidential Power: The Politics of Leadership.* New York: Wiley.

_____. 1990. *Presidential Power and the Modern Presidents: The Politics of Leadership from Roosevelt to Reagan.* New York: Free Press.

Polsby, Nelson W. 1983. *Consequences of Party Reform.* Oxford: Oxford University Press.

Popkin, Samuel, John W. Gorman, Charles Phillips, and Jeffrey A. Smith. 1976. "Comment: What Have You Done for Me Lately? Toward an Investment Theory of Voting". *American Political Science Review* 70 (September): 779–805.

Ranney, Austin. 1975. *Curing the Mischiefs of Faction: Party Reform in America.* Berkeley and Los Angeles: University of California Press.

Rohde, David W. 1989. "Something's Happening Here: What It Is Ain't Exactly Clear": Southern Democrats in the House of Representatives. In *Home Style and Washington Work: Studies of Congressional Politics,* ed. Morris P. Fiorina and David W. Rohde, pp. 137–163. Ann Arbor: University of Michigan Press.

_____. 1991. *Parties and Leaders in the Postreform House.* Chicago: University of Chicago Press.

Schlesinger, Joseph A. 1966. *Ambition and Politics: Political Careers in the United States.* Chicago: Rand McNally.

_____. 1975. "The Primary Goals of Political Parties: A Clarification of Positive Theory". *American Political Science Review* 69 (September): 840–49.

_____. 1985. The New American Political Party. *American Political Science Review* 79 (December): 1152–69.

Wattenberg, Martin P. 1990. *The Decline of American Political Parties: 1952–1988.* Cambridge: Harvard University Press.

12-2 Partisanship and Voting Behavior, 1952–1996

Larry M. Bartels

Many Americans consider themselves to be Democrats or Republicans, and a few iden-
tify with some other party. In the late 1960s and 1970s the number of Americans willing
to call themselves Democrats or Republicans declined, leading political scientists to speak
of a dealignment and worry about the declining importance of parties. Then partisanship
appeared to rebound in the 1990s. In this essay political scientist Larry M. Bartels
describes these trends and explains the importance of partisanship for the voting behav-
ior of Americans. He argues that party identification increased in the 1980s and 1990s
and that the correlation between party identification and presidential voting increased
even more. He concludes by observing that changes in the behavior of elected partisans—
greater partisanship among presidents and members of Congress—may have contributed
to resurgent partisanship in voting in the electorate.

The "decline of parties" is one of the most familiar themes in popular and scholarly discourse about contemporary American politics. One influential journalist has asserted that "the most important phenomenon of American politics in the past quarter century has been the rise of independent voters." . . . The most persistent academic analyst of partisan decline has argued that "For over four decades the American public has been drifting away from the two major political parties," while another prominent scholar has referred to a "massive decay of partisan electoral linkages" and to "the ruins of the traditional partisan regime."

I shall argue here that this conventional wisdom regarding the "decline of parties" is both exaggerated and outdated. Partisan loyalties in the American public have rebounded significantly since the mid-1970s, especially among those who actually turn out to vote. Meanwhile, the impact of partisanship on voting behavior has increased markedly in recent years, both at the presidential level (where the overall impact of partisanship in 1996 was almost 80 percent greater than in 1972) and at the congressional level (where the overall impact of partisanship in 1996 was almost 60 percent

greater than in 1978). . . . My analysis suggests that "partisan loyalties had at least as much impact on voting behavior at the presidential level in the 1980s as in the 1950s"—and even more in the 1990s than in the 1980s.

The Thesis of Partisan Decline

Almost forty years ago, the authors of *The American Voter* asserted that

Few factors are of greater importance for our national elections than the lasting attachment of tens of millions of Americans to one of the parties. These loyalties establish a basic division of electoral strength within which the competition of particular campaigns takes place. . . . Most Americans have this sense of attachment with one party or the other. And for the individual who does, the strength and direction of party identification are facts of central importance in accounting for attitude and behavior.

The so-called "Michigan model," with its emphasis on the fundamental importance of long-standing

Source: Larry Bartels, "Partisanship and Voting Behavior, 1952–1996," *American Journal of Political Science* 44, no. 1 (January 2000): 35–50. *American Journal of Political Science* by Midwest Political Science Association (U.S.) Reproduced with permission of Blackwell Publishing, Inc. in the format Republish in a book via Copyright Clearance Center. Notes and bibliographic references appearing in the original have been deleted.

partisan loyalties, dominated the subsequent decade of academic research on voting behavior. However, over the same decade, changes in the political environment seemed to be rendering the "Michigan model" increasingly obsolete. By the early 1970s, political observers were pointing to the increasing proportion of "independents" in opinion surveys and the increasing prevalence of split-ticket voting as indications of significant partisan decline. By the mid-1970s, some political scientists were extrapolating from a decade-long trend to project a permanent demise of partisan politics. . . .

The "increase in the number of independents" in the 1960s and early '70s . . . —and the corresponding decrease in the proportion of the public who identified themselves as Democrats or Republicans—constitute the single most important piece of evidence in support of the thesis of partisan decline. These and subsequent trends are displayed in the two panels of Figure 1, which show the proportions of party identifiers (including "strong" and "weak" identifiers) and independents (including "pure" independents and "leaners"), respectively, in each of the biennial American National Election Studies from 1952 through 1996.

. . . The proportion of "strong" identifiers in the population increased from 24 percent in 1976 to 31 percent in 1996, while the proportion of "pure" independents—those who neither identified themselves as Democrats or Republicans nor "leaned" to either party in response to the traditional Michigan follow-up question—declined from 16 percent in 1976 to only 9 percent in 1996.

A Summary Measure of Partisan Voting

What significance should we attach to the shifts in the distribution of party identification documented in Figure 1? . . . To the extent that our interest in partisan loyalties is motivated by an interest in voting behavior, we would seem to need (at least) two kinds of additional information to interpret the electoral implications of changing levels of partisanship. First, are the shifts documented in Figure 1 concentrated among voters or among nonvoters?

Declining partisanship among nonvoters may leave the distribution of party identification in the voting booth unchanged. And second, has the electoral *impact* of a given level of partisanship declined or increased over time? Declining *levels* of partisanship might be either reinforced or counteracted by changes in the *impact* of partisanship on electoral choices.

The first of these two questions is addressed by Figure 2, which shows separate trend lines for the proportion of ("strong" or "weak") party identifiers among voters and nonvoters in presidential elections since 1952. Not surprisingly, nonvoters are less partisan than voters in every year. But what is more important to note here is that the gap in partisanship between voters and nonvoters has widened noticeably over time, from about ten percentage points in the 1950s to about twenty percentage points by the 1990s. Indeed, it appears from these results that the decline in partisanship evident in Figure 1 has been almost entirely reversed among voters: the proportion of party identifiers in the presidential electorate was 77 percent in 1952, 76 percent in 1956, and 75 percent in 1996, while the proportion among nonvoters was almost fifteen points lower in 1996 than in the 1950s. Thus, while the trend lines shown in Figure 1 suggest that the erosion of party loyalties underlying the "partisan decline" thesis has ended and probably even reversed in the last two decades, the results presented in Figure 2 suggest that these developments have been especially pronounced among actual voters.

The erosion of party loyalties among nonvoters evident in Figure 2 is of importance for any general account of the role of partisanship in contemporary American politics. It is especially important in view of evidence suggesting that declining partisanship is, at least in modest part, *responsible* for the substantial decline in turnout over the period covered by Figure 2, and that individual turnout decisions are increasingly sensitive to the strength of prospective voters' preferences for one candidate or the other, which derive in significant part from long-term partisan attachments. However, given my narrower aim here of documenting changes in the impact of partisanship

Figure 1   The Distribution of Party Identification, 1952–1996

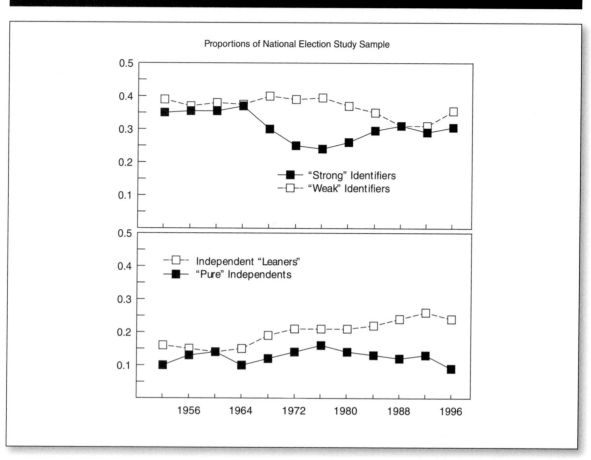

Proportions of National Election Study Sample

on voting behavior, the most important implication of Figure 2 is that the distribution of partisan attachments *among those citizens who actually got to the polls* was not much different in the 1990s from what it had been in the 1950s.

Of course, the significance of partisanship in the electoral process depends not only upon the level of partisanship in the electorate, but also upon the extent to which partisanship influences voting behavior. How, if at all, has that influence changed over the four and a half decades covered by the NES data? . . . . [Editors: Bartels estimates the impact of party identification on voting by taking advantage of the survey from which respondents are coded as strong Republican, weak Republican, leaning Republican, independent, leaning Democrat, weak Democrat, and strong Democrat. For each category, a statistical estimate is calculated for the effect of being in that category on voting for the alternative presidential or congressional candidates. The statistical estimate, called a probit coefficient, is averaged for the partisan categories to yield an overall measure "partisan voting." Figure 3 presents the result for elections in the 1952–1996 period.]

Figure 2   Party Identification among Presidential Voters and Nonvoters

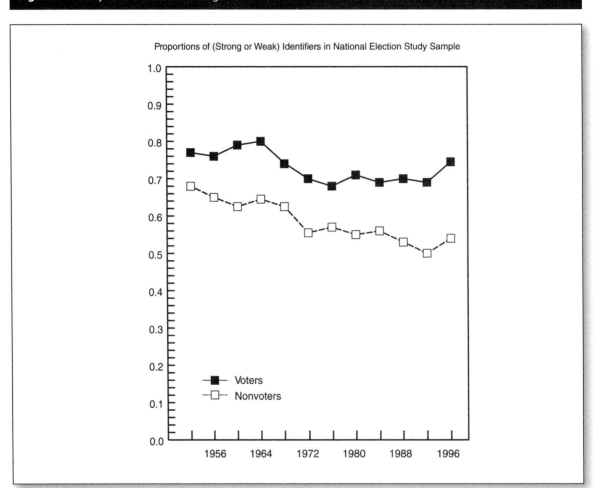

The Revival of Partisan Voting in Presidential Elections

. . . Figure 3 shows noticeable declines in the level of partisan voting in the presidential elections of 1964 and, especially, 1972. These declines primarily reflect the fact that Republican identifiers in 1964 and Democratic identifiers in 1972 abandoned their parties' unpopular presidential candidates by the millions, depressing the estimated effects of partisan loyalties on the presidential vote in those years. However, an even more striking pattern in Figure 3 is the monotonic increase in partisan voting in every presidential election since 1972. By 1996, this trend had produced a level of partisan voting 77 percent higher than in 1972—an average increase of 10 percent in each election, compounded over six election cycles—and 15 to 20 percent higher than in the supposed glory days of the 1950s that spawned *The American Voter.*

... One possible explanation for the revival of partisan voting evident in Figure 3 is the sorting out of partisan attachments of southerners following the civil rights upheavals of the early and middle 1960s. As national party elites took increasingly distinct stands on racial issues, black voters moved overwhelmingly into the Democratic column, while white southerners defected to conservative Republican presidential candidates. What is important here is that many of these conservative white southerners only gradually shed their traditional

Democratic identifications—and Democratic voting behavior at the subpresidential level—through the 1980s and '90s. Thus, it may be tempting to interpret the revival of partisan voting at the presidential level largely as a reflection of the gradual reequilibration of presidential votes and more general partisan attachments among white southerners in the wake of a regional partisan realignment.

As it happens, however, the steady and substantial increases in partisan voting over the past quarter-century evident in Figure 3 are by no means confined

Figure 3   Partisan Voting in Presidential Elections

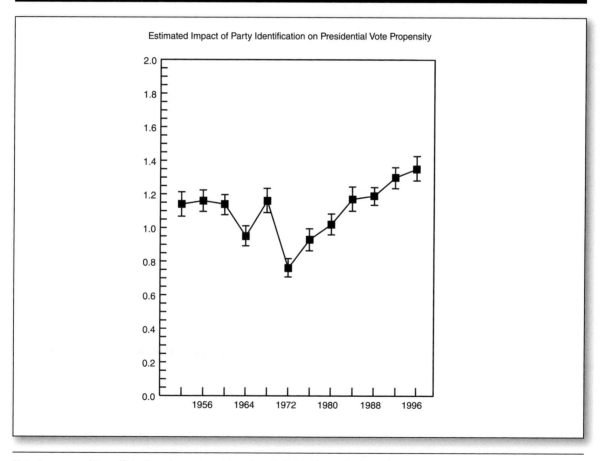

Note: Average probit coefficients, major-party voters only, with jackknife standard error bars.

Figure 4   Partisan Voting in Presidential Elections, White Southerners and White Nonsoutherners

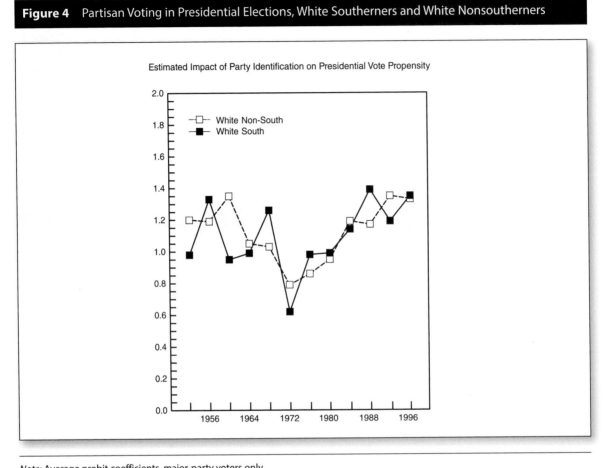

Estimated Impact of Party Identification on Presidential Vote Propensity

Note: Average probit coefficients, major-party voters only.

to the South. This fact is evident from Figure 4, which displays separate patterns of partisan voting for white southerners and white nonsoutherners. The trend lines are somewhat more ragged for these subgroups than for the electorate as a whole, especially in the South (where the year-by-year estimates are based on an average of fewer than 300 southern white voters in each election); nevertheless, the general pattern in Figure 3 is replicated almost identically in both subgroups in Figure 4. The absolute level of partisan voting in the 1964 and 1972 elections is only slightly lower among southern whites than among nonsouthern whites, and the substantial increase in partisan voting since 1972 appears clearly (indeed, nearly monotonically) in both subgroups.

It should be evident from Figure 4 that the revival of partisan voting in presidential elections documented in Figure 3 is a national rather than a regional phenomenon. Indeed, additional analysis along these lines suggests that the same pattern is evident in a wide variety of subgroups of the electorate, including voters under 40 and those over 50 years of age, those with college educations and those without high school diplomas, and so on. Thus, any convincing explanation of this partisan revival will presumably have to be based upon broad changes in the national political environment, rather than upon narrower demographic or generational developments.

Partisan Voting in Congressional Elections

My analysis so far has focused solely on the impact of partisan loyalties on voting behavior in presidential elections. However, there are a variety of reasons to suppose that the trends evident in presidential voting might not appear at other electoral levels. For one thing, I have already argued that the significant dips in partisanship at the presidential level evident in Figure 3 are attributable primarily to the parties' specific presidential candidates in 1964 and 1972. If that is so, there is little reason to expect those dips—or the subsequent rebounds—in levels of partisan voting to appear at other electoral levels.

In any case, analysts of congressional voting behavior since the 1970s have been more impressed by the advantages of incumbency than by any strong connections between presidential and congressional votes—except insofar as voters may go out of their way to split their tickets in order to produce divided government. Thus, it would not be surprising to find a longer, more substantial decline in the level of partisan voting in congressional elections than in the analysis of presidential voting summarized in Figure 3.

. . . Figure 5 clearly shows a substantial decline in partisan voting in congressional elections from the early 1960s through the late 1970s. Indeed, the level of partisan voting declined in seven of the eight congressional elections between 1964 and 1978; by 1978, the average impact of partisanship on congressional voting was only a bit more than half what it had been before 1964. Although the overall impact of partisanship at the presidential and congressional levels was generally similar for much of this period, the declines at the congressional level were less episodic and longer lasting than those at the presidential level.

What is more surprising is that the revival of partisanship evident in presidential voting patterns since 1972 is also evident in congressional voting patterns since 1978. While the trend is later and less regular at the congressional level than at the presidential level, the absolute increases in partisan voting since 1980 have been of quite similar magnitude in presidential and congressional elections. While partisan voting remains noticeably less powerful in recent congressional elections than it was before 1964—or than it has been in recent presidential elections—the impact of partisanship on congressional votes in 1996 was almost60 percent greater than in 1978.

An interesting feature of the resurgence of partisan voting in congressional elections documented in Figure 5 is that it appears to be concentrated disproportionately among younger and better-educated voters. For example, voters under the age of 40 were noticeably less partisan in their voting behavior than those over the age of 50 in almost every election from 1952 through 1984, but virtually indistinguishable from the older voters in the late 1980s and 1990s. Similarly, levels of partisan voting were distinctly lower among voters with some college education than among those without high school diplomas before 1982, but not thereafter. These patterns suggest that the resurgence of partisan voting reflects some positive reaction by younger and better-educated voters to the political developments of the past two decades, rather than simply a "wearing off" of the political stimuli of the 1960s and 1970s.

Discussion

If the analysis presented here is correct, the American political system has slipped, with remarkably little fanfare, into an era of increasingly vibrant partisanship in the electorate, especially at the presidential level but also at the congressional level. How might we account for this apparent revival of partisan voting?

One plausible hypothesis is that increasing partisanship in the electorate represents a response at the mass level to increasing partisanship at the elite level. "If parties in government are weakened," [political scientist Martin] Wattenberg argued, "the public will naturally have less of a stimulus to think

Figure 5   Partisan Voting in Presidential and Congressional Elections

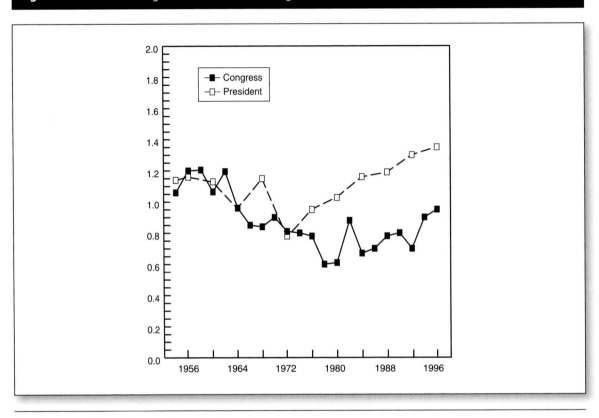

Note: Average probit coefficients, major-party voters only.

of themselves politically in partisan terms." But then the converse may also be true: in an era in which parties in government seem increasingly consequential, the public may increasingly come to develop and apply partisan predispositions of exactly the sort described by the authors of *The American Voter.*

Why might parties in government seem more relevant in the late 1990s than they had a quarter-century earlier? The ascensions of two highly partisan political leaders—Ronald Reagan in 1981 and Newt Gingrich in 1995—may provide part of the explanation. So too may the increasing prominence of the Religious Right in Republican party nominating politics over this period. At a more structural

level, the realignment of partisan loyalties in the South in the wake of the civil rights movement of the 1960s may be important, despite the evidence presented in Figure 4 suggesting that the revival of partisan voting has been a national rather than a regional phenomenon.

Regional realignment in the South and the influence of ideological extremists in both parties' nominating politics have combined to produce a marked polarization of the national parties at the elite level. By a variety of measures . . . votes on the floor of Congress have become increasingly partisan since the 1970s. . . . These changes in the composition of the parties' congressional delegations have been "reinforced by the operation of those reform provisions that were intended to enhance collective control" by party leaders in Congress, including a strengthened Democratic caucus and whip system. The new Republican congressional majority in 1995 produced further procedural reforms "delegating more power to party leaders than any House majority since the revolt against Joe Cannon in 1910."

We know less than we should about the nature and extent of mass-level reactions to these elite-level developments. However, the plausibility of a causal link between recent increases in partisanship at the elite and mass levels is reinforced by the fact that the decline in partisan voting in the electorate in the 1960s and 1970s was itself preceded by a noticeable decline in party voting in Congress from the 1950s through the early 1970s. Moreover, some more direct evidence suggests that citizens have taken note of the increasing strength of partisan cues from Washington. For example, the proportion of NES survey respondents perceiving "important differences" between the Democratic and Republican parties increased noticeably in 1980 and again in 1984 and reached a new all-time high (for the period since 1952) in 1996.

Even more intriguingly, [political scientist John] Coleman has documented a systematic temporal relationship between the strength of partisanship in government and the strength of partisanship in the electorate. Analyzing data from 1952 through 1990, Coleman found a strong positive correlation across election years (.60) between the strength of partisanship in NES surveys and the proportion of House budget votes with opposing party majorities—and an even stronger correlation (.66) between mass partisanship and opposing party majorities on budget authorization votes. While the detailed processes underlying this aggregate relationship are by no means clear, the strength of the correlation at least suggests that students of party politics would do well to examine more closely the interrelationship of mass-level and elite-level trends. . . .

12-3 Parties as Problem Solvers

Morris P. Fiorina

Political parties receive conflicting reviews. Some people view parties as self-serving entities that generate unnecessary conflict, make essential compromise more difficult, and serve as obstacles to solving important national problems. Others view party competition as the means for aggregating a variety of interests, generating policy alternatives, coordinating action across branches of government, and holding elected officials accountable. In this essay, political scientist Morris Fiorina evaluates the role of parties in addressing the nation's problems in the first decade of the new millennium.

Some twenty-five years ago I wrote an article entitled "The Decline of Collective Responsibility in American Politics." In that article (henceforth referenced as DOCR), I updated the classic arguments for party responsibility in light of which the politics of the 1970s looked seriously deficient. . . . . [I] noted that in the 1970s party cohesion had dropped to a level not seen since before the Civil War. As a result, national politics had degenerated into a free-for-all of unprincipled bargaining in which participants blithely sacrificed general interests in their pursuit of particularistic constituency interests. The unified Democratic government of President Jimmy Carter that failed to deal with national problems such as runaway inflation and successive energy crises exemplified the sorry state of national politics. Moreover, not only had policy failure become more likely, but because voting for members of Congress increasingly reflected the particularistic activities and personal records of incumbents, members had little fear of being held accountable for their contribution to the failures of national politics. In that light, I sympathetically resurrected the arguments of early to midcentury political scientists who advocated more responsible parties. Although not all problems were amenable to government solution, unified political parties led by strong presidents were more likely to act decisively to meet

the challenges facing the country, and when they took their collective performance records to the electorate for ratification or rejection, the voters at least had a good idea of whom to reward or blame.

Looking back at these essays, the 1980s clearly was the decade of party responsibility for me. But . . . . the prevalence of divided government in the late twentieth century had raised doubts in my mind about the arguments articulated a decade earlier. These doubts cumulated into a change of position explicated at length in *Divided Government* and later writings. In brief, as the parties became more distinct and cohesive during the 1980s, voters seemed to show little appreciation for the changes. Rather than entrust control of government to one unified party, Americans were increasingly voting to split control of government—at the state as well as the national level. And whether that was their actual goal or not—a matter of continuing debate—polls showed that majorities were happy enough with the situation, whatever political scientists thought of the supposed programmatic inefficiency and electoral irresponsibility of divided government. By the early 1990s, I had come to appreciate the electorate's point of view.

Moving from one side of an argument to the other in a decade suggests that the protagonist either was wrong earlier or (worse!) wrong later. But there is

Source: Morris P. Fiorina, "Parties as Problem Solvers," in *Promoting the General Welfare: New Perspectives on Government Performance,* eds. Alan S. Gerber and Eric M. Patashnik (Washington, D.C.: Brookings Institution Press, 2006), 237–253. Reproduced with permission of Brookings Institution Press in the format Republish in a book via Copyright Clearance Center. Notes appearing in the original have been deleted.

another less uncomplimentary possibility—namely, that the shift in stance did not reflect blatant error in the earlier argument so much as changes in one or more unrecognized but important empirical premises, which vitiate the larger argument. . . . . By 1990 I had come to believe that in important respects the parties we were observing in the contemporary era were different in composition and behavior from the ones described in the political science literature we had studied in graduate school. Parties organized to solve the governance problems of one era do not necessarily operate in the same way as parties organized to solve the problems of later eras.

This chapter considers the capacity of the contemporary party system to solve societal problems and meet contemporary challenges. I do so by revisiting DOCR and reconsidering it against the realities of contemporary politics. I begin by briefly contrasting American politics in the 1970s and the 2000s.

Politics Then and Now

DOCR reflected the politics of the 1970s, a decade that began with divided government (then still regarded as something of an anomaly), proceeded through the resignations of a vice president and president followed by the brief administration of an unelected president, then saw the restoration of the "normal order"—unified Democratic government—in 1976, only to see it collapse at the end of the decade in the landslide rejection of a presidency mortally wounded by international humiliation, stagflation, and energy crises. Contemporary critics placed much of the responsibility for the "failed" Carter presidency at the feet of Carter himself—his obsession with detail, his inability to delegate, his political tin ear, and so forth—but I felt then that the critics were giving insufficient attention to larger developments and more general circumstances that would have posed serious obstacles for presidents who possessed much stronger executive and political skills than Carter.

Political Conditions in the 1970s

Not only did Jimmy Carter's 1976 victory restore the presidency to the Democrats, but large Democratic majorities also controlled both the House and Senate. It seemed that the great era of government activism that had been derailed by the war in Vietnam would resume. Such was not to be. After four years of political frustration Carter was soundly defeated, the Republicans captured the Senate with a remarkable gain of twelve seats, and the Democrats lost thirty-three seats in the House. What happened?

Basically, the country faced a series of new problems, and the Democratic Party failed to deal with them in a manner satisfactory to electoral majorities in the nation as a whole and in many states and districts. Gas lines in particular, and the energy crisis in general, were something new in modern American experience, as were double-digit inflation and interest rates near 20 percent. Middle-class tax revolts were a startling development that frightened Democrats and energized Republicans, and a succession of foreign policy setbacks led many to fear that the United States was ill prepared to deal with new challenges around the world. In the face of such developments Democratic majorities in Congress failed to deliver. Indeed, they seemed fixated on old, ineffective solutions like public works spending and trade restrictions. The honeymoon between Carter and congressional Democrats ended fairly quickly, and the partnership was under strain for most of Carter's administration. Members worked to protect their constituencies from the negative effects of the new developments and worried much less about the fate of Carter or the party as a whole. As Figure 1 shows, this was a period of low party cohesion, and although cross-party majorities were not as common as in the late 1960s, Figure 2 shows that they still were common.

The generation of congressional scholars who contributed to the literature of the 1950s and 1960s had defended the decentralized Congresses of the period against the centralizing impulses of presidential scholars and policy wonks. True, Congress did not move fast or efficiently, nor did it defer to presidential leadership, but most scholars would have characterized this as pragmatic incrementalism rather than the "deadlock of democracy." Congress reflected and was responsive to the heterogeneity of interests in the country. . . .

Figure 1   The Decline and Resurgence of Party in Government Party Unity, 1954–98

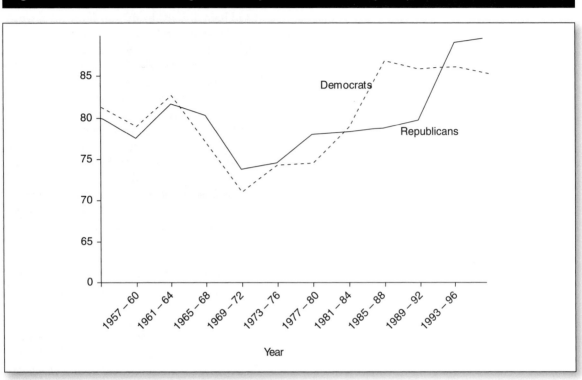

Year

Source: Harold W. Stanley and Richard G. Niemi, eds., *Vital Statistics on American Politics, 2005–2006* (Washington, DC: CQ Press, 2005), Table 5.8.

To a younger generation of scholars, however, the failings of the decentralized Congresses and disorganized parties were cause for concern. Serious problems faced the country, presidents were held responsible for solving these problems, but incumbent members of Congress seemingly could win reelection by abandoning their presidents and parties in favor of protecting parochial constituency interests. By emphasizing their individual records, members of Congress had adapted to an era of candidate-centered politics. Historically speaking, they had far less to gain or lose from the effects of presidential coattails, nor need they be very concerned about midterm swings against their president's party.

Collective responsibility traditionally provided by the political parties was at a low ebb. *Pluribus* was running rampant, leaving *unum* in the electoral dust.

Political Conditions Now

In retrospect, the trends decried in DOCR had already bottomed out by the Carter presidency. The cross-party majorities that passed President Reagan's budget and tax cuts may have obscured the fact, but party unity and party differences already were on the rise and continued rising in succeeding years (Figures 1 and 2). In a related development, the electoral advantages accruing to incumbency already were beginning to recede as

Figure 2   The Decline and Resurgence of Party in Government Party Votes, 1953–98

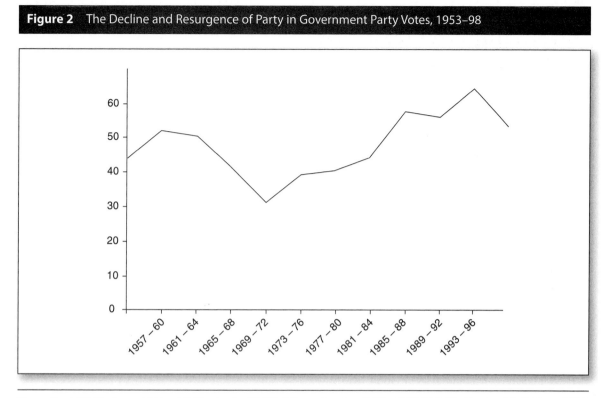

Source: Harold W. Stanley and Richard G. Niemi, eds., *Vital Statistics on American Politics, 2005–2006* (Washington, DC: CQ Press, 2005), Table 5.7.

national influences in voting reasserted themselves. And a new breed of congressional leaders emerged to focus the efforts of their parties in support of or opposition to presidential proposals. In 1993 President Clinton's initial budget passed without a single Republican vote in the House or Senate, and unified Republican opposition contributed greatly to the demise of the administration's signature health care plan.

And then came 1994, when the Republicans finally had success in an undertaking they had sporadically attempted for a generation—nationalizing the congressional elections. In the 1994 elections, personal opposition to gun control or various other liberal policies no longer sufficed to save Democrats in conservative districts whose

party label overwhelmed their personal positions. The new Republican majorities in Congress seized the initiative from President Clinton to the extent that he was asked at a press conference whether he was "still relevant." When congressional Republicans overreached, Clinton reasserted his relevance, beating back Republican attempts to cut entitlement programs and saddling them with the blame for the government shutdowns of 1995–96.

At the time, the Republican attempt to govern as a responsible party struck many political scientists as unprecedented in the modern era, but, as Baer and Bositis pointed out, politics had been moving in that direction for several decades. Indeed, a great deal of what the 1950 APSA [American Political Science Association] report called for already had come to pass (Table 1). Now, a decade later, it is apparent that the Congress elected in 1994 was only the leading edge of a new period in national politics. Party unity and presidential support among Republicans hit fifty-year highs during the first term of President George W. Bush, and in 2002 the president pulled off the rare feat of leading his party to seat gains in a midterm election. After his reelection in 2004, President Bush spoke in terms clearly reminiscent of those used by responsible party theorists. On the basis of a 51 percent popular majority, he claimed a mandate to make his tax cuts permanent and transform Social Security. Moreover, early in 2005 when the president was asked why no one in his administration had been held accountable for mistakes and miscalculations about Iraq, he replied in words that should have warmed the hearts of responsible party theorists: "We had an account-ability moment, and that's called the 2004 election. And the American people listened to different assess-ments made about what was taking place in Iraq, and they looked at the two candidates, and chose me, for which I'm grateful." No president in living memory had articulated such clear statements of collective party responsibility legitimized by electoral victory.

In sum, the collective responsibility DOCR found wanting in the 1970s seems clearly present in the 2000s. Why, then, am I troubled by the operation of something I fervently wished for in the 1970s?

The Problems with Today's Responsible Parties

In 2002 a Republican administration ostensibly committed to free enterprise endorsed tariffs to pro-tect the U.S. steel industry, a policy condemned by economists across the ideological spectrum. Also in 2002 Congress passed and President Bush signed an agricultural subsidy bill that the left-leaning *New York Times* decried as an "orgy of pandering to special interest groups," the centrist *USA Today* called "a congressional atrocity," and the right-leaning *Economist* characterized as "monstrous." In 2003 Congress passed and the president signed a special interest–riddled prescription drug plan that was the largest entitlement program adopted since Medicare itself in 1965, a fiscal commitment that immediately put the larger Medicare program on a steep slide toward bankruptcy. In 2004 congres-sional Republicans proposed and President Bush supported a constitutional amendment to ban gay marriage, a divisive proposal that had no chance of passing. After his reelection, President Bush declared his highest priority was to avert a crisis in a Social Security system he insisted was bankrupt, by estab-lishing a system of personal accounts, while disin-terested observers generally pronounced the situation far from crisis and in need of relatively moderate reform—especially compared to Medicare.

Table 1 APSA Report after Forty Years			
Fate of proposal	**Democrats**	**Republicans**	**System**
Full implementation	13	6	5
Partial implementation	7	5	5
De facto movement	8	9	5
No change	3	10	3
Negative movement	2	3	2

Source: Grossly adapted from Denise Baer and David Bositis, *Politics and Linkage in a Democratic Society* (Upper Saddle River, N.J.: Prentice-Hall, 1993), appendix.

In 2005 the Republican Congress passed and President Bush signed a pork-filled transportation bill that contained 6,371 congressional earmarks, forty times as many as contained in a bill vetoed by an earlier Republican president in 1987. Meanwhile, at the time of this writing Americans continue to die in a war of choice launched on the basis of ambiguous intelligence that appears to have been systematically interpreted to support a previously adopted position.

The preceding are only some of the more noteworthy lowlights of public policies adopted or proposed under the responsible party government of 2000–05. All things considered, if someone wished to argue that politics in the 1970s was better than today, I would find it hard to rebut them. Why? Are today's problems and challenges so much more difficult than those of the 1970s that the decentralized, irresponsible parties of that time would have done an even poorer job of meeting them than the more responsible parties of today? Or are today's responsible parties operating in a manner that was not anticipated by those of us who wished for more responsible parties? In the remainder of this chapter, I will focus on the latter possibility.

What Didn't DOCR Anticipate?

With the benefit of hindsight, one potentially negative effect of political competition by cohesive, differentiated parties is to raise the stakes of politics. Certainly, majority control of institutions always is valuable; committee chairs, agenda control, staff budgets, and numerous other benefits go to the majority. But if majority control of the House or Senate means relatively little for policymaking because moderate Republicans and Democrats hold the balance of power, which party formally holds control means less than when policy is decided within each party caucus. Similarly, the knowledge that the president's program either will be rubber-stamped by a supportive congressional majority or killed by an opposition majority makes unified control of all three institutions that much more valuable. The fact that the parties have been so closely matched in the past decade makes the competition that much more intense.

With the political stakes ratcheted upward, politics naturally becomes more conflictual. The benefits of winning and the costs of losing both increase. Informal norms and even formal rules come under pressure as the legislative majority strives to eliminate obstacles to its agenda. Meanwhile, the minority is first ignored, then abused. House Democrats under Jim Wright marginalized House Republicans in the 1980s, and the Republicans have enthusiastically returned the favor since taking control in 1994. Meanwhile Senate Majority Leader Bill Frist threatens the minority Democrats with the "nuclear option"—a rules change that effectively eliminates the filibuster on presidential appointments. In sum, the increasing disparity between majority and minority status further raises the electoral stakes and makes politics more conflictual.

In retrospect, it is probable that the development of more responsible parties was a factor—certainly not the only one—that contributed to the rise of the permanent campaign. With majority status that much more valuable, and minority status that much more intolerable, the parties are less able to afford a hiatus between elections in which governing takes precedence over electioneering. All else now is subordinated to party positioning for the next election. Free trade principles? Forget about them if Pennsylvania and Ohio steel workers are needed to win the next election. Budget deficits? Ignore them if a budget-busting prescription drug plan is needed to keep the opposition from scoring points with senior citizens. Politics always has affected policies, of course, but today the linkage is closer and stronger than ever before.

A second problem with cohesive parties that offer voters a clear choice is that voters may not like clear choices. The APSA report asserted that responsible parties would offer voters "a proper range of choice." But what is "proper"? Voters may not want a clear choice between repeal of *Roe v. Wade* and unregulated abortion, between private Social Security accounts and ignoring inevitable problems, between launching wars of choice and ignoring developing threats. Despite much popular commentary to the contrary, the issue positions of the electorate as a whole are not polarized; voters today remain, as always, generally moderate, or, at least, ambivalent. But candidates and their parties are polarized, and the consequence is candidate evaluations and votes that are highly polarized, which is what we have seen in recent elections.

Even if voters *were* polarized on issues and wished the parties to offer clear choices, they would still be dissatisfied if there were more than one issue and the opinion divisions across issues were not the same. For example, contemporary Republicans are basically an alliance between economic and social conservatives, and Democrats an alliance between economic and social liberals. So, in which party does someone who is an economic conservative and a social liberal belong? An economic liberal and a social conservative? Such people might well prefer moderate positions on both dimensions to issue packages consisting of one position they like a great deal and another they dislike a great deal.

The bottom line is that the majoritarianism that accompanies responsible parties may be ill suited for a heterogeneous society. With only one dimension of conflict a victory by one party can reasonably be interpreted to mean that a majority prefers its program to that of the other party. But with more than one dimension a victory by one party by no means guarantees majority support for its program(s). Indeed, . . . given variations in voter intensity on different issues, a party can win by constructing a coalition of minorities—taking the minority position on each issue.

American politics probably appeared to have a simpler and clearer structure at the time the APSA report was written. Race was not on the agenda. Social and cultural issues were largely dormant in the midcentury decades, their importance diminished by the end of immigration in the 1920s, the Great Depression, and World War II. A bipartisan consensus surrounded foreign and defense policy. Under such conditions it is understandable that a midcentury political scientist could have felt that all

the country needed was two parties that advocated alternative economic programs. For example, in 1962 political historian James McGregor Burns wrote, "It is curious that majoritarian politics has won such a reputation for radicalism in this country. Actually it is moderate politics; it looks radical only in relation to the snail-like progress of Madisonian politics. The Jeffersonian strategy is essentially moderate because it is essentially competitive; in a homogeneous society it must appeal to the moderate, middle-class independent voters who hold the balance of power."

To most contemporary observers the United States looks rather less homogeneous than it apparently did to observers of Burns's era. Compared to 1950, our present situation is more complex with a more elaborate political issue space and less of a tendency to appeal to the moderate voter, as we discuss below.

Burns's contention that majoritarian politics is moderate politics is quite interesting in light of the contemporary discussion of the polarization of American politics. Although the electorate is not polarized, there is no question that the political class—the variegated collection of candidates, activists, interest group spokespersons, and infotainment media—is polarized. And, where we can measure it well, there is little doubt that the political class has become increasingly polarized over the past several decades. Figure 3 illustrates the oft-noted fact that moderates have disappeared from Congress: the area of overlap where conservative Democrats and liberal Republicans meet has shrunk to almost nothing, and it has done so at the same time as the parties were becoming more responsible—indeed, figures like these often are cited as indicators of party responsibility.

Why would polarization accompany party responsibility? Logically it need not. Indeed, the APSA report asserted that "[n]eeded clarification of party policy in itself will not cause the parties to differ more fundamentally or more sharply than they have in the past." But as I have argued elsewhere, today's parties are not the same as the parties described in midcentury textbooks. The old distinctions between

Figure 3 Polarization of Congress since the 1960s

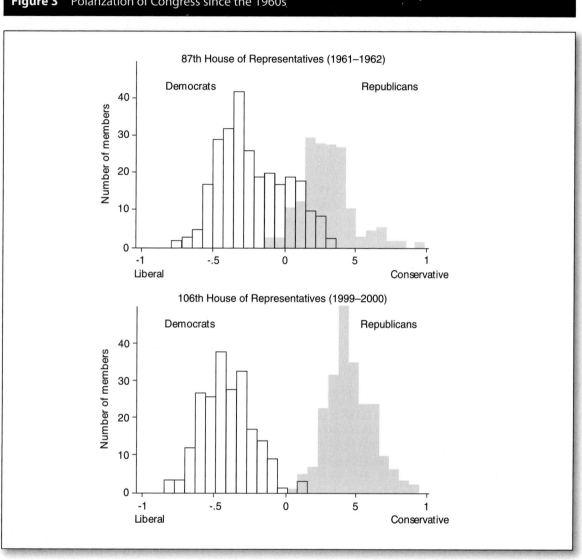

Source: Keith Poole, http://voteview.com/dwnomin.htm.

"amateurs" and "professionals" or "purists" and "professionals" no longer have the same conceptual value because the amateurs have won, or perhaps more accurately, the professionals now are purists. At the time the responsible party theorists wrote, parties nominated candidates on the basis of their service to the party and their connections to party leaders, or, in more competitive areas, their electability. Aside from times when a party was bitterly divided, issue positions were seldom a litmus test of a candidate's suitability. Material motivations—control of offices, patronage—were dominant, but civil service, public sector unionization, conflict of interest laws, social welfare programs, and other developments have lessened the personal material rewards that once motivated many of those active in politics. Today, ideological motivations are relatively more important than previously. Candidates must have the right set of issue stances to attract support, and many of the potential supporters would prefer to lose with a pure ideological candidate than to win with a mushy moderate. Some candidates themselves no doubt feel the same.

These developments have contributed to a basic shift in party electoral strategy in the contemporary United States. At midcentury, the conventional wisdom expressed by Burns was in accord with political science theory—that two-party competition induces parties to move toward the center to capture the median voter. But in the last decade of the century we saw a shift to what now seems to be the prevailing strategy of concentrating on the party base—doing whatever is necessary to maximize loyalty and turnout by core party constituencies. Thus, the aforementioned forcing of a Senate vote on gay marriage was an entirely symbolic gesture toward the evangelical Christian base of the Republican Party. It had nothing to do with governing; it was a costly signal that the Bush administration was on their side.

Seemingly, today's parties no longer strive to maximize their vote, only to suffice—to get more votes than the other party. At one time a maximal victory was desirable because it would add credibility to the victors' claim that the voters had given them a mandate. But as the previously quoted remarks of President Bush indicate, at least some of today's politicians consider any victory, narrow or not, a mandate.

Parties composed of issue activists and ideologues behave differently from the parties that occupied the political science literature of the mid-twentieth century. At midcentury, each party appealed to a different swath of the American public, Democrats primarily to blue-collar workers and Republicans to middle-class-professionals and managers. Because such large social groupings were far from homogeneous internally, the party platform had to tolerate internal heterogeneity to maintain itself and compete across a reasonably broad portion of the country. As Turner put it, "[Y]ou cannot give Hubert Humphrey [liberal Democratic Senator from Minnesota] a banjo and expect him to carry Kansas. Only a Democrat who rejects part of the Fair Deal can carry Kansas, and only a Republican who moderates the Republican platform can carry Massachusetts."

Although both parties continue to have support in broad social groupings like blue-collar workers and white-collar professionals, their bases now consist of much more specifically defined groups. Democrats rely on public-sector unions, environmentalists, prochoice and other liberal cause groups. Republicans rely on evangelicals, small business organizations, prolife and other conservative cause groups. Rather than compromise on a single major issue such as economics, a process that midcentury political scientists correctly saw as inherently moderating, parties can now compromise across issues by adding up constituency groups' most preferred positions on a series of independent issues. Why should conservative mean prolife, low taxes, procapital punishment, and preemptive war, and liberal mean just the opposite? What is the underlying principle that ties such disparate issues together? The underlying principle is political, not logical or moral. Collections of positions like these happen to be the preferred positions of groups that now constitute important parts of the party bases.

At one time political scientists saw strong political parties as a means of controlling interest groups. Parties and groups were viewed as competing ways of organizing political life. If parties were weak, groups would fill the vacuum; if parties were strong, they would harness group efforts in support of more general party goals. Two decades ago, I was persuaded by this argument, but time has proved it suspect. Modern parties and their associated groups now overlap so closely that it is often hard to make the distinction between a party activist and an issue activist. As noted above, the difference between party professionals and purists does not look nearly so wide as it once did.

Although more speculative, I believe that unbiased information and policy effectiveness are additional casualties of the preceding developments. The APSA report asserts, "As a means of achieving responsibility, the clarification of party policy also tends to keep public debate on a more realistic level, restraining the inclination of party spokesmen to make unsubstantiated statements and charges." Recent experience shows just the opposite. Policies are proposed and opposed relatively more on the basis of ideology and the demands of the base, and relatively less on the basis of their likelihood of solving problems. Disinformation and outright lies become common as dissenting voices in each party leave or are silenced. The most disturbing example comes out of congressional passage of the 2003 Medicare prescription drug add-on bill. Political superiors threatened to fire Medicare's chief actuary if he informed Congress that the add-on would be 25–50 percent more costly than the administration publicly claimed. The administration apparently was willing to lie to members of its own party to assure passage of a bill whose basis was mostly political. More recently, President Bush introduced his campaign to add personal accounts to Social Security by claiming that Social Security was bankrupt and that personal accounts were a means of restoring the system to fiscal solvency. Although many experts see merit in the idea of personal savings accounts, most agreed that implementing them would increase Social Security's fiscal deficits in the coming decades. Even greater agreement surrounded rejection of the claim that Social Security was bankrupt. Although politically difficult, straightforward programmatic changes in the retirement age, the tax base, or the method of indexing future benefits would make Social Security solvent for as long as actuaries can reasonably predict.

Moreover, because parties today focus on their ability to mobilize the already committed, the importance of performance for voting declines in importance relative to ideology and political identity. It was telling that in 2004 John Kerry frequently was criticized for not having a plan to end the war in Iraq that was appreciably different from President Bush's. This seems like a new requirement. In 1952 did Dwight Eisenhower have a specific plan to end the war in Korea that differed from President Truman's? "I will go to Korea" is not exactly a plan. In 1968 did Richard Nixon have a specific plan to end the war in Vietnam that differed from President Johnson's? A "secret plan" to end the war is not exactly a precise blueprint that voters could compare to the Johnson policy. Some decades ago voters apparently felt that an unpopular war was sufficient reason to punish an incumbent, regardless of whether the challenger offered a persuasive "exit strategy."

A final consideration relates to the preceding ones. Because today's parties are composed relatively more of issue activists than of broad demographic groupings, they are not as deeply rooted in the mass of the population as was the case for much of our history. The United States pioneered the mass party, but, as Steven Schier has argued, in recent decades the parties have practiced a kind of exclusive politics. The mass-mobilization campaigns that historically characterized American elections gave way to the high-tech media campaigns of the late twentieth century. Voter mobilization by the political parties correspondingly fell. Late-century campaigns increasingly relied on television commercials, and there is some evidence that such ads demobilize the electorate. In a kind of "back to the future" development, the two most recent presidential elections have seen renewed party effort to get out the vote, with a significant impact, at least in 2004. But modern computing capabilities and rich databases enable the parties to practice a kind of targeted mobilization based on specific issues that was more difficult to do in earlier periods. It is not clear that such activities make the parties more like those of yesteryear, or whether they only reinforce the trends I have previously discussed. One-third of the voting age population continues to eschew a party identification, a figure that has not appreciably changed in three decades.

Discussion

In sum, the parties today are far closer to the responsible party model than those of the 1970s, a development that some of us wished for some decades ago, but it would be difficult to argue that today's party system is more effective at solving problems than the disorganized decentralized party system that it replaced. Rather than seek power on the basis of coherent programs, the parties at times throw fundamental principles to the wind when electoral considerations dictate, just as the decentralized parties of the mid-twentieth century did. At other times they hold fast to divisive positions that have only symbolic importance—President Bush reiterated his support for a constitutional amendment to ban gay marriage in his 2005 State of the Union address—for fear of alienating ideologically committed base elements. On issues like Social Security and the war in Iraq, facts are distorted and subordinated to ideology. Mandates for major policy changes are claimed on the basis of narrow electoral victories.

To be sure, I have painted with a broad brush, and my interpretations of recent political history may prove as partial and inaccurate as some of those advanced in DOCR. In particular, I am sensitive to the possibility that unified Democratic government under present conditions might be significantly different from the unified Republican government we have experienced—Nils Gilman argues that the features of responsible parties discussed above are really Republican features. But even if true, this implies that an earlier generation of political scientists failed to appreciate that Republican and Democratic responsible party government would be significantly different, let alone identify the empirical bases for such differences. What this reconsideration has demonstrated to me is the difficulty of making broad recommendations to improve American politics, even when seemingly solid research and argument underlie many of the component parts, which is the reason I will venture no such recommendations here. It is possible that this paper is as much a product of its temporal context as DOCR was. As Aldrich argues, the political parties periodically reinvent themselves better to deal with the problems they face. That, in fact, is my hope—that the next reinvention of the parties results in organizations that are better than the current models at dealing with the problems our society faces.

Chapter 13

Interest Groups

13-1 The Scope and Bias of the Pressure System

E. E. Schattschneider

> *In the mid-twentieth century, many observers believed that James Madison's vision of America—as a multitude of groups or factions, none of which dominated the government—had been realized. E. E. Schattschneider provided an alternative view. In the following essay, which was originally published in 1960, Schattschneider argued that moneyed interests dominated mid-twentieth-century politics. In his view the dominance of moneyed interests limited the scope of government action and created a bias in the pressures placed on policymakers. Early in the twenty-first century, the issues raised by Schattschneider remain relevant to debates over the influence of organized and moneyed interests in American government and politics.*

The scope of conflict is an aspect of the scale of political organization and the extent of political competition. The size of the constituencies being mobilized, the inclusiveness or exclusiveness of the conflicts people expect to develop leave a bearing on all theories about how politics is or should be organized. In other words, nearly all theories about politics have something to do with the question of who can get into the fight and who is to be excluded. . . .

If we are able . . . to distinguish between public and private interests and between organized and unorganized groups we have marked out the major boundaries of the subject; *we have given the subject shape and scope. . . .* [W]e can now appropriate the piece we want and leave the rest to someone else. For a multitude of reasons *the most likely field of study is that of the organized, special-interest groups.* The advantage of concentrating on organized groups is that they are known, identifiable, and recognizable. The advantage of concentrating on special-interest groups is that they have one important characteristic in common; they are all exclusive. This piece of the pie (the organized special-interest groups) we shall call the *pressure system.* The pressure system has boundaries we can define; we can fix its scope and make an attempt to estimate its bias.

It may be assumed at the outset that all organized special-interest groups have some kind of impact on politics. A sample survey of organizations made by the Trade Associations Division of the United States Department of Commerce in 1942 concluded that "From 70 to 100 percent (of these associations) are

Source: E. E. Schattschneider, "The Scope and Bias of the Pressure System," in *The Semi-Sovereign People* (New York: Holt, Rinehart, Winston, 1960), 20–45. © 1975 Wadsworth, a part of Cengage Learning, Inc. Reproduced by permission. Www.cengage.com/permissions. Some notes appearing in the original have been deleted.

planning activities in the field of government relations, trade promotion, trade practices, public relations, annual conventions, cooperation with other organizations, and information services."

The subject of our analysis can be reduced to manageable proportions and brought under control if we restrict ourselves to the groups whose interests in politics are sufficient to have led them to unite in formal organizations having memberships, bylaws, and officers. A further advantage of this kind of definition is, we may assume, that the organized special-interest groups are the most self-conscious, best developed, most intense and active groups. Whatever claims can be made for a group theory of politics ought to be sustained by the evidence concerning these groups, if the claims have any validity at all.

The organized groups listed in the various directories (such as *National Associations of the United States,* published at intervals by the United States Department of Commerce) and specialty yearbooks, registers, etc., and the *Lobby Index,* published by the United States House of Representatives, probably include the bulk of the organizations in the pressure system. All compilations are incomplete, but these are extensive enough to provide us with some basis for estimating the scope of the system.

By the time a group has developed the kind of interest that leads it to organize, it may be assumed that it has also developed some kind of political bias because *organization is itself a mobilization of bias in preparation for action.* Since these groups can be identified and since they have memberships (i.e., they include and exclude people), it is possible to think of the *scope* of the system.

When lists of these organizations are examined, the fact that strikes the student most forcibly is that *the system is very small.* The range of organized, identifiable, known groups is amazingly narrow; there is nothing remotely universal about it. There is a tendency on the part of the publishers of directories of associations to place an undue emphasis on business organizations, an emphasis that is almost inevitable because the business community is by a wide margin the most highly organized segment of society.

Publishers doubtless tend also to reflect public demand for information. Nevertheless, the dominance of business groups in the pressure system is so marked that it probably cannot be explained away as an accident of the publishing industry.

The business character of the pressure system is shown by almost every list available. *National Associations of the United States* lists 1,860 business associations out of a total of 4,000 in the volume, though it refers without listing to 16,000 organizations of businessmen. One cannot be certain what the total content of the unknown associational universe may be, but, taken with the evidence found in other compilations, it is obvious that business is remarkably well represented. Some evidence of the overall scope of the system is to be seen in the estimate that 15,000 national trade associations have a gross membership of about one million business firms. The data are incomplete, but even if we do not have a detailed map this is the shore dimly seen.

Much more directly related to pressure politics is the *Lobby Index, 1946–1949* (an index of organizations and individuals registering or filing quarterly reports under the Federal Lobbying Act), published as a report of the House Select Committee on Lobbying Activities. In this compilation, 825 out of a total of 1,247 entries (exclusive of individuals and Indian tribes) represented business. A selected list of the most important of the groups listed in the *Index* (the groups spending the largest sums of money on lobbying) published in the *Congressional Quarterly Log* shows 149 business organizations in a total of 265 listed.

The business or upper-class bias of the pressure system shows up everywhere. Businessmen are four or five times as likely to write to their congressmen as manual laborers are. College graduates are far more apt to write to their congressmen than people in the lowest educational category are.

The limited scope of the business pressure system is indicated by all available statistics. Among business organizations, the National Association of Manufacturers (with about 20,000 corporate members) and the Chamber of Commerce of the United States (about as large as the N.A.M.) are giants.

Usually business associations are much smaller. Of 421 trade associations in the metal-products industry listed in *National Associations of the United States,* 153 have a membership of less than 20. The median membership was somewhere between 24 and 50. Approximately the same scale of memberships is to be found in the lumber, furniture, and paper industries, where 37.3 percent of the associations listed had a membership of less than 20 and the median membership was in the 25 to 50 range.

The statistics in these cases are representative of nearly all other classifications of industry.

Data drawn from other sources support this thesis. Broadly, the pressure system has an upper-class bias. There is overwhelming evidence that participation in voluntary organizations is related to upper social and economic status; the rate of participation is much higher in the upper strata than it is elsewhere. The general proposition is well stated by [political scientist Paul] Lazarsfeld:

> People on the lower SES levels are less likely to belong to any organizations than the people on high SES (Social and Economic Status) levels. (On an A and B level, we find 72 percent of these respondents who belong to one or more organizations. The proportion of respondents who are members of formal organizations decreases steadily as SES level descends until, on the D level only 35 percent of the respondents belong to any associations.)[1]

The bias of the system is shown by the fact that even non-business organizations reflect an upper-class tendency.

Lazarsfeld's generalization seems to apply equally well to urban and rural populations. The obverse side of the coin is that large areas of the population appear to be wholly outside the system of private organization. A study made by Ira Reid of a Philadelphia area showed that in a sample of 963 persons, 85 percent belonged to no civic or charitable organization and 74 percent belonged to no occupational, business, or professional associations, while another Philadelphia study of 1,154 women showed that 55 percent belonged to no associations of any kind.[2]

A *Fortune* farm poll taken some years ago found that 70.5 percent of farmers belonged to no agricultural organizations. A similar conclusion was reached by two Gallup polls showing that perhaps no more than one third of the farmers of the country belonged to farm organizations, while another *Fortune* poll showed that 86.8 percent of the low-income farmers belonged to no farm organizations. All available data support the generalization that the farmers who do not participate in rural organizations are largely the poorer ones. . . .

The class bias of associational activity gives meaning to the limited scope of the pressure system, because *scope and bias are aspects of the same tendency.* The data raise a serious question about the validity of the proposition that special-interest groups are a universal form of political organization reflecting *all* interests. As a matter of fact, to suppose that everyone participates in pressure-group activity and that all interests get themselves organized in the pressure system is to destroy the meaning of this form of politics. The pressure system makes sense only as the political instrument of a segment of the community. It gets results by being selective and biased; *if everybody got into the act, the unique advantages of this form of organization would be destroyed, for it is possible that if all interests could be mobilized the result would be a stalemate.*

Special-interest organizations are most easily formed when they deal with small numbers of individuals who are acutely aware of their exclusive interests. To describe the conditions of pressure-group organization in this way is, however, to say that it is primarily a business phenomenon. Aside from a few very large organizations (the churches, organized labor, farm organizations, and veterans' organizations) the residue is a small segment of the population. *Pressure politics is essentially the politics of small groups.*

The vice of the groupist theory is that it conceals the most significant aspects of the system. The flaw in the pluralist heaven is that the heavenly chorus sings with a strong upper-class accent. Probably about 90 percent of the people cannot get into the pressure system.

The notion that the pressure system is automatically representative of the whole community is a myth fostered by the universalizing tendency of modern group theories. *Pressure politics is a selective process* ill designed to serve diffuse interests. The system is skewed, loaded, and unbalanced in favor of a fraction of a minority.

On the other hand, pressure tactics are not remarkably successful in mobilizing general interests. When pressure-group organizations attempt to represent the interests of large numbers of people, they are usually able to reach only a small segment of their constituencies. Only a chemical trace of the fifteen million Negroes in the United States belong to the National Association for the Advancement of Colored People. Only one five-hundredth of 1 percent of American women belong to the League of Women Voters, only one sixteen-hundredth of 1 percent of the consumers belong to the National Consumers' League, and only 6 percent of American automobile drivers belong to the American Automobile Association, while about 15 percent of the veterans belong to the American Legion.

The competing claims of pressure groups and political parties for the loyalty of the American public revolve about the difference between the results likely to be achieved by small-scale and large-scale political organization. Inevitably, the outcome of pressure politics and party politics will be vastly different. . . .

. . . Everything we know about politics suggests that a conflict is likely to change profoundly as it becomes political. It is a rare individual who can confront his antagonists without changing his opinions to some degree. Everything changes once a conflict gets into the political arena—*who* is involved, *what* the conflict is about, the resources available, etc. It is extremely difficult to predict the outcome of a fight by watching its beginning because we do not even know who else is going to get into the conflict. The logical consequence of the exclusive emphasis on the determinism of the private origins of conflict is to assign zero value to the political process.

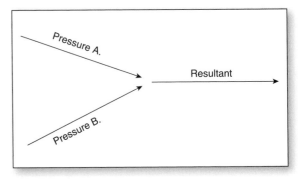

The very expression "pressure politics" invites us to misconceive the role of special-interest groups in politics. The word "pressure" implies the use of some kind of force, a form of intimidation, something other than reason and information, to induce public authorities to act against their own best judgment. [This is reflected in the famous statement by political scientist Earl Latham, in his 1952 book *The Group Basis of Politics*, that] the legislature is a "referee" who "ratifies" and "records" the "balance of power" among the contending groups.[3]

It is hard to imagine a more effective way of saying that Congress has no mind or force of its own or that Congress is unable to invoke new forces that might alter the equation.

Actually the outcome of political conflict is not like the "resultant" of opposing forces in physics. To assume that the forces in a political situation could be diagramed as a physicist might diagram the resultant of opposing physical forces is to wipe the slate clean of all remote, general, and public considerations for the protection of which civil societies have been instituted.

Moreover, the notion of "pressure" distorts the image of the power relations involved. Private conflicts are taken into the public arena precisely because someone wants to make certain that the power ratio among the private interests most immediately involved shall not prevail. To treat a conflict as a mere test of the strength of the private interests is to leave out the most significant factors. This is so true that it might indeed be said that the only way to preserve private power ratios is to keep conflicts out of the public arena.

The assumption that it is only the "interested" who count ought to be reexamined in view of the foregoing discussion. The tendency of the literature of pressure politics has been to neglect the low-tension force of large numbers because it *assumes that the equation of forces is fixed at the outset.*

Given the assumptions made by the group theorists, the attack on the idea of the majority is completely logical. The assumption is that conflict is monopolized narrowly by the parties immediately concerned. There is no room for a majority when conflict is defined so narrowly. It is a great deficiency of the group theory that it has found no place in the political system for the majority. The force of the majority is of an entirely different order of magnitude, something not to be measured by pressure-group standards.

Instead of attempting to exterminate all political forms, organizations, and alignments that do not qualify as pressure groups, would it not be better to attempt to make a synthesis, covering the whole political system and finding a place for all kinds of political life?

One possible synthesis of pressure politics and party politics might be produced by *describing politics as the socialization of conflict.* That is to say, the political process is a sequence: conflicts are initiated by highly motivated, high-tension groups so directly and immediately involved that it is difficult for them to see the justice of competing claims. As long as the conflicts of these groups remain *private* (carried on in terms of economic competition, reciprocal denial of goods and services, private negotiations and bargaining, struggles for corporate control or competition for membership), no political process is initiated. Conflicts become political only when an attempt is made to involve the wider public. Pressure politics might be described as a stage in the socialization of conflict. This analysis makes pressure politics an integral part of all politics, including party politics.

One of the characteristic points of origin of pressure politics is a breakdown of the discipline of the business community. The flight to government is perpetual. Something like this is likely to happen wherever there is a point of contact between competing power systems. It is the *losers in intrabusiness conflict who seek redress from public authority. The dominant business interests resist appeals to the government.* The role of the government as the patron of the defeated private interest sheds light on its function as the critic of private power relations.

Since the contestants in private conflicts are apt to be unequal in strength, it follows that *the most powerful special interests want private settlements* because they are able to dictate the outcome as long as the conflict remains private. If A is a hundred times as strong as B he does not welcome the intervention of a third party because he expects to impose his own terms on B; he wants to isolate B. He is especially opposed to the intervention of public authority, because public authority represents the most overwhelming form of outside intervention. Thus, if A/B = 100/1, it is obviously not to A's advantage to involve a third party a million times as strong as A and B combined. Therefore, it is the weak, not the strong, who appeal to public authority for relief. It is the weak who want to socialize conflict, i.e., to involve more and more people in the conflict until the balance of forces is changed. In the schoolyard it is not the bully but the defenseless smaller boys who "tell the teacher." When the teacher intervenes, the balance of power in the schoolyard is apt to change drastically. It is the function of public authority to *modify private power relations by enlarging the scope of conflict.* Nothing could be more mistaken than to suppose that public authority merely registers the dominance of the strong over the weak. The mere existence of public order has already ruled out a great variety of forms of private pressure. Nothing could be more confusing than to suppose that the refugees from the business community who come to Congress for relief and protection *force* Congress to do their bidding.

Evidence of the truth of this analysis may be seen in the fact that the big private interests do not necessarily win if they are involved in public conflicts with petty interests. The image of the lobbyists as primarily the agents of big business is not easy to support on the face of the record of congressional hearings, for example. The biggest corporations in the country tend to avoid the arena in which pressure groups and lobbyists fight it out before congressional committees. To describe this process exclusively in terms of an effort of business to intimidate congressmen is to misconceive what is actually going on.

It is probably a mistake to assume that pressure politics is the typical or even the most important relation between government and business. The pressure group is by no means the perfect instrument of the business community. What does big business want? The *winners* in intrabusiness strife want (1) to be let alone (they want autonomy) and (2) to preserve the solidarity of the business community. For these purposes pressure politics is not a wholly satisfactory device. The most elementary considerations of strategy call for the business community to develop some kind of common policy more broadly based than any special-interest group is likely to be.

The political influence of business depends on the kind of solidarity that, on the one hand, leads all business to rally to the support of *any* businessman in trouble with the government and, on the other hand, keeps internal business disputes out of the public arena. In this system businessmen resist the impulse to attack each other in public and discourage the efforts of individual members of the business community to take intrabusiness conflicts into politics.

The attempt to mobilize a united front of the whole business community does not resemble the classical concept of pressure politics. The logic of business politics is to keep peace within the business community by supporting as far as possible all claims that business groups make for themselves. The tendency is to support all businessmen who

have conflicts with the government and support all businessmen in conflict with labor. In this way *special-interest politics can be converted into party policy*. The search is for a broad base of political mobilization grounded on the strategic need for political organization on a wider scale than is possible in the case of the historical pressure group. Once the business community begins to think in terms of a larger scale of political organization the Republican party looms large in business politics.

It is a great achievement of American democracy that business has been forced to form a political organization designed to win elections, i.e., has been forced to compete for power in the widest arena in the political system. On the other hand, *the power of the Republican party to make terms with business rests on the fact that business cannot afford to be isolated*.

The Republican party has played a major role in *the political organization of the business community,* a far greater role than many students of politics seem to have realized. The influence of business in the Republican party is great, but it is never absolute because business is remarkably dependent on the party. The business community is too small, it arouses too much antagonism, and its aims are too narrow to win the support of a popular majority. The political education of business is a function of the Republican party that can never be done so well by anyone else.

In the management of the political relations of the business community, the Republican party is much more important than any combination of pressure groups ever could be. The success of special interests in Congress is due less to the "pressure" exerted by these groups than it is due to the fact that Republican members of Congress are committed in advance to a general probusiness attitude. The notion that business groups coerce Republican congressmen into voting for their bills underestimates the whole Republican posture in American politics.

It is not easy to manage the political interests of the business community because there is a perpetual stream of losers in intrabusiness conflicts who go to the government for relief and protection. It has not been possible therefore to maintain perfect solidarity, and when solidarity is breached the government is involved almost automatically. The fact that business has not become hopelessly divided and that it has retained great influence in American politics has been due chiefly to the overall mediating role played by the Republican party. There has never been a pressure group or a combination of pressure groups capable of performing this function.

Notes

1. Paul F. Lazarsfeld, Bernard Berelson, and Hazel Gaudet. *The People's Choice* (New York: Columbia University Press, 1948), p. 145.

2. Ira Reid and Emily Ehle, "Leadership Selection in the Urban Locality Areas," *Public Opinion Quarterly* (1950), 14:262–284. See also Norman Powell, *Anatomy of Public Opinion* (New York: Prentice Hall, 1951), pp. 180–181.

3. Earl Latham, *The Group Basis of Politics* (Ithaca: Cornell University Press, 1952), pp. 35–36.

13-2 Issue Advertising and Legislative Advocacy in Health Politics

Richard L. Hall and Richard Anderson

Advertising in the media by special interests seeking to influence the public and policymakers has grown in recent decades. Focusing on the politics of health policy in recent decades, political scientists Richard L. Hall and Richard Anderson describe recent trends and outline the efforts of special interest groups to frame issues and mobilize public support for their causes. Less clear is the effect of issue advertising on legislators and policy outcomes. In the case of health policy prior to the Obama administration, the authors demonstrate that the advertising was heavily stacked against health policy reform. That changed to a more equal balance in the early Obama administration, after it made significant concessions to business, when health care reform was adopted.

In the fall of 1993 President Bill Clinton announced his plan for comprehensive health care reform, and an unremarkable political commercial appeared on American television screens in a handful of states. The ad portrayed a conversation "sometime in the future." A middle-class couple named Harry and Louise sit at their kitchen table discussing how good their health insurance coverage used to be and how bad it had become. With a discordant piano refrain playing in the background, the foreboding voice of the narrator intones that "the government may force us to pick from a few health care plans designed by government bureaucrats." "If they choose," Harry begins, "we lose," Louise concludes. A simple admonition, "Get the Facts," then appears on the television screen, while the narrator tells the viewer: "For reforms that protect what we have, call toll free. . . ."

Fast-forward fifteen years. Similarly ominous music plays in the background, and we again see the characters Harry and Louise sitting at their kitchen table, this time dressed for work. Harry has been reading the newspaper and lays it open in front of Louise: "Health care costs are up again. Small companies are being forced to cut their plans." Displeased but not surprised, Louise mentions a family friend who has just been diagnosed with cancer. "He's covered, right?" Harry worriedly asks. "No," responds Louise, "He just joined a start-up and he couldn't afford a plan." "Just too many people are falling through the cracks," Harry opines; then Louise concludes that the next president needs to "make something happen."

These two examples represent a form of political advocacy typically referred to as "issue advertising." Issue advertisements are mass-media appeals intended to promote an interest group's favored policy, much as business firms use commercials to promote retail products. Indeed, many of the Madison Avenue techniques for influencing consumers are used by political consultants to influence citizens. And like conventional commercials, issue advertisements appear through a variety of media: newspapers,

Source: Richard L. Hall and Richard Anderson, "Issue Advertising and Legislative Advocacy in Health Politics," in *Interest Group Politics,* 8th ed., ed. Allan J. Cigler and Burdett A. Loomis (Washington DC: CQ Press, 2012), 221–242.

television, radio, the Internet, even highway billboards. Unlike commercials selling retail products, however, issue ads typically exhibit one or both of two purposes: to alter or intensify viewers' beliefs about a particular public policy and/or to induce viewers to communicate those beliefs to elected officials that represent them.

Achieving these purposes, in turn, is a means to a more distant, Washington-centered end: changing the behavior of those officials in order to influence the policy being advertised. In fact, the first Harry and Louise ads were widely credited with having killed the Clinton health care plan.[1] Subsequent research has shown that claim to be greatly exaggerated,[2] but politicians are a risk-averse lot. They ignore communications from constituents—mail, e-mail, phone calls, comments or protests during "town hall" meetings—at their peril, and a good issue ad campaign can produce a flurry of messages. Such a campaign can also "prime" a legislator's constituents for subsequent appeals.[3] And spending on an ad campaign itself, independent of its effect on citizens' behavior, signals a group's willingness to reward legislators who help it and punish those who don't.

Issue advertising is not new in the practice of advocacy, of course, but its use has expanded substantially in the two decades since Harry and Louise first appeared on our television screens, and that trend shows no signs of slowing. In this chapter, we examine issue advertising, treating it as a particular form of grassroots lobbying. We describe briefly the rapid expansion of issue advertising in US national politics. We review what we know about the effectiveness of issue ads in changing citizens' beliefs and behavior: How do interest groups frame their messages? How do they evoke emotions to best effect? We then explore the relationship between issue advertising strategies and legislative strategies: Which legislators do interest groups target when making their advertising buys, and why? What effects do targeted advertising campaigns have on congressional policy making? In addressing these questions, we focus on the role of issue advertising in health policy making, one of the

most contentious policy domains of our time and a site of some of the most intense issue advertising campaigns in recent memory.

Issue Advertising as Outside Lobbying

As we use the term here, *issue advertising* is a particular form of grassroots advocacy or "outside" lobbying.[4] Outside lobbying occurs when organized interests attempt to influence elected representatives indirectly by influencing the attitudes and/or behavior of citizens whose subsequent votes the reelection-minded representative will seek. Our definition thus focuses on advertising that is about specific issues and occurs between elections, not during them. In applying this definition, we hasten to emphasize, this chapter employs a distinction that is becoming increasingly blurry in American politics: namely, between legislative advocacy and campaign advocacy, or between "pure" issue ads and "sham" issue ads. The latter are campaign ads that, until very recently, had to masquerade as issue ads to escape Federal Election Commission (FEC) regulation. We come back to that distinction in the concluding section in order to speculate about the legal and practical future of issue advertising. For now, we focus on issue advertising that is distinguishable from candidate-centered advertising and draw on cases and data that encompass almost exclusively the former.

Like other forms of outside lobbying, most issue advertising aims to influence politicians by mobilizing citizens. Thus, most ads contain admonitions that the viewer contact his or her representative(s) in Washington and contain information that facilitates such contacts.[5] Alleging that special interest groups were misleading the public on health care reform, for example, one 2009 AARP ad urged viewers to "tell Congress not to let myths get in the way of fixing what's broken with health care." The ad then directed them to the group's Web site, where they would find links to congressional Web sites. On the opposing side, one ad in a $1.5 million campaign by The 60 Plus Association alleged that reformers wanted government to decide "if older patients are worth the cost." It then ended with the plea: "Tell Congress: Don't Pay for Health Care Reform On the Backs of Our Seniors."[6] The final frame displayed a phone number. The viewers who called it were patched through to their own representatives' offices.

Some issue ads are tailored to more specific audiences, sometimes identifying particular legislators for praise or scorn. For example, a 2009 ad run by Health Care for America Now (HCAN) charged that the Republicans were blocking health care reform because of $14.3 million dollars they allegedly received from the health care industry. The ad opened with photos of the Republican leadership, including the respective chambers' minority leaders, Senator Mitch McConnell and Rep. John Boehner. Similarly, a conservative ad that likened health care reform to a prescription drug with bad side effects was repeated in selected districts and identified their specific representatives: "Call Collin Peterson (202–225 . . .). Tell him to oppose a government takeover of health care." Peterson, a moderate House Democrat from Minnesota, had already announced that he would vote against his party's reform package when it came to the House floor, but he never got the chance to vote against a government takeover of health care. No such measure was proposed by either party in either chamber.

Not all issue ads are intended to incite immediate action by the audience, however. Some ads simply call attention to the larger policy problem, raising its salience in the minds of the voters. In the year-long lead-up to health care reform in 2009, AARP broadcast hundreds of spots in a multi-million-dollar "Divided We Fail" campaign, "demanding" that Congress reform the health care system. Appearing in television, radio, and print media, the ads featured average citizens highlighting the problems they faced because of rising costs and declining coverage. The ads for this campaign said nothing about what sorts of reforms AARP supported, so at first glance, they might seem strategically ill conceived; media strategies that have no actionable message are unlikely to generate much action.[7] However, such ads might prove effective in priming citizens for subsequent messages or signaling legislators about interest group resolve, mechanisms that we discuss below.[8]

The Rise of Issue Advertising

Issue advertising in the United States has a rich and varied history. As citizens of England, colonial agitators used petitions to protest excessive taxes and the quartering of British troops. The first antislavery petitions date at least to 1783, when several hundred Pennsylvania Quakers signed a resolution urging the young Congress to abolish slavery. Petition drives are still useful instruments of grassroots activism, but issue advocacy has changed more than it has stayed the same, both in scope and technology. For example, telephone campaigns conducted through "robo-calls" can reach pre-programmed quotas of citizens at a relatively low cost, encouraging them to "let Washington know" how strongly they support or oppose a piece of legislation. Almost all grassroots organizations active today develop their own Internet networks. When an organization has a priority that is ripe for action, it can quickly send out to attentive sympathizers an "action alert"—a well-timed message asking them to contact their respective representatives.

Comprehensive data on the full variety, number, and cost of issue advertisements are not available, but most agree that this category of interest group spending has been rising rapidly since the mid-1990s. The most extensive and systematic analysis to date comes from two studies by the Annenberg Public Policy Center.[9] The reports focus on the 107th (2001–02) and 108th (2003–04) Congresses, respectively, and they only examine advertising within the Washington, D.C., media markets. Nonetheless, they show that interest groups are spending remarkable sums on issue advertising. The study of the 107th Congress estimated that $41 million was spent on television issue ads. The study of the 108th Congress found that that number had increased over five-fold—to $225 million. Combining both broadcast and print totals for the Washington area, issue ad expenditures went from $105 million in the 107th Congress to $404 million in the 108th.[10]

The Annenberg reports also break down spending by topic. Over the two Congresses, health care ranked second among the twenty-eight policy areas that generated nonnegligible advertising buys. In the 108th Congress, Medicare prescription drug legislation, not comprehensive reform, was on the agenda. Yet in that two-year period advocacy groups spent $80.4 million in and around Washington, D.C., a sum greater than spending for the entire country on the 1993 Clinton reforms, which would have affected every health sector. By way of comparison, all campaign contributions by all health PACs to all federal candidates during the 108th Congress totaled just $31.6 million, less than 40 percent of issue advertising costs in the Washington media market. We should note, too, that the Annenberg categorizations exclude from the health category several health-related areas: tort reform ($5.9 million), substance abuse ($1.6 million), and abortion ($0.7 million).

Data from several sources permit a rough comparison of issue ad spending on the Clinton health care reform bill in 1993–94 with the Obama reform bill considered in 2009–10. On the 1993 Harry and Louise issue ads alone, one study found that the insurance industry spent approximately $14 million in 1993–94.[11] Summing across all groups that were contacted, in turn, the same study estimated interest group spending on television issue advertisements at $60 million, with the lion's share spent by groups against the Clinton bill.[12] Compare this to the 2009–10 debate over comprehensive health care reform. In March 2010 a *Time* article reported that in the single week leading up to the final House vote, television spending on issue ads was about $24 million, and that sum came on top of approximately $200 million that had already been spent during the yearlong debate over the bill.[13] Millions more were spent on radio and print advertising during both fights, so these estimates are undoubtedly low.[14] Nonetheless, they suggest that in the fifteen years between health care reform initiatives, issue advertising increased substantially, perhaps dramatically. "From both the left and the right," a 2009 *Time* article concludes, " . . . political campaign ads are

saturating our television screens with arguments for and against President Obama's health-care-reform effort."[15] The *Washington Post* echoes this sentiment, observing that the "heated fight over health-care legislation is saturating the summer airwaves, with groups on all sides of the debate pouring tens of millions of dollars into advertising campaigns."[16]

Omitted from the above numbers is the increasingly important use of issue advertising on the Internet.[17] In the health care reform fight of 2009–10, groups from both ends of the political spectrum placed issue ads on such websites as *Politico, The Drudge Report, Talking Points Memo,* and others whose audiences included politically attentive individuals who are most easily mobilized. Internet ads were also used to mount old-style petition drives with new technology. For instance, the antireform group, the Association of American Physicians and Surgeons, used Google search ads to generate signatories to their petition to "Fight Obama Health Care."[18] MoveOn, HCAN, and AARP likewise purchased Google search ads in 2009 to dispel a false claim propagated by Sarah Palin and Rush Limbaugh that the Obama plan would create government "death panels" to advise seniors when to end their lives. The *Los Angeles Times* reported that the Palin allegation generated far more Internet advertising than any public policy issue to date, including the Iraq War. At one point in September 2009, over ninety different organizations had purchased Google ads related to the health care reform debate.[19]

Targeting the Legislator's Audience

Interest groups do not often spend huge sums on issue advertising absent a larger strategy about how to achieve their policy objectives. As we have noted, the two-step purpose of most ads is to influence the attitudes and/or behavior of citizens, who will then influence the behavior of their Washington, D.C., representatives. However, even the richest groups running the most expensive campaigns cannot cover the entire country. How do interest groups decide at whom they will target their advertising buys?

The receptivity of citizens to an advertising appeal counts as one important factor; in this respect, issue advertisements are like most types of outside lobbying.[20] Issue ads that advocate a major expansion of Medicaid are unlikely to play well in highly conservative areas, where most citizens want the size of the welfare state to contract, not expand. Similarly, ads about gaps in Medicare prescription drug coverage will mobilize more viewers in districts that have disproportionately high numbers of senior citizens.

Antireform groups followed this logic in 1993–94, encouraging individuals predisposed to dislike President Clinton's "Health Security for All" proposal to participate politically. The insurance companies' media consultant, Ben Goddard, would later report that they "targeted involved Americans, people who were registered to vote, wrote letters to editors or public officials, attended meetings and made political contributions."[21] But the only media venue that Goddard mentioned other than the major news networks was Rush Limbaugh,[22] whose far-right audience hated "Hillary-Care." Ken Goldstein's interviews with lobbyists active on the same bill also found an interest group tendency to target "reliable supporters."[23]

Unfortunately, no data are available on the incidence and placement of issue ads directed at the Clinton reform bill, but we do have systematic evidence about a related and more recent case. The data come from the Wisconsin Advertising Project, which catalogued the number of television issue advertisements in the top 100 media markets that dealt with the Medicare Prescription Drug and Modernization Act (hereafter, the MMA). Enacted by Congress in 2003, the MMA created for the first time government-funded prescription drug coverage for Medicare recipients. Early polls showed that seniors had misgivings about a new government plan, but by the time the legislation was adopted, their attitudes had changed in the bill's favor. Moreover, senior citizens meet all of the criteria for good targets that Goddard had applied in 1993–94. They are disproportionately more likely to vote, write letters, and otherwise participate in politics.

Figure 1 reports the average number of advertisements that ran in each state according to the number of prescriptions written for individuals over age sixty-five. As the bar graph shows, the greater the prescription drug demand generated by a state's retirees, the more television ads health advocacy groups ran in that state. In fact, groups on both sides followed this pattern. Groups promoting the new coverage anticipated major political benefit once coverage began for the bill's beneficiaries. The Association of Retired Americans (ARA), which ran issue ads opposing the bill, did so not because it opposed the new coverage; rather it thought the new benefit was not generous enough.[24]

A second factor in determining which audiences to target is the degree to which a group has an organizational presence in the member's constituency. Unions and other federated organizations may have one or more chapters or locals in a district or state, which provide a group with greater access to the press, better developed networks within the area, and a base for political mobilization around specific issues. Similarly, corporations enjoy connections to a geographic constituency to the extent that they have headquarters, offices, or manufacturing plants and therefore employees among a member's constituents. In such areas, issue ads should prove more effective in that a subset of citizens will have a predisposition—perhaps a self-interested incentive—to contact their representatives.

How much does a group's connection to a member's constituency affect the number of issue ads it will run there? In his study of advocacy on the Clinton health care bill, Goldstein asked interest group strategists about their organization's outside lobbying activities, one of which was issue advertising. He found that a group's connectedness to a district mattered a good deal. For example, a group of pharmaceutical companies hired a political consultant to fashion a message that would appeal to its stockholders and employees. Using that message in a telephone campaign, "nineteen thousand retired workers and stockholders were patched through to twenty different congressional offices."[25] Goldstein also cites a newspaper report that large corporations opposed to reform

Figure 1   Targeting Interested Constituents: Issue Advertising on the MMA of 2003

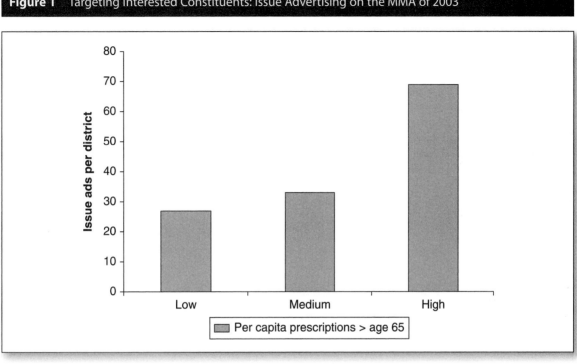

Source: Based on data provided by the Wisconsin Advertising Project, http://wiscadproject.wisc.edu/project.php.

developed similar communication strategies to influence their employees in key congressional districts.[26] A spokesperson for one of the organizations behind the 2009 Harry and Louise campaign explained: "Most of [the advertising buys] will come in targeted congressional districts where our companies have a significant economic presence, or in districts where members [of Congress] can still be persuaded to support comprehensive health-care reform."[27]

Do such patterns hold for other health policies and health advocacy groups? To help answer this question, we return to the Wisconsin Advertising Project's data on the Medicare prescription drug legislation. For each of the five groups that ran television ads regarding the MMA, we counted the number of organizational sites—for example, headquarters or regional offices, state or local chapters, research sites, manufacturing plants—in each state. These groups ran advertisements in 46 states for a total of 230 group-state observations. The relationship between organizational presence (sites per congressional district) and issue advertisements is shown in Figure 2. The pattern is striking. On average, the five groups that advertised on the MMA ran about 25 ads per congressional district in states where they had a low number of sites (the lowest third), about 80 ads where their presence ranked in the middle, and over 180 ads per district in states where their presence was high (the top third).

Targeting Legislators

From the previous section, we can conclude that groups tend to advertise in areas where the public is likely to be attentive or can be made attentive and

Figure 2 Issue Advertising Close to Home: Targeted Ads on the MMA of 2003

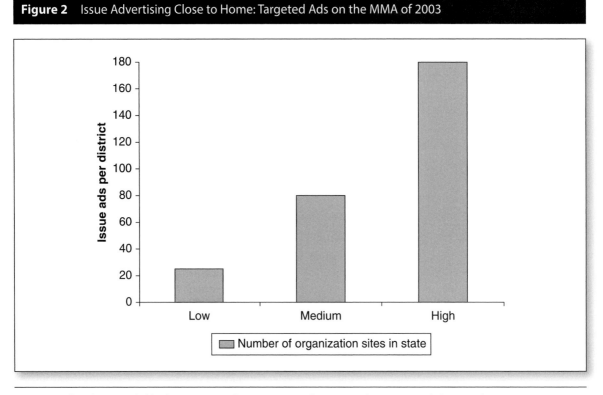

Source: Based on data provided by the Wisconsin Advertising Project, http://wiscadproject.wisc.edu/project.php.

where the citizenry (or some significant subset of it) is receptive to the group's position, precisely the two factors that Ken Kollman concludes are important for all outside lobbying.[28] But influencing constituents is not an end in itself. Ad campaigns outside of Washington are ineffectual inside Washington if they neglect the districts of (potentially) influential legislators.[29]

Most accounts of outside lobbying, both academic and journalistic, characterize it as an instrument for swaying pivotal legislators to support the interest group's position. In fact, legislators take positions in several ways that can affect a bill's progress. A member might cosponsor the bill (or a competing bill), either before or after it is formally introduced; she might sign (or dissent from) a committee report; she

might sign a "Dear Colleague" letter or issue a statement supporting (opposing) it. But the most visible and important position taking occurs when the roll is called—when members must vote yea or nay on a bill, any amendments to it, and any procedural choices that affect it.

In his study of the Clinton health care fight, Goldstein interviewed interest group strategists to identify the members they targeted using outside tactics, one of which was issue advertising. He found that outside lobbying campaigns mainly targeted "persuadable" legislators, that is, the members in the middle.[30] Because the Clinton reforms never came to the floor in either chamber, Goldstein found, most of these targets were in the committees of jurisdiction, and most groups—sixteen of twenty-one or 67 percent—focused on "undecided" legislators.[31] One of Goldstein's respondents commented, "We figured out who was for us and who was against us and threw the kitchen sink at everyone in the middle."[32]

The American Medical Association (AMA) applied similar tactics in the summer of 2008 when the Senate was considering legislation to increase doctor reimbursement rates under Medicare.[33] The governing statute set rates according to a long-outdated formula, but because Congress had not devised a better one, it had been adopting year-to-year adjustments. Absent such an adjustment, reimbursement rates would drop steeply in July of 2008. By a ratio of six to one, the House passed a one-year fix giving doctors a 1 percent increase rather than the formula's 10.6 percent cut, but the bill stalled in the Senate due to opposition by key Republicans. The AMA responded by launching an aggressive issue advertising campaign. One television ad warned that the government would "slash physician Medicare payments," forcing doctors to cut back on medical care for seniors. Applauding the House for "doing the right thing," the ad charged that a group of senators had committed "an outrage," conspiring with insurance company lobbyists to maintain the industry's inflated payments under Medicare Advantage plans. The AMA ran the ads in the states of ten senators who were holding up the bill.[34]

The AMA's strategy in this last case also suggests that groups tend to focus on members of Congress who are electorally vulnerable. Of senators targeted by the AMA in 2008, 70 percent were up for reelection in the 2008 cycle as opposed to the one-third up in any given cycle. More generally, the prospect of a close election concentrates the mind of ambitious politicians, making them especially hesitant to alienate single-issue voters. Interest group advocates understand that tendency and put their knowledge to strategic use whenever possible. Returning to the MMA case, the number of Medicare prescription drug issue ads in 2003 ran more than 30 percent higher in states that had a senator up for reelection. So too in the Obama health care case: the conservative group 60

Plus ran a series of ads against the reform package, announcing that it was going after eighteen electorally vulnerable Democrats.[35]

The advertising data from the 2003 MMA debate provide additional evidence of the importance that groups attach to approaching floor votes. In the 2003 time-series of group advertising buys, the number of ads spiked at three times. The first was April 2003, when the House committees held the first hearings of the 108th Congress on Medicare prescription drug coverage. But the other two spikes appeared, respectively, in the two weeks before the July floor votes and the two weeks prior to the November votes on the conference report. From February through early June, the number of Medicare issue ads averaged about 1,000 per week nationwide. In the two weeks before the first floor votes in June, the number of ads jumped to 3,000 per week. In the two weeks before the November votes on the conference report, the weekly incidence of ads dropped to about 500. But in the two weeks before adoption of the conference report, the number of ads shot up to almost 6,000 per week.

In sum, advertising buys can increase dramatically as important floor votes approach. But do those ads therefore target only the swing legislators? Not entirely. Patterns of issue advertising in the MMA case indicate that winning over undecided legislators directly was not the only or even the most important goal served by issue ad campaigns. Groups also targeted states heavily represented by members already friendly to their cause. In states where the percentage of allies in a delegation was high, for example, the number of ads was approximately twice the number as in states where the percentage of swing members was high and four times the number in states with a high percentage of opponents.

Why would groups focus on members whose positions one doesn't need to change? One possible explanation is that a group does so strategically—that is, it mounts an advertising campaign to anticipate or offset (advertising-induced) pressure on its allies from the other side, a strategy analogous to "counteractive lobbying" inside Congress.[36] But a more complete answer depends on the importance of legislative activities other than voting. Influence in Congress goes to those who work at it. It comes from labor-intensive efforts, such as drafting and introducing legislation, offering amendments, planning strategy, trading favors, and otherwise spending scarce time and political capital.[37] One of the most important of these activities, in fact, may be the legislator lobbying his or her colleagues on how to vote. Issue ads provide incentives for group-friendly members to do such lobbying and other work on an issue where the group and legislator share a common purpose. By raising the salience of an issue among a friendly member's constituents, issue ads can increase the political credit that that member can then claim for effective work in Washington.

Conversely, groups can and sometimes do use ads to lay blame at the feet of legislators who were steadfastly opposed to the advertising group's position. Running negative ads about a bill can short-circuit subsequent attempts by the member to claim credit for helping to pass it. They may even "prime" a member's constituents for subsequent issue ads that blame the legislator for promoting an unpopular bill.[38] Were they to work in this way, negative issue ads could thus "demobilize" a member by turning visibility on an issue into a political liability.

In the MMA case, blame-focused ads were relatively rare. Of the issue ads that named a particular member, in fact, the vast majority were laudatory, not accusatory. In the 2009–10 health care reform debate, no systematically collected data are available, but even during this unusually negative, strident debate, many of the leading advocacy groups ran ads expressing praise or appreciation for the actions of their legislative allies as the fight unfolded. The AFL-CIO, Americans for Health Care Reform, Americans United for Change, Catholics United, Families USA, the Pharmaceutical Research Manufacturers Association (PhRMA), Healthcare for America Now (HCAN), and the Service Employees International Union (SEIU) together spent tens of millions of dollars on ad campaigns crediting key Democrats for their actions in supporting health care reform. Conservative groups, including the 60 Plus Association and the Susan B. Anthony List, likewise ran ads praising specific antireform members. Other antireform groups spent millions of advertising dollars on ideologically right-wing Internet sites, talk radio, and television that reached conservative audiences represented by conservative members.

Journalistic reports on the issue ad campaigns suggest that positive ads targeted at legislative allies were much less frequent than ads targeting undecided legislators or legislators opposed to the group's position. Numerous organizations on both sides aggressively targeted wavering legislators and publicly announced that they were doing so. The pharmaceutical spokesperson quoted above stated they were doing so with the latter-day Harry and Louise ads. Similarly, the pro-reform groups Health Care for America Now and MoveOn.org and the antireform groups U.S. Chamber of Commerce and 60 Plus announced campaigns that would focus on undecided legislators or legislators whose electoral vulnerability might make them so.[39]

However, most stories in the press reported on television ads that attacked legislators either for their support for or their opposition to the bill. Such ads were especially common from ideological groups that opposed reform, such as the Club for Growth. Indeed, these ads continued to run after the bill's passage. Emboldened by opinion polls that showed much of the public dissatisfied with the Obama legislation, antireform groups went after Democratic incumbents who had voted for the bill by supporting their challengers who vowed to repeal it.

In general, we do not know the degree to which either side targeted allies, undecided members, or opponents during the 2009–10 health care reform fight, but issue advertising on this issue broke all records. Given the tens of millions spent on health care reform ads, it should come as no surprise that some groups could use their advertising capacity to reward friends, attack opponents, and pressure undecided members.

Issue Advertising Messages and the Political Psychology of Citizens

To this point we have examined the nature and purpose of interest group advertising strategies. That many groups spend millions of dollars on issue ad campaigns suggests that they think their strategies bear fruit. But are they right? To what extent do issue ads induce citizens to change their views? And what features of issue advertisements make them more or less effective?

Research in political psychology provides some insight into the process by which political advertisements can influence voters. We have already referred to one mechanism, what the political psychologists refer to as "priming."[40] In this context, priming refers to the way in which previous, often repetitious, ads affect a viewer's implicit memory in such a way that some aspects of a complex issue are more easily retrieved. In the year leading up to the Obama administration's health care reforms, for example, AARP ran an expensive advertising campaign that characterized the current health care system as broken in ways that could no longer be ignored. When the legislative debate over reform got underway in 2009, aspects of the debate that reflected the "broken status quo" might then be evoked more easily.

Research also shows how features of advertisements as subtle as the background music will cue different emotional reactions from viewers.[41] Ominous music with discordant chords arouses listener fear or anxiety, but those emotions also increase individuals' willingness to consider new information and reassess their opinions. Advertisements with patriotic or inspirational music that evoke enthusiasm, on the other hand, cause experimental subjects to report higher likelihood of participation, an effect that should be important if the purpose is to mobilize citizens to contact their representatives.

We can see these tactics in action by comparing the two advertisements that opened this chapter. The first is from the original Harry and Louise ad campaign, which was aired by the Health Insurance Association of America (HIAA).[42] In 1993, when these ads were run, public support for Clinton's health care reform was high. To undercut this support, the insurance industry ad needed citizens to rethink their positions. The ad imagines a Harry and Louise conversation after reform about how bad their health insurance has become. The negative message is thus clear, but the music reinforces the effectiveness at an emotional level. A discordant piano refrain plays in the background as the foreboding voice of the narrator warns viewers that they will lose control of their own health care.

In the second commercial, Harry and Louise return to the airwaves, this time representing a pro-reform message.[43] In 2008, support for healthcare reform was high, but the form it should take was being contested in the presidential campaign. The pro-reform advocates thus needed to do two things: warn the public about how bad the private health care system had become, but also deliver a positive message about what reform could do. The music in the ad reflects the two-part nature of the ad's purpose. In the first half, the actors are asking viewers to rethink their satisfaction with the current system, so the music is ominous and discordant. But near the end of the ad, the music shifts to uplifting, resonating chords as Louise looks to the future and the importance of the issue in the next election: "Whoever the next president is, health care should be at the top of his agenda, bringing everyone to the table and making it happen." The implicit emotional cue to the viewer is to get out and vote, and vote with health policy reform in mind.

Of course, issue ads are designed to work through message as well as emotion. Both scholars and practitioners emphasize the potential for issue ads to *frame* a policy message in terms that, if internalized by the public, advantages one side. In research on political communication, framing is a psychological concept that refers to one's perception about "what the debate is about."[44] Is health care reform about government bureaucrats denying choice to average

Americans, as the first Harry and Louise suggested? Or is it about expanding insurance coverage to the "too many people" who are "slipping through the cracks," as the latter-day Harry and Louise characterized it?

Ben Goddard, the head of the media consulting firm for the insurance industry in 1993–94, described the development of the original ads that cast Harry and Louise as two average Americans whom health care reform would hurt:

> The key thing in advertising is finding the right message and messenger. In putting together the materials, we tested as spokespersons high-profile celebrities, doctors, and academic experts. Bill Gradison then gave a speech and said, 'this issue is going to be decided around people's kitchen tables.' My first reaction was skepticism, but we tried it with a couple around a kitchen table and it was a huge success over other formats. People respond to a familiar environment. The kitchen is a symbol for family decisions. Our research told us that people would respond to the message and that they would like the messenger.[45]

Of course, media consultants such as Goddard were not the first to discover the importance of framing in health politics. Analyzing a century of failed attempts to adopt universal health insurance in the United States, historian Colin Gordon emphasizes the skill of the American Medical Association in framing all reform proposals as "socialized medicine," a mischaracterization that in 2009–10 once again gave opponents of reform good traction.[46]

Work in psychology and political science also shows that citizens are not indiscriminate in the messages they accept. The source of the message matters. If a viewer is exposed to an advertisement sponsored by a group whose ideology they know and disagree with, that viewer will discount that information. Likewise, ads that contain messages reflecting the self-interest of the sponsor are considered less trustworthy.[47] Groups interested in running advertising

campaigns recognize this, however, and often select ambiguous and nonoffensive names that mask the policy biases of the group.[48] In one study, for instance, participants were presented with advertisements sponsored either by the "United Seniors Association," a highly active group financed largely by pharmaceutical interests, or by "pharmaceutical or drug companies." Respondents held the innocuously named "United Seniors Association" in much higher esteem, reporting a 5 percent disapproval rating, compared to the 58 percent disapproval rating given to the generic "pharmaceutical or drug companies."[49]

This tactic was evident again in the health care debates of 2009–10. Working this time on the pro-reform side, for instance, the pharmaceutical industry ran issue ads using the name "Americans for Stable and Quality Care." Other groups with unrevealing monikers included the Alliance for Health, Americans United for Change, and the Alliance to Improve Medicare.

Issue Advertising and Health Policy Making

The assumption that the insurance industry won the media wars in 1993 is one reason that Clinton and his advisers listed special interest influence on public opinion as a primary cause of their defeat.[50] Other observers at the time agreed. The HIAA Harry and Louise ads were widely credited with having contributed to the administration's defeat.[51] Some academic studies later echoed the point. Goldsteen et al. attribute the precipitous drop in support for the Clinton plan in 1993 to the Harry and Louise advertising campaign, which "captured public opinion" and reversed the trend in public opinion that was undercutting the insurance industry's position.[52] Kathleen Hall Jamieson likewise reports that the health insurance industry's Harry and Louise ads attacking the Clinton bill cost $12 million and generated a remarkable 300,000 calls, the effect of which was inflated by the fact that the ads themselves attracted a great deal of free media attention.[53]

Subsequent analysis by Larry Jacobs suggests that the influence on public opinion attributed to HIAA's Harry and Louise ads has been significantly overstated, in part because the public's latent discomfort with new federal programs was already strong.[54] The poll numbers supporting health care reform were thus artificially high in 1993 and likely to come down even if HIAA had stayed off of the airwaves. The point that issue advertising is most effective when one side dominates the airwaves remains valid, however. Jacobs and Shapiro make precisely this point in their analysis of public opinion regarding Clinton's reform bill.[55] In Jacob and Shapiro's view, however, both sides used "crafted speech" in an attempt to manipulate public opinion in their favor, although the pro-reform message was promoted by the White House, for the most part, and not through issue ads. The presence of conflicting messages, Jacobs and Shapiro argue, limited the impact of either side on the attitudes of individual citizens.

In another important case a few years later, however, Jamieson emphasizes the paucity of competing messages. In 1997, the tobacco industry mounted a multimedia ad campaign against legislation that would impose higher cigarette taxes, Food and Drug Administration (FDA) regulation of tobacco, and a $500 billion multistate settlement of cases against the industry for reimbursement of Medicaid costs.[56] Four tobacco companies joined together to spend $40 million in advertising over a five-month period. An industry spokesperson later reported that the ads generated 400,000 calls and telegrams to congressional offices. The American Cancer Society and the Campaign for Tobacco-Free Kids, in contrast, mounted a belated, bare-bones ad campaign targeted at a handful of senators. The tobacco industry's campaign, Jamieson concludes, was "a textbook example of the power of saturation advertising," which "allowed the industry to reshape the debate."[57]

Press accounts likewise point to the success of the AMA's issue ads urging Congress to correct the Medicare reimbursement rates for physicians in June of 2008, which we discuss above. The ads targeted ten senators who were blocking adoption of the reimbursement readjustment, and the AMA had the advertising airwaves to itself. Shortly after the July 4 recess, nine of the ten senators who had voted to block the bill changed their votes, more than enough to invoke cloture on the measure and move it toward passage.[58]

As in the case of tobacco regulation, evidence of advertising's influence in the doctor reimbursement matter is specific to the case, but that is not its main limitation. The problem is that any inference that the issue ads caused any senator's vote to change is more than a little tenuous. As we have seen, interest groups tend to target constituents already inclined to support their policies. And if group strategists can anticipate that reaction, so can senators. In fact, members do pay attention to constituent mail and other expressions of issue-specific opinions, such as e-mail, phone calls, and postcards. As constituent-initiated contacts increase, the probability that a sincerely undecided member will vote in the interest group's favor will probably go up. But because members of Congress *do* pay attention to constituents, and do so over long periods with good political intelligence, it is always possible that an interest group advertiser will push them where they were already likely to go.

Had the AMA not advertised, would the senators have done anything different? (Nine of ten, after all, is a good batting average in any league.) In fact, the answer is probably not. Republican support in Congress for AMA-favored policies is consistently strong; the organization's PAC gives to Republican over Democratic Senate candidates at a ratio greater than two to one. In fact, it had given generous contributions to every one of the ten senators in question in their previous election cycle (an average of $7,500 out of a maximum $10,000). The ten Republican senators did not want to cut payments to doctors, it turns out; instead they held out to protest the cuts in Medicare Advantage that the Democratic bill used to pay for the increase. Even for this simple case, the legislative effects of issue advertising are unclear.

It will be especially hard to assess whether the ubiquitous advertising about health care reform in

2009–10 had any effect on its eventual adoption. That the votes were so close in both chambers suggests that any number of factors might have made the difference. At the same time, no one voice, nor even one side of the issue, had a major advertising advantage in the print or broadcast media, much less traffic on the Internet.[59] The extraordinary frequency and diversity of ads created a political disharmony, the effects of which will require difficult research and very good data to sort out.

Conclusion: Issue Advertising and Democratic Practice

In summary, issue ads may be strategically clever instruments of political advocacy, they may command media budgets in the millions of dollars, and they may reach into the households of millions of Americans. Many of those Americans may actually watch them, and many who do watch may be influenced by them. But that does not mean that the ads have a net effect on the behavior of lawmakers, much less the shape of the laws that get made. That advertising campaigns launched by special interests can push around members of Congress is a disturbing assertion with modest empirical backing. But so would be the assertion that the millions of dollars spent on issue advertising are legislatively inconsequential. The fact is that we don't really know how much policy influence issue advertising generates.[60]

Even if one cannot show that issue advertising matters legislatively, however, it still matters democratically. In the practice of representation, we care not only who wins in the end but who participates in the process that leads to that end. Free speech and broad participation by diverse voices promote democratic deliberation and lend legitimacy to the policy process. As West and Francis point out, in fact, one of the main advantages of paid advertising is that a group can promote its perspective with the public without its views being screened and interpreted by the regular news media or political elites.[61] Other things equal, interest group participation in public policy debates is a good thing.

Issue advertising appears more democratically problematic, however, when one considers that in its most common forms it is highly expensive. Relevant here is E. E. Schattschnider's critique of American democracy, now a half century old: "The flaw in the pluralist heaven is that the heavenly chorus sings with a strong upper-class accent."[62] Social scientists since then have often found that narrow, resource-rich interests organize with relative ease, and they deploy their resources to magnify their voices in Congress. If this is also the case with issue ads, the public might hear a multitude of voices but only within a limited range. The Annenberg study for the 108th Congress found that nearly 80 percent of issue ads that ran in the Washington, D.C., media market were sponsored by corporations.[63] Within that set of groups, the vast majority of spending was done by a handful of private sector interests. The Annenberg study likewise reported an issue ad spending ratio of 5 to 1 by corporations relative to cause or citizen groups and a gigantic 100 to 1 business-to-union ratio.[64] A study of issue ads reported in the *New York Times* found a less severe bias in favor of corporations, though corporate ads were twice as common as those from nonprofit groups, some of which were themselves advocates for, and financed by, business organizations.[65] That study also found a smaller but still substantial business-to-union ratio of fourteen to one.

These patterns appear more democratically disturbing in light of the social scientific literature on framing, discussed above. Successful framing strategies structure the set of choices considered in public debate, and they are most successful when one viewpoint or one side controls the message. For the most part, antireform ads dominated the paid media during the Clinton health care debate, and almost all of those ads were financed by business interests that stood to lose from the proposed reforms. In the Medicare prescription drug case in 2003, only one organization ran any ads against the bill, and its ads were outnumbered by the insurance industry and other pro-business groups by more than ten to one. In the fight over tobacco legislation,

Jamieson concludes, the tobacco industry prevailed in part because of the meager and belated public interest group effort and "a lack of counterbalancing information in the news."[66]

Of the cases we have examined here, only the debate over the Obama health care reforms in 2009–10 elicited substantial issue advertising by both sides. In this respect, the competition of ideas generated in the paid media was robust. At the same time, two important features of that competition warrant mention. First, the range of the debate was framed narrowly very early in the process. A single-payer system was never on the table, not because it lacked merit on policy grounds but because it was dead on arrival on special interest grounds. Even its diminutive cousin, a "public option" for health insurance that would compete with private plans, was gasping its last breath before the Senate Finance Committee markup had begun. Likewise omitted from the Democrats' agenda were provisions that they had championed during the MMA debate only a few years before: reimportation of pharmaceuticals and government bargaining over the pharmaceutical prices passed through to Medicare and Medicaid. Either provision would have lowered the bill's cost by billions of dollars, but neither was tolerable to the pharmaceutical industry, whose support the White House thought crucial.[67]

The second feature of the issue ad competition regarding the Obama health care reforms follows from the first. It was because the Obama administration had made major concessions to business interests at the beginning of the process that so many ads appeared on both sides of the bill. The insurance industry and U.S. Chamber of Commerce antireform advertising campaigns, for instance, were countered in part by multimillion dollar campaigns promoting the bill by the pharmaceutical industry and by health provider groups, including the American Medical Association—the nemesis of every comprehensive health care proposal for almost a century. That strong business interests weighed in on the pro-reform side may be the most important reason that comprehensive health care reform passed in 2010

after almost a century of failure. But those groups did not do it for nothing.

Notes

1. See, e.g., Darrell M. West, Diane Heith, and Chris Goodwin, "Harry and Louise Go to Washington: Political Advertising and Health Care Reform," *Journal of Health Politics, Policy and Law* 21, no. 1 (1996): 35–68.

2. See Lawrence R. Jacobs and Robert Y. Shapiro, *Politicians Don't Pander* (Chicago: University of Chicago Press, 2000); Lawrence R. Jacobs, "Questioning the Conventional Wisdom on Public Opinion Toward Health Reform," *PS: Political Science and Politics,* 27, no. 2 (1994): 208–14.

3. Kenneth Goldstein, "Understanding Interest Group Targeting" (unpublished manuscript, University of Wisconsin, 2001).

4. See Allan Cigler and Burdett Loomis, "Contemporary Interest Group Politics: More than 'More of the Same,'" in *Interest Group Politics,* 4th ed., eds. Allan Cigler and Burdett Loomis (Washington, DC: CQ Press, 1996): 393–406; Kathleen Hall Jamieson, *Everything You Think You Know About Politics—and Why You're Wrong* (New York: Basic Books, 2000): chap. 18. The two major works on outside lobbying on which we draw in this chapter are Ken Kollman, *Outside Lobbying* (Princeton, NJ: Princeton University Press, 1998); and Kenneth Goldstein, *Interest Groups, Lobbying, and Participation in America* (Cambridge, UK: Cambridge University Press, 1999).

5. *Time* magazine ran a story in 2009 identifying the "Top 10 Fight Ads on Health Reform," providing links to the videos of each one. We refer to those ads several times in this chapter. We recommend that the reader view some of these ads as a supplement to the discussion below. See Michael Scherer, "Top 10 Health-Care-Reform Fight Ads," *Time,* August 20, 2009, http://www.time.com/time/nation/article/0,8599,1917690,00.html#ixzz12fTFXK8w/.

6. Scherer, "Top 10 Health-Care-Reform Fight Ads."

7. See especially Lawrence Wallack, Katie Woodruff, Lori Dorfman, and Iris Diaz, *News for a Change: An Advocate's Guide to Working with the Media,* Thousand Oaks, CA: Sage, 1999.

8. On priming constituents, see Goldstein, "Understanding Interest Group Targeting." On signaling by interest groups, see Kollman, *Outside Lobbying,* chap. 3.

9. Erika Falk, "Legislative Issue Advertising in the 107th Congress," a report to the Annenberg Public Policy Center of the University of Pennsylvania, Washington, DC, July 2003, http://www.annenbergpublicpolicy center.org/Downloads/Political_Communication/ LegIssueAds107Congress/2003_APPC_IssueAd s107th.pdf; Erika Falk, Erin Grizard, and Gordon McDonald, "Legislative Issue Advertising in the 108th Congress: Pluralism or Peril? *The Harvard International Journal of Press/Politics* 11, no. 4 (2006): 148–64.

10. Falk, Grizard, and McDonald, "Legislative Issue Advertising in the 108th Congress."

11. West, Heith, and Goodwin, "Harry and Louise Go to Washington."

12. West, Heith, and Goodwin, "Harry and Louise Go to Washington."

13. Michael Scherer, "Heated Health-Reform Ads Give Taste of Fall Campaign." *Time.* March 15, 2010, http://www.time.com/time/politics/article/0,859 9,1972364,00.html.

14. No clean comparison is possible, because the Clinton bill never came to the floor, whereas the reform package in 2009–10 saw floor action in both House and Senate and subsequent floor action on a package of amendments adopted through budget reconciliation.

15. Scherer, "Top 10 Health-Care Reform Fight Ads," para. 1.

16. Ben Pershing, "Groups Take Health-Reform Debate to Airwaves," *Washington Post,* August 5, 2009, http://www.washingtonpost.com/wp-dyn/content/ article/2009/08/04/AR2009080401447.html.

17. See "Healthcare Reform Advertisers Warming Up Big Guns," *ClickZ,* November 10, 2009, http://www .clickz.com/clickz/news/1707122/healthcare-reform- advertisers-warming-up-big-guns/.

18. "Healthcare Reform Advertisers Warming Up Big Guns."

19. Peter Wallsten, "Health Care Campaigns Connect with Internet Search Terms," *Los Angeles Times,* September 4, 2009.

20. Kollman, *Outside Lobbying,* see esp. chaps. 2–3.

21. West, Heith, and Goodwin, "Harry and Louise Go to Washington," 43.

22. West, Heith, and Goodwin, "Harry and Louise Go to Washington," 43.

23. Goldstein, *Interest Groups, Lobbying, and Participation in America,* 86.

24. Besides ARA and AARP, three other groups mounted issue ad campaigns on the MMA: Alliance to Improve Medicare (AIM), Pfizer, and United States Action.

25. Goldstein, *Interest Groups, Lobbying, and Participation in America,* 86.

26. Goldstein, *Interest Groups, Lobbying, and Participation in America,* 86.

27. Pershing, "Groups Take Health-Reform Debate to Airwaves."

28. Kollman, *Outside Lobbying.*

29. Goldstein, *Interest Groups, Lobbying, and Participation in America.*

30. Goldstein, *Interest Groups, Lobbying, and Participation in America,* 42.

31. Goldstein, *Interest Groups, Lobbying, and Participation in America.* However, Goldstein's definition of "undecided" includes both "soft" supporters and "soft" opponents. See 83, n. 4.

32. Goldstein, *Interest Groups, Lobbying, and Participation in America,* 84.

33. See Robert Pear, "Doctors Press Senate to Undo Medicare Cuts, *New York Times,* July 7, 2008, http:// www.nytimes.com/2008/07/07/health/policy/07medi care.html.

34. Pear, "Doctors Press Senate to Undo Medicare Cuts."

35. Jeffrey Young, "Conservative Seniors Group Launches Ads Against Healthcare Reform," *The Hill,* February 17, 2010, http://thehill.com/blogs/blog-briefing- room/news/81767-conservative-seniors-group-launc hes-ads-against-healthcare-reform.

36. David Austen-Smith and John R. Wright, "Counteractive Lobbying," *American Journal of Political Science* 38, no. 1 (1994): 25–44.

37. See Richard L. Hall, *Participation in Congress* (New Haven, CT: Yale University Press, 1996): chap. 1.

38. Goldstein, "Understanding Interest Group Targeting."

39. Young, "Conservative Seniors Troup Launches Ads Against Healthcare Reform"; Rachel Slajda, "HCAN Targets 11 House Dems in new TV Ads," *Talking Points Memo,* March 16, 2010, http://tpmdc.talking- pointsmemo.com/2010/03/hcan-targets-11-house- dems-in-new-tv-ads.php; Michael Scherer, "Heated Health-Reform Ads Give Taste of Fall Campaign,"

Time, March 16, 2010, http://www.time.com/time/politics/article/0,8599,1972364,00.html.

40. Priming is especially significant for the study of the news media's effects on citizen attitudes and behavior. See Shanto Iyengar and Donald R. Kinder, *News that Matters* (Chicago: Chicago University Press, 1987).

41. Brader, Ted, *Campaigning For Hearts and Minds: How Emotional Appeals in Political Ads Work* (Chicago: University of Chicago Press, 2006).

42. Video available at http://www.youtube.com/watch?v=Dt31nhleeCg.

43. Video available at http://www.youtube.com/watch?v=fOr17a4ZOIU.

44. The classic work on the subject is Amos Tversky and Daniel Kahneman, "The Framing of Decisions and the Psychology of Choice," *Science* 211, no. 4481 (1981): 453–58.

45. Quoted in West, Heith, and Goodwin, "Harry and Louise Go to Washington," 48.

46. Colin Gordon, *Dead on Arrival: The Politics of Health Care in Twentieth-Century America* (Princeton, NJ: Princeton University Press, 2003).

47. Eric W. Groenendyk and Nicholas A. Valentino. "Of Dark Clouds and Silver Linings: Effects of Exposure to Issue Versus Candidate Advertising on Persuasion, Information Retention, and Issue Salience," *Communication Research,* 29, no. 3 (2002): 295–319.

48. See, e.g., Kathleen Hall Jamieson, *Everything You Think You Know About Politics.*

49. David G. Magleby and J. Quin Monson, "The Non-candidate Campaign: Soft Money and Issue Advocacy in the 2002 Congressional Elections," *PS: Political Science & Politics* 36, no. 3 (2003): 401–03.

50. Haynes Johnson and David S. Broder, *The System: The American Way of Politics at the Breaking Point* (Boston: Little, Brown, 1996).

51. Johnson and Broder, *The System.*

52. Raymond L. Goldsteen, Karen Goldsteen, James H Swan, and Wendy Clemeña, "Harry and Louise and Health Care Reform: Romancing Public Opinion," *Journal of Health Politics, Policy, and Law* 26, no. 6 (2001): 1325–52.

53. Jamieson, *Everything You Think You Know About Politics.*

54. Jacobs, "Questioning the Conventional Wisdom on Public Opinion Toward Health Reform."

55. Jacobs and Shapiro, *Politicians Don't Pander.*

56. Jamieson, *Everything You Think You Know About Politics,* 136.

57. Jamieson, *Everything You Think You Know About Politics,* 136.

58. "Senate Passes Doctor Reimbursement Bill," *USA Today,* July 9, 2008.

59. As we discuss below, however, one reason for the diversity of the ads was that major business interests received concessions very early in the process and thus ran issue ads on the bill's behalf.

60. On this general point, see Frank Baumgarter, M. Berry, Marie Hojnacki, David C. Kimball, and Beth L. Leech, *Lobbying and Policy Change* (Chicago: University of Chicago Press, 2009). Baumgartner et al. conclude that resource-rich groups seldom win new policies when they want them. Instead their power comes in protecting a status quo that already favors their interests.

61. Darrell M. West and Richard Francis, "Electronic Advocacy: Interest Groups and Public Policymaking." *PS: Political Science and Politics* 29, no 1 (1996): 25–29. See also Jamieson, *Everything You Think You Know About Politics,* 125–131.

62. E. E. Schattschneider, *The Semisovereign People: A Realist's View of Democracy in America* (Chicago: Holt, Rinehart and Winston, 1960): 37.

63. Falk, Grizard, and McDonald, "Legislative Issue Advertising in the 108th Congress," 157.

64. Falk, Grizard, and McDonald, "Legislative Issue Advertising in the 108th Congress," 155–157.

65. Clyde Brown, Herbert Waltzer, and Miriam B. Waltzer, "Daring to Be Heard: Advertorials by Organized Interests on the Op-Ed Page of *The New York Times,* 1985–1998," *Political Communication* 18, no. 1 (2001): 23–50.

66. Jamieson, *Everything You Think You Know,* 136.

67. See Andrea Seabrook and Peter Overby, "Drug Firms Pour $40 Million Into Health Care Debate," National Public Radio, *All Things Considered,* July 23, 2009, http://www.npr.org/templates/story/story.php?storyId=106899074.

13-3 Gridlock Lobbying: Breaking, Creating, and Maintaining Legislative Stalemate

Jennifer Nicoll Victor

The policy views of Americans and their policymakers are often characterized as locations on a liberal-to-conservative continuum. Political scientists take advantage of this description to predict the behavior of policymakers and the policy outcomes. Even a simple model can yield important insights about the policymaking process and the strategies of the key players. In this essay, political scientist Jennifer Victor shows how such a model works. She uses it to help understand how lobbyists for interest groups adjust their strategies to the policy preferences of legislators and presidents.

Interest groups are permanent players in the policy making process. They seek legislative outcomes and provide a means of representation for subsets of citizens. According to The Center for Responsive Politics, a watchdog organization that monitors lobbying and archives public data on lobbying disclosures, interest groups spent $3.27 billion lobbying the U.S. Congress in 2008. This is up from $1.45 billion in 1998, when the data were first recorded.[1] The amount of money that firms, groups, and individuals spent on lobbying in 2008 was roughly equivalent to the $3.2 billion that all congressional and presidential candidates raised in the 2008 election. Lobbying is therefore a massive presence in the U.S. Congress, but what exactly do organized interests hope to achieve through their lobbying expenditures?

In this essay, I show how we can understand interest groups' lobbying strategies through the basic legislative spatial model. Because groups and lobbyists are ultimately interested in policy outcomes, they, like members of Congress, are strategic actors in a policy making game. Congressional scholars have used the legislative spatial model to describe many of the strategic actions of members of Congress. I argue that interest groups act in this policy space and that we can use the legislative spatial model as a framework to understand the behavior of groups. To do so, I first describe legislative spatial models, and then I add interest groups as non-decisive players in the spatial model, which provides a platform to describe interest groups' persuasion-oriented lobbying tactics.

The Basic Legislative Spatial Model

It is commonplace to use spatial terms to describe politics (*e.g.*, Obama is *left* of McCain). Legislative scholars have applied the spatial model of politics to a variety of aspects of legislative decision-making, such as elections, committee decision-making, legislators' ideological preferences, and congressional parties.[2] In particular, models of legislative gridlock have recently been used to describe policy change in Congress. For example, Brady and Volden argue that Congress only successfully changes policy when the median members of the House and Senate prefer some policy alternative to the status quo.[3] Their

Source: Jennifer Nicoll Victor, "Gridlock Lobbying: Breaking, Creating, and Maintaining Legislative Stalemate," in *Interest Group Politics,* 8th ed., ed. Allan J. Cigler and Burdett A. Loomis (Washington DC: CQ Press, 2012), 243–263.

argument is not based on interest group lobbying, election politics, or party manipulations; rather, they argue that one can explain policy change by examining the uni-dimensional preferences of members of Congress, particularly those near the median.[4]

In the basic legislative spatial model legislators exist in a one-dimensional linear space (a line) that is assumed to be a liberal-to-conservative scale that represents players' preferences over a particular policy. Each legislator has an ideal point in the policy space and individual legislators prefer points closer to their ideal points to points further away.[5] Using the theorem developed by Black known as the median voter theorem, the model produces a single equilibrium outcome.[6] On any one-dimensional scale (with an odd number of players) a median voter will exist and the policy that corresponds with her preference will always be an equilibrium.[7]

We can use a hypothetical committee, such as that displayed in Figure 1, to describe three important consequences of the median voter theorem as applied to group decision making: 1) determining whether a motion will pass or fail; 2) identifying the median voter; and 3) identifying the set of policies that can defeat the status quo. The hypothetical committee in Figure 1 has seven voters who are voting between a proposal called "Motion" and the status quo (Q). Each voter has an ideal point—or the point at which each individual receives the most utility. Each voter evaluates whether this ideal point is closer to "Motion" or to "Q," and casts a vote for the alternative closest to her ideal point. Contests are decided by simple majority rule.

To determine (1) whether any given motion will pass or fail, we simply look at the model and ascertain for each voter whether (s)he is closer to "Q" or to "motion." In this example, the motion would pass because David, Elaine, Faith, and Gerald prefer the motion to Q because it is closer to their ideal points than is Q.

Also, we can identify the median voter (2) by simply finding the voter whose preference is in the middle of the spectrum, when each voter is aligned along the one-dimensional scale. In this case, David has exactly three voters to his left and three voters to

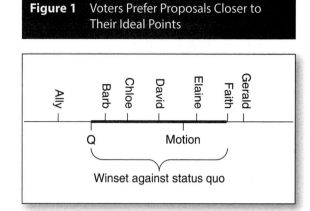

Figure 1   Voters Prefer Proposals Closer to Their Ideal Points

his right; David is the median voter. As the median voter, David's preference for "Motion" over Q will prevail.

Finally, we can find the set of policies that could defeat the status quo (3) by identifying the set of policies that the median voter, "David," prefers to the status quo. David will prefer all policies that are closer to him than the status quo. We call this set of policies the "winset" against the status quo, or the set of policies that could defeat the status quo. In Figure 1 this winset is highlighted in black. The winset against the status quo in this case extends from David's ideal point to the status quo, and a distance on the other side of David's ideal point (away from the status quo) that is equal to the distance from David to Q. One could use the median voter theorem to describe the passage and failure of bills in the chambers of the U.S. Congress, but the U.S. Congress does not operate by simple majority rule.

Two super-majority rules are particularly relevant for understanding legislative gridlock—the filibuster and the veto. Each of these rules involves a key lawmaker (called a pivot player) who is different from the chamber median voter. In the US Senate, 60 (of 100) of the members are needed to break a filibuster and allow a vote to proceed on a policy. A minority of at least 41 senators can therefore prevent a bill from coming to a vote. Figure 2 illustrates this point. Here, *M* represents the median member of the Senate and Q represents the status quo. The senators at F_L and F_R represent filibuster pivots. There are 20 senators between F_L and F_R, with 40 senators to the left of F_L and 40 to the right of F_R. Either of these groups of forty, plus the pivot senator, could successfully filibuster a bill. When the status quo is between F_L and F_R, gridlock occurs. That is, if a senator proposed to enact a policy just to the right of Q, the 40 senators to the left of and including F_L would object and prevent a vote on such a change. The same is true for those to the right of F_R if a proposal was put forth left of Q. Therefore, Brady and Volden call the range between F_L and F_R the "gridlock region."[8]

The gridlock region is made larger by the institutional veto. A 2/3 vote is required in each chamber to override a Presidential veto. The member in each chamber whose vote is pivotal to meet the 2/3 threshold is called the veto pivot. When the President is liberal, the veto pivot is the member who has 1/3 of the chamber to his left and 2/3 of the chamber to his right. When the President is conservative, the veto pivot has 1/3 of the chamber to his right and 2/3 to his left. Figures 3 and 4 demonstrate this, respectively. The veto pivot can effectively determine whether or not a bill will pass, in much the same way the median voter does. For example, given a liberal President (as in Figure 4), if a bill is proposed to the right of Q, say at M, the President (P) will veto such a bill and the chamber will not be able to muster the 2/3 supermajority to override a presidential veto.[9] The veto will be sustained by V_L and the 33 senators

to her left (notice that all policies right of Q are outside of P and V_L's winset against the status quo). If the bill is proposed to the left of Q and the president vetoed then V_L and the 66 senators to her right could override the veto.

The complete gridlock region is bounded by the filibuster pivot and the veto pivot. Figure 5 illustrates this point using a hypothetical senate chamber (because 100 is an easy number of players to work with). If the president is liberal, a gridlock region will exist from the 33rd senator (from the left) to the 59th senator (from the left). If the status quo is in this region of 26 senators, between the veto pivot and the filibuster pivot, the chamber will not be able to agree to make a policy change, even when a majority exists who seek change. The supermajority veto and filibuster rules cause this legislative gridlock. Note that the President himself could be the edge of the gridlock region if the President were more conservative (centrist) than the veto pivot. Because players who form the boundary of the gridlock region change, it is important to talk about the "pivotal players," rather than specifically refer to F, V or M. Below, when I refer to pivotal players I am referring to the pivots that form the boundary of the gridlock region; these are the filibuster pivot, veto pivot, median voter, or president.

To summarize, *legislative gridlock occurs when the status quo is already near the ideal policy preference of the median legislator.* The gridlock theory predicts that gridlock will persist when the status quo is

Figure 2   Gridlock with Filibuster Pivots

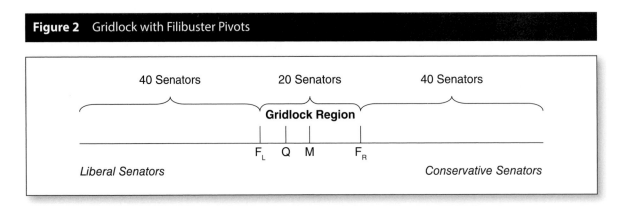

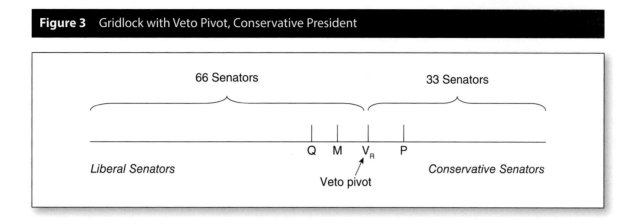

Figure 3 Gridlock with Veto Pivot, Conservative President

Figure 4 Gridlock with Veto Pivot, Liberal President

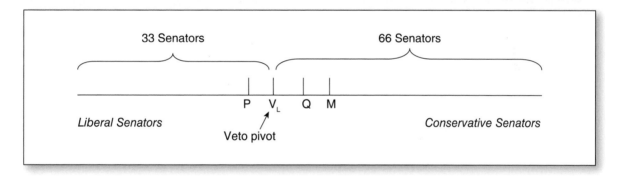

within the gridlock region. If the status quo is outside of the gridlock region, policy will be amended to move it inside the region, thus achieving a stable equilibrium. This theory presumes that every legislator has equal power to filibuster, propose legislation or to override a veto—there is no agenda setter. Moreover, legislators are presumed to act as individual utility maximizers, not party loyalists. Under this theory, gridlock occurs often and under many different government circumstances (liberal/conservative President, unified/divided government). When gridlock does not occur, policies tend to pass by supermajorities because of the existence of supermajority rules like vetoes and filibusters. For example, the health care reform bill (H.R. 3590, Patient Protection

and Affordable Care Act), which was signed into law in March 2010, passed the Senate with a supermajority of 60 votes. It passed the House with a bare majority of 219 votes, because there was no Presidential veto threat. Next, it is important to understand the roles that interest groups play in the creation, maintenance and disruption of gridlock.

Interest Groups in the Spatial Model

The legislative process is characterized by many uncertainties. Members of Congress are uncertain about how a policy might work in the "real world," how constituents and voters will respond to policy changes, and about the policy preferences of their colleagues. All of this uncertainty creates a ripe

Figure 5 Complete Gridlock Region with Filibuster and Veto Pivots

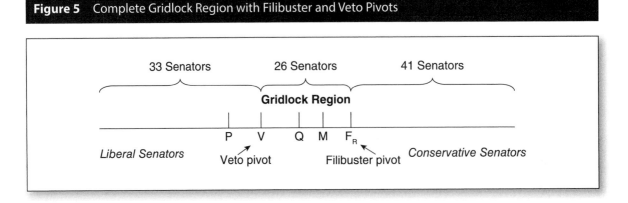

breeding ground for interest groups. We know that interest groups are seen as purveyors of information in Washington, DC and one of their main goals is to reduce the uncertainties of members of Congress.[10] John Wright argues that interest groups "achieve influence through the acquisition and *strategic* transmission of information that legislators need to make good public policy and to get reelected."[11] I argue that groups attempt to reduce uncertainty for members of Congress by strategically providing information that may alter their preferences over policy or change their beliefs about the dimensionality of the policy space. Ultimately, groups want to move policy closer to the group's ideal point—to do so, they may need to move legislators' ideal points. Lobbyists and groups attempt to do this, at least in part, by changing legislators' preferences over policy.

Based on the gridlock model, or pivotal politics model, two observations are immediately clear. First, if gridlock exists (the status quo lies between the filibuster pivot and veto pivot) a policy proposal is likely to fail because of the institutional supermajority requirements of the filibuster and veto override, as demonstrated above. Second, an interest group will prefer those policy proposals that are closer to its ideal point than the status quo, and oppose those proposals that are further from its ideal point than the status quo. The set of policies an actor prefers to the status quo is the actor's "winset." An interest group will support any bill in the interest group's

winset and oppose any bill outside of the group's winset. These two features—the existence of gridlock and a group's preferences for policy proposals—provide the basis for understanding group behavior.

In order to determine how interest groups affect the spatial model of legislative policy making we must consider the relative positions of the interest group, a proposed policy, and the status quo. The systematic consideration of these positions leads to four general scenarios in which interest groups will act and four expectations about the behavior of interest groups in legislative politics. I refer to this as the spatial model of interest group lobbying. The model shows that interest groups will engage in three general strategies when they seek to affect the outcome of a proposed policy: to break legislative gridlock, maintain gridlock, or create gridlock.[12] The model presented in Table 1 explains these strategies in the context of each scenario.

The upper-left cell of Table 1 describes what an interest group should do when legislative gridlock exists and the proposed bill falls within the interest group's winset. In such a situation, the group (*IG*) wants the bill (*b*) to pass, but it is likely to fail. The example provided in Table 1 highlights the interest group's winset—the interest group prefers the bill to the status quo; however, the proposal is likely to fail because the President (*P*) will veto the bill and it will not be overridden by the veto pivot (*V*) (the bill is

Table 1

	Bill (b) is IN Interest Group's Winset	**Bill (b) is OUT of Interest Group's Winset**
Legislative Gridlock Exists	• Interest group supports a bill that is likely to fail. • Interest group will try to BREAK gridlock by targeting the FAR PIVOT. • Example: IG F b SQ V P	• Interest group opposes a bill that is likely to fail. • Interest group seeks to MAINTAIN gridlock to kill the bill by targeting BOTH PIVOTS. • Example: b P V IG SQ F
Legislative Gridlock does NOT Exist	• Interest group supports a bill that is likely to pass. • Interest group will target the MEDIAN of the chamber in an attempt to pass a bill as close to the group's ideal point as possible. • Example: SQ F b M IG V P	• Interest group opposes a bill that will likely pass. • Interest group will try to CREATE gridlock to kill the bill by targeting the NEAR PIVOT. • Example: F B V P IG SQ

In each example, gridlock is created when the status quo (*SQ*) is between the filibuster pivot (*F*) and the veto pivot (*V*). The winset of policies that the Interest Group (*IG*) prefers to the status quo is highlighted in bold. When the proposed bill (*b*) falls inside the interest group's winset, the group favors the bill; when the proposed bill (*b*) falls outside of the interest group's winset, the group opposes the bill.

outside the veto pivot's winset). The interest group can anticipate this outcome and attempt to change legislators' policy preferences in an attempt to *break* the gridlock that exists. To do so, the interest group would have to target the *far pivot*, or in this case V, to move to the other side of the status quo. The only way to break gridlock is to move one of the pivots to the other side of the status quo (in one dimension—I consider the two-dimensional case below). It would be illogical for the interest group to target the near pivot because the group would have to try to move the pivot *away* from the group. Rather, the group can target the pivot that is on the opposite side of the status quo relative to the group, and attempt to change enough legislators' preferences such that the pivot moved to the other side of the status quo.[13] In the example in Table 1, this would amount to the

President vetoing the bill, but the override vote would be successful if the bill was in the veto pivot's winset. Thus, it can be proposed that:

Proposition 1: When legislative gridlock exists and a policy proposal is within an interest group's winset, the group will seek to BREAK gridlock by targeting the policy preferences of the pivot on the opposite side of the status quo, relative to the interest group.

The upper-right cell of Table 1 describes a scenario in which legislative gridlock exists, but the proposed bill is outside of the interest group's winset. In such a case, the interest group opposes a bill that is likely to fail—an advantageous position for the group. In such a case, the group would seek to *maintain* the existing gridlock in order to ensure that the bill dies. The group could do this by targeting both pivotal players, and the legislators near them, to encourage them to hold their positions. This would be akin to counteractive lobbying, where groups lobby allies in an attempt to counteract the lobbying by their adversaries.[14] In the example shown in Table 1, the group's winset is highlighted. The bill (*b*) clearly falls outside the group's winset; however, it is also clear that the bill will be opposed by the filibuster pivot (*F*). Any proposal to the left of the status quo in such a case, would be filibustered in the Senate because it is too far from the policy ideal points of the forty senators to the right of *F*.

Proposition 2: When legislative gridlock exists and a policy proposal is NOT within an interest group's winset, the group will seek to MAINTAIN gridlock by targeting the policy preferences of both pivots.

The lower-left cell of Table 1 describes a case in which legislative gridlock does not exist and a proposed bill falls within an interest group's winset. In this case, the interest group supports a bill that is likely to pass—an advantageous position for the group.[15] The example shown in this cell of Table 1 indicates that the interest group has a large winset, because its ideal point is far from the status quo. However, the status quo is far from most players' ideal points and is to the left of the filibuster pivot (*F*), veto pivot (*V*), and median voter of the chamber (*M*). The policy proposal at *b* is likely to pass, and effectively would move the status quo closer to the interest group's ideal point. While the group is pleased with such an outcome, we should expect the interest group to lobby the median voter of the chamber in this case. The bill is likely to pass at the median voter's ideal point and the closer that point is to the interest group's ideal point, the better off the interest group is.

Proposition 3: When legislative gridlock does NOT exist and a policy proposal is within an *interest group's winset, the group will target the median voter of the chamber.*

The lower-right cell of Table 1 depicts a scenario in which legislative gridlock does not exist and a proposed bill falls outside of an interest group's winset. In such a case, the interest group is opposed to a bill that is likely to pass.[16] The interest group would attempt to change legislators' preferences in an attempt to *create* gridlock to kill the bill. As the example in Table 1 shows, the bill is well outside the interest group's winset, but the bill is likely to pass because the legislative incentives are to move the status quo into the gridlock region. In its attempt to prevent that from happening, the group would target the *near pivot*, in this case *V*. If the interest group could persuade enough legislators to change the policy positions to the right such that the veto pivot moved to the opposite side of the status quo, gridlock would be created and the proposed bill would fail.

Proposition 4: When legislative gridlock does NOT exist and a policy proposal is NOT within an interest group's winset, the group will seek to CREATE gridlock by targeting the policy preferences of the pivot on the same side of the status quo, relative to the interest group.

One might ask whether it is reasonable to assume that legislators' policy preferences can change. Might Senator Orrin Hatch (R-UT) be convinced that abortion is acceptable? Not likely. Legislators' policy goals are assumed to be fixed; but, groups may be able to change legislators' beliefs about how to achieve those goals.[17] For example, suppose a legislator has a preference for low crime rates and a derived preference for capital punishment because she believes it will deter crime. The derived preference is based on a belief linking capital punishment to lower crime rates. It is this belief that interest groups attempt to affect. An anti-capital punishment group might attempt to change the derived preference of the legislator by presenting evidence that capital punishment does not deter crime. In this instance, the interest group tries to affect the member's beliefs about the connection between her stable preference and her policy preference.

We should not expect each of the four spatial scenarios outlined in Table 1 to occur with equal frequency. The gridlock theory of legislative politics recognizes that gridlock is a common occurrence. We are therefore more likely to observe scenarios described in the top row of Table 1 than in the bottom row. When groups are supportive of policy proposals in the case of legislative gridlock (upper-left cell), groups seek to break gridlock (Proposition 1). However, shifting enough legislators' preferences to break gridlock is likely to be an expensive and often unlikely outcome.

Case Studies

Empirically, no metric exists that allows us to examine the relative positions of legislators, interest groups and bills in the same policy space, on the same scale. While testing the propositions stated above poses significant challenges, empirical evidence does exist to support them. Two recent case studies exemplify the scenarios described above. The first is an example of lobbying on a policy in gridlock. The case involves a bill in the 110th Congress (2007–2008) that would move regulation of tobacco products to the jurisdiction of the Food and Drug Administration over the Department of Agriculture. The second is an example of lobbying on a policy not in gridlock. The case involves a bill in the 109th Congress (2005–2006) that would make it a federal crime to transport a minor across state lines to obtain an abortion in order to circumvent state parental notification and consent laws.

Tobacco Case—Gridlock

In 2007 and 2008 the House of Representatives and Senate separately considered legislation that would change how tobacco and tobacco products are regulated in the United States. The proposed legislation would have given jurisdiction over tobacco to the Food and Drug Administration (FDA) instead of the Department of Agriculture, which has long regulated in the U.S.[18] Democrats won a majority of seats in both chambers after the 2006 elections for the first time in 12 years and promised to make a strong push to grant the FDA broad new powers to regulate tobacco, including packaging, sales, marketing, and nicotine levels.[19]

In the House, several committees fought for jurisdiction over the bill (H.R. 1108), including the House Ways and Means Committee (which has jurisdiction over tax and revenue raising bills) and the Natural Resources Committee (which has jurisdiction over Indian Affairs issues included in the bill). The bill was sponsored in the House by Henry Waxman (D-CA), who chaired the Oversight and Government Reform Committee. In July, Chairman Waxman and Chairman John Dingell (D-MI), of the Energy and Commerce Committee, reached a compromise that allowed the bill to move forward, in a form that did not require the consent of the Natural Resources Committee.[20] The House passed the bill in July by a veto-proof vote of 326–102.[21]

The Senate bill (S. 625) was sponsored by a liberal stalwart, Sen. Edward Kennedy (D-MA) and a conservative pillar, Sen. John Cornyn (R-TX). This team of odd bedfellows gave supporters hope that a bill would pass, but President George W. Bush had promised to veto any bill that won approval. Kennedy's position as chair of the Health, Education, Labor, and Pensions Committee (HELP Committee), which had jurisdiction of the bill in the Senate, helped to push the bill forward. However, Senator Richard M. Burr (R-NC) strongly opposed the bill and permanently stalled it.[22]

Organized groups that opposed the proposed change in regulatory scheme included medium and small tobacco producers, such as Lorillard Tobacco, R.J. Reynolds Tobacco, the Cigar Association of America, and U.S. Smokeless Tobacco. These groups coordinated their efforts to oppose this bill, and lobbied on few other issues during this Congress.[23]

Supporters of this bill included a surprising mix. Major tobacco producer Philip-Morris supported the bill because the marketing restrictions would give it a strong advantage over its competitors. The American College of Cardiology supported the bill because of the health ramifications of having tobacco regulated as a drug rather than purely an agricultural product.[24]

To test the predicted behavior described in the model above, I require a spatial representation of the pivotal players, the status quo, the bill, and the lobbying interest groups who seek to influence the outcome of the bill. I can determine the positions of pivotal players using Poole and Rosenthals' DW-NOMINATE scores.[25] These scores provide a one-dimensional measure of each legislator's ideology based on all votes taken over the course of a Congress. A limitation of this test is that I am assuming that the ideological scores for legislators over the course of a Congress is equivalent to legislators' preferences on tobacco legislation. In addition, it is impossible to pinpoint the location of the bill, status quo and interest groups on the same scale as the NOMINATE scores. I use journalistic accounts of the lobbying and legislative procedure on this bill to help me infer the locations of these features of the model. Figure 6 depicts the spatial setup of this bill.

Here, with the benefit of hindsight I infer that the bill is in the gridlock region between the filibuster pivot and the veto pivot in the Senate. We know that the bill was ultimately filibustered, or at least blocked

by the efforts of Senator Burr. Democrats had been trying to pass a bill of this type since 1995 and had been thwarted by Republicans in each attempt during previous congresses. This is strong evidence to suggest that the bill was in gridlock. We also know that the smaller tobacco producers opposed the bill, while hundreds of health organizations supported it.[26] Given this setup, we should expect that the opposing interest groups, or smaller tobacco producers, should understand that the bill was in gridlock and lobby both the veto and filibuster pivots in order to preserve the gridlock on the bill, thereby killing the legislation (this amounts to the upper-right corner of Table 1). Meanwhile, we should observe the supporting interest groups, such as the health organizations, targeting the far pivot, or in this case, the veto pivot (upper-left cell of Table 1).

It is difficult to observe the actual lobbying behavior of interest groups, especially the exact targets of their campaigns. To overcome this challenge, I analyze the contribution behavior of the political action committees (PACs) associated with the major groups that lobbied on these bills. Using publicly available data from the Federal Election Commission and compiled by the Center for Responsive Politics, I can identify the targets of groups' PAC donations.[27] A PAC is an organization designed solely to raise money to contribute to candidates. This is a limited test because PAC contributions are not the same as

Figure 6 Tobacco Regulation in the 110th Senate

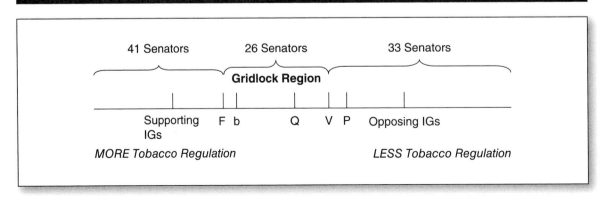

lobbying. I expect the interests of a group's PAC to be broader and more diverse than the associated interest group's position on a single piece of legislation. In this way, using PAC contribution behavior should provide a *conservative* test of these propositions.

Another limitation of these data is that evidence exists that suggests campaign donations do not buy votes.[28] Rather, campaign donations are thought to buy access and serve as a legislative subsidy.[29] It might therefore be questionable to use campaign donations as evidence of groups targeting particular legislators for the purpose of persuading them to change their policy preferences on a particular bill. While I agree with the shortcomings of this method, I argue that given the absence of measures of interest group's lobbying targets for the purpose of persuasion, campaign contribution behavior provides a telling window that may reveal groups' favored legislators. While campaign contributions cannot be a perfect substitute for lobbying targets, the extent to which PAC contributions provide a signal of legislators with whom groups would like to maintain avenues of contact, relationships, and access, these data can help reveal groups' lobbying targets without providing a causal link between donations and legislators' votes.[30]

Also, because I do not expect groups to attempt to identify and target a single pivotal player, I examine the data for pivotal ranges of players. First, I arrange Senators on a left-right scale according to their NOMINATE scores. To identify players in the veto pivot range, for example, I identify the 33rd Senator from the right (in this case it is Sen. Mel Martinez (R-FL)) and include the Senators whose NOMINATE scores fall within one standard deviation of the single pivotal player I identified. For the 110th Senate, the range of NOMINATE scores for 102 Senators is −1.093 on the left (Sen. Russ Feingold (D-WI)), to 0.89 on the right (Sen. Tom Coburn (R-OK)). The standard deviation of Senators' NOMINATE scores is 0.476. The range of veto pivot players, in this case then, extends from Sen. Jim DeMint (R-SC, score = 0.75) to Sen. Ben Nelson (D-NE, score = −0.068).

In Table 2 I summarize the mean contributions of four organizations opposed to the tobacco bill and two organizations in favor of it. The opponents include Lorillard Tobacco, R.J. Reynolds Tobacco, Cigar Association of America, and US Smokeless Tobacco. The proponents include Altria, the parent company of Philip-Morris and the American College of Cardiology.

The results provided in Table 2 generally support my expectations, despite the limitations of this analytic approach. I expected that supporters of the bill, including Philip-Morris and the health organizations, would anticipate the gridlock problem and target the veto pivot in an attempt to break gridlock by changing the preferences of the veto pivot players. The contribution data show that the PACs of the pro-regulatory groups gave significantly more donations to Senators in the veto pivot range than Senators outside of the veto pivot range ($2,656.90 versus $1,352.90, respectively). The difference is statistically significant using a student's T distribution difference of means one-tailed test. Moreover, the pro-regulation interests do *not* significantly target Senators around the filibuster pivot over those outside the filibuster pivot range ($1,509.30 versus $2,562.50, respectively). Senators around the veto pivot appear to be the primary target of the groups who support the legislation. This behavior is particularly telling since it suggests that groups with a liberal leaning preference over this bill are targeting conservative leaning Senators with their PAC donations. This provides strong support for the most counterintuitive theoretical claim laid out above.

I also find support for the behavior of the groups that opposed the tobacco regulation. Here, I expected groups to target both the veto and filibuster pivots in order to try to maintain the existing legislative gridlock. The results show that these groups targeted Senators in the veto pivot range, but not in the filibuster pivot range. Table 2 shows that anti-regulation interest groups save significantly more campaign donations to Senators within the veto pivot range ($3,441 versus $568, respectively). However, the anti-regulation groups also gave significantly to groups

Table 2

	Pro-Regulation of Tobacco Groups				Anti-Regulation of Tobacco Groups			
	Contribution				Contribution			
	Mean	N	T	Pr(T)<0	Mean	N	T	Pr(T)<0
Donations *within* Veto Pivot range	2656.9 (567.3)	51	−1.95	0.027	3441 (918.4)	51	−2.97	0.0018
Donations *outside* of Veto Pivot range	1352.9 (356.5)	51			568.6 (300.3)	51		
			T	Pr(T)~=0			T	Pr(T)>0
Donations *within* Filibuster Pivot range	1509.3 (362.3)	54	1.56	0.122	611.1 (290.99)	54	3.06	0.0014
Donations *outside* of Filibuster Pivot range	2562.5 (589.6)	48			3572.9 (970.8)	48		

Standard errors in parentheses.

not in the filibuster pivot range ($611 to Senators in the filibuster pivot range versus $3,573 to Senators outside the filibuster pivot range). This finding goes against my expectation. According to the spatial model, these groups should seek to maintain gridlock by targeting both the filibuster and veto pivots to stay the course and ultimately kill the bill. However, these conservative groups concentrated their campaign donations to Senators on the right side of the spectrum.

Overall, I find strong, but not unequivocal, support for the spatial model of lobbying in this single gridlock case. I make reasonable estimations of the spatial representation of the case of tobacco regulation in the 110th Senate and find that liberal groups that sought to break gridlock indeed targeted the far pivot. I also found the conservative groups that sought to maintain gridlock targeted one, but not both, of the pivots that made up the bounds of the gridlock region. Next, I examine a test case of the lower two cells of Table 1—a case without gridlock.

Abortion Case—No Gridlock

To test the behavior of groups lobbying when gridlock does not exist, I look at Republicans' attempt to tighten rules relating to abortion in the 109th Congress (2005–2006). The political context of the 109th Congress was quite a bit different from the 110th. In the 109th Republicans held majorities in both chambers of Congress and had control of the White House. President Bush had just won his second term as President and Republicans generally felt buoyant about the possibility of making good progress on passing a conservative agenda. During the 109th both the House and Senate passed different versions of a bill known as the Child Interstate Abortion Notification Act that would have criminalized the act of an adult helping to transport a minor across state lines to seek an abortion in avoidance of parental notification laws in the minor's home state. The bill enjoyed widespread support from conservatives. Republicans held a majority of seats in both the House and Senate in the 109th Congress, and then President George W. Bush favored the proposal.

Pro-life organizations supported the bill, and pro-choice organizations opposed it.

Ultimately, this bill failed to make it to President Bush's desk, despite the fact that both chambers passed some version of the bill. The House approved a broad version of the bill (HR 748) in April of 2005. More than a year later, the Senate passed a version of this bill (S. 403), but Democrats thwarted efforts to form a conference to settle the differences between the chambers. Republicans in the House then decided to take up S. 403, but the House added a last minute amendment to penalize doctors who perform abortions on out-of-state minors who live in states with parental notification laws. The House passed this bill, but the Senate was unable to muster the 60 votes for cloture on the amended bill.[31] Evidence suggests that conservatives were confident the bill would pass: "Social conservative appeared poised during the summer to score another win in a campaign to incrementally restrict abortions. In late July a filibuster-proof majority of 65 senators voted to pass a parental consent bill (S. 403), introduced by Nevada Republican John Ensign."[32] A lobbyist for the National Right-to-Life Committee, the premier anti-abortion organization, was quoted as being "cautiously optimistic"[33] and believing that "the measure probably will pass."[34] This optimism was likely based on the Republican majority in the Senate and the fact that the Senate leadership had made passage of this bill a high priority. These descriptive accounts suggest that lobbyists at least believed gridlock did not exist.[35]

Assuming that the bill was *not* in gridlock—or at least that the key players did not believe the bill to be in gridlock—I use the same procedure as outlined above to test the propositions about groups lobbying on bills out of gridlock outlined in Table 1 above. In this case, I expect the pro-life organizations to support the bill and target the chamber median in an attempt to move the final bill as close to the group's ideal point as possible (the lower-left cell of Table 1). In addition, I expect pro-choice groups to seek to *create* gridlock by targeting the near pivot, or in this case the filibuster pivot (the lower-right cell of Table 1). To assess the behavior of interest groups on the left, I collected the PAC contribution behavior of Planned Parenthood, National Abortion Rights Action League (NARAL), and People for the American Way. On the right, I collect the PAC contributions and individual lobbying donations of the PAC and lobbyists associated with the National Right-to-Life Committee. Each of these groups filed disclosure reports that indicate they lobbied on this bill.[36] Figure 7 lays out the spatial setup of this case.

Figure 7 shows the status quo (Q) to be outside the gridlock region. This is the scenario that provided conservative groups with their "cautious"

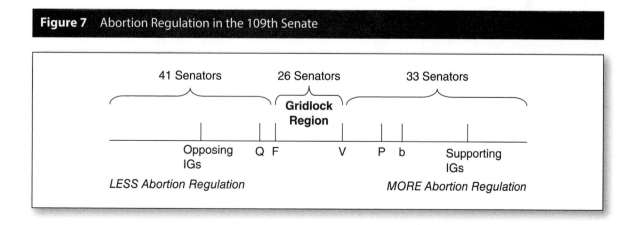

Figure 7 Abortion Regulation in the 109th Senate

confidence that the bill would likely pass and that policy would probably move to the right.[37]

Table 3 summarizes the contribution behavior of the pro-life and pro-choice PACs and lobbyists. I find evidence to support the spatial account of this case and the theoretical expectations noted above. Pro-life organizations are expected to target the Senate median voter. Indeed, the National Right-to-Life Committee gave significantly more to Senators around the median than to those on the ends ($16,773 versus $706, respectively). Likewise, there is no evidence that this organization was concerned about the filibuster or targeted those in the filibuster range during their campaign. The National Right-to-Life Committee gave an amount to Senators in the filibuster pivot range ($5,249) that is considerably less than to those outside of it ($14,903), but the difference is not *statistically* significant. This evidence suggests that this organization perceived the lack of legislative gridlock and sought to take advantage of

that scenario in their favorable disposition for the bill.

Likewise, pro-choice organizations should seek to *create* gridlock by targeting the near pivot, or in this case the filibuster pivot. Evidence suggests they did this. Pro-choice groups in fact, *only* gave money to Senators in the filibuster range ($1,245 versus $0). Also, it appears that these groups were not targeting the median voter. Pro-choice groups gave a statistically similar amount of money to Senators within the Median voter range ($345) as to those outside of it ($1,040).

The campaign contribution behavior by interest groups that lobbied for and against the so-called "transporting minors" bill demonstrates the utility of the spatial model of interest group lobbying. Pro-life and pro-choice groups exerted interest group "influence" in the manner predicted by the theoretical model laid out above: pro-life groups sought to influence the median voter because they believed the bill they favored was likely to pass, while pro-choice groups

Table 3

	Pro-Choice Groups				Pro-Life Groups			
	Contribution				Contribution			
	Mean	N	T	Pr(T)~=0	Mean	N	T	Pr(T)<0
Donations *within* Median Voter Range	344.9 (239.1)	58	1.36	0.177	16773.1 (7901.3)	58	−1.75	0.042
Donations *outside* Median Voter Range	1040.7 (500.96)	43			706.5 (706.5)	43		
			T	Pr(T)<0			T	Pr(T)~=0
Donations *within* Filibuster Pivot range	1245.2 (481.6)	52	−2.51	0.007	5249.23 (5249.23)	52	1.05	0.297
Donations *outside* of Filibuster Pivot range	0 0	49			14903.2 (7666.7)	49		

Standard errors in parentheses.

sought to create gridlock where none seemed to exist by targeting the near (in this case, filibuster) pivot.

Conclusion

There is no shortage of evidence that interest groups are strategic actors in the legislative policy-making game. Groups have preferences for particular outcomes and possess limited resources to spend in affecting those outcomes. The challenge for scholars is to be precise about *how* interest groups exert their lobbying influence. Under what conditions do interest groups act? How do they decide which type of action to take? The legislative spatial model provides a foundation from which to understand interest group activity, because legislation is the primary target of lobbying activity. While interest groups are not decision makers in the legislative game, and "persuasion lobbying" is not the only activity in which groups engage, they are interested actors who attempt to influence policy outcomes in predictable ways.

The spatial model outlined above shows that two features of the legislative environment explain the lobbying behavior of interested groups: the spatial context of a particular bill and groups' preferences over proposed legislation. The presence or absence of legislative gridlock (which occurs when the status quo lies between pivotal players' ideal point) is a key feature of the model. When gridlock exists, interest groups that favor a bill seek to break gridlock by attempting to change the policy preferences of the pivotal player furthest from the group's ideal point. If a group can change enough legislators' minds to successfully move the far pivot to the opposite side of the status quo, gridlock will be broken and the group may have an opportunity to see a preferred bill passed. When a group opposes legislation that is in gridlock, the group seeks to maintain gridlock and does so by targeting both pivots to encourage them to stay right where they are. If gridlock can be maintained on a bill that a group opposes, the bill will die and the group will have achieved their preferred outcome.

When legislative gridlock does *not* exist, a group that favors a bill will target the legislative median voter. The group is in an advantageous position under this scenario because it supports a bill that is likely to pass. At this point, the group can only add icing to their proverbial cake by moving the bill even closer to its ideal point. If a group opposes a bill out of gridlock the group will try to create gridlock by targeting the pivot closest to its ideal point and attempting to move it to the other side of the status quo.

The relative positions of groups to the status quo, and the status quo to pivotal players in the legislative game help us to glean insights into the lobbying behavior of organized interests. I examined a case of legislative gridlock in the 110th Congress where a tobacco regulation bill was ultimately filibustered (or at least killed in the senate due to inaction). The groups that supported the bill behaved as anticipated and targeted the veto pivot, but not the filibuster pivot, in an attempt to break gridlock. The groups that opposed the bill behaved partially as expected and targeted one, but not both, of the pivotal players in an attempt to maintain gridlock. In the abortion case in the 109th congress, I analyzed a case without legislative gridlock and found that groups that supported an abortion-restrictions bill targeted the median voter, as expected, in an attempt to help move a bill that was expected to pass even closer to the group. I also found that groups that opposed the bill targeted the near pivot (filibuster pivot) in an attempt to create gridlock where none existed.

The cases of tobacco regulation in the 110th and abortion restrictions in the 109th are not particularly special cases. There is no reason to believe that the findings that support the spatial model of lobbying in these cases would not generalize to other Congresses and other bills. I selected these cases because of the ease of developing measures from these high profile cases. There are limitations with the empirical approach used here, and it provides a limited test of the theoretical model. It is problematic to identify the exact locations of key players and items in the spatial model, to identify the population of groups that lobby for and against bills, and to identify the targets of lobbying that is aimed at persuasion; however, the drawbacks of the analytical approach generally should make it *less* likely to find support for my claims and be a conservative test of the propositions.

Notes

1. The Center for Responsive Politics, [ON LINE] "Lobbying Database," *Opensecrets.org*, April-June 2009, http://www.opensecrets.org/lobby/index.php.

2. On elections see Anthony Downs, *An Economic Theory of Democracy* (New York: Harper and Row, 1957), and David R. Mayhew, *Congress: The Electoral Connection* (New Haven: Yale University Press, 1974), and Richard Fenno, *Home Style: House Members in Their Districts* (Boston: Little-Brown, 1978). On committee decision making see Duncan Black, *The Theory of Committees and Elections* (Cambridge: Cambridge UP, 1958), and Richard Fenno, *Congressmen in Committees* (Boston: Little-Brown, 1974) and Keith Krehbiel, *Information and Legislative Organization* (Ann Arbor: University of Michigan Press, 1991). On legislators' ideological preferences see Keith T. Poole and Howard Rosenthal, *Congress: A Political-Economic History of Roll Call Voting* (Oxford: Oxford UP, 1997), and Keith T. Poole and Howard Rosenthal, *Ideology and Congress* (New Brunswick: Transaction Publishers, 2007). On congressional parties see John Aldrich, *Why Parties? The Origin and Transformation of Party Politics in America* (Chicago: University of Chicago Press, 1995), and David W. Rohde, *Parties and Leaders in the Postreform House* (Chicago: University of Chicago Press, 1991), and Gary Cox and Mathew D. McCubbins, *Legislative Leviathan: Party Government in the House* (Berkeley: University of California Press, 1993).

3. David W. Brady and Craig Volden, *Revolving Gridlock: Politics and Policy From Jimmy Carter to George W. Bush*, 2nd ed. (Cambridge: Westview Press, 2006).

4. Keith Krehbiel, *Pivotal Politics: A Theory of U.S. Lawmaking* (Chicago: University of Chicago Press, 1998).

5. In the parlance of formal theory, we would say that legislators' utility functions are symmetrical and single-peaked.

6. See Duncan Black, *The Theory of Committees and Elections* (Cambridge: Cambridge University Press, 1958). Also, for detailed and accessible descriptions of one and two dimensional spatial models of legislative voting see Keith Krehbiel, *Pivotal Politics: A Theory of U.S. Lawmaking* (Chicago: University of Chicago Press, 1998), and Charles Stewart, III, *Analyzing Congress* (New York: W.W. Norton & Co., 2001).

7. An equilibrium is the stable outcome that occurs when each player plays the strategy that maximizes her outcome, given that she believes every other player is also playing the strategy that maximizes their outcome. In equilibrium, no individual player can benefit by unilaterally changing her strategy, given that other players' strategies are unchanged.

8. David W. Brady and Craig Volden, *Revolving Gridlock: Politics and Policy From Jimmy Carter to George W. Bush*, 2nd ed. (Cambridge: Westview Press, 2006), 16.

9. You can prove this by drawing a *winset* for P. A winset is the set of policies a player prefers to the status quo. P's winset is therefore any policy between P and Q and policies to the left of P that extend a distance equivalent to the distance P-Q. The policy M is clearly outside this winset because it lies on the opposite side of Q from P.

10. Lester W. Milbrath, *The Washington Lobbyist* (Chicago: Rand McNally, 1963); John W. Kingdon, *Congressmen's Voting Decisions*, 3rd ed. (Ann Arbor: University of Michigan Press, 1989); Richard L. Hall and Frank W. Wayman, "Buying Time: Moneyed Interests and the Mobilization of bias in Congressional Committees," *American Political Science Review* 84 (March 1990): 797–820; John Mark Hansen, *Gaining Access: Congress and the Farm Lobby, 1919–1981* (Chicago: University of Chicago Press, 1991); Gregory A. Caldeira and John R. Wright, "Lobbying for Justice: Organized Interests Supreme Court Nominations, and United States Senate," *American Journal of Political Science* 82 (1998): 1109–27.

11. John R. Wright, *Interest Groups and Congress: Lobbying, Contributions, and Influence* (Boston: Allyn & Bacon, 1996), 2.

12. Of course, interest groups engage in many activities that are not aimed at affecting policy outcomes. Much of what some groups do has nothing to do with lobbying for or against proposed legislation. Groups expend considerable resources trying to get specific

policies proposed in Congress, or trying to keep policies from being proposed. Such lobbying efforts are outside the scope of this model. The model is intended to explain interest group *reactions* to proposed bills, not their *proactive* attempts to affect legislation.

13. Notice that changing the preferences of a single senator makes no difference even if that senator happens to be the pivot. To effectively change the location of the pivot and move it to the other side of the status quo enough senators would have to change their policy preferences to shift the location of the veto pivot. The status quo does not move, but senators can. To change the location of a pivot, it is likely that many senators' preferences have to change.

14. David Austin-Smith and John R. Wright, "Counteractive Lobbying," *American Journal of Political Science* 38 (February 1994): 25–44; David Austin-Smith and John R. Wright, "The Multiple Ambiguities of Counteractive Lobbying," *American Journal of Political Science* 40 (November 1996): 543–64; Frank R. Baumgartner and Beth L. Leech, "Theory and Evidence for Counteractive Lobbying," *American Journal of Political Science* 40 (November 1996): 521–42.

15. It is theoretically possible, although realistically unlikely, for a policy to be proposed outside the gridlock region. In such a case the interest group would support the proposal but the bill would be likely to fail because of its location outside the gridlock region. Such a bill would like be killed or amended to something inside the gridlock region. The group would lobby for an amended bill that falls inside its winset.

16. Again, it is theoretically possible, although realistically unlikely, for a policy to be proposed outside the gridlock region. In such a case the interest group would oppose a bill that would be likely to fail or likely to be amended to something within the gridlock region. The group would then lobby for an amended bill that falls within its winset. However, when gridlock does not exist, policy proposals are more likely to be within the gridlock region, as described in the lower-right cell of Table 1.

17. In his book, Keith Krehbiel argues that decision makers' utilities are based on their preferences over outcomes (basic preferences) but that they make decisions over policies. It is preferences over policies that are potentially moveable (derived preferences)

Krehbiel, *Information and Legislative Organization* (Ann Arbor: University of Michigan Press, 1991): 66–77.

18. A. Lee Fritschler and James M. Hoefler, *Smoking and Politics: Policy Making and the Federal Bureaucracy* (Englewood Cliffs, NJ: Prentice Hall, 1996).

19. Drew Armstrong, "2008 Legislative Summary: Tobacco Regulations," *CQ Weekly* (December 2008), 3284.

20. Drew Armstrong, "2008 Legislative Summary: Tobacco Regulations," *CQ Weekly* (December 2008), 3284.

21. Drew Armstrong, "Tobacco Regulation Bill Passes House," *CQ Weekly* (August 2008), 2132

22. Drew Armstrong, "2008 Legislative Summary: Tobacco Regulations," *CQ Weekly* (December 2008), 3284.

23. The Center for Responsive Politics, [ON LINE] "Lobbying Database," *Opensecrets.org*, April-June 2009, http://www.opensecrets.org/lobby/index.php.

24. The Center for Responsive Politics, [ON LINE] "Lobbying Database," *Opensecrets.org*, April-June 2009, http://www.opensecrets.org/lobby/index.php.

25. Keith T. Poole and Howard Rosenthal, *Congress: A Political-Economic History of Roll Call Voting* (Oxford: Oxford UP, 1997).

26. Shawn Zeller, "Public Health Doctors Take On Tobacco Control Bill," *CQ Weekly* (July 2008), 1952.

27. The Center for Responsive Politics, [ON LINE] "Lobbying Database," *Opensecrets.org*, April-June 2009, http://www.opensecrets.org/lobby/index.php.

28. Richard L. Hall and Alan V. Deardorff, "Lobbying as Legislative Subsidy," *American Political Science Review* 100 (2006): 69–84; Gregory Wawro, "A Panel Probit Analysis of Campaign Contributions and Roll-Call Votes," *American Journal of Political Science* 45 (July 2001):563–79; Gregory Wawro, *Legislative Entrepreneurship in the U.S. House of Representatives* (Ann Arbor: University of Michigan Press, 2000); also see James B. Kau and Paul H. Rubin, *Congressmen, Constituents, and Contributors: Determinants of Roll Call Voting in the House of Representatives* (Boston: Martinus Nijhoff, 1992); Sam Peltzman, "Constituent Interest and Congressional Voting," *Journal of Politics and Economics* 27 (1984): 181–210; Lawrence S. Rothenberg, *Linking Citizens to Government: Interest Group Politics at Common*

Cause (New York: Cambridge University Press, 1992); John R. Wright, "PACs, Contributions, and Roll Calls: An Organization Perspective," *American Political Science Review* 79 (1985): 400–414; John R. Wright, "Contributions, Lobbying, and Committee Voting in the U.S. House of Representatives," *American Political Science Review* 84 (1990): 417–438; John R. Wright, *Interest Groups and Congress: Lobbying, Contributions, and Influence* (Boston: Allyn & Bacon, 1996); Janet M. Grenzke, "Shopping in the Congressional Supermarket: The Currency Is Complex," *American Journal of Political* Science 33 (1989): 1–24.

29. Regarding campaign donations as access, see Richard L. Hall and Frank W. Wayman, "Buying Time: Moneyed Interests and the Mobilization of Bias in Congressional Committees," *American Political Science Review* 84 (1990): 797–820; John Mark Hansen, *Gaining Access: Congress and the Farm Lobby, 1919–1981* (Chicago: University of Chicago Press, 1991). Regarding campaign donations as legislative subsidy see Richard L. Hall and Alan V. Deardorff, "Lobbying as Legislative Subsidy," *American Political Science Review* 100 (2006): 69–84; Richard L. Hall and Kristina C. Miler, "What Happens After the Alarm? Interest Group Subsidies to Legislative Overseers," *Journal of Politics* 70 (2008): 990–1005.

30. Jennifer Victor and Gregory Kroger, "The Beltway Network: A Network Analysis of Lobbyists' Decisions to Donate to Members of Congress," Presented at the annual meeting of the Midwest Political Science Association, Chicago, IL. April 2–5, 2009.

31. Keith Perine, "2006 Legislative Summary: Transporting Minors," *CQ Weekly* (December 2006), 3336.

32. Keith Perine, "2006 Legislative Summary: Transporting Minors," *CQ Weekly* (December 2006), 3336.

33. Sheryl Gay Stolberg, "House Tightens Parental Rule for Abortions," *The New York Times*, April 28, 2005.

34. Amy Fagan, "House approve abortion limits," *The Washington Times*, April 28, 2005.

35. Even if gridlock did exist, lobbyists' beliefs about the spatial context of a bill are more important than the latent true state of the world since these beliefs will inform lobbying strategies.

36. The Center for Responsive Politics, [ON LINE] "Lobbying Database," *Opensecrets.org*, April-June 2009, http://www.opensecrets.org/lobby/index.php.

37. This model also explains why the bill ultimately failed as the bill (*b*) is clearly outside of the winset of the filibuster pivot.

Chapter 14

News Media

14-1 The Market and the Media

James T. Hamilton

> *With good reason, the news media have long been called the "fourth branch" of government. In a democracy citizens need news to monitor the performance of their representatives. Conversely, officeholders and those who wish to replace them need to be able to communicate with their constituencies. Moreover, with officeholders needing to coordinate with one another across the institutions that divide them, "news," as Woodrow Wilson aptly observed, "is the atmosphere of politics." The First Amendment to the Constitution recognizes the news media's special role by placing freedom of the press alongside freedoms of speech and religion as deserving categorical protection from government infringement. More than in any other Western democracy, the news media developed in America as private business enterprises virtually free of government regulation or investment. Modern news, James Hamilton reminds us, is as much a product of business as it ever was. As technology creates new audiences and products, the business of news has undergone significant market adjustment.*

Since market forces have played the most decisive role in transforming the delivery of news, the history of the American press from the 1970s to the present is economic history. Although journalists may not explicitly consider economics as they cover the day's events, the stories, reporters, firms, and media that ultimately survive in the marketplace depend on economic factors. The decisions of producers and editors are driven by supply and demand: Who cares about a particular piece of information? What is an audience willing to pay for the news, or what are advertisers willing to pay for the attention of readers, listeners, or viewers? How many consumers share particular interests in a topic? How many competitors are vying for readers' or viewers' attention, and what are these competitors offering as

news? What are the costs of generating and transmitting a story? Who owns the outlet? What are the owners' goals? What are the property rights that govern how news is produced, distributed, and sold? News is a commercial product.

News outlets that cover public affairs have always struggled with the tension between giving people what they want to know and giving them what they need to know. The low probability that any reader has of influencing the outcome of a policy debate leaves many readers "rationally ignorant" about the details of governing.[1] From an investment perspective, why learn about global warming if your actions have little chance of affecting policy? News outlets do face strong demand for entertaining news, or information that helps people in their role as consumers or

Source: James T. Hamilton, "The Market and the Media," in *The Institutions of American Democracy: The Press,* edited by Geneva Overholser and Kathleen Hall Jamieson, pp. 351-370. Copyright © 2005 Oxford University Press, Inc. By permission of Oxford University Press, Inc. Some notes appearing in the original have been deleted.

workers. Some people may also express a demand for news about politics, though the set of viewers that prefers politics covered as a sport or drama may exceed that which prefers detailed analysis.

In this essay I argue that since the 1970s news coverage has shifted to an increasing emphasis on what people want to know and away from information that they may need as voters. I identify three economic factors that help account for this shift: changes in technology, product definition and differentiation, and media ownership. I will examine in detail how each has affected news content over time. I then focus on network evening news programs in a case study that demonstrates how these economic factors have shaped news coverage. After providing a snapshot of current media coverage, I conclude with a section analyzing the implications of these alterations in the ways in which news is defined, distributed, and consumed.

What's Different: Technology, Products, and Owners

Three technological changes have affected the way in which images and information have entered households since 1970: the growth of cable television; the advent of the Internet; and the increased use of satellite technology to transmit news across continents and into homes. The spread of cable television in the 1980s and 1990s and introduction of direct-broadcast satellite delivery meant that by 2003 at least 85 percent of television households subscribed to multichannel delivery systems. The average number of channels per home went from 7.1 in 1970 to 71.2 in 2001. The average number of channels viewed weekly for at least ten minutes went from 4.5 to 13.5 channels per television household.[2] This proliferation of channels meant that news on cable could focus on specific niches. Rather than attempting to garner 10 million viewers (the audience attracted by the *NBC Nightly News* in 2003), a cable news program could be successful by attracting less than 1 million viewers. The result is that cable channels can focus their products on particular types of news: sports stories on ESPN; business news on CNBC; storm data on the Weather Channel; and

news that appeals to a conservative audience on FOX News Channel. Both the network evening news programs and daily newspapers have broader audiences than cable channels. If survey respondents are asked to rate themselves on an ideological scale of liberalism and conservatism, the average rating for consumers of the network evening news programs and daily newspapers is the same as the national sample average. The regular consumers of the FOX News Channel, however, have the most conservative ideological rating in the survey. Cable political shows such as *Crossfire* and *Hardball*, in contrast, attract audiences more likely to rate themselves as liberal.

The relatively small audiences of some cable news programs yield profits because of low production budgets. Since talk can be cheap, cable news programs often feature journalists acting as political pundits. Political pundits, who offer a mixture of fact and opinion, face many market constraints. Since readers have the freedom to sample and ignore stories across the portfolio of topics covered in a paper, those writing for newspapers can aim for a relatively educated audience and afford to write about topics that may not be of interest to many. Television pundits, in contrast, operate in a medium where viewers of a particular program all consume the same story. If these pundits pick topics of little interest, they risk losing viewers, who may be less educated (than newspaper readers) and more likely to search for entertainment than enlightenment from television. The result is that pundits choose different languages to talk about politics, depending on the avenue of expression.

To see these differences, consider the case of George Will, who writes a syndicated column and appears as a commentator on ABC News programming.[3] As I demonstrate in my book *All the News That's Fit to Sell*, the print George Will uses a greater variety of terms and longer words than the television George Will. When composing for a print audience, Will uses more abstract terms such as those relating to inspiration, as well as more numeric terms. He writes about groups rather than individuals, as reflected in a greater focus on core values and institutions. In television appearances, Will changes expression to comply with the greater demands for entertainment. He uses more human-interest language. He makes more self-references. He simplifies and summarizes, and at the same time hedges his bets through qualifications (higher use of ambivalent language). His statements on television focus more on the present and emphasize motion. On television, Will offers opinions that are marked by greater activity and realism. Although George Will has developed a brand name for expression, he changes the delivery of his product to suit the audience demands and cost constraints of the medium. . . .

A second technological change affecting news markets is the spread of the Internet. Competition for attention across sites has driven the price of news on nearly all Internet sites to zero (the marginal delivery cost of the information). This explosion of free information has many ramifications. Consumption of high-quality newspapers, for example, is now possible around the world. If one looks at the top one hundred newspapers in the United States, the circulation of the top five (the *Wall Street Journal, USA Today,* the *New York Times, Los Angeles Times,* and *Washington Post*) accounted for 21.5 percent of the total newspaper circulation in 1999.[4] If you look at the links generated on the Internet by these top one hundred newspapers, however, the top five papers in terms of links (which included *USA Today,* the *New York Times,* and the *Washington Post*) accounted for 41.4 percent of the total links. In part this reflects the advantages of established brands on the Internet, since familiarity with a product's existence and reputation can lead to its consumption. . . .

The low cost of entry to placing information on the Internet has had many effects on news. The ability of news outlets, and columnists such as Matt Drudge, to post instantly during any time of the day has extended news cycles and created additional pressure on traditional news outlets to run with breaking news.[5] The lack of large investment in sites means that news provided may not be heavily edited or screened, which can give rise to a spread of rumor

and gossip. The archiving of data on the Internet and easy accessibility make it easier for errors in reporting to propagate, as journalists access information collected by others and incorporate it into stories. The widespread existence of government and nonprofit Web sites lowers the cost of information generation and analysis for reporters. Journalists writing about campaign finance, for example, can readily locate data at the individual contributor level at the Federal Election Commission Web site or at Opensecrets.org. Similarly, reporters writing about the environment can use government data aggregated by the nonprofit Environmental Defense, which posts detailed pollution data by the zip code level at Scorecard.org.

Widespread use of satellite technology to beam images across the country and the world marks a third change in news reporting. During the 1970s the three evening network news programs had an "oligopoly of image," where viewers tuned in the programs in part to see the first pictures of the day's breaking stories. The deployment of satellite technology across the country, however, soon meant that local television stations had the ability to import stories quickly from other parts of the country and to go live to events in their own city. The ability of local stations to share in network feeds or tap into other sources of pictures meant that local news programs began to offer viewers images of national or international stories, which in turn put pressure on the evening news to offer a differentiated product (including more interpretative or contextual material). The existence of satellite technology also meant that international coverage could take place in real time, including the coverage of the Iraq War by embedded reporters.

These technological changes have put increased pressures on traditional news outlets to compete for readers and viewers. The growth in cable channels and cable/direct broadcast satellite subscription has eroded the market share of the network evening news programs and focused attention on retaining viewers. The network evening news programs have a core audience of faithful viewers and a set of marginal viewers, those who may tune in to the news or choose another program depending on what has happened in the world or what types of news the networks choose to focus on. News directors will select a mix of stories aimed at capturing the marginal viewers while not alienating the average or regular viewers. The result of competition from cable is a mix of stories that leaves average viewers somewhat frustrated and marginal viewers somewhat placated.

Survey data from the Pew Center for the People and the Press in 2000 show the tension between the interests of the average (i.e., regularly view) and marginal (i.e., sometimes view) consumers of the network nightly news programs.[6] A majority of the regular viewers are over fifty (54.8 percent) and female (53.9 percent). The marginal viewers are much younger. Females aged eighteen to thirty-four account for 20.6 percent of those who sometimes view the national news, and males aged eighteen to thirty-four account for 17.5 percent of these sometime viewers. In contrast, eighteen-to-thirty-four-year-old females are only 9.1 percent of the regular audience, and males of that age group only 9.2 percent of the regular viewers. These demographic differences translate into predictable and sharp differences between the interests of marginal and average viewers. Marginal viewers are not as attached to the news. When asked whether they enjoyed keeping up with the news, 68.1 percent of average viewers responded that they did "a lot" versus only 37.0 percent for the marginal viewers. A majority of marginal viewers said that they followed national or international news closely "only when something important or interesting is happening." Marginal viewers also were more likely to report that they watched the news with "my remote in hand" and switched channels when they were not interested in a topic.

What captures the interests of occasional viewers differs from the type of news favored by loyal viewers. The marginal and average viewers have the same top two news interests, crime and health, which may explain the prevalence of these news categories on the network evening news. The two sets of viewers differ markedly, however, in their interest in politics. For the average viewer of network news, news about political figures and events in Washington ranked fifth out of thirteen news types. This same category of news ranked tenth among marginal viewers. Political news about Washington was followed very closely by 28.4 percent of the average viewers, versus 12.3 percent of the marginals. Sports ranked sixth and entertainment news ranked twelfth among the regular viewers. These topics ranked much more highly among marginal viewers, who ranked them third and eighth among the thirteen news topics.

Viewers who are younger than fifty may also merit attention for another reason—they are more highly valued by advertisers. Reasons offered for why advertisers pay more for viewers under fifty include a belief that their brand preferences are not as fixed and the fact that they watch less television and hence are harder to reach. The rewards for capturing relatively younger viewers offer another reason for news directors to pay less attention to the (older) loyal watchers. One way to forge a compromise between the interests of average and marginal viewers is to cover the political issues of interest to younger viewers. The January 2000 Pew survey asked respondents to indicate the priority they attached to twenty political issues. When I examined the number of minutes or number of stories devoted on each network to these issues in 2000, I found that the higher the priority attached to an issue at the start of the year by the eighteen-to-thirty-four set, the more attention devoted over the year by the network news. The priorities of older viewers had no impact or a negative effect on coverage devoted by the networks. The survey data indicate that females in the [above] age range care relatively more about issues such as dealing with the problems of families with children and strengthening gun control laws. Searching for marginal viewers and those valued by advertisers may thus lead the networks to talk about issues often associated with the Democratic Party. The competition generated by technology, and the influence of advertiser values, thus generate pressure to provide network stories that may give rise to perceptions of media bias. Among those identifying themselves as very conservative, 37.4 percent reported in 2000 that they viewed the national nightly network news as very biased. Among survey respondents who labeled themselves as very liberal, only 16.6 percent saw network news programs the same way.

Product Changes

In print and broadcast, there has been a substantial change in the content and style of news coverage since 1970. These product changes are numerous: a decrease in hard news (e.g., public-affairs coverage) and an increase in soft news (e.g., entertainment, human-interest stories); an increase in negative tone to cover elections; less focus on watchdog stories (e.g., those dealing with the operation of government); and an increase in the mix of opinion and interpretation in news coverage. These product changes also have many origins. Emphasis on cost cutting and profits has led to declines in international coverage. Competition across media and the pressure for product differentiation within a market have led some outlets to specialize in soft news. The drive to entertain can transform political coverage into horse-race coverage, with a focus on who is ahead in the polls and a tone that is often critical of candidates and events. In publicly traded companies, pressures to meet market earnings expectations can mean more focus on pleasing readers and viewers and less room for journalists to exercise their own news judgment. Changes in rules by the Federal Communications Commission (FCC) have reduced station worries about whether views expressed on air are "fair" and removed specific requirements that broadcasters provide a minimum amount of public-affairs coverage. In this section I describe the dimensions of news product changes since 1970. These changes in product attributes result from an interplay of demand and supply factors, though I do not attempt here to specify which factors generate particular product alterations.

Content analysis by the Committee of Concerned Journalists (CCJ) in 1998 captured broad changes in the media by examining for 1977, 1987, and 1997 one month of coverage on the three network evening news programs, each cover story during the year for *Time* and *Newsweek*, and each front-page story for the *New York Times* and *Los Angeles Times*. For this sample of 3,760 stories, the CCJ found that straight news accounts (e.g., what happened yesterday) went from 52 percent of stories in 1977 to only 32 percent in 1997. Story topics in traditional hard-news areas (i.e., government, military, and domestic and foreign affairs) went from 66.3 percent of all reports to 48.9 percent. Feature stories such as those about entertainment, celebrities, lifestyle, and celebrity crime grew from 5.1 percent in 1977 to 11.1 percent in 1997. Crime stories went from 8.4 percent to 11.4 percent and personal health from 0.7 percent to 3.5 percent. Attention also grew for stories about science (2.7 percent to 5.9 percent) and religion (0.5 percent to 3.7 percent).[7]. . .

As hard-news coverage declined, the tone of many stories about elections grew more critical. Assessing coverage of major-party presidential nominees in *Time* and *Newsweek* from 1960 to 1992, [Thomas] Patterson found that unfavorable references to the candidates grew from approximately 25 percent in 1960 to 60 percent in 1992. Studying front-page election stories in the *New York Times*, he found that in the 1960s the candidates and other partisan sources set the tone of nearly 70 percent of the articles. By 1992, journalists set the tone for the reports about 80 percent of the time. Kiku Adatto documented similar patterns of a shrinking role for the candidate and increasing role for the reporter on network television coverage of presidential campaigns. She found that in 1968 the average sound bite for a presidential candidate on the network evening news was 42.3 seconds. By the 1988 campaign this figure dropped to 9.8 seconds (and decreased further to 8.4 seconds in the 1992 general election). What replaced the words of the candidates was strategy coverage provided by reporters, who gave viewers their assessment of why the candidate was engaged in a particular strategy and how the candidate was faring in the horse race. Critical coverage also greeted the eventual winners. A study for the Council for Excellence in Government found that in the first year of the presidencies of Ronald Reagan (1981), Bill Clinton (1993), and George W. Bush (2001), coverage of the administration on network television news was negative in tone by a ratio of nearly two to one. The critical eye reporters used in covering government emerged in part from journalists' experience with government deception during both the Vietnam War and Watergate.[8]. . .

Product changes are evident too in the percentage of journalists saying that a particular media role was extremely important. In 1971 76 percent of journalists said investigating government claims was an extremely important mass media role, 61 percent said the same for providing analysis of complex problems, and 55 percent for discussing national policy. These figures dropped in 1992 to 67 percent for investigating government, 48 percent for analysis of complex problems, and 39 percent for national problems. Journalists in 1992 were much more likely (69 percent) to say that getting information to the public quickly was an extremely important role, versus 56 percent in 1971.[9]

In extended interviews with journalists, Howard Gardner, Mihaly Csikszentmihalyi, and William Damon also found that journalists were frustrated: 51 percent said changes in the media were negative, versus 24 percent indicating that the changes were positive. Sixty-four percent of the journalists they interviewed said the demands to comply with business goals in journalism were increasing, and 63 percent said there was a perceived drop in ethics and values in the media. Many of those interviewed pointed to the drive for market share as a prime force undercutting the performance of journalists.[10]

Changes in government regulation also affected the extent and kind of information provided. Prior to 1987, the FCC's fairness doctrine required broadcasters to provide free and equal time to parties that dissented from controversial views that stations chose to air. While the policy may have promoted perceptions of fairness, empirical evidence indicates that the policy may have chilled speech by discouraging stations from presenting viewpoints that might trigger demands for free response time on air.[11] Once the fairness doctrine was abolished by the FCC, the genre of informational programming immediately expanded on radio. This radio genre, which includes news programming and the talk-radio format made famous by Rush Limbaugh, became both a popular and controversial force in public-affairs debates in the 1990s.

Ownership

Change in ownership of news media outlets is a third factor affecting content. There are many theories about why ownership matters: publicly traded firms could be more likely to focus on profits than journalism properties (e.g., newspapers) owned by individuals or families; outlets owned by groups, whether a newspaper in a chain or a broadcast station owned by a network may be less likely to identify with the problems of a specific city; and the concentration of ownership in a small number of firms may crowd out a diverse set of views.

Calculating how ownership has changed over time requires defining a medium and a market. Between 1970 and 1998, the number of daily newspapers declined from 1,748 to 1,489 and average circulation dropped from 62,202 to 56,183. The number of weekly newspapers, however, grew from 7,612 to 8,193 and average circulation jumped from 3,660 to 9,067. The number of cities with two or more fully competing dailies with different ownership declined from 37 in 1973 to 19 in 1996. The number of newspaper groups dropped from 157 in 1970 to 129 in 1996. In the same period, the percentage of dailies owned by chains grew from 50.3 percent to 76.2 percent and the percentage of daily circulation accounted for by these group-owned papers increased from 63.0 percent to 81.5 percent. The fifteen largest newspaper chains generated slightly more than half of the daily circulation of newspapers in the United States in 1998.[12]

At a broad level, the media have not become significantly more concentrated (in terms of the concentration of sales in a specific number of firms) over this time period. It is estimated that in terms of revenues, the top fifty media firms (which include newspaper, broadcast, cable, publishing, music, and film companies) accounted for 79.7 percent of all media industry revenues in 1986 and 81.8 percent in 1997; the share of the top four firms grew from 18.8 percent to 24.1 percent.[13] ... One study looked at how ownership had changed between 1960 and 2000 for ten local media markets in the United States. After counting for each local market the number of broadcast outlets, cable systems, direct-broadcast satellite systems, and daily newspapers available, the study found that the percentage growth in the total number of media outlets available averaged more than 200 percent between 1960 and 2000. The percentage increase in the number of owners in the market averaged 140 percent.[14]

The actual impact of group or chain ownership in media outlets is a topic of spirited empirical debate. Reviewing the social science evidence on the impact of chain ownership on newspaper operation in 1994, Edwin Baker concluded, "Chain ownership's primary documented effects are negative. However, the findings seem tepid, hardly motivating any strong critique of chain ownership or prompting any significant policy interventions." Lisa George found that as the number of owners in a local newspaper market goes down, product differentiation between newspapers increases and the number of topical reporting beats covered in the market overall goes up. The Project for Excellence in Journalism found that in local television markets, stations affiliated with networks produced higher-quality news programs than those actually owned and operated by the networks, that stations owned by a company also operating a newspaper in the market generated higher-quality local television news programs, and that locally owned stations were not obviously superior to other stations in news production.[15]

The Changing Nature of Network News

The transformation of the network evening news programs since 1970 offers a case study of the impact of changes in technology, news definitions, and ownership.[16] In 1969 the daily debates among network news executives and reporters about what stories to include in the evening news broadcasts centered around which domestic politics and foreign policy stories to cover. Each television network was part of a media company. For each of the three networks, the founder or an early leader was still involved and identified with the operation of the organization. Network news operations were expected to generate prestige, part of which reflected back on the owners and broadcasters. The FCC routinely examined the number of hours of public-affairs programming provided when stations had their licenses renewed. A reputation for covering public affairs well in the news provided added security when licenses were up for renewal. If viewers did not enjoy the hard-news stories provided in the evening news programs, they had few other options on the dial. The average television household received seven channels. At the dinner hour more than one-third of all television households watched the network evening news. The stories they saw were news to most viewers. National news programs were not on earlier in the afternoon, and local news programs lacked the technology and time to cover national events on their own. Decision makers on network news programs felt a responsibility to provide viewers with information they needed as citizens. The large audience share and focus on politics attracted significant scrutiny of the programs, which were a frequent target of criticism from the White House.[17]

In 2000 the daily debates in network story conferences centered on whether to include domestic political stories or softer news items about health and entertainment topics. Foreign coverage was not often on the agenda, except in cases of military action. Each network was part of a publicly traded conglomerate. Network news operations were expected by corporate managers and Wall Street analysts to generate profits. The FCC no longer scrutinized public affairs coverage and license renewals were virtually assured. Television households received an average of sixty-three channels. Viewers at the dinner hour could watch sitcoms, entertainment news, sports news, and news on PBS. The three major network news programs combined captured only 23 percent of all television households. Viewers often came to the network news programs with a sense of the day's headline stories, after watching news on cable channels or local television programs containing stories and footage from around the nation. Network decision-makers felt pressure to gain ratings, which translated into a competition to discover and serve viewers' interests. Anchors and reporters were promoted as celebrities. Political criticisms of news coverage focused more on the content of cable news programs, though press critics faulted the network evening news shows for an increasing shift to soft-news stories.

To see the shift in news content, consider how the network evening news treated a consistent set of stories over time. Each year, *People* magazine selects its "25 Most Intriguing People" of the year, which consist of a set of soft-news personalities (i.e., television stars, movie actors, sports figures, persons involved in famous crimes, and royalty) and a set of famous figures from business and politics. In 1974–78, 40 percent of the soft-news personalities on the *People* list were covered in stories on at least one of the three major network evening news programs. In 1994–98, this figure rose to 52 percent. For those soft-news personalities that generated coverage over the course of the year they were listed by *People*, on ABC the "Intriguing" person averaged 9.9 stories and 1,275 seconds in coverage per year in 1974–78. This grew to 17.2 stories and 2,141 seconds of annual average coverage by 1994–98. NBC's reputation of providing more soft news than the other two networks is confirmed by its average of 25.6 stories and 3,238 seconds of coverage in 1994–98.

By many measures hard-news coverage dropped over this period. Each year, *Congressional Quarterly* identifies the key votes that take place in the U.S. Senate and House. In 1969–73, 82 percent of these major votes were covered on at least one of the network evening news programs on the day of or day after the congressional action. Yet for the period

1994–98, only 62 percent of the *CQ* votes generated network stories. A similar pattern holds for the key legislative votes identified each year by two ideological interest groups, the Americans for Democratic Action (ADA) and the American Conservative Union (ACU). The percentage of key interest-group votes in Congress that generated stories on the nightly news dropped from 64 percent in 1969–73 to 44 percent in 1994–98. The shift on the network news away from a headline service toward more background reporting is evident in the fact that those bills that were covered got more time on the evening news programs. On ABC, for example, the mean overage length for *CQ* bills went from 117 seconds in 1969–73 to 211 seconds in 1994–98.

Statistical analysis shows that many factors contributed to these changes in coverage. *People*'s intriguing personalities were more likely to be covered over the course of a year on the network evening news in the era (i.e., 1984 or later) when the FCC had deregulated much of broadcast television. Coverage of *CQ* votes declined in election years (when they were probably crowded out by campaign stories) and dropped as cost cutting became more prominent in network news operations. Interest-group vote coverage declined on each network as the percentage of households with cable increased, indicating how broadcast television shifted away from some forms of hard news as competition increased from cable. In the period 1969 to 1999, the number of network evening news stories mentioning soft-news terms such as *actor, sex,* or *movie* increased along with the percentage of households with cable. In the post-deregulation era, stories about hard-news topics such as education or Medicaid or NATO declined.

Network evening news anchors not only covered celebrities, they became them. News products have always been what economists call experience goods, which means that companies have always sought ways to signal to potential customers what today's version of events will look like in their papers or programs. The pressure for journalists to become part of the news product, however, is increasing as the number of news outlets expands. In a world of four broadcast television channels, a consumer can easily switch among viewing options to sample content. In a world where channels can number in the hundreds, sampling becomes more time-consuming.[18] If viewers recognize and enjoy watching a particular journalist on television, they may be more likely to watch a given channel because of this familiarity. The personalities of those who present the information become shortcuts for viewers to find their news niche. The changing salary rewards in network evening news programs provide evidence of how journalists have become part of the product in news.

Although network anchors deliver the news, they are rewarded in the marketplace for delivering viewers to advertisers. The salary patterns for network evening news anchors suggest that the value attached to the personal ability of these stars to deliver viewers increased markedly during the 1990s. . . . When consumers have many more choices, the value of a known commodity can increase. Network anchors become a way for channels to create a brand image in viewers' minds. If anchors become more important in drawing viewers to programs, this may translate into higher returns for anchors in salary negotiations. . . . The amount in salary that an anchor received for attracting a thousand viewing households increased from a range of $0.13 to $0.31 (in 1999 dollars) in 1976 to a range of $0.86 to $1.07 in 1999. Another way to view this is to look at the ratio of the anchor's salary to the ad price on the evening news programs. In 1976 anchors such as Walter Cronkite and John Chancellor were paid the equivalent of 28 ads per year, while in 1999 this had grown to 149 ads for Dan Rather and Tom Brokaw. The marked increase in the amount paid per viewing household, salary expressed in ad revenues, and the absolute magnitude of the salary took place in the 1990s. This was a time of declining absolute audiences, but rising importance of anchors in attracting viewers. The increased value placed on anchors is consistent with these personalities playing a growing role in attracting viewers in a multichannel universe.

Current News Markets

The expanding opportunities for individuals to consume media products has meant declining market shares for most traditional news media outlets. The percentage of survey respondents saying that they were regular consumers of a specific news outlet dropped substantially between May 1993 and April 2002 in Pew surveys: from 77 percent to 57 percent for local television news; 60 percent to 32 percent for nightly network news; and 52 percent to 24 percent for network television news magazines. Between 1994 and 2002, Pew surveys indicated drops in regular consumption from 47 percent to 41 percent for radio and 58 percent to 41 percent for newspapers. Respondents reporting regular consumption of online news grew from 2 percent in April 1996 to 25 percent in April 2002; NPR's figures also increased during that period, from 13 percent to 16 percent. In April 2002, 33 percent of survey respondents reported that they were regular consumers of cable television news. . . .

The multiplication of news outlets on cable and the Internet means [also] that an individual is more likely today than in the 1970s or 1980s to find a news outlet closer to his or her ideal news source. The creation of niche programming and content means that individuals may be more likely to find what they want. But the division of the audience into smaller groups also means that any one channel may be less likely to attract viewers, less likely to amass advertiser revenue, and hence less able to devote resources to programming. There may be a trade-off between cable channels' catering to individual topical interests and the quality of programming that can be supported by the audience size. On the Internet, the drive of competition means that price eventually equals marginal costs (zero), so sites are searching for ways to generate revenue. This means that breaking news becomes a commodity essentially offered for free. The lack of revenue may mean that sites simply repeat readily available information rather than generate their own coverage. In a study of Internet content during the 2000 presidential primaries, the Committee of Concerned Journalists found that one-quarter of the political front pages on Internet sites they studied had no original reporting.[19] The time pressure to provide news generated by the Internet and the lack of resources to do original reporting may increase the likelihood that information cascades occur. When initial news reports get facts wrong, the tendency of reporters to rely on the work of others and the quick multiplication effects can mean that bad information propagates. . . .

An additional dilemma for hard-news consumers is the economic pressures that may push some outlets away from offering the type of news they prefer. If advertisers value younger viewers and younger viewers demonstrate a higher willingness to switch channels, then broadcast programs may end up at the margins, putting more soft-news topics into previously hard-news programs. This explains in part the increased emphasis on entertainment and human-interest stories on the network news broadcasts. Media bias can also emerge as a commercial product, in at least two forms. If networks are targeting relatively younger female viewers, and these viewers express more interest in issues such as gun control and the problems of families with children, the network news programs may focus on traditionally Democratic (liberal) issues out of economic necessity. The development of niche programs on cable can also generate programs targeted at viewers with a particular ideology. The FOX News Channel. for example, attracts a relatively conservative audience and offers the cable news program with the largest audience—*The O'Reilly Factor*. The added variety arising from the expansion of cable programming means that viewers uninterested in politics can more readily avoid it. In 1996 viewers with cable who had low levels of political interest (i.e., had low levels of political information) were much less likely to watch presidential debates than viewers who had broadcast channels.[20] Those who were not interested in politics but had only broadcast television did end up watching these debates, since their options were limited. The greater entertainment options provided by cable television also appear to affect who votes. Among viewers with high interest in entertainment programming, those with cable are much less likely to vote (perhaps because they are able to avoid political programming by watching the many entertainment channels offered on cable). . . .

Changes in news markets from 1970 to today have brought new media, generated more diverse offerings, and added opportunities to find both hard and soft news. In pushing for the deregulation of broadcast television in the 1980s, FCC chairman Mark Fowler declared famously, "The public's interest . . . defines the public interest." [21] The competition for interested audiences has clearly driven many of the recent changes in journalism. Whether the aggregation of individuals pursuing the stories they want to know about yields the type of information they need to know about as citizens and voters is a question pursued further in other chapters in this volume.

Notes

1. Anthony Downs, *An Economic Theory of Democracy* (New York: Harper Books, 1957). Downs coined the term *rational ignorance* to refer to the fact that the small probability that an individual has of influencing public policy decisions means that it may be rational to remain ignorant of current affairs, if one views information only as an instrument in making decisions and calculates the personal payoffs from keeping up with public affairs. There may still be a demand expressed for political coverage, from those who feel a duty to be informed, people who find the details of politics and policies inherently interesting, or people who derive entertainment from politics as drama, horse race, or scandal. The logic of rational ignorance may help explain why Delli Carpini and Keeter find that "despite the numerous political, economic, and social changes that have occurred since World War II, overall political knowledge levels in the United States are about the same today as they were forty to fifty years ago" (*What Americans Know about Politics and Why It Matters.* New Haven, Conn.: Yale University Press, 1996, 270).

2. For data on channel availability and consumption, see Ed Papazian, ed., *TV Dimensions 2002* (New York: Media Dynamics, 2002).

3. To study the market for pundits, I analyzed a sample of the print offerings and broadcast transcripts of fifty-six pundits in 1999 using the text analysis software DICTION. See chapter 8 in Hamilton, *All the News That's Fit to Sell,* (Princeton, N.J.: Princeton University Press, 2004).

4. For analysis of news markets on the Internet, see chapter 7 in Hamilton, *All the News That's Fit to Sell.*

5. See Kovach and Rosensteil, *Warp Speed* (New York: Century Foundation Press, 1999), and Kalb, *One Scandalous Story* (New York: Free Press, 2001), for discussions of the time pressures on journalists created by the speed of information transmission and the Internet.

6. See chapter 3 in Hamilton, *All the News That's Fit to Sell*, for an analysis of the network news audience.

7. Committee of Concerned Journalists, *Changing Definitions of News* (Washington, D.C.: Committee of Concerned Journalists, 1998), available from www.journalism.org.

8. Patterson, *Out of Order* (New York: Knopf, 1993); Adatto, *Picture Perfect* (New York: Basic Books, 1993); Council for Excellence in Government, *Government: In and Out of the News*, study by the Center for Media and Public Affairs, 2003, available at http://www.excelgov.org/displaycontent.asp?keyword=prnHomePage. Patterson's *Out of Order* also includes a discussion of distrust between reporters and politicians.

9. Weaver and Wilhoit, *The American Journalist in the 1990s* (Mahwah, N.J.: Lawrence Erlbaum, 1996).

10. Gardner, Csikszentmihalyi, and Damon, *Good Work* (New York: Basic Books, 2001).

11. Thomas W. Hazlett and David W. Sosa, "Was the Fairness Doctrine a 'Chilling Effect'?: Evidence from the Post-Deregulation Radio Market," *Journal of Legal Studies* 26, no. 1 (1997): 279–301.

12. For data on newspaper markets, see Compaine and Gomery, *Who Owns the Media?* 3rd ed. (Mahwah, N.J.: Lawrence Erlbaum, 2000).

13. Ibid.

14. Scott Roberts, Jane Frenette, and Dione Stearns, "A Comparison of Media Outlets and Owners for Ten Selected Markets: 1960, 1980, 2000" (working paper, Media Ownership Working Group, Federal Communications Commission, Washington, D.C., 2002).

15. For discussion of the impact of media ownership and concentration on content, see Peter O. Steiner, "Program Patterns and Preferences, and the Workability of Competition in Radio Broadcasting," *Quarterly Journal of Economics* 66 (1952): 194-223; Demers, *The Menace of the Corporate Newspaper* (Ames: Iowa State University Press, 1996); Bagdikian, *The Media Monopoly* (Boston: Beacon Press, 1997); McChesney, *Rich Man, Poor Democracy* (Urbana: University of Illinois Press, 2000); Jeff Chester, "Strict Scrutiny: Why Journalists Should Be Concerned about New Federal and Industry Media Deregulation Proposals," *Harvard International Journal of Press/Politics* 7, no. 2 (2002): 105–15; and Roberts and Kunkel, eds., *Breach of Faith* (Fayetteville: University of Arkansas Press, 2002). The quotation on ownership studies comes from C. Edwin Baker, "Ownership of Newspapers: The View from Positivist Social Science" (research paper, Joan Shorenstein Center on the Press, Politics and Public Policy, Kennedy School of Government, Harvard University, Cambridge, Mass., 1994), 19. See also Lisa George, "What's Fit to Print: The Effect of Ownership Concentration on Product Variety in Daily Newspaper Markets" (working paper, Michigan State University, East Lansing, Mich., 2001), and Project for Excellence in Journalism, *Does Ownership Matter in Local Television News? A Five-Year Study of Ownership and Quality*, updated April 29, 2003, http://www.journalism.org/resources/research/reports/ownership/default.asp.

16. This section excerpts and summarizes analysis from chapters 6 and 8 of Hamilton, *All the News That's Fit to Sell*.

17. In 1969 the founders or early leaders of each network still served as the chairman of the board: William S. Paley (CBS); David Sarnoff (RCA, which owned NBC); and Leonard Goldenson (ABC). For an overview of the networks that focuses on the 1980s, see Auletta, *Three Blind Mice* (New York: Random House, 1992). Data on channels per television household come from Ed Papazian, ed., *TV Dimensions 2001* (New York: Media Dynamics, 2001), which indicates (on p. 22) that averages were 7.1 for 1970 and 63.4 for 2000. Larry M. Bartels and Wendy M. Rahn, in "Political Attitudes in the Post-Network Era" (paper prepared for the Annual Meeting of the

American Political Science Association, Washington, D.C., September, 2000), report that the sum of the Nielsen ratings for the three network evening news programs was close to 36 in 1970–71 and 23 in 1999–2000. For the text of Vice President Spiro Agnew's speech attacking network television news on November 13, 1969, see James Keogh, *President Nixon and the Press* (New York: Funk & Wagnalls, 1972).

18. In summer 2001 DirecTV, a digital satellite service, offered subscribers more than 225 channels (see www.directv.com). The average number of channels received in U.S. television households grew from 28 in 1988 to 49 in 1997. Households clearly have favorites among these channels. The average number of channels viewed per household, where viewing is defined as "10 or more continuous minutes per channel," was 12 in 1997. See Nielsen Media Research, *1998 Report on Television* (New York: Nielsen Media Research, 1998), 19.

19. Committee of Concerned Journalists, *ePolitics: A Study of the 2000 Presidential Campaign on the Internet* (Washington, D.C.: Committee of Concerned Journalists, 2000), available from www.journalism.org.

20. See Matthew A. Baum and Samuel Kernell, "Has Cable Ended the Golden Age of Presidential Television?" *American Political Science Review* 93, no. 1 (1999): 99–114.

21. See Hamilton, *All the News That's Fit to Sell*, 1.

14-2 Red Media, Blue Media: Evidence of Ideological Selectivity in Media Use

Shanto Iyengar and Kyu S. Hahn

The extent to which the American public has become polarized into conservative Republican and liberal Democratic camps is a lively issue among political scientists. Public attitudes on most policies have not changed much over the years. What does appear to have changed, however, is voters' ability to identify those politicians who favor policies closer to their own views. Shanto Iyengar and Kyu S. Hahn report experiments suggesting that this development reflects the availability of diverse news sources offered by cable television networks. The public seeks news from producers who adopt an ideological stance with which they agree. Conservatives strongly trust Fox News, while liberals (and self-described) moderates are more inclined to trust NPR and cable news producers MSNBC and CNN.

... The division of the United States into predictably "red" and "blue" states and the gradual decline in the number of genuine "battlegrounds" (Abramowitz & Saunders, 2006) where either party has a genuine chance of victory suggests that American politics today is more polarized than in eras past. The standard explanation for polarized politics is the tendency for candidates to cater to the preferences of political activists. Because activists on both sides represent the far ideological wings of the parties . . . , rational candidates avoid middle-of-the-road appeals. . . .

Political activists are polarized, but at the level of the mass public there is considerable debate. Some scholars believe that increased polarization is only an illusion, stemming from the tendency of the media to treat conflict as more newsworthy than consensus (Fiorina et al., 2005). Alternatively, the impression of mass polarization may reflect the nomination of extreme rather than centrist candidates, and an electorate that votes along party lines (Layman & Carsey, 2002). Other researchers,

however, point to evidence that increasing numbers of ordinary citizens have migrated to the opposite ends of the liberal-conservative scale. Between 1972 and 2004, for instance, the average difference in ideological self-placement between non-activist Democrats and Republicans more than doubled (Abramowitz & Saunders, 2006).

An alternative indicator of political polarization—and one that also suggests increased polarization at the mass level—is the intensification of partisan attitudes. There is a wealth of time series data tracking Americans' evaluations of the incumbent president. These data show that on balance, Democrats' and Republicans' negative evaluations of a president of the other party have steadily intensified (Abramowitz & Saunders, 2006; Jacobson, 2006). The approval data document a widening partisan chasm between Republicans and Democrats; the percentage of partisans who respond at the extremes ("strong approval" or "strong disapproval") has increased significantly over time. In fact, polarized assessments of presidential performance are higher today than at any other

Source: Shanto Iyengar and Kyu S. Hahn, "Red Media, Blue Media: Evidence of Ideological Selectivity in Media Use," *Journal of Communication* 59, no. 1 (March 2009). *Journal of Communication* by National Society for the Study of Communication; International Communication Association; Annenberg School of Communications (University of) Reproduced with permission of Blackwell Publishing, Inc in the formation Republish in a book via Copyright Clearance Center.

time in recent history, including the months preceding the resignation of President Nixon. In this sense at least, mass public opinion is polarized.

Media Consumption as an Antecedent of Polarization

It is no mere coincidence that the trend toward a more divided electorate has occurred simultaneously with the revolution in information technology. Forty years ago, the great majority of Americans got their daily news from one of three network newscasts. These newscasts offered a homogeneous and generic "point-counterpoint" perspective on the news, thus ensuring that exposure to the news was a common experience. The development of cable television and the explosion of media outlets on the Internet have created a more fragmented information environment in which cable news, talk radio, and 24-hour news outlets compete for attention. Consumers can access—with minimal effort—newspapers, radio, and television stations the world over. Given this dramatic increase in the number of available news outlets, it is not surprising that media choices increasingly reflect partisan considerations. People who feel strongly about the correctness of their cause or policy preferences seek out information they believe is consistent rather than inconsistent with their preferences.

The Revival of Selective Exposure

The argument that people prefer to approach supportive over nonsupportive information precedes the onset of new media and dates back to the heyday of cognitive consistency theories in the 1950s. . . . The theory predicted that as a means of minimizing dissonance, people would seek out information they expected to agree with. Given the nonpartisan, "objective" content of mainstream American press coverage, early tests of this hypothesis focused on exposure to political campaigns rather than news and documented the tendency of partisan voters to report greater exposure to appeals from the candidate or party they preferred. . . . This pattern of exposure to in-party appeals was considered the principal explanation for the reinforcing effects of campaigns. . . .

An important theoretical limitation of the early work on selective exposure was that it failed to distinguish between deliberate or motivated exposure and "de facto" exposure that was a by-product of voters' personal networks or social context. High-income voters, for instance, might have encountered more pro-Republican messages not because they actively screened out information about the Democrat, but because their friends and neighbors were disproportionately Republican (Cotton, 1985; Sears & Freedman, 1967).

More direct tests of whether people deliberately avoid exposure to disagreeable information yielded mixed results suggesting that dissonance avoidance was a relatively weak motive for the acquisition of information (McGuire, 1968; Sears, 1968). Although some controlled studies uncovered traces of motivated exposure to in-party sources . . . , others did not. . . . Moreover, the preference for congenial information seemed to occur under limited circumstances. . . . For example, people first asked to make a decision and then presented with information choices tended to select information consistent with their decision (Jonas, Schulz-Hardt, Frey, & Thelen, 2001).

The fact that researchers have been hard pressed to detect consistent traces of partisan selective exposure among American voters is attributable in part to the evolving institutional context of campaigns. As political campaigns became less controlled by political parties and more media based . . . voters found it increasingly difficult to encounter partisan messages or messengers (Mutz & Martin, 2001). Instead, they encountered the same "point-counterpoint," unbiased media coverage no matter where they turned (Allen & D'Alissio, 2000). But, this overtly neutral media environment changed dramatically with the diffusion of cable television and the Internet. The new, more diversified information environment makes it not only more possible for consumers to seek out news they might find agreeable but also provides a strong economic incentive for news organizations to cater to their viewers' political preferences (Mullainathan & Schleifer, 2005). The emergence of Fox News as the leading cable news provider is testimony to the viability of this "niche news" paradigm. Between 2000 and 2004, although Fox News increased the size of its regular audience by some 50%, the other cable providers showed no growth (Pew Research Center for the People and Press, 2004).[1]

A growing body of evidence suggests that consumers are in fact exercising greater selectivity in their news choices. In the first place, in keeping with the well-known "hostile media" phenomenon . . . partisans of either side have become more likely to impute bias to mainstream news sources (Smith, Lichter, & Harris, 1997). Cynical assessments of the media have surged most dramatically among conservatives; according to a Pew Research Center for the People and the Press survey, Republicans are twice as likely as Democrats to rate major news outlets including the three network newscasts, the weekly news magazines, NPR, and PBS as biased (Pew Research Center for the People and Press, 2004). As indicated by the recent furor over *The New York Times'* front-page story suggesting an inappropriate relationship between Senator John McCain and a female lobbyist (Rutenberg, Thompson, & Kirkpatrick, 2008), critical coverage from a source viewed as biased becomes a rallying event for supporters of the targeted candidate. In the immediate aftermath of the publication of the report, the McCain campaign set a record for the amount of money raised online (Bumiller, 2008).

In response to their perceptions of hostile bias in the mainstream media environment, partisans of both sides have begun to explore alternative sources of news. A study of self-reported media exposure during the 2000 and 2004 campaigns uncovered significant evidence of differential media use among Republicans and Democrats (Pfau, Houston, & Semmler, 2007). Republicans gravitated to talk radio, radio news, and television advertising, whereas Democrats avoided talk radio and tuned in to television news magazines and late-night entertainment television (Pfau et al., 2007, pp. 36–38).

In short, there is growing evidence that in the new media environment, partisans attribute bias to mainstream news outlets and gravitate to alternative sources perceived as more congenial to their preferences. But are these perceptions grounded in reality? Put differently, is there evidence that "new" media do in fact deliver more slanted or biased news? At least in the case of Fox News, the answer is in the affirmative.

In its relatively short life span, Fox News has staked out a distinctive reputation for delivering a proconservative perspective on issues and events. A systematic comparison of Fox News' coverage of national issues with the coverage provided by other new media and two "old" media (AP and UPI) demonstrated that Fox News' reputation was deserved—the outlet's news coverage showed a consistently pro-Republican slant (Groeling & Baum, 2007). Despite the fact that real-world conditions generated significantly more "bad news" stories about Republican candidates contesting the 2006 congressional elections (due mainly to the series of lobbying-related scandals involving Republican incumbents), Fox News was the only news outlet in which negative stories about Republicans did not outnumber balanced or positive stories. Unlike previous studies of media bias in which the key indicator of bias is not news content per se but some proxy for content . . . , this study provides direct content-based evidence of ideological slant in Fox News. The availability of Fox News, in fact, makes it possible for Republicans and conservatives to seek out a more sympathetic perspective and, conversely, to avoid exposure to discordant points of view.

Given the evidence concerning partisans' perceptions of Fox News and the actual slant conveyed by the outlet, we may anticipate significant behavioral (as opposed to self-reported) differences between partisan groups in exposure to Fox News: Conservatives and Republicans should seek it out while Democrats and liberals do the opposite. Moreover, given the current political environment, we further anticipate that an "approach-avoidance" behavioral pattern will vary across the subject matter of news reports. In a world of polarized news consumers, conservatives should most prefer exposure to Fox News when the subject of the news is some controversial policy issue (e.g., the war in Iraq). They might also prefer Fox coverage when the news focuses on less politicized subjects (e.g., healthcare or travel), but to a lesser degree.

Method

Experimental Design

We designed an online experiment to investigate the extent to which partisans on the right treat Fox News as a preferred provider. More specifically, we observed whether attention to the identical news story was increased or decreased when the story was attributed to Fox News, NPR, CNN, or the BBC.

Using the MSNBC daily news feed (which includes reports from a wide variety of news organizations), we randomly assigned news stories to one of four sources—Fox, NPR, CNN, or BBC. We attained the maximum level of realism by providing participants with the most recent news stories in real time. Study participants were provided with a brief headline accompanied by the logo of the news organization and asked to indicate (by clicking a box) which of four reports displayed on the screen they would like to read. Because respondents could also click a "Can't Say" box, each respondent had a choice between *five alternatives*. They repeated this task across six different subject matter categories evenly divided between "hard" and "soft" topics. The former included reports on American politics (e.g., the relations between President Bush and Democrats in Congress), the war in Iraq, and race relations. The soft topics included crime, travel, and sports. We also included a baseline or control condition in which all source logos were deleted; here participants could only choose between the reports based on the text of the accompanying headlines.

In the analyses that follow, the control condition formed the baseline to which the selection rate of news stories in the treatment condition was compared. Any difference in the rate of selecting a particular story between the control and treatment conditions can only be attributed to the presence or absence of the source label because the same set of stories were provided to both groups.

All other aspects of the presentation were equalized across the different conditions. For instance, the placement of a particular story or news source on the screen was randomized so that no particular source gained from being the first or last on the screen. Stories and sources were randomly matched. Thus, the design was fully counterbalanced on order, story headline, and news logo. The study was run between March 30 and April 16, 2006. The total sample of news stories was 383. Because the MSNBC feed features more rapid daily replacement of stories on political issues (i.e., Iraq and politics), the sample included more stories on Iraq and politics (60 and 71, respectively) than the more specialized topics of race and travel (40 and 11, respectively).

The Sample

Using the services of Polimetrix—an opinion research firm—we administered the experiment on a nationally representative sample of 1,023 (772 and 251 assigned to the treatment and control conditions, respectively) registered voters. Polimetrix has developed a new methodology for sampling from pools of opt-in respondents (the sampling methodology is available at www.polimetrix.com). Their two-stage procedure first draws a conventional probability sample a large-scale random digit dialing (RDD) sample (the target sample).[2] Next, for each member of the target sample, Polimetrix selects one or more matched members from their pool of opt-in Internet respondents. This is called the matched sample. Polimetrix implements matching—searching for an available opt-in respondent who is as similar as possible to the corresponding member of the target sample—sing the variables of race, gender, age, education, and imputed party identification and ideology. The end result is a sample of opt-in respondents with equivalent characteristics as the target sample on the matched characteristics listed above; under most conditions, the matched sample will converge with a true random sample (Rivers, 2005).[3]

Hypotheses

Given the lineup of news sources, we naturally hypothesized that the demand for news stories would be heightened among Republicans and those with conservative political views when stories were labeled as Fox reports. Conversely, we expected participants on the left of the political spectrum to show greater interest in stories assigned to CNN or NPR. Even though CNN and NPR both claim to be committed to nonpartisan and objective reporting (as does Fox), in the context of the four sources available to study participants, the content provided by CNN and NPR more closely matched the preferences of Democrats than the content provided by Fox. And since the BBC is a foreign news source with a well-known reputation for independent journalism, we expected uniform indifference for the BBC label among Democrats, Republicans, and nonpartisans alike.

We further hypothesized that the effects of the source manipulation would be stronger for political subject matter where partisan divisions are intense, but weaker when the news dwelled on nonpolitical subjects such as travel destinations or sporting events.

Based on the polarization literature, we also hypothesized that the source manipulation would be weakened among less attentive partisans and those with no party preference since they are likely to be unaware of the partisan slant of particular news outlets, while more attentive partisans are well aware of the partisan location of Fox, NPR, or CNN. Thus, we expected that the interaction of political interest and ideology/partisanship would significantly affect news selection—more interested conservatives, for instance, would display stronger preferences for Fox.

. . .

Our dependent variable consisted of five "unordered" choices. An unordered choice situation is one in which outcomes cannot be scaled, that is, outcome A does not necessarily denote more of the underlying concept than outcome B, and B more than C for all observation. . . .

Results

Overall Effects of News Labels

Prior to assessing the degree of partisan polarization in news selection, we begin by considering the simple main effects of the source labels. We constructed four dummy variables (coded 0 or 1) denoting each of the four news sources: (a) FOX, (b) CNN, (c) NPR, and (d) BBC. We further included an indicator variable denoting those who answered "can't say" (ABST). Table 1 displays the coefficient estimates from a conditional logit model predicting the selection of news stories with the individual-level data. As noted above, the selection rate of "unlabeled" news stories forms the baseline in our analysis. Thus, the four dummy variables—FOX, NPR, CNN, and BBC—capture differences in the selection rate associated with the presence of each label in any given matter dimension.

Overall, the results suggest that news source labels are an important cue for readers. . . .

The Fox label had the strongest impact on story selection in five of the six issue dimensions examined, . . . for the categories of politics, race relations, Iraq, sports, and crime, the Fox label increased the likelihood of respondents selecting news stories beyond that of nonlabeled stories. . . .

. . . On the other hand, in the case of travel news where CNN proved to be the most popular source . . . the null hypothesis . . . could not be rejected . . . indicating that CNN was *not* necessarily more popular than Fox in the case of travel news. All told, these results indicate that among the four news organizations included in the current study, the Fox label was the most appealing. Clearly, Fox's strategy to cater to a conservative audience has worked to increase its market share.

Evidence of Selective Exposure in News Selection

Next, we turn to assessing the role of respondent attributes in news story selection, that is, who chose which news stories to read? Of course, our primary

Table 1   Baseline Versus Labeled Conditions (conditional logit estimates)

	Hard News Dimension			Soft News Dimension		
	Politics	**Race Relations**	**Iraq**	**Sports**	**Crime**	**Travel**
FOX	.613 (.267)*	.743 (.201)*	.981 (.229)**	.645 (.166)**	.767 (.203)**	.360 (.168)*
NPR	.223 (.271)	.373 (.206)	.407 (.236)	.083 (.184)	.451 (.207)*	.375 (.167)*
CNN	.306 (.270)	.380 (.206)	.643 (.233)**	.403 (.173)*	.438 (.207)*	.435 (.166)**
BBC	.125 (.272)	.346 (.206)	.469 (.235)*	-.280 (.201)	.438 (.207)*	.287 (.169)
ABST	-.908 (.219)**	-.056 (.160)	-.401 (.180)*	1,933 (.131)**	-.56 (.160)	1,057 (.128)**
N	1,023	1,023	1,023	1,023	1,023	1,023
Likelihood ratio x^2	155.88**	47.84**	128.75**	765.89**	48.16**	138.10**
Pseudo R^2	.047	.015	.039	.233	.015	.042

Notes: Cell entries are given as conditional logit estimates with their standard errors (SE) in parenthesis. Coefficient estimates show deviations in news selection rates from the baseline in labeled conditions
*p < .05, **p < .01.

focus was to assess whether respondents' ideological leanings induced a polarizing effect in news selection. As a first-cut at the data, we plotted *story selection rates* with and without source labels for Republicans, Independents, and Democrats (Figure 1). Here, the unit of analysis is the individual news story and the selection rate is the proportion of respondents clicking on this story. As described earlier, one-quarter of the study participants were provided with the news reports without source labels. Therefore, we can compare the fraction of the study participants who selected *the same story* when it was either unlabeled, or attributed to Fox, CNN, or NPR.

Figure 1 provides considerable evidence of political selectivity: The very same news story on crime or Iraq or politics or racial issues attracts a different audience when labeled as a Fox, CNN, or NPR report. Consistent with our expectations, the effects of the Fox label were weakened for nonpolitical news. Nonetheless, the effects of the Fox label nearly doubled the selection rate for travel and sports stories among Republicans. While Republicans were drawn to the Fox label, they avoided CNN and NPR. On average, the probability that a Republican would select a CNN or NPR report was around 10%. As for the Democrats, they were just as averse to Fox as the Republicans were to CNN and NPR. But unlike the Republicans, they did not seem to converge on a particular news source. Although the CNN and NPR labels boosted interest among Democrats, the effects appeared somewhat weak.

Figure 1   Effects of Story Label on Story Selection

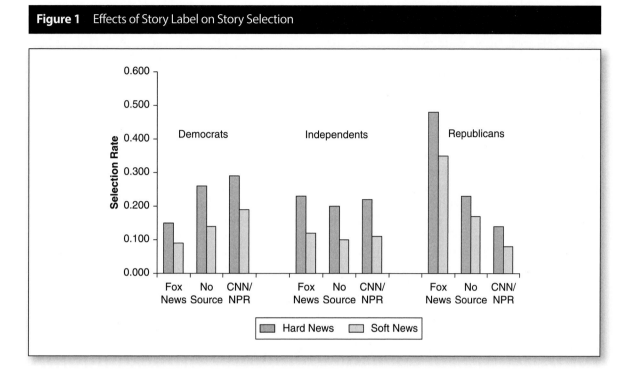

Conclusion

No matter how we sliced the data—either at the level of individuals or news stories—the results demonstrate that Fox News is the dominant news source for conservatives (the results presented above are equally strong if we substitute party identification for ideology). Although Fox's brand advantage for conservatives is especially strong when the news deals with politicized subjects, it also applies to subject matter typically not associated with partisan division. Indeed, the most surprising of our findings is the substantial level of polarization in exposure to soft news.

The emergence of Fox News as the cable ratings leader suggests that in a competitive market, politically slanted news programming allows a new organization to create a niche for itself. Recent theoretical work in economics shows that under competition and diversity of opinion, newspapers will provide content that is more biased: "Competition forces newspapers to cater to the prejudices of their readers, and greater competition typically results in more aggressive catering to such prejudices as competitors strive to divide the market" (Mullainathan & Schleifer, 2005, p. 18).

Thus, as the audience become polarized over matters of politics and public policy, rational media owners stand to gain market share by injecting more rather than less political bias into the news (Gentzkow & Shapiro, 2006). The recent experience of MSNBC is revealing. The network's most popular evening *Countdown with Keith Olbermann*—conveys an unabashedly anti-Bush Administration perspective. The network now plans to "to showcase its nighttime lineup as a welcome haven for viewers of a similar mind" (Steinberg, 2007). When the audience is polarized, "news with an edge" makes for market success.

A further implication of voters' increased exposure to one-sided news coverage is an "echo chamber" effect—the news serves to reinforce existing beliefs and attitudes. During periods of Republican governance, for instance, criticisms of the incumbent administration conveyed by mainstream news organizations can be dismissed as evidence of "liberal bias" thus further increasing partisan polarization. After the revelations in the news media that the Bush Administration's prewar intelligence claims were erroneous, Democrats (when asked whether the U.S. had found weapons of mass destruction (WMD) in Iraq), switched to the "no WMD" response by a factor of more than 30%. Independents also switched, by more than 10 percentage points. But Republicans remained steadfast in their beliefs affirming the presence of WMD—between June 2003 and October 2004 the percentage of Republicans acknowledging that the United States had not found WMD increased by less than five points (Iyengar & McGrady, 2007; Kull, Ramsay, & Lewis, 2003).

The importance of source cues to news exposure and the resulting "reinforcement of priors" effect will only grow as technology diffuses and consumers increasingly customize their online news menus. Our results are consistent with the argument that Internet technology will, in practice, narrow rather than widen users' political horizons. Although an infinite variety of information is available, individuals may well limit their exposure to news or sources that they expect to find agreeable. Over time, this behavior is likely to become habituated so that users turn to their preferred sources automatically no matter what the subject matter. The observed behavior of Republicans in this study may be attributed, in part, to their 20 years of experience with a favored news provider, thus reinforcing their information-seeking behavior. As Democrats and politically inclined independents also begin to establish media preferences, consumers will be able to "wall themselves off from topics and opinions that they would prefer to avoid" (Sunstein, 2001, pp. 201–202). The end result is likely to be a less informed and more polarized electorate.

Selective exposure is especially likely in the new media environment because of information overload. New forms of communication not only deliver much larger chunks of campaign information, but they also facilitate consumers' ability to attend to the information selectively. The audience for conventional news programs is hard pressed to avoid coverage of the candidate they dislike because news reports typically assign equal coverage to each. But when browsing the web, users can filter or search through masses of text more easily. Thus, as candidates, interest groups, and voters all converge on the Internet, the possibility of selective exposure to political information increases. As we have found, people prefer to encounter information that they find supportive or consistent with their existing beliefs.

Notes

1. Of course, it is possible that there are also nonpolitical reasons for the competitive edge enjoyed by the Fox Network.

2. The target sample is drawn from the 2004 American Community Study, conducted by the U.S. Bureau of the Census, which is a probability sample of size 1,194,354 with a response rate of 93.1 percent.

3. The fact that the Polimetrix (PMX) sample was matched according to a set of demographic characteristics does *not* imply that the samples are unbiased. All sampling modes are characterized by different forms of bias and opt-in Internet panels are no exception. Systematic comparisons of PMX matched samples with RDD (telephone) samples and face-to face interviews indicate the online samples appear biased in the direction of politically attentive voters. For instance, in comparison with National Election Study respondents (interviewed face-to-face), PMX respondents were more likely by eight percentage points to correctly identify the Vice President of the U.S.

References

Abramowitz, A. I., & Saunders, K. L. (2006). Exploring the bases of partisanship in the American electorate: Social identity vs. ideology. *Political Research Quarterly, 59*, 175–187.

Allen, M., & D'Alissio, D. (2000). Media bias in presidential elections: A meta-analysis. *Journal of Communication, 50*, 133–156.

Bumiller, E. (2008, February 23). McCain gathers support and donations in aftermath of article in *The Times. The New York Times*, p. A13.

Cotton, J. L. (1985). Cognitive dissonance in selective exposure. In D. Zillman & J. Bryant (Eds.), *Selective exposure to communication* (pp. 11–33). Hillsdale, NJ: Erlbaum.

Fiorina, M. P., Abrams, S. J., & Pope, J. C. (2005). *Culture wars? The myth of polarized America.* New York: Pearson Longman.

Gentzkow, M., & Shapiro, J. M. (2006). Media bias and reputation. *Journal of Political Economy, 114*, 280–316.

Groeling, T., & Baum, M. A. (2007, August). *Barbarians inside the gates: Partisan news media and the polarization of American political discourse.* Paper presented at the annual meeting of the American Political Science Association, Chicago, IL.

Iyengar, S., & McGrady, J. (2007). *Media and politics: A citizen's guide.* New York: W. W. Norton.

Jacobson, G.C. (2006). *A divider, not a uniter: George W. Bush and the American people.* New York: Pearson.

Jonas, E., Schulz-Hardt, S., Frey, D., & Thelen, N. (2001). Confirmation bias in sequential information search after preliminary decisions: An expansion of dissonance theoretical research on 'selective exposure to information.' *Journal of Personality and Social Psychology, 80*, 557–571.

Kull, S., Ramsay, C., & Lewis, E. (2003). Misperceptions, the media, and the Iraq war. *Political Science Quarterly, 118*, 569–598.

Layman, G. C., & Carsey, T. M. (2002). Party polarization and 'conflict extension' in the American electorate. *American journal of Political Science, 46*, 786–802.

McGuire, W. J. (1968). Selective exposure: A summing up. In R. Abelson, E. Aronson, W. J. McGuire, T. M. Newcomb, M. J. Rosenberg, & P. H. Tannenbaum (Eds.), *Theories of cognitive consistency: A sourcebook* (pp. 788–796). Chicago: Rand McNally.

Mullainathan, S., & Schleifer, A. (2005). The market for news. *American Economic Review, 95*, 1031–1053.

Mutz, D. C, & Martin, P. S. (2001). Facilitating communication across lines of political difference: The role of the mass media. *American Political Science Review, 95*, 97–114.

Pew Research Center for the People and Press. (2004). *Online news audience larger, more diverse: News audience increasingly polarized.* Washington, DC: Pew Research Center for the People and Press.

Pfau, M. J., Houston, B., & Semmler, S. M. (2007). *Mediating the vote: The changing media landscape in U.S. presidential campaigns.* Lanham, MD: Rowman and Littlefield.

Rivers, D. (2005). Sample matching: Representative sample from internet panels. Retrieved February 29, 2008, from http://www.polimetrix.com/documents/Polimetrix_Whitepaper_Sample_Matching.pdf

Rutenberg, J., Thompson, M. W., & Kirkpatrick, D. D. (2008, February 21). For McCain, self-confidence on ethics poses its own risk. *The New York Times*, p. A1.

Sears, D. O. (1968). The paradox of de facto selective exposure without preference for supportive information. In R. P. Abelson, E. Aronson, W. J. McGuire, T. M. Newcomb, M. J. Rosenberg, & P. H. Tannenbaum (Eds.), *Theories of cognitive consistency: A sourcebook* (pp. 777–787). Chicago: Rand McNally.

Sears, D. O., & Freedman, J. F. (1967). Selective exposure to information: A critical review. *Public Opinion Quarterly, 31*, 194–213.

Smith, T. J., III, Lichter, S. R., & Harris, T. (1997). *What the people want from the press.* Washington, DC: Center for Media and Public Affairs.

Steinberg, J. (2007, November 6). Cable channel nods to ratings and leans left. *The New York Times*, p. A1.

Sunstein, C. R. (2001). *Republic.com.* Princeton, NJ: Princeton University Press.

CONSTITUTION OF THE UNITED STATES

We the People of the United States, in Order to form a more perfect Union, establish Justice, insure domestic Tranquility, provide for the common defence, promote the general Welfare, and secure the Blessings of Liberty to ourselves and our Posterity, do ordain and establish this Constitution for the United States of America.

Article I

Section 1. All legislative Powers herein granted shall be vested in a Congress of the United States, which shall consist of a Senate and House of Representatives.

Section 2. The House of Representatives shall be composed of Members chosen every second Year by the People of the several States, and the Electors in each State shall have the Qualifications requisite for Electors of the most numerous Branch of the State Legislature.

No Person shall be a Representative who shall not have attained to the age of twenty five Years, and been seven Years a Citizen of the United States, and who shall not, when elected, be an Inhabitant of that State in which he shall be chosen.

[Representatives and direct Taxes shall be apportioned among the several States which may be included within this Union, according to their respective Numbers, which shall be determined by adding to the whole Number of free Persons, including those bound to Service for a Term of Years, and excluding Indians not taxed, three fifths of all other Persons.][1] The actual Enumeration shall be made within three Years after the first Meeting of the Congress of the United States, and within every subsequent Term of ten Years, in such Manner as they shall by Law direct. The Number of Representatives shall not exceed one for every thirty Thousand, but each State shall have at Least one Representative; and until such enumeration shall be made, the State of New Hampshire shall be entitled to chuse three, Massachusetts eight, Rhode-Island and Providence Plantations one, Connecticut five, New-York six, New Jersey four, Pennsylvania eight, Delaware one, Maryland six, Virginia ten, North Carolina five, South Carolina five, and Georgia three.

When vacancies happen in the Representation from any State, the Executive Authority thereof shall issue Writs of Election to fill such Vacancies.

The House of Representatives shall chuse their Speaker and other Officers; and shall have the sole Power of Impeachment.

Section 3. The Senate of the United States shall be composed of two Senators from each State, [chosen by the Legislature thereof,][2] for six Years; and each Senator shall have one Vote.

Immediately after they shall be assembled in Consequence of the first Election, they shall be divided as equally as may be into three Classes. The Seats of the Senators of the first Class shall be vacated at the Expiration of the second Year, of the second Class at the Expiration of the fourth Year, and of the third Class at the Expiration of the sixth Year, so that one third may be chosen every second Year; [and if Vacancies happen by Resignation, or otherwise, during the Recess of the Legislature of any State, the Executive thereof may make temporary Appointments until the next Meeting of the Legislature, which shall then fill such Vacancies.][3]

No Person shall be a Senator who shall not have attained to the Age of thirty Years, and been nine

Source: U.S. Congress, House, Committee on the Judiciary, *The Constitution of the United States of America, as Amended,* 100th Cong., 1st sess., 1987, H Doc 100-94.

Years a Citizen of the United States, and who shall not, when elected, be an Inhabitant of that State for which he shall be chosen.

The Vice President of the United States shall be President of the Senate, but shall have no Vote, unless they be equally divided.

The Senate shall chuse their other Officers, and also a President pro tempore, in the Absence of the Vice President, or when he shall exercise the Office of President of the United States.

The Senate shall have the sole Power to try all Impeachments. When sitting for that Purpose, they shall be on Oath or Affirmation. When the President of the United States is tried, the Chief Justice shall preside: And no Person shall be convicted without the Concurrence of two thirds of the Members present.

Judgment in Cases of Impeachment shall not extend further than to removal from Office, and disqualification to hold and enjoy any Office of honor, Trust or Profit under the United States: but the Party convicted shall nevertheless be liable and subject to Indictment, Trial, Judgment and Punishment, according to Law.

Section 4. The Times, Places and Manner of holding Elections for Senators and Representatives, shall be prescribed in each State by the Legislature thereof; but the Congress may at any time by Law make or alter such Regulations, except as to the Places of chusing Senators.

The Congress shall assemble at least once in every Year, and such Meeting shall [be on the first Monday in December],[4] unless they shall by Law appoint a different Day.

Section 5. Each House shall be the Judge of the Elections, Returns and Qualifications of its own Members, and a Majority of each shall constitute a Quorum to do Business; but a smaller Number may adjourn from day to day, and may be authorized to compel the Attendance of absent Members, in such Manner, and under such Penalties as each House may provide.

Each House may determine the Rules of its Proceedings, punish its Members for disorderly Behaviour, and, with the Concurrence of two thirds, expel a Member.

Each House shall keep a Journal of its Proceedings, and from time to time publish the same, excepting such Parts as may in their Judgment require Secrecy; and the Yeas and Nays of the Members of either House on any question shall, at the Desire of one fifth of those Present, be entered on the Journal.

Neither House, during the Session of Congress, shall, without the Consent of the other, adjourn for more than three days, nor to any other Place than that in which the two Houses shall be sitting.

Section 6. The Senators and Representatives shall receive a Compensation for their Services, to be ascertained by Law, and paid out of the Treasury of the United States. They shall in all Cases, except Treason, Felony and Breach of the Peace, be privileged from Arrest during their Attendance at the Session of their respective Houses, and in going to and returning from the same; and for any Speech or Debate in either House, they shall not be questioned in any other Place.

No Senator or Representative shall, during the Time for which he was elected, be appointed to any civil Office under the Authority of the United States, which shall have been created, or the Emoluments whereof shall have been encreased during such time; and no Person holding any Office under the United States, shall be a Member of either House during his Continuance in Office.

Section 7. All Bills for raising Revenue shall originate in the House of Representatives; but the Senate may propose or concur with Amendments as on other Bills.

Every Bill which shall have passed the House of Representatives and the Senate, shall, before it become a Law, be presented to the President of the United States; If he approve he shall sign it, but if not he shall return it, with his Objections to that House in which it shall have originated, who shall enter the Objections at large on their Journal, and proceed to reconsider it. If after such Reconsideration two thirds of that House shall agree to pass the Bill, it shall be sent, together with the Objections, to the other House, by which it shall likewise be reconsidered, and if approved by two thirds of that House, it shall become a Law. But in all such Cases the Votes of both Houses shall be determined by yeas and Nays, and the Names of the Persons voting for and against the Bill shall be entered on the Journal of each House respectively. If any Bill shall not be returned by the President within ten Days (Sundays excepted) after it shall have been presented to him, the Same shall be a Law, in like Manner as if he had signed it, unless the Congress by their Adjournment prevent its Return, in which Case it shall not be a Law.

Every Order, Resolution, or Vote to which the Concurrence of the Senate and House of Representatives may be necessary (except on a question of Adjournment) shall be presented to the President of the United States; and before the Same shall take Effect, shall be approved by him, or being disapproved by him, shall be repassed by two thirds of the Senate and House of Representatives, according to the Rules and Limitations prescribed in the Case of a Bill.

Section 8. The Congress shall have Power To lay and collect Taxes, Duties, Imposts and Excises, to pay the Debts and provide for the common Defence and general Welfare of the United States; but all Duties, Imposts and Excises shall be uniform throughout the United States;

To borrow Money on the credit of the United States;

To regulate Commerce with foreign Nations, and among the several States, and with the Indian Tribes;

To establish an uniform Rule of Naturalization, and uniform Laws on the subject of Bankruptcies throughout the United States;

To coin Money, regulate the Value thereof, and of foreign Coin, and fix the Standard of Weights and Measures;

To provide for the Punishment of counterfeiting the Securities and current Coin of the United States;

To establish Post Offices and post Roads;

To promote the Progress of Science and useful Arts, by securing for limited Times to Authors and Inventors the exclusive Right to their respective Writings and Discoveries;

To constitute Tribunals inferior to the supreme Court;

To define and punish Piracies and Felonies committed on the high Seas, and Offences against the Law of Nations;

To declare War, grant Letters of Marque and Reprisal, and make Rules concerning Captures on Land and Water;

To raise and support Armies, but no Appropriation of Money to that Use shall be for a longer Term than two Years;

To provide and maintain a Navy;

To make Rules for the Government and Regulation of the land and naval Forces;

To provide for calling forth the Militia to execute the Laws of the Union, suppress Insurrections and repel Invasions;

To provide for organizing, arming, and disciplining, the Militia, and for governing such Part of them as may be employed in the Service of the United States, reserving to the States respectively, the Appointment of the Officers, and the Authority of training the Militia according to the discipline prescribed by Congress;

To exercise exclusive Legislation in all Cases whatsoever, over such District (not exceeding ten Miles square) as may, by Cession of particular States, and the Acceptance of Congress, become the Seat of the Government of the United States, and to exercise like Authority over all Places purchased by the Consent of the Legislature of the State in which the Same shall be, for the Erection of Forts, Magazines, Arsenals, dock-Yards, and other needful Buildings;—And

To make all Laws which shall be necessary and proper for carrying into Execution the foregoing Powers, and all other Powers vested by this Constitution in the Government of the United States, or in any Department or Officer thereof.

Section 9. The Migration or Importation of such Persons as any of the States now existing shall think proper to admit, shall not be prohibited by the Congress prior to the Year one thousand eight hundred and eight, but a Tax or duty may be imposed on such Importation, not exceeding ten dollars for each Person.

The Privilege of the Writ of Habeas Corpus shall not be suspended, unless when in Cases of Rebellion or Invasion the public Safety may require it.

No Bill of Attainder or ex post facto Law shall be passed.

No Capitation, or other direct, Tax shall be laid, unless in Proportion to the Census or Enumeration herein before directed to be taken.[5]

No Tax or Duty shall be laid on Articles exported from any State.

No Preference shall be given by any Regulation of Commerce or Revenue to the Ports of one State over those of another; nor shall Vessels bound to, or from, one State, be obliged to enter, clear, or pay Duties in another.

No Money shall be drawn from the Treasury, but in Consequence of Appropriations made by Law; and a regular Statement and Account of the Receipts and Expenditures of all public Money shall be published from time to time.

No Title of Nobility shall be granted by the United States: And no Person holding any Office of Profit or Trust under them, shall, without the Consent of the Congress, accept of any present, Emolument, Office, or Title, of any kind whatever, from any King, Prince, or foreign State.

Section 10. No State shall enter into any Treaty, Alliance, or Confederation; grant Letters of Marque and Reprisal; coin Money; emit Bills of Credit; make any Thing but gold and silver Coin a Tender in Payment of Debts; pass any Bill of Attainder, ex post facto Law, or Law impairing the Obligation of Contracts, or grant any Title of Nobility.

No State shall, without the Consent of the Congress, lay any Imposts or Duties on Imports or Exports, except what may be absolutely necessary for executing it's inspection Laws: and the net Produce of all Duties and Imposts, laid by any State on Imports or Exports, shall be for the Use of the Treasury of the United States; and all such Laws shall be subject to the Revision and Controul of the Congress.

No State shall, without the Consent of Congress, lay any Duty of Tonnage, keep Troops, or Ships of War in time of Peace, enter into any Agreement or Compact with another State, or with a foreign Power, or engage in War, unless actually invaded, or in such imminent Danger as will not admit of delay.

Article II

Section 1. The executive Power shall be vested in a President of the United States of America. He shall hold his Office during the Term of four Years, and, together with the Vice President, chosen for the same Term, be elected, as follows

Each State shall appoint, in such Manner as the Legislature thereof may direct, a Number of Electors, equal to the whole Number of Senators and Representatives to which the State may be entitled in the Congress: but no Senator or Representative, or Person holding an Office of Trust or Profit under the United States, shall be appointed an Elector.

[The Electors shall meet in their respective States, and vote by Ballot for two Persons, of whom one at least shall not be an Inhabitant of the same State with themselves. And they shall make a List of all the Persons voted for, and of the Number of Votes for each; which List they shall sign and certify, and transmit sealed to the Seat of the Government of the United States, directed to the President of the Senate. The President of the Senate shall, in the Presence of the Senate and House of Representatives, open all the Certificates, and the Votes shall then be counted. The Person having the greatest Number of Votes shall be the President, if such Number be a Majority of the whole Number of Electors appointed; and if there be more than one who have such Majority, and have an equal Number of Votes, then the House of Representatives shall immediately chuse by Ballot one of them for President; and if no Person have a Majority, then from the five highest on the list the said House shall in like Manner chuse the President. But in chusing the President, the Votes shall be taken by States, the Representation from each State having one Vote; A quorum for this Purpose shall consist of a Member or Members from two thirds of the States, and a Majority of all the States shall be necessary to a Choice. In every Case, after the Choice of the President, the Person having the greatest Number of Votes of the Electors shall be the Vice President. But if there should remain two or more who have equal Votes, the Senate shall chuse from them by Ballot the Vice President.][6]

The Congress may determine the Time of chusing the Electors, and the Day on which they shall give their Votes; which Day shall be the same throughout the United States.

No Person except a natural born Citizen, or a Citizen of the United States, at the time of the Adoption of this Constitution, shall be eligible to the Office of President; neither shall any Person be eligible to that Office who shall not have attained to the Age of thirty five Years, and been fourteen Years a Resident within the United States.

In Case of the Removal of the President from Office, or of his Death, Resignation, or Inability to discharge the Powers and Duties of the said Office,[7] the Same shall devolve on the Vice President, and the Congress may by Law provide for the Case of Removal, Death, Resignation or Inability, both of the President and Vice President, declaring what Officer shall then act as President, and such Officer shall act accordingly, until the Disability be removed, or a President shall be elected.

The President shall, at stated Times, receive for his Services, a Compensation, which shall neither be encreased nor diminished during the Period for which he shall have been elected, and he shall not receive within that Period any other Emolument from the United States, or any of them.

Before he enter on the Execution of his Office, he shall take the following Oath or Affirmation:—"I do solemnly swear (or affirm) that I will faithfully execute the Office of President of the United States, and will to the best of my Ability, preserve,

protect and defend the Constitution of the United States."

Section 2. The President shall be Commander in Chief of the Army and Navy of the United States, and of the Militia of the several States, when called into the actual Service of the United States; he may require the Opinion, in writing, of the principal Officer in each of the executive Departments, upon any Subject relating to the Duties of their respective Offices, and he shall have Power to grant Reprieves and Pardons for Offences against the United States, except in Cases of Impeachment.

He shall have Power, by and with the Advice and Consent of the Senate, to make Treaties, provided two thirds of the Senators present concur; and he shall nominate, and by and with the Advice and Consent of the Senate, shall appoint Ambassadors, other public Ministers and Consuls, Judges of the supreme Court, and all other Officers of the United States, whose Appointments are not herein otherwise provided for, and which shall be established by Law: but the Congress may by Law vest the Appointment of such inferior Officers, as they think proper, in the President alone, in the Courts of Law, or in the Heads of Departments.

The President shall have Power to fill up all Vacancies that may happen during the Recess of the Senate, by granting Commissions which shall expire at the End of their next Session.

Section 3. He shall from time to time give to the Congress Information of the State of the Union, and recommend to their Consideration such Measures as he shall judge necessary and expedient; he may, on extraordinary Occasions, convene both Houses, or either of them, and in Case of Disagreement between them, with Respect to the Time of Adjournment, he may adjourn them to such Time as he shall think proper; he shall receive Ambassadors and other public Ministers; he shall take Care that the Laws be faithfully executed, and shall Commission all the Officers of the United States.

Section 4. The President, Vice President and all civil Officers of the United States, shall be removed from Office on Impeachment for, and Conviction of, Treason, Bribery, or other high Crimes and Misdemeanors.

Article III

Section 1. The judicial Power of the United States, shall be vested in one supreme Court, and in such inferior Courts as the Congress may from time to time ordain and establish. The Judges, both of the supreme and inferior Courts, shall hold their Offices during good Behaviour, and shall, at stated Times, receive for their Services, a Compensation, which shall not be diminished during their Continuance in Office.

Section 2. The judicial Power shall extend to all Cases, in Law and Equity, arising under this Constitution, the Laws of the United States, and Treaties made, or which shall be made, under their Authority;—to all Cases affecting Ambassadors, other public Ministers and Consuls;—to all Cases of admiralty and maritime Jurisdiction;—to Controversies to which the United States shall be a Party;—to Controversies between two or more States;—between a State and Citizens of another State;[8]—between Citizens of different States;—between Citizens of the same State claiming Lands under Grants of different States, and between a State, or the Citizens thereof, and foreign States, Citizens or Subjects.

In all Cases affecting Ambassadors, other public Ministers and Consuls, and those in which a State shall be Party, the supreme Court shall have original Jurisdiction. In all the other Cases before mentioned, the supreme Court shall have appellate Jurisdiction, both as to Law and Fact, with such Exceptions, and under such Regulations as the Congress shall make.

The Trial of all Crimes, except in Cases of Impeachment, shall be by Jury; and such Trial shall be held in the State where the said Crimes shall have been committed; but when not committed within any State, the Trial shall be at such Place or Places as the Congress may by Law have directed.

Section 3. Treason against the United States, shall consist only in levying War against them, or in adhering to their Enemies, giving them Aid and Comfort. No Person shall be convicted of Treason unless on the Testimony of two Witnesses to the same overt Act, or on Confession in open Court.

The Congress shall have Power to declare the Punishment of Treason, but no Attainder of Treason shall work Corruption of Blood, or Forfeiture except during the Life of the Person attainted.

Article IV

Section 1. Full Faith and Credit shall be given in each State to the public Acts, Records, and judicial Proceedings of every other State. And the Congress may by general Laws prescribe the Manner in which such Acts, Records and Proceedings shall be proved, and the Effect thereof.

Section 2. The Citizens of each State shall be entitled to all Privileges and Immunities of Citizens in the several States.

A Person charged in any State with Treason, Felony, or other Crime, who shall flee from Justice, and be found in another State, shall on Demand of the executive Authority of the State from which he fled, be delivered up, to be removed to the State having Jurisdiction of the Crime.

[No Person held to Service or Labour in one State, under the Laws thereof, escaping into another, shall, in Consequence of any Law or Regulation therein, be discharged from such Service or Labour, but shall be delivered up on Claim of the Party to whom such Service or Labour may be due.][9]

Section 3. New States may be admitted by the Congress into this Union; but no new State shall be formed or erected within the Jurisdiction of any other State; nor any State be formed by the Junction of two or more States, or Parts of States, without the

Consent of the Legislatures of the States concerned as well as of the Congress.

The Congress shall have Power to dispose of and make all needful Rules and Regulations respecting the Territory or other Property belonging to the United States; and nothing in this Constitution shall be so construed as to Prejudice any Claims of the United States, or of any particular State.

Section 4. The United States shall guarantee to every State in this Union a Republican Form of Government, and shall protect each of them against Invasion; and on Application of the Legislature, or of the Executive (when the Legislature cannot be convened) against domestic Violence.

Article V

The Congress, whenever two thirds of both Houses shall deem it necessary, shall propose Amendments to this Constitution, or, on the Application of the Legislatures of two thirds of the several States, shall call a Convention for proposing Amendments, which, in either Case, shall be valid to all Intents and Purposes, as Part of this Constitution, when ratified by the Legislatures of three fourths of the several States, or by Conventions in three fourths thereof, as the one or the other Mode of Ratification may be proposed by the Congress; Provided [that no Amendment which may be made prior to the Year One thousand eight hundred and eight shall in any Manner affect the first and fourth Clauses in the Ninth Section of the first Article; and][10] that no State, without its Consent, shall be deprived of its equal Suffrage in the Senate.

Article VI

All Debts contracted and Engagements entered into, before the Adoption of this Constitution, shall be as valid against the United States under this Constitution, as under the Confederation.

This Constitution, and the Laws of the United States which shall be made in Pursuance thereof; and all Treaties made, or which shall be made, under the Authority of the United States, shall be the supreme Law of the Land; and the Judges in every State shall be bound thereby, any Thing in the Constitution or Laws of any State to the Contrary notwithstanding.

The Senators and Representatives before mentioned, and the Members of the several State Legislatures, and all executive and judicial Officers, both of the United States and of the several States, shall be bound by Oath or Affirmation, to support this Constitution; but no religious Test shall ever be required as a Qualification to any Office or public Trust under the United States.

Article VII

The Ratification of the Conventions of nine States, shall be sufficient for the Establishment of this Constitution between the States so ratifying the Same.

Done in Convention by the Unanimous Consent of the States present the Seventeenth Day of September in the Year of our Lord one thousand seven hundred and Eighty seven and of the Independence of the United States of America the Twelfth. IN WITNESS whereof We have hereunto subscribed our Names,

	George Washington,
	President and
	deputy from Virginia.
New Hampshire:	John Langdon,
	Nicholas Gilman.
Massachusetts:	Nathaniel Gorham,
	Rufus King.
Connecticut:	William Samuel Johnson,
	Roger Sherman.
New York:	Alexander Hamilton.
New Jersey:	William Livingston,
	David Brearley,

	William Paterson,
	Jonathan Dayton.
Pennsylvania:	Benjamin Franklin,
	Thomas Mifflin,
	Robert Morris,
	George Clymer,
	Thomas FitzSimons,
	Jared Ingersoll,
	James Wilson,
	Gouverneur Morris.
Delaware:	George Read,
	Gunning Bedford Jr.,
	John Dickinson,
	Richard Bassett,
	Jacob Broom.
Maryland:	James McHenry,
	Daniel of St. Thomas Jenifer,
	Daniel Carroll.
Virginia:	John Blair,
	James Madison Jr.
North Carolina:	William Blount,
	Richard Dobbs Spaight,
	Hugh Williamson.
South Carolina:	John Rutledge,
	Charles Cotesworth Pinckney,
	Charles Pinckney,
	Pierce Butler.
Georgia:	William Few,
	Abraham Baldwin.

[The language of the original Constitution, not including the Amendments, was adopted by a convention of the states on September 17, 1787, and was subsequently ratified by the states on the following dates: Delaware, December 7, 1787; Pennsylvania, December 12, 1787; New Jersey, December 18, 1787; Georgia, January 2, 1788; Connecticut, January 9, 1788; Massachusetts, February 6, 1788; Maryland, April 28, 1788; South Carolina, May 23, 1788; New Hampshire, June 21, 1788.

Ratification was completed on June 21, 1788.

The Constitution subsequently was ratified by Virginia, June 25, 1788; New York, July 26, 1788; North Carolina, November 21, 1789; Rhode Island, May 29, 1790; and Vermont, January 10, 1791.]

Amendments

Amendment I

(First ten amendments ratified December 15, 1791.)

Congress shall make no law respecting an establishment of religion, or prohibiting the free exercise thereof; or abridging the freedom of speech, or of the press; or the right of the people peaceably to assemble, and to petition the Government for a redress of grievances.

Amendment II

A well regulated Militia, being necessary to the security of a free State, the right of the people to keep and bear Arms, shall not be infringed.

Amendment III

No Soldier shall, in time of peace be quartered in any house, without the consent of the Owner, nor in time of war, but in a manner to be prescribed by law.

Amendment IV

The right of the people to be secure in their persons, houses, papers, and effects, against unreasonable searches and seizures, shall not be violated, and no Warrants shall issue, but upon probable cause, supported by Oath or affirmation, and particularly describing the place to be searched, and the persons or things to be seized.

Amendment V

No person shall be held to answer for a capital, or otherwise infamous crime, unless on a presentment or indictment of a Grand Jury, except in cases arising in the land or naval forces, or in the Militia, when in actual service in time of War or public danger; nor shall any person be subject for the same offence to be twice put in jeopardy of life or limb; nor shall be compelled in any criminal case to be a witness against himself, nor be deprived of life, liberty, or property, without due process of law; nor shall private property be taken for public use, without just compensation.

Amendment VI

In all criminal prosecutions, the accused shall enjoy the right to a speedy and public trial, by an impartial jury of the State and district wherein the crime shall have been committed, which district shall have been previously ascertained by law, and to be informed of the nature and cause of the accusation; to be confronted with the witnesses against him; to have compulsory process for obtaining witnesses in his favor, and to have the Assistance of Counsel for his defence.

Amendment VII

In Suits at common law, where the value in controversy shall exceed twenty dollars, the right of trial by jury shall be preserved, and no fact tried by a jury, shall be otherwise re-examined in any Court of the United States, than according to the rules of the common law.

Amendment VIII

Excessive bail shall not be required, nor excessive fines imposed, nor cruel and unusual punishments inflicted.

Amendment IX

The enumeration in the Constitution, of certain rights, shall not be construed to deny or disparage others retained by the people.

Amendment X

The powers not delegated to the United States by the Constitution, nor prohibited by it to the States, are reserved to the States respectively, or to the people.

Amendment XI (Ratified February 7, 1795)

The Judicial power of the United States shall not be construed to extend to any suit in law or equity, commenced or prosecuted against one of the United States by Citizens of another State, or by Citizens or Subjects of any Foreign State.

Amendment XII (Ratified June 15, 1804)

The Electors shall meet in their respective states and vote by ballot for President and Vice-President, one of whom, at least, shall not be an inhabitant of the same state with themselves; they shall name in their ballots the person voted for as President, and in distinct ballots the person voted for as Vice-President, and they shall make distinct lists of all persons voted for as President, and of all persons voted for as Vice-President, and of the number of votes for each, which lists they shall sign and certify, and transmit sealed to the seat of the government of the United States, directed to the President of the Senate;—The President of the Senate shall, in the presence of the Senate and House of Representatives, open all the certificates and the votes shall then be counted;— The person having the greatest number of votes for President, shall be the President, if such number be a majority of the whole number of Electors appointed; and if no person have such majority, then from the persons having the highest numbers not exceeding three on the list of those voted for as President, the House of Representatives shall choose immediately, by ballot, the President. But in choosing the President, the votes shall be taken by states, the representation from each state having one vote; a quorum for this purpose shall consist of a member or members from two-thirds of the states, and a majority of all the states shall be necessary to a choice. [And if the House of Representatives shall not choose a President whenever the right of choice shall devolve upon them, before the fourth day of March next following, then the Vice-President shall act as President, as in the case of the death or other constitutional disability of the President.—][11] The person having the greatest number of votes as Vice-President, shall be the Vice-President, if such number be a majority of the whole number of Electors appointed, and if no person have a majority, then from the two highest numbers on the list, the Senate shall choose the Vice-President; a quorum for the purpose shall consist of two-thirds of the whole number of Senators, and a majority of the whole number shall be necessary to a choice. But no person constitutionally ineligible to the office of President shall be eligible to that of Vice-President of the United States.

Amendment XIII (Ratified December 6, 1865)

Section 1. Neither slavery nor involuntary servitude, except as a punishment for crime whereof the party shall have been duly convicted, shall exist within the United States, or any place subject to their jurisdiction.

Section 2. Congress shall have power to enforce this article by appropriate legislation.

Amendment XIV (Ratified July 9, 1868)

Section 1. All persons born or naturalized in the United States, and subject to the jurisdiction thereof, are citizens of the United States and of the State wherein they reside. No State shall make or enforce any law which shall abridge the privileges or immunities of citizens of the United States; nor shall any State deprive any person of life, liberty, or property, without due process of law; nor deny to any person within its jurisdiction the equal protection of the laws.

Section 2. Representatives shall be apportioned among the several States according to their respective numbers, counting the whole number of persons in each State, excluding Indians not taxed. But when the right to vote at any election for the choice of electors for President and Vice President of the United States, Representatives in Congress, the Executive and Judicial officers of a State, or the members of the Legislature thereof, is denied to any of the male inhabitants of such State, being twenty-one years of age,[12] and citizens of the United States, or in any way abridged, except for participation in rebellion, or other crime, the basis of representation therein shall be reduced in the proportion which the number of such male citizens shall bear to the whole number of male citizens twenty-one years of age in such State.

Section 3. No person shall be a Senator or Representative in Congress, or elector of President and Vice President, or hold any office, civil or military, under the United States, or under any State, who, having previously taken an oath, as a member of Congress, or as an officer of the United States, or as a member of any State legislature, or as an executive or judicial officer of any State, to support the Constitution of the United States, shall have engaged in insurrection or rebellion against the same, or given aid or comfort to the enemies thereof. But Congress may by a vote of two-thirds of each House, remove such disability.

Section 4. The validity of the public debt of the United States, authorized by law, including debts incurred for payment of pensions and bounties for services in suppressing insurrection or rebellion, shall not be questioned. But neither the United States nor any State shall assume or pay any debt or obligation incurred in aid of insurrection or rebellion against the United States, or any claim for the loss or emancipation of any slave; but all such debts, obligations and claims shall be held illegal and void.

Section 5. The Congress shall have power to enforce, by appropriate legislation, the provisions of this article.

Amendment XV (Ratified February 3, 1870)

Section 1. The right of citizens of the United States to vote shall not be denied or abridged by the United

States or by any State on account of race, color, or previous condition of servitude.

Section 2. The Congress shall have power to enforce this article by appropriate legislation.

Amendment XVI (Ratified February 3, 1913)

The Congress shall have power to lay and collect taxes on incomes, from whatever source derived, without apportionment among the several States, and without regard to any census or enumeration.

Amendment XVII (Ratified April 8, 1913)

The Senate of the United States shall be composed of two Senators from each State, elected by the people thereof, for six years; and each Senator shall have one vote. The electors in each State shall have the qualifications requisite for electors of the most numerous branch of the State legislatures.

When vacancies happen in the representation of any State in the Senate, the executive authority of such State shall issue writs of election to fill such vacancies: *Provided,* That the legislature of any State may empower the executive thereof to make temporary appointments until the people fill the vacancies by election as the legislature may direct.

This amendment shall not be so construed as to affect the election or term of any Senator chosen before it becomes valid as part of the Constitution.

Amendment XVIII (Ratified January 16, 1919)[13]

Section 1. After one year from the ratification of this article the manufacture, sale, or transportation of intoxicating liquors within, the importation thereof into, or the exportation thereof from the United States and all territory subject to the jurisdiction thereof for beverage purposes is hereby prohibited.

Section 2. The Congress and the several States shall have concurrent power to enforce this article by appropriate legislation.

Section 3. This article shall be inoperative unless it shall have been ratified as an amendment to the Constitution by the legislatures of the several States, as provided in the Constitution, within seven years from the date of the submission hereof to the States by the Congress.

Amendment XIX (Ratified August 18, 1920)

The right of citizens of the United States to vote shall not be denied or abridged by the United States or by any State on account of sex.

Congress shall have power to enforce this article by appropriate legislation.

Amendment XX (Ratified January 23, 1933)

Section 1. The terms of the President and Vice President shall end at noon on the 20th day of January, and the terms of Senators and Representatives at noon on the 3d day of January, of the years in which such terms would have ended if this article had not been ratified; and the terms of their successors shall then begin.

Section 2. The Congress shall assemble at least once in every year, and such meeting shall begin at noon on the 3d day of January, unless they shall by law appoint a different day.

Section 3.[14] If, at the time fixed for the beginning of the term of the President, the President elect shall have died, the Vice President elect shall become President. If a President shall not have been chosen before the time fixed for the beginning of his term, or if the President elect shall have failed to qualify, then the Vice President elect shall act as President until a President shall have qualified; and the Congress may by law provide for the case wherein neither a President elect nor a Vice President elect shall have qualified, declaring who shall then act as President, or the manner in which one who is to act shall be selected, and such person shall act accordingly until a President or Vice President shall have qualified.

Section 4. The Congress may by law provide for the case of the death of any of the persons from whom the House of Representatives may choose a President whenever the right of choice shall have devolved upon them, and for the case of the death of any of the persons from whom the Senate may choose a Vice President whenever the right of choice shall have devolved upon them.

Section 5. Sections 1 and 2 shall take effect on the 15th day of October following the ratification of this article.

Section 6. This article shall be inoperative unless it shall have been ratified as an amendment to the Constitution by the legislatures of three-fourths of the several States within seven years from the date of its submission.

Amendment XXI (Ratified December 5, 1933)

Section 1. The eighteenth article of amendment to the Constitution of the United States is hereby repealed.

Section 2. The transportation or importation into any State, Territory, or possession of the United States for delivery or use therein of intoxicating liquors, in violation of the laws thereof, is hereby prohibited.

Section 3. This article shall be inoperative unless it shall have been ratified as an amendment to the Constitution by conventions in the several States, as provided in the Constitution, within seven years from the date of the submission hereof to the States by the Congress.

Amendment XXII (Ratified February 27, 1951)

Section 1. No person shall be elected to the office of the President more than twice, and no person who has held the office of President, or acted as President, for more than two years of a term to which some other person was elected President shall be elected to the office of the President more than once. But this Article shall not apply to any person holding the office of President when this Article was proposed by the Congress, and shall not prevent any person who may be holding the office of President, or acting as President, during the term within which this Article become operative from holding the office of President or acting as President during the remainder of such term.

Section 2. This article shall be inoperative unless it shall have been ratified as an amendment to the Constitution by the legislatures of three-fourths of the several States within seven years from the date of its submission to the States by the Congress.

Amendment XXIII (Ratified March 29, 1961)

Section 1. The District constituting the seat of Government of the United States shall appoint in such manner as the Congress may direct:

A number of electors of President and Vice President equal to the whole number of Senators and Representatives in Congress to which the District would be entitled if it were a State, but in no event more than the least populous State; they shall be in addition to those appointed by the States, but they shall be considered, for the purposes of the election of President and Vice President, to be electors appointed by a State; and they shall meet in the District and perform such duties as provided by the twelfth article of amendment.

Section 2. The Congress shall have power to enforce this article by appropriate legislation.

Amendment XXIV (Ratified January 23, 1964)

Section 1. The right of citizens of the United States to vote in any primary or other election for President or Vice President, for electors for President or Vice President, or for Senator or Representative in Congress, shall not be denied or abridged by the United States or any State by reason of failure to pay any poll tax or other tax.

Section 2. The Congress shall have power to enforce this article by appropriate legislation.

Amendment XXV (Ratified February 10, 1967)

Section 1. In case of the removal of the President from office or of his death or resignation, the Vice President shall become President.

Section 2. Whenever there is a vacancy in the office of the Vice President, the President shall nominate a Vice President who shall take office upon confirmation by a majority vote of both Houses of Congress.

Section 3. Whenever the President transmits to the President pro tempore of the Senate and the Speaker of the House of Representatives his written declaration that he is unable to discharge the powers and duties of his office, and until he transmits to them a written declaration to the contrary, such powers and duties shall be discharged by the Vice President as Acting President.

Section 4. Whenever the Vice President and a majority of either the principal officers of the executive departments or of such other body as Congress may by law provide, transmit to the President pro tempore of the Senate and the Speaker of the House of Representatives their written declaration that the President is unable to discharge the powers and duties of his office, the Vice President shall immediately assume the powers and duties of the office as Acting President.

Thereafter, when the President transmits to the President pro tempore of the Senate and the Speaker of the House of Representatives his written declaration that no inability exists, he shall resume the powers and duties of his office unless the Vice President and a majority of either the principal officers of the executive department or of such other body as Congress may by law provide, transmit within four days to the President pro tempore of the Senate and the Speaker of the House of Representatives their written declaration that the President is unable to discharge the powers and duties of his office. Thereupon Congress shall decide the issue, assembling within forty-eight hours for that purpose if not in session. If the Congress, within twenty-one days after receipt of the latter written declaration, or, if Congress is not in session, within twenty-one days after Congress is required to assemble, determines by two-thirds vote of both Houses that the President is unable to discharge the powers and duties of his office, the Vice President shall continue to discharge the same as Acting President; otherwise, the President shall resume the powers and duties of his office.

Amendment XXVI (Ratified July 1, 1971)

Section 1. The right of citizens of the United States, who are eighteen years of age or older, to vote shall not be denied or abridged by the United States or by any State on account of age.

Section 2. The Congress shall have power to enforce this article by appropriate legislation.

Amendment XXVII (Ratified May 7, 1992)

No law varying the compensation for the services of the Senators and Representatives shall take effect, until an election of Representatives shall have intervened.

Notes

1. The part in brackets was changed by section 2 of the Fourteenth Amendment.
2. The part in brackets was changed by the first paragraph of the Seventeenth Amendment.
3. The part in brackets was changed by the second paragraph of the Seventeenth Amendment.
4. The part in brackets was changed by section 2 of the Twentieth Amendment.
5. The Sixteenth Amendment gave Congress the power to tax incomes.
6. The material in brackets has been superseded by the Twelfth Amendment.
7. This provision has been affected by the Twenty-fifth Amendment.
8. These clauses were affected by the Eleventh Amendment.
9. This paragraph has been superseded by the Thirteenth Amendment.
10. Obsolete.
11. The part in brackets has been superseded by section 3 of the Twentieth Amendment.
12. See the Nineteenth and Twenty-sixth Amendments.
13. This Amendment was repealed by section 1 of the Twenty-first Amendment.
14. See the Twenty-fifth Amendment.

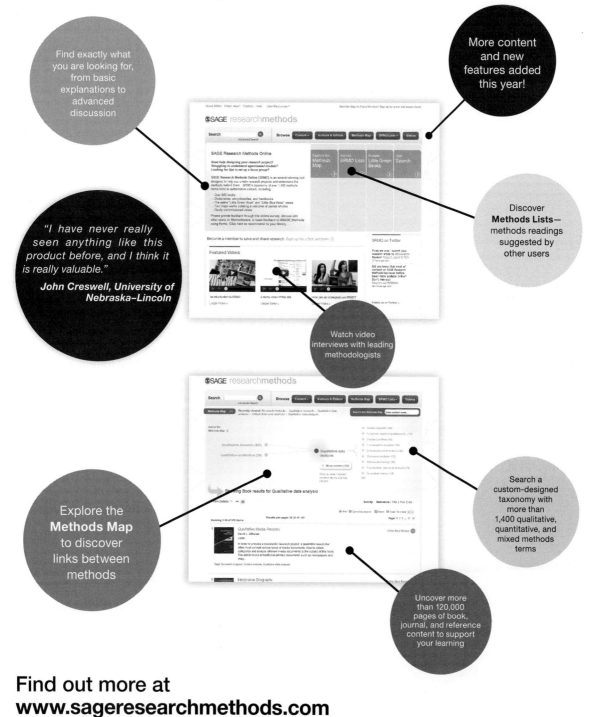

SAGE researchmethods

The essential online tool for researchers from the world's leading methods publisher

Find exactly what you are looking for, from basic explanations to advanced discussion

More content and new features added this year!

"I have never really seen anything like this product before, and I think it is really valuable."

John Creswell, University of Nebraska–Lincoln

Discover **Methods Lists**— methods readings suggested by other users

Watch video interviews with leading methodologists

Explore the **Methods Map** to discover links between methods

Search a custom-designed taxonomy with more than 1,400 qualitative, quantitative, and mixed methods terms

Uncover more than 120,000 pages of book, journal, and reference content to support your learning

Find out more at
www.sageresearchmethods.com